SIGNIFICANCE TEST	=	SIZE OF EFFECT	×	SIZE OF STUDY
t	=	d	×	$\dfrac{\sqrt{df}}{2}$
F	=	$\dfrac{r^2}{1-r^2}$	×	df
F	=	$\dfrac{eta^2}{1-eta^2}$	×	$\dfrac{df_{\text{error}}}{df_{\text{means}}}$
F	=	$\dfrac{S^2_{\text{means}}}{S^2}$	×	n
t^*	=	$\dfrac{r}{\sqrt{1-r^2}}$	×	$\sqrt{df}$
t^*	=	$\dfrac{\bar{D}}{S_D}$	×	$\sqrt{n}$
t^*	=	d	×	$\sqrt{df}$

*Correlated observations.

ESSENTIALS OF BEHAVIORAL RESEARCH
Methods and Data Analysis

ESSENTIALS OF BEHAVIORAL RESEARCH
Methods and Data Analysis

Second Edition

Robert Rosenthal
Harvard University

Ralph L. Rosnow
Temple University

McGraw-Hill, Inc.

New York   St. Louis   San Francisco   Auckland   Bogotá   Caracas   Hamburg
Lisbon   London   Madrid   Mexico   Milan   Montreal   New Delhi   Paris
San Juan   São Paulo   Singapore   Sydney   Tokyo   Toronto

This book was set in Times Roman by Beacon Graphics Corporation.
The editors were Maria E. Chiappetta, Jane Vaicuna, and Margery Luhrs;
the production supervisor was Louise Karam.
New drawings were done by J & R Services, Inc.
Arcata Graphics/Halliday was printer and binder.

ESSENTIALS OF BEHAVIORAL RESEARCH
Methods and Data Analysis

1 2 3 4 5 6 7 8 9 0 HAL HAL 9 0 9 8 7 6 5 4 3 2 1

ISBN 0-07-053929-4

Library of Congress Cataloging-in-Publication Data

Rosenthal, Robert, (date).
    Essentials of behavioral research: methods and data analysis/
    Robert Rosenthal, Ralph L. Rosnow.—2nd ed.
        p.   cm.—(McGraw-Hill series in psychology)
    Includes bibliographical references and index.
    ISBN 0-07-053929-4
    1. Psychology—Research—Methodology.   I. Rosnow, Ralph L.
    II. Title.   III. Series.
        [DNLM: 1. Behavior.   2. Research—methods.   3. Statistics.   BF
    76.5 R815e]
    BF76.5.R629   1991
    300'.72—dc20
    DNLM/DLC
    for Library of Congress   90-13424

To our students
past, present, and future

CONTENTS

Random Digits 600/   B.10 Significance Levels of ρ, the Spearman
Rank-Correlation Coefficient 607/   B.11 Significance Levels of
$F_{MAX} = S^2_{MAX}/S^2_{MIN}$ in a Set of k Independent Variances, Each Based on
$n - 1$ Degrees of Freedom 608/   B.12 Significance Levels of
Cochran's $g = S^2_{MAX}/\Sigma S^2$ in a Set of k Independent Variances, Each
Based on $n - 1$ Degrees of Freedom 610/   B.13 Arcsin Transformation
$(a = 2 \arcsin \sqrt{X})$ 612

PREFACE

As with the first edition of this book, this second edition evolved out of our lectures at Harvard University and Temple University, and many of the chapters were originally handouts that were used in our research methods classes. Thus much of the material has been undergoing a process of development and refinement for years, primarily in our graduate and advanced undergraduate psychology classes but also with graduate students in communication research, school psychology, business, and marketing. These students had at least one course in statistics as a prerequisite, and we assume that our readers will also have had one course in quantitative methods, although we do review elementary topics (Chapters 13–15) as a brushup for those who may have forgotten some of their basic statistics. In Chapter 2, we also review basic concepts (such as the null hypothesis in significance testing, statistical power and effect size) in order to establish a common ground of understanding for the later discussions. In these reviews, as much as in our more advanced discussions later on, we have included some conceptually less common material to make this material of interest to more experienced students and researchers. For example, in talking about experimental design we include a brief discussion of the philosophical evolution of the concept of causality, and in addressing the topic of descriptive statistics we include material that will be of interest to researchers trained before the advent of exploratory data-analytic procedures.

Readers familiar with the first edition will, we believe, find this second edition to be a more integrated synthesis of research methods and data analysis. The intended audience includes advanced undergraduate students (e.g., honors students, advanced psychology majors who plan to enter graduate school), graduate students at all levels in the behavioral sciences, and researchers themselves (who may be interested in a refresher as well as a conceptually integrated introduction to recent developments in statistical data analysis. With this audience in mind, Appendix A ("Writing Literature Reviews and Original-Study Papers") is focused on preparing articles for publication, and the style and format that are recommended follow the standard American Psychological Association guidelines (but in a much more abbreviated presentation here). What if highly motivated graduate or undergraduate students with no prior work in statistics wanted to go through this book on their own? They could do it, but it might be useful for them to read a more introductory text before (or while) consulting ours. For advanced graduate students and more experienced researchers, we have also written a brief supplementary textbook on the very central and flexible procedures of contrasts—*Contrast Analysis: Focused Comparisons in the Analysis of Variance* (Cambridge University Press). In our graduate classes, we have usually substituted it for Chapter 21, inasmuch as the introductory material in that chapter is reviewed (along with more detailed information) in *Contrast Analysis.*

Recently, we have characterized the dominant discursive pattern of the intuitions and inductive inferences that characterize the scientific outlook by the slogan "Think Yiddish, write British" (Rosnow and Rosenthal, 1989b). Beginning in Chapter 1 we pick up on this idea, and throughout this book we endeavor to look beneath the surface rhetoric of behavioral science (the "write British" aspect) to reveal the deeper structure of behavioral research methodology. In the second half of this book, following the thrust of that recent article, we expose some problems of what are later described as matters of methodological spirit and substance, which in the past have been resistant to attempts to correct them. We view this as a continuation of our discussion of the rhetoric of justification, which in part depends on statistical data analysis to shore up facts and inductive inferences. In the data-analytic chapters, a recurring theme is the general relationship between tests of significance and the size of the effect under investigation, i.e., significance test = size of effect × size of study. The front inside cover shows effect size and study size components of familiar significance tests, providing a handy summary of the application of this theme. The back inside cover, which provides a summary of some easily computed measures of effect size, further underscores the view that a test of significance without an effect size estimate is an incomplete story under almost all conditions.

Our approach to the teaching of data analysis is intuitive, concrete, and arithmetic rather than rigorously mathematical. There are two reasons for this: First, we ourselves are not rigorously mathematical in our approach to data analysis. Second, experience in teaching young researchers from the sophomore to the postdoctoral level convinces us that we can be more effective in our preferred mode. We pay a price for this. When we have a mathematically sophisticated student, he or she will miss out on something valuable, and we encourage such a student to take course work in a department of mathematical statistics. We would still advise such a student to read this book, since our approach will prove complementary, not contradictory. As a further pedagogic aid, the statistical examples we employ are in most cases hypothetical, constructed specifically to illustrate the logical bases of the computational procedures. The numbers were chosen to be clear and instructive; therefore, they are neater than real-life numbers tend to be. There are also fewer of them in any single example than we would find in an actual data set. Readers who have looked at the primary literature of the behavioral sciences will know that most real-life examples involve more observations than are found in our statistical examples, and all readers should keep that in mind.

We are indebted to Russell Knoth and Robert Bauserman for preparing the instructor's manual that accompanies this text, and to Mary Lu Rosenthal for preparing the indexes in this book. We also thank the following colleagues for their comments and suggestions concerning the drafts of the second edition of this book: Frank Bernieri, Oregon State University; Kenneth Bordens, Indiana University-Purdue University; Stephen Davis, Emporia State University; Bella DePaulo, University of Virginia; Robin DiMatteo, University of California, Riverside; Howard Friedman, University of California, Riverside; Charles Judd, University of Colorado; David Kenny, University of Connecticut; Sheldon Solomon, Skidmore College; and Richard Williams, Brigham Young University. The first author also thanks William G. Cochran, Jacob Cohen, Paul W. Holland, Frederick Mosteller, and Donald B. Rubin, who were influential in developing his philosophy of research, and the National Science Foundation for its support of much of the research leading to the methodological developments described in this book and our supplementary volume on contrasts. The second author is grateful for the support that has been forthcoming from Temple University in the form of the Thaddeus Bolton Professorship and a National Institute of Health Biomedical Research Support Grant. At the time at which this manuscript was completed, Rosenthal was a Fellow at the Center for Advanced Study in the Behavioral Sciences with financial support from the John D. and Catherine T. MacArthur Foundation, and Rosnow was a Visiting Professor at Harvard University. We wish to thank these institutions for the generous support provided us, and we both express our appreciation to Blair Boudreau and to Deanna Knickerbocker for their superb manuscript preparation. We also thank the following authors, journals, and publishers for generously granting permission to adapt tables, figures, excerpts, and illustrations: Freed Bales, Earl Baughman, Arnold Buss, Donald Campbell, Jacob Cohen, Peter Crabb, W. Grant Dahlstrom, Jack Friedman, John Haviland, Howard Kahane, Louise Kidder, Joseph Lev, Irwin Mahler, Conrad Smith, Alan Sockloff, Academic Press, the *Alberta Journal of Educational Research,* the American Educational Research Association, the American Psychological Association, the American Sociological Association, the American Statistical Association, Elsevier Scientific Publishing Company, Heldref Publications, Houghton Mifflin, Iowa State University Press, the *Journal of Communication,* the Journal Press, Alan R. Liss, Inc., McGraw-Hill Publishing Company, Oxford University Press, Prentice-Hall, Inc., *Psychological Reports,* the Rand Corporation, the University of Chicago Press, Wadsworth Publishing Company, and John Wiley & Sons Publishers. Finally, we thank Mary Lu Rosenthal and Mimi Rosnow for their helpful suggestions and particularly for their tireless support.

A wise researcher, Edward Tolman, once said that in the end the only sure criterion is to have fun. Writing this revision, as with the first edition, has been a labor of love, and we hope that the thrill of research discovery and justification we have experienced in our own work is reflected in this book. This is our eighth book together, and we have had terrific fun throughout the course of this long collaboration.

Robert Rosenthal
Ralph L. Rosnow

ESSENTIALS OF BEHAVIORAL RESEARCH
Methods and Data Analysis

PART

I

EMPIRICAL INQUIRY AND DECISION CRITERIA

THE NATURE
OF BEHAVIORAL
RESEARCH

THE SCIENTIFIC METHOD

The history of science is a story of the continuous attempt to use the *scientific method* to arrive at a rational comprehension of the world in which we live and to construct a logically consistent picture of that world (see Sambursky, 1975). Yet, as one eminent researcher put it, "Ask a scientist what he conceives the scientific method to be, and he will adopt an expression that is at once solemn and shifty-eyed: solemn, because he feels he ought to declare an opinion; shifty-eyed, because he is wondering how to conceal the fact that he has no opinion to declare" (Medawar, 1969, p. 11). The problem, as this chapter shows, is that "the scientific method" is more of a philosophical outlook than a single fixed procedure.

What is the nature of this outlook? That, too, is a matter of some controversy. Some philosophers have made a career of attempting to describe how scientists think and what they do, but the philosophers of science have not developed a unified formulation and are in considerable disarray at this time (see Kourany, 1987). Looking back over the history of science, another noted scholar observed that any metaphor that might characterize the scientific method would have to be a mixed one. "It is *not* an explanatory web, a predictive network, a descriptive grammar, an experiential map, a technological abacus, a practical almanac, or a moral calculus. It is *not* an arsenal of methods—logical, mathematical, or instrumentative" (Koch, 1959, p. 2). We will see that the scientific method is not any *one* thing, but is *all of these things*—and much more.

SOME CHARACTERISTICS OF SCIENCE

Foremost, science involves reliance not on armchair theorizing, political persuasiveness, or personal position, but instead on methods of *empirical inquiry* (external observation) independently available to anyone as a means of opening up the world for scrutiny. Trying to unlock a door with a set of previously untried keys, a person says, "If this key fits the lock, then the lock will spring when I turn the key." The same is true in science. The scientist has a choice of empirical procedures, decides on one, and then says in essence "let's try it and see" (Conant, 1957, p. xii).

Second, this outlook is characterized by the particular *rhetoric* (or language) of any given field or discipline. It involves the use of technical definitions, quantitative analysis, hypotheses, and theories. These elements must satisfy methodological standards, developed on the basis of logic and practical experience, that have come to be regarded as good scientific practice. As shown later, the rhetoric of science does not constitute an exact representation of the intuitions and hunches, the illogical as well as the logical ideas that scientists use in creating ideas and in planning their research. It has been said, with tongue in cheek, that the dominant discursive pattern (i.e., the pattern of reasoning and argument) in science during this century is "Think Yiddish, write British" (Jaeger and Rosnow, 1988). The inventive ways in which scientists think often seem to resemble the "*bubbeh*-psychology" of an astute Jewish grandmother, but the tightly logical outcome of this "thinking Yiddish" is expressed within the traditions of British empiricist philosophy.

Third, in spite of the concern with logic, the scientific outlook is also characterized by a number of "hidden" assumptions that are not strictly logical, but are intuitive presuppositions about the nature of reality—philosophers call them *regulative principles* (see Apel, 1982; Rosnow, 1983). These assumptions, though hidden, still influence the way in which scientists conceptualize empirical findings. In the past, one such regulative principle was that of *strict determinism,* the notion that there is a causal law for every behavior or action. The idea was a carryover from classical physics, which stressed that there is a causal law for everything in heaven and on earth. Isaac Newton, the great English physicist, believed that if we know the present exactly, then we can calculate the future. In this century, discoveries by Werner Heisenberg and other physicists have revealed that changes that atoms undergo from one energy level to another are *not* strictly deterministic. Using rules of probability, modern physicists refer to the average behavior of a large number of atoms, but they cannot predict with certainty which of several possible actions will occur within an individual atom (Russell, 1957, p. 109). Most behavioral scientists now also accept the idea that behavior is not governed by strict causal laws, but is influenced by conscious events and voluntary decisions that vary from person to person and at different moments within individuals.

Fourth, the history of ideas teaches that the explanatory act, to be influential in science, must perforce reflect a way of thinking in which *perceptibility* has a hand (Miller, 1978). We mean that relationships, as explained, are perceptible in a way that has to "make sense" given the accepted truths. The quantum theorists initially had a terrible time persuading the physical determinists of how it should be possible, given a very great many atoms, all capable of certain definite changes, to tell what proportion will undergo each change, yet impossible to tell which particular changes any given atom will undergo. "God does not play dice with the world"—is the way one great critic, Albert Einstein, responded. He could not accept as common sense that, at the level of simple atomic processes, activity could be ruled by blind chance (Clark, 1971). Only after the mainstream of physicists were able to accept this idea as sensible did it enter the textbooks as a precise model of knowledge.

Fifth, although it would be wrong to claim that art and poetry are the same as science, scientists and philosophers have long been aware of the basic unity of the creative act as found in the arts and poetry and that in the sciences (e.g., Garfield, 1989a, 1989b; Nisbet, 1976). Twenty-five hundred years ago, Plato likened the creative work of the astronomer to that of the painter. Just as art and poetry are grounded in *aesthetics* (i.e., a sense of the beautiful), scientists are conscious of the "beauty" and "poetry" of their theoretical conceptualizations and empirical relationships. The chemist Primo Levi (1984, p. 41) writes in his autobiography that "Mendeleev's Periodic Table . . . was poetry, loftier and more solemn than all the poetry we had swallowed . . . ; and come to think of it, it even rhymed!" Scientists, as much as artists and writers, love beauty and strive for it as they attempt to envisage some aspect of the world.

Sixth, in spite of the fact that most scientists search for universal truths, there are limits or boundaries of scientific truths, as much as there are limits and boundaries of the scientific enterprise itself. One way in which science is limited is by our cognitive capacity to visualize and express our experiences fully. By analogy, we can bend our arms forward at the elbow, but not backward; nature has imposed a limit on how far the human forearm can be bent. Language enables us to bend our experiences into prose, but nature has imposed a limit on our cognitive capacity to process the world's richness of information—which is a prerequisite to expressing what we experience in theoretical language. Another way in which science is limited derives from the logical and temporal boundaries of particular empirical methods. Were physicists to insist that the only lawful generalizations are those based on direct observation, they would be unable to accept some very fundamental laws of science. Newton's first law of motion states that a body not acted on by any force will continue in a state of rest or uniform motion in a straight line forever. But no scientist has ever seen a "body not acted on by any force" (e.g., friction or gravity), much less observed its "motion in a straight line forever" (see Cohen, 1959). The scientific outlook concedes that there are always aspects of reality that are beyond the bounds of particular empirical methods. It is important that we recognize the limitations of the scientific method so that we do not credit it with properties it does not have.

Given these six characteristics, is it any surprise that scholars equivocate when asked to define "the scientific method"? Paul Feyerabend (1975), a modern philosopher, has said that success in science occurs only because scientists break every methodological rule and adopt the motto "anything goes." Feyerabend and others (Knorr-Cetina, 1981; Mitroff, 1974) have offered evidence that suggests that scientists repeatedly violate the norms or canons usually called "scientific." One contemporary philosopher, Abraham Kaplan, when asked to define the scientific method, answered that the "scientist has no other method than doing his damndest" (Kaplan, 1964, p. 27). Not all philosophers or scientists would accept Kaplan's answer, but instead would call for a new, unified model of scientific rationality that recognizes the subjective nature of discovery and proof (e.g., Laudan, 1977). We will have more to say about this in Chapter 12.

BEHAVIORAL SCIENCE DEFINED

The term *behavioral science* is used in this book as an "umbrella" concept to refer to many fields of inquiry (or disciplines) that have been traditionally grouped together in many academic institutions. The behavior of early primitive humans, humans as political animals, economic animals, social animals, talking animals, humans as logicians—these are *heuristic* expressions which serve to "indicate or point out" some particular aspects or relationships concerning human nature. Such aspects or relationships are the concern of psychologists, communication and educational researchers, sociologists, anthropologists, economists, psycholinguists, behavioral biologists, and even some statisticians.

While for many purposes it probably makes little difference whether we can distinguish among the various disciplines, there are differences nonetheless. Table 1.1 illustrates one major difference, which is that the scientific objective is defined at different levels in specific fields. For example, the objective of personality psychologists is defined as "explaining the influence of traits and personal dispositions on individual behavior," which is the "most micro" (or diminutive) aspect of individual and interpersonal actions. Cultural anthropologists, on the other hand, would define their scientific objective as "explaining the structure and function of societal systems as influencing agents," which is the "most macro" (or largest) aspect of human relations. Between these two extremes, we see that the focus of social psychologists is on "explaining the interactions among individuals" (less micro than the object of study of personality psychologists) and that sociologists are interested in "explaining the relationships among groups" (less macro than cultural anthropology).

There are also traditional differences in the particular tactics used to pursue these scientific objectives in specific disciplines. The sociologists use ques-

TABLE 1.1
Some of the different fields of behavioral science

Field	Focus	Object of explanation
Cultural anthropology	Most macro	Societal systems
Sociology	More macro	Relationships among groups
Social psychology	More micro	Interpersonal behavior
Personality psychology	Most micro	Traits, dispositions

tionnaires and survey sampling procedures more than do the psychologists in order to study people's reactions, but many psychologists also use these procedures in their research. The social psychologists, particularly those trained in a psychology graduate program, prefer to conduct controlled experiments to simulate interactions in laboratory as well as natural settings, although some sociologists and others also like to run laboratory and field experiments.

Thus, in spite of the traditional boundaries indicated in this table, behavioral scientists find it useful to borrow from one another's storehouse of methods and concepts. The boundary lines, in other words, are by no means rigid. Another example: the sociologists study the relationships among specific groups, but if reductionistic goals are accepted, they will often turn to aspects of interpersonal behavior to explain those interactions (McMillin, 1970). The psychologists have borrowed concepts from the sociologists to explain the societal functioning of rumors as so-called improvised news, i.e., as public communications that reflect private hypotheses about how the world works (see Rosnow, 1980; Rosnow and Fine, 1976; Shibutani, 1966). These psychologists have used both traditional experimental procedures and sampling and questionnaire procedures borrowed from the sociologists to study when, why, and how rumors spread in communities (Rosnow, 1988).

In many fields, the scope of theorizing has evolved considerably during the past two decades in order to reflect a more "multiplistic" viewpoint (e.g., Houts, Cook, and Shadish, 1986). That is, there is an emphasis on the use of multiple methods of observation and explanation instead of an emphasis on a single method of observation or a single theoretical explanation. Thus we see many interdisciplinary research projects at the present time, as researchers strive to develop a theoretically "ecumenical" picture of human nature (see Jaeger and Rosnow, 1988). Sometimes a whole new field is created when the researchers combine methods and theories from different fields. Examples would include behavioral medicine, mathematical psychology, sociobiology, psychochemistry, ethnopsychology, and psychological anthropology. The researchers hope that these boundary-melting fields will show the same vigor and potential for breakthrough that has been evident when other sciences have combined to form a new "species."

A final point: the term "behavioral science" is not just another synonym for the philosophical doctrine known as *methodological behaviorism*, which insists that scientists confine their analyzing to fully observable behavior. This latter view, sometimes called "pure empiricism," would disallow cognitive functioning (i.e., the way the mind functions) as a legitimate area of scientific analysis, unless we agreed to define mind as "what the body does" (Skinner, 1987, p. 784). In recent years, a new wave of thinking has swept over "neobehaviorists" and "radical behaviorists" (e.g., Hayes, 1987, 1988; Morris, 1988), in part a reaction against the development of cognitive science as a competing orientation (cf. Gardner, 1986). Leading methodological behaviorists call for abandonment of "behaviorism" as a methodological label for their scientific enterprise, and call instead for a liberalization in pronouncing what is analyzable by the scientific method (Hayes, 1988). We will have much more to say about this idea in Chapter 12, in which we discuss the new label of "contextualism," which a number of behavioral scientists in different areas have adopted (see Rosnow and Georgoudi, 1986).

We will also advocate a liberalized definition of behavioral science and throughout this book will describe the major methods employed by researchers in quite different fields (e.g., psychologists, educational researchers, communication researchers, sociologists, and anthropologists). While the methods are different, the basic problem is the same—to describe and explain how and why people behave the way they do, including how and why they feel and think about things as they do. William James, the great American philosopher (and founder of experimental psychology in the United States), viewed the field of psychology as the science of "mental life," but he viewed it as concerned with the nature of reality as revealed by how people feel, think, and behave. The job of behavioral science, as James said of psychology, is to describe and explain consciousness in the context of behavior and processes in the body. Another task of behavioral research is to deal with questions concerning the nature of language, planning, problem solving, and imagination in the context of mind, thinking, intentions, and mental representations (e.g., Kimble, 1989).

WORKING METHODS, REALISM, AND ANTIREALISM

Painters, novelists, philosophers, and theologians are also quite interested in how people feel, think, and behave. These specialists, certainly, have much of consequence to suggest to the behavioral scientist, but they themselves are not behavioral scientists (nor would they wish to be considered as such). It is not easy to say just how the behavioral scientist's interest in feeling, thinking, and behaving differs from anyone else's, but it is possible to differentiate the *working methods* of the behavioral scientist from those of others who share such interests. As noted, these methods are characterized by the use of empirical inquiry to open up the world of motivation and consciousness for scrutiny and investigation.

In other fields, such as literature and art, empirical inquiry is not a *necessary* part of the "road to truth." Another famous American philosopher, Charles Sanders Peirce, whose ideas also flourished early in this century, discussed four paths to understanding and gave his opinion as to the best way to create a storehouse of verifiable knowledge. The poorest of these paths he called the "method of tenacity," in which the person stubbornly clings to a familiar idea just because this familiarity brings peace of mind. A second path, the "method of authority," referred to the idea that some beliefs are held to be true merely because they are advocated by someone who calls himself or herself an "expert" or who possesses power and authority. The perception of who is an authority, surely, is in the eye of the beholder; someone who seems an expert to one person may not seem so expert to another person. Peirce thought that the method of authority made up for some of the shortcomings of the method of tenacity, but he argued that neither approach encouraged critical reasoning.

On the third path, which he called the "a priori method," the person uses his or her critical reasoning powers to decide what is true. The term *a priori* is defined as "from cause to effect," and as used by Peirce, it referred to the idea that the person reasons from cause to effect independently of observation or experiment. Peirce believed this approach to be more reliable than the preceding two; that is, if the person thinks hard and critically. But it is still not much of an improvement, because it makes inquiry a matter of taste or fashion, he argued. It is only the fourth path, the scientific method, that Peirce believed to be the most satisfactory approach, because it lets nature answer the questions we ask.

There are some problems with Peirce's idealization. As we said, scientists do not subscribe to one method but to many different methods. Also, modern philosophers disagree on what the term "truth" means, or even whether there are such things as "objectively verifiable" truths. In ancient times truth was defined as an "adequate conception of, or correspondence with, reality." But what is reality? In philosophy of science, a distinction is drawn between realist and antirealist explanations. The *realists* (names such as Rudolf Carnap, Ronald Giere, and Karl Popper) claim that scientific theories give (or probably give) a literally true account of the way the world is; the *antirealists* (such as Pierre Duhem, Thomas Kuhn, and Imre Lakatos) argue that scientific theories do not give a literally true account of the world (see Kourany, 1987). There may be no adequate resolution of this difference of opinion, and in this book we borrow ideas and assumptions from both camps, the realists and the antirealists.

Thus antirealism should not be equated with antiempiricism. Empirical inquiry (as we have repeatedly stated) is *the* essential characteristic of the scientific method, having entered into behavioral science during the late nineteenth century. At that time researchers first demonstrated the possibility of bringing within the empirical domain of science questions concerning behavior until then thought to lie completely outside its competence (see Medawar, 1969). One pioneering researcher was the English scientist and writer Francis Galton. In a famous study he perceived a way of establishing "objective" grounds for empirically testing the belief that prayers are answered.

In England, the health and longevity of the royal families is prayed for weekly on a national scale. Galton developed the hypothesis that if prayers are answered, then members of royal families should live longer as a result of prayers on their behalf. To perform an empirical test, he computed the mean age attained by various groups of adult males (excluding deaths by accident or violence) and compared these figures with the mean age attained by the adult members of royal houses. Finding that the average longevity of members of royal houses was 64 years, while clergymen lived to be 69 and lawyers to be 68, he concluded that, within the objective arena in which he had examined this question, a belief in the efficacy of prayer was unjustified. This was not to say that prayers could not strengthen resolution and bring serenity, but only that the weight of empirical evidence suggested that in the area of longevity, royalty fared worse than people of humbler birth.

Empirical research methods in behavioral science, most investigators would agree, include a wide variety of laboratory and nonlaboratory procedures. Taking a broader view we might say that the procedures that are available are employed in three general kinds of empirical investigations: (1) descriptive research investigations, (2) relational research investigations, and (3) experimental research investigations.

THREE PERSPECTIVES IN EMPIRICAL INQUIRY

By *descriptive research* we mean an investigatory focus that tends to have as its goal the careful mapping out of a situation or set of events in order to describe what is happening behaviorally. This focus does not, by definition, directly concern itself with causal explanations, except perhaps speculatively. For example, the educational psychologist who is interested in the study of children's failure in school may spend a good deal of time observing the classroom behavior of children who are doing poorly. The researcher can then describe as carefully as possible what was observed. Careful observation of failing pupils might lead to some revision of the concepts of classroom failure, to suggestions as to factors that may have contributed to the development of failure, and even perhaps to speculative ideas for the remediation of failure.

This type of focus is usually considered a necessary first step in the development of a program of research, because it establishes the basis or cornerstone of any future undertaking. But it is rarely regarded as sufficient, because sooner or later someone will want to know *why* something happens or *how* what happens is related to other events. If our interest is in children's failure, we are not likely to be satisfied for very long with even the most careful description of that behavior. Sooner or later, we will want to know the antecedents of failure and the outcomes of various procedures designed to reduce classroom failure. Even if we were not motivated directly by the practical implications of knowing the causes and cures of failure, we would believe our understanding of it to be considerably improved if we knew the conditions that increase and decrease its likelihood. For us to learn about the increase or decrease of failure, or any other behavior, our observations must focus on at least two variables at the same time. Two sets of observations must be made that can be related to one another.

That is what is meant by *relational research*, which has as its focus the description of how what happens changes along with changes in some other set of observations. Research is relational when two or more variables or conditions are measured and related to one another. Continuing with the classroom example, let us suppose the researcher noted that many of the scholastically failing students were rarely looked at or addressed by their teachers and were seldom exposed to new academically relevant information. At this stage the researcher might have only an impression about the relation between learning failure and teaching behavior. Such impressions, or *broad working hypotheses,* are a frequent, and often valuable, byproduct of descriptive research. But if they are to be taken seriously as a relational principle, they cannot be left at the impressionistic level for very long.

Our educational psychologist, or perhaps another observer who wanted to find out whether the psychologist's impressions were accurate, might then arrange to make a series of "coordinated" observations on a sample of pupils in classrooms that adequately represented the population of pupils about whom some conclusion was to be drawn. For each pupil it could be noted (1) whether the student was learning anything or the degree to which the student had been learning and (2) the degree to which the teacher had been exposing the student to material to be learned. From the coordinated observations it should then be possible to make a quantitative statement concerning the degree of correlation between the amount of pupils' exposure to material to be learned and the amount of such material they did in fact learn. The scientist would indicate not just (1) whether "X and Y are significantly related" (i.e., whether this nonzero relationship is likely to emerge consistently on repeating the research), but also (2) the form of the relationship (e.g., linear or nonlinear, positive or negative) and (3) the strength of the relationship, or "effect size" (a concept defined in the next chapter).

To carry the illustration one step further, suppose that pupils exposed to less information were also those who tended to learn less. On discovering this relation, there might be a temptation to conclude that children learn less because they are taught less. Such an *ad hoc hypothesis* (i.e., one developed "for this" special result), while plausible, would not be warranted by the relation reported. It might be that teachers teach less to those they know to be less able to learn. Differences in teaching behavior might be as much a result of the pupils' learning as a determinant of that learning. To pursue this working hypothesis we could make further observations that would allow us to infer whether differences in information presented to pupils, apart from any individual differences among them, affected the pupils' learning. Such questions are best answered by manipulating the conditions that one believes to be responsible for the effect. That is, some change is introduced into the situation, or it is interrupted or terminated in order to identify some causes.

That is what is generally meant by *experimental research*, the focus of which is the identification of causes, i.e., *what* leads to what. Relational research can only rarely provide such information, and then only under very special conditions (discussed in Chapter 5). The difference between the degree of focus on causal explanation of relational and experimental research can be expressed in the difference between the two statements "X is related to Y" (relational research) and "X is responsible for Y" (experimental research). In our example, teaching is X and learning is Y. Our experiment is designed to reveal the effects of teaching on pupil learning. We might select a sample of youngsters and, by tossing a coin or by means of some other random method of selection, divide them into two equivalent groups. One of these groups (the *experimental group*) would have more information given them by their teachers than the other group (the *control group*) would. We could then assess whether the experimental group surpassed the control group in learning achievement. If we found this result, we could say that giving the experimental group more information was *responsible* for this outcome.

There might still be a question of what it was about the better procedure that led to the improvement. In the case of increased teaching, we might wonder whether the improvement was due to the nature of the additional material; the increased attention from the teacher while presenting the additional material; any accompanying increases in eye contact, smiles, warmth; or other possible correlates of increased teaching behavior. In fact, these various hypotheses have already been investigated. The results indicate that the amount of new material that teachers present to their pupils is sometimes predicated not so much on the children's learning ability, but on the teachers' beliefs or expectations about their pupils' learning ability. The teachers' expectations about their pupils' performance can come to serve as a *self-fulfilling prophecy,* in which the expectations are essentially responsible for the outcome in behavior (Rosenthal, 1985b; Rosenthal and Rubin, 1978).

We have described a series of hypothetical studies, and we now turn to a series of actual research studies. In practice, the term "experimental" can also be said to describe goals, i.e., *why* the researchers did the study. In the following examples we will see that, no matter whether the research study is primarily descriptive, relational, or experimental, it can be guided toward a number of secondary goals as well. Another purpose of the following examples is to introduce some additional key concepts in the vernacular language of behavioral science.

DESCRIPTIVE RESEARCH

The first investigation to be discussed was done under the auspices of the Office of Strategic Services (OSS), this nation's first organized nonmilitary espionage and sabotage agency, which came into being in World War II. Under the directorship of Gen. William ("Wild Bill") Donovan, the OSS was charged with tasks such as intelligence gathering, sabotage behind enemy lines, mobilization of guerrilla groups to resist the Nazi occupation of Europe, and preparation and dissemination of propaganda (OSS Assessment Staff, 1948). The organization was a forerunner of today's Central Intelligence Agency. The assessment studies done by OSS investigators will illustrate what we characterized as descriptive research.

Thousands of men, drawn from both military and civilian life, were recruited to carry out the often hazardous missions of the OSS. Initially it was not known what type of personnel to select for each of the various missions, and a group of psychologists and psychiatrists was assembled to aid in the assessment of the special agents. The chief contribution of these researchers was to set up a series of situations that would permit more useful and relevant descriptions of the personalities of the candidates. The original intent of the assessment staff had been more ambitious. It had been hoped that in the long run it would be possible to lower appreciably the error rate in the selection of recruits for the OSS and to increase the likelihood of assignment of agents to those missions they could best perform. Unfortunately, several factors made impossible the development of a screening and placement system that could be fairly and properly evaluated. Chief among these factors were the assessment staff's not knowing what particular mission would finally be assigned to a recruit and, most importantly, several weaknesses in the final appraisal of how good a job an agent had actually done.

From December 1943 to August 1945, more than 5,000 recruits were studied by the assessment staff. The primary assessment station was located about an hour's ride from Washington, D.C., in a rustic setting of rolling meadows and stately trees. It was here that the recruits were sent for a $3\frac{1}{2}$-day period, during which they were given identical clothes to wear and assigned pseudonyms so that colonels and privates and college professors would be indistinguishable to the assessment researchers. Besides a false name, each recruit had to invent a cover story giving himself a new occupation, new residence, new place of birth, and new educational background. Candidates were warned that the assessment researchers would try to trick them into breaking cover and giving away their true identities.

Virtually everything that a recruit did from the moment he arrived at the station was observed and assessed: how he got off the truck that brought his group of recruits, the manner in which he asked questions of the staff members who explained procedures to the candidates, what he said during the first dinner, and what he chose to do after dinner when he was free to read or talk or withdraw. The first evening, the candidates filled out a great many paper-and-pencil tests of personality and ability and also answered questions concerning personal background information. The next few days were filled with many situational tests in which the staff had the opportunity to evaluate each man's level of initiative, leadership, functioning intelligence, social relationships, and physical ability. For example, a group of four to seven men had to move a log and a rock across an 8-foot-wide brook. The situation was rigged so that either a bridge or an overhead cable system could be constructed to solve the problem. The achievement of a solution was not the main purpose of the exercise, however. Instead, it was to give the researchers an opportunity to observe the different roles the men assumed in the team effort required to solve the problem.

One of the most trying, and probably most revealing, situations was a task in which the candidates were to direct the efforts of two helpers in building a 5-foot cube out of a giant Tinkertoy set. To the candidates the task seemed to be another assessment of their leadership abilities, but it was actually a test of stress tolerance. "Kippy" and "Buster," the two helpers, were really two members of the research staff. Kippy was a passive sort who did nothing unless ordered to, except occasionally to get in the way. Buster offered useless suggestions, griped repeatedly, and harped on the candidates' weaknesses. Kippy and Buster were sufficiently obstructive that, in the whole history of the OSS assessment program, no recruit was ever able to complete the task in the allotted 10 minutes.

Some of the candidates perceived immediately that the two "helpers" were confederates of the researchers. That insight sometimes, but not always, helped the candidates to contain their tempers and persist in trying to get the job done. Other candidates wondered why the OSS could not afford better farmhands around the estate and admitted that the obstreperousness and insolence of the helpers tempted them more than once to lay an uncharitable hand upon one or the other of them. On more than one occasion a fight did ensue. Some candidates learned enough about themselves from this experience that they asked to be excused from the program, realizing that the kind of stress involved would be too much for them.

As this project unfolded, its primary objective was descriptive, but it should be noted again that description had not been the only goal of the research staff. They had also hoped to correlate the assessments made of the men with their performance in the field, thus, using a relational strategy as well as a descriptive one. Such correlations would define the adequacy of the selection procedures. If these correlations were high, they would tell the researchers that the assessment (the *predictor variable*) did its job of predicting actual task performance (the *criterion variable*, or outcome). Because the researchers had only the vaguest (and probably many erroneous) ideas about the nature of the jobs for which the candidates were being selected, there was no satisfactory evaluation of just how good a job had been done by agents in the field. It would be impractical to think that one could select people for the performance of unspecified functions. However, it seems unlikely that, either before or since, have so many people been observed and described so carefully by so many behavioral researchers.

RELATIONAL RESEARCH

The OSS assessment researchers had been in a position to make many detailed observations relevant to many of the candidates' motives. However, there was not a "systematic" or organized attempt to relate the scores or ratings on any one of these variables to the scores or ratings on some subsequently measured variable which, on the basis of theory, should show a strong correlation with the predictor variable. For our next example, we will show how relational research was used in another classic investigation to develop a personality construct and then to validate a psychological scale to measure this construct, the "need for social approval." This research also illustrates the utility of replications that vary slightly from one another ("varied replications"), which can help us to pinpoint the relationships of interest; we will have more to say about replications in Chapter 3.

The term *construct* refers to an abstract idea that is used as an explanatory concept (we will have much more to say about this in later chapters). The construct "need for social approval" was investigated by Douglas Crowne and David Marlowe, who performed this research at Ohio State University in the late 1950s. The concept refers to the idea that people differ in their need for approval and affection from respected others. Crowne and Marlowe were interested in developing a scale to measure the degree to which people vary on this personality dimension. They wanted their scale to measure the respondent's social desirability independent of his or her level of psychopathology and began by considering hundreds of personality test items that could be answered in a true-false format. To be included, an item had to be one that would reflect socially approved behavior but yet be almost certain to be untrue, i.e., behavior too good to be true. In addition, answers to the items could not have any implications of psychological abnormality or psychopathology. By having a group of psychology graduate students and faculty judge the social desirability of each item it was possible to develop a set of items that would reflect behavior too virtuous to be probable, but would not be primarily influenced by personal maladjustment.

The final form of the test, the Marlowe-Crowne social desirability scale, included 33 items (Crowne, 1979; Crowne and Marlowe, 1964). In about half the items a "true" answer reflected the socially desirable (i.e., the higher need for approval) response, and in the remainder a "false" answer reflected this type of response. An example of the former type of item might be "I have never intensely disliked anyone," whereas the latter item might be "I sometimes feel resentful when I don't get my way."

The items, combined to form a psychological scale, showed a high degree of relation with those measures with which the scale was expected to show high correlations. First, it correlated well with itself, which is to say an impressive statistical relation was obtained between the two testings of a group of subjects who were tested one month apart. Thus the test seemed to be measuring what it measured in a *reliable* (consistent) manner. In addition, although the test did show moderate correlations with measures of psychopathology, there were fewer of these and they were smaller in magnitude than was the case for an earlier developed scale of need for social approval. These were promising beginnings for the Marlowe-Crowne scale, but it remained to be shown that the concept of need for social approval (and the scale developed to measure it) was useful beyond predicting responses to other paper-and-pencil measures. As part of their program of further validating their new scale and the construct that was its basis, the researchers undertook an ingenious series of varied replications relating scores on their scale to subjects' behavior in a number of non-paper-and-pencil test situations.

In the first of these studies, subjects began by completing various tests, including the Marlowe-Crowne scale, and then were asked to get down to the serious business of the experiment. This "serious business" required them to (1) pack a dozen spools of thread into a small box, (2) unpack the box, (3) repack the box, (4) re-unpack the box, and so on for 25 minutes while the experimenter appeared to be timing the performance and making notes about them. After these dull 25 minutes had elapsed, subjects were asked to rate how "interesting" the task had been, how "instructive," and how "important to science," and were asked how much they wanted to participate in similar experiments in the future. Results of this study showed quite clearly that those subjects who scored above the mean on desire for social approval said they found the task more interesting, more instructive, and more important to science, and were more eager to participate again in similar studies than those subjects who had scored below the mean. In other words, just as we would have predicted, subjects higher in the need for social approval were more ingratiating and said nicer things to the experimenter about the task that he had set for them.

Next, the investigators conducted a series of studies using the method of verbal conditioning. In one variant of this procedure the subject is asked to say all the words he or she can think of to the listening experimenter. In the *reward* condition, every time the subject utters a plural noun the experimenter responds affirmatively by saying "mm-hmm." In the *punishment* condition, every time the subject utters a plural noun the experimenter responds negatively by saying "uh-uh." Researchers who use this procedure then define the magnitude of verbal conditioning by the amount of increase in the production of plural nouns from the pre-reinforcement level to some subsequent time block after the subject has received the reward or punishment. Magnitude of verbal conditioning is theorized to be a good indicator of susceptibility to social influence. Subjects who are more susceptible to the experimenter's reinforcements are hypothesized to be more susceptible to other forms of elementary social influence.

In the first of their verbal conditioning studies the investigators found that subjects higher in the need for social approval responded with far more plural nouns when rewarded than did subjects lower in this need. They also found that subjects higher in the need for social approval responded with fewer plural nouns when punished than did subjects lower in this personality characteristic. In this particular study those subjects who saw the connection between their utterances and the experimenter's reinforcement were dropped. In this way the relation obtained was between subjects' need for approval as measured by the Marlowe-Crowne scale and subjects' responsivity to the approval of their experimenter, but only when they were not explicitly aware (or said they were unaware) of the role of the experimenter's reinforcement.

In the second of their verbal conditioning studies the investigators wanted to use a task that would be more lifelike and engaging than producing random words. They asked subjects to describe their own personality, and every positive self-reference was reinforced by the experimenter's saying "mm-hmm" in a flat monotone. A positive self-reference was operationalized as any statement that reflected favorably on the subject, and two judges working independently showed a very high degree of consistency in identifying positive self-references. Results of this study indicated that subjects above the mean in need for social approval made significantly more positive self-references when reinforced for doing so than did subjects scoring lower in the need for social approval. It now appeared that, regardless of whether the subjects' responses were as trivial as the production of random words or as meaningful as talking about themselves, this behavior could be increased much more by subtle social reinforcement in people who were higher rather than lower in their measured need for social approval.

In their third verbal conditioning study the investigators used a *vicarious* (substitute) reward method. The subject was not rewarded for a given type of response, but insead watched someone else receive a reward. The real subjects of the study observed a *pseudosubject* (confederate of the experimenter) make up a series of sentences using one of six pronouns (I, you, we, he, she, they) and a verb given by the experimenter. Whenever the pseudosubject began a sentence with the pronoun "I" or "we," the experimenter responded with the word "good." Before and after the observation interval the subjects themselves made up sentences using one of the same six pronouns. Results of this study indicated that subjects higher in the need for social approval showed a significantly greater increase in their use of the reinforced pronouns (I, we) from their preobservational to their postobservational sentence-construction session than did subjects lower in the need for social approval. Once again, Crowne and Marlowe had demonstrated that subjects, on the average, can be successfully predicted to be more responsive to the approving behavior of an experimenter when they have scored higher on a test of need for social approval.

The term *validity* (discussed in later chapters) can be defined in several different ways. One way of defining it refers to the degree to which a test measures what it purports to measure (*test validity*), and another way refers to whether a particular construct is an appropriate image or idea as an explanatory term (*construct validity*). In another set of studies the investigators sought to extend these concepts of validity with regard to the Marlowe-Crowne scale and the construct of need for social approval. The method used was a derivative of a conformity procedure pioneered by social psychologist Solomon Asch (1952). A group of subjects were required to make judgments on specific issues. Each judgment was to be stated aloud, as the purpose of this procedure was to permit an assessment of the effects of earlier subjects' judgments on the judgments of subsequent subjects. In order to control the judgments made earlier, accomplices of the experimenters served as pseudosubjects. All the pseudosubjects made the same uniform judgment, but it was one that was quite clearly in error. Conformity was defined as the real subject's "going along with" (conforming to) the majority in his or her own judgment rather than giving the objectively correct response.

In one of Crowne and Marlowe's variations on this procedure the subjects listened to a tape recording of knocks on a table and then reported their judgment of the number of knocks they had heard. Each subject was led to believe that he or she was the fourth participant. To create this illusion the subject heard the tape-recorded responses of three prior subjects to each series of knocks that were to be judged. The earlier three subjects were the pseudosubjects, and they all agreed with one another by consistently giving an incorrect response on 12 of 18 trials. For each real subject it was therefore possible to count the number of times out of 12 that he or she yielded to the wrong but unanimous majority. Results showed that the subjects who scored higher in the need for social approval conformed more to the majority judgment than did the subjects who scored lower in the need for social approval.

In these studies the majority presence was simulated by having the real subject hear a taped response. In followup studies the researchers investigated whether the same effect would result with the accomplices actually present. This time the task was a discrimination problem in which the subjects had to judge which of two clusters of dots was larger. Pseudosubjects were again used to give responses that were clearly wrong but unanimous, and as before, the results showed that the subjects who scored above the mean on social desirability yielded more often to the unanimous but erring majority than did the subjects who scored below the mean.

We have seen a number of studies that support the validity of the Marlowe-Crowne scale and the construct of the need for social approval (or social desirability). Like almost any well-researched problem in behavioral science, there are many additional, relevant studies (not cited here) that support and do not support these findings. An exhaustive literature review would turn up these additional results, but our purpose was not to be exhaustive but rather to illustrate the goal of relational research by a series of varied replications, and also to introduce some technical concepts.

Experimental research is characterized by the controlled arrangement and manipulation of one or more conditions in order to identify the causes of resulting variations in one or more other conditions. In the research by Crowne and Marlowe there were instances in which some condition was controlled and manipulated by the investigators. Even though we used the terms "experiment" and "experimenter" to describe some aspects of this research, we still do not regard it as "experimental research" in its broad purpose. It was not experimental, because its goal was not to identify the causes of the need for social approval, nor was need for approval a manipulated variable in these studies. Instead the purpose of this research was to measure this variable and then relate it to behavior in order to decide whether the Marlowe-Crowne scale measured the construct the researchers had in mind when creating it. We now turn to an example from the field of comparative psychology to illustrate the nature of varied replications in the work of Harry and Margaret Harlow dealing with affection in primates.

EXPERIMENTAL RESEARCH

There are few personality theories that do not consider early life experiences to be of special importance in the development of personality. Among the early life experiences often given special attention are those involving mother-child relationships. A generally posed proposition might be "loving mother-child relationships are more likely to lead to healthy adult personalities than hostile, rejecting mother-child relationships." To investigate this hypothesis experimentally, we would be required to assign half our sample of young children to loving mothers and half to rejecting mothers and then follow up the development of each child's adult personality. Such an experimental plan is an ethical absurdity in our culture's value matrix, although there are no special problems of experimental logic involved. Does this mean that behavorial scientists can never do experimental work on important questions of human development and human personality? One approach to the problem has capitalized on the biological continuities between nonhuman organisms and human beings. Primates especially have been shown to share some attributes with humans sufficiently to make primates valuable, if far from exact or even very accurate, models for human behavior. We cannot, for the sake of furthering our knowledge of personality development, separate a human baby from its mother, but the important lessons we might learn from such separation make it seem rational, if not easily (or readily) justifiable, to separate a nonhuman primate from its mother. (In Chapter 11, we will discuss ethical issues of research that have implications for nonhuman as well as human subjects.)

In their extensive research program at the University of Wisconsin, the Harlows and their coworkers used arrays of procedures and approaches of both the psychologist and the biologist, which is typical in the field of comparative psychology. Much of their research on the affectional system of monkeys was of the descriptive type (e.g., young monkeys become attached to other young monkeys) and of the relational type (e.g., male monkeys become more forceful with age, and female monkeys become more passive). However, our interest here is on their experimental research, although we will be able to describe only a fraction of it in this limited space.

As part of that research program, infant monkeys were separated from their mothers just a few hours after birth and were then raised by bottle with great success. The Harlows had been advised by another researcher, Gertrude van Wagenen, to have available for their infant monkeys some soft pliant surfaces, and folded gauze diapers were consequently made available to all the baby monkeys. The babies became very much attached to these diapers, so much so that the diapers could be removed for laundering only after great difficulty. These observations led to an experiment designed to show more systematically the shorter- and longer-term effects of access to a soft material. Also the research was planned to shed light on the question of the relative importance to the development of the infant's attachment to its mother of being fed by her as opposed to being in close and cuddly contact with her (Harlow, 1959; Harlow and Harlow, 1966).

Accordingly, two "pseudomothers" were built: one, a bare welded-wire cylindrical form with a crude wooden head and face attached and the other, a similar apparatus covered with soft terry cloth. Eight newborn monkeys were given equal access to the wire and to the cloth mother figures, but four were fed at the breast of the wire mother and four were fed at the breast of the cloth mother. Results showed that when the measures were of the amount of milk consumed or the amount of weight gained, the two pseudomothers made no difference. The monkeys fed by them drank about the same amount of milk and gained about the same amount of weight. However, regardless of which mother had fed them, baby monkeys spent much more time climbing on the cloth mother and clinging to her than they did the wire mother. This finding not only demonstrated the importance of contact comfort, but showed that an earlier formulation of love for mother was really much too simple. That earlier theory held that mothers become prized because they are associated with the reduction of hunger and thirst. The Harlow results showed quite clearly that being the source of food is not nearly so good a predictor of a baby's subsequent preference as is being a soft and cuddly mother. When the monkeys were about 100 days old, they spent an average of approximately 15 hours a day on the cloth mother but only about 1.5 hours on the wire mother, regardless of whether it had been the cloth or wire mother that had fed the baby monkey.

Later experiments showed that when the infant monkey was placed into a fear-arousing situation, it was the cloth mother that was sought out for comfort and reassurance. A frightened monkey, confronted by a mechanical bear that advanced while beating a drum, would flee to the cloth mother, secure a dose of reassurance, and then gradually explore the frightening object and turn it into a toy. When the cloth mother was not in the room, the infant monkeys hurled themselves to the floor, clutched their heads and bodies, and screamed in distress. The wire mother provided the infant with no greater security or reassurance than no mother at all.

Robert A. Butler, a coworker, had discovered that monkeys enclosed in a dimly lit box will spend hour after hour pressing a lever that opens a window in the box and gives them a chance to see something outside. Monkeys barely able to walk will press the lever for a brief peek at the world outside. One of the variables that determines how hard the monkey will work to look out the window is what there is to be seen. When the monkey infants we have been discussing were tested in the "Butler box," it turned out that they worked as hard to see their cloth mothers as to see another real monkey. However, they worked no harder to see the wire mother than to see nothing at all outside the box. Not only in this experiment, but to a surprising degree in general, a wire mother is not much better than no mother at all, but a cloth mother comes close to being as good as the real thing.

A number of female monkeys became mothers themselves, although they had not had any monkey mothers of their own and no physical contact with agemates during the first year of their life (Harlow and Harlow, 1965). Compared with normal monkey mothers, these unmothered mothers were usually brutal to their firstborn offspring, hitting, kicking, and crushing them. Those motherless mothers who were not brutal were indifferent. The most cheerful result of this experiment was that those motherless monkeys who went on to become mothers for a second time treated their second babies in a normal or even overprotective manner.

A very important series of studies required that infant monkeys be raised in social isolation (Harlow and Harlow, 1970). When the isolation is total, the young monkey is exposed to no other living human or nonhuman animal. All the monkey's physical needs are met in automated fashion. A major influencing factor is length of isolation since birth: 0, 3, 6, or 12 months. All the monkeys raised in isolation were physically healthy, but when placed into a new environment, they appeared to crouch in terror. Those monkeys that had been isolated only 3 months recovered from their neurotic fear within a month or so. Those monkeys that had been isolated for 6 months never did quite recover. Their play behavior, even after 6 months, was minimal and isolated. Their social activity, when it did occur, was directed only to monkeys that had been raised in isolation. Those monkeys that had been isolated for 12 months showed the most severe retardation of play and of the development of aggression. Apathetic and terrified, these monkeys were defenseless against the attacks of the healthy control group monkeys.

Longer-term effects of early social isolation have also been discovered. Several years later, the monkeys that had been isolated for 6 months showed a dramatic change in orientation to other monkeys. Whereas earlier they had been attacked by other monkeys and had not defended themselves, they had by now developed into pathological aggressors, attacking other monkeys large and small, acts virtually never occurring among normal monkeys of their age. Another long-term effect of early social isolation can be seen in the inadequacy of the sexual behavior of these monkeys. Even females who have been only partially isolated in infancy avoid contact with breeding males; do not groom themselves; engage in threats, in aggression, in clutching themselves, biting themselves; and often fail to support the male should mounting occur. Normal females rarely engage in any of these behaviors. Male monkeys who have been isolated show even more serious sexual inadequacy than do the isolated females. When contrasted with normal males, they groom less, threaten more, are more aggressive, initiate little sexual contact, engage in unusual sex behavior, and almost never achieve intromission.

PROBABILISTIC ASSERTIONS, DEDUCTIVE AND INDUCTIVE REASONING

Out of the results of the investigations we have described there have emerged a number of *empirical principles,* i.e., accepted truths justified on the basis of empirical observations. For example, there were many other experiments done in the extensive research program of the Harlow group. Some monkeys were raised without mothers but with access to age-mates, while other monkeys were raised by their mothers but without access to age-mates (Harlow and Harlow, 1966). Overall results, while complicated, suggested the empirical principle that both normal mothering and normal age-mate contact are important to normal social development, but to some extent each can substitute or compensate for some deficits in the other. That is, both types of experience are better than either alone, but either alone appears to be very much better than neither. We characterize such generalizations as *probabilistic assertions* and view them in terms of the model of logic that philosopher Carl Hempel called *inductive-statistical reasoning.*

Hempel made a classical distinction between the kinds of assertions that are based on either deductive or inductive reasoning (e.g., Hempel and Oppenheim, 1965). One kind, that called *deductive-statistical explanation,* is the model for what scientists term "universal laws." The second kind, *inductive-statistical explanation,* is the model for what we mean by probabilistic assertions. To illustrate, if we make the following two arguments (or *premises*): (1) all the coins in Ralph's piggy bank are pennies and (2) Ralph has shaken a coin out of his piggy bank, it logically follows that (3) the coin Ralph has shaken out of his piggy bank is a penny. This example (suggested by Kourany, 1987) illustrates the deductive-statistical explanation model, inasmuch as arguments of this kind result in a conclusion that *has* to be true (if the premises are true). Such conclusions in science are represented as universal in their lawfuless, i.e., principles that are *always* true. On the other hand, if we make the following two arguments (premises): (1) 95 percent of the coins in Bob's piggy bank are pennies and (2) Bob has shaken a coin out of his piggy bank, it logically follows that (3) the coin Bob has shaken out of his piggy bank is very likely to be a penny. This second example illustrates the inductive-statistical model, because arguments of this kind result in a conclusion that is *probably* true (if the premises are true). Such conclusions, in our terminology, are probabilistic assertions.

As we see, the word "probability" refers to the mathematical chance of an event's occurring. At a racetrack, for instance, we may see a horse that is a "20-to-1 shot." This information implies that in the eyes of the odds setters that particular long shot will win about once in every 21 races, given the conditions (the premises) under which the horse is currently running. Why should a horse ever beat other horses that are faster than it is? Because of the relative uncertainty in the actions that determine the outcome of a horse race. The lead horse might stumble, or the jockey on the second horse might fall off, and so forth. Unlikely? Yes, but that is why the track management is willing to pay 20-to-1 odds.

This example (suggested by H. Wainer, in Lana and Rosnow, 1972) illustrates two ideas about probabilistic assertions, implicit in Hempel's conception of inductive-statistical reasoning: (1) they deal with uncertainty and (2) they are not absolute or "invariant" rules of nature. In physics the laws that govern the changes that atoms undergo from one energy level to another can be viewed as probabilistic assertions. Is this situation analogous to throwing dice? With three dice there are 216 possibilities ($6 \times 6 \times 6 = 216$), and each of the 216 possibilities will occur about equally often in a very large number of throws. In the same way with atoms, given a very great many atoms, all capable of certain definite changes, physicists can tell what proportion will undergo each change but cannot tell what particular changes any given atom will undergo (Russell, 1957). The behavior of an individual atom, like the behavior of an individual human or non-human animal, is also best described as statistically probabilistic.

Typically, empirical principles in behavioral science are not sufficient to determine with exactitude what an individual person will do at a given moment. That is because the phenomena of interest are influenced by (1) human values and the individual's state of mind, (2) the unique nature of the situation, which is usually not static, and (3) historical and sociocultural factors (which are not very predictable). This introduces variability and uncertainty (into our premises) and is the reason we characterize the empirical rules or principles of behavioral science as probabilistic assertions (rather than as universal laws). For example, the Harlows also found that "young monkeys become attached to other young monkeys" (descriptive empirical principle) and that "male monkeys become more forceful with age and female monkeys become more passive" (relational empirical principle). Such accepted rules are presumed to have a high likelihood of applying to average behavior in monkeys—but any individual monkey *may not* behave like the average monkey.

As a handy summary of what we have said about descriptive, relational, and experimental research, Table 1.2 gives some further examples of empirical principles at each of these levels in three different fields. We see that (1) descrip-

TABLE 1.2
Further examples of empirical principles

Research area	Descriptive	Relational	Experimental
Primate behavior	Baboon groups vary in size from 9 to 185 (DeVore and Hall, 1965)	Baboon groups found at higher elevations tend to have fewer members (DeVore and Hall, 1965)	Monkeys separated from their mothers prefer cloth-covered mother surrogates to wire-mesh-type surrogates (Harlow, 1959)
Behavioral study of obedience	A majority of research subjects were willing to administer an allegedly dangerous level of electric shock to another person when requested to do so by a person in authority (Milgram, 1963)	Research subjects who are more willing to administer electric shocks to other persons report themselves as somewhat more tense during their research participation than do subjects who are less willing to apply electric shocks to others (Milgram, 1965)	Research subjects are less obedient to orders to administer electric shocks to other persons when they are in close rather than remote contact with these persons (Milgram, 1965)
Speech behavior	When people are being interviewed for civil service positions, the length of their utterances tends to be short in duration, with only a few lasting as long as a full minute (Matarazzo, Wiens, and Saslow, 1965)	In interviews with both normal subjects and mental patients, it was found that average speech durations were longest with normals and shortest with the most disturbed patients (Matarazzo, Wiens, and Saslow, 1965)	In interviews with applicants for civil service positions, the length of the applicants' utterances could be approximately doubled simply by the interviewers' approximately doubling the length of their utterances (Matarazzo, Wiens, and Saslow, 1965)

tive rules tell "how things are," (2) relational rules tell "how things are in relation to other things," and (3) experimental rules tell "how things are and how they got to be that way." In each case, the principle is presumed to have a high likelihood of applying to average behavior under the conditions specified.

GOOD RESEARCH PRACTICES

We started out by reflecting on the scientific method as a philosophical outlook. It is fitting that we conclude by saying something about the scientist's own psychological outlook as he or she engages in the practice of research. Judith Hall (1984a), a social psychologist, has listed nine habits or attributes that seem to make for a good researcher and, in turn, for sound scientific practice:

1. *Enthusiasm.* Another wise researcher, Edward C. Tolman, summed this up best: "In the end, the only sure criterion is to have fun" (Tolman, 1959, p. 152.) He did not mean that research is just fun and games, but that the activity of research should be as absorbing as any game requiring skill and concentration that fills the researcher with enthusiasm.

2. *Open-mindedness.* The practice of good research, as we see in the next chapter, requires that the scientist observe with a keen, attentive, inquisitive, and open mind, because many great discoveries are made by accident. The Harlows began to study the influence of different pseudomothers only after discovering that their baby monkeys became very much attached to some soft diapers. Open-mindedness also allows us to learn from our mistakes and from the advice and criticisms offered by others.

3. *Common sense.* There is an axiom of science called the *principle of the drunkard's search:* A drunkard lost his house key and began searching for it under a street lamp even though he had dropped the key some distance away. Asked why he didn't look where he had dropped it, he replied, "There is more light here!" This principle teaches that all the book learning in the world cannot replace good sense in the planning and conduct of research. Much effort is lost or vitiated when the researcher fails to use common sense and looks in a convenient place, but not in the most likely place, for the answers to his or her research questions.

4. *Role-taking ability.* Think of yourself as the user of the research, not just as the person who has generated it. In order to anticipate criticisms, researchers must be able to cast themselves in the role of the critic or objective observer. The subjects being studied constitute yet another group inextricably connected with the research, and their unique role is part and parcel of the conclusions to be reached. It is important to be able to empathize with them and to examine the research procedures and results from this subjective viewpoint.

5. *Inventiveness.* Aspects of creativity are required in the good researcher. The most crucial is the ability to develop good hypotheses, which we discuss again

in the next chapter. But inventiveness also encompasses other aspects of sound scientific practice: finding solutions to problems of financial resources, laboratory space, equipment, recruitment and scheduling of research participants; responding to emergencies during the conduct of research; finding new ways to analyze data, if called for; and coming up with convincing interpretations of results.

6. *Confidence in one's own judgment.* Tolman also said, "It seems to me that very often major new scientific insights have come when the scientist . . . has been shaken out of his up-until-then approved scientific rules. . . . Since all the sciences, and especially psychology, are still immersed in such tremendous realms of the uncertain and the unknown, the best that any individual scientist, especially any psychologist, can do seems to be to follow his own gleam and his own bent, however inadequate they may be" (Tolman, 1959, pp. 93, 152).

7. *Consistency and care about details.* Taking pride in one's work will provide a constructive attitude with which to approach what might seem like the relentless detail work involved in doing good research. There is no substitute for accuracy and the hours of care needed to keep complete records, organize and analyze data accurately, state facts precisely, and proofread carefully.

8. *Ability to communicate.* Whether or not one subscribes to the notion that writing is an "unnatural act" (as procrastinators joke), the ability to communicate is basic to the practice of good research. It has been stated, "The literature of science, a permanent record of the communication between scientists, is also the history of science: a record of truth, of observations and opinions, of hypotheses that have been ignored or have been found wanting or have withstood the test of further observation and experiment. Science is a continuing endeavor in which the end of one investigation may be the starting point for another. *Scientists must write,* therefore, so that their discoveries may be known to others" (Barrass, 1978, p. 25).

9. *Honesty.* Scientists respect integrity and scholarship, and abhor dishonesty and sloppiness. However, there is evidence that fraud in science is not uncommon and exists in many parts of the scientific community, e.g., "rigged" experiments, the presentation of faked results (Bridgstock, 1982). As a consequence, various institutions, including leading scientific organizations, are currently seeking ways of policing the scientific community for fraud and misconduct (see American Association for the Advancement of Science, 1988). Fraud is devastating to science, because it undermines the basic respect for the literature on which the advancement of science depends (Koshland, 1988).

CHAPTER 2

DEVELOPMENT AND TESTING OF RESEARCH IDEAS

DISCOVERY AND JUSTIFICATION IN SCIENCE

In the behavioral sciences there are a number of distinctive theories and hypotheses that researchers have formulated to arrive at a rational comprehension of the psychological world in which we live. In this chapter we are concerned with the logic and rules governing the development and testing of these research ideas—ideas that have been characterized as "happy guesses" and "felicitous strokes of inventive talent" (see Grinnell, 1987). By tradition, these two processes—the development and the testing of ideas for research—are also called "discovery" and "justification" by philosophers of science.

In general, *discovery* refers to the origin, creation, or invention of research ideas in the form of, derived from, or inspired by theories and hypotheses. The philosophers of science make three further distinctions regarding what are viewed as three (not necessarily discrete or invariant) steps in this process (Kordig, 1978). The first step, called *initial thinking,* is the point at which the scientist "hits upon" an idea. The idea may be quite vague and difficult to articulate, and may involve introspection, hunches, and intuition. In step 2, *plausibility,* the scientist thinks about whether the idea is worthy of further consideration and testing, i.e., whether there are plausible reasons to support that initial ideal as valid. In step 3, *acceptability,* the scientist accepts the plausibility of the idea and proceeds to mold it into a testable theory or hypothesis for empirical confrontation.

The term *justification* refers in general to the evaluation, defense, and confirmation of the scientist's research ideas. In behavioral science this process traditionally involves *statistical significance testing,* i.e., the use of statistics and probabilities to evaluate a data base of relevant observations in the real world. In the field of psychology it appears to involve one or two further steps for many researchers as they gradually develop their own level of confidence in the research observations (Nelson, Rosenthal, and Rosnow, 1986). In step 1 (the traditional step), confidence is initially earned by the rejectability of what is termed a "null hypothesis" (defined later in this chapter), with particular attention paid to a level of probability that serves as the basis of that decision. In step 2 (which is newer and not yet traditional), given a level of probability low enough to ensure confidence in step 1, the scientist's confidence is increased by the practical importance of the observed results as reflected by the magnitude of the effect. In the third step (which is taken only if the null hypothesis is not rejected in step 1), the scientist considers what is called the "power of the statistical test" (also defined later) used to assess the data base.

As we will see in a moment, while justification is governed by an explicit set of rules, in the process of "discovering" theories and hypotheses almost anything goes (see Stanovich, 1986).

NATURE OF THEORIES AND HYPOTHESES

What do the terms *theory* and *hypothesis* mean in science? In what ways are theories and hypotheses similar, and in what ways are they different? Both questions can be best answered by an illustration.

In the field of social psychology, the study of attributions is concerned with how people explain the causes of interpersonal events. The distinguished theorist Fritz Heider originally argued that people have a "commonsense" psychology by which they explain the significance of causal relationships in everyday life (Heider, 1944, 1958). One goal of this explaining is to assign responsibility for the perceived causal relationships: "Was it my fault or yours?" or "Did he intend to hurt me or not?" Heider noted that people will attribute behavior either to external causes (such as the weather) or to internal causes (such as personality traits and moods). There would seem to be two alternatives: you can attribute the occurrence to an external event (e.g., you might tell your friend that you were late because you were caught in a traffic jam), or you can attribute it to an internal event (e.g., you might tell your friend that you forgot the time).

Led by two later theorists, Edward Jones and Harold Kelley, the social psychologists who study the significance of *causal attributions* have formulated a number of specific hypotheses. For example, Jones and Nisbett (1972) speculated on the ways that people change their preferences for attributions depending on who is being judged. When we ourselves are "on the spot," we should tend to attribute responsibility for our actions to the situation, especially if we have behaved questionably. When we make attributions to others, however, we should tend to place emphasis on those others (the "actors"). Underlying these two hypotheses is a theory that asserts that we literally do not *see* ourselves as actors when we behave; we see only whatever is around us. When we watch others, our attention is focused on the persons and not on their surroundings.

This example suggests two ways in which theories and hypotheses differ from one another. First, a theory is like a large-scale map, with the different areas representing general principles and the connections between them being sets of logical rules. Hypotheses, on the other hand, are like small sectional maps, which focus only on specific areas glossed over by the larger map. Second, hypotheses (being more focused) are more directly amenable to empirical confrontation.

There are conceptual similarities between theories and hypotheses. First, both range from being very explicit (e.g., "frustration leads to aggression") to very vague (e.g., "something will happen if I frustrate the subjects by interfering with their expectations"). Second, both fall back on hidden assumptions, or regulative principles (Chapter 1). Attribution theory, for instance, proceeds on the principle that human beings are constantly deciding what kinds of traits or attitudes people have (see West and Wicklund, 1980). Third, theories and hypotheses give direction to our observations. By analogy, an eminent professor once told his students, "Take pencil and paper; carefully observe, and write down what you have observed!" They, of course, immediately asked *what* it was he wanted them to observe, because observation needs a chosen object, a definite task, an interest, a point of view, and a problem (Popper, 1934, 1963). Theories and hypotheses, at a molar and a molecular level, select what is to be observed by the researcher.

THE ART OF ORIGINAL DISCOVERY

How do scientists hit upon original ideas that can then form the basis of theories and hypotheses? William McGuire (1973, 1976) has identified a number of different situations in which an inventive research idea first saw the light of day.

One source of ideas listed by McGuire is the *intensive case study* situation, in which the researcher carefully documents certain variables or conditions as a prerequisite for theoretical analysis. Raymond Firth, an anthropologist, spent time in a Polynesian community watching and recording the everyday activities of people. From this intensive case study, he developed the theory that gossip is not "idle" talk, but is purposive communication directed at the achievement of concrete goals in the community (Firth 1956). Other studies of gossiping have confirmed that, indeed, it is both functional and purposive: it is described as an exchange process in which a message is traded for specific "social commodities" such as esteem, affection, attention, information, and so forth (e.g., Foa and Foa, 1974; Levin and Arluke, 1987; Paine, 1970; Rosnow and Georgoudi, 1985).

Another source of original ideas is the *paradoxical incident* situation, i.e., a situation that exhibits a contradictory nature. Psychologists Bibb Latané and John Darley were puzzled by contradictory aspects of the circumstances surrounding a lurid murder in the Queens section of New York City. A nurse was coming home from work at 3 A.M. when she was set upon by a man who stabbed her repeatedly. More than three dozen of her neighbors came to their windows to see what was happening. However, not one of them went to her aid when they heard her cries of terror, even though it took the stalker over a half hour to murder her. The psychologists were struck by the paradox that, even though there were so many opportunities, no one bothered to call the police. They wondered whether the large number of onlookers could be the key to explaining these failures of intervention. The reason why *so many* people failed to intervene, they theorized, was that each individual believed someone else was likely to respond. They called this relationship the "diffusion of responsibility," and studied it experimentally (Latané and Darley, 1970).

A third source of original ideas noted by McGuire is the *metaphor* (words or phrases applied to a situation they do not literally denote) that stimulates our thinking. Expressions like "her life was an uphill climb" and "he is between a rock and a hard place" are examples of metaphors: each suggests a comparison with another situation. Whether used in everyday speech or in science, such comparisons can often bring the situation to life by making us think about one thing in terms of another (Billow, 1977). For example, McGuire developed a program of research based on the analogy of "inoculating" people against the effects of harmful propaganda. He hypothesized, and then demonstrated empirically, that exposing people to a small fragment of the propaganda would stimulate them to build up their defenses against any larger doses in the future (McGuire, 1964).

The *rule of thumb* refers to a fourth source of original ideas, in which a rule or procedure based on practice or experience (rather than on scientific knowledge) becomes the inspiration for a hypothesis or theory. Yale University researcher Irving Janis and his coworkers were inspired by the sales representative's rule of thumb: soften up clients by discussing business over a good lunch (Dabbs and Janis, 1965; Janis, Kaye, and Kirschner, 1965). Hungry Yale students were given soda pop and peanuts at the same time that they were given a persuasive message to read. Results were that they became more receptive to the persuasive message, in comparison with a control group that read it but did not receive any soda pop or peanuts. The empirical relationship has been called the "things go better with Coke" effect.

A fifth source of ideas flows from the effort to *account for conflicting results*. Robert Zajonc neatly integrated a body of conflicting data to explain the psychological effects upon one's work of the presence of other people, his *social facilitation hypothesis* (Zajonc, 1965). Prior results showed that performance in humans and animals improves when passive observers are present, but other results showed it becoming poorer in the presence of others. To tie together the conflicting data, Zajonc explained that a high drive level causes people to give the dominant response, i.e., one fixed by or resulting from habit. When the task is familiar and well-learned, the dominant response is usually the correct one. When the task is new, the correct response is usually less likely than the incorrect response. He reasoned that the presence of others must serve to increase the subject's drive level, and the increase in drive then leads to dominant responses. Thus the presence of others will inhibit the learning of new responses and facilitate the performance of well-learned responses. The practical implication for exams on material that can be learned by rote would seem to be that (1) a student should study the new material alone, preferably in an isolated place, but (2) after the material is well-learned, the student should take the exam with as many other students as possible, preferably on a stage before a large audience.

The variety of situations indicated above suggests that the different circumstances in which research ideas are discovered is virtually limitless. Creativity does not necessarily involve great leaps of imagination or the need to be possessed of some special characteristic, called "genius" (Weisberg, 1986). It might be compared to the energy that excites a neuron in the human nervous system. The energy used to excite the neuron is nonspecific. The same nerve impulse occurs whether you hit your finger with a hammer, slam it in a car door, or have it bitten by a dog. So long as the excitation is there, the result will be the same— ignition. In science, it also seems to make little difference as to what circumstances provide the inspiration to light the fuse of creativity. So long as the situation is sufficiently stimulating to excite thought in the scientist, there will be "ignition."

SERENDIPITY AS A SOURCE OF IDEAS

Luck, as much as planning and determination, can also play a significant role in the creative process, in everyday life as in science. One day in May 1984, a young artist named J. S. G. Boggs was sitting in a Chicago diner having a doughnut and coffee and doodling on a napkin (Weschler, 1988). As the waitress kept refilling his cup, the doodle evolved into an abstracted $1 bill. Fascinated, the waitress asked if she could buy it, causing Boggs to wonder why anyone would want a greasy napkin covered with coffee stains and perspiration. "Tell you what," he said, "I'll pay you for my doughnut and coffee with this drawing." To his astonishment, she took the "dollar" and gave him a dime's change. Inspired by this lucky incident, Boggs began a career of drawing fairly exact representations of existing denominations of actual currency and successfully "spending" his drawings for goods and services.

When luck plays the decisive role in a discovery, the term for it is *serendipity*. It comes from Serendip, once the name for Sri Lanka; it was claimed that the three princes of Serendip were always making discoveries by good luck. Serendipity has often played a decisive role in science (Cannon, 1945; Medawar, 1969, 1979; Merton, 1968). A famous case occurred in 1967, when pulsars (pulsating radio sources) were discovered at Cambridge University, in the United Kingdom. A research student, whose task it was to analyze charts of extraterrestrial noises, noticed a "bit of scruff" in the sky. At first she thought it was an anomaly (accidental deviation), but then noticed a pattern. What she had observed by luck were the remnants of rapidly spinning neutron stars that resulted from the collapse of stars in supernova explosions. The breakthrough might never have been made at this time had it not been for the student's watchful eye and lucky finding (Dean, 1977).

Murray Sidman has mentioned another example of serendipity in behavioral science, in the behind-the-scenes story of a series of experiments that came to be known as the "ulcer project" (Sidman, 1960). Psychologist Joseph V. Brady, working at Walter Reed Army Hospital, was running experiments with monkeys, using long-term conditioning, electric shocks, food reinforcements, and brain stimulation. There was an unusually high mortality rate among the monkeys, which he might have continued to treat simply as an unavoidable problem were it not for a lucky discovery. A pathologist, R.W. Porter, was working at Walter Reed and, when he heard about the large number of deaths, asked Brady for permission to do a postmortem on the next five monkeys that became available. During the next few months, Porter would occasionally appear in Brady's office holding a piece of freshly excised monkey gut. Somewhere in the tissue there would be a clear round hole, which (Porter explained to Brady) was a perforated ulcer.

One day, Porter remarked that of several hundred monkeys he had examined before coming to Walter Reed, not one had shown any sign of a normally occurring ulcer. Brady thought about Porter's accidental finding, and it changed the course of Brady's research. He asked, Could the ulcers have had something to do with the role the monkeys were obliged to play in the stress situation? He then began doing experiments in which monkeys were subjected to electric shock avoidance training and were paired with other monkeys who received the same shocks but without the opportunity to avoid them. When the monkeys were finally sacrificed, there were the stomach ulcers in the monkeys who had been called on to make "executive" decisions in the stress situation, but the "subordinate" monkeys showed no unusual pathology (Brady, 1958; Brady, Porter, Conrad, and Mason, 1958). Porter's serendipitous finding led to research to pinpoint the precise factors influencing ulcers in this situation, and later to studies leading to additional empirical data and new explanations by Brady and others.

CRITERIA OF GOOD RESEARCH IDEAS

How do scientists distinguish good research ideas from not-so-good ones? Traditionally, three criteria are used to assess the "goodness" of theories and hypotheses: (1) correspondence with reality, (2) coherence and parsimony, and (3) falsifiability.

The first criterion refers to the extent to which the idea agrees with what is accepted as true. It is usually assumed that speculative ideas that correspond most closely with accepted truths will have a higher *payoff potential*, i.e., can be expected to be more readily validated. Unfortunately, some researchers have spent weary and scientifically profitless years pursuing some pet research idea that, while it seemed plausible to the researchers at the time, later proved groundless (see Medawar, 1979). How can one tell whether an idea will pay off? There is no sure way, but scientists use common sense, critical feedback from respected colleagues, and a familiarity with the relevant literature to try to ensure that their efforts will not be wasted ones.

Scientists also usually act on the strong presumption that speculative ideas that contradict accepted truths should be disregarded. However, as long ago as the seventeenth century, Francis Bacon noted that accepted "truths" are not always actually true (e.g., the classical notion of the Earth as the center of the universe). In this case they can instead act as blinders, and not increase the payoff potential but rather limit the chance for a scientific breakthrough. Bacon called these invalid accepted truths "phantoms" and underscored how they may cloud our minds and make it very difficult for even valid ideas to penetrate.

The twentieth century has seen its versions of such phantoms, such as the myths and superstitions about the occult, which are deeply rooted in the past. In science, too, there are phantoms in the form of certain facts and theories previously learned, common sense and hearsay, methodological biases, and professional norms, which when we fail to realize their limitations can also be misleading (see Barber, 1961; Beveridge, 1957; Hurvich, 1969; Mahoney, 1976). To illustrate: Michael Polanyi (1963) described an experience of his, in 1914, when he published his theory of the adsorption (adhesion) of gases on solids. Within a few years of its publication he had gotten what he considered to be convincing empirical evidence to support the theory, but the then-current conception of atomic forces made his findings unacceptable. Invited to state his position publicly, Polanyi was chastised by Albert Einstein for showing a "total disregard" for what was then "known" about the structure of matter. Polanyi, of course, was later credited with having been correct, and given the Nobel prize. In evaluating the payoff potential of research ideas, it is essential not to be blinded by phantoms that masquerade as truths.

Second are the joint criteria of coherence and parsimony. *Coherence* refers to whether the idea "sticks together," and *parsimony* to how "sparing" or "frugal" it is. A research idea should not be any more complicated than necessary. A parsimonious idea is one that has been subjected to the scientist's intellectual ruminative and winnowing process to "cut away" what is superfluous. This winnowing process employs *Occam's razor*, after William of Occam, the fourteenth-century Franciscan philosopher, who insisted that we "cut away" what is unnecessary or unwieldy. "What can be explained on fewer principles is explained needlessly by more," he stated.

Another word of caution is necessary, however. It is important to realize that Occam's razor is not a description of nature (because nature is often very complicated) but is instead a prescription for science. It is important not to cut off too much—i.e., "beards" but not "chins." In the analysis of data, Occam's razor has been mistakenly used to justify the dictum that the analysis should be carried no further than is necessary to obtain a simple result. The analysis of experience is not necessarily connected in fact or in logic only with simplicity (see Battig, 1962; Luchins and Luchins, 1965).

The third criterion, *falsifiability* (refutability), is the most important one in the eyes of most scientists. It was proposed by Karl Popper, a leading realist philosopher, who argued that a theory or hypothesis not refutable by any conceivable observation is nonscientific (Popper, 1934). The reason, he argued, is that it is possible for those with a fertile imagination to discover "facts" or "observations" to validate almost any claims. Imagine that humans were theorized to be direct descendants of extraterrestrials who, thousands of years ago, arrived in flying saucers to colonize Earth. The problem with this "theory" from a scientific point of view is that it is not refutable by any conceivable observation. On the other hand, it should not be too difficult for an active intellect to uncover or fabricate all sorts of previously unexplained "data" to validate the earthly existence of intelligent creatures from outer space. In the same way, for example, astrology is the "prophecy that never fails," because people believe what they want to believe and interpret the prophecies only in ways that support their biases and gratify their superstitions (see Bunge, 1982; Weimann, 1982).

FALSIFICATIONISM AND THE BUCKET THEORY OF SCIENCE

Before Popper proposed the concept of falsifiability, the *logical positivist* view reigned supreme. Developed under British empiricists during the fourteenth to seventeenth centuries, it was stated as "positivism" by the nineteenth-century social philosopher Auguste Comte and later propounded by followers of the Vienna Circle (Carnap, Schlick, and others) as "logical empiricism" (Simon, 1972). It entered behavioral science in the ninteenth century and continued strong up until rather recently. Indeed we still find strong remnants of positivist philosophy in some areas of psychology and other fields (Rosnow, 1981). As one writer has stated, however, "the word 'positivist,' like the word 'bourgeois,' has become more a derogatory epithet than a useful descriptive concept, and consequently has been largely stripped of whatever agreed meaning it may once have had" (Giddens, 1974, p. ix).

Essentially, positivism was developed to provide a new foundation for knowledge on the basis of Cartesian skepticism (*cogito ergo sum*: "I think, therefore I am"—the basic philosophical principle of René Descartes). The idea was to use sensory experience as a positive basis of knowledge that "cannot be doubted" (Stockman, 1983). It is only by shoring up our explanations with empirical facts that we can arrive at an exact understanding of objective reality, it was argued by the positivists.

In 1919–1920, while still a student, Popper was led to certain "inescapable conclusions," which he reformulated as a profoundly antipositivist view, now know as *falsificationism*. Interestingly, he originally perceived his own ideas as almost trivial and did not realize their full scientific implications (or their philosophical significance) until a fellow student suggested that they should be published. In the 1940s, he presented a lecture in which he compared the logical positivist view of science to a bucket into which the wine of knowledge was presumed to flow pure and simple from patiently and industriously gathered facts (the *bucket theory of science*). The problem with this theory, he argued, is that it is possible to find empirical facts to support even the most ridiculous claims.

To illustrate: Franz Mesmer, an eighteenth-century Viennese physician, observed that his patients who touched a magnetized wand or tube during a seance immediately fell into a trancelike sleep. Believing that, somehow, an invisible "fluid" had literally rearranged parts of their brains, he claimed that "magnetic current" was the basis of this mysterious phenomenon. He was treating a young female patient, nicknamed "Franzl," who was suffering from a form of hysteria (fainting, temporary paralysis, agonizing aches and pains). From observing the periodicity of her attacks, he believed it plausible to stem their ebb and flow by having her swallow a preparation containing iron and then placing magnets of assorted shapes and sizes on different parts of her body. Just as he expected, by changing the "magnetic current" inside her body he could "control" her symptoms for several hours at a time.

Antoine Lavoisier, the great eighteenth-century French chemist, said, "The human mind gets creased into a way of seeing things. Those who have envisaged nature according to a certain point of view during much of their career rise only with difficulty to new ideas" (see Hurvich, 1969). So it seems with Mesmer, who then found that he could produce the same effects without the use of iron magnets. Touching a piece of cloth or wood, his patients immediately became "magnetized" (or so he perceived). They were magnetized because he, Mesmer, had touched them, and therefore *he* was the source of "animal magnetic" energy. A patient who had suffered hearing loss during a thunderstorm was miraculously cured when Mesmer held his hands over the patient's ears. Another patient lost his stomachache when Mesmer gently stroked away the spasms. Of course, *something* was happening, even though Mesmer's explanation was rather farfetched. What he had observed, we now realize, was the powerful effect of suggestibility on the human mind (Buranelli, 1975; Hilgard, 1980).

The problem with Mesmer's pseudoscientific theory is that it was not "risky," i.e., falsifiable by any observations he would accept as relevant. Popper noted the Marxist theory of history, psychoanalysis, and Alfred Adler's individual psychology as his own pet examples of the bucket theory approach to justification. He writes, "As for Adler, I was much impressed by a personal experience. Once, in 1919, I reported to him a case which to me did not seem particularly Adlerian, but which he found no difficulty in analyzing in terms of his theory of inferiority feelings, although he had not even seen the child. Slightly shocked, I asked him how he could be so sure. 'Because of my thousandfold experience,' he replied; whereupon I could not help saying, 'And with this new case, I suppose your experience has become thousand-and-one-fold'" (Popper, 1963).

Popper's falsificationism has for some years been the standard in science against which other views of the justification of knowledge are compared (Simon, 1983)—although in philosophy of science, it is considered but one of several alternative views that have superseded the outmoded approach of the logical positivist position. To be considered scientific, according to falsificationism, conjectures must be stated in such a way that they can, if incorrect, be falsified by some finite set of observations. If one theory, T', is more falsifiable than another theory, T, and if T' has survived more severe testing than has T, scientists will presumably conclude that T' is a better theory than T (see Kordig, 1978).

CONVENTIONALISM AND THE LIMITS OF FALSIFICATION

Critics such as Pierre Duhem—whose position is known as *conventionalism*—make the argument that theories evolve by convention, on the basis of considerations like simplicity, not merely on the basis of their ability to withstand falsification. In fact, crucial experiments are impossible, he argues; there can be no such thing as a completely decisive falsifying test because when a refutation occurs, it merely tells us that the general formulation needs to be adjusted, not that it needs to be discarded (Duhem, 1954). This argument, called the *Duhem-Quine thesis* (after the modern philosopher, W. V. O. Quine), essentially rejects the idea that a theory can be logically refuted by any body of evidence. Popper, on the other hand, clearly believes that new theories simply replace old theories, rather than being additions to old theories. The evolution of one famous theory in psychology—Leon Festinger's *cognitive dissonance theory*—would seem to support Duhem's viewpoint (see Greenwald and Ronis, 1978).

Festinger got his initial idea in the 1950s, when he was puzzled as to why people in a village several miles away from an earthquake in India were swamped in rumors of impending disaster (Festinger, 1957). It did not make sense, because the rumors predicting calamity were being spread by those who had not been harmed by the earthquake. To explain it, Festinger argued that, having no concrete grounds for their anxiety, people had to manufacture reasons in order to be consistent in their thinking and reduce their cognitive dissonance. This drive, dissonance reduction, then became the basis of one of the most influential theories in social psychology and, in the 1960s, stimulated an enormous amount of research to test its specific claims. Presumably, the dissonance produced by discrepant cognitions will function as would any biological drive: if we are hungry, we do something to reduce our discomfort; if we experience cognitive dissonance, we also do something to reduce our discomfort.

Hundreds of experiments followed, resulting in a series of revisions of Festinger's original theory. As a result, it is now theorized that being responsible for one's actions is essential for dissonance reduction to occur. But how could earthquake survivors feel responsible for surviving? The disaster must have come as a complete surprise to them; their survival was essentially beyond their control. The theory of cognitive dissonance, as it is currently formulated, can no longer explain the situation that inspired Festinger in the first place!

Accepting the tenets of falsificationism, most scientists would agree (1) that a theory (to be considered "scientific") must be stated so that it can be falsified by a finite set of observations and (2) that a scientific theory can only be falsified, never proved correct. Consistent with the tenets of conventionalism, most would also agree (3) that (in actuality) scientific theories can evolve as additions to, as well as replacements of, outmoded formulations. And finally, they would add (4) that if a hypothesis does not receive support, it means the theory in its current form *may* be wrong, (5) that if a theory is repeatedly not supported, despite every attempt by researchers to produce good tests of the theory and powerful research designs, then it should be discarded or revised, but (6) that if a hypothesis based on a theory *is* supported, the theory on which it is based is not proved to be correct, because another theory (waiting to be discovered) might account for all the existing results.

DEFINING TERMS

In the final step of discovery, the precise meanings of the terms to be used in theories and hypotheses are specified as a prerequisite to molding the initial hunches into testable research ideas. Two kinds of definitions are traditionally employed: operational and theoretical. An *operational definition* (a concept proposed by the physicist Percy W. Bridgman) assigns the meaning of a term on the empirical basis of the conditions or operations needed to measure or to manipulate it. A *theoretical definition* assigns the meaning of a term more abstractly.

For example, the term "aggression" has been theoretically defined by one investigator, Saul Rosenzweig, as "generic assertiveness which includes both constructive and destructive behaviors" of various kinds (Rosenzweig, 1977). He has also proposed his own operational definition: scores on the Rosenzweig picture-frustration test. The test consists of a series of 24 cartoonlike pictures depicting everyday frustrating situations. The figure at the left of each picture is shown saying certain words which either describe the frustration of the individual on the right or which of themselves actually frustrate that individual. The figure on the right is always shown with a blank caption box (balloon) above his or her head, and the subject is instructed to write in the balloon the first reply of that figure that occurs to him or her. The responses are then scored to reveal the type and degree of aggressive personality of the subject (Rosenzweig, 1981).

In proposing a distinction between operational and theoretical definitions, Bridgman argued that in science the "concept [the term requiring definition] is synonymous with the corresponding set of operations" (1927, p. 5). Subsequently, he concluded that not every concept can be, or need be, defined in directly empirical terms (Bridgman, 1945). For example, physicists speak meaningfully of the "weight of an object while it is falling" even though the only instruments for measuring its weight would require that its motion be stopped (see Easley, 1971; Easley and Tatsuoka, 1968). Theoretical definitions do not force thinking into a rigid empirical mold or lead to abandonment of useful terms that may not be completely definable empirically (see Cronbach and Meehl, 1955; Cronbach and Quirk, 1971).

Aggression is a good example of a concept that many people continue to find hard to pin down operationally. Table 2.1 gives various other definitions of aggression, but all imply motive or intent as a necessary defining characteristic (e.g., "intended to inflict pain," "goal of harming or injuring," "drives toward change"). How can we objectively measure motive or intent empirically? We cannot enter people's intentions in order to measure their motivations directly. We can ask people to describe their motives and feelings, but there is no guarantee they will not withhold sensitive information or lie to us when responding on a picture-frustration test. Some researchers attempt to circumvent this difficulty by defining aggression in very general terms: "the delivery of some measurable injury to another organism" (Baenninger, 1980)—but, it could be argued, that would include surgeons and dentists as aggressive, and leave out aggressive threat displays of the kind that some comparative psychologists study (e.g., threat displays in Siamese fighting fish). Another definition states, "the actual or threatened delivery of either physical or psychological injury to another organism— to be aggressive there must be conscious or unconscious intent to injure" (Baenninger, 1988). By this notion, an aggressor need not actually do anything, and the victim need not show any actual effect of the interaction (or even be aware of the aggression).

TABLE 2.1
Some definitions of aggression

"A response intended to inflict pain or discomfort" (Averill, 1982, p. 30)

"Any form of behavior directed toward the goal of harming or injuring another living being who is motivated to avoid such treatment" (R. A. Baron, 1977, p. 7)

"Drives toward change, even against the will of others" (Galtung, 1972, p. 85)

"The fighting instinct in beast and man which is directed *against* members of the same species" (Lorenz, 1971, p. ix)

"The use or threat of force, in territory not clearly one's own, without clear evidence that a majority of the emotionally involved people in that territory want such intervention" (White, 1984, p. 14)

"Any and every activity of an animal that is directed toward another animal and that inflicts partial or complete destruction upon that animal or that is associated with a high probability of so doing" (Zillman, 1979, p. 16)

The logical positivist approach, which dominated behavioral science for decades, led to a search for universal, context-free laws and to the use of context-stripping definitions (see Mishler, 1979). However, as illustrated, trying to describe aggression in context-stripping definitions is like trying to imagine smiles alongside of faces—quite impossible (see Bhaskar, 1983). Indeed, world bodies—from the 1915 Congress of Vienna, The Hague and Versailles peace conferences, to the United Nations—have forever struggled with the definition of aggression. One French law expert, after exhaustive review, concluded that he was like the person told to define an elephant; he did not know how to do it, but he knew it was something big (Shenker, 1971). Aggression, like any other aspect of human behavior, does not simply occur in a vacuum, but is like a message that takes its meaning from the total context in which it occurs (see Crabb and Rosnow, 1988; Rosnow and Georgoudi, 1986). The definition of aggression must also be circular, because any definition is basically a verbal equation in which the term on the left of the equals sign must be *the same* as the definition on the right of the equals sign (Kimble, 1989). In practice, by using multiple operational and theoretical definitions, scientists attempt to zero in on the concept of interest (e.g., Houts, Cook, and Shadish, Jr., 1986), and they would concede that "circular definitions are not a scientific sin" (Kimble, 1989, p. 495).

In the examples in Table 2.1, we see some of the definitions of aggression as stated in prose form (phrases and sentences). Scientific definitions can also sometimes be stated in the form of an equation or quantitative equality (e.g., $PV = nRT$, the definition of the ideal gas law in physics, where $P =$ pressure, $V =$ volume, $n =$ number of moles of gas, $R =$ universal gas constant, and $T =$ temperature). In psychology, a classical example was Clark L. Hull's equations for conditioning or learning, which defined the "habit strength" of stimulus-response connections in symbolic quantitative terms. Another approach to prose definition is to define the various types in terms of a prose typology; Table 2.2 gives such an illustration. It shows one researcher's definitions of the

TABLE 2.2
A typology of aggression to show all possible classes of aggressive behaviors in humans

		Physical aggression	Verbal aggression
Active aggression	Direct aggression	Punching someone	Insulting someone
	Indirect aggression	Playing a practical joke on someone	Maliciously gossiping about someone
Passive aggression	Direct aggression	Blocking someone's passage	Refusing to talk to someone
	Indirect aggression	Refusing to do some necessary task	Refusing to give one's consent

Source: A. H. Buss, "Aggression Pays," in J. L. Singer (ed.), *The Control of Aggression and Violence,* Academic Press, New York, 1971. Adapted by permission of the author and Academic Press.

various types of aggression that he hypothesized, and avoids the problem of trying to reduce this complex concept to a single phrase or sentence (Buss, 1971). Models such as this one can be developed intuitively, or developed empirically by using quantitative methods such as multidimensional scaling and factor analysis (discussed in Chapter 24).

THE NULL HYPOTHESIS IN SIGNIFICANCE TESTING

Traditionally, statistics and probabilities (statistical significance testing) are employed to evaluate the data base the researcher has collected to provide justification for his or her theory or hypothesis. This testing helps the researcher, as well as the research consumers, to decide between (1) believing that a relationship between two (or more) variables exists in the population from which sample data are drawn and (2) believing that no such relationship exists in the population from which sample data are drawn. Critics argue that statistical significance testing carries too much of the burden of scientific inference in some of the behavioral sciences (e.g., psychology) and is credited with properties it does not have (see Bakan, 1967; Danziger, 1985; Pollard and Richardson, 1987; Rosenthal and Rubin, 1985). We will look at two ancillary criteria for appraising sample data: statistical power and effect size.

An analogy (suggested by H. Wainer, in Lana and Rosnow, 1972, pp. 434–437) illustrates the basic logic: Suppose you were walking along the street and a shady character approached and whispered he had a quarter to sell for only five dollars. He claimed this was a quarter with some extraordinary properties. When properly used, this quarter could win you fame and fortune because it does not come up heads and tails with equal regularity. Instead, one outcome is more likely than the other. A shrewd bettor could, when flipping the coin, simply predict the alternative that occurred more frequently, he tells you. Would you believe him? To help you in your decision you could test whether the probability of heads equals the probability of tails. Suppose you flip the coin once and a head appears. You flip the coin again, and again it comes up heads. Suppose you flip the coin 10 times and each time it comes up heads. Would you believe him at this point? If you answered "yes," then would you believe him if after 10 tosses there were 9 heads and 1 tail? This is the essential problem in significance testing. We can be as stringent as we like in setting rejection criteria, but we may eventually pay for this decision by rejecting what we perhaps should not.

The classical ideas involved in this process evolved out of the arguments of different statisticians (for discussions, see Gigerenzer, 1987; Gigerenzer and Murray, 1987; Gigerenzer, Swijtink, Porter, Daston, Beatty, and Krüger, 1989), and let us state more precisely these ideas. Initially we stated a hypothesis—that the quarter was fair. We then matched this hypothesis with an alternative one, which was that the coin was not fair. The "experiment" we performed was to determine which of the two alternatives we could not logically reject. In classical statistical terms we would state the two alternatives as follows:

H_0 (called the *null hypothesis*): The coin is fair (the probability of heads equals the probability of tails).

H_1 (called the *alternate hypothesis*): The coin is not fair (the probability of heads is not equal to the probability of tails).

Note that the two hypotheses we propose to test must be *mutually exclusive*; i.e., when one is true the other must be false. And we see that they must be *exhaustive*; i.e., they must include all possible occurrences. Experimenters who do significance testing are usually interested in testing the specific H_0 against a general H_1. They will try to see if they can reject H_0 and yet be reasonably sure that when they do, they will not be wrong in doing so. In our example, this testing would presumably lead us to buy the quarter from the entrepreneur—assuming we felt no pangs of conscience about gambling with a crooked coin. We come back to this example in a moment, but there are two other important terms: type I error and type II error.

TYPE I AND TYPE II ERRORS

By analogy, the college admissions officer when faced with a candidate for his or her school must decide between two alternatives: the prospective student can do the work required in the school and will succeed if admitted (the null hypothesis), or the student cannot do the required work and will flunk out (the alternate hypothesis). If the admissions officer rejects a student and the student could have done well, he commits what is called a *type I error*; that is, the null hypothesis is true. If, on the other hand, the admissions officer accepts a student and the student flunks out, he has committed a *type II error*; that is, the null hypothesis is false. In statistics the probability of making a type I error is called by a number of different names: *alpha, significance level, p value*. The probability of making a type II error is known by one name: *beta*.

Let us return to the street entrepreneur and examine his coin with this newfound knowledge. Let us say that we do not want to be wrong more than 1 time out of 20. We then flip the coin 9 times and get 8 heads and 1 tail. What are the chances of obtaining these results if the null hypothesis is true? If this probability is less than .05, then we shall reject the null; if not, then we shall not.

Keep in mind at this point that if we had obtained all heads, all tails, or 8 tails and 1 head, we would consider them in the same light, because all these events will occur with equal or smaller probability than the obtained result. The probability of all heads (and also all tails) is $(1/2)^9$, or 1/512; the probability of having exactly 1 head (or 1 tail) is 9/512. The reason this event is 9 times as likely as the event of having all heads or all tails is that it can occur in 9 different ways, whereas having all heads or all tails can occur in only 1 way. Adding together all the possibilities, we obtain $1/512 + 9/512 + 1/512 + 9/512 = .039$ (rounded to .04). Because this is less than .05, we may reject the null hypothesis and be sure that we would be incorrect not more than 40 times in 1,000 (on average) were we to repeat our 9 tosses that many times.

WEIGHING THE RISKS OF GULLIBILITY AND BLINDNESS

This example is overly simplified to illustrate basic ideas in probability; in behavioral science the researcher is usually interested in more complex questions. For example, experimenters are usually interested in estimating the probability of claiming that two variables are related. The type I error would then be defined as claiming a relationship that truly does not exist, and the type II error would be defined as failing to claim a relationship that truly does exist. The coin example was a descriptive rather than a relational observation inasmuch as there was only one variable, the result of the coin toss. Later in this book, we show how researchers determine probabilities for different statistical tests.

As our example implied, when behavioral scientists do significance testing, they focus on the question "What is the probability of a type I error?" That does not mean they are indifferent to the probability of making a type II error, but the fact is that (in most circumstances) they have traditionally attached greater psychological importance to the risk of making a type I error. In everyday life as well, we often give greater weight to some decision risks as opposed to others. Imagine that a man is being tried for having committed a brutal murder, with hanging the likely penalty if convicted. As a member of the jury, you have to vote on whether he is innocent or guilty of the charges against him. If you vote "guilty" but in fact he is not, you could be sending an innocent man to the gallows. If you vote "innocent" but in fact he is not, you could be turning a murderer loose in the community. Just as these two risks are not usually weighted equally, type I and type II errors are also not weighted equally.

Table 2.3 illustrates an underlying notion in the simplified terms of the shady character with the coin for sale. It characterizes the risk of making a type I error as an inferential mistake involving "gullibility" and that of making a type II error as an inferential mistake involving "blindness to a relationship." Traditionally, scientists believe it is worse to risk being gullible than it is to be blind to a relationship—which the philosophers of science characterize as the "healthy skepticism" of the scientific outlook (see Axinn, 1966; Kaplan, 1964).

In Table 2.4, we see these ideas translated into the scientist's tactical language. Recall that for experimenters the *null hypothesis* refers to the assumption that no "relationship" between two variables is present in the population from which a sample was drawn. The experimenter considers the possibility of making a type I error whenever a true null hypothesis is tested. As this table shows, type I errors occur when researchers mistakenly reject the null hypothesis (by claiming a relationship that does not exist). Type II errors occur when they mistakenly fail to reject the null hypothesis (by failing to claim a relationship that does exist). We will have more to say about this later in this book but it is also essential to understand the role of statistical power and effect size estimation in this process.

TABLE 2.3
Example to illustrate definitions of type I and II errors

	Actual state of affairs	
Your decision	The coin is fair	The coin is not fair
The coin is not fair (i.e., it can win you fame and fortune, since it will not come up heads and tails equally).	Type I error ("gullibility")	No error
The coin is fair (i.e., it cannot win you fame and fortune, since it is an ordinary coin).	No error	Type II error ("blindness")

TABLE 2.4
Implications of the decision to reject or not to reject the null hypothesis

Scientist's decision	Actual state of affairs	
	Null hypothesis is true	Null hypothesis is false
Reject null hypothesis	Type I error (claiming a relationship that does not exist)	No decision error
Do not reject null hypothesis	No decision error	Type II error (failing to claim a relationship that does exist)

STATISTICAL POWER AND EFFECT SIZE

To review, in significance testing we estimate the probability of making a type I error whenever a true null hypothesis is tested. As we show later, scientists do this by computing a statistical test (e.g., t, F, chi-square, Z) the value (or magnitude) of which they enter in a table (see Appendix B for examples) to see the probability that the statistical test result could have been that large or larger if the null hypothesis of no relationship were really true. The larger the test value, the smaller is the probability of making a type I error. In Chapter 15 we discuss t tests in detail, but here it will suffice to say that, given similar conditions of testing, a t test of magnitude 2.4 might run less than a 5 percent risk of false rejection of the null hypothesis (i.e., $p < .05$), but a t test of half this magnitude ($t = 1.2$) might run an approximately 25 percent risk of false rejection of the null hypothesis (i.e., $.20 < p < .30$).

The *effect size* refers to the strength (or magnitude) of the relationship in the population, or the degree of departure from the null hypothesis. This is a valuable piece of information, which allows us to appraise the strength of the evidence about a research hypothesis and guides our judgment about the nature of the next study we might conduct. One reason this information is valuable is that significant statistical tests do not necessarily imply large effects, nor do nonsignificant statistical tests imply small effects. Furthermore, even statistically small effects may be of considerable practical importance.

For example, a major biomedical research study reported in 1988 that heart attack risk in the population is cut by aspirin (Steering Committee of the Physicians' Health Study Research Group, 1988). This conclusion was based on the results of a 5-year study of a sample of 22,071 physicians, approximately half of whom (11,037) were given an ordinary aspirin tablet every other day while the remainder (11,034) were given a placebo. Part of the results of this study are shown in Table 2.5, regarding whether 325 mg of aspirin taken every other day reduces heart attack risk (part A) and mortality after a myocardial infarction (part B).

TABLE 2.5
Aspirin's effect on heart attack
A. Myocardial infarctions in aspirin and placebo conditions

Condition	No heart attack	Heart attack
Aspirin	10,933	104
Placebo	10,845	189

B. Fatal and nonfatal myocardial infarctions

Condition	Lived	Died
Aspirin	99	5
Placebo	171	18

Source: Steering Committee of the Physicians' Health Study Research Group, "Preliminary Report: Findings from the Aspirin Component of the Ongoing Physicians' Health Study," *New England Journal of Medicine,* 1988, vol. 318, pp. 262–264.

Part A shows the number of participants in each condition who did or did not suffer a heart attack. We see that 1.3 percent experienced a heart attack, and this event occurred more frequently in the placebo condition than in the aspirin condition. Testing the statistical significance of these results yields a p value which is *considerably* smaller than .05 (p even much less than .0001), indicating that the results were not a fluke or lucky coincidence. However, the effect size computed on these results is quite small, and would be considered quantitatively "unimpressive" by methodological convention in behavioral science ($r = .03$).

Part B gives a breakdown of the number of participants whose heart attack was fatal or nonfatal. In the aspirin condition 4.8 percent experienced a fatal heart attack, whereas in the placebo condition 9.5 percent experienced a fatal heart attack. It appears that mortality from heart attack decreases by half as a result of a regimen of 325 mg of aspirin taken every other day. This difference is not statistically significant by the customary .05 standard, but it is nearly significant ($p < .08$). The effect size, while nearly three times larger ($r = .08$) than that in part A, would still be labeled as "quite small" by methodological convention in psychology. The lesson? Even a quite small population effect can have great practical benefit when the criterion is who lives and dies.

We also see that sample size seems to have a great deal to do with whether or not we achieve an "acceptable" level of statistical significance. To clarify this relationship it is necessary to understand what is meant by the concept of *statistical power*. Defined as 1 minus beta, statistical power refers to the probability of rejecting the null hypothesis when it is false, and needs rejecting. As we show in this book, for any given statistical test of a null hypothesis (e.g., t, F, chi-square, Z), the power of the statistical test (i.e., the probability of not making a type II error) is determined by (1) the level of risk of drawing a spuriously positive conclusion (i.e., the *p* level), (2) the size of the study (i.e., the sample size), and (3) the effect size. These three factors are so related that when any two of them are known, the third can be determined. Thus, if we know the values for factors 1 and 3, we can easily figure out how big a sample we need to achieve any desired level of statistical power.

INFERENTIAL ERRORS
AND REPLICABILITY

In the next chapter, we shall have something to say about *replicability*, i.e., the ability to repeat or duplicate a research result. Briefly, suppose that researcher Smith conducts an experiment with 80 learning-disabled children: half undergo special training (the experimental group), whereas the others receive no special training (the control group). She reports that the experimental group improved significantly more than the control group (i.e., $p < .05$). Researcher Jones is skeptical about Smith's results and attempts to repeat this experiment with 40 learning-disabled children (20 in the experimental group and 20 in the control group). His results, while in the same direction as Smith's, show alpha greater than 3 in 10 (i.e., $p > .3$), and he reports that Smith's results are unreplicable. That is,

Smith's results	Jones's results
$t(38) = 2.21$	$t(18) = 1.06$
$p < .05$	$p > .3$
$r = .24$	$r = .24$
power = .33	power = .18

Consumers of research relying on *p* values alone to tell them whether Smith's research has been replicated would be seriously misled by Jones's conclusion of nonreplication, because we see the size of effect was identical in both studies ($r = .24$). It appears the major difference is that Smith's sample was large enough to reveal a significant effect at $p < .05$, but Jones's sample was too small to reveal it: Smith was working with nearly double the power as was Jones (.33 vs. .18, respectively).

This hypothetical example illustrates the importance of always examining the effect size, not only when *p* values are "significant" but also when they are reported as "not significant." If the reported results of a study always include both an estimate of effect size and a test of significance (or a related quantity such as a confidence interval), we can better protect ourselves against the inferential invalidity of type I and type II errors (e.g., concluding that *X* and *Y* are unrelated when they really are related). In behavioral science, there is little doubt that type II errors are far more likely than type I errors (Cohen, 1962, 1977, 1988). The frequency of type II errors can be reduced drastically by our attention to the magnitude of the estimated effect size. If that estimate is large and we find a nonsignificant result, we would do well to avoid deciding that variables *X* and *Y* are not related, i.e., that "nothing happened." Only if the pooled results of a good many replications point to a very small effect size (on the average), and to a combined test of significance that does not reach our favorite alpha level, are we justified in concluding that no nontrivial relationship exists between X and Y.

Table 2.6 summarizes inferential errors and some possible consequences as a joint function of the results of significance testing and the population effect size (Rosenthal, 1983, 1984). Suppose a nonsignificant but large effect—what should this tell us? Low power may have led to failure to detect the true effect, and this line of investigation should probably be continued with a larger sample size before concluding that nothing happened. Had the medical researchers in the aspirin study worked with a much smaller sample, they would not have gotten statistical significance—it would have been like trying to read in a very dim light, harder to make out the information. On the other hand, suppose a significant but small effect—what should this tell us? The answer depends on what we consider to be the practical importance of the small estimated population effect. In the aspirin study, even a "quite small" effect was considered to be important, because the criterion was who lives or dies.

The essential conclusion is that a test of significance without an effect size estimate fails to tell the whole story. Fortunately, as we shall see later, it is the case that from the information that many journals require scientists to report, effect sizes can usually be directly derived. Another important conclusion is that it is very useful to consider the power of the statistical test, and we will have much more to say on this subject in Chapters 19–21.

TABLE 2.6
Population effect sizes and results of significance testing as determinants of inferential errors

Population effect size	Results of significance testing	
	Not significant	**Significant**
Zero	No error	Type I error
Small	Type II error*	No error[†]
Large	Type II error[‡]	No error

*Low power may lead to failure to detect the true effect; however, if the true effect is quite small, the costs of this error may not be too great.

[†]Although not an inferential error, if the effect size is very small and N is very large, we may mistake a result that is merely very significant for one that is of practical importance.

[‡]Low power may lead to failure to detect the true effect, and with a substantial true effect the costs may be very great.

CHAPTER 3

STANDARDS
OF RELIABILITY
AND VALIDITY

ERRORS OF MEASUREMENT

All measurements, including measurements of behavior, are subject to fluctuations (also called *error*) that can affect reliability and validity. In general terms, *reliability* refers to consistency or stability (e.g., can what we measure or observe be confirmed by further competent measurements or observations?), and *validity* refers to appropriateness or meaningfulness (e.g., are our measurements or observations a true representation of reality?). To be sure, among some philosophers and researchers, the phrase "a true representation of reality" would not go unchallenged. In this chapter, in order to avoid getting mired in metaphysics, we will proceed on a methodological convention. As empiricists, we find (or hope to find) that our observations increasingly converge on a particular "real" value—although we do not take the idiom too literally (see Kaplan, 1964).

Suppose we wanted to measure the relative merits of several teachers on factors such as nonverbal warmth, empathy, nurturance, and so forth. We might compute reliability coefficients based on having expert judges rate the teachers at different times. The term *reliability coefficient* is a generic name for the degree to which what is measured is relatively free from measurement fluctuations. For instance, the correlation between ratings based on observations made by different judges at the same time would give a (reliability) coefficient of *observer agreement*: it would tell us something about the objectivity or repeatability of our rating procedure (Medley and Mitzel, 1963). A correlation between ratings based on observations made by the same judge at different times would give a *stability* (reliability) coefficient: it would tell us something about the consistency of the behavior from time to time, or the consistency of the judge from time to time, or both (Medley and Mitzel, 1963).

A distinction can be made between two kinds of measurement fluctuations, called random and systematic errors. *Random errors* cancel out, on the average, over repeated measurements on a single person or over a group of people measured on some attribute. *Systematic errors*, on the other hand, do not cancel out, but rather cause the mean value to be too big or too small. Imagine that we weigh a child several times at short intervals on an ordinary scale. We would not get exactly the same value each time, but we assume the small variations are random errors that cancel out—we estimate the child's "real" weight by averaging the values. But what if the scale is always 3 pounds too high? Taking the average will not cancel this systematic error, but we can compensate for it by subtracting 3 pounds from the average.

In the next chapter we shall see that systematic errors (also known as *biases*) are the main concern of internal validity—which refers to the degree of validity of statements made about whether X causes Y. In some cases a little bias may be better than a lot of random error, particularly when the direction and magnitude of the bias are known and can be compensated for (Stanley, 1971). In a later chapter we discuss the way in which biases due to subject role and experimenter behavior constitute systematic errors, because they may serve to influence the behavior of research participants in ways that can lead to type I and type II inferential errors (Chapter 6). We shall also be discussing the sources of rating errors and the ways in which they are traditionally controlled (Chapter 8). In this chapter we are concerned with the standards used by behavioral researchers to assess reliability and validity in different situations. As in the preceding chapters, we will be reviewing some basic ideas (which may be known to many readers) while also introducing some more advanced topics which may not be well known.

RELIABILITY CRITERIA IN PSYCHOLOGICAL TESTING

One situation in which reliability is a major concern is when a psychological test or questionnaire is used to measure some attribute or behavior. If we are to understand the functioning of a test, we must understand its reliability, i.e., the extent to which it *consistently* discriminates individuals at one time or over the course of time. The principal criteria of test reliability in current usage include (1) test-retest reliability and (2) the reliability of test components, or internal consistency.

Test-retest reliability refers to the temporal stability of a test from one measurement session to another. It is arrived at by administering the test to a group of individuals and then administering the same test later. The correlation between scores on the identical test administered at different times operationally defines its test-retest reliability. When we plan to use a test to make predictions, it is important to know this type of reliability, inasmuch as it gives an estimate of the dependability (or *stability*) of the test from one administration to another.

A difficulty involved in test-retest coefficients resides in the problem of distinguishing between effects of memory and those of real change (see Remmers, 1963). If the interval between the two sessions is too short, the test-retest coefficient may be inflated by the effect of memory in increasing the consistency of responses. On the other hand, if the interval is too long, there may be real changes in the characteristic being measured, which may lower the test-retest co-efficient. Standards for educational and psychological testing insist that test manuals should attempt to specify the optimal interval as well as the kinds of real changes (e.g., effects of counseling, career moves, psychotherapy) that the persons being tested may have experienced that could affect the test-retest coef-ficient (American Psychological Association, 1985).

Knowing that real changes have taken place can be used to our advantage if we want to assess whether the test is *sensitive,* i.e., whether changes in the real value invariably lead to changes in the measured value (Martin and Bateson, 1986). If we know that the behavior being measured is consistently undergoing change, a high test-retest coefficient would indicate an insensitive test that has failed to measure change (Lindzey and Borgatta, 1954).

The second criterion, *internal-consistency reliability* (also called *reliability of components*), depends on the average of the intercorrelations among all the single test items. Coefficients of internal consistency increase as the number of test items goes up (if the newly added items are positively correlated with the old items). To help us see this we can use a traditional equation, the *Spearman-Brown formula*—named after Charles Spearman and William Brown, who in 1910 reported it independently (Walker and Lev, 1953):

$$R = \frac{n\bar{r}}{1 + (n - 1)\bar{r}}$$

where R is the reliability coefficient, n is the factor by which the test is length-ened (or shortened), and $\bar{r}$ is the mean correlation among all the items.

Suppose on a certain test the mean correlation of the scores on item 1 with the scores on item 2, on item 1 with item 3, on item 1 with item 4, and so on equals .50. We want to know how reliable a comparable form of the test with twice as many items will be. Employing this formula we obtain $2(.50)/[1 + (2 - 1).50] = .667$. By doubling the length of the test, we will have increased its reliability from .50 to .667 (if other relevant factors remain the same). What if we tripled the number of items—$3(.50)/[1 + (3 - 1).50] = .75$. By tripling the length of the test, we will presumably increase its reliability by half. The more items, the more internally consistent the test and, in turn, the higher the Spearman-Brown coefficient. A problem, however, is that "other relevant factors" are not always the same in tests of different lengths. The more items, the more likely that fatigue and boredom can result in *attenuation* (reduction) in the consistency of accurate responding.

ALTERNATIVE PROCEDURES FOR RELIABILITY OF COMPONENTS

There are a number of other formulas for computing internal-consistency reli-abilities that are also in widespread use, and we shall describe them briefly in order to familiarize readers with what the results, when found in journal articles and monographs, tell us. A second classical procedure is the *Kuder-Richardson formula 20* (*K-R 20*):

$$r_{tt} = \left(\frac{n}{n-1}\right)\left(\frac{\sigma_t^2 - \Sigma PQ}{\sigma_t^2}\right)$$

in which r_{tt} is the reliability coefficient, n = number of items in the test, σ_t^2 = total variance of the test (a measure of the amount of fluctuation, or error), P = proportion of correct responses to each item in turn, $Q = 1 - P$, and ΣPQ instructs us to sum the products of P and Q for each individual item.

K-R 20 is used to measure internal consistency when the items of the test are scored "1" if marked correctly and "0" otherwise (Kuder and Richardson, 1937). The value of r_{tt} can vary from as low as 0 to as high as 1 (if all items are of exactly the same difficulty). Table 3.1 illustrates its application in a case in which four persons responded correctly (1) or incorrectly (0) to three test items ($n = 3$). Not shown is the calculation of the variance (indicated as 2.25 in this example), which we save for a more detailed discussion in Chapter 13. The proportion of correct responses ($P = .5$) and incorrect responses ($Q = .5$) was the same for each item, and the sum of the products gives $\Sigma PQ = [(.5)(.5) + (.5)(.5) + (.5)(.5)] = .75$. Plugging these values into K-R 20, $r_{tt} = 1.0$—indicating perfect internal-consistency reliability, which is exactly what one should get with these data.

TABLE 3.1
Internal consistency by the Kuder-Richardson formula

A. Responses of four persons on three items

	Items		
Persons	A	B	C
a	1	1	1
b	1	1	1
c	0	0	0
d	0	0	0
P	.5	.5	.5
Q	.5	.5	.5
PQ	.25	.25	.25

B. Computation of K-R 20

$$r_{tt} = \left(\frac{n}{n-1}\right)\left(\frac{\sigma_t^2 - \Sigma PQ}{\sigma_t^2}\right)$$

$$= \left(\frac{3}{2}\right)\left(\frac{2.25 - .75}{2.25}\right) = 1.00$$

Another popular internal-consistency coefficient, which is similar to K-R 20, is Lee J. Cronbach's *alpha coefficient* (Cronbach, 1951). We presume that readers are already familiar with the rudiments of analysis of variance, and we discuss these and more advanced topics in later chapters. It is worth noting that Cronbach and his coworkers have also employed the use of analysis of variance procedures for estimating the reliability of test components (Cronbach, Gleser, Nanda, and Rajaratnam, 1972)—an approach pioneered by Jackson (1939) and Hoyt (1941). When employing this technique, Cronbach coined the term *generalizability coefficient* as a reliability statistic to refer to the applicability of obtained scores as an estimate of "true" scores if all possible tests or all possible scores were available. We shall have a little more to say about the analysis of variance approach to reliability in a moment.

In later discussions (e.g., Chapter 24) we shall also be discussing the various uses of multivariate procedures, and we might mention here that one such use is in reliability analysis. David J. Armor (1974) developed an index, *theta*, that is based on the data from a correlational matrix that has been subjected to a particular multivariate statistical analysis. This approach, like the others mentioned, can be used to assess the reliability of test items, or even judges or observers of behavior (to which we turn in a moment).

WHAT IS ACCEPTABLE RELIABILITY?

The practical benefit of studying reliability is that it enables us to evaluate whether a low validity might be due to reliability that is too low and could be improved by adding items (or, as we see in the next section, judges). An important question is, What is an acceptable range of reliability?

The answer would seem to depend on the situation and the nature of the variable being measured. For purposes of clinical testing, reliability coefficients of approximately .85 or higher may be considered as indicative of dependable psychological tests, whereas in experimental research, instruments with much lower reliability coefficients may be accepted as satisfactory. Because the reliability of a test reflects both real individual differences and measurement fluctuations, if everyone were alike, the only measurable differences among them would be due to error variations (Graham and Lilly, 1984). Thus the same intelligence test should have a lower reliability when used at a highly selective university where the students are more similar (i.e., there are fewer individual differences) than in a public university where we find less restriction of range of real individual difference.

We can begin to get a general idea of what convention dictates as acceptable in psychological testing by looking at the reliabilities of some major tests used in this field. Parker, Hanson, and Hunsley (1988) have estimated the average internal-consistency reliability, test-retest stability, and validity of the Minnesota Multiphasic Personality Inventory (MMPI), Rorschach inkblot test, and Wechsler Adult Intelligence Scale (WAIS). They tabulated the reports of research results in two primary journals between 1970 and 1981 in order to collect the basic information. The MMPI and the Rorschach are two of the most frequently used personality tests, and also are among the most widely researched psychological tests. The WAIS served as a "control" with which to compare these two tests, inasmuch as it is usually considered one of the most reliable and valid tests used in clinical assessment.

In the internal-consistency category, Parker and the others included results reporting K-R 20, alpha, and related internal-consistency coefficients. On the basis of an analysis of 12 studies with a total of 1,759 subjects, they estimated the average internal consistency of the WAIS as .87. From their analysis of 33 studies with a total of 3,414 subjects, they estimated the MMPI internal consistency to be .84. On the basis of four studies with a total of 154 subjects, they estimated the average internal consistency of the Rorschach as .86. All three tests had acceptable internal-consistency reliability.

In the stability category, Parker and the others included results between repeated administrations of the same test. There were far fewer studies available, only four for the WAIS (total $N = 93$), five for the MMPI (total $N = 171$), and two for the Rorschach (total $N = 125$). On the basis of this information, the investigators calculated the average stability of the WAIS as .82, MMPI as .74, and Rorschach as .85. The value for the Rorschach is larger than that for the WAIS, but the difference was not statistically significant. The difference between the Rorschach and MMPI, on the other hand, was highly significant as was the difference between the WAIS and MMPI. Internal-consistency values are generally expected to be higher than test-retest values, and the results of this investigation are consistent with that expectation (although in the case of the Rorschach the difference is hardly noticeable). The average values are all quite respectable by psychometric standards of internal consistency and stability. (We turn to the validity findings in a moment.)

EFFECTIVE RELIABILITY OF JUDGES

Test reliability procedures are also applicable when we are using judges or raters and want to assess their "aggregate" internal consistency. Suppose a counseling psychologist interested in assertiveness training has two judges rate 20 subjects who are administered a counseling treatment. The correlation between the ratings made by the two judges is .60, which tells us not the reliability of *both* judges, but the reliability of *either single* judge in this situation. If we want to know the *aggregate* reliability (i.e., the composite reliability of both judges) — what we term *effective reliability* — we can approach this question the same way we approached that of "How many items?" in the previous discussion. Using the Spearman-Brown formula, with notation redefined, we can estimate the effective reliability (assuming the reliability of individual judges is similar; see Overall, 1965):

$$R = \frac{n\bar{r}}{1 + (n - 1)\bar{r}}$$

where R is the effective reliability, i.e., reliability of the *total* set of judges, n is the number of judges, and $\bar{r}$ is the mean correlation among all the judges. Applying this formula we obtain $2(.60)/[1 + (2 - 1).60] = .75$. The reliability of a single judge (i.e., judge-to-judge reliability) was .60, and the effective reliability (the "upped" Spearman-Brown reliability) was .75. In reporting his results the counseling psychologist would give both reliabilities and label each in order to avoid reader misunderstandings.

Let us try another example: A developmental psychologist uses three judges (A, B, and C) to rate five children in an observational child study, with the results shown in part A of Table 3.2. For the set of five children we can compute the correlation between each pair of judges: A with B, A with C, and B with C. These results are given in part B of this table—the mean correlation was computed as $\bar{r} = (.645 + .800 + .582)/3 = .676$. Substituting in the effective reliability formula, we obtain $3(.676)/[1 + (3 - 1).676] = .862$. The investigator reports that the effective (or aggregate) reliability of three judges' ratings is .862 and that the estimated reliability of the average individual judge (mean reliability) is .676.

Table 3.3 is a useful summary table based on our adaptation of the Spearman-Brown formula (Rosenthal, 1987a). It gives the effective reliability R for values of n ranging from 1 to 100 judges or raters. We see that the effective reliability (R) is equivalent to the reliability of a single judge $(\bar{r})$ when $n = 1$. The table can be used to help us obtain approximate answers to questions such as the following:

1. Given an obtained or estimated mean reliability $\bar{r}$ and a sample of n judges, what is the approximate effective reliability R of the mean of the judges' ratings? The value of R is read from the table at the intersection of the appropri-

TABLE 3.2
Ratings and intercorrelations for three judges
A. Judges' ratings

Persons	Judges		
	A	B	C
a	5	6	7
b	3	6	4
c	3	4	6
d	2	2	3
e	1	4	4

B. Judge-to-judge correlations

$$r_{AB} = .645$$
$$r_{AC} = .800$$
$$r_{BC} = .582$$
$$\bar{r} = .676$$

TABLE 3.3
Effective reliability of the mean of judges' ratings

Number of judges (n)	Mean reliability ($\bar{r}$)																				
	.01	.03	.05	.10	.15	.20	.25	.30	.35	.40	.45	.50	.55	.60	.65	.70	.75	.80	.85	.90	.95
1	01	03	05	10	15	20	25	30	35	40	45	50	55	60	65	70	75	80	85	90	95
2	02	06	10	18	26	33	40	46	52	57	62	67	71	75	79	82	86	89	92	95	97
3	03	08	14	25	35	43	50	56	62	67	71	75	79	82	85	88	90	92	94	96	98
4	04	11	17	31	41	50	57	63	68	73	77	80	83	86	88	90	92	94	96	97	*
5	05	13	21	36	47	56	62	68	73	77	80	83	86	88	90	92	94	95	97	98	*
6	06	16	24	40	51	60	67	72	76	80	83	86	88	90	92	93	95	96	97	98	*
7	07	18	27	44	55	64	70	75	79	82	85	88	90	91	93	94	95	97	98	98	*
8	07	20	30	47	59	67	73	77	81	84	87	89	91	92	94	95	96	97	98	*	*
9	08	22	32	50	61	69	75	79	83	86	88	90	92	93	94	95	96	97	98	*	*
10	09	24	34	53	64	71	77	81	84	87	89	91	92	94	95	96	97	98	98	*	*
12	11	27	39	57	68	75	80	84	87	89	91	92	94	95	96	97	97	98	*	*	**
14	12	30	42	61	71	78	82	86	88	90	92	93	94	95	96	97	98	98	*	*	**
16	14	33	46	64	74	80	84	87	90	91	93	94	95	96	97	97	98	98	*	*	**
18	15	36	49	67	76	82	86	89	91	92	94	95	96	96	97	98	98	*	*	*	**
20	17	38	51	69	78	83	87	90	92	93	94	95	96	97	97	98	98	*	*	*	**
24	20	43	56	73	81	86	89	91	93	94	95	96	97	97	98	98	*	*	*	**	**
28	22	46	60	76	83	88	90	92	94	95	96	97	97	98	98	98	*	*	*	**	**
32	24	50	63	78	85	89	91	93	95	96	96	97	98	98	98	*	*	*	*	**	**
36	27	53	65	80	86	90	92	94	95	96	97	97	98	98	*	*	*	*	**	**	**
40	29	55	68	82	88	91	93	94	96	96	97	98	98	98	*	*	*	*	**	**	**
50	34	61	72	85	90	93	94	96	96	97	98	98	98	*	*	*	*	**	**	**	**
60	38	65	76	87	91	94	95	96	97	98	98	98	*	*	*	*	*	**	**	**	**
80	45	71	81	90	93	95	96	97	98	98	98	*	*	*	*	*	**	**	**	**	**
100	50	76	84	92	95	96	97	98	98	*	*	*	*	*	*	**	**	**	**	**	**

Note: Decimal points omitted. * = approximately .99; ** = approximately 1.00.

ate row (n) and column ($\bar{r}$). Suppose an investigator wants to work with a variable believed to show a mean reliability of .50 and can afford only four judges. The investigator believes he should go ahead with his study only if the effective reliability will reach or exceed .75. Shall he go ahead? The answer is yes, because the table shows R to be .80 for an n of 4 and an $\bar{r}$ of .50.

2. Given the value of the obtained or desired effective reliability R and the number of judges actually available n, what will be the approximate value of the required mean reliability, $\bar{r}$? The table is entered in the row corresponding to the n of judges available and is read across until the value of R closest to the one desired is reached; the value of $\bar{r}$ is then read as the corresponding column heading. Suppose an investigator who will settle for an effective reliability no less than .90 has a sample of 20 judges available. In the investigator's selection of variables to be rated by these judges, what should be their minimally acceptable average individual reliability? From this table we see the answer is $\bar{r} = .30$.

3. Given an obtained or estimated mean reliability $\bar{r}$ and the obtained or desired effective reliability R, what is the approximate number of judges n required? The table is entered in the column corresponding to the mean reliability $\bar{r}$ and is read down until the value of R closest to the one desired is reached; the value of n is then read as the corresponding row title. For example, we know our choice of variables to have a mean reliability of .40 and want to achieve an effective reliability of .85 or higher. How many judges must we allow for in our preparation of a research budget? The answer is nine judges.

PERCENT AGREEMENT AND RELIABILITY

A practice among many researchers is to represent interrater consistency in terms of percent agreement as an index of interrater reliability. In this case the number of agreements A and the number of disagreements D among the judges are counted, and the researcher then computes (1) the percentage agreement as $[A/(A + D)] \times 100$ or (2) the net agreements as $[(A - D)/(A + D)] \times 100$. However, *percent agreement is a misleading index* inasmuch as it fails to differentiate between accuracy and variability (see Cohen, 1960; Robinson, 1957; Rosenthal, 1987a; Tinsley and Weiss, 1975).

Table 3.4 shows why it is inappropriate to employ such indices of "reliability" as percentage agreement. Smith and Jones independently have two judges evaluate the same 100 film clips of children for the presence or absence of frowning behavior, with the results as shown. Smith computes the percentage agreement between judges A and B as $[98/(98 + 2)] \times 100 = 98$ percent; Jones computes the percentage agreement between judges C and D as $[98/(98 + 2)] \times 100 = 98$ percent. The percentages are identical, yet we see clearly that the original data are quite different. The results suggest that the judges in Smith's study shared the same bias, but those in Jones's study were consistently unbiased.

A better procedure would be to report the product-moment correlation (e.g., phi). It can be computed from the chi-square (χ^2) statistic (discussed in detail later), which is employed to test the degree of agreement between the data

TABLE 3.4
Two cases of 98 percent agreement

Smith's results			Jones's results		
	Judge A			Judge C	
Judge B	Frown	No frown	Judge D	Frown	No frown
Frown	98	1	Frown	49	1
No frown	1	0	No frown	1	49
Agreement = 98%			Agreement = 98%		
r (phi) = −.01*			r (phi) = .96†		

*$\chi^2(1)$ = 0.01 (testing the significance of r).
†$\chi^2(1)$ = 92.16 (testing the significance of r).

actually obtained and that expected under the null hypothesis. The formula that would be used to calculate the product-moment correlation is r (phi) = $\sqrt{\chi^2/N}$. For Smith's results we obtain $r = \sqrt{.01/100} = -.01$; for Jones's results we obtain $\sqrt{92.16/100} = .96$.

RELIABILITY AND ANALYSIS OF VARIANCE

In certain situations, researchers need to use more than two or three judges, such as when they are constructing an attitude scale (Chapter 8) or when they are piloting stimuli for a later study.

An excellent approach to reliability when there are more than two judges for comparison is based on the analysis of variance. Suppose we want to know both the average and the aggregate reliability of our judges. We could use the approach described previously, but it can be tedious to average a large number of correlations. Fortunately, there is an easier way, and it involves the analysis of variance (Rosenthal, 1987a). In our discussion of effective reliability, we presented a hypothetical example involving a developmental psychologist who had three judges (A, B, C) rate five children in an observational child study (see Table 3.2). With the correlational approach, the mean reliability was $\bar{r}$ = .676 and the effective (aggregate) reliability was R = .862. Using standard procedures (illustrated in later discussions), we now compute an analysis of variance on the judges' ratings, with the results shown in part B of Table 3.5. Our computations require the use of only the last column, that labeled "MS" (mean squares) (Guilford, 1954). From these data, we can assess how well the judges were able to discriminate among the sampling units (children, or "persons") minus the judges' disagreements controlling for rating bias or main effects (e.g., MS persons − MS residuals), divided by a standardizing quantity.

Effective reliability is estimated as follows:

$$R_{est} = \frac{MS \text{ persons} - MS \text{ residual}}{MS \text{ persons}}$$

TABLE 3.5
Judges' ratings and analysis of variance of ratings

A. Judges' ratings

Persons	Judges		
	A	B	C
a	5	6	7
b	3	6	4
c	3	4	6
d	2	2	3
e	1	4	4

B. Analysis of variance

Source	SS	df	MS
Persons	24.0	4	6.00
Judges	11.2	2	5.60
Residual	6.8	8	0.85

from which we obtain $(6.00 - 0.85)/6.00 = .858$. To obtain an estimate of the reliability of a single judge, we compute:

$$\bar{r}_{est} = \frac{MS \text{ persons} - MS \text{ residual}}{MS \text{ persons} + (n - 1)(MS \text{ residual})}$$

which gives $(6.00 - 0.85)/[6.00 + (3 - 1)0.85] = .669$. We see that the effective reliability obtained by the correlational procedure ($R = .862$) differs by only .004 from the estimate (.858) obtained by the analysis of variance approach, and the mean intercorrelation obtained by the correlational procedure ($\bar{r} = .676$) differs by only .007 from the estimate (.669) obtained by analysis of variance. In general, the differences obtained between the correlational approach and the analysis of variance approach are quite small (see Guilford, 1954). A final point: in this simple example the correlational approach was not an onerous one to use, with only three correlations to compute. As the number of judges increases, we should find it increasingly convenient to employ the analysis of variance approach.

REPLICATION AND RELIABILTY

Reliability in research, as noted briefly in Chapter 1, implies generalizability as indicated by the *replicability* (repeatability) of the results, which we might now say is akin to reliability in test evaluation. The undetected equipment failure, the possibly random human errors of procedure, observation, recording, computation, or report are well enough known to make scientists wary of the unreplicated study. Thus, generalizability is sought in the replication of research results across time (*test-retest reliability*) and across different measurements, observers, or manipulations (*reliability of components*). However, whereas replicability is universally accepted as one of the most important criteria of the establishment of true constants (e.g., the speed of light), even in the natural sciences it is not possible to repeat and authenticate every observation at will or with perfect precision.

To illustrate: Larry V. Hedges (1987) did a comparison of a number of literature reviews in behavioral and social science with those in physics in order to assess the consistency of replicated research results in the so-called soft and hard sciences. The reviews in behavioral science came from relatively "hard" areas of psychology (e.g., the study of sex differences in cognitive abilities), relatively "soft" areas of educational psychology and evaluation research (e.g., studies of the effectiveness of open education programs and studies of the effects of school desegregation on academic achievement), and a middle ground between hard and soft areas of educational psychology (viz., studies of the validity of student ratings of instruction and the effect of teacher expectancies on student IQ). The reviews in physics came from an international group of physicists who had collected experimental results on the properties of elementary particles. Hedges chose the particle physics area because it is one of the most elite branches of physics—many of the best physicists work in this area, the research is expensive and well supported, many particle properties are well understood, and the research reviews are accessible and complete.

Hedges computed a reliability coefficient (called *Birge's ratio*) on both sets of results; it gives an estimate of the degree to which measurement estimates differ from one another by more than random errors (the smaller the ratio, the more consistent the results). To his surprise, he found the consistency of the research results varied as much in physics as it did in behavioral and social science (Birge's ratio of 2.11 in physics and 2.09 in behavioral and social science, based on an average of 13 reviews in each field). In fact, he found a number of striking examples of serious discrepancies in measurements in the reference data on thermodynamics. Of 64 values reported for 64 elements in 1961, 25 of them (as of 1975) were later found to be in error by over 10 percent, 16 by over 30 percent, 8 by over 50 percent, 2 by over 100 percent, and 1 by 245 percent! Interestingly, he also reported the methodological practice in physics of omitting a relatively large proportion of the studies to obtain a more consistent sample for data analysis.

In behavioral science, as in physics, some of the difficulty in replication is undoubtedly due to measurement fluctuations, but it might also be said to be due to the limitations of our conventional mode of expression, language. In Chapter 1 we spoke of the fact that journal articles and research reports do not always reflect the intuitions, hunches, and illogical as well as logical ideas that scientists carry in their heads ("think Yiddish, write British"). The term *tacit knowledge* refers to "unvoiceable" wisdom, i.e., facts, truths, or principles that we cannot easily communicate verbally (Polanyi, 1966). For instance, Jane knows from experience how to ride a bicycle, but she knows more about the skill involved than she can say in words. John is an aborigine who finds an abandoned bicycle in the Australian outback; he has never seen anyone ride a bicycle, and there are no intructions to accompany this one. Noticing it has wheels, he tries to ride it, but after taking a spill, he concludes that no one can ride this contraption—it must be designed for some other purpose, he thinks.

This analogy helps us to understand why there are sometimes difficulties encountered when replication is attempted without the benefit of direct experience. For example, in the 1970s, British scientists were trying to replicate a certain form of laser experiment (Collins, 1978). The laser was invented in the 1960s, but details were not made public for several years. This laser experiment turned out to be very difficult to replicate without the benefit of previous work at the source of the original laser. With access only to written information, it was like trying to ride a bicycle without the benefit of having *seen* this skill demonstrated.

Behavioral scientists who fail to replicate an experiment may conclude that the claimed effect is not reliable. It is also possible, however, that the scientists who failed to replicate it did not carry out the experiment "properly," because they did not have the benefit of tacit knowledge.

FACTORS AFFECTING THE UTILITY OF REPLICATIONS

Clearly the *same* experiment can never be repeated by a different worker. Indeed, it can never be repeated by even the same experimenter, because at the very least the subjects and the experimenter are older. But to avoid the not very helpful conclusion that there can be no replication, we can speak of *relative* replications. We might, for example, rank experiments on how close they are to each other in terms of subjects, experimenters, tasks, and situations, and then agree that *this* experiment, more than *that* one, is like a given standard experiment. When researchers speak of replication, then, they are referring to a "relatively" exact repetition of a research result. Three factors affecting the utility of any particular replication as an indicator of reliability are (1) *when* the replication is conducted, (2) *how* the replication is conducted, and (3) *by whom* the replication is conducted.

The first factor—*when* the replication is conducted—is important because replicated studies conducted early in the history of a particular research question are usually more useful than replications conducted later in the history of that question. The first replication essentially doubles our information about the research issue; the fifth replication adds 20 percent to our information level; and the fiftieth replication adds only 2 percent to our information level. Once the number of replications grows to be substantial, our need for further replication is likely to be due not to a real need for repetition of results but to a real need for the more adequate evaluation and summary of the replications already available (discussed in Chapter 22).

How the replication is conducted is another important factor to keep in mind. It has already been noted that replications are possible only in a relative sense. Still, there is a distribution of possible replications in which the variance is generated by the degree of similarity to the standard (i.e., the original study) that characterizes each possible replication. If we choose our replications to be as similar as possible to the standard study being replicated, we may be more true to the original idea of replication but we also pay a price in terms of generalizability. If we conduct a series of replications as exactly like the standard as we can, and if their results are consistent with the results of the original study, we have succeeded in "replicating" but not in extending the generality of the underlying relationship investigated in the original study. The more imprecise the replications, the greater is the generalizability of the results if they support the relationship tested. If the results do not support the original finding, however, we cannot tell whether the lack of support stems from the instability of the original result or from the imprecision of the replications.

The third factor—*by whom* the replicated research is conducted—is important because of the problem of *correlated replicators*. So far in our discussion we have assumed that the replications are independent of one another, but what does "independence" really mean? The usual minimal requirement for independence is that the subjects of the replications be different persons. What about the independence of the replicators? Are a series of 10 replications conducted by a single investigator as independent of one another as a series of 10 replications each conducted by a different investigator? An investigator who has devoted her life's work, for example, to the study of vision is less likely to carry out a study of verbal conditioning than is an investigator whose interests have always been in the area of verbal learning. To the extent that researchers with different interests are different kinds of people, and as such are likely to obtain different data from their subjects, we are forced to the conclusion that, within any area of science, researchers come "precorrelated" by virtue of their common interests and any associated characteristics (i.e., they are correlated replicators). Thus, there is a limit placed on the degree of independence we may expect from workers or replications in a common field. However, for different fields, the degree of correlation or of similarity among its workers may be quite different. Certainly, we all know of researchers in a common field who obtain data quite dissimilar from that obtained by others in that field. The actual degree of reliability, then, may not be very high, and may even be represented by a negative correlation.

A common situation in which research is conducted nowadays is with a team of researchers. Sometimes these teams consist entirely of colleagues; often they comprise one or more faculty members and one or more students at various stages of progress toward the Ph.D. degree. Researchers within a single research group may reasonably be assumed to be even more highly intercorrelated than any group of workers in the same area of interest who are not within the same research group. Students in a research group are perhaps more correlated with their major professor than would be true of another faculty member of the research group. There are two reasons for this likelihood: *selection* and *training*. First, students may elect to work in a given area with a given investigator because of their perceived or actual similarity of interest and associated characteristics. Colleagues are less likely to select a university, area of interest, and specific project because of a faculty member at that institution. Second, students may have had a larger proportion of their research training under the direction of a single professor. Other professors, though collaborating with their colleagues, are more often trained in research elsewhere by other persons. While there may be exceptions, it seems reasonable, on the whole, to assume that student researchers are more correlated with their adviser than another professor might be.

The correlation of replicators that we have been discussing refers directly to a correlation of *attributes* and indirectly to a correlation of the *data* the investigators will obtain from their subjects. The issue of correlated replicators is by no means a new one: the British statistician Karl Pearson, over 80 years ago, spoke of the "high correlation of judgements [suggesting] an influence of the immediate atmosphere, which may work upon two observers for a time in the same manner" (Pearson, 1902, p. 261). He believed the problem of correlated observers to be as critical for the physical sciences as for the behavioral sciences. Out of this discussion a simple principle evolves: it is that replications yielding consistent results are maximally informative and maximally convincing if they are maximally separated from the first study and from each other along such dimensions as time, physical distance, personal attributes of the researchers, expectancies on the part of the researchers and subjects, and the degree of personal contact between the researchers. So far we have talked about reliability, and we now turn to the major methods used by researchers to assess validity.

VALIDITY CRITERIA IN PSYCHOLOGICAL TESTING

Determining the *validity* of a psychological test or questionnaire for use in research means finding out the degree to which it measures what it is supposed to measure. It is the most important consideration in test evaluation and involves accumulating evidence in three categories: content-related validity, criterion-related validity, and construct-related validity (American Psychological Association, 1985).

Content validity requires that the test or questionnaire items represent the kinds of material (or content areas) they are supposed to represent. In developing standardized educational and psychological tests, the subjective evaluations of expert judges are usually required to assess this factor. Less formal methods are used in other situations, e.g., if we were making up a final exam in a research methods course and wanted it to have content validity. We might start by asking ourselves "What kinds of material should students be able to master after studying the textbooks and taking this course?" We would make a list of all the material the exam would be expected to sample, and then make up questions to represent this material. Tests and questionnaires are regarded as more content-valid the more they cover all the relevant material. This type of validity is usually expressed either as a global, nonquantitative judgment or in terms of the adequacy of sampling of the contents to be covered.

Criterion validity refers to the degree to which the test or questionnaire correlates with one or more outcome criteria. If we were developing a test of college aptitude, we might employ as our criterion the successful completion of the first year of college or maybe grade-point average after each year of college. If we were developing a test to measure anxiety, we might use as our criterion the pooled judgments of a group of highly trained clinicians who rate (e.g., on a scale of anxiety) each person to whom we have administered the test. In testing for criterion validity we try to select the most sensitive and meaningful criterion in the past, present, or future.

When the criterion is in the present, we speak of *concurrent validity*. Clinical diagnostic tests are ordinarily assessed for criterion validity by this procedure, since the criterion of the patients' "real" diagnostic status is in the present with respect to the tests being validated. Shorter forms of longer tests are also often evaluated with respect to their concurrent validity, using the longer test as the criterion. It could be reasonably argued in such cases that it is not validity but reliability that is being assessed. Indeed, while reliability and validity are conceptually distinguishable, it is sometimes difficult to separate them in practice.

Another type of criterion-related evidence is when we attempt to predict the future. Tests of college aptitude are normally assessed for *predictive validity*, inasmuch as the criteria of graduation and grade-point average are events that will occur in the future. The aptitude-test scores are saved until the future-criterion data become available and are then correlated with them. The resulting correlation coefficient serves as another statement of criterion validity. Grade-point average tends to be a fairly reliable criterion, but clinicians' judgments, e.g., about complex behavior, may be a less reliable criterion. Previously, we showed how the reliabilty of pooled judgments can be increased by adding more judges (see Table 3.3); we can increase the reliability of pooled clinical judgments by adding more clinicians to the group whose pooled judgments will serve as our criterion (Rosenthal, 1973a, 1982).

Sometimes we must be concerned about the validity of the criterion itself. Suppose that we want to develop a short test of anxiety that will predict the scores on a longer test of anxiety. The longer test serves as our criterion, and the new short test may be relatively quite valid with respect to the longer test. But the longer test may be of dubious validity with respect to some other criterion, e.g., clinicians' judgments. Sometimes, criteria must be evaluated with respect to other criteria, and there are no firm rules (beyond the consensus of the researchers in that area) as to what shall constitute an ultimate criterion.

More sophisticated views of the validation of tests, or of observations generally, require that we be sensitive not only to the correlation between our measures and some appropriate criterion, but also to the correlation between our measures and some inappropriate criterion. Suppose we developed a measure of adjustment and found that it correlated positively and substantially with our criterion of the pooled judgment of expert clinicians. That would be an attractive outcome of a concurrent validation effort. Imagine, however, that we administer a test of intelligence to all our subjects and find that the correlation between our adjustment scores and intelligence is also positive and substantial. Would our new test be a reasonably valid test of adjustment, of intelligence, of both, or of neither? That question is difficult to answer, but we could not claim on the basis of these results to understand our new test very well. It was not intended, after all, to be a measure of intelligence. In short, our test has good concurrent validity but fails to discriminate—it does not correlate differentially with criteria for different types of observation.

CONVERGENT AND DISCRIMINANT VALIDITY

This ability to discriminate is a characteristic of construct-validation evidence. The term *construct validity* refers to the degree to which the test or questionnaire score is a measure of the psychological characteristic of interest (cf. Cronbach and Meehl, 1955). Strictly speaking, a construct (like a theory) can never be verified or proved, because we could never complete every possible check on it (Cronbach and Quirk, 1971). In a widely cited paper, Donald T. Campbell and Donald W. Fiske (1959) sought to formalize this process on a statisitical basis by proposing two kinds of construct-validation evidence: (1) the testing for "convergence" across different measures or manipulations of the same trait or behavior and (2) the testing for "divergence" between measures or manipulations of related but conceptually distinct behaviors or traits.

Imagine that we were developing a new test to assess people's ability to read other people's emotions from still photographs. We would want the test to correlate highly with other tests of sensitivity to nonverbal cues—if it did so, we would have achieved *convergent validity*. However, we would not want our new test to correlate very highly with ordinary intelligence as measured by some standard IQ test. If it did correlate highly, it could be argued that what we had developed was simply one more test of general intelligence. The lack of divergence would argue for poor *discriminant validity*. We want our measures to correlate highly with the measures that our construct implies they should correlate highly with (convergent validity), but to correlate less with the measures our construct implies they should not correlate so highly with (discriminant validity).

Campbell and Fiske proposed that a *multitrait-multimethod matrix* of intercorrelations be constructed to help us triangulate (i.e., zero in) on the convergent and discriminant validity of a construct. In this case we pair different methods (A, B, C, D, E) with different trait variables (1, 2, 3, 4, 5), e.g.,

	Method A	Method B	Method C	Method D	Method E
Traits	1 2 3 4 5	1 2 3 4 5	1 2 3 4 5	1 2 3 4 5	1 2 3 4 5

The idea behind using multiple methods to measure the same and differing traits is that it avoids the difficulty that high or low correlations may be due not to convergent or discriminant validity, but to their common basis in the same method of measurement. Campbell has also advocated the use of multiple perspectives and triangulation in research in general, on the assumption that multiple vantage points permit fixing on a real effect in a way that is impossible from a single perspective (cf. Brewer and Collins, 1981).

However, it has also been argued that an inherent lack of independence among traits and methods can produce spurious intercorrelations that, in turn, lead to inflated assessments of validity by Campbell and Fiske's now classical approach (Alwin, 1974; Jackson, 1969). Similarly, it has been argued that the "hidden hand of common influence" makes it uncertain whether scientists ever have independently arrived at conclusions (Skagestad, 1981). Philosophers and methodologists continue to wrestle with this problem at different levels (e.g., Brewer and Collins, 1981; Browne, 1984; Campbell and O'Connell, 1967, 1982; Fiske, 1982; Kalleberg and Kluegel, 1975), but on one point they all agree: given fallible measurements, our recourse must be to multiple operations (cf. Houts, Cook, and Shadish, Jr., 1986; Rosnow and Georgoudi, 1986).

Earlier, we asked the question, What is an acceptable level of reliability?—and we turned to convention for the answer. The same question can be asked about the validity of psychological tests, and we can again turn to convention for help in arriving at an answer. In the study by Parker, Hanson, and Hunsley (1988), the convergent validity of the WAIS, MMPI, and Rorschach was assessed along with their reliability and stability. The criteria against which the WAIS—the standard of comparison in this investigation—was validated were typically measures such as other intelligence tests. Those other tests generally had higher validity and reliability than did the measures against which the MMPI and the Rorschach were validated (e.g., clinical diagnoses). As a result, we would expect higher validity coefficients for the WAIS than for the MMPI or Rorschach, and that is what Parker and the others observed. For the WAIS, based on 26 studies with a total of 3,441 subjects, the estimated average validity was .62. For the MMPI, with 30 studies and 4,980 subjects, it was .46. And for the Rorschach it was .41, based on 5 studies and 283 subjects.

The results are also of interest because of the low esteem in which the Rorschach is held by many clinicians. It has been characterized as an intriguing but unscientific instrument, whereas the MMPI has been portrayed as the "standard of psychological assessment" (Kendall and Norton-Ford, 1982, p. 310). One writer states, "The rate of scientific progress in clinical psychology might well be measured by the speed and thoroughness with which it gets over the Rorschach" (Jensen, 1965, p. 238). The results of the investigation by Parker, Hanson, and Hunsley show, however, that the Rorschach and MMPI are very similar on the psychometric ground of internal consistency and convergent validity, and that the Rorschach surpasses the MMPI in stability. The results for all these tests are generally considered acceptable for research purposes, so long as researchers know what they are looking for and use the tests appropriately.

VALIDITY CRITERIA IN EXPERIMENTATION

In the next chapter we turn to the logic of demonstrating causal connections in experimental relationships. Four kinds of validity-related evidence are given special consideration: evidence for statistical conclusion validity, internal validity, construct validity, and external validity (Campbell and Stanley, 1966; Cook and Campbell, 1979). Each kind bears a relationship to a different question in the unfolding of the experimental research process.

First, *statistical conclusion validity* refers to the question of whether the presumed causal variable X and its effect Y are statistically related, inasmuch as an essential requirement of a causal connection is that the cause and effect can be shown to *covary* (i.e., variations in one variable are related to variations in the other variable). If they are statistically unrelated (i.e., if they do not covary), then the changes in the one variable cannot have been a cause of the changes in the other variable.

To know whether X and Y covary involves three further questions: (1) Is the study sufficiently *sensitive* (i.e., able to detect small differences) to permit definite statements about covariation? (2) Given that it is sensitive enough, what is the evidence that X and Y covary? (3) Given this evidence, how strongly do X

and Y covary? In order to answer these questions we need to take into consideration the power of the statistical test (Chapters 2 and 19) as well as the stability of the experimental manipulation of X. Imagine that different experimenters are responsible for manipulating the causal condition; we must be sure the manipulation does not differ very much from one experimenter to another. If the same experimenter is responsible for manipulating this condition, then we must be sure there are no differences from occasion to occasion. We could do pilot testing to see whether there were any differences, and could then make changes in the procedures to make them more rigorously standardized.

Second, *internal validity* refers to the degree of validity of statements made about whether X causes Y. Suppose a male student and a female student decide to conduct, as a team, an experiment on verbal learning. Their particular interest is in the effect of stress, in the form of loud noise, on the learning of prose material. In order to divide the work fairly, the experimenters flip a coin to determine which of them will run the subjects in the stress condition and which of them will run the subjects in the no-stress condition. Let us say they find that better learning occurred in the stress condition. Can we confidently ascribe the effect to the experimental stress? We cannot, because we have a *plausible rival hypothesis* to the working hypothesis of "result is due to stress." Our plausible rival hypothesis is "result is due to experimenter differences (e.g., personality and gender differences)." This rival hypothesis could have been fairly well ruled out in this experiment by having each of the two experimenters contact half the subjects of the stress condition and half the subjects of the no-stress condition. Such a plan would avoid the "confounding" (or intermixing) of the effects of stress and the effects of experimenter differences. Thus we see that internal validity is primarily concerned with ruling out plausible rival hypotheses.

Third, *construct validity* (discussed in the previous section) is here concerned with the psychological qualities constituting the relationship between X and Y (Cronbach and Meehl, 1955). For example, in Chapter 1 we discussed the construct of "need for social approval" and some of the procedures used by Crowne and Marlowe to validate it. The term "validate" is perhaps too strong because, as we noted before, a construct cannot be verified or proved, but can only be falsified. Constructs are considered a "kind of temporary scaffolding" in theory construction, since one could never complete every possible validation check (Cronbach and Quirk, 1971, p. 173).

Fourth, *external validity* refers to the generalizability of a causal relationship beyond the circumstances under which it was studied or observed by the scientist. Let us say we have been successful in establishing the validity of our construct. Having gotten to this point we might now ask: How robust is the causal relationship between X and Y? We can address this question in terms of generalizability across both persons and settings.

To illustrate: some classical results have shown that people are *more* persuaded by scary messages the more threatening they are, whereas other classical results have shown that people are *less* persuaded by scary messages the more threatening they are (Rosnow and Robinson, 1967). Irwin A. Horowitz (1969) believed this difference might be indirectly due to the fact that volunteer subjects participated in the former studies, whereas "captive" subjects (samples consisting of available subjects) participated in the latter studies. To test his idea that the results of both sets of studies might be seriously limited in terms of external validity, he performed an experiment in which he assigned volunteers and non-volunteers to two groups, in one of which there was a high level of fear aroused and in the other, a low level of fear. The high-fear group read pamphlets on the abuse and effects of drugs and watched two films that depicted the hazards of LSD and other hallucinogens and the dangerous effects of amphetamines and barbiturates. The low-fear group did not see the films, but instead read pamphlets on the hazards of drug abuse that omitted the vivid verbal descriptions of death and disability to which the high-fear group was exposed. The subjects were then given a questionnaire asking them to respond on opinion scales corresponding to statements contained in the pamphlets. To check on the effectiveness of the fear manipulation, they were also given another scale that asked them to tell the extent, if any, to which they had been concerned and upset (called an *internal manipulation check*). The results of this check confirmed that the high-fear manipulation had been more distressing than the low-fear manipulation. More to the point, Horowitz's results indicated that the volunteer subjects had been more persuaded by the high-fear than by the low-fear message, and the nonvolunteer subjects had been more persuaded by the low-fear than by the high-fear message.

The lesson? It is important to consider the interdependence of the subjects' volunteer status and the X variable of interest, if our conclusions are to have external validity. We shall have more to say about the volunteer subject problem, and the ways to deal with it effectively, in Chapter 10. However, we now want to consider the research implications of internal validity, construct validity, and external validity in more detail.

PART
II

NATURE
AND LIMITATIONS
OF CONTROL
PROCEDURES

STRUCTURE
AND LOGIC
OF EXPERIMENTAL
DESIGNS

RANDOMIZATION IN TRUE EXPERIMENTS

The *research design*, including both the true experimental type (discussed in this chapter) and the quasi-experimental type (discussed in the following chapter), can be thought of as a blueprint that provides the scientist with a detailed outline or plan for the collection and analysis of the data. Textbooks of experimental methods usually present a series of designs one after another for discussion, but we believe it is more useful to understand the basic ideas in the structure and logic of research designs in general, because no list of experimental and quasi-experimental designs could exhaust all the possible variants. Nevertheless, we will also illustrate these basic ideas within some prototypical cases in order to bring them to life in this, and the next, chapter. In the second half of this book we turn to the data analysis of both true experimental and quasi-experimental research examples, and another purpose of this and the following discussion is to set the stage for the later chapters.

In this discussion we are primarily interested in the basic ideas behind causal inferences within true experimental designs in which the *sampling units* (e.g., the research participants) are exposed to one treatment condition each; such statistical research designs are called *between-subjects designs*. This category of designs can be contrasted with another category of statistical research designs in which the sampling units receive two or more treatments, called *within-subjects designs* or *repeated-measures designs*. True experimental designs, depending on the particular plan for the collection and analysis of the data, can fall into either one of these categories. However, as we shall see in the next chapter, not all between-subjects or within-subjects designs are necessarily "true" experimental designs.

What defines a *true* experimental design? There are a number of answers, including the controlled arrangement and manipulation of the conditions (or "treatments") of the experiment. However, the primary characteristic that distinguishes a research design as a true experiment is the *random assignment* of treatments to the sampling units, also called *randomization*. A blueprint for the collection and analysis of research data that approximates that of a true experimental design in other ways, but fails to allocate the treatments to the sampling units at random, would not be a true experimental design, but a *quasi-experimental design*. Because randomization is a vital characteristic that differentiates true from quasi-experimental designs, it is important that we understand its purpose as well as the mechanics of randomly assigning treatments to sampling units.

Simply stated, the purpose of randomization is to decide by some unbiased procedure (such as the flip of a coin or looking into a table of random digits) how the treatments will be allocated in order to protect against unsuspected sources of bias. As originally conceived by the statisticians who invented it, it was meant to be a safeguard against the possibility that the experimenter might subconsciously let his or her opinions and preferences influence which sampling units received any given treatment condition (see Gigerenzer, Swijtink, Porter, Daston, Beatty, and Krüger, 1989). Randomization does not guarantee to balance out the differences between the characteristics of the subjects participating in the different treatment groups, but the idea is to give each treatment an equal chance of being allocated to any research participant.

There are a number of alternative randomization techniques that can be used in order to increase the likelihood that the groups receiving different treatments are not systematically different from one another in terms of personal attributes (Snedecor and Cochran, 1980). One conventional procedure, used when pairs have been formed by matching, is to toss a coin in order to decide which member of a pair will receive the experimental treatment and which will receive the control treatment. Another conventional technique, also alluded to above, is to use a random digits table (see Appendix B-9). In this case we might choose a number and then start to read across the row or down the column, with odd or even digits determining which member of the pair will receive the experimental treatment. With independent samples, the subjects would be numbered in sequence, and we might proceed down a column of random digits choosing one subject at a time until each condition is filled with an equal number of subjects.

In sum, randomization is the sine qua non of true experimental designs, and it makes no difference whether the sampling units consist of human participants, laboratory-bred animals, or even argicultural crops. For example, animals are used in biomedical research as models of the human species in order scientifically to test the validity of new drugs and surgical procedures, biological assays, the etiology of diseases, and a wide range of other research questions. The rationale is that, if an appropriate animal species is chosen, the animal model should generalize to the human species as well as be more readily available for independent replications (Sechzer, 1983). It is possible one might think that laboratory-bred animals within the same species are so similar in personal attributes that randomization is unnecessary. However, some animals inevitably give an unusually good or an unusually poor response. Without randomization it would be difficult to protect against any systematic bias, conscious or unconscious, that could result in their being in one group and not another. The essential point is that, when random assignment of treatments to subjects is impossible or impractical, systematic error may be introduced by unknown subject attributes.

INDEPENDENT AND DEPENDENT VARIABLES

In Chapter 1 we noted that true experiments have as their focus the identification of causes, i.e., "how things are and how they got to be that way." The characterization of experimentation as causal investigation has a long philosophical tradition. With the rise of positivistic thinking, however, it became unpopular for a time to speak of causes, and instead more fashionable to speak of "effects" only, or the "effects of X on Y," or the "functional correlations" between X and Y (Gigerenzer, 1987; Wallace, 1972). By X and Y, the scientist means what are called the *variables* of the study, a concept derived from the notion that the things that researchers observe or measure or plan to investigate are "liable to variation" (or change). The idea of a variable was then qualified by means of a distinction drawn between the dependent variable (symbolized as Y) and the independent variable (symbolized as X).

The *dependent variable* refers to the status of the "effect" (or outcome) in which the researcher is interested; the *independent variable* refers to the status of the presumed "cause," changes in which lead to changes in the status of the dependent variable. In the statement "jogging makes you feel better," the independent variable (X) would be jogging status (i.e., jogging or not jogging), and the dependent variable (Y) would be feeling status (i.e., feeling better or not feeling better). Thus, even though researchers (who wish to avoid speaking of causes) may sometimes refer to the "functional" relationship between X and Y, the implicit assumption is that X has or serves a utilitarian purpose in relation to the outcome measure, Y.

Of course, any event or condition can be conceptualized as either an independent or a dependent variable. For example, it has been observed that rumor-mongering can sometimes cause a riot to erupt, but it has also been observed that riots can cause rumors to surface. Rumors are variables that can be conceived of as causes (independent variables) and as effects (dependent variables). One can also conceive of more complex relationships between X and Y, and we will explore some of these possibilities in the next chapter. To illustrate: rumor-mongering can trigger needs which, in turn, instigate new rumors, which then trigger new needs, and so on (Rosnow, 1980). A further implication is that the distinction made between an independent and a dependent variable can apply as much to causal relationships between X and Y variables outside of laboratory experimental situations.

When the researcher feels a need to make such a distinction in nonlaboratory research of the relational kind, but there is doubt about the dependence of a variable, the logical temporal sequence might serve as a probable basis for this decision. Suppose we found a relationship between gender and height, and we wanted to say which is the independent variable and which is the dependent variable. Common sense leads us to conclude that gender is more likely to determine height than that height is to determine gender, because a person's gender is biologically established at conception. Similarly, in explaining the "causal" relationship between birth order and volunteering to participate in behavioral research, we would logically think of birth order as the independent variable inasmuch as it is unreasonable to think that volunteering to be a research participant could be a determinant of one's order of birth.

CLASSES OF INDEPENDENT VARIABLES

There is no single, agreed-upon way of classifying independent and dependent variables, in the way, for example, that chemists can always turn to the periodic table to see how a particular element is classified. However, one way to conceptualize independent variables is in terms of the following five categories: (1) biological events, (2) environmental conditions, (3) hereditary factors, (4) previous training and experience, and (5) maturity. These should not be thought of as either exhaustive or mutually exclusive categories of independent variables, but only as convenient categories to help us see some of the possibilities in a brighter light.

Suppose we were interested in the general topic of eating behavior. An obvious *biological* independent variable could be the status of the hunger drive in an organism (i.e., high versus low state of arousal). By comparing food-deprived animals (high arousal) with others who were already quite satiated (low arousal), this independent variable could be studied experimentally for its effect on any given outcome (dependent variable) related to eating behavior.

The *social environment* constitutes a second class. It could include factors ranging from the nature of the experimental setting to sociocultural pressures and the demographics of social systems in quasi-experimental research. For example, anthropologist Michael J. Harner (1970) developed a scale for measuring population pressures in agricultural societies. He then used the scale in relational research to test the theory that growth of population pressure (the independent variable) is a major determinant of human social evolution (the dependent variable) through the process of competition for increasingly scarce subsistence resources (a *mediating*, or "linking," *variable* between X and Y).

Hereditary factors represent a third class of independent variables. A famous case involved a little boy who was born with corticoadrenal insufficiency, who showed an enormous and continual craving for salt (Wilkins and Richter, 1940). His malfuntioning adrenals were not discovered until his death. When his perplexed parents brought him to the hospital to find a cure for his unusual salt-craving drive, the unsuspecting dietician kept the child on a normal hospital diet and he died within a few days. His great appetite for salt (unbeknownst to his parents or the dietician in charge) was what had been instrumental in keeping him alive. In this case the status of the adrenals would be the independent variable (X), and health status the dependent variable (Y).

The fourth class, *previous training and experience,* can be illustrated by experiments done by psychologist Paul Rozin (1967, 1969). He demonstrated that rats maintained on a diet that is deficient in thiamine will prefer one that is supplemented by this vitamin over one that is not. The rat eats the more favorable diet because of its more favorable consequences, not because the animal "knows" what is good for it, Rozin found. Given a choice of several diets, only one of which contains the nutrient it lacks, the hungry rat will consume one of the diets for several days until its effects are felt. If it is not a healthy diet, the rat will experiment with another, and so on until it learns which diet has the most favorable consequences. The status of previous training and experience, as reflected by the maintenance schedule or diet (of thiamine), would represent X, the independent variable, and the status of the rat's eating behavior the dependent variable, Y.

Maturity constitutes a fifth class, which could include the age of subjects, their level of social maturity, and similar kinds of variables. Previously, we cautioned that these five classes of independent variables should not be viewed as mutually exclusive categories, and maturity is a good illustration of the need for caution. Suppose we found a relationship between subjects' ages and food preferences. Because factors of aging are sometimes correlated with biological development and deterioration (as much as with social factors), it would be difficult to determine whether changes in eating behavior were a simple function of age or a function of biological events associated with age. It would be prudent in this situation, as indeed in most situations, to regard the organism's behavior as *multiply* determined.

CLASSES OF DEPENDENT VARIABLES

As in the case of independent variables, there are many dependent variables and no consensual agreement as to how to classify them. There are many possibilities, indeed, and we will give only a flavor of some of them. In animal learning or conditioning studies, for example, three dependent variables that sometimes serve as outcome measures are (1) the *direction* of the observed change in behavior, (2) the *amount* of this change, and (3) the *ease* with which the change is effected. In a learning experiment that consists of teaching a thirsty rat to run through a complex maze toward a thimbleful of water, the measurements might focus on (1) the direction the rat chooses on each trial (i.e., whether it turns toward or away from the water), (2) the amount of change as reflected by how long the rat persists in the correct response when the water is no longer available at the end of its run, and (3) the ease with which the rat reacquires the correct response when the reward is again made available.

A number of researchers working with human subjects have devised their own human variants of these animal experimental measures. An experimental-social psychologist who is interested in opinion change could measure people's reactions after they were randomly exposed to a message treatment or to a control condition. Among the outcome measures employed could be (1) the direction of each person's opinion (in order to determine whether results in the experimental group were different from those in the control condition), (2) the persistence of any observed changes over time in each group, and (3) the ease with which the subjects are able to express their newly acquired opinion after participating in the condition to which they were assigned.

Literally thousands of specific measures of dependent variables have been described by behavioral scientists. To mention two further general classes, Uriel G. Foa, a social psychologist trained in sociology, referred to diffusion effects and hierarchical variations (Foa, 1968).

First, *diffusion* means that changes in the primary reaction to a stimulus situation have a tendency to "fan out" onto other events or behaviors that are close in time to the primary one. This "irradiation" effect has been demonstrated in research on the ways in which mood-inducing communications can affect opinion reactions to other communications (Rosnow, 1968). One such experiment dealt with the opinions of high school students about Pablo Picasso, the famous artist, when the students were in a good or bad mood (Corrozi and Rosnow, 1968). Four sets of arguments were prepared: two were pro and con positions on the genius of Picasso, and two others were pro and con positions on the question "Should we have a longer school week?" The argument for a longer school week was intended to put the students in a bad mood, and the argument for a shorter school week was designed to put them in a good mood. The experimental design consisted of having them read both the pro and con Picasso arguments in conjunction with one or the other of the school week arguments, varying the sequence and timing of the presentations, and measuring the resulting shifts in opinions about Picasso. The results were that their opinions changed in the direction of whichever Picasso argument was closer in time to the "good mood" event (argument for a shorter school week) or farther in time from the "bad mood" event (argument for a longer school week).

Second, Foa's notion of *hierarchical variations* in dependent variables refers to changes in a system in which one thing is ranked above another. In group psychotherapy, for example, the so-called marathon group involves a continuous meeting lasting as long as three or four days. It provides an intensive experience in group processes, and could result in changes in friendship hierarchies among the participants and their acquaintances. Suppose that person A (a participant) increased his liking for person C (another participant) and decreased his liking for person B (a nonparticipant)—this friendship hierarchy changes from ABC to ACB.

EVOLUTION OF THE CONCEPT OF CAUSALITY

So far, we have sampled some of the kinds of independent and dependent variables that are studied by behavioral researchers in their efforts (implicit or explicit) to identify causal relationships. But what does it mean, logically speaking, to say that X is the *cause* of Y, or to say that X and Y are *causally* related? For example, what "causes" a new skyscraper to be built? From the beginning of civilization all the way up to the present time, philosophers, logicians, scientists, methodologists, statisticians—all borrowing from one another—have dissected the concept of causality from different perspectives.

More than 2,300 years ago, the Greek philosopher Aristotle differentiated four kinds of causes: material, formal, efficient, and final. The *material cause* can be said to refer to the substance or material out of which something results. When an architect builds a skyscraper, the concrete, bricks, steel, etc., represent the material cause. The *formal cause* refers to the image or idea that gives meaning to the effect—it is the architect's idea in the form of a blueprint of the finished structure. The *efficient cause* refers to the activating event that is close in space and time to the effect; in this case it might be said to be the work of the architect, the laborers, and their tools. The *final cause* refers to the objective toward which the effect is focused, e.g., to provide a workplace for personnel, or perhaps to provide public recognition for the architect (see Wheelwright, 1951).

Philosophers into the Middle Ages consistently associated science (*scientia*) with causal knowledge (Wallace, 1972). By the eighteenth century, however, science had come to be regarded largely as the search for efficient causes, in the sense that physicists (and others who emulated the natural sciences) looked for mechanical connections between variables (see Rosnow, 1978, 1981). To change the position of a body at rest, we push it, lift it, or let other bodies act upon it—all mechanical connections. The difficulty with this view, when it is applied to behavior, is it implies that, like a machine that runs with clockwork precision, behavior is exactly predictable—we return to this difficulty in Chapter 12.

In the eighteenth century, David Hume, the Scottish philosopher, observed that when people speak in terms of efficient causality, they really have no other notion than that two events are "conjoined together" in space and time. It is, of course, impossible to see into this "conjunction"—in the way, for instance, we can see into a cell through a microscope. How, then, do we justify our belief that X causes Y? Hume answered by way of a set of proofs, or "rules" (shown in Table 4.1), which he believed to be all the logic necessary to justify that something is the "cause" of something else.

In this century, scientists have traditionally boiled down Hume's classical rules to three imperatives. First, it must be demonstrated that the cause is positively correlated with the effect (*covariation rule*). Second, it must be proved that the effect did not occur until after the cause (*temporal-precedence rule*). Third, it must be possible to rule out plausible alternative explanations of the causal relationship that is claimed to exist (*internal-validity rule*). Even working within this more limited framework, however, researchers find that they must settle for the best evidence available of causality, even if it is inconclusive.

SETTLING FOR THE BEST AVAILABLE EVIDENCE

Suppose we discover an outbreak of strange psychological symptoms and want to explain them in causal terms. We might begin by interviewing all or some of the

TABLE 4.1
Hume's "rules by which to judge of causes and effects"

1. The cause and effect must be contiguous in space and time.
2. The cause must be prior to the effect.
3. There must be a constant union betwixt the cause and effect.
'Tis chiefly this quality, that constitutes the relation.

4. The same cause always produces the same effect, and the same effect never arises but from the same cause. This principle we derive from experience, and is the source of most of our philosophical reasonings. For when by any clear experiment we have discover'd the causes or effects of any phenomenon, we immediately extend our observation to every phenomenon of the same kind, without waiting for that constant repetition, from which the first idea of this relation is deriv'd.

5. There is another principle, which hangs upon this, viz. that where several different objects produce the same effect, it must be by means of some quality, which we discover to be common amongst them. For as like effects imply like causes, we must always ascribe the causation to the circumstances, wherein we discover the resemblance.

6. The following principle is founded on the same reason. The difference in the effects of two resembling objects must proceed from that particular, in which they differ. For as like causes always produce like effects, when in any instance we find our expectation to be disappointed, we must conclude that this irregularity proceeds from some difference in the causes.

7. When any object encreases or diminishes with the encrease or diminution of its cause, 'tis to be regarded as a compounded effect, deriv'd from the union of the several different effects, which arise from the several different parts of the cause. The absence or presence of one part of the cause is here suppos'd to be always attended with the absence or presence of a proportionable part of the effect. This constant conjunction sufficiently proves, that the one part is the cause of the other. We must, however, beware not to draw such a conclusion from a few experiments. A certain degree of heat gives pleasure; if you diminish that heat, the pleasure diminishes; but it does not follow, that if you augment it beyond a certain degree, the pleasure will likewise augment; for we find that it degenerates into pain.

8. The eighth and last rule I shall take notice of is, that an object, which exists for any time in its full perfection without any effect, is not the sole cause of that effect, but requires to be assisted by some other principle, which may forward its influence and operation. For as like effects necessarily follow from like causes, and in a contiguous time and place, their separation for a moment shews, that these causes are not compleat ones.

Source: D. Hume, *A Treatise of Human Nature*, Oxford University Press, England, 1978 (originally published 1739–1740), pp. 173–175. Reprinted by permission of the publisher.

afflicted with the aim of finding some common event among those afflicted. Suppose our interviews suggest that, for all of them, a new drug has been pre-scribed whose side effects are not yet fully established. We now suspect the drug may, for some persons at least, be the cause of the strange symptoms. Shall we take a sample of patients and arrange to give half of them the suspected drug? That would allow us to compare two groups of people to see whether those given the drug were more likely to develop the strange symptoms. However, the ethical cost of such experimental research would be too high—we would not be willing to expose people to a drug we had good reason to believe to be harmful.

As a practical alternative, we might want to compare those persons who were given the new drug by their physicians with those persons whose physicians did not prescribe the new drug. If only those given the drug developed the new symptoms, the drug would be more seriously implicated—but its causal role would still not be fully established. It might have been that those patients given the new drug differed in a number of ways from those who were not given the drug by their physicians. Not the new drug, but a correlate of being given the drug could be the causal variable.

However, among those patients given the drug some will very likely have been given large dosages, whereas others will have been given small dosages. If it turns out that persons on larger dosages suffer more severely from the new symptoms, this evidence will implicate the drug more strongly. Of course, we still cannot be certain about the causal role of the drug, because it might be the case that those who were judged to be more ill by the physicians were given larger dosages. In this case, it is the illness for which the drug is prescribed that could be the "cause" rather than the drug.

How have we satisfied our three imperatives? "Not very well," you might answer. The temporal-precedence rule insisted that we show that the drug preceded the symptoms in time. Unless our medical records went back far enough, however, we would be unable to prove that the symptoms did not occur until after the drug. The covariation rule stated that we show statistically that the drug was related to the symptoms. Even if we could show that taking the drug was correlated with the mysterious symptoms, it might be argued that in order to be susceptible to the drug, a person had to be already in a given state of distress. It was not the drug, or *not only* the drug, that was related to the symptoms, according to this argument.

If we have not done very well in trying to satisfy these two imperatives, it is even more difficult to satisfy the internal-validity requirement. What we need, it would seem, is a comparison group of subjects who were in a similar state of distress but not given the drug. The name for this condition is a *control group*, but "control" (as we see next) also has at least three other meanings in behavioral science: (1) constancy of conditions, (2) control series, and (3) behavior control (Boring, 1954, 1969).

DIFFERENT MEANINGS OF CONTROL

In its orginal usage, the term *control* referred to a master list or duplicate register (called a "counter-roll") that was used to verify the accuracy of a later roll. By the late nineteenth century, it had also come to refer to a check or test observation in scientific parlance. In current usage one meaning of control refers to the *constancy of conditions* in the experimental research situation. That is, it refers to the importance of maintaining (or "controlling") the extraneous conditions that might affect the variables of the research. For example, unless a scientist wanted to study the effect of extreme temperature variations in a particular situation, it would not be good scientific practice to allow the temperature in a laboratory to vary capriciously from very chilly to very hot. If such variation occurred, the scientist would be unable to claim the "constancy of conditions" that allows statements of X and Y relationships to be made, because the extremes of ambient temperature might be a confounding variable. To avoid this, the scientist would control the room temperature by holding it constant, in order to eliminate the possibility of systematic error variability leading to spurious conclusions about the relationship between X and Y.

Another usage of control refers to the calibration of various elements of the research situation, particularly in psychophysical investigations, also called a *control series*. In psychophysical research the subjects may be asked to judge whether their skin is being touched by one or two fine compass points. If subjects know that two points will always be applied, they may never report the sensation of being stimulated by only one point. Because it is known that when two points are sufficiently close to one another they are invariably perceived as only one point, a control series might consist of applying only one point on a certain percentage of the trials. If the subjects do not know when they are receiving one or two points, their responses are less likely to be influenced by their *expectation* of what they are receiving.

Still another usage of control refers to the manipulation (or "shaping") of behavior based on a particular schedule of reinforcement that could be said to elicit the behavior in question, also called *behavior control* (e.g., Hineline, 1986). B. F. Skinner (1980) discussed a remarkable illustration of behavior control involving two brothers, the Colliers, who were found dead in a house completely filled with rubbish—he called it behavior control "by a worsening schedule." The Collier brothers, he explained, had been inveterate collectors of string, newspapers, and boxes. The collection slowly became aversive as it grew, because the addition of one more piece of string, or one more newspaper or box, could hardly have been as rewarding to the brothers as when they began their collection. It would have required a monumental effort for them to clean up their house; they would have had to call outsiders, who no doubt would have ridiculed the Colliers. Their compulsive behavior was shaped or "controlled" by saving or collecting, but in a curious way, because reinforcement must have been very rare. We see that behavior control implies an organism's (the Colliers, in this case) dependency on obtaining rewards by acting in certain ways; we will have more to say about research designs based on this approach in the next chapter.

The final meaning, *control condition*, is of primary concern to us. Although the term is of relatively recent origin, the notion goes far back into antiquity (Jones, 1964; Ramul, 1963). The story is told of a magistrate in ancient Egypt who sentenced some criminals to be executed by being exposed to poisonous snakes. It was reported back to him that none of the criminals had died, despite the care in carrying out the sentence. He learned that the prisoners, just before they were bitten, had been given some citron to eat by an old woman who took pity on them. Suspecting it was the citron that saved their lives, he then had citron fed to one of each pair of prisoners and nothing to the others. This time when they were bitten by the poisonous snakes, those who had been given the citron suffered no harm but the untreated ones died instantly. The story illustrates the early use of control conditions (Jones, 1964).

MILL'S METHODS OF ESTABLISHING NECESSARY AND SUFFICIENT CAUSES

This fourth sense of control also embodies certain "methods" of experimental inquiry developed by John Herschel (an eminent English astronomer born in Germany) centuries later. Popularized by John Stuart Mill (the English philosopher and economist) in his *A System of Logic, Ratiocinative and Inductive* of 1843, they came to be known as "Mill's methods." There are four such methods—the method of agreement, the method of difference, the method of residues, and the method of concomitant variation—the purpose of which is to provide a logical basis for the justification of claimed causal relationships between variables. One of the four, the method of residues, need not concern us here.

The *method of agreement* states simply, "If X, then Y"—in which X symbolizes the cause and Y the effect. It means that if we find two or more instances in which Y occurs, and only X is present on each occasion, then it can be said that X is a *sufficient* condition of Y. That is, X is adequate for bringing about the effect. In the game of baseball, we would say that the cause (X) of getting on base (Y) is a "sufficient" condition because it might be brought about by getting a hit ($X1$), walking ($X2$), or being struck by the pitch ($X3$).

The *method of difference* states: "If not-X, then not-Y." It means that if Y does not occur when X is absent, then it can be said that X is a *necessary* condition of Y. That is, X is essential for bringing about the effect. To win in baseball (Y), it is "necessary" to score the most runs (X); not scoring any runs (not-X) will result in not winning (not-Y).

If follows that using both methods, agreement and difference (called the *joint method*), should lead to better, more highly justified conclusions about the necessary and sufficient conditions of Y than either method separately can. Table 4.2 helps to illustrate this assumption (Kahane, 1986). Imagine we were trying to track down the cause of food poisoning in five people (Mimi, Nancy, Michele, John, and Sheila). Initially, we learn that they all ate at the same fast-

TABLE 4.2
Illustration of agreement and difference methods

Persons	Ate burger	Ate fries	Ate salad	Drank shake	Got food poisoning
Mimi	Yes	Yes	No	No	Yes
Connie	No	Yes	No	No	No
Greg	No	No	Yes	Yes	No
Nancy	Yes	Yes	Yes	No	Yes
Jeffrey	No	Yes	No	No	No
Michele	Yes	Yes	Yes	Yes	Yes
John	Yes	Yes	Yes	No	Yes
Sheila	Yes	No	No	No	Yes

Source: H. Kahane, *Logic and Philosophy: A Modern Introduction* (5th ed.), Wadsworth Publishing Company, Belmont, Calif., 1986. Adapted by permission of the author and publisher.

food restaurant. We discover that one of them drank a milk shake (which *may* have contained spoiled ingredients, but we are not sure), three of them ate a salad (which *may* have had spoiled dressing, but we are not sure), four of them ate greasy french fries, and all five of them ate a greasy hamburger. What shall we conclude?

On the surface, the one common factor is the greasy hamburger. However, the owner tells us that the food handler was feeling ill the day these persons were served. He worked for a while, but then asked to be excused after he said he felt dizzy and nauseous. Is it possible the food handler was the culprit? Suppose he touched some of but not all the foods eaten that day—maybe he passed on his germs in this way. If he handled Mimi's and Sheila's burger, Nancy's salad dressing, and Michele's and John's fries, that would be another factor common to all the cases. It is possible, in other words, that all these foods were *sufficient* to bring about poisoning (Y), but the food handler's handling of them (X?) was the *necessary* condition.

We think we can safely rule out the food handler, because he must have touched many more items than just these. If he were the cause (X), then others who ate at the restaurant should have become ill (Y). However, this table shows that Connie, Greg, and Jeffrey did not get food poisoning (not-Y) even though they ate some of the same things the others ate (X?)—except for the greasy hamburger (the true X). Only the suspected factor of the burger was absent in every case in which there was no food poisoning. On the basis of this evidence, we now believe that the greasy hamburger was the necessary and sufficient condition (X) that brought about food poisoning (Y).

And finally, the *method of concomitant variation* refers to related changes in amount or degree between two factors. It states: $Y = f(X)$, which means that the variations in one factor (Y) are functionally related to the variations in another factor (X). In our previous example involving the mysterious symptoms, many scientists would be willing to be convinced by strong evidence in terms of the variations in amount or degree between the new drug and the appearance of the symptoms. Thus, if persons taking the drug were more likely to show the symptoms, and if those taking more of the drug show more of the symptoms, and if those taking it over a longer period of time show more of the symptoms, a prudent scientist would be cautious about deciding the drug *was not* the cause of the symptoms. Even if an investigator were unwilling to conclude that the drug was surely at the root of the symptoms, at least not on the basis of the type of evidence discussed, he or she might well decide that it would be wisest to act *as though* it were.

PRACTICAL APPLICATION OF THE
JOINT METHOD

In practice, it is exceedingly rare to find a situation in which X and Y covary perfectly (i.e., $r = 1.0$), or in which it is possible to rule out every plausible rival hypothesis. It is also true that only experience in a given area is likely to teach the researcher what will constitute an adequate control condition.

Suppose that X represents a new and highly touted tranquilizer that can be obtained without prescription, while Y represents a change in measured tension. We give a group of subjects who complain of tension a certain dosage of X (the experimental group), and they show a reduction in measured tension. Could we conclude from this single observation that it was the tranquilizer that led to the reduction in tension? Not yet, because we have established only that X is a sufficient condition of Y, i.e., Mill's method of agreement. What we seem to require is a *control group* against which to compare the reaction in the experimental group. For our control, we use a group of comparable subjects to whom we do not give drug X. If these subjects show no tension reduction, we have established that X is a necessary condition of Y, i.e., Mill's method of difference.

We can diagram this two-group design as follows, and we quickly see that it corresponds precisely to the joint method.

Experimental group	Control group
If X, then Y	If not-X, then not-Y

Could we now conclude that taking the drug is what led to tension reduction? Yes—but with the stipulation that "taking the drug" means something quite different from getting a chemical into the blood system. "Taking the drug" means among other things (1) having someone give the subject a pill, (2) having someone give the subject the attention that goes with pill giving, (3) having the subject believe that relevant medication has been administered, and (4) having the ingredients of the drug find their way to the blood system of the subject.

Usually, when testing a new drug, the researcher is interested only in the subject's physical reaction to the active ingredients of the medication. The researcher does not care to learn that subjects will get to feel better if they *believe* they are being helped, because this fact (i.e., the power of suggestion) is already established. But if the researcher knows this, then how is he or she to separate the effects of the drug's ingredients from the effects of pill giving, subject expectations of help, and other psychological variables that may also be sufficient conditions of Y? The answer is by the choice of a different (or an additional) control group.

This time, we will use not a group given nothing, but instead a group given something that differs only in terms of the ingredients whose effects we would like to establish. The need for this type of control is so well established in drug research that virtually all trained investigators routinely use *placebo control groups*—a "placebo" being a substance without any pharmacological benefit, but given as a pseudomedicine to a control group. The general finding is that placebos are often effective, and sometimes even as effective as the far more expensive drug for which they serve as the relevant control.

We see that it is not always immediately evident what control group or groups to employ, but instead experience in a given area teaches one what will constitute adequate controls. In this research we first used a no-pill control group and then a placebo control (probably a sugar pill). Assuming that there is often a choice of control groups, how can the researcher decide on the most appropriate control groups? That question is not a simple one; two major factors to be taken into account are (1) the specific question of greatest interest to the researcher and (2) what is known generally about the research area. Even a very experienced scientist, however, may go astray in choosing control groups when he or she makes a major shift of research areas or makes misleading analogies that lead to faulty conclusions (cf. Lieberman and Dunlap, 1979; Peek, 1977; Rosenthal, 1985a; Shapiro and Morris, 1978; Wilkins, 1984).

INTERNAL VALIDITY OF PREEXPERIMENTAL DESIGNS

To deal with this problem in a systematic fashion, Donald Campbell and his coworkers, Julian Stanley and Thomas Cook (Campbell and Stanley, 1966; Cook and Campbell, 1976, 1979), attempted to standarize the choice of control groups. Their approach was to isolate the potential sources of invalidity that may be inherent in particular experimental (and quasi-experimental) designs. It is recognized, however, that there is no magic potion to guard against all the sources of invalidity discussed in the previous chapter (Brinberg and Kidder, 1982).

The logic of this particular approach is illustrated in Table 4.3, which shows the relationship between a number of representative sources of internal invalidity and three one-treatment designs. Internal validity is traditionally viewed as the most important of the four types of validity (i.e., statistical conclusion validity, internal validity, construct validity, and external validity), but it is never completely satisfied. A major objective of true experimental designs is to avoid confounding, which is achieved by controlling for the identifiable sources of internal invalidity. *Confounding*, as defined in this context, means that the treatment effect and some other effect cannot be separated. In this table we see four sources of internal invalidity that have been identified as relevant to the preexperimental and true experimental designs shown.

We begin our analysis by defining briefly each of the terms and symbols that appear in this table, and we return to them in more detail in a moment. The sources of internal invalidity are designated as (1) history, (2) maturation, (3) instrumentation, and (4) selection. *History* refers to an event or incident which takes place between the premeasurement (if any) and the postmeasurement, and which may have the effect of contaminating the results indicated by the postmeasurement. *Maturation* usually refers to the research participants' having grown older or wiser or stronger or more experienced between the pre- and postmeasurement. *Instrumentation* refers to the possibility that the effect observed is due to changes in the measuring instrument, e.g., deterioration of instrumentation over time. *Selection* refers to the nature of the participants in the group or groups being compared, i.e., whether the researcher has control over the assignment of subjects. The first two designs are indicated as *preexperimental*, which refers to the fact that the total absence of control makes them of minimal value in establishing causality. The various symbols are defined as follows: "X" denotes the exposure of a group to an experimental variable or event; "O" denotes

TABLE 4.3
Sources of internal invalidity for two preexperimental designs and the Solomon four-group experimental design

	Sources of invalidity			
	History	**Maturation**	**Instrumentation**	**Selection**
1. Preexperimental: one-shot case study X O	−	−	Not relevant	−
2. Preexperimental: one-group pre-post O X O	−	−	−	+
3. True experimental: four-group design I R O X O II R X O III R O O IV R O	+	+	+	+

Note: An X symbolizes the exposure of a group to an experimental variable or event, the effects of which are measured by O (which represents an observation or measurement). An R symbolizes random assignment to separate treatment groups. A minus (−) indicates a definite weakness, a plus (+) that the source of invalidity is controlled.

Source: D.T. Campbell and J.C. Stanley, *Experimental and Quasi-experimental Designs for Research,* Rand McNally, Chicago, 1966 (republished by Houghton Mifflin). Copyright 1963, American Educational Research Association, Washington, D.C. Adapted by permission of the first author, Houghton Mifflin Co., and the American Educational Research Association.

an observation or measurement; "R" represents the random assignment of subjects to separate treatment groups; a negative sign (−) indicates a definite weakness in terms of internal validity; and a positive sign (+) indicates that the source of internal invalidity is presumably well controlled.

Design 1, characterized as a "one-shot case study," consists of observing or measuring some behavior or event after the independent variable of interest has occurred. For example, following the introduction of a new educational treatment designed to improve students' concentration, the students might be tested on a standard achievement test. In preexperimental designs of this type, no allowance is made for a comparison with the reactions of other students who were not subjected to the new treatment. The negative signs indicate that the design is clearly deficient in terms of any reasonable controls for internal invalidity. However, instrumentation is not a relevant factor inasmuch as there is no premeasurement against which the postmeasurement could be compared.

Design 2, characterized as a "one-group pre-post" study, is also deficient in terms of any basic controls for internal invalidity. It makes a slight improvement on the first design, in that the students would be measured both before and after exposure to the treatment that represents the independent variable. Still, no allowance is made for a comparison with the reactions of other students who were not exposed to that treatment. Before turning to design 3, let us examine in more detail the four sources of invalidity.

First, history may be considered to be a plausible rival explanation in designs 1 and 2 because specific contaminating events occurring before the post-measurement cannot be controlled and assessed by either design. Suppose that a sudden snowstorm resulted in an unexpected cancellation of classes. Neither design allows us to isolate the effects on motivation of a school closing, and to assess that factor apart from the effects of the new educational treatment that was designed to improve concentration.

The second type of error, maturation, could refer to the students' concentration improving as a result of getting older. If they became better at the task, we could not tell whether the gains were due to their having grown older or to the fact that they were subjected to a particular educational treatment.

The third type of error, instrumentation, is relevant only to design 2. This type of error could be accounted for by a change in the calibration of the measuring instrument or by changes in the observers or scorers, rather than by changes due to the impact of the treatment. Observers might over time become better judges of student concentration, resulting not in instrument deterioration but instrument improvement (i.e., improved precision).

The fourth type of error, selection, refers to the particular characteristics of the participants themselves. In design 1 there is no way of knowing beforehand anything about the state of the participants, because they are observed or measured only after the treatment has been administered. The addition of a pre-observation in design 2 results in an improvement over design 1; it enables us to ascertain the prior state of the participants.

We turn to design 3 next, but this table shows that all four classes of potential errors are well controlled in this four-group experimental design, also called the "Solomon design" (named after the experimental psychologist, Richard L. Solomon, who introduced it in the 1940s). It is not the only four-group experimental design (see, e.g., Marlatt, Demming, and Reid, 1973; Rosenthal, 1966, 1976; Ross, Krugman, Lyerly, and Clyde, 1962), nor is it as commonly used as some other four-group experimental designs. However, it provides an elegant illustration of the logic of control in true experimental designs (see Solomon, 1949). To set the stage for this discussion, we first review the nature of a research problem that Solomon and his coworker, Michael Lessac, set out to study (Lessac and Solomon, 1969).

BACKGROUND OF THE SOLOMON DESIGN

Previous research by other investigators had led to their formulation of the "critical period" concept in postnatal behavioral development. The notion, with historical roots in William James and earlier (Columbo, 1982), states that there are optimum periods in the life of an infant during which it learns to make adaptive responses to its environment. The possibility that such periods may exist in human development provides the rationale for early intervention in education (e.g., Head Start) as well as other areas. In past research it was believed that withholding some kinds of stimulation early in the organism's development would impede the learning of sensory and motor associations important to adult behavior. However, Solomon and Lessac questioned this idea because it ignores two rival explanations for the critical period effect. One is that early deprivation destroys not the opportunity to learn, but an already formed perceptual-motor pattern for triggering further development. A second alternative is that early deprivation results in unusual patterns that interfere with already formed perceptual-motor patterns.

In other words, the original idea was that deprivation kept normal perceptual-motor patterns from forming. However, Solomon and Lessac's alternative explanations both assumed that normal perceptual-motor capabilities exist at birth, but are either destroyed or interfered with by the experience of deprivation. To enable them to rule out these rival explanations it was necessary for them to evaluate the organism's capabilities before it underwent an isolation treatment. At the same time, it was necessary to control for the possible confounding of this pretesting, because it constitutes extraneous stimulation that may interfere with the subjects' reactions to the isolation treatment.

This is an easy problem to deal with logically, but it presents an insurmountable ethical problem with human subjects. Logically, all we need do is randomly assign a sample of newborn infants to two groups, in one of which they are tested on perceptual-motor capabilities at birth and in the other of which they are placed in isolation. Later, we use the pretest results from the former group as an estimate of how the latter "would have" responded had they been pretested. Randomization would maximize the likelihood that the two groups are comparable by giving each child an equal opportunity of being assigned to either group by chance. However, it is ethically absurd even to consider working with human subjects. An alternative approach—assuming we can justify it on ethical grounds—would be to work with an animal model. This is what Solomon and Lessac chose to do, working with beagle pups—though readers may have ethical objections to this method.

In their investigation, the researchers were also interested in learning what the effect of measuring an animal is on its subsequent responding in respect to the isolation condition. That is, they wanted to find out whether there is a confounding of pretesting and X, the independent variable of interest (isolation versus no isolation). The term for this confounding is *pretest sensitization*, and the Solomon design enables us to tease out evidence of whether X affects the outcome measure only when a pretest measure also is administered (e.g., Braver and Braver, 1988; Lana, 1969; Rosnow and Suls, 1970).

To obtain answers to their various research questions, Solomon and Lessac employed design 3 shown in Table 4.3. They assigned beagle pups at random to the four groups shown in this table (Lessac and Solomon, 1969). Those assigned to groups III and IV were raised normally in the way they would have been raised in a kennel, whereas those assigned to groups I and II were raised in isolation in $18 \times 24 \times 30$-inch aluminum cages through which light entered by a $2\frac{1}{2}$-inch space between the bottom tray and the door. All the pups were fed and medicated at the same time, and the dependent variables (measures of psychomotor skills such as testing each pup's response to pain, how it responded to its physical environment, and various tests of learning) were observed for all groups after one year had passed.

ANALYZING THE SOLOMON FOUR-GROUP DESIGN

In Table 4.4 we see the Solomon design recast in part A as a 2 × 2 table; the recast model shown in this table corresponds exactly to design 3 in Table 4.3. Group I, for example, is pretested on whatever dependent variables are theoretically meaningful, then subjected to a state of isolation, and finally retested on the dependent variables. Group II is not pretested but undergoes the same isolation treatment and is given the same posttest as in group I. Group III is pretested and posttested, but is treated normally instead of being subjected to a period of isolation. Group IV gets only the posttest.

What can this four-group design tell us? First, we use the pretest performance scores in groups I and III to estimate the pretest performance scores in groups II and IV without contaminating the latter by pretesting them. This requires a leap of faith, however. Even if the value of the pretest in group I is identical with that in group III, we can only *assume* that the values would be close to those of the pretests in groups II and IV. If the pretest values in groups I and III

TABLE 4.4
The Solomon four-group research design
A. Displayed as 2 × 2 table

Pretest procedure	Treatment conditions	
	Isolation	**Control**
Pretested	Group I	Group III
Not pretested	Group II	Group IV

B. Plausible causal events

Causal events	Outcome measures			
	$\overline{Y}_I$	$\overline{Y}_{II}$	$\overline{Y}_{III}$	$\overline{Y}_{IV}$
Pretest-posttest effect	+	−	+	−
Experimental treatment effect	+	+	−	−
Pretest and X sensitization	+	−	−	−
Extraneous effects	+	+	+	+

differed greatly, it is still possible that the unknown pretest values in groups II and IV could be exactly equal to the mean of I and III.

Traditionally, the statistical assessment of the effect of the experimental treatment (the isolation) and the effect of the pretesting calls for a factorial analysis of variance of the posttest performance scores (discussed in Chapter 16). Because we already have an estimate of the pretest performance scores in groups II and IV (without having contaminated them by pretesting), we may use this information to enrich our comparison of these two groups. Other analyses have also been suggested (see Braver and Braver, 1988).

Third, this design can tell us whether there is any confounding of pretesting and X (e.g., the isolation treatment). If, using the analysis of variance, there is statistical evidence of such a result, we will want to know whether the pretesting *enhanced* or *reduced* the effect of the treatment. Solomon showed how this question can be answered by a "subtractive difference" procedure, in which we examine the differences between the performance outcomes in the four groups. This procedure can be best illustrated by referring to part B of Table 4.4.

Part B lists four plausible causal events affecting the performance outcomes in groups I, II, III, and IV. The columns are headed by $\overline{Y}$ in order to represent the mean outcome value in a particular group. A positive sign (+) indicates that the event noted (the pretest, the treatment, pretest sensitization, or extraneous events) is considered to be a plausible causal event; a negative sign (−) indicates that it is not considered to be relevant. Thus, the performance outcome in group I ($\overline{Y}_I$) may be affected by the pretest, the treatment, pretest sensitization, and extraneous events. The performance outcome in group II ($\overline{Y}_{II}$) may be affected only by the treatment and any extraneous events, since there was no pretest to produce a pretest-sensitization effect. The performance outcome in group III ($\overline{Y}_{III}$) may be affected by the pretest and any extraneous events, but by no other conditions, because there was no treatment to produce a pretest sensitization effect. The performance outcome in group IV ($\overline{Y}_{IV}$) may be affected by extraneous events, but by no other conditions. To tease out whether pretest sensitization enhanced or reduced the effect of the experimental treatment, we compute: $(\overline{Y}_I - \overline{Y}_{III}) - (\overline{Y}_{II} - \overline{Y}_{IV})$ = pretest sensitization effect. A positive effect will tell us that pretest sensitization enhanced the effect of the treatment; a negative effect will tell us that pretest sensitization reduced the effect of the treatment.

In a number of studies no pretest sensitization effect was obtained (see Lana, 1969), but in other investigations different directions of pretest sensitization were demonstrated or suggested by the results. For example, Solomon (1949) conducted an experiment in which grammar school classes were equated for spelling ability by teacher judgment. Different groups of children were pretested on a list of words of equal difficulty by having the children spell the words. The children were then given a lesson on the rules of correct spelling and afterward were tested on the same list of words. The results suggested that taking the pretest made the children more resistant to the spelling lesson. Doris R. Entwisle (1961) conducted a study in which she investigated the subjects' abilities to learn about state locations of large U.S. cities. The results suggested that pretest sensitization aided recall for high-IQ subjects and was "mildly hindering" for average-

IQ subjects. In an experiment involving attitude measurements, Rosnow and Suls (1970) employed the Solomon four-group design to study pretest sensitization to a persuasive message treatment. They found that pretest sensitization enhanced receptivity to the treatment for volunteer subjects and reduced receptivity for nonvolunteer subjects.

INTERNAL AND EXTERNAL VALIDITY OF EXPERIMENTAL DESIGNS

Table 4.5 provides a validity analysis (internal and external validity) of three one-treatment experimental designs. Design 3 is the Solomon four-group design, and designs 4 and 5 are two-group designs derived from carving up the Solomon design. Added to the four sources of internal invalidity (defined previously), we see two sources of external invalidity noted. One source of external invalidity, the "confounding of pretesting and X," refers to the pretest sensitization question. The other source of external invalidity, the "confounding of selection and X," refers in this example to the possible confounding of the subjects' volunteer status and the status of the independent variable (e.g., Rosnow and Suls, 1970).

Design 4, characterized as a "pre-post control group" design, is composed of groups I and III of the Solomon design. Design 5, referred to as a "posttest-only control group" design, consists of groups II and IV of the Solomon design. Except for the two sources of external invalidity noted, there is no loss in the relative validities of the two-group designs as compared with the Solomon four-group design. Design 4, however, is deficient as to control of the possible confounding of pretest sensitization, which (as noted previously) could be a problem in attitude change and learning experiments. Design 5 is not flawed in this respect, because the subjects are measured only after the manipulation of X. Design 5, even though unconfounded in this respect, would not have been a good choice in the Solomon and Lessac study, since they raised specific questions that could be answered only by estimating the state of the pups' psychomotor skills before the isolation began. Design 5, while perhaps less precise and less powerful than design 4, would be clearly preferable when the situation does not warrant pretesting.

All three designs are subject to concerns about the possible threat to external validity resulting from the confounding of "selection and X," e.g., confounding of the subjects' volunteer status and the status of the independent variable. In Chapter 10 we turn to ways of addressing this problem. This table is by no means an exhaustive list of the sources of internal and external invalidity identified by Campbell and others. Interested readers will find more detailed discussions in Brinberg and Kidder (1982), Campbell and Stanley (1966), and Cook and Campbell (1976, 1979).

INTRODUCTION TO WITHIN-SUBJECTS DESIGNS

We now briefly focus on within-subjects experimental and quasi-experimental designs, e.g., those in which each subject (or sampling unit) receives all treat-

TABLE 4.5
Some sources of internal and external invalidity for three true experimental designs

Designs	Sources of internal invalidity				Sources of external invalidity	
	History	Matu-ration	Instru-mentation	Selection	Confounding of pretesting and X	Confounding of selection and X
3. Solomon four-group design I R O X O II R X O III R O O IV R O	+	+	+	+	+	?
4. Pre-post control group design I R O X O III R O O	+	+	+	+	−	?
5. Posttest-only control group design II R X O IV R O	+	+	+	+	+	?

Note: An X symbolizes the exposure of a group to an experimental variable or event, the effects of which are measured by O (which represents an observation or measurement). An R symbolizes random assignment to separate treatment groups. A minus (−) indicates a definite weakness, a plus (+) that the source of invalidity is controlled. A question mark (?) indicates a possible source of concern.

Source: D.T. Campbell and J.C. Stanley, *Experimental and Quasi-experimental Designs for Research*, Rand McNally, Chicago, 1966 (republished by Houghton Mifflin). Copyright 1963, American Educational Research Associaton, Washington, D.C. Adapted by permission of the first author, Houghton Mifflin Co., and the American Educational Research Association.

ments in turn. In Chapter 18 we deal with the statistical analysis of such "repeated-measures" designs. They have found widespread use in a number of research areas such as human learning and memory, drug research, and clinical research. In the 1880s, for example, experimental psychologist Hermann Ebbinghaus used a repeated-measures procedure to develop a curve of forgetting. In fact, Ebbinghaus himself was his only subject, as he learned and relearned over a thousand lists of a baker's dozen of nonsense syllables and then plotted learning and forgetting curves (Ebbinghaus, 1885). In the next chapter we describe alternative designs of this "single-case" repeated-measures type as illustrations of quasi-experimental designs.

There are advantages but also some difficulties with the use of within-subjects experimental designs. One advantage is that the same number of subjects can be used more efficiently in a within-subjects design than in a between-subjects design, because in the former, one is making use of the same subjects repeatedly. Each sampling unit serves as its own control in a within-subjects design, although this does not prevent us from using a mixed design including both between-subjects and within-subjects factors. A second advantage in animal research is that we can save some of the animals from being sacrificed by using a "group sequential" design. In this particular within-subjects design the researchers divide up the available number of animals into several equal-sized groups and perform the repeated measures in stages (Geller, 1983). Some animals are saved until later stages; if the results are statistically significant at an early stage, then the research is concluded and the animals that were saved are never used. A third advantage, useful in the study of developmental problems, is that we can examine relations longitudinally—discussed in the next chapter.

A difficulty when employing within-subjects experimental designs is the sensitization problem referred to above. Another difficulty is that the order in which the treatments are administered may produce differences between successive measurements. For example, in developmental research, the children may be nervous when first measured, and they may perform poorly; later on they may be less nervous, and they may perform better. To deal with problems of systematic differences between successive measurements, *counterbalancing* is used. Some subjects are randomly administered treatment A before treatment B, and the others receive treatment B before treatment A (see, e.g., Rosnow, 1968). In Chapter 18 we discuss these and more complex examples of counterbalancing in within-subjects designs.

In concluding this chapter, we do not want to leave the reader with an oversimplified picture of what is possible in controlling for sources of internal invalidity (or other threats to validity). For example, a particular threat to internal validity in longitudinal repeated-measures designs is what is called *regression toward the mean*—about which considerable confusion seems to exist. The term is a mathematical concept that refers to the relationship between two paired variables, X and Y, for which cases at one extreme on X (the independent variable) will, on the average over time, be less extreme on the other variable. That is, when the variables consist of the same measure taken at two points in time, the predicted score on Y will always be nearer to the sample mean than is the value of X whenever the linear relation between X and Y is imperfect (see Cohen and Cohen, 1983). Thus, on the average, overweight people will appear to lose weight, low IQ children will appear to become brighter, and rich people will appear to become poorer when the variables are measured longitudinally. To deal with this problem, methodologists often recommend that subjects be selected not for their extremeness, but for their representativeness and then assigned to groups by randomization.

However, even in an initially representative sample, one can end up with extremeness if attrition of average subjects occurred over the course of the research. Later in this book, we discuss regression and the nature of standard scores in detail, but readers who are familiar with these concepts will quickly see why regression toward the mean is a mathematical necessity whenever two variables, X and Y, correlate less than perfectly. To review, a *standard score,* or *Z score*, is a raw score from which the sample mean has been subtracted and the difference then divided by the standard deviation. Briefly, the regression equation, expressed in standard scores, is $Z_Y = r_{XY}Z_X$ where the estimated standard score of Y is predicted from the product of the XY correlation (r_{XY}) times the standard score of X. Given a perfect correlation between X and Y (i.e., $r_{XY} = 1.0$), it follows that Z_Y must be equivalent to Z_X. Given $r_{XY} < 1$, however, then Z_Y cannot be equivalent to Z_X. For example, given $r_{XY} = .4$, then Z_y can be only 0.4 as large as Z_X (Cohen and Cohen, 1983). Thus regression toward the mean will always be observed when the variables consist of the same measure taken at two points in time and $r_{XY} < 1$.

The design of experiments, as the design of all research, requires familiarity with statistical analysis because mastering research design involves knowing how to optimize statistical efficiency. In the second half of this book we deal with this aspect of behavioral research in considerable detail. However, research design also requires a realization of the logical constraints imposed on interpretation by practical limitations, such as the fact that subjects cannot always be randomly assigned and that control conditions do not always make it possible for us to tease out precise effects.

CHAPTER
5

MODELS OF QUASI-EXPERIMENTAL DESIGNS

NONRANDOM ASSIGNMENT IN QUASI EXPERIMENTS

Random assignment to treatment is not always possible in human subject research, and researchers have employed a number of alternative approaches that could—under ideal conditions of implementation—serve as an approximation of true experimental designs. *Quasi* means "resembling," and (as noted previously) these quasi-experimental approaches resemble true experiments in that both types have treatments, outcome measures, and sampling units. However, also as noted, quasi experiments do not use randomization to create the comparisons from which treatment-caused change is inferred in true experimental designs (see Cook and Campbell, 1979). The various true experimental designs in Chapter 4 would then fall into the category of quasi-experimental designs if the treatment conditions were not assigned to the sampling units at random. In this chapter we are concerned with three classes of quasi-experimental approaches: nonequivalent-groups designs, interrupted time-series designs, and correlational designs.

NONEQUIVALENT-GROUPS DESIGNS

The *nonequivalent-groups design* is the most widely used quasi-experimental method. It refers to nonrandomized research in which responses of a treatment group and a control group are compared on measures collected at the beginning and end of the research. For example, in a traffic safety project to reduce drink-ing and driving, a court-ordered treatment program is to be evaluated by the re-searchers (Vaught, 1977). Four conditions are to be compared: (1) drug therapy using Antabuse (which causes an unpleasant reaction if alcohol is consumed), (2) group psychotherapy administered by clinical psychologists, (3) a volunteer pro-gram along the lines of Alcoholics Anonymous, and (4) a zero-control condition (i.e., no treatment of any kind). In using a nonequivalent-groups design a basic requirement is a pretest and a posttest that measure the same construct.

Basically a "pre-post between-subjects" design up to this point, the study falls into the quasi-experimental category because in attempting randomly to as-sign treatments to the sampling units a number of difficulties are encountered. First, the volunteer program will accept only individuals who attend of their own accord. However, many of them are not "willing" participants—inasmuch as this is a court-mandated program—and the volunteer program refuses to work with them. Second, the judge feels a legal or moral obligation to assign the worst offenders to the drug or group psychotherapy conditions, not to the volunteer program or the control condition. Third, an administrator at the institution con-ducting this research is worried about the risks inherent in random assignment. He believes the institution could be sued by repeat offenders who find them-selves assigned to a condition not to their liking, or sued by future victims of participants assigned to the control condition.

Difficulties such as these are typically encountered in field experiments. The essential problem is that, in employing a nonequivalent-groups design, the researcher can expect subjects in the different groups to differ because assign-ment to the experimental and comparison groups cannot be controlled. There are alternative methods that researchers employ to increase the likelihood that the comparison group is really comparable to the treated group (see Judd and Kenny, 1981). They are not without problems, however.

One alternative is to try to overcome objections against random assignment by proposing randomization *after* assignment (Vaught, 1977). In our example the assignment would be made to "experimental" groups I, II, and III on the basis of some decision process presumably involving the judge, the institutional adminis-trator, the volunteer program coordinator, and the researchers. Afterward, each group of participants would be randomly divided into experimental and control subgroups; the former subgroups receive the experimental treatment assigned and the controls receive nothing. Within groups, the experimental and control subgroups should be comparable because each experimental subgroup is natu-rally paired with its own control subgroup. The problem with this approach is that the reasons we cannot randomize to begin with may also prevent randomiz-ing after assignment, e.g., legal and ethical constraints.

A second alternative that is sometimes employed is to match the groups as closely as possible on demographic variables such as age, sex, and socioeconomic status of subjects. The problem with this approach is that matching implies biased dropping of subjects if the groups differ on the matching variables. In our ex-ample the judge would no doubt find this alternative unacceptable. However, if the researchers think that subjects need to be dropped from certain conditions in order to facilitate matching, but the judge thinks that the researchers are morally bound to include those subjects in the experimental programs, then the subjects could be included in the treatment but not in the data analysis.

A third alternative, sometimes employed when the participants who receive the treatment condition are volunteer subjects, is to assign the nonvolunteers to a "wait list" group. The wait list group is then conceptualized as an untreated control condition to be compared with the treatment group of volunteers. The problem with this approach is that nonvolunteers are often different from volunteers in ways that are related to the outcome measures. We will have more to say about volunteer and nonvolunteer subjects in Chapter 10, but another possibility might be to divide all the subjects—volunteer and nonvolunteer—into wait list and nonwait list groups.

A fourth alternative, recalling the method of concomitant variation (discussed in Chapter 4), would be to compare those subjects who received large amounts of the treatment with those who received small amounts. The problem with this approach is that the subjects who received the larger amounts may be initially different from those subjects who received the smaller amounts. If the groups are not comparable to begin with, it is problematic whether we can draw any generalizable conclusions based on their different reactions.

There is an element of inferential risk in any investigation, true experimental or quasi-experimental. In nonequivalent-groups designs the risk is that assumptions must be made about an unknown variable, inasmuch as the assignment rule is neither known nor random in most cases.

INTERRUPTED TIME-SERIES DESIGNS

The *interrupted time-series design* is that in which the effects of a treatment are inferred from comparing outcome measures obtained at different time intervals before and after the treatment is introduced. In the previous chapter we alluded to such designs within the context of single-case research (which we discuss in a moment), but interrupted time-series designs are also employed by sociologists and applied researchers for evaluating the effects of social interventions with large numbers of sampling units. The data structure is called a "time series" because there is a single data point for each point in time, and it is called an "interrupted" time series because, presumably, there is a clear dividing line at the beginning of the "experimental" treatment, or *intervention* (Judd and Kenny, 1981).

To illustrate: Diana DiNitto, a social welfare professor, employed an interrupted time-series design to evaluate the effects of government-mandated changes in the food stamp purchase requirement in 1977 (DiNitto, 1983). One change, intended to increase the number of qualified participants, consisted of awarding them a bonus equivalent to the monthly value of the stamps for which they were eligible. DiNitto focused on food stamp program participation in one state, Florida, in order to study the impact of the new law. There were three steps involved in her interrupted time-series analysis.

The initial step was to define the period of observations in this interrupted time-series design. DiNitto selected for her analysis the period from March 1972 to December 1981. This enabled her to examine food stamp participation prior to, during, and following the new law's initiation.

The next step was to obtain the data to be analyzed, but there were four considerations. First, there had to be a sufficient number of observations and time points—no fewer than 50 in order to use the data-analytic method she chose (the Box-Jenkins procedure, which we turn to in a moment). Second, the same units had to be employed throughout the analysis in order to ensure that observations and time points were equally spaced. She could not, for example, take monthly observations one year and then quarterly observations for another year. Third, the time points had to be sensitive to the particular effects being studied. If there were a drop of food stamp recipients one week each month, the time points chosen must reflect such variations. Fourth, the measurements should not fluctuate very much as a result of intrumentation changes; i.e., observations had to be reliable.

The final step was to use the Box-Jenkins (1970) procedure, also called *ARIMA* (*autoregressive integrated moving average*), as a technique to assess change (cf. Gottman, 1981; Judd and Kenny, 1981; Ostrom, 1978).

BOX-JENKINS PROCEDURE TO ASSESS CHANGE

The Box-Jenkins procedure is oriented toward identifying an underlying model of serial effects, and DiNitto considered three possibilities. One alternative was that there was an abrupt change in the level of participation followed by maintenance of the new level. Given a hypothetical mean of 3 for the pretreatment series, we can visualize this model as 3, 3, 3, 5, 5, 5, 5. That is, there would be a sharp increase level following the intervention after the third observation, and this heightened effect would continue. Another alternative was that there were gradual, constant changes in the level of participation. This may be visualized as 3, 3, 3, 4.5, 4.5, 5, 5, 5.5, in which the series after intervention shows a drift upward. A third alternative was that there was an abrupt change—called a *pulse function*—but lasting only a short time. This might be 3, 3, 3, 5, 4, 3, 3, 3, in which the effect pulses upward but then reverts to the pretreatment level.

Traditionally, the Box-Jenkins procedure calls for testing of the efficacy of each model in turn. There were some technical considerations to deal with first. In later chapters we refer to the "IID normal" assumptions that underlie use of the t and F tests, and there are similar kinds of assumptions underlying the use of the Box-Jenkins procedure. We will present two considerations in order to familiarize readers with the terminology of this procedure.

One important assumption is that a series of observations must be *stationary*; i.e., the integer values of the observations must fluctuate normally about the mean, as opposed to systematically drifting upward or downward. Most time-series observations, however, do show systematic increases or decreases in the level of the series, referred to as a *secular trend*. For statistical purposes, a secular trend can be made stationary by *differencing*, which consists of subtracting the first observation from the second, the second from the third, and so forth. For example, in the series 2, 3, 4, 5, 6, differencing would give us: $3 - 2 = 1$; $4 - 3 = 1$; $5 - 4 = 1$; $6 - 5 = 1$—which has no secular trend (i.e., 1, 1, 1, 1). Mathematically, differencing does not affect the actual pattern of the results, only the manner in which the data are entered into the time-series analysis (see, e.g., Cook and Campbell, 1979). A problem, however, is that we forfeit an observation in this series; i.e., differencing results in a loss of some data.

Another consideration concerns what is termed *autocorrelation*. This concept refers to whether the observations are dependent on one another (autocorrelated), or instead can be assumed to be independent data points. In time-series analysis a distinction is made between two kinds of autocorrelations: *regular*, which describe the dependency of adjacent observations on one another, and *seasonal*, which describe the dependency of observations separated by one period or cycle, e.g., biannual separation (Cook and Campbell, 1979). In this example we expect that food stamp recipients this month probably received them last month and the month before that, which suggests that the observations are regularly autocorrelated. Mathematically, the data analyst must allow for (or "correct") this autocorrelation, or else risk the increased likelihood of making a type I error, i.e., rejecting the null hypothesis when it should not be rejected.

After doing all this, DiNitto was able to conclude that model 1 provided the "best fit" of her interrupted time-series data. Actual results in this study were that the new law led to a sharp increase of 5 percent (12,117 households) to Florida's food stamp program, a change that DiNitto found to be statistically significant at $p < .05$. But even though statistically significant, it might be questioned whether a 5 percent increase would be regarded as "practically significant" by policy analysts. That is, would a gain of this many households be considered a reasonable gain in view of the bottom-line (i.e., cost-benefit) requirements of policy analysts, or would it be seen as a trivial gain? The difference between statistical significance and practical significance is an important issue, and we turn to it in Chapter 14.

SINGLE-CASE AND SMALL-*N* RESEARCH DESIGNS

In the preceding chapter we referred to a repeated-measures method employed by Hermann Ebbinghaus in which he himself was the only subject. This use of a single case is considered to be the prototype of what has come to be known as *small-N* or *N-of-one* or *single-case* "experimental" research. It is widely used to evaluate the effects of behavior control treatments, such as in conditioning studies of the Skinner-type employing programmed instruction and continuous assessment of performance. Because randomization is not usually a consideration in these studies, it is problematic whether to characterize them as experimental—

which is the way in which they are described in the behavior control literature. As we now see, they fit better into the category of time-series quasi-experimental designs.

The researchers who favor this approach argue that when subjects serve as their own controls, any ongoing behavior can be continuously monitored as the treatment effects are replicated within the same subjects over time. Changes in the patterns of performance are taken as the basis for drawing inferences about the treatment (Kazdin and Tuma, 1982). The researchers start by establishing a *behavioral baseline* (i.e., a comparison base), operationally defined as the "continuous, and continuing, performance of a single individual" (Sidman, 1960, p. 409). If there is any variability of the baselines of different subjects (usually rats, mice, rabbits, etc.), the procedure is to search for previously overlooked or ignored sources of differences in order to impose comparability on the data. This approach has found widespread acceptance in some areas of animal behavioral research, in which the vast majority of studies use partially or fully inbred strains of animal subjects and genetic differences are minimized by the breeding schedule.

In recent years, single-case designs have found a niche in human subject research as a quasi-experimental tool for evaluating the effects of clinical, counseling, and educational interventions (Hersen and Barlow, 1976; Kazdin and Tuma, 1982). The prototype procedure, called the "A-B-A design," has many variants and is popular among behavioral psychologists who do clinical evaluations of therapeutic treatments. It evolved out of the so-called "A-B design," which is the simplest of the strategies used for studying behavior change by single-case designs. The "A phase" refers to a baseline or pretreatment period, and the "B phase" denotes introduction of the independent variable. In an A-B design the dependent variable is measured repeatedly throughout the pretreatment and treatment phases of the study. In the A-B-A design the treatment is withdrawn at the end, and the behavior is measured; i.e., there are repeated measures before the treatment, during the treatment, and then with the treatment withdrawn.

There are a number of other variants of single-case designs that fall into this category. None is unambiguous in terms of internal validity, even though each presents certain improvements over the traditional A-B design (e.g., Barlow and Hayes, 1979; Thyer and Curtis, 1983; Watson and Workman, 1981). The "A-B-BC-B design," for example, is one in which B and C refer to two therapeutic conditions. In this case there are repeated measurements: (1) before the introduction of either treatment, (2) during treatment B, (3) during the combination of B and C, and (4) during B alone. The purpose of this design is to tease out the effect of B both in combination with C and apart from C.

Still another variant is the "A-B-A-B design." Here, the strategy is again to end on a treatment phase of B, but this quasi-experimental design provides for two occasions (B to A and then A to B) for demonstrating the positive effects for the treatment variable (Hersen and Barlow, 1976). The researchers who employ these single-case designs seldom report elaborate statistical analyses, instead insisting that a good graphical representation will usually suffice.

CROSS-LAGGED PANEL DESIGNS

We turn now to the third class of quasi-experimental designs, called *correlational*, a catchall category for odds and ends of relational methods. The term "correlational" is really a misnomer, because correlations are what one looks for in true experiments as well as in quasi-experiments, i.e., evidence that the cause and effect covary (see Cook and Campbell, 1979). In the second half of this book we discuss various techniques of correlational study in the statistical sense, but here we are interested in illustrating the structure and logic of the quasi-experimental kinds.

For our first example we examine a design that has in the past been employed with some frequency but is now treated with "skeptical advocacy" by Donald Campbell, one of its originators (see Cook and Campbell, 1979, p. 309) — the *cross-lagged panel design*. It is called "cross-lagged" because, while basically another variant of a time-series design, some data points are treated as temporally "lagged" values of the outcome variable. It is called a "panel" design because, in social survey terms, a panel study is another name for a longitudinal study, and the original idea of this design has roots in longitudinal investigations in sociological survey research. Longitudinal designs, which we discuss again in this chapter, have two principal motivations: (1) to increase the precision of the treatment comparisons by observing each subject under all the different conditions to be compared and (2) to examine the individual's changing response over time (Cook and Ware, 1983).

When the cross-lagged panel design was developed, the assumption was that longitudinal measurements of the same two variables, A and B, should potentially provide information about any causal relationships between them (Lazarsfeld, 1978). Stated another way, the cross-lagged panel model was originally intended as a method for choosing among competing causal hypotheses (Campbell, 1963; Campbell and Stanley, 1966; Lazarsfeld, 1978; Pelz and Andrew, 1964; Rozelle and Campbell, 1969).

Figure 5-1 diagrams the simplest model, in which A and B denote two variables each of which is measured individually at two successive time periods. Three sets of paired correlations are represented: *test-retest correlations* (r_{A1A2} and r_{B1B2}), *synchronous correlations* (r_{A1B1} and r_{A2B2}), and *cross-lagged correlations* (r_{A1B2} and r_{B1A2}). Test-retest correlations indicate the reliability of A and B over time. Synchronous correlations, when compared with one another, indicate the reliability of the relationship between A and B over time. Cross-lagged correlations show the relationships between two sets of data points, in which one is treated as a lagged value of the outcome variable. The question addressed by this design is whether A is a stronger cause of B than B is of A. The logic is that, given reliable test-retest and synchronous correlations, comparing the cross-lagged correlations should enable one to answer this question. The answer is "yes" if r_{A1B2} is higher than r_{B1A2}, but it is "no" if r_{B1A2} is higher than r_{A1B2} (i.e., B is a stronger cause of A than A is of B).

Figure 5-2a shows some hypothetical test-retest, synchronous, and cross-lagged correlations at three successive time periods. In this idealized case we see

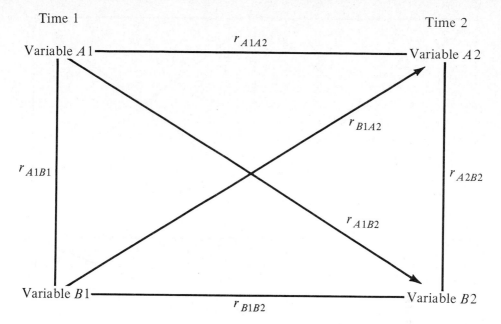

FIGURE 5-1
Design for cross-lagged and other correlations between variables A and B.

that A and B are highly reliable variables, with a consistent test-retest correlation of .85. The synchronous correlation between A and B is also remarkably consistent—.40 at times 1, 2, and 3. The cross-lagged correlations are also precisely the same within each level throughout the investigation. Since $r_{A1B2} > r_{B1A2}$ and $r_{A2B3} > r_{B2A3}$, one is led to the conclusion that the data are symptomatic of an $A \rightarrow B$ rather than a $B \rightarrow A$ causal path.

Interpretability is considered maximum when the r's remain the same at each period, as in this case. In actuality, relationships are seldom stationary but instead are usually lower over longer lapses of time, called *temporal erosion* (Kenny, 1973). Suppose the test-retest correlation of A eroded from .85 between two successive periods (i.e., $A1$ with $A2$, and also $A2$ with $A3$) down to .765 between periods 1 and 3 (i.e., $A1$ with $A3$). And suppose the same temporal rate occurred with variable B, i.e., down from .85 to .765. This 10 percent *attenuation* (reduction) in test-retest reliability leaves us with a 90 percent leftover, or *residual* effect per unit of time (shown in Figure 5-2b), i.e., $(.765/.85) \times 100 = 90$ percent. After making necessary statistical corrections, we might use this figure to estimate the attenuation of the cross-lagged correlations. In this idealized case we multiplied the 90 percent residual times each of the cross-lagged r's in Figure 5-2a. The results are given as idealized values in (b) of this figure, e.g., $.65 \times .90 = .585$.

In real life the correlations are rarely, if ever, this reliable or clear-cut. Thus there is seldom a firm and clear inference that can be made even in the

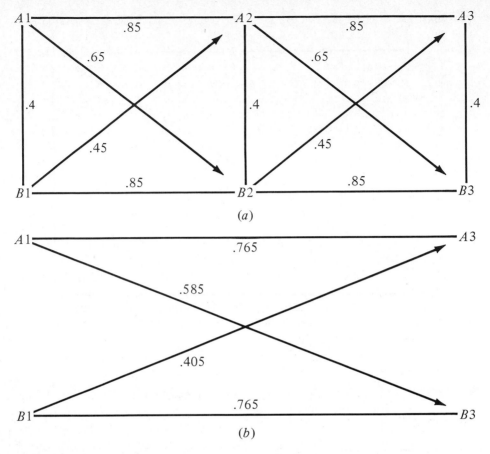

FIGURE 5-2
Hypothetical panel correlations between variables A and B measured at three successive time periods: (*a*) test-retest, synchronous, and cross-lagged correlations at two successive periods; (*b*) estimated test-retest and cross-lagged correlations based on a given temporal erosion rate.

simplest real case (see Mayer and Carroll, 1987). We turn now to real data in order to illustrate (1) some actual values of *r* and (2) another correlational method, called *path analysis*, which we discuss again in Chapter 24. This method, widely employed in sociology, economics, and political science, deals with estimating *path coefficients* from correlation coefficients. Cross-lagged panel analysis, which is much less widely used than path analysis, can be presented in path analysis form (Cook and Campbell, 1979), and in the following case we introduce the logic of this approach.

PATH ANALYSIS IN THE CONTEXT OF A CROSS-LAGGED DESIGN

In this study the researchers were interested in the increasing prominence of violence in American society (Eron, Huesmann, Lefkowitz, and Walder, 1972). In particular, they turned their attention to television programming, with its heavy emphasis on violence and lawlessness, as a plausible cause of violence in our society. A number of laboratory experiments had in the past demonstrated an immediate effect on the extent of aggressive behavior of subjects who witnessed aggressive displays on film. In the minds of these researchers, however, the applicability of these results to nonlaboratory situations seemed questionable because of what they perceived as a lack of correspondence with real-life television viewing habits. To deal with this problem the researchers in this study collected longitudinal data on several hundred teenagers of an original group of children who had participated in a study of third-grade children in 1960 (Eron, 1963; Eron, Walder, and Lefkowitz, 1971). The research design was essentially that shown in Figure 5-1.

So far in our discussion of the cross-lagged panel design we have considered only the possibility that $A \rightarrow B$ or $B \rightarrow A$. However, a causal relationship can be either positive or negative and can also take a more circuitous causal path involving, for example, $A1 \rightarrow A2 \rightarrow B2$ or $B1 \rightarrow A1 \rightarrow B2$. Figure 5-3 shows the results obtained by these researchers in their attempt to examine the relationship between television viewing habits in children and their subsequent behavior. The information collected in both time periods, 1960 and 1970, fell into two classes: (1) measures of aggression (such as asking students "Who starts a fight over nothing?" and "Who takes other children's things without asking?") and (2) potential predictors of aggression (in particular, preference for violent television programs, e.g., by asking each mother for her child's three favorite television programs).

The results shown in Figure 5-3 indicate the correlations between a preference for violent television, labeled as A, and peer-rated aggression, labeled as B,

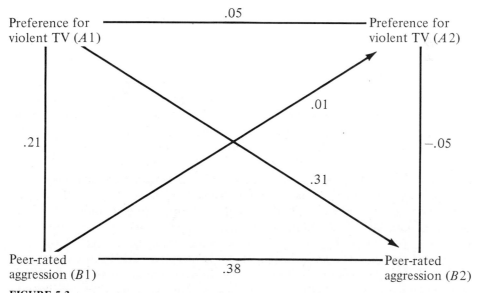

FIGURE 5-3
Correlations between a preference for violent television and peer-rated aggression for 211 boys in 1960 and 1970 (after Eron, Huesmann, Lefkowitz, and Walder, 1972).

for boys over a 10-year lag (Eron, Huesmann, Lefkowitz, and Walder, 1972, p. 257). In contrast to the mock data shown in Figure 5-2, these real data indicate some not very reliable relationships. We see, first of all, that the relationship between A and B in the third grade is positive ($r = .21$) but 10 years later is negative and quite small ($r = -.05$). We also observe the test-retest correlations are only .05 for a preference for violent TV and .38 for aggression. We find a statistically significant relationship between a preference for violent television in the third grade and aggressive habits 10 years later ($r = .31$). But we see that the alternative causal pattern is quite negligible ($r = .01$). The challenge is to make inferences about a childhood preference for violent TV and teenage aggression with this temporal information.

It is not possible to demonstrate that a particular hypothesis is true, but it is possible to reject untenable hypotheses and in this way to narrow down the plausible rival explanations. In this study the results established that there exists a statistically significant relationship between a preference for violent television in the third grade and aggressive habits 10 years later. The researchers considered five plausible hypotheses for this result, which are shown in Figure 5-4 as five different causal paths.

Path 1, the major hypothesis of this study, was that preferring to watch violent television is a direct cause of aggressive behavior. Results of both the synchronous correlation between $A1$ and $B1$ (.21) and the cross-lagged correlation between $A1$ and $B2$ (.31) seem logically consistent with this hypothesis. The low test-retest reliability of variable A might be explained by the notion that the subjects, by the time they were teenagers, were more likely to turn to other, more overtly aggressive activities (e.g., stealing and fighting) rather than getting their "kicks" vicariously by watching violent TV. That might explain the vanishing correlation between $A2$ and $B2$. The researchers also recognized four rival hypotheses to account for the results, represented as paths 2 to 5 in this figure.

Path 2 hypothesizes that a preference for violent TV as a young child stimulates the child to be aggressive, and this aggressive behavior carries over into the teenage years. The researchers ruled out this hypothesis on the grounds that the correlation between the end points (previously indicated in Figure 5-3 as $r = .31$ between $A1$ and $B2$) is much higher than the product of the intermediate correlations. They reasoned that, if the hypothesis were true, the relationship between the end points (i.e., $A1$ and $B2$) would have been no stronger than the product of the relations between all adjacent intermediate points (i.e., $.21 \times .38 = .08$).

Path 3 hypothesizes that aggressive children prefer aggressive television, and a preference for aggressive TV then leads to aggressive behavior as teenagers. The researchers eliminated this hypothesis on similar grounds as for the second hypothesis. The strength of the relationship between the end points, i.e., $B1$ and $B2$ ($r = .38$ in Figure 5-3) is much greater than the product of the relationships between all adjacent intermediate points shown in Figure 5-4.

Path 4 is not so easily rejected. It hypothesizes that aggressive children are both (1) more likely to enjoy watching aggressive television and (2) more likely to become aggressive teenagers. The researchers reasoned that if this were the complete explanation of the relationship between $A1$ and $B2$, then adjusting for

Path 1:

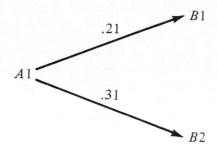

Path 2:

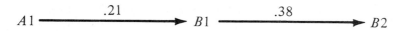

Path 3:

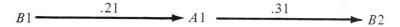

Path 4:

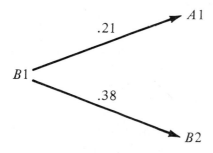

Path 5:

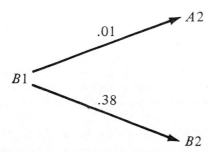

FIGURE 5-4
Five plausible causal paths to explain the correlations presented in Figure 5-3 (after Eron, Huesmann, Lefkowitz, and Walder, 1972).

third-grade aggression would result in a near-zero relation between $A1$ and $B2$. They tested this idea by computing a *partial correlation*, i.e., a correlation between two variables when the influence of other variables on their relationship has been eliminated. The partial correlation computed was between $A1$ and $B2$ while controlling for $B1$; the result was a partial correlation of .25. Because this is only .06 below the original correlation between $A1$ and $B2$ (.31 in Figure 5-3), they concluded that path 4 is implausible as a "complete" causal explanation.

Path 5 is that early aggression causes both (1) a weaker preference for TV violence as a teenager and (2) a penchant for continuing to be aggressive. To assess this hypothesis the researchers decided they needed an "unattenuated" cross-correlation (i.e., a correlation not reduced by the passage of time) as a comparison base to evaluate the .01 r between $B1$ and $A2$. Without going into detail, it will suffice to say that they found that .01 was very close to that comparison base, leading them to reject this fifth hypothesis (cf. Rozelle and Campbell, 1969).

Having eliminated the various rival hypotheses, they concluded that path 1 could best account for the observed results. That is, watching violent television has a direct causal link to aggressive behavior in some viewers, they concluded.

UTILITY OF COHORT RESEARCH DESIGNS

Previously, we stated that one purpose of longitudinal designs (e.g., the cross-lagged panel procedure) is to examine the individual's response over an extended period of time. We turn now to a wider category of longitudinal designs, consisting of two general classes: *pure longitudinal designs*, in which a "cohort" is followed over time, and *mixed longitudinal designs*, in which several cohorts are followed and age effects, time effects, and cohort effects are examined periodically (cf. Cook and Ware, 1983). The *cohort* refers to a collection of people who were born in the same period (Ryder, 1965), and we begin by illustrating the utility of cohort designs for longitudinal analysis.

Some years ago, it was believed that the age curve for intelligence increased to a maximum at 30 years of age and then declined. The bases of this accepted relationship were the results of cross-sectional studies in which IQ tests had been given at the same time to younger and older persons whose scores were then compared as a function of their calendar ages. The term "cross-sectional" refers to the fact that the research took a slice of time in order to observe variables (in this case, the subject's chronological age and his or her IQ test score) as they existed at one brief period in time. Another name for cross-sectional investigations is *synchronic research*, i.e., research having reference to the facts as they exist at one point in time. Later, a very different picture of the relationship between chronological age and intelligence began to emerge when a comparison was made of the cross-sectional results of the IQ testing of military draftees during World Wars I and II.

It was observed that the average IQ of young adults tested in the early 1940s (World War II) coincided with the 82d percentile of young adults tested 24 years earlier (World War I). That is, the World War I recruits, when they were the same age as the World War II recruits, scored much lower in IQ. The new picture was based on a reinterpretation of the earlier cross-sectional results as being in error owing to the confounding of cohort and age of subjects. It seemed plausible that cohort effects (i.e., differences in the life experiences of the different generations of people) could account for differences in the status of their IQ test results. In other words, it was not that IQ decays after age 30, but that 20 or 30 years is a dividing line between the experiences of one generation and another (e.g., education, child-rearing practices, cultural advantages). Thus, if both cohorts had been tested at the same time (as in the earlier studies), it would have "looked as if" the older generation had lost some intelligence points over the intervening period (24 years). In actuality, of course, the older generation would not have performed as well on the tests even when they were the same age as the younger generation.

This example illustrates how the relationship between age and IQ can be misinterpreted by relying on the results of cross-sectional studies instead of on the results of longitudinal studies of cohorts. Cohort designs for longitudinal research are an example of what are called *diachronic* research designs, i.e., research designs in which a phenomenon or variable is observed in such a way as to uncover changes that occur during successive periods of time. Thus, this example implies the utility of cohort designs as procedures for uncovering relationships that can only remain shrouded in synchronic research designs. We have seen that synchronic research designs come in a variety of experimental and quasi-experimental forms. Diachronic research designs of the cohort type, which are inherently relational, also come in a variety of different forms, as we see next (cf. Schaie, 1965; Wohlwill, 1970).

LIMITATIONS OF DIFFERENT FORMS OF COHORT DESIGNS

One way to begin to visualize the various forms and combinations of cohort designs is with the help of what is called a *cohort table*. Table 5.1 provides the basic data and enables us to see the basic differences between synchronic and diachronic designs for age, period, and generational (cohort) analyses. The values in the body of this table, adapted from a more complete cohort design reported by sociologists Jacques A. Hagenaars and Niki P. Cobben (1978), give the percentages of women in the Netherlands with no religious affiliation, according to age and time period. The results are shown for seven different cohorts (or "generations") of respondents.

The analysis of one particular column would be comparable to the "one-shot case study" design noted in Chapter 4, i.e., a cross-sectional survey. An example is shown with reference to period 4; Figure 5-5 shows the shape of the cross-sectional age curve in 1969. These data seem to support the conclusion that, with the passing of years and the approach of the end of life, religious observance increases (i.e., percentage of nonaffiliation decreases).

The analysis of one particular cohort would be equivalent to a longitudinal survey carried out periodically to follow the life course of that generation of in-

TABLE 5.1
Percentages of women in the Netherlands with no religious affiliation, according to age and time period

	Period 1 (1909)	Period 2 (1929)	Period 3 (1949)	Period 4 (1969)
Age 20–30	Cohort 4 4.8%	Cohort 5 13.9%	Cohort 6 17.4%	Cohort 7 23.9%
Age 40–50	Cohort 3 3.1%	Cohort 4 11.9%	Cohort 5 17.2%	Cohort 6 22.0%
Age 60–70	Cohort 2 1.9%	Cohort 3 6.7%	Cohort 4 11.9%	Cohort 5 19.4%
Age 80–	Cohort 1 1.2%	Cohort 2 3.8%	Cohort 3 6.6%	Cohort 4 12.2%

Note: An example of a cross-sectional design is shown by the vertical analysis (Period 4), and an example of a longitudinal design is shown by the diagonal analysis (Cohort 4).

Source: J. A. Hagenaars and N. P. Cobben, "Age, Cohort and Period: A General Model for the Analysis of Social Change," *Netherlands Journal of Sociology,* 1978, *14,* 59–91. Reprinted by permission of Elsevier Scientific Publishing Co.

dividuals. An example is shown with reference to cohort 4 (on the diagonal of Table 5.1), and Figure 5-5 shows the shape of the age curve from 1909 to 1969. Here, we clearly see that the conclusion based on the cross-sectional survey *cannot* be correct.

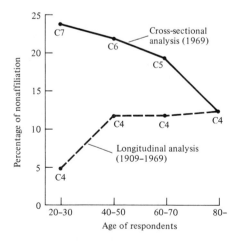

FIGURE 5-5
Percentages of women in the Netherlands not affiliated with a church, as shown by a cross-sectional design in 1969 and a longitudinal design from 1909 to 1969 (after Hagenaars and Cobben, 1978). Cohorts are symbolized as C7 (cohort 7), C6 (cohort 6), and so forth.

When we have an adequate cohort table, such as that in Table 5.1, other relevant analyses are also possible. For example, we could improve on the one-shot analysis by plotting all the cross-sectional curves, as shown in Figure 5-6a. We now see that the exact percentages of affiliation and the slopes of the age curves are different for different periods. We could also plot the values according to cohort of women, as shown in Figure 5-6b, which helps us to avoid the mistake of assuming that the results of an analysis of one particular time period are generalizable to other periods (called the *fallacy of period centrism*).

This design can also be used with survey data to study age trends by re-examining not the same persons, but a particular age group (persons aged 21 to 29 in 1963) several years later (persons aged 30 to 38 in 1972). It approximates a true longitudinal design because the sampling units are based on random selection.

It should be noted that the concepts of age, cohort, and period are defined differently in different fields. In the literature on counseling and student development, "age" is often taken to mean the subject's year in school rather than chronological age (Whiteley, Burkhart, Harway-Herman, and Whiteley, 1975). Similarly, in research on social change, "period" is often defined as some environmental effect or cultural change that is the result of lengthy historical processes such as industrialization or urbanization (Hagenaars and Cobben, 1978). In general, (1) the *age effect* represents changes in the average response due to the natural aging process, (2) the *time of measurement effect* refers to the impact of events in chronological time that occur at the points of measurement, and (3)

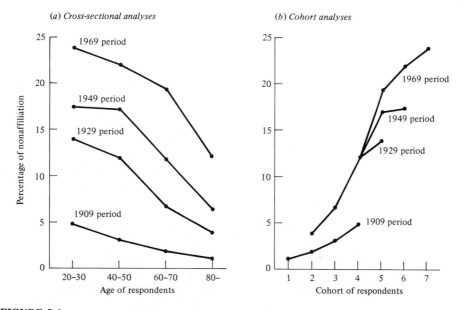

FIGURE 5-6
Percentages of women in the Netherlands not affiliated with a church, according to (a) age of women and (b) cohort of women (after Hagenaars and Cobben, 1978).

the *cohort effect* represents "past history" specific to a particular generation and contributes to all measurements of the generation (Cook and Ware, 1983).

Table 5.2 provides a comparison of different longitudinal and cross-sectional designs in which age, time of measurement (period), and cohort are the major variables (Schaie, 1965; Wohlwill, 1970). The three effects cannot be estimated simultaneously in any of the designs:

First, in the *simple cross-sectional design*, subjects at different ages are observed at the same time. The limitation of this design is that it confounds the age of the subject and the cohort. That is, 20-year-olds would be from only one generation.

TABLE 5.2

Five sampling designs according to "age" (grades 1–6), period (history or time of measurement), and cohort (C1 to C11)

Simple cross-sectional design (1980)

Age	Period					
	1975	1976	1977	1978	1979	1980
G1	C6	C7	C8	C9	C10	C11
G2	C5	C6	C7	C8	C9	C10
G3	C4	C5	C6	C7	C8	C9
G4	C3	C4	C5	C6	C7	C8
G5	C2	C3	C4	C5	C6	C7
G6	C1	C2	C3	C4	C5	C6

Simple longitudinal design

Age	Period					
	1975	1976	1977	1978	1979	1980
G1	C6					
G2		C6				
G3			C6			
G4				C6		
G5					C6	
G6						C6

Cohort-sequential design

Age	Period					
	1975	1976	1977	1978	1979	1980
G1						
G2						
G3	C4	C5	C6			
G4		C4	C5	C6		
G5			C4	C5	C6	
G6				C4	C5	C6

Time-sequential design

Age	Period					
	1975	1976	1977	1978	1979	1980
G1				C9	C10	C11
G2				C8	C9	C10
G3				C7	C8	C9
G4				C6	C7	C8
G5				C5	C6	C7
G6				C4	C5	C6

Cross-sequential design

Age	Period					
	1975	1976	1977	1978	1979	1980
G1	C6					
G2	C5	C6				
G3	C4	C5	C6			
G4			C4	C5	C6	
G5				C4	C5	
G6					C4	

Note: Each sampling design is accentuated by dotted lines. Only the first subtable is completely labeled to show all possible cohorts; in addition it shows the simple cross-sectional design for the 1980 period (set off by dotted lines).

Second, in the *simple longitudinal design*, subjects of the same cohort are observed over several periods. The deficiency in this case is that the design does not control for the effect of history (or period). That is, different results might have been obtained if people from different time periods had been studied.

Third, in the *cohort-sequential design*, several cohorts are studied, with the initial measurements taken in successive years. The design takes into account cohort and age, but does not take time of measurement (period) fully into account. That is, different results might have been obtained if all the blank spaces representing time of measurement were filled in.

Fourth, in the *time-sequential design*, subjects at different ages are observed at several different times. This design considers age and time of measurement, but as the blank spaces indicate, it does not take cohort fully into account.

Fifth, in the *cross-sequential design*, several different cohorts that are observed over several periods are initially measured in the same period. This design takes into account the time of measurement and the cohort but (again as indicated by the blank spaces) does not take age fully into account.

Even though the more complex designs are a distinct improvement over the simple cross-sectional design when studying maturational processes, we see that each design is limited in some way. This is not a startling revelation, inasmuch as all empirical research (as noted in Chapter 1) has its limitations. This table also reminds us that, in order to achieve an optimum level of understanding, it is best whenever possible to employ a variety of different methods each of which has its own but different limitations.

CHAPTER
6

SUBJECT-EXPERIMENTER ARTIFACTS AND THEIR CONTROL

NATURE OF THE ARTIFACT PROBLEM

The term *artifact* is used in this chapter to refer, generally, to findings resulting from factors other than the one intended by the experimenter, usually factors quite extraneous to the intent of the experimenter. However, it does not refer simply to serendipitous findings, but to findings resulting from uncontrolled factors which could jeopardize the validity (construct, internal, or external) of the researcher's conclusion about what went on in the study, or the implications of the findings. In particular, we will be interested in this chapter in *subject-experimenter artifacts*, by which we mean the threats to validity that reside in one or both sides of the psychological equation involving the interaction between the experimenter and the subject. The *experimenter* is used here as a general concept that refers to an investigator who *tests* or *tries* some observational method in behavioral science, i.e., experimental *or* quasi-experimental research.

To the extent that experimenters hope for dependable knowledge in behavioral science, they must have dependable knowledge about the experimenter-subject equation. Without an understanding of the data collection situation, behavioral researchers can no more hope to acquire accurate information for their disciplines than astronomers and zoologists could hope to acquire accurate information without their understanding of the operation of their telescopes and microscopes. In behavioral science it is the experimenter himself or herself who is frequently the "instrument" of observation, which makes the artifact problem intriguing as an area of study, called the "social psychology of the psychological experiment." We are interested in various aspects of this problem, but with particular emphasis on its control.

We shall begin by discussing the subject side of the data collection situation. Much of the complexity of human activity described by behavioral researchers is in the nature of the human organism that serves as our model—the research subject. We know, for example, that no two research subjects behave identically. Thus we also know that the "same" careful experiment conducted in one place at one time can often yield results very different from one conducted in another place at another time. While it is generally accepted that much of this complexity is due to the endless intricacies of human nature, it is also recognized that most subjects know perfectly well that they are to be research participants and this role is to be played out in interaction with another human being, the experimenter. Considerable evidence has been gathered to suggest that the role of the research subject is well understood by the majority of normal adults who find their way into the behavioral scientists' subject pools (see Adair, 1973; Rosenthal and Rosnow, 1969; Silverman, 1977). As a consequence, what one researcher interprets as a causal relationship between X and Y may be seen by another researcher as the relationship between some role variable and Y.

We shall also examine the opposite side of the data collection equation— the experimenter. The systematic errors generated by the experimenter are usually unintentional, and it is convenient to think of them as falling into two classes: noninteractional and interactional. *Noninteractional errors* are biases that do not affect the actual response of the human or animal subject; they are in the mind, the eye, or the hand of the experimenter. *Interactional errors* are biases that do affect the actual response of the research subject. We shall see that there are several kinds of noninteractional and interactional experimenter effects. One in particular, the experimenter expectancy effect, is of special interest to us, and we discuss how it can be assessed or possibly reduced.

The term "control" will again refer to the use of a comparison condition to isolate some effect or the use of a procedure to serve as a check on validity. In this discussion it can also refer to ways of exercising restraint or direction, or of holding certain events in check, which thus enable the experimenter to avoid some particular artifact. There has been considerable research into the social psychology of the psychological experiment, but it was not until the 1960s that it began in earnest. To learn why it took so long to happen, and also to give further insight into the critical process in science, we will have something to say about the history of the artifact problem.

HISTORY OF THE ARTIFACT PROBLEM IN BEHAVIORAL SCIENCE

Interestingly, three events during the first three decades of this century could conceivably have sparked interest in isolating, measuring, and possibly eliminating or circumventing subject and experimenter artifacts, but they did not do so. Foremost among these events was the case of Clever Hans, a horse known throughout Europe for his remarkable "intellectual" feats. Hans could tap out the answers to mathematical problems or the date of any day mentioned, aided ostensibly by a code table in front of him. Visitors from all over Europe came to examine Hans. One visitor, the psychologist Oskar Pfungst, discovered in careful observations made over a 6-month period that Hans was responding to the unintentional cues of his questioners (Pfungst, 1911/1965). For instance, someone would ask Hans a question that required a long tapping response, and then the questioner would lean forward as if settling in for a long wait. Hans responded to the questioner's forward movement, not to the actual question, and kept tapping until the questioner unwittingly communicated the expectancy that Hans would stop tapping. This the questioner might do by beginning to straighten up in anticipation that Hans was about to reach the correct number of taps.

Pfungst's unraveling of the mystery of Clever Hans dramatically demonstrated the potentially contaminating influence of the inadvertent cues elicited by a questioner's expectations. Given the influence on animal subjects, might not the same phenomenon hold for human subjects who were interacting with experimenters oriented by their own theoretical expectations and hypotheses? Though Pfungst's results were widely circulated and dutifully cited by other researchers, the wider methodological implications of his discovery did not strike a resonant chord in behavioral science during this period. To be sure, a number of leading behavioral researchers, including Hermann Ebbinghaus and Ivan Pavlov, voiced their suspicion that experimenters might unwittingly influence their subjects (Ebbinghaus, 1885, 1913; Gruenberg, 1929). However, their concerns, along with the wider methodological implications of Pfungst's discovery, went largely unheeded for several decades.

In a pioneering series of studies that began in 1924 and continued for a number of years, another major discovery occurred in the Western Electric Company's Hawthorne works, located on the boundary between Chicago and Cicero, Illinois (Roethlisberger and Dickson, 1939). A team of researchers, led by Elton Mayo, F. J. Roethlisberger, and W. J. Dickson, studied how workers' productivity and job satisfaction were affected by workplace conditions such as light, temperature, and rest periods. In the illumination study the workers were taken from their regular jobs to be placed in a test room. Workers in the experimental condition worked under decreasing levels of illumination, while the lighting received by workers in the control condition was a constant illumination. The striking result was that both sets of subjects increased their performance until it was virtually impossible for those in the experimental condition to see what they were doing.

The results of these studies were later talked about as being due to the inadvertent changes made in order to create a controlled experiment. For example, special privileges were allowed the participants, and it was suggested by textbook writers and methodologists that the workers' performance increased because they were "flattered" to participate, or were more keenly aware and responsive to task-orienting cues than would be expected in "real-life" work situations. The term *Hawthorne effect* was coined by the contributor of a chapter in a popular research methods textbook in the 1950s (French, 1953) and was soon picked up and widely quoted in other books and articles in psychology and sociology. In recent years the Hawthorne effect seems to have become synonymous with "placebo effect" as a tag label for the power of suggestion in experimental research (Sommer, 1968).

Recent examinations of the original investigation have revealed numerous inaccuracies in standard textbook interpretations of what occurred at the Hawthorne plant. Because excellent discussions of the original results, as well as of the later misinterpretations and reinterpretations of them, are available (see Adair, 1984; Gillespie, 1988), it will suffice to say that, as in the case of Clever Hans, the official account of the Hawthorne experiments, as echoed by researchers and textbook writers, provoked informal interest but failed to spark any systematic research on the artifact problem.

This is not to say that behavioral researchers were, without any exception, complacent about the wider theoretical implications of the data collection situation. The third in this trilogy of historical events occurred in 1933. Saul Rosenzweig, a young psychologist who had just gotten his Ph.D. degree, published what (with hindsight) is generally recognized as a landmark paper, in which he argued that the experimental situation is a psychological problem in its own right (Rosenzweig, 1933). In large measure on the basis of his interpretation and application of psychoanalytic concepts, he developed a methodological analysis of what transpires in the human interaction of the psychological laboratory and introduced a taxonomy of certain types of interaction (Rosenzweig, 1986). He contended, for instance, that subjects might try to guess the purpose of the experiment and then give the results that they thought were desired by the experimenter—now called the *good subject effect*. Further, the experimenter might unwittingly influence the results (not unlike the questioners of Clever Hans). Rosenzweig suggested that these concerns might be profitably investigated and ways found to avoid or minimize the problems.

RESISTANCE TO THE ARTIFACT PROBLEM

Although published in the prestigious *Psychological Review*, Rosenzweig's theoretical analysis was largely ignored. It took until the 1960s for the concept to be rediscovered by researchers working in the area of the social psychology of the psychological experiment. Before we turn to this work, it is interesting to ask why it took so long for systematic research on subject and experimenter artifacts to begin in earnest. In light of Pfungst's dramatic discovery, the Hawthorne study, and Rosenzweig's prescient analysis, it might be expected that research on artifacts would have been high on the behavioral scientists' agendas. Why should the early researchers tend to ignore or fail to appreciate what, in retrospect, were clearly serious issues? Three reasons for this resistance or oversight have been suggested (Suls and Rosnow, 1988).

First, the phenomenon of artifacts that stem from playing a subject role presupposes the active influence of conscious cognition. Until the 1950s, such a presupposition was largely inconsistent with behavioristic tenets (noted in Chapter 1). Those tenets emphasized the use only of observable responses as data and dismissed cognition as a variable of less than scientific significance (Watson, 1913).

Second, concerns about pervasive biases that may be part and parcel of human research were possibly viewed as impeding the emergence and growing influence of behavioral research and its status as a science in the United States.

For instance, there was tremendous growth of academic psychology departments and an increasing role for experimental psychologists in the government, military, and industry because of widespread optimism about the likely benefits to be achieved by a scientific psychology. Concerns about the possible weaknesses of experimental research—upon which major psychological facts and theories were based—might promote doubts about the field and undermine its growing influence.

Third, owing in large part to its scientific aspiration, the psychologists and others believed strongly in philosophical ideas gleaned from classical physics and biology. By the 1930s, these behavioral researchers were finding support for the major assumptions of the classical mechanistic approach in assertions of the logical positivist view (Toulmin and Leary, 1985). This approach placed great faith in the impartiality (or "objectivity") of experimental research, but the case of Clever Hans and the Hawthorne study raised the possibility that impartiality was an illusion.

For all these reasons, then, behavioral researchers were simply unprepared to take the methodological implications of Pfungst's study of Clever Hans, the Hawthorne effect, or Rosenzweig's conceptual analysis as seriously as they might have. The situation began to change in the late 1950s, as positivistic and logical empiricist tenets began to lose their hold on behavioral researchers with the rise of cognitive science and the sprouting of a more liberalized notion of science in general. By the 1960s, scientists in all fields were talking about the critical limits of empirical inquiry, instead of treating science as an endless frontier. In almost every field—from physics and mathematics to philosophy, biomedicine, and sociology—there seemed to be a crisis of confidence brewing, at the center of which was an erosion of trust in traditional assumptions (Rosnow, 1981). We return to these developments in Chapter 12, but we now examine some of the artifact work that was conducted starting in the 1950s.

DEMAND CHARACTERISTICS AND THE GOOD SUBJECT EFFECT

Martin T. Orne, a psychiatrist and clinical and social psychologist, was in the first wave of contemporary researchers to initiate a program of empirical investigation into the social psychology of the psychological experiment. He came to realize the need for systematic research on this problem as a consequence of observations he made in his research on hypnosis. In the 1950s, he performed a number of experiments that suggested that the trance manifestations a volunteer subject exhibits on entering hypnosis might be determined in part by the subject's motivation to "act out" the role of a hypnotized person. Both the subject's preconceptions of how a hypnotized person ought to act and the cues communicated by the hypnotist were conceptualized by Orne as plausible determinants of the subject's expectations concerning how this role was to be enacted (Orne, 1970).

Orne wondered, if subjects participating in hypnosis research wanted to give the hypnotist what he or she was looking for, might not subjects in other kinds of psychological research be doing the same thing? His answer proceeded on the assumption that research participants, surely, are sensitive to any task-orienting cues that are unwittingly communicated to them by means of campus scuttlebutt, the experimenter's instructions, the research setting, and other aspects of the experimental situation. He hypothesized that research subjects would be prone to act out the role of the "good" subject, i.e., to give the experimenters what they presumably wanted to find. The phrase *demand characteristics of the experimental situation* was coined by Orne to refer to the mixture of various hints and cues that govern the subject's perceptions of his or her role and of the experimenter's hypothesis (Orne, 1962). In an elegant series of studies, he then proceeded to test this interesting hypothesis.

In one representative study, he tested whether subjects in experimental hypnosis will behave in whatever ways that they are led to believe are characteristic of hypnotized subjects (Orne, 1959). He first concocted a novel characteristic of hypnosis, "catalepsy of the dominant hand," which he demonstrated to a large college class using volunteers in a lecture on hypnosis. The volunteers were given the posthypnotic suggestion that on entering a "trance" they would manifest catalepsy (rigidity) of the dominant hand. The class was instructed that catalepsy of the dominant hand was a "classical" reaction of the hypnotized subject, and attention was called to the fact that the right-handed subject exhibited catalepsy of the right hand and the left-handed subject exhibited catalepsy of the left hand. In another lecture section, designed to serve as a control condition, the demonstration of hypnosis was also performed, but there was no discussion or display of catalepsy of the dominant hand. A few weeks later, students from both classes were invited to serve as the research subjects in a study of hypnosis. When they arrived at the laboratory and were hypnotized, catalepsy of the dominant hand was found to be present in almost all the subjects who attended the previous lecture asserting that the response was characteristic of the hypnotized state. None of the subjects in the control condition exhibited the catalepsy response.

On the basis of similar observations in a series of followup studies, Orne theorized that the typical subject is attentive to demand characteristics and attempts to behave "altruistically," i.e., in a way that confirms what he or she believes to be the experimenter's scientific hypothesis. However, as we see next, the subject's behavior is probably influenced by a variety of motivations, including this kind of altruistic role behavior, but which are not easy to fathom in advance.

ALTRUISM, EVALUATION APPREHENSION, AND OBEDIENCE AS MOTIVATORS

Orne theorized that subjects in psychology experiments have a predilection to enact the good subject role. There is, in fact, evidence to indicate that students as early as high school will tend to associate the role of the psychological research subject with characteristics such as being cooperative, alert, and observant, i.e., attributes of the good subject (Rosenthal and Rosnow, 1975). In the early 1960s, it became clear to a number of artifact researchers (including Orne) that subjects do not always enact the "altruistic" role; that is, they do not always make an attempt to fulfill the experimenter's scientific expectations. Other motivations besides wanting to be cooperative, alert, and observant may be operative in the subjects' minds as they approach the research situation.

Figure 6-1 illustrates the relationships between three kinds of hypothesized subject motivations—altruism (i.e., helping the cause of science), obedience to authority, and evaluation apprehension—and being in a psychology experiment (Aiken and Rosnow, 1973; in Rosenthal and Rosnow, 1975). It also serves to introduce another correlational procedure, called *multidimensional scaling* (MDS), which we turn to again in a later chapter. Briefly, MDS is a set of mathematical techniques for constructing a pictorial representation of the "hidden structure" of the relations among data points. By analogy, if we were given a map showing the locations of different cities, we could easily construct a table of distances between them. We would measure the distance between pairs of cities with a ruler, convert the distances into some scalar unit (e.g., miles or kilometers), and then make a table in which the rows and columns showed the names of the cities and the cells showed the distance between each pair. If we reverse this situation, we see the essential nature of MDS. What it does is to make a "map" out of a table of psychological distances (Kruskal and Wish, 1978).

The map shown in this figure was developed by having college students indicate how similar or different they perceived the 11 situations to be. Three kinds of motivations were represented by two related situations in a kind of "projective" technique. Orne's conception of the good subject as altruistically motivated is reflected in "giving anonymously to charity" and "working free as a laboratory assistant." Another type of subject motivation, called *evaluation apprehension* by Milton J. Rosenberg (1966), refers to the notion that subjects are concerned about being observed and judged while in the experimental setting. Here, the idea is that the subjects will develop hypotheses about how to win positive evaluation and how to avoid negative evaluation, clinically reflected in the analogous situations of "taking a final exam" and "being interviewed for a job." The third subject motivation, *obedience to authority*, refers to the idea that, like "obeying a No Smoking sign" or "not arguing with the professor," the research subject dutifully wants to go along with what he or she is told to do (Fillenbaum, 1966; Kelman, 1972; Sigall, Aronson, and Van Hoose, 1970).

Each statement was paired with every other statement until all possible combinations were exhausted. Using a 15-point rating scale, the subject was asked to say how similar or different two situations were, using any personal standard. The key situation, for purposes of this discussion, was "being a subject in a psychology experiment" (no. 11). In this figure, the closer the data points are to one another, the more similar the situations were perceived. Arrows show the psychological distance from the mean of each of the paired situations representing altruism (1 and 2), obedience (3 and 4), and evaluation apprehension (5 and 6) to the key situation (11). Labels on the vertical and horizontal axes indicate how the two dimensions were named by the researchers after examining the results.

What do we learn from this map? First, we see that being a subject in a psychology experiment was most closely associated with the good subject role (Orne's original hypothesis). Second, we find that the other hypothesized motivations, obedience and evaluation apprehension, also entered into these potential subjects' thinking. Third, we learn that the college students who participated in this study viewed the idea of research participation not as onerous, but as a mildly

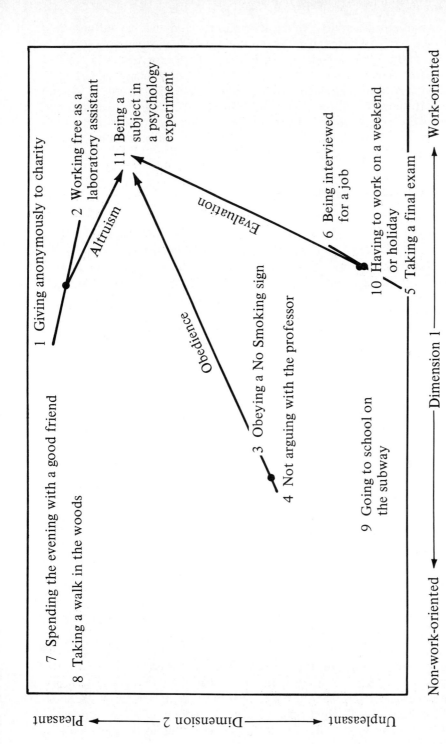

FIGURE 6-1

Multidimensional map of subjects' perceptions of the relative distances between three kinds of subject motivations (altruism, obedience to authority, and evaluation apprehension) and the key situation of being a subject in a psychology experiment. The proximity of any pair of situations reflects the perceived similarity in role expectations for the pair members.

pleasant, work-oriented activity. Before leaving this study we should note that the results were based on respondents' perceptions *before* participating in an actual research study. What would happen if the subject experienced a conflict of motives after having begun to participate in a psychology experiment? That question has been addressed experimentally, and the results of several studies (e.g., Rosnow, Goodstadt, Suls, and Gitter, 1973; Sigall, Aronson, and Van Hoose, 1970) indicate that evaluation apprehension (i.e., "looking good") is likely to emerge as the predominant motivation of many subjects, as opposed to helping the cause of science ("doing good").

METHODS OF DETECTING
TASK-ORIENTING CUES

How can researchers detect the demand characteristics possibly lurking in their experiments and quasi experiments? Orne proposed the use of *quasi-control subjects* as a possible way to get the subjects themselves to figure out what is going on just by thinking about it (Orne, 1962, 1969). Quasi controls are subjects who step out of their traditional roles and serve as "coinvestigators" rather than as "objects of study" for the experimenter to manipulate. Such subjects, Orne advised, should be drawn from the same population as the other subjects, but the experimenter specifically instructs the quasi controls to reflect "clinically" on the context in which the experiment is being conducted. They then speculate on the ways in which the situation might influence their behavior if they were in the experimental group. Orne described three specific quasi-control techniques.

One approach is to have the experimental subjects function as their own quasi controls. This would involve eliciting from the subjects, by judicious and exhaustive inquiry in a postexperimental interview or in an interview conducted after a pilot study, their perceptions and beliefs about the experimental situation, without making them unduly suspicious or inadvertently cuing them about what to say.

A second approach, called *preinquiry*, employs quasi-control subjects who are told to *imagine* that they are the real research subjects. The quasi controls never actually take part in the experiment but are given the same information about it that is provided the research subjects. After being informed of all significant details of the experiment, the quasi controls predict how they might behave if they were the real subjects. Similarity between the data from the quasi controls and the real subjects would imply that the experimental results *could* have been affected by the real subjects' guesses about how they should respond, i.e., rather than by the experimental manipulation.

The third approach is to use *blind controls*, who are unaware of their status. The researcher compares the reactions of these "blind" subjects with the quasi controls who were told to imagine that they were the real research subjects. This is sometimes accomplished by using a *sacrifice group* of blind subjects. Some subjects' participation at different points during the course of an experiment is terminated ("sacrificed"), and they are then questioned about their perceptions of the experiment up to that point (Orne, 1970).

In addition to the use of quasi controls, another technique to ferret out demand characteristics involves observing the dependent variable more than once in different contexts (Rosnow and Aiken, 1973). In a study on hypnosis, the hypnotized subjects and a control group of subjects who simulated being hypnotized were given the suggestion that for the next two days every time they heard the word "experiment" mentioned, they would respond by touching their forehead (Orne, Sheehan, and Evans, 1968). Initially, the researchers tested the suggestion in the original experimental setting. They then tested it when the situation was changed. They had a secretary in the waiting room confirm the time of the subject's appointment "to come for the next part of the *experiment*." Later, she asked the subject if she could pay him "now for today's *experiment* and for the next part of the study tomorrow." On the following day, she met the subject with the question "Are you here for Dr. Sheehan's *experiment*?"

In this way it was possible to observe the critical response both outside and inside the laboratory setting. We know the subjects were aware of being observed, but it is assumed that they did not connect the fact of being observed by the secretary with the demand characteristics of the experimental situation. In fact, no simulating subjects responded to the secretary's suggestion in the waiting room on both days, but 5 out of 17 hypnotized subjects did so. The results of this experiment supported the hypothesis that posthypnotic behavior is not limited to the experimental setting.

Quasi controls and sacrifice groups were recommended by Orne as *supplementary* control methods. That is, they should be employed in addition to the requisite standard controls, he argued. Techniques such as these, however, do not automatically enable us to avoid the confounding effects of demand characteristics, because not even the person who designs a study is always aware of the ways in which they come up and have their effect. What is interesting and challenging about demand characteristics is their subtlety and the difficulty of teasing them out.

THEORETICAL OVERVIEW OF SUBJECT-ARTIFACT PROBLEM

In the 1970s, there were allusions to the idea of trying to integrate the findings concerning the social psychology of the experiment within the framework of a single comprehensive theory. It was thought that such a theory might then provide a rationale for weighing the various ways of estimating, even possibly eliminating, these biasing effects. We will turn briefly to one model that was proposed, but it was meant to be a preliminary statement and not a final theory of the social psychology of the experiment (Rosenthal and Rosnow, 1975; Rosnow and Aiken, 1973; Rosnow and Davis, 1977). Its basic assumption was that research subjects, no less than other socialized human beings, are also sensitive to the coercive demands of whatever propriety norms may be operating in the psychological experiment. Instead of attempting to categorize dozens of specific artifact-producing variables, this model focused on a few intervening variables on the further assumption that the artifact-producing variables generalized to a few mediatory factors.

The nature of these mediatory factors, and the end states that might theoretically result, is shown in Table 6.1. We see that it lists three end states of "demand-compliant" behavior: compliance, noncompliance, and countercompliance. The first, *compliance* (symbolized as B^+; see part B of this table), refers to the subject's being cooperative or capitulating to the demand characteristics of the situation. *Noncompliance* (B^0) refers to behavior that is overtly unaffected by the demand characteristics of the situation. *Countercompliance* (B^-) refers to behavior that is antithetical to the demand characteristics of the situation. It is theorized that these three behavioral states are the end products of the mediating variables defined in part A of this table.

Thus, a subject could adequately receive the demand characteristics operating in an experimental situation (R^+), or he or she could be unreceptive or unclear about what demands were operating (R^0). Second, the subject's motivation to comply with such demands could be based on acquiescence (A^+), counteracquiescence (A^-), or simply not caring (A^0). Third, the subject might (C^+), or might not (C^0), have the capability of responding to the demand characteristics that he or she received.

The theoretical sequences leading to the three behavioral outcomes are depicted in part B in the form of a "tree diagram." There is only one branch of the tree that leads to compliance with demand characteristics. This branch, labeled 1, requires adequate reception, a positive motivation, and the capability to pursue that motivation. There is also only one branch that leads to countercompliance with demand characteristics. This branch, labeled 3, requires adequate reception, a counteracquiescent motivation, and the capability to express that negative motivation behaviorally. All the remaining paths lead to noncompliance. Path 6 is limited by the receptivity state; path 5, by the motivational state; and paths 2 and 4, by the capability state. If the subject accurately perceived demand characteristics, was motivated by acquiescence, and yet was unable to comply, then demand characteristics could not influence his or her experimental behavior (path 2). Neither could demand characteristics distort the subject's experimental reaction if he or she received them, was motivated in a counteracquiescent direction, but lacked the capacity to manifest this negative motivation behaviorally (path 4).

PREDICTING AND CONTROLLING SUBJECT ARTIFACTS

We said that, in proposing this model, the authors had two objectives: (1) to enable experimenters to visualize more systematically how demand characteristics will theoretically operate in a given situation and (2) to provide experimenters with a blueprint with which to lay out particular strategies for reducing or eliminating these subject artifacts. This model is also useful in that it allows us to generate theoretical predictions concerning the ways in which any particular artifact-producing event might operate in a given situation.

For example, imagine a situation in which we were interested in hypothesizing about the relationship between the "clarity" (or distinctiveness) of the de-

TABLE 6.1

Theoretical model of the subject-artifact problem

A. Mutually exclusive and exhaustive states for each of three mediating variables: receptivity, motivation, and capability

Mediator	State	Notation	Description
Receptivity	Adequate	R^+	Subject understands what is expected by the experimenter
	Inadequate	R^0	Subject does not understand what is expected by the experimenter
Motivation	Acquiescent	A^+	Subject is cooperatively motivated as regards demand characteristics
	Nonacquiescent	A^0	Subject is neither cooperatively or uncooperatively motivated as regards demand characteristics
	Counteracqui-escent	A^-	Subject is uncooperatively motivated as regards demand characteristics
Capability	Capable	C^+	Subject is capable of acting in accordance with his or her motivations
	Incapable	C^0	Subject is incapable of acting in accordance with his or her motivations

B. Sequences of determining states leading to compliance, noncompliance, and countercompliance with demand characteristics

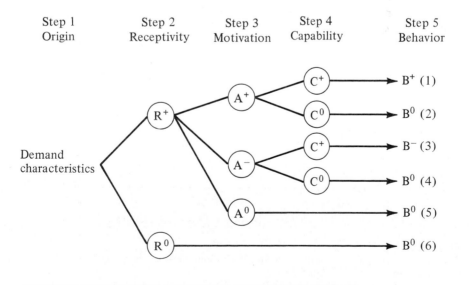

mand characteristics and the subjects' behavior as a result. We could begin by assuming there are only two mediating factors to consider, receptivity and motivation, because subjects are hardly ever *incapable* of responding to the demand characteristics. Figure 6-2 shows what we might want to hypothesize in this situation. It also proceeds on the assumption that when someone's freedom is threatened, this will result in a motivational state (called *psychological reactance* by social psychologists) in which the person attempts to do the opposite of what is demanded (Brehm, 1966; Wicklund, 1974).

We can begin by hypothesizing that when demand characteristics are so patently obtrusive that they tend to restrict the subject's freedom of action, this should theoretically have a dampening effect on the subject's willingness to comply with them. However, we might also hypothesize that the more straightforward the demand characteristics are, the more opportunity there will be for them to be adequately received. These two hypotheses are represented by the dashed lines in this figure, which indicate that the subject's motivation is expected to be negatively related to demand clarity and the subject's receptivity is expected to be positively related to demand clarity. Insofar as the subject who does not receive the demand characteristics, or one who is not motivated to respond to them, can neither acquiesce nor counteracquiesce to them, the relationships with motivation and receptivity should cancel one another when the demand clarity is very low or very high. The combination of these actions gives

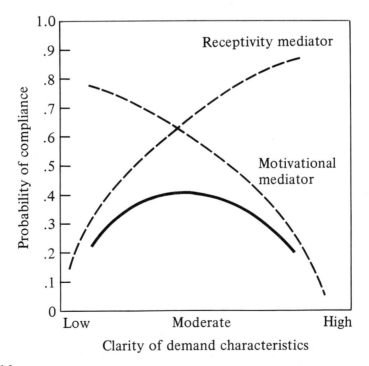

FIGURE 6-2
Theorized curvilinear relationship (shown by solid line) between demand clarity and behavioral compliance with demand characteristics.

the curve shown by the solid line in this figure (after Rosnow and Davis, 1977, p. 305).

To understand how the solid line was arithmetically derived from the dashed lines, we need to understand a little about two particular rules of probability, the conjunctive and the disjunctive. The height of the solid curve was determined by multiplying the point of intersect on the vertical axis of the receptivity curve times that for the motivational curve. The underlying assumption is that the relationship between the receptivity mediator and the motivation mediator is *conjunctive,* i.e., both events must occur to produce the solid curve. If, on the other hand, motivation *or* receptivity were predicted as necessary events, but not both, the situation would be described in statistics as *disjunctive.* Probabilities are used to predict conjunctive and disjunctive events. In throwing dice, for example, the probability of throwing a 6 on the first die *and* a 1 on the second is a conjunctive event. The probability of throwing a 6 on the first die *or* a 1 on the second is a disjunctive event. The difference between the two cases is the difference between "and" and "or." This difference indicates that the individual probabilities of the receptivity and the motivational mediator are *multiplied* in order to determine the height of the solid line.

We said that one important reason for generating this theoretical model was to help us lay out particular strategies for reducing or eliminating these subject artifacts, and Table 6.2 lists nine such strategies (Rosnow and Davis, 1977, p. 307). The strategy chosen by an experimenter will depend on the significance attached

TABLE 6.2
Strategies for reducing subject-artifact influences in experimental settings

Receptivity manipulations to minimize demand clarity
1. Measure the dependent variable in a setting not obviously connected to the treatment or employ unobtrusive measurements.
2. Measure the dependent variable removed in time from the treatment.
3. Employ the Solomon design (see Chapter 4) or else avoid pretesting, especially in attitude-change experiments, and instead employ after-only designs.
4. Standardize and restrict the experimenter's communication with the subjects.
5. Use "blind" procedures in testing and experimental manipulations.
Receptivity manipulation to generate alternative demands
6. Elicit false hypotheses about the purpose of the research, i.e., deception strategies.
Motivational manipulations to encourage honest responding
7. Give feedback of compliant behavior in a set of preexperimental tasks in order to bring the subject to a state of nonacquiescence.
8. Make the experimental setting and procedures low-keyed and nonthreatening; in particular, employ subject anonymity or confidential responding procedures if possible.
9. Encourage honest responding through self-monitoring, e.g., bogus pipeline procedure.

to this problem and the path in Table 6.1 (part B) that is implicitly emphasized by the researcher. The implication of Figure 6-2, however, is that the control or elimination of subject artifacts primarily revolves around two mediatory variables, receptivity and motivation. The nine strategies are as follows:

1. In the ideal experiment, no demand characteristics are received. This can be approximated by field studies using unobtrusive measures. Because the subjects are unaware that they are participating in an experiment, receptivity to demand characteristics is nil.

2. Unfortunately, the ideal in the first strategy cannot be met in most studies, and the reception of demand characteristics is unavoidable. However, because demand characteristics are often transmitted by means of the relationship between the treatment and the measurement procedures, the separation of these in space and time should reduce demand clarity and, therefore, lower the probability of reception. For example, we could have one person run the experiment and, if it were possible, have another person administer the measurements, preferably elsewhere and at another time.

3. In Chapter 4 we noted that pretest sensitization effects were isolated in an attitude-change experiment employing the Solomon four-group design (Rosnow and Suls, 1970). Pretest sensitization enhanced the effect of the treatment with the volunteers and reduced its effect with the nonvolunteers, because of the different ways in which the volunteers and the nonvolunteers processed or responded to the experimenter's implicit wish to change their attitudes. Thus elimination of pretesting in favor of posttest-only designs, or the use of the Solomon four-group design in order to control for pretest sensitization, is suggested as another strategy for addressing subject artifacts.

4. Experimenters are typically the main channel for communicating demand characteristics. Presumably, the more standardized and restricted their communication with the subjects, the less likely the experimenters will be to communicate demands associated with aspects of the experiment. One way to achieve this is by running experiments with a computerized presentation of the instructions.

5. In "blind" procedures, experimenters are unaware of as many vital aspects of the experiment as possible and yet able to perform their task. The less they know, the less they will be able to transmit consciously or unconsciously.

6. Deception strategies in effect replace the "true" expectations with a set of contrived demands; we will have more to say about deception in Chapter 11.

7. Manipulation of motivation is much more difficult, and there is less confidence in the exact influence of the manipulation. For example, an experiment by Gustafson and Orne (1965) indicates that eliciting compliant behavior and giving feedback of this to the subject may reduce acquiescence in later trials. This points to the possibility that experiments be preceded by a set of procedures that bring the subject to a state of nonacquiescence with regard to demand characteristics only. In effect, the subject is given the opportunity to cooperate with and be favorably evaluated by the experimenter before the

true experiment. Presumably, this results in satiation, and when the experiment begins, the subject is nonacquiescent.

8. Another motivational approach would be to make the setting and procedures low-keyed, i.e., as nonthreatening as possible, in order to avoid arousing evaluation apprehensions in the subjects. For example, the mere asking of sensitive questions might arouse a desire in respondents to protect their privacy and thus to withhold information about the unacceptable behavior or, if they answer at all, to distort personal details in a socially desirable direction. There is research evidence to suggest that ensuring the subject's anonymity or confidentiality, inasmuch as it protects the privacy of the information provided by individual participants, may be an effective way to deal with this evasive-answer bias (Esposito, Agard, and Rosnow, 1984; Thomas, Hall, Miller, Dewhirst, Fine, Taylor and Rosnow, 1979). Insofar as the research data cannot be linked back to the individual subject, the protection of privacy by means of ensuring anonymity or confidentiality should promote cooperation and honest disclosures of research participants.

9. In the *bogus pipeline strategy*, conceived by Edward E. Jones and Harold Sigall (1971), the subject is told that a physiological monitoring device can detect lying. The idea here is that the subjects will give truthful rather than compliant answers because they think the machine will know it if they do not. This procedure is also not without risk, because it relies on the subject's naïveté and initial state of acquiescence, but it is another interesting way of looking at the subject-artifact problem.

Some experimental investigators believe that one of the best ways to avoid a lot of these artifacts is to construct an experimental scenario that is sufficiently credible and involving that the subjects rarely have the time or the inclination to, for example, try to figure out what's "really" going on—they are too engrossed in the task. However, none of the techniques mentioned here can really be thought of as an infallible method to reduce or circumvent demand-compliant behavior. The purpose of the model, as it was originally conceived, was to stimulate researchers to think more deeply about the subjects' possible perceptions of the research setting, and thus to bring a fresh perspective to both the design phase and the data interpretation phase of the research process.

NONINTERACTIONAL EXPERIMENTER EFFECTS

Where some researchers have focused on the subject's perceptions and reactions to demand characteristics, other researchers have been concerned with the types of systematic errors that reside in the experimenter side of the experimenter-subject equation. Previously, we made a distinction between noninteractional and interactional experimenter effects, and we begin by noting some examples of the former, i.e., the kind that operate, so to speak, in the mind, in the eye, or in the hand of the experimenter. The three types to be discussed are observer effects, interpreter effects, and intentional effects (Rosenthal, 1977).

In any science, the experimenter must make provision for the careful observation and recording of the events under study. It is not so easy to be sure that
one has, in fact, made an accurate observation, and *observer effects* refer to systematic errors of observation. This source of error was focused on originally by
astronomers near the end of the eighteenth century. The royal astronomer at the
Greenwich Observatory in England, a man named Maskelyne, discovered that
his assistant, Kinnebrook, was consistently "too slow" in his observations of the
movement of stars across the sky. Maskelyne cautioned Kinnebrook about his
"mistakes," but they continued unabated. Kinnebrook was fired.

The person who might have saved Kinnebrook's job was a German astronomer at Königsberg, a man named Bessel. Unfortunately, Bessel's discovery
came about 20 years too late to help Kinnebrook. It was not until then that Bessel
arrived at the conclusion that Kinnebrook's "mistake" was probably not willful.
Bessel studied the observations of stellar transits made by a number of senior astronomers. Differences in observation, he discovered, were the rule, not the exception (Boring, 1950). That early observation of the scientist on the observations
of science made Bessel perhaps the first student of the "psychology of scientists."

A second noninteractional effect is called an *interpreter effect*, because it
refers to systematic error that resides in the interpretation of data. A glance at
any of the technical journals in behavioral science will suggest strongly that while
researchers only rarely debate the observations made by one another, they often
debate the interpretation of those observations. It is as difficult to state the rules
for accurate interpretation of data as it is for accurate observation, but the variety
of interpretations offered in explanation of the same data imply that many researchers must turn out to be wrong.

The history of science generally, and the history of behavioral science more
specifically, suggests that more researchers are wrong longer than they need to
be because they hold their theories in too tight a grip. The common practice of
"theory monogamy"—as we refer to this one source of interpreter error—has its
advantages, however. It does keep researchers motivated to make more crucial
observations. In any case, interpreter effects seem less serious than observer effects, because the former are public while the latter are private. Given a set of
reported observations, the interpretations become generally available to the scientific community. We are free to agree or disagree with any specific interpretation—not so in the case of the actual observations. Often, those observations are
made by a single investigator, so that we are not free to agree or disagree. We
can hope only that no observer errors occurred, and we can (and should) replicate the observations when that is possible.

A third noninteractional effect is called an *intentional effect*, and it implies
dishonesty or at least sloppiness. The dishonesty happens sometimes in undergraduate laboratory science courses when students "collect" and report data too
beautiful to be true. (That probably happens most often when students learning
science are told what results they must get to do well in the course, instead of
being taught the logic of scientific inquiry and the value of being quite open-eyed
and open-minded.) Unfortunately, the history of science teaches us that not only
undergraduates have been dishonest in science (Weinstein, 1979). A famous case

is that of the late Cyril Burt, a leading British psychologist whose work on twins figured prominently in the public debate about racial differences in intelligence.

Burt, who was greatly influenced by the eugenics movement in England, hypothesized that intelligence is irredeemably determined by heredity, and he produced overwhelming amounts of data to support this conclusion. But it is now believed that he fabricated his data, a suspicion that was first voiced when Leon Kamin, an American psychologist, became skeptical of Burt's published findings on the basis of Kamin's discovery of internal implausibilities and basic methodological oversights in the data (Kamin, 1974). Because Burt is dead, we may never know whether statistical distortions in his data were due only to his carelessness or, as it has also been argued, to outright faking of research evidence (cf. Cohen, 1980; Dorfman, 1978; Gillie, 1978, 1979; Hearnshaw, 1979; Jensen, 1978; McAskie, 1978). The point is that researchers need to have a strong sense of ethics and honesty (see Rosnow, 1990).

INTERACTIONAL EXPERIMENTER EFFECTS

This second major category includes biosocial effects, psychosocial effects, situational effects, modeling effects, and expectancy effects. What distinguishes them from the previous three types is that these five all operate by affecting the actual response of the research subject.

First, *biosocial effects* include the sex, age, and race of the experimenter, all of which have been found to affect the results of research. It appears that subjects respond differently simply to the presence of experimenters varying in these biosocial attributes (Barnes and Rosenthal, 1985). That is, experimenters varying in these attributes behave differently toward their subjects and therefore obtain different responses from them because they have, in effect, altered the experimental situation for their subjects. So far, the evidence suggests that male and female experimenters conduct the "same" experiment quite differently, so that the different results they obtain may well be due to the fact that they have unintentionally conducted different experiments.

For example, male experimenters have been found to be more friendly to their subjects (Rosenthal, 1977). Biosocial attributes of the subject can, in turn, affect the experimenter's behavior, which in turn affects the subject's responses. In one study the interactions between the experimenters and their subjects were recorded on sound films. The researchers found that only 12 percent of the experimenters ever smiled at their male subjects, but 70 percent of the experimenters smiled at their female subjects. Smiling by the experimenters, it was also found, affected the results of the experiment (Rosenthal, 1967). The moral is clear. Before claiming a gender difference in the results of behavioral research, we must first be sure that males and females were treated identically by the experimenter. If they were not, then gender differences might be due not to constitutional or socialization factors, but simply to the fact that males and females did not participate in the "same" experiment; i.e., they were treated differently.

Second, *psychosocial effects* include such factors as the personality and temperament of the experimenter. Experimenters who differ in anxiety, need for approval, hostility, authoritarianism, status, and warmth tend to obtain different responses from their subjects. For instance, experimenters higher in status tend to obtain more conforming responses from their subjects, and experimenters who are warmer in their interaction with their subjects tend to obtain more pleasant responses from their subjects. Warmer examiners administering standardized tests of intelligence are likely to obtain better intellectual performance than are cooler examiners or examiners who are more threatening or more unfamiliar to their examinees.

Third, *situational effects* refer to the context or situation as a factor moderating the experimenter's interactions with the subjects. Experimenters who are more experienced at performing a given experiment will often obtain different responses from their subjects than will their less experienced colleagues. Experimenters who are acquainted with their subjects obtain different responses than do their colleagues who have never met their subjects. The things that happen to experimenters during the course of their experiments, including the responses they obtain from their first few subjects, can all influence their behavior, and in turn these changes can lead to changes in their subjects' further responses. When the first few subjects of their experiments tend to respond as they are expected to respond, the behavior of the experimenters often changes in such a way as to influence their subsequent subjects to respond too often in the direction of their hypothesis (see Rosenthal, 1976).

A fourth type of interactional bias is a *modeling effect*. It sometimes happens that before experimenters conduct their studies, they try out the tasks they will later have their research subjects perform. Though the evidence on this point is not all that clear, it would seem that, at least sometimes, the investigator's own performance becomes a factor in the subjects' performance. When the experimental stimuli are ambiguous, for instance, subjects' interpretations of their meaning may too often agree with the investigator's own interpretations of the stimuli. The problem is that the experimenter's behavior, rather than the hypothesized psychological processes, may have been producing the results (see Rosenthal, 1976).

A fifth interactional bias would be the effects of the researcher's expectancy or hypothesis on the results of the research. Some expectation of how the research will turn out is virtually a constant in science. In the behavioral sciences, the hypotheses held by investigators can lead them unintentionally to alter their behavior toward their subjects in much the way that the questioners of Clever Hans unintentionally affected his actions. We are speaking, then, of the investigator's hypothesis as a *self-fulfilling prophecy*, but not exactly in the way this term was originally defined. Robert Merton, its originator, defined it as a "*false* definition of the situation evoking a new behavior which makes the originally false conception come *true*" (Merton, 1948, p. 195). As defined here, one prophesies an event (true *or* false), and the expectation of the event then changes the behavior of the prophet in such a way as to make the prophesied event more likely.

In the following discussion we focus on how the investigator's expectation can come to serve as a self-fulfilling prophecy, also called an *experimenter-expectancy effect* (Rosenthal, 1966). Speaking in more general terms, experimenter-expectancy effects can be seen as one type of *interpersonal expectancy effect*, by which we mean that a person, acting in accordance with a set of expectations, treats another person in such a manner as to elicit behavior that tends to conform to the original expectations (Rosenthal, 1966, 1976). For example, a teacher who believes that certain pupils are especially bright may act more warmly toward them, teach them more material, and spend more time with them. Over time, such a process could result in greater gains in achievement for those students than would have occurred in the absence of this interpersonal expectancy effect (Rosenthal and Jacobson, 1968).

EXPERIMENTER-EXPECTANCY EFFECTS

To demonstrate the effects of the investigators' expectancy on the results of their research, at least two groups of experimenters are needed, each group with a different hypothesis or expectancy regarding the outcome of its research. One approach might be to conduct a kind of census or poll of actual or potential experimenters in a given area of research in which opinions as to relationships between variables are divided. Some experimenters expecting one type of result and some experimenters expecting the opposite type of result might then be asked to conduct a standard experiment. If each group of experimenters obtained the results expected—results opposite to those expected by the other group of experimenters—we could conclude that the expectation of the experimenter does indeed affect the results of the research. Or could we? A problem would be that experimenters who differ in their theories, hypotheses, or expectations might very well differ in a number of important related ways as well. The differences in the data they obtained from their subjects might be due not to the differences in expectations about the results, but to other variables correlated with expectancies. A better strategy than trying to find two groups of experimenters differing in their hypotheses would be to "create" two groups of experimenters differing only in the hypotheses or expectations they held about the results of a particular experiment.

In one early study, for example, 12 experimenters were each given five rats that were to be taught to run a maze with the aid of visual cues (Rosenthal and Fode, 1963). Half the experimenters were told their rats had been specifically bred for maze brightness; half the experimenters were told their rats had been bred for maze dullness. Actually, there were no differences between the rats assigned to each of the two groups. At the end of the experiment the results were clear. Rats run by experimenters expecting brighter behavior showed significantly superior learning compared with rats run by experimenters expecting dull behavior.

The study was repeated, this time employing a series of learning experiments, each conducted in Skinner boxes (Rosenthal and Lawson, 1964). Half the experimenters were led to believe their rats were "Skinner box bright" and half were led to believe their animals were "Skinner box dull." Once again, there were not really any differences in the two groups of rats, at least not until the results were analyzed at the end of the study. Then, the allegedly brighter animals really were brighter, and the alleged dullards really duller.

In the period since these two studies were conducted, literally hundreds of additional studies have examined the possible occurrence of expectancy effects both inside and outside the laboratory (see Harris and Rosenthal, 1985; Rosenthal and Rubin, 1978). This work has been, and continues to be, the basis of considerable pro and con discussion and careful scrutiny (see, e.g., Rosenthal, 1987b, for a summary). However, the existence of expectancy effects is no longer in doubt. One literature summary reported the results of a meta-analysis of 345 studies of expectancy effects (Rosenthal and Rubin, 1978). (*Meta-analysis*, discussed in the next chapter and in more detail in Chapter 22, is the quantitative assessment of the results of a group of studies of a given topic.) This meta-analysis showed that the probability that there is no relation between experimenters' expectations and their subjects' subsequent behavior is much smaller than even .0000001! The mean effect size (r) of expectancy bias in these 345 studies was .33.

This meta-analysis also examined the occurrence of expectancy effects in a wide range of research domains, including reaction-time experiments, inkblot test situations, animal learning, psychophysical judgment studies, learning and ability experiments, person perception investigations, and so forth. Although effect sizes varied across categories, it was clear that expectancy effects occurred to some considerable degree in each category. More recently, expectancy effects have also been documented in other domains besides research settings, such as teacher-student and therapist-client interactions. Thus there can be little doubt that interpersonal expectancy effects are widespread.

How are these expectancy effects communicated? The results of further meta-analyses point to a number of different conditions that mediate interpersonal expectancies (Harris and Rosenthal, 1985). In particular, it appears that the psychological climate, physical distance between the interactants, frequency and duration of interactions, eye contact and smiling, verbal rewards and punishments all play a significant role as mediating factors that influence the degree to which expectancy effects are communicated.

CONTROLLING FOR EXPERIMENTER-EXPECTANCY BIAS

How can such effects be controlled in experiments and quasi experiments in behavioral science? Table 6.3 lists six different strategies for the reduction of experimenter-expectancy effects and, in each case, also lists some consequences of the employment of such a strategy (Rosenthal, 1979b; Rosenthal, Hall, DiMatteo, Rogers, and Archer, 1979).

First, by increasing the number of experimenters, it is possible to reduce the likelihood of expectancy effects in various ways. It decreases the learning of influence techniques. If, for example, an experimenter learns on an unconscious

TABLE 6.3
Strategies for the reduction of experimenter-expectancy effects

1. Increasing the number of experimenters:
   - Decreases learning of influence techniques
   - Helps to maintain "blindness"
   - Randomizes expectancies
   - Increases generality of results

2. Observing the behavior of experimenters:
   - Sometimes reduces expectancy effects
   - Permits correction for unprogrammed behavior
   - Facilitates greater standardization of experimenter behavior

3. Analyzing experiments for order effects:
   - Permits inference about changes in experimenter behavior

4. Maintaining "blind" contact:
   - Minimizes expectancy effects

5. Minimizing experimenter-subject contact:
   - Minimizes expectancy effects

6. Employing expectancy control groups:
   - Permits assessment of expectancy effects

level, then expectancy effects should be minimized by having each experimenter interact with fewer subjects. It helps to maintain "blind" contact between the experimenters and the subjects. Experimenters will be less likely to figure out what treatment a given subject is receiving if the experimenter interacts with only a few subjects. It also randomizes expectancies; that is, experimenters may have different expectancies that will cancel out if there are enough experimenters. And finally, even beyond the issue of expectancy effects, increasing the number of experimenters increases the generality of the results. We can be more confident of a result if it were obtained by a larger number of researchers than if only one researcher produced it.

Second, observing the behavior of experimenters will not by itself eliminate expectancy effects, but it will help in identifying unprogrammed, differential experimenter behaviors. Experimenters will probably also make greater efforts to keep their behavior constant and standardized if they know they are being observed.

Third, analyzing experiments for order effects enables us to compare early results with later results. Experimenter-subject contact may be quite different as the experiment progresses. The climate of the interaction may simply change as the experimenter sees the end of the research in sight, or the experimenter may become more adept at instituting the experimental manipulation with experience.

Fourth, maintaining "blind" contact was mentioned above, but it is more than a salutary convenience. If the experimenters do not know what treatment the subject is receiving, they will be unable to communicate differential expectancies for the efficacy of that treatment. The necessity of keeping the experimenters blind is fully recognized in the area of biochemical research; no pharmacological study is taken seriously unless it has followed elaborate double-blind procedures. In behavioral science, blind contact is a definite way of minimizing expectancy effects.

Fifth, minimizing experimenter-subject contact, along with keeping the experimenters blind, is one of the best ways of assuring that expectancy effects will not occur. For example, it may be possible to employ automated instructions and data collection, e.g., videotaped treatment manipulation. Some experiments consist only of greeting the subjects and seating them in front of the monitor—the computer does all the rest. When employing this strategy, it is important to ask oneself whether it reduces the "realism" of the manipulations. Reducing experimental realism might jeopardize generalizability, and one would ask oneself whether the trade-off is worthwhile in this case.

Sixth, if the wish is to design a study that will not only assess whether an expectancy effect was present but also will allow the direct comparison of the magnitude of expectancy effects versus the phenomenon of interest, then there is only one logical choice—the use of an *expectancy control design* (Rosenthal, 1966). In this design, experimenter expectancy becomes a second independent variable that is systematically varied along with the variable of theoretical interest. It is easiest to explain this design with a concrete example.

In Table 6.4 we see the results of a study performed by J. R. Burnham (1966). There were 23 experimenters, who each ran one rat in a T-maze discrimination problem. Approximately half the rats had been lesioned by surgical removal of portions of the brain. The remaining rats had received only sham surgery, which involved cutting through the skull but with no damage to brain tissue. The purpose of the study was explained to the experimenters as an attempt to learn the effects of lesions on discrimination learning. Expectancies were manipulated by labeling each rat as lesioned or unlesioned. Some of the really lesioned rats were labeled accurately as lesioned, but some were falsely labeled as unlesioned. Similarly, some of the really unlesioned rats were labeled accurately as unlesioned, but others were falsely labeled as lesioned.

By comparing the margin totals and the differences between these totals we get an idea of the relative effectiveness of the two manipulations: (1) manipu-

TABLE 6.4
Expectancy control design used by Burnham (1966) to study discrimination learning in rats as a function of brain lesions and experimenter expectancy

	(b) Expectancy		
(a) Brain state	Lesioned	Unlesioned	Totals
Lesioned	46.5	49.0	95.5
Unlesioned	48.2	58.3	106.5
Totals	94.7	107.3	

lation of the brain state of the animals and (2) manipulation of the experimenters' expectancies concerning the brain state of the animals. The higher the scores, the better were the rats' performances. We see that rats that had been lesioned did not perform as well as those that had not been lesioned, and we also see that rats that were believed to be lesioned did not perform as well as those that were believed to be unlesioned. What makes this experiment of special interest is that the magnitude of the effect of experimenter expectancy was similar to the magnitude of the effect of actual removal of brain tissue.

If an experimenter interested in the effects of brain lesions on discrimination learning had employed only the two most commonly used conditions, the researcher could have been seriously misled by the results. Had he or she employed experimenters who believed the rats to be lesioned to run the lesioned rats and compared the results with those obtained by experimenters running unlesioned rats and believing them to be unlesioned, the experimenter would have greatly overestimated the effects on discrimination learning of brain lesions. Thus, for investigators interested in assessing for their area of research the likelihood and magnitude of expectancy effects, there is no substitute for the employment of expectancy control groups. For the investigator interested only in the reduction of expectancy effects, the other strategies listed in Table 6.3 will probably suffice (see also Kleinmuntz and McLean, 1968; McGuigan, 1963; Miller, Bregman, and Norman, 1965; Rosenthal, 1966).

NOTE ON THE LIMITATIONS OF KNOWLEDGE

We began by referring to the complexity of the research subject. Sometimes we change the research subject's world ever so slightly and observe enormous changes in his or her behavior. Other times, we change this world greatly and observe hardly any changes as a result (e.g., Lamberth and Byrne, 1971). A spectacular example in the latter vein was a study of the efficiency of subject performance under bizarre measurement conditions (Hovey, 1928). Two forms of an intelligence test were administered to 171 subjects. One form was administered in a quiet room. The second form was administered in a room with 7 bells, 5 buzzers, a 550-watt spotlight, 2 organ pipes of varying pitches, 3 metal whistles, a 55-pound circular saw mounted on a wooden frame, a photographer taking pictures, and 4 students doing acrobatics! Remarkably, the group did as well in the second situation as in the first situation. What is the lesson to be learned? Even though we know a great deal about the nature of our model of human behavior, the research subject, there is much that goes beyond current understanding.

We do not want to leave the reader with a sense of desperation or frustration about the limitations of empirical research in behavioral science. A wise researcher, Herbert Hyman, once stated,

> All scientific inquiry is subject to error, and it is far better to be aware of this, to study the sources in an attempt to reduce it, and to estimate the magnitude of such errors in our findings, than to be ignorant of the errors concealed in the data. One

must not equate ignorance of error with the lack of error. The lack of demonstration of error in certain fields of inquiry often derives from the nonexistence of methodological research into the problem and merely denotes a less advanced stage of that profession (Hyman, 1954, p. 4).

With rare exceptions, progress does not occur in science simply as a result of "crucial" experiments. It occurs because competent observers, aware of the errors in the data, employ different strategies, replicate and cross-validate, do experiments and quasi experiments, perform studies in the laboratory and in naturalistic settings. Research results, over the long run, may point in a particular direction, but in the short run the research will always be mixed and call out for further investigation and analysis. The scientist's job is never done. As Boring (1969) put it, scientific truth remains forever tentative, subject always to possible disconfirmation. It is this undeniable aspect of science that is a source both of intellectual challenge and of frustration. But whatever is the momentary disappointment, there is always some interesting, elusive question waiting to be asked—and then answered. Subject-experimenter artifacts do not destroy our opportunities to do good research, but instead make us aware of the errors in the data—and, of course, the limitations of all human understanding.

PART
III

DATA
COLLECTION
AND MEASUREMENT
PROCEDURES

FURTHER STRATEGIES FOR GATHERING DATA

SYSTEMATIC PLURALISM IN UNDERSTANDING

One of the themes of this book is methodological pluralism. It means that, given the limitations of any particular strategy of inquiry, more than one approach to understanding is a logical necessity. To be effective, methodological pluralism is also tempered by being systematic. That is, it is essential not to proceed in a haphazard fashion, but instead to have a plan of action with particular objectives. The bulk of our previous discussion, as of that in other methods textbooks, gives ample testimony to the scope and variety of methods of data gathering that are possible in behavioral science, including experiments, case studies, narratives, survey questionnaires, interviews, participant observations, and so forth. In this and the following chapter we illustrate variants of these approaches (and introduce some new terms) within the conceptual framework of descriptive, relational, and experimental research. The main purpose of this chapter is to communicate a sense of the wide variety of research strategies available and to give a flavor of the ins and outs of using these methods.

To review, descriptive research tells "how things are" but can also carry implications of relationships. Relational research tells "how things are in relation to other things," thereby revealing how variables are associated or correlated. Experimental research, by manipulating specific independent variables, tells "how things get to be the way they are." When the same question can be answered by experimental and nonexperimental means, behavioral scientists usually prefer to do controlled experiments because of the greater strength of causal inference that is generally associated with this approach. But as we saw in Chapter 5, researchers do not always have this option open to them. They conduct research of a descriptive or relational nature because it may be all that they can conduct. They also conduct nonexperimental research because that is what seems most urgently needed at that stage of their knowledge in a given area.

In Chapter 1 we discussed the OSS study as a paradigm case of descriptive inquiry. In this chapter we begin by illustrating three further descriptive possibilities: the enumerative survey, the descriptive analysis of secondary records, and descriptive (and relational) meta-analysis. Next, we focus more specifically on relational research, with emphasis on the analytic survey, the participant observation method, and the quantitative method of historical comparisons. And finally, we examine the strong inference study, the role play experiment, and the naturalistic experiment as representative of the variety of strategies possible in testing for causal relationships inside or outside the laboratory situation. As noted previously, while it is often possible to classify a study as being *primarily* descriptive, relational, or experimental, most studies have characteristics of more than one type. Thus we sometimes suspect a higher-order relationship even when the data are employed in a generally descriptive manner (illustrated by the OSS study discussed in Chapter 1).

ENUMERATIVE SURVEYS

Descriptive research is not restricted to narrative descriptions of behavior, such as the behavior of the OSS recruits during World War II. It can also involve an *enumerative* type of survey, the purpose of which is to count (enumerate) a representative sample (when it cannot count everyone) and then to make inferences about the frequencies of occurrence in the population as a whole. A *sample* refers to a small part of something, and a *population* refers to the total number of parts from which the sample was taken. The enumerative survey is one important way of sampling a population in its normal surroundings. This type of research is not meant to explain a causal relationship, or even to show the relationships between one variable and another, but only to tell how many members of a population have a specified attribute or how often certain events occur (Oppenheim, 1966). Even though it is primarily descriptive, there can also be relational aspects that are implicit in the findings. Research done by R. E. Peterson (1968a, 1968b) on the scope of organized student protests in the 1960s illustrates what we mean.

During the 1960s, student activism was rampant on many college campuses in the United States, and sociologists and psychologists considered various reasons to explain the unrest. Although the activists appeared, outwardly at least, to be rejecting or rebelling against parental values and ideologies, many researchers believed that the students were in fact closer to their parents' ideals than the nonactivist students were (Flacks, 1967; Keniston, 1967). Peterson's research approached this problem from the descriptive rather than from the causal perspective (though there were also relational aspects to it) and simply enumerated the clear-cut, consistent, and growing trends.

The data were obtained from questionnaires that Peterson sent out in 1965 and again in 1968 to college deans at more than 800 of all regionally accredited, 4-year, degree-granting institutions in the United States. As a working definition, he described organized student protest as "planned, public expressions of disapproval." The responses were then coded in summary categories based on whether the deans reported that they had experienced organized protests in connection with instruction and curriculum issues, faculty concerns, freedom of expression, student-administration problems, or extracurricular activities. The responding institutions were divided into four geographical areas in order to identify regional differences in regard to particular social issues. The type of educational institution in which protest was most frequent was also coded, e.g., public liberal arts college, public university, independent liberal arts college. Thus, although the objective of this research was *primarily* descriptive, there were relational aspects. That is, it was possible to relate protest events to protest issues, type of school, or region of the country.

Results of this investigation were used to establish an institutional and national profile of the types of schools that had experienced organized student protests during these periods (1964–1965 and 1967–1968). It showed, for instance, that some issues were consistently more salient than others throughout the country, but that in certain regions, such as the south, the unrest was not so active as in other areas. It also showed an increase from 1964 to 1968 in organized dissent about U.S. policies in Vietnam, but a decrease in civil rights protests during the same period. The inner mood of dissension may not have changed very much, but the outward display of behavior was focused on entirely different issues as time passed.

Particularly interesting in this investigation was the observation that only a small minority of college students actually participated in organized dissent, yet to many Americans it seemed that the majority of students were involved in the dissent. One explanation for this difference between the reality of the situation and people's impressions was that the student activists were unusually talented at making themselves and their causes highly visible (Keniston, 1969). The results of this survey showed that protests were most likely to occur in the largest universities, those where student populations were most mixed and the faculty had many celebrities. These high-protest campuses were generally superactive places, in which everyone was more intense, more active, and more involved. They were also the type of educational institution that was most likely to be publicized by the mass media (Hodgkinson, 1970).

DESCRIPTIVE ANALYSES OF SECONDARY RECORDS

Peterson collected his data directly, but it is also possible to use "secondary records" as a basis of a descriptive study. Examples of secondary records used by behavioral researchers include the federal census and the kinds of raw data depositories available at the Human Relations Area Files at Yale University and elsewhere, the University of Chicago's National Opinion Research Center (NORC), and the University of Michigan's Survey Research Center. For instance, the Roper Center of the University of Connecticut offers survey data collected by NORC going back to the early 1950s. Data are available from personal interviews administered to national samples employing a standardized questionnaire with the same questions appearing in every survey or according to a rotation pattern. All the data are in the public domain and are readily accessible to researchers for duplication, analysis, and publication without clearance from NORC. A wide range of variables is tapped, including demographic, sociopsychological, political, socioeconomic, and other aspects of behavior.

In Chapter 5 we noted some of the ways in which such data might be employed in cohort designs. There are many other kinds of public data that are available for other kinds of analyses, from the simple birth, wedding, and death entries in town hall ledgers to various census records. To illustrate: there are extensive records and documents in research libraries that are available on variables such as population growth, race, industrialization, urbanization, migration, and fertility. Using those records, it is possible to generate historical profiles of regional and metropolitan areas going back over a century. Then, switching again to a relational mode of research, one can look for trends and growth patterns of old urban centers and the multiplication of new ones as a consequence of industrialization's drawing more and more of the rural population toward the city. One can also see how, over the past 100 years, this country has grown more native-born and more female, and then (doing further relational research) correlate the records with others to highlight the relationships between one variable and another (cf. Warner and Fleisch, 1977).

In another example, Ronald Baenninger (1987), a comparative and physiological psychologist, did a survey of paintings from major museums in Europe and North America, in order to study changes in the presence of animals in western art. He hypothesized a decline in the appearance of animals in serious paintings over the centuries, on the premise that animals, having come to play a less significant role in daily life, are also less salient as art objects. Without funding to support travel to museums all over the world, he instead turned to secondary records. He used illustrated books that showed the collections of major museums and in this way tracked down nearly 1,700 paintings. There was, as hypothesized, evidence of a steady decline of animals as art objects over the last 2,500 years in the paintings of the western world.

DESCRIPTIVE AND RELATIONAL META-ANALYSES

The reanalysis of someone else's data is known as *secondary analysis*. One type of secondary analysis is called *meta-analysis*, which is a widely used set of statistical procedures for comparing and combining results from different studies. Discussed in detail in Chapter 22, it literally means the "analysis of analyses." One benefit of meta-analytic procedures is that by combining the results of a number of studies we increase the power of our statistical analysis. That enables us to identify effects that could escape our scrutiny in a single study with much lower statistical power (Wachter, 1988).

Meta-analysis is used as both a descriptive and a relational tool in behavioral science. It was used in one study to answer the questions (1) how often do recording or observer errors occur in psychological experimentation and (2) are the errors that do occur likely to be biased in favor of the observer's hypothesis (Rosenthal, 1978b)? The investigation began with a literature search for research reports that gave an estimate of the frequency of recording errors and the degree to which those errors were biased in the observer's favor. Only 21 studies that satisfied either criterion were found, but the data from the studies were based on over 300 observers making about 140,000 observations. Since almost all the studies were designed (at least in part) to permit the quantitative assessment of error rates, they cannot be regarded as truly representative of behavioral research in general, nor can we have any way of knowing whether the studies give overestimates or underestimates of the rates of error making in the population of psychological experiments as a whole. But given these limitations, it was found (1) that about 1 percent of all observations were wrong and (2) that of the observational errors, about two-thirds supported the observer's hypothesis. The latter finding clearly reflects the operation of a bias, because only half should do so by chance if the observers were unbiased.

In another study, social psychologist Alice H. Eagly (1978) used the meta-analysis approach to examine the literature in the area of sex differences in influenceability. Textbooks in her field had long asserted that women were more easily influenced, and therefore more persuasible and conforming, than men. The traditional theoretical interpretation was that this sex difference was due to socialization processes that had taught men to be independent thinkers, a cultural value that was seldom suggested as suitable for women. Eagly uncovered a pronounced difference in the distribution of experimental findings when she compared the results of studies published before 1970 with those published during the period of the women's movement in the 1970s. In contrast to the older experiments, which showed significantly greater influenceability among females, the newer studies showed few if any statistically significant sex differences in influenceability. Results of this very interesting analysis suggested that the historical period during which an experiment on sex differences in influenceability was conducted was a major factor influencing the likelihood that the findings would show that women are more influenceable than men.

ANALYTIC SURVEYS

We referred to Peterson's use of an enumerative survey to study the scope of organized student protest in the 1960s. It is possible to distinguish between two types of surveys, and Peterson's is illustrative of the primarily descriptive type. The purpose of that kind of survey is to count, and therefore it is essentially fact-finding and actuarial, i.e., used to describe or uncover certain facts. The second type is the *analytic* survey, which is designed to explore the relations among variables (Oppenheim, 1966). This type is usually less oriented toward representativeness (which we discuss in Chapter 10) and more oriented toward finding associations and explanations that can tell us "what goes with what."

The analytic survey is another example of *naturalistic observation*, i.e., observation of behavior in the "real world" as compared with observation of it in the more tightly controlled situation of the psychological laboratory.

The construction of questionnaires and interview schedules (discussed in Chapter 9) usually (but not always) involves many weeks of planning prior to the actual carrying out of the survey. During those weeks, *pilot work* (i.e., preliminary testing of materials) is done to improve the various materials to be used. This piloting may involve doing lengthy, unstructured interviews with subjects in order to get a better sense of the problem being investigated. Once the pilot work is completed, the questionnaire or the interview schedule is pretested on a sample chosen for its similarity to the final sample. Only after the researchers are satisfied that they have developed a sound measuring instrument is the survey ready to be undertaken.

A good analytic survey will incorporate controls to help in the analysis of relationships. Suppose we decided to do an analytic survey of children's bedtime behavior (snacking behavior, time to doze off, etc.). We might try to control some variables by excluding them, by holding them constant, or by using random samples. We know that children usually go to bed later in the summer and on school holidays, and we might control these variables by collecting the data during one short period in the school term. We also know that children with older brothers or sisters usually go to bed later, and we might control this variable by random sampling. We would make sure that children with older brothers or sisters were randomly distributed throughout the sample.

Not all analytic surveys permit this much advance scheduling and pilot testing. Sudden, unexpected events can present opportunities for survey studies in which the window of research opportunity does not remain open very long. A recent case involved an analytic survey of students in the immediate aftermath of the murder of a graduate student in a campus dormitory at the University of Pennsylvania (Rosnow, Esposito, and Gibney, 1988). The investigators were interested in studying the factors influencing rumor spreading after an unexpected event, in order to see whether the relationships that they had observed in previous experimental and quasi-experimental studies could be replicated in this naturalistic setting. Items from questionnaires previously tested were pulled together to develop a new questionnaire specifically designed for this particular situation. The new questionnaire was then administered to residents of the murdered student's dormitory as they were returning from a holiday break. To serve as a control group, dormitory students at Temple University were administered the questionnaire on the same day that the target group received it. The results of this questionnaire survey were quite consistent with the investigators' previous findings. They supported the theory that rumors are likely to be launched and sustained in an atmosphere of anxiety and uncertainty, and that credulity (belief or trust in the rumor) mediates and fosters rumor transmission.

PARTICIPANT-OBSERVER STUDIES

It has been said that only a visitor from another planet could get an objective fix on human nature unfettered by the anxieties and self-deceptions of human soci-

ety. The research approach known as *participant observation* is said by its propo-
nents to be the next best bet. A group or community is studied from within by a
researcher who makes careful observations of the behavior as it proceeds. This
strategy is believed to be more appropriate than the analytic survey for studying
people in their normal surroundings when the project involves an examination of
complex social relationships or intricate patterns of interaction that cannot be
precisely quantified or anticipated (see Becker and Geer, 1960; Warwick and
Lininger, 1975).

Animal behaviorists employ a variant of this technique when they do participant-observer studies of the social life and customs of wild animals. A
hypothesis-testing study by Ronald Baenninger and his coworkers in east Africa
is illustrative (Baenninger, Estes, and Baldwin, 1977). The researchers patiently
watched and recorded the course of actions taken by a troop of baboons when it
encountered a cheetah drinking in the river. Other researchers had claimed that
adult male baboons will actively defend their troops against predators, but there
were few accepted records of this behavior at the time of this study (cf. DeVore
and Washburn, 1963). Observations made in the east Africa study dispelled any
doubts as to the reality of baboon defensive behavior. As Baenninger and his colleagues watched, two male members of the baboon troop continued to harass the
cheetah until they had successfully chased him far away from the main body of
the troop.

The animal behaviorists who engage in this kind of research employ a
number of methodological distinctions that have been borrowed by, and from,
the sociologists and the cultural anthropologists who do participant-observer
studies of human cultures (Altmann, 1974). For example, a distinction is made
between *events*, which are defined as relatively instantaneous occurrences, and
states, defined as occurrences of more appreciable duration. One can, for instance, record the course of actions of baboons chasing a cheetah (an event) or
the organizational structure of a troop of baboons (a state). Several different
types of data sampling for observational studies have been discussed. One type
involves watching and making field notes based on impromptu or extemporane-
ous sampling, in which case the observers simply record everything they can get
down on paper. Another sampling procedure involves recording all occurrences
of some specified behavior only during a given sample period, using tally sheets
and field notes for the record keeping.

In human research another variation consists of supplementing one's observations with interviews in order to flesh out the data records with narrative responses. For example, cultural anthropologist David D. Gilmore (1987) set up
housekeeping in Andalusia, a region in southern Spain where approximately one-
fifth of the population lives. The purpose of his visit was systematically to study
the dark side of human nature, aggression, as manifested in the passions and
animosities that lie concealed under the thin veil of domestic and social life of
Andalusian culture. He theorized that this form of aggression was not maladap-
tive and disruptive, but was essential to the perpetuation of the feeling of a
shared sense of belonging that bound family groups together in this society.
Characterizing his method as "anthropological snooping" (p. 66), he collected
observations and narratives pertaining to a number of aspects of everyday life.

For instance, he kept careful notes about Carnaval, the Spanish Mardi Gras, a festival of songs, parodies, and mischief. The masks and disguises that people wore as they promenaded up and down the main street chanting ribald ditties and shouting epithets provided a way of seeing without being seen, freeing those participating from the inhibitions imposed by conventions of propriety, Gilmore speculated. The festival gave rise to passion and excitement that in turn led to symbolic aggression as the celebrants used Carnaval to ventilate feelings and set things right. "Shame takes a holiday," so the Andalusians say (p. 7). Every word and deed, Gilmore observed, seemed a paradox of double meanings as people were drawn together by mutual dislikes at the same time that envy and rivalry set them apart.

The duplicity of concealment and voyeurism was, Gilmore theorized, a conflict of love and hate, rivalry and amity, trust and distrust. At one point, he studied the "evil eye and hard looks" in the context of owning a balcony. The balcony, Gilmore inferred, provided the owner with the power and security "to be seen or not to be seen" in this tight, atomistic society (p. 158). Another time, he took notes about an incident one hot evening when he left the window propped open with a book to let in the cool night air. At the market the next morning, the woman at the first vegetable stall he came to asked tersely why he put a book in his window. How did she know, he wondered? "Oh, you know the people, the town," was the reply (p. 76). Keep your shutters tightly closed, your true self concealed—this is the hidden message in Andalusia, Gilmore inferred.

There are many well-known examples of such studies in sociology and cultural anthropology, including the classic work of Ruth Benedict, Raymond Firth, Bronislaw Malinowski, and Margaret Mead. These researchers spent many months, sometimes years, methodically collecting narrative accounts and recording their own impressions and reflections based on fieldwork in a particular culture. In all societies, human beings relate to one another by role and by affect (emotion), and the research diaries of these and other researchers can help us to examine the cultural context of social facts. The scientist who enters a community to record the natural behavior of the group has access to a body of information firsthand. He or she can sense the frustrations and exhilarations of the community in perhaps a way that cannot be felt from the results of an analytic questionnaire alone (cf. Goode and Hatt, 1952).

SYNCHRONIC AND DIACHRONIC RESEARCH

In Chapters 4 and 5 we saw that much empirical investigation is concerned with taking a single cross-sectional slice of time, so that the observations or measures have reference to the relationship between a particular set of variables only as it exists in the here and now. In Chapter 5 this kind of temporal approach—in which the variables are observed as they exist at one brief period in time, not using information about the long-term development or consequences of the relationship—was called "synchronic research." It was distinguished from "diachronic research," in which the data are collected in such a way as to uncover relatively long-term changes that occur during successive periods of time.

Diachronic research is inherently relational inasmuch as it examines descriptions at varying points in time. The descriptions are the dependent variables, and time is the independent variable. This kind of temporal orientation makes it possible, for example, to study stability and social change in behavior (see Barber and Inkeles, 1971). Unlike synchronic research (which forecloses on the temporal dimension), diachronic research enables us to look for long-term trends and growth patterns, on the basis of which it may then be possible to plan further relational (or experimental) research. Diachronic research also allows us the freedom to search for persistent or continual or regularly recurrent patterns of behavior (because change cannot be understood except in reference to stability), which may provide clues about future trends and growth patterns.

An example that is reminiscent of Baenninger's survey of paintings was a study conducted by Stanley Coren and Clare Porac (1977), also employing art records as a secondary data base. They made an analysis of several thousand years of artwork in order to gather evidence as to whether right-handedness is a recent trait or an age-old human characteristic. Previously, it had been hypothesized that the development of right-handedness in humans is a physiological predisposition possibly heritable in nature. A rival hypothesis asserted that social or environmental pressures (or both) led to the high incidence of right-handedness in humans, which was seen as an adaptive response that resulted from the suppression of left-handedness. Coren and Porac submitted these alternative hypotheses to an empirical test by simply counting the instances of unimanual tool usage in available representations of works of art from various cultures and times over many centuries.

More than 12,000 photographs and reproductions of drawings, paintings, and sculpture, dated from approximately 15,000 B.C. to A.D. 1950, extracted from European, Asian, African, and American sources were examined in this study. Each plate or reproduction was carefully coded for figures displaying a clear hand preference, and from these a final sample of 1,180 scorable instances was obtained. Of those, an average of 92.6 percent depicted the use of the right hand, and the geographical and historical distribution of right-handedness tended to be uniformly very high. Because there were no clear differences emerging among the various cultural subgroupings or in different historical epochs, the results seemed to support a physiological interpretation of handedness rather than one that proposes cultural and social determinants of handedness. It is impossible to ensure that the 12,000 photographs and reproductions were representative of the actual (as opposed to idealized) state, or of the diffuse population of artworks as a whole. Nevertheless, it does seem safe to conclude that, as far as this historical record takes us, human beings have forever been "depicted" as primarily right-handed.

Here, we have an example of diachronic research in which secondary records were the basis of the data analysis. This type of approach is called a *historical comparison* when it attempts to show how the *Zeitgeist* ("temper of the times") acts as a mediatory link to the social, political, and economic conditions of society. Various statistical techniques are employed in this kind of research. Quantitative historians refer to their arsenal of quantitative methods as *cliometrics*, comparable to *biostatistics* in biology and biomedicine, *psychometrics* in psychology, *sociometrics* in sociology and anthropology, and *econometrics* in economics. Only the terms are different in these different fields; the quantitative methodologies are essentially the same.

William J. McGuire (1976) did a quantitative historical comparison in which he painstakingly gathered basic demographic information on over 37,000 famous people of all times and places. He used this historical data archive to search for cycles and trends in politics, religion, the arts and literature, the humanities, etc., as a function of historical periods. Working along similar lines, social psychologist Dean Keith Simonton (1984) did a series of quantitative historical comparisons in which he investigated possible causal links among these different variables; we return to this investigator's work in a moment.

STRONG INFERENCE IN EXPERIMENTS AND QUASI EXPERIMENTS

Strong inference studies are recognized from the fact that competing hypotheses vie against one another, the underlying assumption being that this will enable the researcher to make "stronger" conclusions than if he or she were testing only one hypothesis at a time (Platt, 1964). The process is meant to resemble a squirrel climbing a tree, in that at each fork the squirrel chooses to go to the right or to the left branch, until it has finally reached the top. The scientist first devises alternative predictions to represent rival hypotheses, on the basis of prior observation or the nature of known facts. The second step is to design a study with alternative possible outcomes, each of which will (as nearly as possible) exclude one or more of the hypotheses. The third step is to carry out the research so as to get a clean result. The process is then repeated, making and testing new competing hypotheses to refine the possibilities that remain.

The underlying idea has a long history in the natural sciences. Before the turn of this century, T. C. Chamberlin, a geologist, argued that the moment we offer an explanation for a phenomenon, we begin to feel "parental affection" for the idea. The more we think about it, the more this affection grows—and soon we find ourselves pressing the hypothesis to fit the facts and pressing the facts to make them fit the hypothesis. "To avoid this grave danger," Chamberlin (1897) suggested, "the method of multiple working hypotheses is urged. It differs from the simple working hypothesis in that it distributes the effort and divides the affections." Strong inference studies essentially formalize what Chamberlin was alluding to.

There is a problem, however; it is not always possible to get a "clean" (or unequivocal) result in human subject research. When we do not get a clean result, it may simply mean that there is more than one direction of relationship or causal patterning operating. A quasi-experimental study by Simonton illustrates this notion (Simonton, 1976). Two hypotheses were allowed to vie against one another by employing a cross-lagged panel design. One hypothesis was that the ascent and decline of civilizations is a result of changes in personal needs and values, which Simonton developed from the work of psychologist David McClelland (1961). The competing hypothesis, developed from the work that was done by sociologist Pitirim Sorokin (1964), was that personal beliefs are a response to prevailing political and cultural events. Simonton did a series of cross-lagged comparisons of 122 consecutive 20-year intervals from 540 B.C. to A.D. 1900 for which there were archival data available on measures of philosophical beliefs and political contexts. He reasoned that if variation in a political variable always preceded variation in a philosophical variable, then personal beliefs are probably the function of sociocultural context (Sorokin's hypothesis). On the other hand, if variation in a philosophical variable always preceded variation in a political variable, then personal beliefs may possess sociocultural consequences (McClelland's hypothesis). Simonton found support for both causal hypotheses throughout history.

Presumably, the prepotency of a particular causal sequence is tied to the nature of the situation, and in some situations A causes B while in other situations B causes A. A series of strong inference studies should enable us to discover the circumstances in which each of the relationships or causal patterns is more strongly supported. To illustrate: suppose we were subjects in an impression-formation experiment. The characteristics of fictitious individuals are described to us, and we are instructed to report our impressions of them on certain outcome variables. The purpose of the study, from the experimenter's point of view, is to allow two hypotheses—the "adding hypothesis" and the "averaging hypothesis"—to vie against one another. These two hypotheses are considered to be rival explanations for how ideas and perceptions combine into distinct categories and stereotypes. Thus some scientists would argue that the human mind pools information on the basis of an averaging principle, while others would argue that the principle involved conforms to an adding rule. The experimenter theorizes that both principles are correct, but they operate in different contexts.

To test her idea she conducts a strong inference study: she instructs us to imagine that two persons, A and B, each have an income of $100 a day and that a third person, C, has an income of $40 a day. In part 1 she asks us, "Would a *group* consisting of A, B, and C enjoy *higher* or *lower* economic status than a *group* consisting only of A and B?" We answer "lower" because we perceive that the average income of A, B, and C is lower than the average income of A and B. In part 2 she asks, "Would a *family* consisting of A, B, and C enjoy *higher* or *lower* economic status than a *famiy* consisting only of A and B?" We answer "higher" because we now perceive that the total income of A, B, and C is higher than the total income of A and B. The results of her study tell the experimenter that people do both adding and averaging. She must now come up with a construct that names the particular contexts in which each principle applies, and then design followup studies to test her ideas further (cf. Rosnow and Arms, 1968; Rosnow, Wainer, and Arms, 1970).

SIMULATION EXPERIMENTS

In Chapter 1 we described the studies of "mother love" of Harry Harlow and his coworkers. That research illustrates some of the more general kinds of strategies that are possible in experimental research (cf. Kaplan, 1964). The entire program is illustrative of the use of *heuristic experiments*, i.e., experiments conducted to generate ideas, provide leads for further inquiry, and open up new lines of investigation. There were also *methodological experiments*, which served to develop or improve some technique of inquiry—as in the development of the Butler box for studying whether monkeys would work as hard to see their cloth mothers as they would to see another live monkey. There were *exploratory experiments*, which invited serendipity—as in the early stages of Harlow's research, when he began experimenting with the cloth surrogate mothers. There were *fact-finding experiments*, aimed at determining some magnitude or property of the dependent variable. And finally, there were *boundary experiments*, which were designed to fix the range of application (or "boundaries") of relationships.

Another type of experimental strategy involves a *simulation*, also illustrated to some extent by Harlow's research. The purpose of simulations is to learn what will happen under conditions that are designed to mimic the natural environment in some definite way. We simulate, for instance, when more realistic experiments are morally impossible (e.g., Harlow's use of monkeys instead of humans to study the development of personality) or when simulation can serve a training function (e.g., driver simulation or astronaut simulation). We also use simulation in order to "telescope" time and predict future events from present ones, e.g., internation simulations to predict future world events from present "nation" characteristics. And we simulate when the real situation is too costly or when more realistic experiments would be too costly. The fundamental task of simulation is that of scaling down the natural environment to a laboratory size that still contains the key elements thought to account for the dynamics of the real-world phenomenon under investigation.

An example of a simulation is the work of Joseph V. Brady and his associates at Johns Hopkins University, where a programmed environment has been constructed in the medical school for the analysis of individual and social behavior over extended time periods (Brady, Bigelow, Emurian, and Williams, 1974; Brady and Emurian, 1979). This environmental design consists of a complex of rooms for individual living quarters, a larger social-living unit, and a workshop. Volunteers reside in this environment over a continuous period while they are monitored by electromechanical control devices interfaced with a computer. Various activities are programmed (e.g., 10 minutes of light calisthenics, access to reading and art materials, social recreation), and the emotional interactions and reactions within this programmed environment are coded and quantified for statistical analysis of trends and cycles.

In this way, Brady and his coworkers have been able to explore the continuous effects of living in a self-contained programmed environment. The purpose is to extrapolate from this simulation to the daily environment of astronauts, submarine crews, and others who are confined to a self-contained environment.

EXPERIMENTAL REALISM, MUNDANE REALISM, AND INFERENTIAL VALIDITY

It is generally argued by methodology textbook authors that two important criteria for assessing the effectiveness of a laboratory simulation (or indeed any laboratory experiment in behavioral science) are its experimental realism and mundane realism (Aronson and Carlsmith, 1968), but not all researchers or text-book authors would agree. *Experimental realism* refers to its psychological impact on the participants, and *mundane realism* refers to the extent to which the laboratory events are likely to be encountered in an analogous form in a naturalistic setting. When criteria of internal validity (see Chapter 4) and mundane realism are satisfied, this is sometimes referred to as *inferential validity* (Rosnow and Aiken 1973). That is, when a relationship between two variables that is obtained in a laboratory setting is free of confounding (has high internal validity), and when such a relationship would occur outside the laboratory under analogous conditions (has mundane realism), then we may say that the laboratory study has inferential validity.

In some laboratory simulations, the mundane realism is suspect, and, in turn, so is the inferential validity of the study. For example, classic laboratory simulations of rumor spreading were seriously limited in terms of mundane realism (Allport and Postman, 1947). As a means of isolating the kinds of message distortions that can occur in rumormongering, the simulation consisted of projecting a slide depicting a semidramatic scene of a large number of related details. Six or seven participants who were unfamiliar with the picture waited in an adjoining room. The first participant entered and took a position from which he or she could not see the picture. The experimenter or another participant described the picture, giving about 20 details in the account. A second participant then entered the room and stood beside the first, who told the second participant everything that could be recalled about the picture. This "hearsay" account was next communicated to a third participant, and so on. Once the subjects had completed this "rumor" chain, their reports were analyzed and contrasted with the picture on the slide.

Out of this research, it was concluded that the subtle interpenetration of cognitive and emotional processes in rumormongering that leads to the obliteration of some details (called "leveling") and the pointing up of other details ("sharpening") is due to the cognitive effort to assimilate information by twisting new materials to build a better overall structure. Later results suggested that this conclusion was correct, but another conclusion, which stated that the effect of leveling and sharpening is to produce rumors that inevitably become more concise, was an overgeneralization. Rumors in real life can also sometimes "snowball" into a profusion of invented details, thereby becoming more complex not more concise (Rosnow, 1980). A classic case occurred in 1969; there was a rumor that Paul McCartney of the Beatles had been decapitated in a car accident and replaced by a double. This rumor, which swept U.S. college campuses at the height of the Beatles' popularity, kept growing in its complexity as a stream of new "facts" was continually forthcoming. At one point, McCartney denied his death in a cover article in *Life* magazine! But even this denial was interpreted as new evidence in support of the rumor, because belief in it was theory-driven rather than data-driven. On the reverse side of the magazine cover was an automobile advertisement. Held up to the light, it revealed a picture of a car that appeared to be superimposed across McCartney's chest so that the top of his head was blocked out. This "clue" merely added credence to the underlying thesis and caused the rumor to become more diffuse rather than more concise (Rosnow and Fine, 1976).

Thus whether a rumor will shrink or expand is apparently more complex and unpredictable than early simulation studies led researchers to believe (Esposito and Rosnow, 1984). One problem with the simulation was that there was very little emotional or psychological involvement required of the participants. In real life there is usually some ego involvement and concern when passing on or listening to a nice juicy rumor. There is a question, then, as to the simulation's experimental realism. A second problem was that in normal conversation when a person hears a rumor that is not understood, he or she usually asks for clarification. In real life we tend to use our critical faculties to work out the meaning of a rumor, but in this simulation the subjects were always passive receivers. Thus there is also a question as to the simulation's mundane realism, and in turn its weak external validity.

Interestingly, Douglas Mook (1983), in an intriguing "defense of external invalidity" in laboratory experimentation, has argued, however, that the insistence on external validity can sometimes be misguided. The point of many experiments, he suggests, is not to generalize to the real world, but instead to try to make predictions about the real world from the laboratory. He noted the monkey love studies of Harlow as a clear example of experiments lacking in external validity (because using baby monkeys in cages, and wire mesh or cloth-covered mother surrogates, to study human babies falls far short of the ideal), but which nevertheless tell us something theoretically valuable about personality development. Mook has suggested that before condemning any laboratory study as "artificial" it would be better to ask oneself (1) is the investigator really trying to estimate from sample characteristics the characteristics of some population, or is the purpose of the study instead to draw conclusions about a theory that predicts what *these* subjects will do, and (2) is the purpose of the study to predict what would happen in a real-life situation, or is its purpose to test under carefully controlled conditions a predicted causal relationship that is viewed as a universal principle (and should therefore operate in the laboratory as well as in real life)? One may, or may not, agree with the premises of Mook's argument (cf. Banaji and Crowder, 1989); however, the two questions he posed should, at least, help one to avoid a "misplaced preoccupation with external validity [which] can lead us to dismiss good research for which generalization to real life is not intended...." (p. 379).

ROLE PLAY EXPERIMENTS

Earlier, we alluded to research studies in which some form of deception was used to prevent the subjects from guessing the researcher's hypotheses or true intent. A famous example was noted in Chapter 1 (see Table 1.2 on page 23), the behavioral studies done by Stanley Milgram on obedience to authority (Milgram, 1963, 1965, 1975). Volunteers were subjected to an elaborate deception to make them believe that they were giving painful electric shocks to a hapless victim (actually a confederate of the experimenter). Each volunteer was seated in front of a "shock generator" on which there were switches indicating increases in voltage from 15 to 450 volts and was told to administer shocks to a "learner" every time he made a mistake in a simple memory test. The first mistake was punished ostensibly by a 15-volt shock, the second by a 30-volt shock, and so on up the scale.

In Chapter 11 we return to this study for a detailed discussion of ethical considerations and debriefing procedures in human subject research. However, many researchers object to the use of deception, and there have been efforts to develop experimental alternatives. One such strategy is called *role play*, a variant on the simulation experiment, but it is also not without its critics. It consists of having subjects act out a given scenario; i.e., they enact the role of a research subject by improvising with the help of a script devised by the experimenter. Proponents of this strategy argue that it is humanistic and person-centered, that it allows a wide latitude of response, and that it allows complex behavior to be explored (cf. R. M. Baron, 1977; Forward, Canter, and Kirsh, 1976; Geller, 1978; Hamilton, 1976; Mixon, 1971). Critics argue that role play is unscientific because it lacks adequate controls, and that it relies on theoretical terminology that is ambiguous (cf. Cooper, 1976; Freedman, 1969; Miller, 1972; Yardley, 1984)—we return to the criticisms in a moment.

Martin S. Greenberg (1967) did a methodological experiment to assess the utility of role play in a given situation. He simulated an earlier experimental study on anxiety and affiliation (to which we alluded in the previous chapter). In a well-known series of experiments by Stanley Schachter (1959), the subjects had been allowed to wait with others or to wait alone before participating in a research study. For some subjects (the "high-anxiety" group) the anticipated project was described as involving painful electric shocks, while for others (the "low-anxiety" group) it was represented as involving no physical discomfort. Significantly more of the high-anxiety subjects chose to wait with others in a similar plight, i.e., a kind of "misery prefers miserable company" effect. Another of Schachter's findings was that anxious firstborns and only children showed this desire to affiliate with others more than did children not born first. In Greenberg's role play experiment, the participants were instructed to "act as if the situation were real" and were then subjected to a scenario closely modeled after Schachter's original design. While some of the results of Greenberg's role play experiment were not statistically significant, the direction of his major findings was consistent with Schachter's earlier experimental findings.

The qualified success of this study has been interpreted by many proponents of the role play approach as giving support to the idea that role play experiments can play a useful part when the scenario is realistic (and we return to this point below). Other methodological experiments on role play have been done in recent years (e.g., Darroch and Steiner, 1970; Horowitz and Rothschild, 1970; Wicker and Bushweiler, 1970; Willis and Willis, 1970), but opinions continue to be sharply divided on the usefulness of role play as a substitute for more traditional experimental methods (e.g., Hendrick, 1977; Miller, 1972; Yardley, 1984). Critics of role play argue, for example, that the problems are far more serious than the fact that sometimes the terms are not clear, etc. One of the truly serious problems, they assert, is that subjects often cannot predict the most interesting results that come from true experiments; and, in fact, counterintuitive findings are probably exactly what subjects will do terribly at duplicating in role play formats, it is argued. Although it is true that role play experiments will sometimes produce the same, or nearly the same results, as true experiments, what really does them in, the critics argue, is that we simply cannot predict in advance whether the results of such a study would or would not have corresponded to the results of a non-role play study. So when one does such a study, the most that can be said is that the results *might* have occurred if a non-role play methodology had been used. The essential point, of course, is that researchers must go into this methodology with their eyes open.

EMOTIONAL ROLE PLAYING

However, we do not want to leave readers with the idea that we are anti-role play, and the following example will illustrate what is possible when appropriate steps are taken to make this approach realistic by increasing the participants' emotional involvement, also called *emotional role play*. The following research was done by Irving Janis and Leon Mann (1965; Mann, 1967; Mann and Janis, 1968), who were interested in applying the laboratory-demonstrated principle of "saying is believing" to demonstrate how to get people to stop smoking. The volunteer subjects were young women, all between the ages of 18 and 23, none of whom knew that the objective of the research involved modifying their smoking habits and attitudes toward smoking. Before the study began, each subject averaged about a pack of cigarettes a day. Randomly assigned to either an experimental or a control group, the participants were told at the beginning of the study that the research was intended to examine two important problems about the human side of medical practice: (1) how patients react to bad news and (2) how they feel when a physician tells them to quit an enjoyable habit such as smoking.

Each participant in the experimental condition was instructed to imagine that the experimenter was a physician who had been treating her for a persistent cough, and on this third visit he was going to give her the results of x-rays and other diagnostic tests previously carried out. The experimenter then outlined five different scenes, and he instructed the participant to "act out" each scene as realistically as possible. The first scene took place in the doctor's office while the patient awaited the diagnosis. She was asked to imagine and express aloud her thoughts, her concern, her feelings about whether to give up cigarettes. The second scene was the imagined confrontation with the physician. She was told that according to the results of his diagnostic tests, there was a small malignant mass in her right lung. She was also told that there was only a moderate chance for surgical success for treating this condition. She was then encouraged to ask questions. In the next scene she was instructed to express her feelings about her misfortune. The physician could be overheard in the background phoning for a hospital bed. In the fourth scene the physician described details of imminent hospitalization. He told the subject that chest surgery typically requires a long convalescent period, at least 6 weeks. He then raised questions about the woman's smoking history and asked whether she was aware of the relation between smoking and cancer. He stressed the urgent need for her to stop smoking immediately and encouraged her to talk freely about the problems she thought she might encounter in trying to break the smoking habit.

Subjects assigned to the control group were exposed to similar information about lung cancer from a tape recording of one of the experimental sessions. However, they were not given an opportunity to engage in emotional role play.

As Janis and Mann had hypothesized, the immediate impact of the emotional role play condition in producing attitude change was consistently greater than the effect in the control condition. There was greater fear of personal harm from smoking, a stronger belief that smoking causes lung cancer, and a greater willingness and intent to quit smoking in the experimental group. To determine the long-term impact of this role play manipulation, the researchers conducted follow-up interviews at different points over an 18-month interval. The results were essentially as before. On the average, women who had participated in the emotional role play sessions reported that they had reduced their daily cigarette consumption by more than twice the amount of those who participated in the control condition, and this difference persisted even after a year and a half.

NATURALISTIC AND
SOCIAL EXPERIMENTATION

So far, we have looked at experiments and quasi experiments that used various kinds of simulation methods, including the heuristic experiments of Harlow, the environmental simulations of Brady, and the emotional role play experiments of Janis and Mann. Some experimenters believe that the ideal context for behavioral science is not the laboratory but the natural environment, and in recent years there has been a movement by many researchers in social psychology and other areas toward the greater use of field experiments. These researchers believe that field experiments can also be an effective way of circumventing the subject-artifact problems discussed in the previous chapter.

A classic example of this naturalistic approach is a study that was done by psychologist George W. Hartmann in 1935 (Hartmann, 1936). Its purpose was to investigate the relative effects of rational and emotional political propaganda in an election campaign. Hartmann had his own name entered on the ballot in a statewide election campaign in Allentown, Pennsylvania. He then wrote two political leaflets, one designed to appeal to the voters' reason and the other to their emotions. He had the leaflets distributed in different wards matched on the basis of their size, population density, assessed property valuation, previous voting habits, and socioeconomic status. By comparing the election results in the wards that got the rational appeal with those that got the emotional appeal, he inferred that the emotional propaganda must have had the stronger impact. That is to say, the voting results showed that the emotional message was associated with greater increases in voting for Hartmann relative both to the control regions and to the increases in voting for candidates of the other parties.

Another example of field experimentation is a study that was done by Roy E. Feldman (1968) in several countries in order to identify national differences in helping behavior. For many kinds of behavior, the cultural context in which it is enacted can be an important condition. Feldman repeated several standard experiments in Athens, Paris, and Boston using both foreigners and natives of the region as confederates. In one study he had the confederates ask directions from passersby. In another, they asked strangers to mail a letter for them, explaining that they were waiting for someone and could not leave the spot right then. In a third study, confederates overpaid merchants and taxi drivers and then observed whether the people were honest and returned the money. By cross-tabulating the reactions of more than 3,000 subjects, Feldman was able to show that when a difference in helping behavior occurred, Parisians and Bostonians treated compatriots better than they did foreigners. On the other hand, Athenians were more helpful to foreigners than to compatriots.

Another approach to naturalistic research is called *social experimentation* (Riecken, 1975), but it frequently involves the nonrandom assignment of treatments to subjects. It essentially involves the application of experimental and quasi-experimental methods to the analysis of social problems and to the development, testing, and assessment of workable intervention procedures to reduce the problems. For example, one might use a nonequivalent-groups design to evaluate the effects of low-cost public housing or of age-graded penal institutions. It will be recalled from Chapter 5 that a design is called "quasi-experimental" if it resembles an experimental design but there are factors operating that make random assignment of treatments to sampling units impossible. If one were doing a study to evaluate the effects of low-cost public housing, it might be difficult or impossible (for administrative and ethical reasons) to have full control over the assignment of treatments to families.

The technical capacity to carry out social experiments and quasi experiments is not well developed in the United States, but in other countries it has been used quite effectively to develop social programs and social policy. A lingering problem with social experimentation is that there is no guarantee that similar conditions will prevail in the future as obtained in the past. This means that, unless it is possible to develop and apply reliable forecasting techniques, there is an element of risk in attempting to generalize from past experimental or quasi-experimental results to future social conditions (cf. Horowitz, 1979).

SUMMARY OF DIFFERENT FUNCTIONS

The research studies discussed so far in this book help us to see that strategies of descriptive, relational, and experimental inquiry—of which we have sampled but a few—serve a number of different functions. In the case of descriptive research, for example, one function is to provide the "groundwork" by which to take a complex behavioral or organizational structure with which we are unfamiliar and to get a sense of it. When we are thrown into a strange, ambiguous situation, the first thing we do is to try to orient ourselves by making use of reference points, and in this way the nature of the situation is gradually revealed to us. The psychologists and psychiatrists who aided in the assessment of the OSS (Chapter 1) had no idea of what particular missions would be assigned to the recruits. On the basis of descriptive research they were gradually able to perceive ways of dealing with this problem.

A second function of descriptive-level research could be to establish the *parameters* (the population values) of the research problem, once the nature of the situation is revealed. Descriptive research not only serves as a guide in adjusting to new surroundings, but also helps us to clarify the shape and structure of relationships in the population. By methodically establishing frequencies of occurrence of events or of limiting demographic conditions in the sample, we can begin to specify the parameters of the problem under investigation.

A third function of such research could be to raise, by implication, ideas that can be tested in relational or experimental studies. To be sure, the descriptive and the relational can also serve as a "point-counterpoint" to one another in the same study. Peterson's research (in this chapter) was basically descriptive, but it also showed how protest events were related to other variables.

In the case of relational research we see that behavioral science is not merely adding facts. All science requires that we view facts not as isolated or separate, but as related or connected in some systematic and logical ways (cf. Cohen, 1959). Thus, one function of such research would be to uncover the relationships among different variables. From our discussion of Mill's rules for judging causes and effects (in Chapter 4), we know that a fundamental requirement is to show that X and Y are actually related to one another. Relational research lets us see which variables are correlated (and how much), and which are not.

A second function, and a distinct advantage of relational research, is that it enables us to make comparisons in which time is the independent variable. Thus we might search for long-term patterns in order to predict future trends and growth cycles (McGuire's and Simonton's research). This diachronic approach gives us a unique vantage point from which to develop or test models to suggest how social, political, and economic conditions can influence behavior over a long period of time.

A third function of relational research is that, as in Crowne and Marlowe's studies (in Chapter 1), we can begin to establish the validity of our constructs. In behavioral science there are countless examples of these abstract terms that can be validated only by correlating a variety of subjects' behaviors in a variety of situations, and observing the degree to which the behaviors are correlated, as the construct would predict.

Turning to experimental research, the typical one-shot experiment is another example of a synchronic method. There is an important function of experiments that is different from the functions of some other synchronic methods. It is to test for causal patterns in which changes in one variable lead relatively quickly to changes in another. Experimental research enables us to observe changes in behavior after we have introduced conditions relevant to what we expect to observe. By making use of experimental and control groups, we can establish that variable X actually precedes variable Y in time. And by using follow-up testing (e.g., Janis and Mann) we can assess long-term treatment outcomes.

Strong inference experiments enable us to repeat and test rival hypotheses, not only to exclude one or more of the hypotheses but also to discover the particular contexts in which each of them may be valid. Other functions of experiments include the generation of ideas for further investigation (heuristic experiments) and the development of procedures for research applications (methodological experiments), but their essential value is that they allow us to impose controls in a way that nonexperimental studies do not.

CHAPTER 8

SYSTEMATIC OBSERVATION, UNOBTRUSIVE MEASURES, AND RATING FORMATS

METHODS OF CATEGORIZING JUDGMENTS

This chapter continues our discussion of data collection and measurement procedures, with emphasis on the specific methods of categorizing judgments that might be employed in the different approaches introduced in the previous chapters. In the next chapter we will stay with this general topic, but discuss in particular the ins and outs of interviews, questionnaires, and self-recorded diaries. We begin this discussion by presenting a more detailed account of the making of participant-observer records, in which the researchers will categorize their own judgments about their own or others' (the "actors'") behaviors. One's choice of a given method of data collection or measurement will, like everything else under the sun, depend on the context in which it is to be used, and we will continue to illustrate the rich variety of research contexts available in behavioral science.

Previously we gave as an example of participant-observer research the field investigation of a cultural anthropologist. This strategy of research, though largely developed and used by sociologists and anthropologists, has been borrowed by researchers in other fields to investigate variables that could not be realistically manipulated in the laboratory. For example, social psychologist David Rosenhan (1973) was interested in the stigmatization by others of one's being labeled as "mentally ill." A number of volunteers, including Rosenhan himself, feigned psychiatric symptoms in order to be admitted as patients in mental hospitals. During their stay, they kept detailed records of their interactions with psychiatrists, psychologists, and resident physicians. Research such as this involves making judgments about the actions and conversations of individuals, in which the idea is to apprehend the world from the viewpoint of other human beings who live by particular meaning systems (cf. Heritage, 1984; Spradley, 1980). From their detailed records, the researchers concluded that the staff actually seemed to avoid interacting with the mental patients. This, Rosenhan inferred, accounted for the "depersonalization" that he and the other volunteer participants felt, similar to the felt powerlessness of mental patients.

In this study the actors (the psychologists, psychiatrists, and others) were not told that their behavior was being observed by the scientists. However, it is more typically true of participant-observer research in anthropology and sociology that the actors are well aware of the fact that they are being studied. It is possible that, sensitive to the loss of privacy, they may become more selective in cooperating with the researchers. In one case, 40 participant-observers visited a single Indian settlement in the Northwest Territories of Canada in one summer; when another then showed up to research these same Indians, he nearly ended up being thrown in the river (Lotz, 1968). Each person has an individual sense of the loss of privacy and the invasion of his or her personal life, and participant-observers (as much as any researchers) must be properly attuned to this psychological limitation. Some researchers have turned to the use of unobtrusive measures, and we will sample some of these methods once we have concluded our discussion of the making of "obtrusive" participant-observer records.

The unobtrusive methods we will discuss include the use of physical traces, archival records, and various simple and contrived *nonreactive* observations (i.e., those not affecting the reactions of the actors). In the archival category we will examine in some detail the method of categorizing judgments that communication researchers call *content analysis*, defined as the classification of the parts of a text into content categories. This very useful method has also been borrowed by researchers in other areas, and an investigation by sociologist Jack Levin and psychologist Allan Kimmel is illustrative (Levin and Kimmel, 1977). They asked three questions: (1) what kinds of well-known people are the subject of gossip, (2) in what social contexts does this gossiping take place, and (3) to what extent do gossip columns in the news media emphasize norms and values of American society? To answer these questions they developed an elaborate coding sheet on the basis of pilot testing. They then chose a sample of gossip columns from the 1950s to the 1970s and had three judges categorize the contents of each column using the coding sheet. Each category was carefully defined to avoid the possibility of coding errors resulting from ambiguity. For example, one category had to do with the "focus of the gossip." Several alternative judgments were possible, and the judges were instructed to code each alternative that was discussed in a particular gossip column. They were given specific examples to help them in deciding how to code, e.g., "If they say a target person didn't hit someone in a bar, categorize under *fighting and altercation* anyway, because that norm is being discussed."

We will present some general guidelines for employing content analysis, and also offer a number of technical and commonsense recommendations for how to select the judges who will do the content analyzing. The findings that can be obtained by using these procedures are illustrated by Levin and Kimmel's research results. First, they found that for all time periods the well-known subjects of gossiping were usually white males, of whom about two-thirds were in show business. Only a very small percentage of names were those of politicians, although it increased over the periods sampled. Second, they found that half of all the gossip directly pertained to some aspect of the occupational role of the subjects as opposed to their private lives. The mid-1970s was an especially "gossipy" time, judging from the researchers' conclusion that small talk about the private affairs of others was most prevalent in the content of the news media during this period. Romance and relationships, their establishment and dissolution, were also perennial favorites of the gossip columnists, but the representation of romantic tales declined from the early to the later periods sampled. Third, this content analysis revealed that media gossip does have a strong normative bias. Almost half of all the gossip was centrally concerned with the prescription or proscription of some behavior or attitude (cf. Levin and Arluke, 1987; Sabini and Silver, 1982; Spacks, 1985).

We turn then to the subject of rating scales, which are among the most widely used methods of categorizing judgments both in field studies and laboratory research. We will examine three traditional rating formats—the numerical, the forced-choice, and the graphic—as well as discuss the nature of rating "errors" (or biases) and their control. In the past a distinction was made between *rating* scales and *category* scales. The judge who worked with category scales was viewed as a "classifier" and not an "evaluator," inasmuch as it was argued that no assessment was made as to whether one behavior was more appropriate, more effective, etc., than another. It was said that the judge who worked with category scales merely read, listened to, or watched something and then classified it as accurately as possible. The judge who worked with ratings was said to be an evaluator who not only classified or counted frequencies, but also gave a numerical value to certain judgments or assessments. In this discussion we offer a different perspective, and instead will proceed on the premise that classifying and evaluating are characteristic of all judgments (Rosenthal, 1987a). From this simplified perspective one can say that working with category ratings (i.e., categorizing some behavior as present or absent) is just a special case of a two-value (0,1) rating scale, and not a different class of scales.

SYSTEMATIC OBSERVATIONAL RECORDS

In the early development of participant-observer research, scientists had yet to formulate a tradition of how to obtain the most objective results through systematic observation. In recent years, that problem has surfaced in discussions concerning the objectivity of the seminal studies by Margaret Mead and others, and in turn their reliability and validity have been questioned. Modern researchers are seemingly more attuned to the persistent and unique limitations associated with this method, and they frequently employ various controls to try to ensure the reliability and validity of their category records, which we turn to now.

For example, one way in which they attempt to achieve this is by the use of *systematic observation*, which they distinguish from common everyday observation in that the former conforms to a definite plan of action concerning what is to be observed, ignored, and recorded (i.e., categorized) as well as what measurement techniques and instruments are to be used (Michaels, 1983). Secondly, the researchers now frequently work in teams, rather than individually, and employ various checks and balances to control for possible biases in their individual classifications and evaluations. Thirdly, they usually try to establish rapport with a wide range of individuals (men and women, young and old, etc.) by framing questions during interviews in a context of the indigenous folklore of the culture. They then compare one another's observations to ensure that the study has arrived at a sophisticated awareness of the entire culture. Finally, to deal with the "observer as artifact" (i.e., observer interference or bias), the researchers frequently use concealment—but this again brings up the ethical issue of invasion of privacy.

The result of all this work is to produce a meticulous record—called an *ethnographic record* by the sociologists and cultural anthropologists—of what was systematically observed. It typically consists of field notes, tape recordings, pictures, and anything else that documents the situation under study (Spradley, 1980). In making category judgments the participant-observer employs as a basic unit of analysis what is called an *activity*; it refers to any intentional act, behavior, or incident aimed at affecting the status of events. Ethnographic records are usually concerned with the answers to such questions as, "What is happening?" and "What are people doing?" The purpose of classifying and evaluating what is happening or what people are doing is to tell us the objective of the act, behavior, or incident: "They are gossiping" or "They are taking a siesta" or "They are preparing a meal."

The information in Table 8.1 was taken from a study by John Beard Haviland (1977), in which he classified and evaluated the everyday activities involving the use of gossip in Zinacantan, a small village in Mexico. Over a period of 10 years, he and his family set up housekeeping from time to time in the village. Each time, he meticulously observed and tape-recorded the behavior and conversations of the villagers, which he then categorized and analyzed. Shown are fragments of conversations, based on verbatim accounts transcribed from tape recordings and field notes, along with Haviland's interpretation of each fragment. On the basis of his wide sampling of conversations, he reached the conclusion that gossiping was part of a pattern of behaviors that encouraged mutual spying between households at the same time that it isolated households from one another.

In doing this kind of research there are six questions that usually serve as general guideposts for the researchers (Goodenough, 1980):

1. *What is the purpose of the activity?* That is, what are the goals and their justifications? In Haviland's study, several objectives of gossiping were classified,

TABLE 8.1
Translated fragments of Zinacanteco gossip and their interpretation

Examples	Interpretations
"Didn't I hear that old José was up to some mischief?" "Perhaps, but that never became public knowledge. It was a secret affair." "The magistrate settled the whole business in private." "Yes, when a dispute is settled at the townhall, then a newspaper report goes out to every part of town... Ha ha ha." "Yes, then we all hear about it on the radio... Ha ha ha." "But when the thing is hushed up, then there's nothing on the radio. There are no newspapers. Then we don't hear about it. Ha ha ha."	Shows how some villagers even gossip about gossip.
"Is it true that old Maria divorced Manuel?" "Yes. She complained that she awoke every morning with a wet shirt. Old Manuel used to piss himself every night, just like a child." "When he was drunk, you mean?" "No, even when he was sober. 'How it stinks!' she said." "Ha ha ha. She spoke right out at the townhall."	Shows how some gossip trades on a separation, but also on a connection, between the public and the private domain.
"This is what I told him: All right, I'll see how deeply I must go into debt to take this office. But I don't want you to start complaining about it later. If I hear that you have been ridiculing me, saying things like: 'Boy he is just pretending to be a man; he is just pretending to have money to do ritual service. He stole my office, he took it from me...' If you say such things, please excuse me, but I'll drag you to jail. I'll come looking for you myself. I don't want you to tell stories about me, because you have freely given me your ritual office. If there is no dispute, then I too will behave the same way. I won't gossip about you. I won't ridicule you. I won't say, for example. 'Hah, I am replacing him; he has no shame, acting like a man, asking for religious office when he has no money.' I won't talk like that. 'He wanted to serve Our Lord, but he ran away. I had to take over for him.' I won't say things like that, if we agree to keep silent about it..."	Shows a common theme in gossip about shady dealings and how the villagers take pains to ensure that the matter is kept quiet.

Source: J. B. Haviland, "Gossip as Competition in Zinacantan," *Journal of Communication,* 1977, *27,* 186–191. Reprinted by permission of the author and the *Journal of Communication.*

which led him to conclude that, despite fences erected between households, the actors were constantly scrutinizing one another's dealings.

2. *What procedures are used?* What are the operations performed, the media or raw materials used, the skills and instruments involved, if any? The medium of gossip was word of mouth, and Haviland carefully categorized the linguistic and psychological skills required in effective gossipmongering.

3. *What are the time and space requirements?* How much time is needed for each operation, what areas or facilities are required, and are there any obstacles in the way of the activity? Haviland noted when and where the gossiping occurred, as well as what natural obstacles to the transmission of information existed.

4. *What are the personnel requirements?* How many actors participate, and what are their specializations, if any? Haviland classified and evaluated the elaborate conversational devices by which certain people in positions of authority protected themselves against charges of slander.

5. *What is the nature of the social organization?* What are the categories of actors, their rights, duties, privileges, powers, and the types of sanctions used by them? Haviland classified and evaluated the ways in which Zinacanteco gossip was a form of behavior by which villagers managed their social faces and at the same time protected their privacy.

6. *What are the occasions for performance?* When is the activity mandatory, permitted, and prohibited, and what is the relationship of the initiator's role to the roles of others? Haviland noted the occasions that were most and least conducive to gossiping, and categorized and analyzed the particular role interactions of the gossipmongers within those circumstances.

TAKING ACCURATE FIELD NOTES

In taking field notes it is important that the observer indicate whether they were written in the kind of ordinary language he or she uses in everyday situations, or whether they consisted of verbatim quotes (as in Table 8.1). People have a tendency to translate and simplify what they see and hear, and this can introduce an element of bias in the entries or in later evaluations of the written records (Spradley, 1980).

There are different kinds of field notes, beginning with the *condensed account*, in which the observer includes quoted phrases, single words, and unconnected sentences, but embellished by the observer's own transcriptions. The idea is to present an initial, shortened version of what was observed or heard, which can be expanded on later. Second, the *expanded account* is the researcher's addition to the condensed account, which he or she should try to do as soon as possible (before memory becomes cloudy). The observer fills in details and recalls things that were not recorded on the spot. Third, there is the *fieldwork journal*, which is a diary that contains a record of experiences, ideas, fears, mistakes, confusions, problems, and so forth. It represents the personal, or subjective, side of fieldwork, i.e., the observer's reactions to the events of the day (Spradley, 1980).

Another distinction is that between *grand tour observations* and *mini-tour observations* (Spradley, 1980). The former refer to the researcher's general impressions about what is occurring based on some of or all the following dimensions of every social situation: (1) *space* (the physical place or places), (2) *actors* (the people involved), (3) *activity* (an individual action), (4) *objects* (the physical things that are present), (5) *act* (single actions that people do), (6) *event* (the related activities of several people), (7) *time* (the sequencing that takes place over time), (8) *goals* (the things people are trying to accomplish), and (9) *feelings* (the emotions felt and expressed). In contrast, mini-tour observations deal with concrete details of a unit of experience, i.e., an in-depth look at the smaller segments of each activity observed.

We do not want to leave readers with the impression that systematic observation is limited to ethnography (e.g., Haviland's study) or even to fieldwork generally (e.g., Rosenhan's study). In the next section we turn to its application in the classic laboratory research done by Robert F. Bales on interactions in small groups. Before going on to that work, we will give one further example of the participant-observer method. The following example illustrates its use in a very different context from those represented in the previous examples.

Louise H. Kidder, a social psychologist who specializes in descriptive participant-observer research, did a field observation study in which tape recordings, interviews, and participant observation in a hypnosis workshop were used to classify and evaluate the role interactions between the hypnotists and the persons becoming hypnotized (Kidder, 1972). She was curious to learn how the skeptical subject who says, "How do I know if I was hypnotized?" or "I still don't consider it an experience any different from others," ends up being convinced of the reality of the power of hypnosis and the ability of hypnotists to implement and control it. Kidder did her field observations over a 3-day period while attending a workshop given for practicing psychologists who were there to learn the procedures of how to hypnotize someone. Employing a tape recorder and written notes, she made verbatim accounts of the interactions between the hypnotists and their subjects and then categorized and analyzed this data base. Some of her reported results are given in Table 8.2, which shows fragments of some of the conversations she recorded and her interpretation of each. By the end of the workshop the skeptical subjects had become convinced that hypnosis was a real phenomenon and had also lowered their criteria for what could pass as "hypnosis."

CHOOSING JUDGES TO ANALYZE
AND CLASSIFY

Whether we make ethnographic observations and classify and evaluate activities as they proceed, or whether we make film records and then use judges to classify and evaluate what they see, an important question to consider is, "Who should the judges or observers be?" There is usually no special interest in individual differences among observers or judges when we consider issues of interobserver or interjudge reliability. We simply decide on the type of judges or observers we want (college students, clinical psychologists, linguists, mothers, etc.) and then

TABLE 8.2
How skeptics became convinced of the power of hypnosis

Example	Interpretation
Subject: The question in my mind is, how do you know if you were in a trance or not? I mean, I know I did some things, but I think they were all under conscious voluntary control.	
Hypnotist 1: This is the one question that all patients will ask ... And they'll say, "You see, it doesn't work." I think you can tell if someone is in a trance by looking at them .... the facial expressions. I could walk around the room and tell who wasn't and who was, by how they responded. I thought you were, but maybe you didn't think you were.	Shows the ambiguity and the fine line between what one person calls "hypnosis" and what another calls "playing the game."
Hypnotist 2: You were actually the one that I thought went into trance the quickest....The question is not were you in a trance, but why did you feel compelled to do those things. And why did you follow the suggestions?	
Subject: My conscious perception was that I was kind of going along with the thing all the way. I was kind of playing the game the way it's supposed to be. I was trying to achieve something which somehow felt different from just playing the game, and as far as I was consciously aware, I didn't succeed.	

(continued)

regard each observer or judge within that sample as to some degree equivalent to, or interchangeable with, any other observer or judge within the sample.

For example, if we wanted a sample of educated judges, we might be content to select college students. If we wanted judgments of nonverbal cues to psychoses, we might choose experts for our judges, such as clinical psychologists or psychiatrists. If we wanted judgments of nonverbal cues to discomfort in infants, we might select pediatricians, developmental psychologists, or mothers. If we wanted judgments of nonverbal cues of persuasiveness, we might invite trial lawyers, fundamentalist ministers, or salespersons. Of course, to get objective judgments we would want to be careful that they are not relying on stereotypes that may not be accurate; e.g., salespersons recruited to watch people give persuasive messages might rely on their stereotypes to tell us which of the nonverbal cues were most persuasive.

In any of these cases we might do even better by taking a nonrandom selection of judges. However, if we wanted to obtain the highest possible level of general accuracy of judgments of nonverbal cues, we could instead select our judges

TABLE 8.2 *Continued*

Example	Interpretation
Hypnotist: Dr. Z tried to help those of you who weren't able to do the arm lift. He said, "For those for whom this was difficult, the arm can get very heavy" (so persons could let their arms go down instead of up).... He pointed out the successes instead of failures and gave other possibilities for achieving success. *Subject:* You make it sound as if it's the patient's fault instead of yours if he doesn't go into trance. *Hypnotist:* Well, let me say this. Earlier hypnosis was done in an authoritarian fashion—now it is much more permissive and we conceive of hypnosis as the achievement of the subject, in which the hypnotist helps.	Shows how the responsibility for "successes" and "failures" is placed on the subject rather than on the hypnotist.
Subject 1: I'm surprised, most of us don't think it's so different from other things. *Subject 2:* Yes, I guess my expectations have changed. Now if I experience anything like it I'm satisfied. And I'm not sure about what the different depths mean. But now if I'm under I still notice if another person comes over, but I say, "I don't care."	Shows how the subject gives up his original idea that hypnosis is a dramatically different state of being and accepts even mildly different experiences as evidence that he was hypnotized.

Source: L. H. Kidder, "On Becoming Hypnotized: How Skeptics Become Convinced: A Case of Attitude Change?" *Journal of Abnormal Psychology,* 1972, *80,* 317–322. Reprinted by permission of the author and the American Psychological Association.

on the basis of prior research that has identified specific characteristics of people who are more sensitive to nonverbal cues. This research suggests that to optimize overall sensitivity to nonverbal cues we should probably select judges who are (1) female, (2) college-aged, (3) cognitively complex, and (4) psychiatrically unimpaired (Rosenthal, Hall, DiMatteo, Rogers, and Archer, 1979).

Still another way to select judges is on the basis of pilot testing in which one compares all recruits in a pool of potential judges in terms of their accuracy of judgments on some relevant criterion. Suppose we were interested in selecting judges for a future study in which they would have to categorize the emotions expressed by actors in encounter groups. We might begin by showing our pool of potential judges 10 pictures of people who exhibit six different emotions categorized as anger, disgust, fear, happiness, sadness, and surprise. We ask the subjects to select the one emotion that is expressed in each picture, and we then count the correct answers given by each participant.

How do we pick the "really" accurate judges? There is a considerable literature on correcting response measures for guessing and partial information (e.g.,

Link, 1982; Lord and Novick, 1968; Rosenthal, 1987a; Sperling and Melchner, 1976), and we might approach this problem by the same procedure that testers use in estimating the effects of guessing on tests. The number of items that are right after adjustment for guessing (RI-adjusted) is mathematically a function of the number of items that are correctly answered (RI, or "right items"), the number that are incorrectly answered (WI, or "wrong items"), and the number of alternatives for each item (A). The formula for this is RI-adjusted = RI − [WI/(A − 1)]. Our prospective judges were each given 10 pictures to judge, with six multiple-choice alternative responses for each picture. If Smith got five right, substituting in the equation above we find his adjusted accuracy score is $5 − [5/(6 − 1)] = 4$. If Jones got eight items right, her adjusted accuracy score is therefore $8 − [2/(6 − 1)] = 7.6$. Jones is clearly a better judge of emotions than is Smith.

DEVELOPMENT OF CHECKLISTS AND TALLY SHEETS

Another practical question concerns the nature of any particular checklists and tally sheets to be used when making category judgments. To ensure that they are accurate and that we have not omitted any vital information, three steps are taken before going into the field: (1) define each category of behavior that is relevant as specifically as possible (based on experience in pilot studies), (2) decide where and when the observations will be made, and by whom, and (3) select and train judges in the use of the scales to record the particular variables under investigation.

Checklists and tally sheets are used in a variety of other settings, including laboratory settings, to classify what is observed into theoretically meaningful categories. A seminal example is the work of Bales (1950a, 1950b), who developed category scaling procedures to be used by judges to evaluate and classify the behaviors of persons engaged in small-group interactions in the laboratory. This work has been updated by Bales and Cohen (1979), but here we look only at the original system as it is still generally employed in research on interactions in small groups. Figure 8-1 shows the categories developed by Bales and the theorized relationships to one another in terms of the traditional formulation.

In its original usage, trained observers behind a one-way screen recorded every event that occurred among several people who were brought together to have a discussion of some complex human relations problem. The observers were trained to evaluate and classify whether a person asked a question or answered one, gave help or withheld it, agreed or disagreed with someone, and so forth. Using this approach, Bales succeeded in identifying the sequences or patterns employed by the participants when a small group of persons engages in problem solving for a period of time. He found, for example, that there are between 15 and 20 codable interactions a minute, about half of which involve problem-solving activities. The remaining interactions usually consist of positive and negative reactions and questions. Giving information tends to be the most frequent behavior in the first one-third of a problem-solving meeting, and offering suggestions is the most frequent in the last one-third of the meeting.

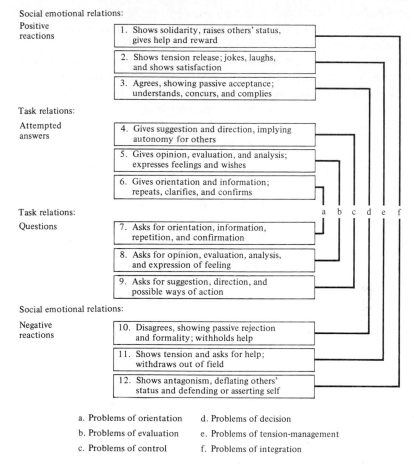

Social emotional relations:

Positive reactions

1. Shows solidarity, raises others' status, gives help and reward
2. Shows tension release; jokes, laughs, and shows satisfaction
3. Agrees, showing passive acceptance; understands, concurs, and complies

Task relations:

Attempted answers

4. Gives suggestion and direction, implying autonomy for others
5. Gives opinion, evaluation, and analysis; expresses feelings and wishes
6. Gives orientation and information; repeats, clarifies, and confirms

Task relations:

Questions

7. Asks for orientation, information, repetition, and confirmation
8. Asks for opinion, evaluation, analysis, and expression of feeling
9. Asks for suggestion, direction, and possible ways of action

Social emotional relations:

Negative reactions

10. Disagrees, showing passive rejection and formality; withholds help
11. Shows tension and asks for help; withdraws out of field
12. Shows antagonism, deflating others' status and defending or asserting self

a. Problems of orientation   d. Problems of decision

b. Problems of evaluation   e. Problems of tension-management

c. Problems of control   f. Problems of integration

FIGURE 8-1

Categories of socioemotional (directed at friendship and emotional needs) and task-related (directed at achieving concrete problem solving) interactions in small groups. (R. F. Bales, "A Set of Categories for Analysis of Small Group Interaction," *American Sociological Review,* 1950, vol. 15, pp. 257–263. Reprinted by permission of the author and the American Sociological Association.)

Other researchers have developed their own checklists or tally sheets based on the particular objectives of their research and the variables of interest. In another example, David Kipnis, an organizational social psychologist, focused on the major tactics of power that people use to influence one another. In his research he has employed checklists to tally the tactics of power used in both field and laboratory situations (Goodstadt and Kipnis, 1970; Grey and Kipnis, 1976; Kipnis and Cosentino, 1969). One category consisted of so-called strong tactics, such as actively criticizing someone's point of view as foolish or childish, or getting angry at someone and demanding that the person give in. A second category, called "rational" tactics, included stating one's point of view and letting the other person decide, or holding mutual talks without arguments. Tally sheets were used by judges to evaluate and classify what they observed, and the data were then analyzed for theoretically predicted relationships. These categories have also been used to code the tactics used by protagonists in dramas, in order to study how actors influence each other in fiction (Kipnis, 1984).

In a representative study, social psychologist Samuel Fung had college students describe, and rate on several scales, incidents they recalled in which they had been either "synthetically benevolent" or "synthetically malevolent" when influencing others (Fung, Kipnis, and Rosnow, 1987). Synthetic benevolence refers to prosocial or otherwise positive actions that are not what they appear or purport to be, whereas synthetic malevolence refers to antisocial or otherwise negative actions that are not what they appear or purport to be (cf. Tunis and Rosnow, 1983). Fung coded his subjects' responses using the categories of power tactics devised by Kipnis. The results were that synthetic benevolence tactics were primarily characterized as involving overt instances of flattery, modeling, and pretending (called "weak" tactics by Kipnis). The synthetic malevolence tactics primarily involved phony threats, false refusals, and fake denials (i.e., "strong" tactics). Most interesting, Fung discovered a tendency for synthetic benevolence to be targeted to higher-status, more powerful others, and a corresponding tendency of synthetic malevolence to be directed against lower-status, less powerful others.

UNOBTRUSIVE INDICATORS OF ATTITUDES AND BEHAVIORS

Behavior is so complicated that there is no single, agreed-upon way of studying or measuring it. In the research we have discussed, other strategies of observation and measurement might also have been used to advantage. One such strategy alluded to previously is the use of *unobtrusive* indicators, including disguised measures, archives, and physical traces. The seminal work on this subject was a synthesis written by a team of interdisciplinary behavioral researchers headed by Eugene J. Webb (Webb, Campbell, Schwartz, and Sechrest, 1966; Webb, Campbell, Schwartz, Sechrest, and Grove, 1981). These authors raised the objection that investigators are overly dependent on single-criterion variables, none of which are ever completely free of error. They underscored the importance of systematic pluralism, in which multiple measures are systematically employed to "triangulate" on the dependent variables of interest. If a relationship or hypothesis can survive the onslaught of a series of imperfect measures, some direct and others unobtrusive, then more confidence can be placed in it.

Unobtrusive measures, while arguably less precise than more direct measures, often have the advantage of being nonreactive instruments. A study by Lawrence S. Wrightsman (1969) is illustrative. He was interested in studying attitudes and behaviors in Davidson County, Tennessee, during the 1969 presidential campaign. The major candidates that year were Nixon and Agnew on the Republican ticket and Humphrey and Muskie on the Democratic side, but there was also a third-party candidate, Governor George Wallace of Alabama, who campaigned using the slogan of "Law and Order." Wrightsman wondered whether the supporters of Wallace were, in fact, more law-abiding than were supporters of the major-party candidates. To answer this question he decided to do an unobtrusive survey of motor vehicles.

He chose to study motor vehicles because an excellent unobtrusive indicator of obeying one law could be readily found in Davidson County. The law that drew his attention mandated that all motor vehicles carry a new tax sticker. Wrightsman and his students made a 5-day survey of parking lots and simply noted for each car whether it had the county tax sticker and also whether it had a bumper sticker supporting Nixon, Humphrey, or Wallace. For a control group, Wrightsman used those cars without a presidential bumper sticker that were parked adjacent to the above cars. On the basis of this informal survey, he found that Wallace supporters obeyed the new tax sticker law proportionately *less* than did supporters of either Nixon or Humphrey, or in comparison with the control cars. In addition, he coded the age of the car (as an unobtrusive indicator of socioeconomic status) and the presence of a tax sticker. The result was that there were almost identical rates of old Wallace cars with the tax sticker on them as new Wallace cars with the tax sticker. On the basis of this finding, Wrightsman felt it was possible to rule out a rival hypothesis that stated that fewer Wallace supporters displayed a tax sticker because they were poorer and less able to pay the $15 tax.

PHYSICAL TRACES, ARCHIVAL RECORDS, SIMPLE AND CONTRIVED OBSERVATIONS

The compendium written by Webb and his coauthors provides us with a veritable mini encyclopedia of unobtrusive measures. They divide them into a number of different categories: physical traces, archival records, simple observations (as in Wrightsman's study), and contrived observations.

First, *physical traces* include the kind of physical evidence that a detective might use as a clue in solving a crime. In a favorite case it was mentioned how a car's radio buttons were clues to the driver's geographic location. By studying the commercial-station frequencies to which the buttons were tuned, it was possible for the detective to triangulate on the place where the car was garaged. In an application of this strategy, radio dial settings were used by a car dealer in an audience-measurement study. The dealer had his mechanics record the position of the dial in all the cars brought in for service, and then used this information to optimize the selection of radio stations to carry his future advertising to old and potentially new customers.

There are many other examples in this category, including measuring the wear and tear (particularly on the corners) of library books as an unobtrusive measure of what is actually being read, not just books checked out but possibly never read or never finished. In one study the relative popularity of children's museum exhibits was measured unobtrusively. The exhibits had glass fronts, and each evening they were dusted for children's noseprints. Those with more noseprints on the glass were more frequently or more closely observed, the researchers speculated. The distance of the noseprints from the floor even provided a crude index of the ages of the children. Other "controlled" measures besides noseprint counting could be keeping track of the wear and tear of the floor tiles in front of each exhibit. Another example in this category would be the study of language behavior by analyzing the content of messages that people composed on floor-sample typewriters and computers in department stores.

Second, *archives* are the ongoing, continuous records of a society. This category includes (1) actuarial records (e.g., birth, marriage, death records in town hall ledgers), (2) political and judicial records (e.g., voting records of legislators and speeches printed in the *Congressional Record*), (3) other government records (e.g., weather reports, invention records, crime reports), (4) the mass media (e.g., stories, news reports, advertising, editorials), (5) sales records (e.g., sales at airport bars, sales of trip-insurance policies, and records of decreased sales of air travel tickets as plausible indicators of increased anxiety over flying), (6) industrial and institutional records (sicknesses and absences from the job, complaints and unsolicited commendations from the public, accident reports), and (7) various other written documents (e.g., diaries and letters from captured soldiers in wartime, letters of protest to large companies, rumors recorded by rumor control centers).

For example, press bias was studied by analyzing the verbs that appeared in sports headlines (Tannenbaum and Noah, 1959). Among the results was that there was a definite hometown bias in the verbs used to report scores (e.g., "Sox Edged 8-7" or "Sox Bludgeon Yankees 8-7"). When archival records are used, it is important to be sensitive to the need for *data transformations* when they are warranted. Suppose we were collecting data regarding the number of votes cast in presidential elections over many years. In using election records we would need to transform the data to take into account the changes in the size of the population from one period to another. In this case the absolute frequencies would be misleading, but the absolute values transformed into percentages would enable us to make more accurate comparisons between successive periods.

Included in this category is what sociologists, theologians, and philosophers call *documentary research*. Basically, such research involves the content analysis of historical documents in order to make clear their interpretation or meaning. The most important concern in doing this research is to establish the authenticity of the documents analyzed. Other concerns involve availability of pertinent documents, problems of sampling, and the problem of how to establish whether the documents are telling the truth. Documentary research is not a clear-cut and well-recognized category, like survey research or experimental research, but it is another example of the use of secondary records. For a detailed discussion containing methodological guidelines, see Jennifer Platt (1981a, 1981b) and the work of others cited by her.

Third, *simple observation* includes the kind of work done by Wrightsman and his students. Webb's group noted an anonymous study that discovered a strong correlation between the methodological disposition of psychologists and the length of their hair. The anonymous authors unobtrusively evaluated and classified the hair styles of psychologists at professional meetings and also categorized the meetings by whether they involved "tough-minded" or "soft-minded" areas of research. They reported that the tough-minded psychologists had shorter hair than the soft-minded psychologists. Another example: in the 1960s, when protesters were planning a mass jail-in, they would wear dungarees as they entered the meeting place. Just as detectives use clothing clues, behavioral researchers might use them as predictor variables in special cases.

Fourth, *contrived observation* is defined by the fact that the observer introduces some variable of interest into a situation and then unobtrusively observes its effect on behavior. For example, we might estimate the degree of fear induced by a ghost story by observing the shrinking diameter of a circle of seated children. Some investigators have "bugged" cocktail parties and recorded the conversations after introducing some variable of interest, e.g., introducing a stranger or an oddly dressed guest. Before the days of audiotapes, Francis Galton, the pioneering English behavioral scientist (noted in Chapter 1), used to carry a paper cross and a little needle point in order to make unobtrusive observations. He used this device to punch holes in the paper in order to keep count of whatever he was at the time observing; a hole at the head of the cross meant "greater," on the arm "equal," and on the bottom "less."

GENERAL GUIDELINES FOR CONTENT ANALYSES

Checklists and tally sheets are also used in *content analysis*, which involves the objective, systematic strategy of decomposing messages and then evaluating and classifying their contents in order to reveal their specific characteristics (e.g., Holsti, 1969; Stone, Dunphy, Smith, and Ogilvie, 1966). Among its early uses, priests burrowed through texts and sermons for evidence of heresy, philosophers through ancient documents for their interpretation ("hermeneutic analysis"), and censors through books and other written documents for hidden meanings (McCormick, 1982). In the 1920s, content analysis was proposed by Harold Lasswell, the political theorist and researcher, as a useful procedure for a program of communication research. But it was not until the 1950s that the first published definitive work on content analysis appeared—Bernard Berelson's *Content Analysis in Communication Research* (1952). Readers interested in using content analysis will find a proliferation of recent work on this subject, including Ole R. Holsti's review in the second edition of the *Handbook of Social Psychology* (Lindzey and Aronson, 1968–1969), Philip J. Stone's computerized strategies (Stone, Dunphy, Smith, and Ogilvie, 1966), and various handbooks by sociologists and communication researchers (e.g., Krippendorff, 1980; Rosengren, 1981; Weber, 1985).

Briefly, the basic procedure consists of making inferences from textual material by counting symbols, words, sentences, ideas, or whatever other category of information is of interest. Traditionally, in doing a content analysis, there are three general guidelines to keep in mind (see Berelson, 1954):

1. It is important that the analyses be consistent among the judges; i.e., different coders should produce the same results. If, for example, two judges are to code the type of gossip and they cannot agree on what constitutes "fighting and altercation," then the resulting analysis cannot be very reliable. If each category and unit of analysis is carefully defined, and if the judges are properly trained, the intercoder reliability should be satisfactorily high.

2. It is essential that the specific categories and units be relevant to the questions or hypotheses of the study. In choosing categories it is a good idea to ask "What is the communication about?" and "How is it said?" This will help to focus the analysis on the substance (the *what*) and the form (the *how*) of the subject matter. It is also well to consider several different units of analysis before settling on any one unit. For example, we might consider coding words and word compounds (or phrases), or perhaps themes (or assertions).

3. And finally, it is important to decide on a good sampling procedure. Because content analysis is so time-consuming, one must be sure that the materials to be analyzed are representative enough to justify the effort.

Although there are limitations of this procedure (cf. Weber, 1985), as there are of all methods, content analysis has at least four distinct advantages when used properly (Woodrum, 1984). First, it requires little more than commonsense logic to develop a coding system and then to implement it (but, of course, common sense in no way guarantees that it will be a *good* one). Second, it is a "shoestring" methodology, in that, though labor-intensive, it requires minimum capital investment. Third, it is a "safe" methodology, because the researcher can add necessary information if it is missed or incorrectly coded (which, if there are changes in what is being measured over time, is not usually possible in the typical experimental or survey study). Fourth, it forces researchers to scrutinize the material that they are evaluating and classifying by specifying category criteria and assessing their success in measuring qualitative phenomena.

In the next chapter we discuss interviews and questionnaires, which can also involve the use of content analysis when open-ended. Recently, interest has been generated in analyzing the narrative reports that participants give in interviews and questionnaires, or in traditional story lines (e.g., Polkinghorne, 1988; Sarbin, 1986). In a representative study, Kenneth J. Gergen and Mary M. Gergen (1986) employed content analysis procedures to identify three logical types of story lines in narratives. One type is the "stability" narrative, in which the protagonist remains essentially unchanged with respect to the goal. A second type is the "progressive" narrative, in which there is steady progress or advancement toward the goal. Third is the "regressive" type, narratives in which the protagonist ends up further away from the goal than when he or she started. Different classifications have been proposed by scholars in other disciplines (e.g., Frye, 1957, 1963).

NUMERICAL, FORCED-CHOICE, AND GRAPHIC RATING SCALES

In interviews and questionnaires, rating scales are often employed to impose a sense of structure on the responses. They are also used in observational studies when the researcher wishes to evaluate the quality of some experience or activity. Whatever objective they are designed to accomplish, they usually take one or a combination of three basic forms: the numerical, the forced-choice, and the graphic rating scale.

First, the *numerical scale* is distinguished by the fact that the raters work with a sequence of defined numbers. The numbers may be quite explicit, as in the following example, which was taken from a behavior rating scale for adolescents (Baughman and Dahlstrom, 1968):

How popular is each of your classmates?
(1) Extremely popular
(2) Above average
(3) About average
(4) Below average
(5) Quite unpopular

In some numerical scales the numbers are implicit rather than explicit, e.g.:

Do you feel that a large-scale civil defense program would tend to incite an enemy to prematurely attack this country, or do you feel that such a program would lessen the chances of an enemy attack? (Check one.)

_____ It would considerably increase the chance of an enemy attack.

_____ It would somewhat increase the chance of an enemy attack.

_____ It would neither increase nor decrease the chance of an enemy attack.

_____ It would somewhat decrease the chance of an enemy attack.

_____ It would considerably decrease the chance of an enemy attack.

In both examples the questions and alternative responses are written in simple, straightforward language. It is very important that the statements not be ambiguous or complexly worded, for that asks the respondent to provide a unidimensional response to a multidimensional question—quite impossible! In the second example, note that the middle alternative ("neither increase nor decrease") represents something like indifference. Many researchers prefer to omit middle categories, so as to push the respondents to one or the other side (Bradburn, 1982).

These numerical scales are also among the easiest to construct and to use, and the simplest in terms of data analysis (Guilford, 1954). However, it is believed that they are more vulnerable to many biases and errors than other forms that have been developed specifically to overcome those problems. An item asking "How popular is each of your classmates?" and giving five alternative possibilities ranging from "quite unpopular" to "extremely popular" may be vulnerable to a particular type of response set called the *halo effect* (Cooper, 1981; Lance and Woehr, 1986)—which we turn to in a moment.

A second basic format, which was specifically developed to overcome the halo effect, is the *forced-choice scale*. An example would be one that presented two equally favorable statements about someone, and asked the rater to choose only one of the statements to describe that person: "X is energetic" and "X is intelligent." The rater is *forced* to say whether X has more of one trait than another of this pair. In an early study by Highland and Berkshire (1951; cited in Guilford, 1954), an extensive analysis was made of six different forms of forced-choice instruments:

1. Form A consisted of two statements per item, both favorable or both unfavorable (i.e., $+$ $+$ or $-$ $-$). The rater was instructed to select the more (or the less) descriptive statement in each pair.
2. Form B consisted of three statements per item, all favorable or all unfavorable (i.e., $+$ $+$ $+$ or $-$ $-$ $-$). The rater was instructed to select the most and least descriptive statements in each triad.
3. Form C consisted of four statements, all favorable (i.e., $+$ $+$ $+$ $+$). The rater was instructed to select the two most descriptive statements in this quadrad.
4. Form D consisted of four statements, like form C (i.e., $+$ $+$ $+$ $+$), but the rater was instructed to select the one most descriptive and the one least descriptive statement in this quadrad.
5. Form E consisted of four statements, two favorable and two unfavorable (i.e., $+$ $+$ $-$ $-$). The rater was instructed to select the most and least descriptive statements in this quadrad (as in form D).
6. Form F consisted of five statements, two favorable, two unfavorable, and one neutral (i.e., $+$ $+$ 0 $-$ $-$), and the rater was instructed to select the one most descriptive and the one least descriptive statement.

The results of this study indicated that, everything considered, form C is perhaps the best choice in many situations. Forms E and F yielded some of the highest coefficients of reliability, but forms C and D tended to give the highest validity results. Forms B and C showed the least tendency to bias, B and D were the least popular methods with the raters, and A and C were the most popular.

The forced-choice method, however, is time-consuming to develop and, whatever the particular format adopted, is sometimes resisted by subjects who object to having to make a choice between equally favorable or equally unfavorable alternatives (Cronbach, 1960). Thus a third basic format is the *graphic scale*, usually a straight line resembling a thermometer and presented either horizontally or vertically:

Unpopular ———————————————	Popular
Shy ———————————————	Outgoing
Solitary ———————————————	Gregarious

When divided into segments, the graphic scale is transformed into a numerical rating scale:

Unpopular —:—:—:—:—:—:—:—:	Popular
Shy —:—:—:—:—:—:—:—:	Outgoing
Solitary —:—:—:—:—:—:—:—:	Gregarious

In these segmented scales the respondent must make a decision that reflects either positively or negatively on the person being rated, because there is no neutral category in any graphic scale divided into an even number of segments. In segmented scales in which there is an uneven number of categories, the implication of the middle category would be "neutrality" (e.g., neither unpopular nor popular).

The implication in the use of segmented scales, as in the case of numerical ratings, is that adjacent segments or categories are psychologically equidistant. That is a problematic assumption in some cases (cf. Surber, 1984), even though it is also a basic one in certain standardized scaling procedures (discussed in the next chapter). Interestingly, one study that compared a number of different procedures (e.g., a numerical rating scale, a checklist, ranking of preferences, a forced choice between paired items) in terms of test-retest reliability found no appreciable differences among them—all the methods, at least in the context of marketing research, generated satisfactory reliability values (Kassarjian and Nakanishi, 1967). The results suggest that the selection of a rating format might best be based on considerations other than concerns about stability. For example, one might decide to use a multipoint scale in order to develop a more precisely defined pattern of what was being rated (King, King, and Klockars, 1983).

How many points or rating segments are optimal in a multipoint scale? Is it better when making a numerical rating scale, for example, to construct a 3-point scale, a 7-point scale, an 11-point scale, etc.? Another study examined the extent to which interrater reliability of a clinical rating scale was affected by the number of scale points from 2 all the way up to 100 (Cicchetti, Showalter, and Tyrer, 1985). The results were that internal-consistency reliability increased steadily up to a 7-point rating scale, beyond which no substantial increases occurred.

In making up *anchor* words, such as "extremely unpopular" and "extremely popular," researchers should try to select terms or short statements that are simple, unidimensional, and unambiguous. The anchors also need to be clearly relevant to the behavior or variables being rated, and consistent with other cues. Figure 8-2 shows a seven-point "mood questionnaire" based on the segmented type of graphic rating scale, in which the same anchor words are relevant to all eight variables (Rosnow, 1968). It is also important that the anchor words be as precise as possible, and that they stay clear of expressions with ethical or moral overtones. In the next chapter we also present several standardized rating scales, most of which incorporate some aspect of one or more of the three basic formats just discussed.

SYSTEMATIC RATING ERRORS AND THEIR CONTROL

The use of rating scales proceeds on the assumption that the person doing the rating is capable of an acceptable degree of precision and objectivity. However, there are a number of potential rating errors that need to be considered by researchers employing these instruments. One type of bias, the *halo effect*, refers to the fact either (1) that a judge who forms a favorable impression of someone with regard to some central trait will then tend to paint a rosier picture of the

Indicate the way you feel *now* by placing a check mark in the appropriate place.

	Not at all		A little		Quite a bit		Extremely
	1	2	3	4	5	6	7
Jittery	_____	_____	_____	_____	_____	_____	_____
Depressed	_____	_____	_____	_____	_____	_____	_____
Troubled	_____	_____	_____	_____	_____	_____	_____
Shaky	_____	_____	_____	_____	_____	_____	_____
Unhappy	_____	_____	_____	_____	_____	_____	_____
Excitable	_____	_____	_____	_____	_____	_____	_____
Downhearted	_____	_____	_____	_____	_____	_____	_____
Anxious	_____	_____	_____	_____	_____	_____	_____
	1	2	3	4	5	6	7
	Not at all		A little		Quite a bit		Extremely

FIGURE 8-2
An illustration of the segmented format of a graphic rating scale.

person on other characteristics or (2) that, if a rater has knowledge of some previous outstanding performance (positive or negative) or trait, this knowledge influences the person's current rating of the ratee for the better or the worse. That is, because we tend to judge a person in terms of a general mental attitude toward him or her, this "halo" will influence our opinions about specific qualities of the individual. For example, a student who is athletic or good-looking might be judged as more popular than is really the case. The halo effect is most prevalent when the trait or characteristic that is being rated (1) is not easily observable, (2) is not clearly defined, (3) involves relations with other people, and (4) is of some moral importance (Symonds, 1925).

As noted, forced-choice rating methods are designed to reduce this tendency of arriving at particular judgments based on a general mental attitude. Suppose the judge is dominated by a desire to make the person being rated "look good" and to avoid making him or her "look bad." In this case the judge would simply pile up favorable ratings using a numerical scale. In using the forced-choice procedure, however, there is no inkling as to which favorable and unfavorable traits receive weight toward the score.

Another type of bias is an *error of leniency*, named from the fact that some judges (i.e., lenient judges) will tend to rate someone who is very familiar, or someone with whom they are ego-involved, more positively than they should. Judges who are made aware of this failing may, however, "lean over backwards" and rate the person more negatively than they should, thus making the opposite type of error. When we anticipate the leniency error, a way to help counteract it is to arrange the rating scale differently. We might give only one unfavorable cue word ("poor") and have most of the range given to degrees of favorable responses ("fairly good," "good," etc.):

Poor	Fairly good	Good	Very good	Excellent

However, we treat or analyze the anchors numerically such that "good" is only a 3 on a five-point scale.

A third type of bias, an *error of central tendency*, occurs when the observer hesitates to give extreme ratings and instead tends to rate in the direction of the mean of the total group. This can usually be controlled in the way that the positive range was expanded in the sample shown above. Thus, in a numerical or a segmented graphic scale, it is usually a good idea to allow for one or two more points than are absolutely essential. If it is essential, for instance, that we have at least five alternative responses or segments, then it would be better to use a seven-point than a five-point rating scale, i.e., if observers are reluctant to use the extremes.

A fourth type of error, a *logical error in rating*, refers to the fact that many judges are likely to give similar ratings for variables or traits that seem logically related in their own minds but may not be related in any given target person. This type of error is similar to the halo effect, in that both increase the intercorrelation of the variables or traits being rated. The difference is that the halo effect results from the observer's favorable attitude about one personality as a whole, whereas the logical error results from the observer's perceptions as to the relatedness of certain variables or traits irrespective of individuals. The way to deal with this problem is to constuct very precise definitions and to make the instructions as explicit as possible.

In general, the most effective strategy for improving ratings is to use multiple judges who have been very carefully trained and to pool their ratings over many different trials employing similar and different rating methods. Observers who have been lectured on rating errors should be more sensitive to the different kinds of biases and also more mindful about how they respond. Training that includes practice sessions followed by discussions of each possible error will teach them what to watch for and how to be more precise and objective in their evaluations (see Cooper, 1981; Guilford, 1954).

CHAPTER 9

INTERVIEWS, QUESTIONNAIRES, AND SELF-RECORDED DIARIES

UTILITY OF SELF-REPORT METHODS

When investigators feel that the research participants have the language and experience to describe their own actions and reactions, then interviews, questionnaires, and self-recorded diaries are frequently employed. Each method has its own distinct advantages, but there is also a family resemblance among them—they are all *self-report methods*. The basic differences are that (1) the interview involves having the researcher ask questions directly of the subjects, (2) the questionnaire has the subjects read and answer the questions themselves, and (3) the self-recorded diary involves having the subjects keep a record at the time an event occurs. Thus only the interview is characterized by an oral exchange between the investigator and the subject, although questionnaires are sometimes used within an interview (e.g., Downs, Smeyak, and Martin, 1980). In this chapter we discuss variants of these conventional self-report methods. We also discuss the advantages and limitations of open-ended and structured items, and the characteristics of particular standardized methods of self-report including the semantic differential, the Q-sort, the Likert and the Thurstone procedures.

As we shall see, among the benefits of the typical interview is that it provides an opportunity to establish rapport with the subject and to stimulate the trust and cooperation often needed to probe sensitive areas. It also provides an opportunity to help the subjects in their interpretation of the questions, and it allows flexibility in determining the wording and sequence of the questions. It achieves this through allowing greater control by the researcher over the situation, e.g., by letting the interviewer determine on the spot the amount of probing required (e.g., Gorden, 1969; Kahn and Cannell, 1965; Ruehlmann, 1977).

Questionnaires have their distinct advantages as well. They are more convenient to use than an interview because they can be administered to large numbers of people, as in mail surveys. For this reason they are more economical than the interview. Mail surveys, for instance, eliminate the cost of travel and travel time. Questionnaires also allow for a type of anonymity not provided by the interview. Instead of a face-to-face exchange of communication, a self-addressed envelope can be provided that is to be sent directly to some research center that has no connection with anyone the subject knows personally.

Many researchers choose to combine the use of the interview and the questionnaire. It may be useful to present some items outside an interview, so the subjects can read them several times and perhaps more easily (e.g., with less embarrassment). On the other hand, it may be helpful to use some interviewing to supplement a questionnaire when the nature of the questions is sensitive and personal contact is needed to elicit a full, frank response (Gorden, 1969).

It is also usually advantageous to use self-recorded diaries, i.e., diaries kept by subjects themselves. An advantage of such diaries is that they should give more reliable data than questionnaires or interviews relying on the subject's recall (e.g., Conrath, 1973; Wickesberg, 1968). We have more to say about this later in this chapter, but we first turn to the particular strategies and techniques that are characteristic of interviews and questionnaires.

OPEN-ENDED VERSUS STRUCTURED
INTERVIEWS AND QUESTIONNAIRES

A basic consideration in interview and questionnaire work is whether to use open-ended or structured questions. The merits and limitations of open-ended and structured items have been debated especially in survey research (e.g., Bradburn, 1983; Dohrenwend and Richardson, 1963).

Open-ended questions offer the respondents an opportunity to expand on their answers, to express feelings, motives, or behavior quite spontaneously (Campbell, 1950). "Tell me, in your own words, how you behaved the day you graduated from high school." This particular example illustrates a technique that has special status in clinical and organizational psychology, also called the *critical incident technique*. Developed by John C. Flanagan (1954), it involves having the subject describe an observable action the purpose of which was fairly clear to the observer, and the consequences sufficiently definite to leave little doubt about its effects.

The critical incident technique is considered to be open-ended because it allows a range of answers not specifically limited by a given range of responses. For instance, in organizational psychology, the following instructions could be used to elicit open-ended replies about a critical incident in the workplace: "Think of the last time you saw one of your subordinates do something that was very helpful to your group in meeting their production schedule." (Pause until the subject indicates that he or she has such an incident in mind.) "What were the general circumstances leading up to this incident?...Tell me exactly what this person did that was so helpful at that time....Why was this so helpful in getting your group's job done?"

In contrast to open-ended questions, *structured* (also called *closed*) questions are those with clear-cut response options. An item such as the following—included in a questionnaire given to junior high school teachers (Baughman and Dahlstrom, 1968)—is illustrative:

> Several things help children to make good grades, of course. Some students seem to make good grades easily, but others have to work hard in order to make their grades. We are interested in knowing how much each child *tries* to do well, even though his grades may or may not be the best.
> (1) tries very, very hard
> (2) tries somewhat more than the average student
> (3) tries about like the average student
> (4) tries somewhat less than the average student
> (5) doesn't try at all

In the view of most experienced researchers, structured questions produce more relevant and comparable responses, whereas open-ended questions (e.g., critical incident questions) produce fuller and "deeper" replies (Bradburn, 1983). The researcher who employs a structured format is looking for responses in which the subjects select a particular choice. The researcher who uses an open-ended format is looking for the nuances of meaning that may not be revealed when the response options are more limited. In a review of methodological studies it was concluded that for nonthreatening topics there is no overall superiority of one format over another; for threatening topics, however, open-ended questions tend to elicit higher levels of reporting by subjects (Sudman and Bradburn, 1974). That is, open-ended questions generally produce more self-revelations by subjects (Dohrenwend, 1965).

Researchers who use open-ended interviews often rely on a tape recorder to capture verbatim the entire reply, which then frees the interviewer to attend to the direction of specific questions and to visual details and impressions that can be filled in later. If this procedure is used, permission should be asked of the subject to record his or her replies and the confidentiality of the interview should be stressed (and ensured) by the researchers. The drawbacks attendant on tape recorders include the fact that they can break, make noise, interrupt the interview, and make some subjects apprehensive.

For practical purposes the researcher may have no choice but to use a structured format. In large-scale interview studies that are not well funded, it would be too costly to employ highly experienced interviewers, but the personal prejudices of neophyte interviewers could bias the results (Pareek and Rao, 1980). In such a situation it is preferable to structure the questions, as well as the sequence in which they are to be asked, in order to exert more control over the situation.

Basically the interview is an oral exchange, and, as in any two-way communication situation, human complexities can facilitate or interfere with this mutual process. Communications will often be guarded when the topics touch on sensitive issues, with research subjects preferring to "look good" rather than to give more revealing answers (discussed in Chapter 6). One study found that white respondents interviewed over the telephone by a black interviewer gave more pro-black responses than did white respondents interviewed by a white interviewer (Cotter, Cohen, and Coulter, 1982). Generally, subjects will share only the information that they want to share (Downs, Smeyak, and Martin, 1980), which unfortunately may tempt some neophyte interviewers to depart from the instructions and provide their own feedback as a way of drawing the sensitive material out.

Figure 9-1 shows what a brief interview schedule might look like. This particular one was used as part of an in-depth study of children in the rural south (Baughman and Dahlstrom, 1968). We see that some items are more structured than others, which is typical of most interview schedules. The more structured items are 2, 4, and 9, and the most unstructured one is 3.

STAGES IN DEVELOPING
INTERVIEW SCHEDULES

There are four basic steps in developing the interview schedule: (1) stating the objective, (2) outlining a plan of attack, (3) structuring the interview schedule, and (4) testing it and making appropriate revisions.

First, the objectives of the interview need to be explicitly stated. What are the research hypotheses? What is the nature of the data that the researchers require to test these hypotheses? What kinds of respondents are needed to produce the relevant responses? We have more to say about this last question in the next chapter, but suppose a researcher's objective were to interview the "opinion leaders" in a community. During the testing phase it would be necessary to locate some of the potential interviewees and try out the questions on them. This requires patience, because it might take a long series of interviews with many randomly selected individuals to lead the researcher to the type of persons that he or she wanted to locate.

Second, we need to develop a plan of attack, i.e., a general strategy for getting the relevant information that is needed to test the research hypotheses. In Chapter 7 we mentioned the rumor about Paul McCartney of the Beatles, and the way it led to an interview study to gather facts about those who spread and did not spread the false allegations (Rosnow and Fine, 1974, 1976). The nature of the rumor essentially took the form of a well-constructed murder mystery in which both clues and allegations were staged so that a stream of new "facts" would be continually forthcoming. It asserted that Paul McCartney had been decapitated in a car accident and replaced by a double, but even his denials were interpreted by the rumormongers as evidence in support of the false allegations. An important objective of this exploratory investigation was to generate leads about whether the rumormongers could be psychologically or demographically different from those who did not spread the rumor but instead "dead-ended" it. The research strategy called for (a) locating the potential interviewees, (b) defining categories of relevant questions and specifying how the replies would be analyzed, (c) planning to pretest the interview schedule, and (d) developing a recruitment and training procedure for the interviewers.

CHILD'S NAME _____ INTERVIEWER _____

DATE _____

We are interested in spending time with your four-year-old child, _____.
We believe there are many things that children can learn when they are young. There are some
things you may be able to tell us about _____ that will help us to know him (her) better.
I will be asking you about what _____ is like and some of the things he (she) may or
may not like to do.

1. Could you tell me what X is usually like?

    a. Happy _____   d. Silly _____
    b. Serious _____   e. Other _____
    c. Sad _____

2. Would you describe him (her) as:

    a. Shy _____   h. Needs encouragement _____
    b. Active _____   i. Always in a hurry _____
    c. Careful _____   j. Plays well alone _____
    d. Fearful _____   k. Would rather play by himself _____
    e. Tries things _____   l. Would rather play with others _____
    f. Shows off _____   m. Does he have to do things just right (just so)? _____
    g. Laughs a lot _____ n. Asks a lot of questions _____

3. Do you have any special concerns about X?

    a. _____

    b. _____

4. Has X had a chance to spend time doing some of these things?

    _____ a. Marking with crayon _____
    _____ b. Marking with a pencil _____
    _____ c. Cutting with scissors _____
    _____ d. Pasting _____
    _____ e. Collecting things _____
    _____ f. Working puzzles _____
    _____ g. Building with blocks or sticks _____
    _____ h. Looking at magazines or catalogs _____

5. Does anyone read story books to him (her)? _____

    (If yes) Does he (she) seem to listen? _____
    (If no) Does he (she) listen to someone tell stories? _____
    Does he (she) seem to enjoy the stories? _____
    What kind does he (she) seem to like most? _____
    Does he (she) ever tell a story that he (she) has heard? _____

    Does he (she) ever make up a story to tell? _____

    Does he (she) ever try to tell a story that he (she) has seen on television? _____

6. Does X get to play with children other than his (her) brothers and sisters? _____

7. Where does he (she) see other children? _____

8. Does he (she) get to spend much time with his (her) daddy? _____

9. Does he (she) like to:

    _____ a. Throw a ball   _____ f. Jump
    _____ b. Run   _____ g. Play games
    _____ c. Climb   _____ h. Make believe (play house, play grown-up)
    _____ d. Dance   _____ i. Other things (list) _____
    _____ e. Sing

    _____

10. Does X try to help around the house or farm? _____

FIGURE 9-1

Example of an interview schedule. (E. E. Baughman and W. G. Dahlstrom, *Negro and White Children: A Psychological Study in the Rural South,* Academic Press, New York, 1968. Reprinted by permission of the authors and Academic Press.)

182

Interestingly, despite the care in planning and executing this strategy, there were hardly any differences found between the rumormongers and the dead-enders. One difference, however, was that the rumormongers were revealed as less popular or less sociable; i.e., their interviews indicated that they dated less often and got together with friends less frequently than did the dead-enders. From this result it was then hypothesized that rumormongering is sometimes an attempt to gain esteem. Someone without many friends might worry about his or her self-esteem and might pass on a titillating rumor in hope of building a new friendship. The recipient of the rumor bestows "status" on the rumormonger merely by accepting the story. In later experimental and relational studies this hypothesis served as a point of embarkation to guide further data collection (Rosnow, 1988).

Third, we must structure the interview schedule. This, in turn, will involve four further considerations: (a) checking that each item is relevant, (b) determining ranges of response for some items, (c) establishing the best sequence of questions, and (d) establishing the best wording of questions:

a. It should be possible to examine each question or item and ask how the answers will be relevant to the particular research hypotheses or exploratory aims of the study. As a consequence, the interview schedule may be found to require an "Occam's razor" kind of pruning to cut away superfluous or undesired items. Researchers also do not want their interviews to be too long—90 minutes seems to be the outermost limit before boredom sets in (Pareek and Rao, 1980). In the study just above, the interview schedule was boiled down to 44 items, but some could be skipped if the respondent answered "no" to a particular question. For instance, the first question asked, "Were you aware of the Paul McCartney rumor even before you agreed to be interviewed?" If the subject answered "yes," the interviewer proceeded to ask a series of related questions ("Would you tell me the substance of that rumor as you remember it?" "Can you recall *when* and *where* you first heard the rumor?" "When you first heard the story, did you believe it, entirely or even partly, or did you think it was a hoax?" "How do you feel *now* about whether or not it was true?" "Did you discuss the rumor very much when you first heard it?" "How many people would you guess you passed the story on to?" "I'm going to show you the jacket now from the Beatle album called *Abbey Road,* and I'd like you to tell me if you recognize any clues either on the cover or on the back side that suggest Paul McCartney's death."). However, if the interviewee responded "no" to the initial question, the interviewer skipped all the items above and went on to other questions.

b. In developing some items, certain ranges of responses were also constructed. There were several purposes: to vary the format and make it more interesting, to enable the interviewee to make a more relevant reply, and to make it easier for the researchers to code and analyze the results. For instance, one item stated, "I'm now going to show you a list of activities, and I'd like you to tell me in which *single* area you find your greatest personal satisfaction as a college student. Remember, I want the one most satisfying area." The subject was then shown a list of activities, including course work, self-discovery, "bull sessions," social life, organized extracurricular activities, getting acquainted, and close friendships. In other research, cues with ranges of response in quantitative terms have been found useful. If we want to know someone's salary, it is well to present ranges of income levels rather than require an exact amount in the answer. For other questions the kinds of rating scales described in the previous chapter may be useful as supplements. A potential problem (which we come back to in a moment) is that some questions may make excessive demands on the cognitive abilities and skills of the subjects by making unrealistic demands on their memory. Even with a range of responses, the subjects may end up making "false negative" reports (i.e., a failure to report information) because of true memory lapses or because of carelessness or unwillingness to make the effort necessary to give a fuller account of past events (Cannell, Miller, and Oksenberg, 1981).

   c. Another consideration in structuring the interview schedule is to establish the best sequence of items. The research literature does not provide any clear-cut or consistent answers to the question of what is the "correct" location in which to pose particular items, but it does seem that there is sometimes a "logical error" (see Chapter 8) in that subjects are apt to give similar answers to related questions when they are contiguous (cf. Bishop, Oldendick, and Tuchfarber, 1982). Separating them by interposing neutral items may help a little, but it does not necessarily eliminate this effect as the answers *should* be relatively similar (Schuman, Kalton, and Ludwig, 1983). In general, specific questions seem to be less affected by what preceded them than are general questions (Bradburn, 1982). One point on which there is agreement is that when sensitive topics are to be discussed, it is usually better to ask these questions at the end of the interview. Questions about an adult's age, education, and income may seem like an invasion of privacy to some interviewees, and when asked at the beginning of an interview, they can interfere with the establishment of trust. Even when asked at the end of the interview, it is helpful to preface such questions by a reassuring statement. In one study the interviewer prefaced them by informing the subject that the information was needed to find out how accurately the interview sample represented U.S. Census estimates of the area population—which, of course, was true. He added, "Some of the questions may seem like an invasion of your privacy, so if you'd rather not answer any of the questions, just tell me it's none of my business" (C. Smith, 1980).

   d. Another consideration at this stage is to establish the best wording of items. It is important to know that the wording can be readily understood in roughly equivalent ways by all subjects. During the pilot stage (the next step) it can be discovered what jargon and expressions are inhibitors and facilitators of communication in the particular circumstances. Especially important is the phrasing of the opening question, because variations in wording can affect how the respondents will interpret later questions (Bradburn, 1982). The opening question should be clearly connected with the explanation of the interview, so that the subject knows immediately that the interviewer is pursuing the stated purpose ("First of all, were you aware of the Paul McCartney rumor even before you agreed to be interviewed?"). Incidentally, research evidence suggests that disclosing as little as possible about the interview in the introduction has no methodological benefits in terms of refusals, rapport, cooperation, or bias (Sobal, 1982). We want to be open and honest in our communications with the subjects, just as we want them to be forthcoming in their responses. Interestingly, however, disclosing the *length* of the interview does seem to have a cost in terms of refusals. In one study it was found that telling the potential respondents that the interview would last 20 minutes resulted in more refusals than telling them it would last "a few minutes" (Sobal, 1982).

Fourth, the final step before going into the field is to pilot the interview schedule and make modifications wherever necessary. At this stage, as much as later on, it is important that the interviewers listen *analytically* to the subjects' responses (Downs, Smeyak, and Martin, 1980). The skilled interviewer does not jump in and interrupt before an idea is sufficiently developed by the subject, but is patient, gets the main ideas, hears the facts, makes valid inferences, hears details, and demonstrates other good listening skills (cf. Weaver, 1972). Having pretested and polished the interview schedule, selected the potential interviewees, and trained the interviewers, the researcher can begin the actual interviews. One final point, however, has to do with whether the training should consist of teaching the interviewers to be neutral (*nondirective*) or teaching them to attempt to motivate the subjects. Motivational procedures, e.g., in the form of selective feedback by a skilled interviewer, can be an effective means of promoting good respondent behavior. Both positive and negative feedback, properly used, can facilitate good performance. Examples of proper positive feedback would be statements such as "Uh huh. I see. This is the kind of information we want." "Thanks. You've mentioned _____ things." "Thanks, we appreciate your frankness." "Uh-huh. We are interested in details like these." Examples of proper negative feedback would include "You answered that quickly." "Sometimes it's easy to forget all the things you felt you noticed here. Could you think about it again?" "That's only _____ things" (Cannell, Miller, and Oksenberg, 1981).

RESEARCH INTERVIEWS BY TELEPHONE

Beginning in the 1960s, various changes in society led many researchers to turn to telephone interviews and mail surveys as substitutes for face-to-face interviews. Among the changes contributing to this shift were (1) the increased costs of conducting face-to-face interviews (because interviewing is a labor-intensive activity), (2) a decrease in the pool of married women seeking part-time employment (a large source of interviewers), (3) rising urban crime rates and fewer people being at home during daylight hours, (4) the invention of random digit-dialing methods for random sampling of telephone households, and (5) the development of computer-assisted methods in which questions are flashed on a cathode-ray screen and the interviewer directly keys in the response for computer scoring (Rossi, Wright, and Anderson, 1983).

In fact, there are both advantages and disadvantages with telephone interviewing (see Downs, Smeyak, and Martin, 1980; Lavrakas, 1987; Miller and Cannell, 1982). Among the advantages are that (1) it allows for a quick turnaround (i.e., information can be gotten more promptly than by the use of face-to-face interviews or mail surveys), (2) refusal rates are usually lower in telephone interviewing (since it is not necessary to allow a stranger into one's home), (3) sample selection is easily facilitated, and (4) follow-up interviewing is generally more efficient for busy people. Among the disadvantages are that (1) interviewing is restricted to households that own a telephone, or those at least that answer their telephones (instead of having an answering machine constantly on duty), (2) visual aids cannot be used as supplements (unless they are mailed out in advance of the call), (3) fewer questions (and less probing questions) can be asked because it is harder to establish rapport and people are more impatient to conclude the telephone interview, and (4) the limited "channel capacity" of the telephone makes it impossible to use facial expressions and gestures as nonverbal cues in analyzing the affective meaning behind the interviewee's words.

Generally speaking, the same procedures are followed in developing an interview schedule and training the interviewers whether telephone or face-to-face interviewing is used. One difference, however, is that telephone interviewers have less time to establish rapport, because the subject can always hang up without listening to the introduction. Various strategies can be employed as a means of impressing upon the subjects the seriousness of the telephone interview and of motivating them to cooperate. One strategy would be to foster *commitment* on the part of the subject by emphasizing the seriousness of the research. The important goals of the research are articulated at various junctures in the interviewing. It is then emphasized that to achieve these goals it is necessary to get complete details, including some that may seem insignificant to the research participants: "In this interview we want to get as much information as we can; this includes things that may seem small and unimportant as well as important things" (Miller and Cannell, 1982, p. 254). Another procedure would be the use of *feedback* to respondents on how well they have carried out the response task, e.g., "As I mentioned, sometimes it's hard for people to remember everything; perhaps if you think about it a little more, you will remember something you missed" (Miller and Cannell, 1982, p. 256). Positive feedback is used as a means of reinforcing good responding: "Thanks . . . this is the sort of information we're looking for in this research . . . it's important to us to get this information . . . these details are helpful" (Miller and Cannell, 1982, p. 256).

PRACTICAL GUIDELINES FOR DEVELOPING RESEARCH QUESTIONNAIRES

Questionnaires are among the most widely used self-report methods of data collection and may be incorporated into an interview schedule (e.g., "I'm now going to show you a list of activities . . ."). As in the writing of an interview schedule the initial steps in the development of a questionnaire will usually be exploratory, including talks with key informants to give a sense of the situation (see Fear, 1978; Kahn and Cannell, 1965; Oppenheim, 1966). Pilot work is required in devising the final wording of questions, which can take several forms to help elicit specific responses. They can be yes-no, either-or, acceptable-unacceptable items. Fill-in-the-blank is another form, useful when more specific responses are sought.

Of course, these structured forms are effective only if answers to the material to be covered can be simplified to this extent.

Piloting will enable us to determine whether the items are worded properly, e.g., whether terms like "approve" and "like" (or "disapprove" and "dislike") are being used as synonyms or whether there are differences in implication. Suppose we wanted to examine people's perceptions of the quality of a mayor's performance, but we phrased the item as follows: "How do you feel about the Mayor? _____ I like him _____ I dislike him." The item is quite useless because it does not distinguish between liking and approving. It is possible, for example, for people to like someone (or something) without approving of him or her (or it), and vice versa (Bradburn, 1982). How might we begin to improve on this item, in order to elicit the kind of information we really want?

We must also be sure that the way in which the items are worded and presented does not lead the respondent into giving an unrealistically narrow answer. A poor question will produce a very narrow range of responses or will be misunderstood by the respondents. Take the following item: "Do you approve of the way the Mayor is handling his duties? _____ Yes _____ No." It is possible that one might approve of the way the mayor handled the "school crisis" but not the "snow removal crisis," or disapprove of the way the mayor handled the "threat by sanitation workers to strike" but not the "threatened tax increase." We see that a number of different items are needed to get at the various issues on which we want an opinion about the mayor's effectiveness, and the issues need to be spelled out in order to avoid any misunderstanding on the part of the respondents. For example, suppose the "school crisis" and the "santitation workers' threat" both involved union confrontations, but the first situation was resolved without a strike and the second involved a protracted strike. We need a separate question, or set of questions, regarding each situation and whether the respondent approved or disapproved of the mayor's handling of it.

We must also avoid a leading question that produces a biased answer: "Do you agree the Mayor has an annoying, confrontational style? _____ Yes _____ No." The way the question is phrased invites the respondents to be overly negative or critical. How should it be phrased to avoid producing a biased set of answers? In coming up with an alternative we also want to be sure that the new question is not worded in such a way as to produce another meaningless answer: "Do you agree with the Mayor's philosophy of city government? _____ Yes _____ No." If someone answered "yes" (or answered "no"), what would that really tell us? We need to do some probing in order to get the kind of information we would consider to be meaningful. Problems such as these can be identified by piloting the questionnaire, and then can usually be corrected by rewording the items or by having a set of probing items instead of a single item.

The methodological question of whether to use open-ended or more structured items, or a combination of both, can also be explored in pilot work. Survey researchers Jean M. Converse and Stanley Presser (1986, p. 52) suggest the following exploratory questions to help identify trouble areas when pretesting the items: "What did the whole question mean to you?" "What was it you had in mind when you said _____ ?" "Consider the same question this way, and tell what you think of it: _____ ." "You said _____ , but would you feel differently if I said _____ ?" Replies to exploratory questions will help us to rewrite items.

As noted, the chief advantage of open-ended items is the flexibility they give to the respondent to let his or her thoughts roam freely and spontaneously. However, while free-response questionnaires are relatively easy to construct, many subjects will find them difficult or cumbersome to respond to in writing because they are often perceived as too wide-ranging and time-consuming (Oppenheim, 1966). One strategy might be to use structured questionnaires but add one or two open-ended questions such that, for example, each 10 percent of the sample gets a different one or two open-ended questions. Thus, overall, we get open-ended data from all, but the number of respondents per question is smaller than for the closed questions. Structured questionnaires require less time to answer, and the answers are easier for the researchers to code. On the other hand, they leave no room for spontaneity and expressiveness. The respondents may feel that the closed format forces them to choose between given alternatives none of which are exactly the best ones. As a resolution of this dilemma, Converse and Presser (1986) suggest that open-ended questions be used to measure the salience of certain behavior and to capture modes of expression.

Another solution to this problem is to use a combination of both types of formats and to order certain questions in a *funnel sequence.* This means the questions begin at the most general level and narrow down to the most specific. Some researchers prefer to use open-ended items at the start of a research project and structured items at the end, when the research hypotheses have become more focused. It is always a good idea to ask multiple questions on a topic, because the idea is to triangulate on the required information. Each item may be beset by a particular problem, but the results should zero in on a particular conclusion. Whatever form and structure the instrument takes, it should be tested before it is actually used in the research study.

It is also important that the information elicited be a reflection of what the subject really feels or believes. As a rule, people have not thought very much about most issues that do not affect them directly, and their replies may reflect only a superficial feeling or understanding. Survey researchers will often ask the respondent how he or she feels about such and such (e.g., "How deeply do you feel about it?") and in this way attempt to determine whether the respondent truly believes what he or she has reported (Labaw, 1980). There is another side to this issue, which is related to the question of rating errors discussed in the previous chapter. It concerns what are called *response sets,* i.e., that type of response bias in which a person's answers to questions or responses to a set of items are determined by a consistent mental set (Cronbach, 1946, 1950).

SOCIAL DESIRABILITY AND ITS CONTROL

In Chapter 1 we discussed the relational research of Crowne and Marlowe (1964) on the approval motive. Other researchers have also studied the influence of a social desirability set on the responses to self-report questionnaires. When the researcher finds a correlation between the scores on a social desirability scale and the responses on another self-report questionnaire, it is usually interpreted to mean that there was a tendency on the part of the subjects to present themselves in a more favorable light on the latter instrument. In one early study it was found that psychiatric patients who scored high on a measure of need for social desirability produced sentence completions that were also high in socially desirable content (Rozynko, 1959). In fact, it has long been observed that scores on self-report personality tests are influenced by factors other than the manifest content of the items. Simply because a person responds "no" to the statement "Once in a while I think of things too bad to talk about" does not mean that the person's thoughts are indeed pure.

Various strategies are employed in interviews and questionnaires to avoid producing a social desirability set. The *randomized response technique* is one procedure that has been used (Warner, 1965). In this approach, an attempt is made to eliminate evasive answers by guaranteeing the confidentiality of the subject's responses. The way this is achieved is to have the subject use a randomizing instrument (such as flipping a coin) to select how to respond concerning a sensitive question. Suppose the question asks, "Have you ever used cocaine?" The subject is instructed to flip the coin out of the researcher's sight and to respond "yes" if it lands heads and to respond truthfully (i.e., answer the question "yes" or "no") if it lands tails. There is no possible way for the researcher to know how each particular respondent answered. However, by knowing that 50 percent of the subjects are expected to get heads to respond "yes," it is then possible to estimate the proportion that actually said they sampled cocaine. There is some evidence that the randomized response technique promotes the reporting of more accurate confidential information (e.g., Boruch and Cecil, 1979; Fidler and Kleinknecht, 1977). However, even in studies not using this procedure, there is evidence that confidentiality (i.e., guaranteeing the privacy of information) can frequently reduce social desirability responding (cf. Esposito, Agard, and Rosnow, 1984).

On the other hand, research on the impact of confidentiality guarantees in interviewing is equivocal in its conclusions. A study by sociologist James H. Frey (1986) used a confidentiality reminder in a telephone survey ("Now, I need to know some information about you for statistical purposes only. *Remember, your responses are confidential.*"). Half the respondents were given both sentences above, and the others were given the first sentence but not the confidentiality reminder. The confidentiality guarantee stimulated *higher* item nonresponse rates than were found in the control group. It is possible the effect of the guarantee was to raise suspicions in the subjects' minds, and thus to undermine any rapport established between the interviewer and the subject. That is, like the pretest in a before-after attitude study (discussed in Chapter 4), the reminder may have had a "sensitizing" effect that alerted the subjects to be careful of their answers to subsequent questions.

In the area of personality research, experimenters have attempted to develop keys for scoring standardized questionnaires and "lie scales," which are used to detect faking by the respondent (Ruch, 1942). One conventional way to develop a "fake key" is to compare the responses of subjects who are instructed to fake with those of subjects who are instructed to respond truthfully. The researcher analyzes the differences in responding and then develops a scoring key using this information as a guideline (Gordon and Gross, 1978; Lautenschlager, 1986).

The Minnesota Multiphasic Personality Inventory (MMPI) is illustrative of how "fakeability" is analyzed in psychological testing. The MMPI contains a "lie" scale (the L Scale) consisting of 15 items to indicate whether the respondent is projecting a falsely perfectionist view of himself or herself. For instance, answering "false" to the statement "I do not like everyone I know" would suggest an evasive response. The subject's replies to the 15 items are interpreted as an indicator of either conscious deception, naive responding, or a highly introspective personality, depending on the particular score (Groth-Marnat, 1984).

YEA-SAYING AND ITS CONTROL

A procedure used for suppressing a rarer response tendency is to vary the direction of the response alternatives when using structured items. This procedure is thought to suppress the response set called *yea-saying,* which refers to the fact that some people like to answer "yes" to almost every statement or question (even to those items with which they disagree!). A famous example came to light in the 1950s as regards the F Scale (for fascism scale), which was developed to study the nature of the authoritarian personality. This research was begun during the 1920s, when a group of investigators at the University of Frankfurt conducted interviews with hundreds of German citizens. The results convinced the investigators that anti-Semitic prejudices were rife in Germany and that the explosion of fascism was imminent. When Hitler came to power, the researchers left Germany and immigrated to the United States. The investigation continued with the emphasis now directed to the dissection of the fascist mentality. Working at the University of California at Berkeley, the researchers developed this personality questionnaire (the F Scale), which included 38 statements such as the following:

1. One should avoid doing things in public that appear wrong to others, even though one knows that these things are really all right.
2. No insult to our honor should ever go unpunished.
3. It is essential for learning or effective work that our teachers or bosses outline in detail what is to be done and exactly how to go about it.

Such statements were thought to go together to form a syndrome of behavior that renders a person receptive to antidemocratic propaganda (Adorno, Frenkel-Brunswik, Levinson, and Sanford, 1950). This authoritarian personality was also seen as having a strong need to align himself or herself with authority figures and protective in-groups, a strong sense of nationalism, rigid moralism, definiteness, and a strong tendency to perceive things in absolutes (i.e., as all good or all bad). Other psychological tests, including the Rorschach, were brought in to flesh out the authoritarian personality.

Although this is regarded as one of the most influential studies done in psychology, it was later recognized that there was a potential problem with the research, concerning the wording of the items making up the F Scale. They had been written in such a way that only by disagreeing with a statement could you obtain a completely nonauthoritarian score. But some amiable, obliging souls, who were not the least bit authoritarian, liked to say "yes" to every statement. In other words, the F Scale was measuring two distinct but not readily distinguishable traits: authoritarianism and the agreeing response set (Couch and Keniston, 1960). To remedy this problem, what was necessary was simply to vary the direction of the statements. Both positive and negative statements would have to be interspersed, preferably in random sequence. To obtain a completely nonauthoritarian score would require that the subject agree with some statements and disagree with others.

As noted in earlier discussions, faking, social desirability bias, and other artifacts are not limited to any particular method of investigation or measurement. Analysis of data from a pre-*glasnost* mail survey in the Soviet Union found evidence to suggest that the responses were falsified to serve the interests of the Soviet officials (Kaplowitz and Shlapentokh, 1982). In interview research in the United States, studies have shown that responding to certain questions is likely to be in a socially desirable direction when the subject and the interviewer are of the same race and social class (Dohrenwend, 1969; Dohrenwend, Colombotos, and Dohrenwend, 1968). The interaction then seems to take on the character of a polite social exchange, in which the subject says only what is socially desirable rather than revealing what is accurate but not desirable. Survey researchers attempt to avoid this problem by using interviewers who have a friendly but professional demeanor rather than ones who are overly solicitous (Weiss, 1970).

BACK-TRANSLATIONS

We turn next to different models for the use of standardized questionnaires. Before going on, however, it should be noted that questionnaires using propositional items (e.g., Likert and Thurstone scales) can run into problems when they are used in different cultures. A main difficulty is that the language used in scale development may mean something different in another culture. For example, Robert LeVine and Donald Campbell faced such a problem when they were conducting fieldwork among the Gusii of western Kenya to try out a preliminary version of a field manual for the cross-cultural study of ethnocentrism (LeVine and Campbell, 1972). LeVine (1981) mentions that many Gusii terms for aggression and hostility had no exact equivalents in English. Furthermore, English terms carry their own connotations and other contextual presumptions, which were not present in Gusii equivalents. LeVine and Campbell's strategy for dealing with this problem involved *back-translation*.

In back-translation the researcher looks beyond the constraints of the source language in order to find a middle ground in which the distinctive meanings and blind spots of the source language and the target language are absent.

To achieve this the researcher has one bilingual person translate the text from source to target language and afterward another bilingual person independently translates it back into the source language. In this way the researcher can compare the original with the twice-translated version (i.e., the back-translation) to see if anything important has been lost in the translation. It may require a number of back-translations to find a middle ground without significant discrepancies.

The methods we discuss in the following sections are in the traditional mode of employing verbal items. We turn first to a time-honored rating method still in widespread use, the *semantic differential* model for the use of multidimensional attitude ratings.

SEMANTIC DIFFERENTIALS FOR THE MEASUREMENT OF MEANING

Developed at the University of Illinois by Charles E. Osgood, George J. Suci, and Percy H. Tannenbaum (1957), this approach proceeds on the idea that the "meaning" of stimuli is best represented by a spatial configuration consisting of more than one dimension. In their research, they repeatedly found that the dimensions of *evaluation, potency,* and *activity* were dominant, appearing in most of the analyses made in different cultures and societies. In statistical terms the evaluative dimension accounts for approximately half of the extractable variance, whereas the potency and activity dimensions (together referred to as *dynamism*) each account for approximately half as much variance as the evaluation dimension. Other dimensions, which account for increasingly less variance, are stability, tautness, novelty, and receptivity. The names were chosen by Osgood and his coworkers, and other researchers might choose different names for the same dimensions. The point, though, is that we presumably use the dimensions of evaluation, potency, and activity—and the other dimensions to a lesser extent—in making attitudinal judgments about the meaning of everyday stimuli (cf. Brinton, 1961; Oskamp, 1977; Triandis, 1964).

In appearance, a semantic differential rating scale would resemble the segmented graphic scale illustrated in the previous chapter. It usually consists of a set of seven-point scales that are anchored at each end by pairs of adjectives, such as:

> bad ____ : ____ : ____ : ____ : ____ : ____ : ____ good
> tense ____ : ____ : ____ : ____ : ____ : ____ : ____ relaxed
> stingy ____ : ____ : ____ : ____ : ____ : ____ : ____ generous

The particular bipolar pairs are chosen on the basis of the underlying dimensions of meaning that are of theoretical interest to the researcher. If the researcher were interested in subjects' evaluative judgments of stimuli, any of the following bipolar pairs could be chosen: bad-good, unpleasant-pleasant, negative-positive, ugly-beautiful, cruel-kind, unfair-fair, and worthless-valuable. If it were the potency dimension the researcher were interested in, then any of the following pairs could suffice: weak-strong, light-heavy, small-large, soft-hard, and thin-heavy. For the activity dimension, any of the following would do: slow-fast, passive-active, and dull-sharp. For the lesser dimensions, still other adjective pairs would be considered: stability dimension (changeable-stable, intuitive-rational, and rash-cautious), tautness dimension (rounded-angular, curved-straight, and blunt-sharp), novelty dimension (old-new, usual-unusual, and mature-youthful), and receptivity dimension (tasteless-savory, boring-interesting, and insensitive-sensitive).

In a given study the scales will not always load on the same dimensions, and many researchers would (and should) check to see that the scales really do cluster in the expected way in their particular study. In practice, however, it seems that most researchers stick with evaluation, potency, and activity. The instructions to the subject are to put a check mark in the appropriate position. The researcher then assigns numbers to the ratings, e.g., +3 extremely good, +2 quite good, +1 slightly good, 0 equally good and bad or neither, −1 slightly bad, −2 quite bad, and −3 extremely bad.

This basic procedure has been put to a wide range of uses (cf. Snider and Osgood, 1969). For instance, one of Richard M. Nixon's first moves in assembling a team for his 1968 presidential campaign was the appointment of advertising researchers who traveled all through the United States asking people to evaluate the presidential candidates on a semantic differential scale. Joe McGinniss (1969) tells in his book *The Selling of the President* how the researchers plotted the "ideal presidential curve" (i.e., the line connecting the points that represented the average rating in each category as applied to the ideal) and then compared this profile with the plotted curves for Nixon, Hubert Humphrey, and George Wallace. The gaps between the Nixon profile and the "ideal line" represented the personality traits that Nixon should try to improve, the advertising researchers believed. It was especially important, they insisted, that he close the "personality gap" between himself and Humphrey.

The semantic differential can be used, for instance, to develop group profiles to show how stereotypes (i.e., the "pictures" in our heads) can be visualized graphically. Figure 9-2 shows two such profiles that were gotten by connecting the points that represented the average ratings of 132 Canadian boys and girls during the early 1960s (Snider, 1962). It is not surprising that the children rated their own Canadian culture more favorably than they did the Russian culture, because there is a tendency to report a more favorable stereotype of one's own nation (e.g., Crabb and Rosnow, 1988).

With a semantic differential in a questionnaire or interview, even three-dimensional graphical representations of the results are possible. Figure 9-3 shows a three-dimensional representation of eight role concepts (self, father, mother, adult, college student, juvenile delinquent, adolescent, and child) that were rated by male and female college students. The instructions to the subjects were first to evaluate the concepts "as you *actually* think they are, in terms of the meanings they have for you" (the two diagrams at the top of Figure 9-3), and then to rate each concept "on the basis of how it should *ideally* be, the way it is supposed to be as opposed to how it actually is" (the two diagrams at the

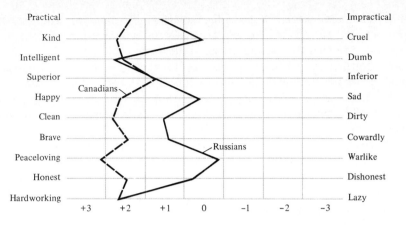

FIGURE 9-2
Profiles for Canadians (*dashed line*) and Russians (*solid line*) in a sample of 132 Canadian ninth graders. (J. G. Snider, "Profiles of Some Stereotypes Held by Ninth-Grade Pupils," *Alberta Journal of Educational Research*, 1962, *8*, 147–156. Adapted by permission of the author and the journal editor.)

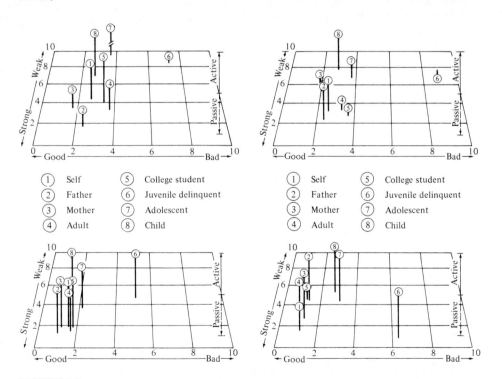

FIGURE 9-3
Actual (*top*) and ideal (*bottom*) locations of eight role concepts on three semantic dimensions for males (*left*) and females (*right*). The three dimensions are the evaluative (bad-good), the potency (weak-strong), and the activity (passive-active). (C. J. Friedman, and J.W. Gladden, "Objective Measurement of Social Role Concept via the Semantic Differential," *Psychological Reports*, 1964, *14*, 239–247. Reprinted by permission of the authors and the journal editor.)

bottom). The subjects were told that there were no right or wrong answers, since this was not a test (Friedman and Gladden, 1964). The various diagrams reveal differences in the three-dimensional spatial relationships, but also some similarities. For instance, we see (1) the general clustering on the left side, with the lone role number 6 ("juvenile delinquent") on the right, (2) the roles "self" and "college student" perceived as somewhat weaker in actuality by men than by women, (3) the role of "father" perceived to be stronger, ideally, by men than by women. The researchers theorized that these differences were due to the influence of learned expectancies regarding role attitudes, an interesting though speculative hypothesis that merits further study.

Q-SORT MODEL FOR SELF-REPORTS

Another time-honored self-report method is the Q-sort. Developed by University of Missouri communication researcher William Stephenson (1953) to study a single individual or a few persons at a time, it takes its name from so-called Q-methodology in factor analysis (we return to factor analysis in Chapter 24). The Q-sort has been shown to be particularly useful in personality assessment research, e.g., to arrive at a comprehensive picture of a person's attitudes, strengths, and weaknesses.

The Q-sort calls for the preparation of a set of stimuli (phrases, pictures, or statements) covering some aspect of behavior or personality. The stimuli will typically differ from one study to the next, because the purpose of the studies is different and stimuli would be chosen depending on the aspect of behavior of interest to the researcher. Each stimulus appears on a separate card, and the subject's job is to sort through the cards and place them into one of a number of different piles to resemble a bell-shaped curve. The number of piles, and the cards allowed in each pile, is determined by a formula for the normal distribution (Stephenson, 1953). For instance, if there were 80 cards, they would be sorted in 11 piles as follows:

Pile number	11	10	9	8	7	6	5	4	3	2	1
Number of cards	2	4	6	9	12	14	12	9	6	4	2

If there were 98 cards, they would be sorted into 13 piles as follows:

Pile numbers	13	12	11	10	9	8	7	6	5	4	3	2	1
Number of cards	2	4	6	8	10	12	14	12	10	8	6	4	2

In a representative study, Stephenson (1980) had children sort through 48 pictures of different faces. They were told to decide which *two* photos they liked *most* and to put them in the extreme favorable pile, and then to decide which *two* they liked *least* and to put them in the extreme unfavorable pile. They then had to decide which *four* photos they liked *next most* and put them in the corresponding pile, and which *four* they liked *next least,* and so forth. In this case there were 9 piles, which were scored from −4 to +4:

Pile number	9	8	7	6	5	4	3	2	1
Number of photos	2	4	5	8	10	8	5	4	2
Score	−4	−3	−2	−1	0	+1	+2	+3	+4

There are several different statistical analyses possible. For instance, the average position of a particular subset of pictures (e.g., pictures of ethnic females) could be calculated and compared with the average positions of other subsets (e.g., pictures of nonethnic females). To evaluate interjudge reliability we could compute the correlations showing how similar one rater is to another in his or her evaluations (discussed in Chapter 3). When the Q-sort is used in assessing personality, statements are prepared covering dozens of specific aspects of behavior. The statements are then judged as fitting or not fitting the individual. A correlation is computed on the scores of each statement to see how closely the two sorters' descriptions correspond (Cronbach, 1960).

LIKERT MODEL OF ITEM ANALYSIS

The term "Likert scaling" (also called the *method of summated ratings*) is among the most misused terms in behavioral science. Many researchers mistakenly call any attitude scale a Likert scale if it instructs the subject to indicate the degree of agreement or disagreement on a five-step numerical scale. To be a true Likert scale, the method known as *item analysis* has to have been used in constructing the questionnaire. Developed by Rensis Likert (1932), this method results in a self-rating attitude questionnaire which, in appearance, is a type of numerical rating scale in that numbers are associated with different response alternatives (e.g., strongly agree, agree, undecided, disagree, strongly disagree) to statements that are easily classifiable as favorable or unfavorable.

The first step in constructing a Likert questionnaire to measure people's attitudes is to gather a large number of statements on the topic of interest. These are given to a sample of subjects from the target population, who indicate their evaluations usually by means of a five-point numerical rating scale. The technique of item analysis is then used to sort through the data in order to select the best statements for the final scale. It consists of calculating the extent to which the responses to individual statements are correlated with the total score (the sum of all the items). Statements that correlate well with the total score are then chosen for the final scale. The rationale is that statements that have low correlations with the total score will not be good at discriminating between those respondents with positive attitudes and those with negative attitudes.

An attitude questionnaire developed along such lines is shown in Figure 9-4 (Mahler, 1953). This particular 20-item scale has been shown to have high internal-consistency reliability. As regards validity, the scale has been found to predict known groups (106 Stanford University students with positive and nega-

Please indicate your reaction to the following statements, using these alternatives:

Strongly Agree = SA   Disagree = D

Agree = A   Strongly Disagree = SD

Undecided = U

*1 The quality of medical care under the system of private practice is superior to that under a system of compulsory health insurance.

SA A U D SD

2 A compulsory health program will produce a healthier and more productive population.

*3 Under a compulsory health program there would be less incentive for young people to become doctors.

4 A compulsory health program is necessary because it brings the greatest good to the greatest number of people.

*5 Treatment under a compulsory health program would be mechanical and superficial.

6 A compulsory health program would be a realization of one of the true aims of a democracy.

*7 Compulsory medical care would upset the traditional relationship between the family doctor and the patient.

*8 I feel that I would get better care from a doctor whom I am paying than from a doctor who is being paid by the government.

9 Despite many practical objections, I feel that compulsory health insurance is a real need of the American people.

10 A compulsory health program could be administered quite efficiently if the doctors would cooperate.

11 There is no reason why the traditional relationship between doctors and patient cannot be continued under a compulsory health program.

*12 If a compulsory health program were enacted, politicians would have control over doctors.

*13 The present system of private medical practice is the one best adapted to the liberal philosophy of democracy.

14 There is no reason why doctors should not be able to work just as well under a compulsory health program as they do now.

15 More and better care will be obtained under a compulsory health program.

*16 The atmosphere of a compulsory health program would destroy the initiative and the ambition of young doctors.

*17 Politicians are trying to force a compulsory health program upon the people without giving them the true facts.

*18 Administrative costs under a compulsory health program would be exorbitant.

*19 Red tape and bureaucratic problems would make a compulsory health program grossly inefficient.

*20 Any system of compulsory health insurance would invade the privacy of the individual.

FIGURE 9-4

Example of a Likert questionnaire that was developed to measure attitudes toward socialized medicine. The response alternatives (SA, A, U, D, SD) would be repeated for each item. The asterisks (*) indicate negative items whose weights must be reversed for purposes of scoring. The same response alternatives are used with all items. (I. Mahler, "Attitudes toward Socialized Medicine," *Journal of Social Psychology,* 1953, *38,* 273–282. Reprinted by permission of the author and The Journal Press.)

tive attitudes about socialized medicine, as established by interviews). In scoring the answers the pro-socialized medicine statements would be weighted from 4 ("strongly agree") to 0 ("strongly disagree"). For the anti-socialized medicine statements (marked by an asterisk) the weighting is reversed. A person's score is the sum of the weighted responses, with a high score indicating an accepting attitude regarding socialized medicine.

THURSTONE EQUAL-APPEARING INTERVAL SCALES

Another traditional approach for developing a self-report attitude questionnaire is based on the *method of equal-appearing intervals,* proposed by L. L. Thurstone (1929), a pioneer in the early development of attitude research. The name of the procedure derives from the assumption that judges, who are asked to sort statements in different piles, are presumed to be able to keep the piles psychologically equidistant. Thurstone also worked on the development of other scaling procedures, but this particular one is most closely associated with him (also frequently called the "Thurstone scale").

The procedure begins with a large number of statements, but this time each statement is typed on a separate slip of paper or index card. Judges (not the subjects to be tested later) then sort the statements into 11 piles numbered from 1 ("most unfavorable statements") to 11 ("most favorable statements"). In this respect the equal-appearing interval method resembles the Q-sort method. Unlike the Q-sort, the judges in Thurstone's approach are allowed to place as many statements as they wish in any pile. A scale value is calculated for each statement, which is simply the average (traditionally the median in this case) of the responses of all judges to that particular item. In selecting statements for the final Thurstone scale, we would choose those (1) that are most consistently rated by the judges and (2) that are spread relatively evenly along the entire attitude range. The former criterion (consistency) refers to any particular item, and the latter criterion (range) refers to the whole set of items.

A questionnaire based on this procedure is shown in Figure 9-5. It is a 22-item self-report questionnaire with reportedly high test-retest reliability. Although this early scale of attitudes toward divorce contains items relevant to the issue today, with the passage of time the original scale positions might be expected to change (Thurstone, 1929–1934). Thus the scale values noted in this figure were more recently obtained from a sample of 26 graduate students in social psychology courses at the University of Florida (Shaw and Wright, 1967). Traditionally, the person's total score would be the median of the scale values of items checked to indicate agreement, with a high score indicating a favorable attitude toward divorce.

UNIDIMENSIONAL AND MULTIDIMENSIONAL ATTITUDE SCALES

There are various other strategies for the development of attitude scales, including both multidimensional and unidimensional scaling procedures. Unidimensional models for the use of attitude scales have attracted considerable attention of late, as a result of the pioneering work of Georg Rasch, a Danish researcher (Rasch, 1960, 1966), and have been the focus of much work in psychology, sociology, and education (e.g., Andrich, 1988; De Jong-Gierveld and Kamphuis, 1985; Wood, 1978; Wright and Master, 1982). However, the researcher who uses an attitude scale to predict behavior should be mindful of the fact that there is not

The following statements express opinions about divorce. Please indicate your agreement or disagreement with each of the statements by marking them as follows:

($\checkmark$) Mark with a check if you agree with the statement.

($\times$) Mark with a cross if you disagree with the statement.

Scale
Value

Scale Value	No.	Statement
3.7	1	Divorce is justifiable only after all efforts to mend the union have failed.
6.6	2	Present divorce conditions are not as discreditable as they appear.
8.5	3	If marriage is to be based on mutual affection, divorce must be easy to obtain.
1.6	4	Divorce lowers the standards of morality.
.5	5	Divorce is disgraceful.
8.4	6	Divorce is desirable for adjusting errors in marriage.
4.8	7	Divorce is a necessary evil.
9.8	8	Divorce should be granted for the asking.
6.2	9	A divorce is justifiable or not, depending on the wants of the persons involved.
10.1	10	A person should have the right to marry and divorce as often as he or she chooses.
.5	11	Divorce is never justifiable.
8.8	12	Easy divorce leads to a more intelligent understanding of marriage.
3.3	13	Divorce should be discouraged in order to stabilize society.
5.8	14	The evils of divorce should not prevent us from seeing its benefits.
9.4	15	The marriage contract should be as easily broken as made.
.8	16	The best solution of the divorce problem is never to grant divorce.
1.2	17	Lenient divorce is equivalent to polygamy.
7.1	18	Divorce should be permitted so long as the rights of all parties are insured.
4.2	19	Divorce should be discouraged but not forbidden.
.8	20	Divorce is legalized adultery.
3.8	21	Long and careful investigation should precede the granting of every divorce.
8.1	22	Permanence in marriage is unnecessary for social stability.

FIGURE 9-5

Example of a questionnaire based on Thurstone's method of equal-appearing interval scaling. This particular questionnaire was developed to measure attitudes toward divorce. In actual practice, the scale values noted would not be shown on the questionnaire administered to the subjects. (After Shaw and Wright, 1967; L. L. Thurstone, *The Measurement of Social Attitudes,* University of Chicago Press, Chicago, Ill., (c) 1931. Reprinted by permission of the University of Chicago Press.)

always a reliable positive correlation between people's social attitudes and their subsequent behavior in a given situation. In the previous chapter we discussed Wrightsman's (1969) law-and-order study, in which he observed that the law-and-order automobile drivers were less likely to obey the new tax sticker law. This does not mean, however, that we should expect a negative correlation between people's attitudes and their public behavior. Research results indicate that behavior can best be predicted from recently expressed intentions (Fishbein and Azjen, 1975).

Many attitude researchers feel that it is necessary to employ a multidimensional strategy as opposed to the unidimensional strategies devised by Likert and Thurstone. A public identity is not only determined by what a person would like to do, but also by what the person thinks is required and by the expected consequences of the behavior (Triandis, 1971). These researchers would argue that attitudes are inherently multidimensional (e.g., Kothandapani, 1971). Thus, if we want to know what a person thinks, we had best measure the belief (or *cognitive*) component of the person's attitude. If we want to know how a person feels about something, then it would be more logical to measure not the belief component but the emotional (or *affective*) component of the person's attitude. And if we want to know how the person will behave, we should measure not just the belief or emotional components, but also the action (or *conative*) component of the person's attitude. The strategy chosen will depend largely on the way in which the researcher conceptualizes the research objective.

MEMORY AND THE USE OF SELF-RECORDED DIARIES

Whatever procedures are used, answering autobiographical questions can run into problems when the subjects are asked questions that rely on aspects of memory, e.g., how often they have done something or how much of something they have bought or consumed. Some examples are "How many weeks have you been looking for work?" and "How much did you pay for car repair expenses over the previous year?" Problems surface because there are many psychological processes that affect accuracy of appropriate recall (e.g., Reed, 1988; Zechmeister and Nyberg, 1982). Several studies have reported inaccuracies in the recall of past actions and patterns of interaction with others (e.g., Bernard and Killworth, 1970, 1980; Webber, 1970).

Not only are there limits of recall, but retrieval of information from memory is often less accurate simply because the question is phrased differently from the way the answer is stored in our minds (Norman, 1973). And in answering questions in interviews and survey questionnaires, people have a tendency to make inferences based on the wording of the items, the sheer number of facts, and the bits of information they do recall. As a result, the answers they give may be biased by the assumptions they apply to the situation and by the limits imposed on human memory (Bradburn, Rips, and Shevell, 1987; Cicourel, 1982).

One alternative that has been proposed is to have the subjects keep a diary in which they record events at the time they occur, called a *self-recorded diary*. Such diaries have been used, for example, in organizational settings as well as in participant-observer studies to supplement the researchers' own records (e.g., Conrath, 1973; Wickesberg, 1968). An assumption that is made is that employing the self-recorded diary should give more reliable data than just using questionnaires or interviews to elicit answers to autobiographical questions.

As a practical illustration of the memory problem, an interview study conducted by Perry London in the 1960s was designed to find out whether there were character traits associated with the extreme heroic acts of Christians who risked their lives to save Jews in Nazi-occupied Europe during World War II (London, 1970). The strategy was to seek out both the rescuers and those who had been rescued, and to do tape-recorded interviews with each person. The interview schedules were constructed using general questions that allowed them to be used across several different samples in the United States and Israel. The answers were then coded, and the content was analyzed to tap a number of autobiographical and psychological variables. In each case the interviews began with the respondents' describing the relevant incidents in their own words, and the interviewer then inquired about the background events that had led up to those incidents. The interviewer, working with a checklist of content areas and questions, would parenthetically ask about personal details, attitudes, and seemingly incidental variables needed to fill in the most sensitive information about character traits.

This was a model interview study in all conventional respects. The design dealt with the impact of memory and inference on recall by using the replies of many respondents residing quite apart from one another. From the respondent's point of view, much of the personal information was communicated spontaneously, and the interview process was formal but friendly in order to stimulate the participant's accurate responding. From the interviewer's point of view, he was able to probe sensitive areas obliquely and tactfully, without being secretive or deceptive and without sacrificing any questions (the sequence was left to the interviewer). As a result, three character traits of heroic helpers were identified: (1) a spirit of adventurousness, (2) a strong sense of identification with a parental model of moral conduct, and (3) a feeling of being a socially marginal individual.

Still, the data are to some degree limited because they rely on the subjects' accurately recalling events from the distant past, which when they occurred must have been surrounded by frightening, uncontrollable anxieties and frustrations. Not surprisingly, few victims of the Holocaust kept (or indeed were able to keep) detailed diaries. Where such information exists (e.g., the diaries of Anne Frank), it is an invaluable supplement to the kind of data collected by London and others based on eliciting personal facts from autobiographical memory.

Is the self-recorded diary itself a reliable record? In a study by David W. Conrath, Christopher A. Higgins, and Ronald J. McClean (1983), data were collected from managers and staff personnel in three diverse organizations (a manufacturer of plastic products, an insurance brokerage company, and a large public utility). Each participant was instructed to keep a diary of 100 consecutive interactions, commencing on a specific date and at a specific time. The instructions were to indicate the other party, the initiator of the activity, the mode of interaction, the elapsed time, and the process involved. The diary was constructed in such a way that the subject could quickly record all this information by no more than 4 to 8 check marks next to particular items. At a later time, each participant was requested to answer a questionnaire in which similar estimates had to be made. For all the participants the data from the self-recorded diary and the standard questionnaire were compared afterward. If a person noted talking to particular others, the responses of those others were checked by the researchers to see whether they reported that activity. In this way a measure of reliability was obtained for the self-recorded diary and the questionnaire data separately, i.e., concerning the reporting of specific events at the time of the events as opposed to a later time. The results were that the questionnaire data (the recalls from autobiographical memory) were less reliable than the self-recorded diary data.

In using the self-recorded diary, it is recommended that only a few minutes (e.g., 5 to 10 minutes) per day be required of the participants (Conrath, 1973). In order to accomplish this the researcher will need to develop checklists or tally sheets that can be answered quickly and accurately by the subjects. The particular times at which the data are to be recorded in the diary also need to be specified precisely. Given adequate preparation, the self-recorded diary can play a useful role as a supplement in almost any research study in which self-report information about events is of interest.

PART
IV

BASIC
ISSUES
IN THE
IMPLEMENTATION
OF RESEARCH

CONSIDERATIONS IN THE SELECTION OF SUBJECTS AND STIMULI

SOME ISSUES OF SAMPLING

Before we implement our research investigation, there are a few more issues to be considered, which we turn to in this and the next couple of chapters. In this chapter we shall examine a number of considerations to be weighed in the selection of the research participants in survey research and experimental research, and in the selection of the stimuli in experimental research when the stimulus is a person. The questions addressed in, as much as the practical limitations of, survey research and experimental research typically require us to use quite different subject selection procedures, and it is important not to play into the intuitive prejudices of people who are naive about experimental research and would dismiss almost any study that did not use random sampling to select the research participants. Nevertheless, experimental researchers have in the past, sometimes almost exclusively, depended on college students as research participants (Higbee and Wells, 1972; Jung, 1969; Schultz, 1969; Smart, 1966), prompting one critic to remark, "The existing science of human behavior is largely the science of the behavior of sophomores" (McNemar, 1946, p. 333).

While these research participants have taught us a tremendous amount about ourselves (and not just about themselves), we do not want to underestimate the limitations of studying individuals who, by virtue of their educational status, may be more sensitive and accommodating to demand characteristics (see Chapter 6) than other people may be. In recent years it has also been observed that these "psychology sophomores," if they are volunteers for psychological research

205

participation, are frequently not representative of even most college sophomores. This, of course, can be a maddening criticism for psychological researchers who intuitively feel the volunteer-subject problem is not a particularly severe one, or who believe it is much less severe because their research participants were recruited from introductory psychology classes and the vast majority of students from those classes did participate. It is important not to exaggerate the problem of using volunteer subjects, or misleadingly characterize their use in behavioral science, but it is also important not to be lulled into the trap of equating ignorance of this problem with the lack of any problem. We discuss a number of aspects of the volunteer-subject question, but without implying that research results are *invariably* going to be different for volunteer than for nonvolunteer subjects. We shall also see that this problem is not unique to psychological experimentation, but represents one side of the *sample selection bias* issue in experimental and survey research.

To set the stage for that discussion, we shall begin by examining the ways in which survey researchers deal with the so-called paradox of sampling. The dilemma involves the fact that, in basing an inference on a sample, the researchers are caught in a paradox, which philosopher Abraham Kaplan described as follows:

> On the one hand, the sample is of no use to us if it is not truly representative of its population, if it is not a "fair" sample. On the other hand, to know that it is representative, we must know what the characteristics of the population are, so that we can judge whether the sample reflects them properly; but in that case, we have no need of the sample at all (Kaplan, 1964, p. 239)

The larger problem, as we quickly recognize, is that all inductive inferences are based on samples. That is to say, we make generalizations about a whole class of cases but have observed only some of them, or we make predictions about future outcomes on the basis of samples of events from the past. In survey research, as we will see, the special way this paradox is resolved is "by the consideration that the representativeness is not a property of the sample but rather of the procedure by which the sample is obtained, the *sampling plan*" (Kaplan, 1964, pp. 239–240). It might not be an exaggeration to say that there is a comparable situation when we look in the dictionary to find out whether a word has been used properly. The dictionary is based on common usage, and so the "proper" usage of words is validated by a method that is based on how the words are actually used (the "paradox of usage").

Thus we shall start by examining the nature of the kinds of sampling plans that are used in surveys. The survey researcher asks a question and then looks for the answer in the replies of the respondents to interviews or questionnaires. *Sampling plans* are the blueprints that specify how those respondents are to be selected in survey studies. In particular, we shall discuss the nature of different *probability sampling plans* employed by researchers. Such plans are essentially specifications of the way in which randomness enters in the selection process at some stage such that the laws of mathematical probability apply. Employing a probability sampling plan enables the survey researcher to know—though never for sure—that the sample is representative of its population, without already knowing what it was that he or she was trying to find out, the characteristics of the population.

Sampling plans are primarily relevant to surveys, not to laboratory research. As noted above, we shall also be examining the nature of the subject selection process in experimental studies, with particular emphasis on the volunteer-subject problem. When the potential recruits have a choice of whether to participate, not everyone will be willing to serve as a research subject. The investigators who have studied this issue have addressed the question of whether research studies that are based on the behavior of people who *are* willing to serve as subjects are any different in their results from research studies in which the subjects were not volunteers but "captive" participants (i.e., required to participate). In survey research the opportunity *not* to play the role of the respondent can produce *nonresponse bias*, the name for the opposite side of the sample selection bias issue.

Another potential contributor to biased results, also examined in this chapter, could be the nonrepresentativeness of the stimulus that is employed. In the classical design all the variables on the stimulus side are held constant except for the independent variable X, and effects upon the dependent variable Y are then observed on the subject side. In a final discussion we shall turn to the generalizability of the results of experimental studies in which X is defined in terms of the experimenter as stimulus. We shall see that in some situations it is absolutely vital to sample from among stimuli and situations, i.e., if we want to make generalizations about whole classes of stimuli and situations.

BIASEDNESS AND INSTABILITY
IN SURVEYS

Probability sampling plans are the survey researcher's way of dealing with the paradox of sampling. They are characterized by the fact that every element in the population has a known nonzero probability of being selected. In deciding on a specific probability sampling plan to use when doing a survey, there are practical considerations to weigh, such as the kinds of resources that are available. There are also two important statistical requirements of sampling that have to be considered. One of them is that the sample values must be *unbiased*, and the other is that there be *stability* in the samples.

What does bias tell us? It indicates that the general sampling plan produces an estimate of the population values that is systematically too high or too low. A related concept in probability sampling is stability, which is inversely related to the degree of variability of the sample values. To illustrate, Figure 10-1 shows various hypothetical outcomes in which the sampling units are designated by O's and the true population mean is shown by an X. The amount of instability is constant within each row, going from a high amount of instability in row 1 to no instability in row 3. The amount of biasedness is constant in each column, going from a high amount in column 1 to zero bias in column 3. Thus, in the three cases in column 3, the sample values are balanced around the population mean,

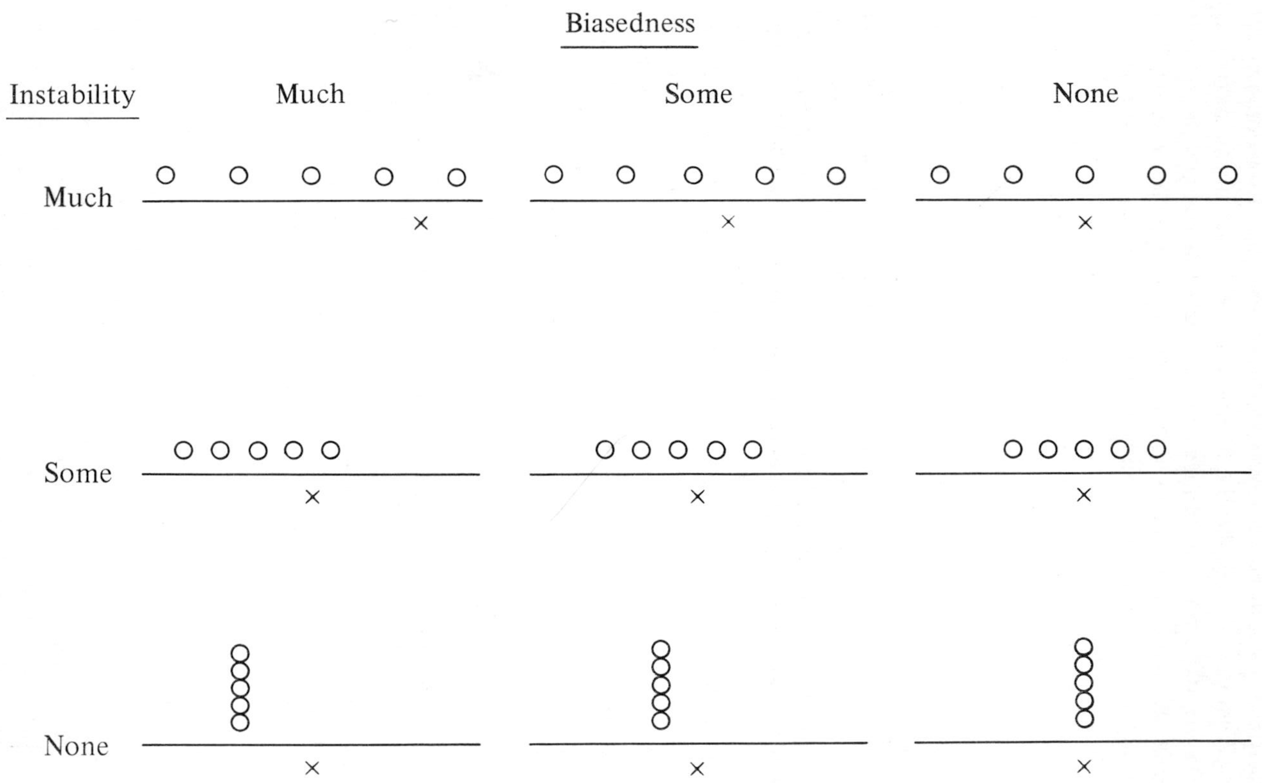

FIGURE 10-1
Illustrations of biasedness and instability in sampling. An O denotes a particular sampling unit, X represents the true population mean, and the horizontal line indicates the underlying continuum on which the relevant values are determined. The distance between the true population mean and the midpoint of the sampling units indicates the amount of biasedness. The spreading (variability) among the sampling units indicates their degree of instability.

but with much instability in row 1, some in row 2, and none in row 3. In the three cases in row 3 there is no instability, but there is much biasedness in column 1, some in column 2, and none in column 3. The case illustrated at the intersection of row 3 and column 3 would appear to represent the best of all situations.

Generally speaking, instability results when the sample size is too small, even if the sampling units have been chosen without bias. On the other hand, the more alike (*homogeneous*) the members of the population (the sampling units), the fewer of them need to be sampled. If all members of the population were exactly alike, then we could choose any sampling unit to provide complete information about the population as a whole. Of course, instability is characteristic of human subject populations. The more unlike (*heterogeneous*) the members of the population are, the more sampling units that will be needed (Kish, 1965).

Can we ever *really* know whether there is, or is not, biasedness in the general sampling plan? Sometimes it is said that election forecasting allows us to know, since we can compare the predicted results against the obtained ones. Even in this case we cannot know for sure, however, since there could be true change from poll to election. As Kaplan (1964) noted, the only way to know for sure would be to examine every member of the population at the same time that the sampling was conducted. If the pattern of replies in the sample duplicated the pattern of replies in the population, then we would know there was no biasedness in the general sampling plan. This procedure is obviously impractical, because we would have no need of a sample if we knew everyone's response in the population (the paradox of sampling). The point is that, unless enough is known about a population to make sampling unnecessary, we can never say for certain that a general sampling plan, random or other, is unbiased (cf. Wallis and Roberts, 1956).

SIMPLE RANDOM SAMPLING PLANS

The concept of randomness, as in *simple random sampling*, means that the sample was chosen by a process that gave each sampling unit in the population the same chance of being selected as any other. This type of general sampling plan, as the name implies, is the least complicated probability sampling method. The method of selection might consist of throwing dice, spinning a roulette wheel, or drawing capsules out of an urn.

The implementation of these procedures is not foolproof, however. A famous example of inadequate randomization occurred in 1970. The previous year, while the Vietnamese war was still in progress, Congress passed a bill allowing a random lottery to be used in selecting conscripts for the armed forces. To make the lottery appear as fair as possible the planners decided to have individuals pick birthdays out of an urn. The 365 days of the year were written on slips of paper that were placed inside tiny cylindrical capsules. The urn was shaken for several hours and the capsules then chosen, one by one, from the urn. However, the results were not random. Birthdates in December tended to be drawn first, those in November next, then those in October, and so on. It seems the January capsules were put in the urn first, the February capsules next, and so forth, and layers were formed, with the December capsules on top. Even though the urn was shaken for several hours, it takes much longer to mix capsules up (Broome, 1984; Kolata, 1986). Interestingly, a similar problem occurred at the beginning of World War II, when capsules containing slips of paper were drawn from a bowl as a "fair" method of selecting men for the draft. Those results also showed marked departures from randomness (Wallis and Roberts, 1956).

Randomness should not be confused with "aimlessness" or "hit-or-miss" sampling, which in fact seldom can be called random. You can prove this to yourself by writing down several hundred 1-digit numbers from 0 to 9 in an "aimless" manner. Afterward, tabulate the 0's, 1's, 2's, and so on. If the numbers are truly random, there should be no obvious sequences and each digit should occur approximately 1/10 of the time. You will find, however, that the results are inconsistent with the hypothesis of randomness (Wallis and Roberts, 1956).

An effective way to avoid the problem of inadequate randomization is to use a table of random digits. To illustrate how to select a simple random sample, we refer to Table 10.1, which was extracted from Table B.9 in Appendix B. The more complete table is actually a small segment of a much larger one that was generated by an electronic roulette wheel programmed to produce a random frequency pulse every tiny fraction of a second (RAND Corporation, 1955). A million random digits were generated, and afterward as a check on the hypothesis of randomness the computer counted the number of 0's, 1's, 2's, and so on. Each digit from 0 to 9 occurred 10 percent of the time in the overall table of a million random digits.

For our example, imagine we want to select 10 men and 10 women individually at random from a population totaling 96 men and 99 women. We begin by numbering the men in the population consecutively from 01 to 96 and the women in the population consecutively from 01 to 99. We are now ready to use the 5 × 5 blocks of random digits in Table 10.1. Ignore the reference numbers in

TABLE 10.1
Random digits

Line	Random digits					
000	10097	32533	76520	13586	34673	54876
001	37542	04805	64894	74296	24805	24037
002	08422	68953	19645	09303	23209	02560
003	99019	02529	09376	70715	38311	31165
004	12807	99970	80157	36147	64032	36653
005	66065	74717	34072	76850	36697	36170
006	31060	10805	45571	82406	35303	42614
007	85269	77602	02051	65692	68665	74818
008	63573	32135	05325	47048	90553	57548
009	73796	45753	03529	64778	35808	34282

Note: This abbreviated table is taken from Table B.9 in Appendix B. The left-hand column is for reference only, while the other columns contain random digits in sets of five (RAND Corporation, 1955).

the left-hand column, which are there to help us refer to any particular line. We do our simple random sampling by putting our finger blindly on some starting position. We can start anywhere in the table and move our finger in any direction, so long as we do not pick some set of numbers because they look right, or avoid some set of numbers because they do not look right. Suppose we put our finger on the first five-digit number on line 004—that would be 12807. We read across the line two digits at a time, then across the next line, and so forth, until we have chosen individually at random the 10 male subjects. We do the same thing, beginning at another blindly chosen point, until we have selected the 10 female subjects. Beginning with the number 12807, we would select men numbered 12, 80, 79, and so on.

In simple random sampling, two options are sampling with replacement and sampling without replacement. In *sampling with replacement* the selected names are placed in the selection pool again and may be reselected on subsequent draws. Thus every element in the population continues to have the same probability of being chosen every time a number is read. Tossing a coin would also be sampling with replacement, in this case from a population consisting of two elements, heads and tails (Kish, 1965). In *sampling without replacement* a previously selected name cannot be reselected and must be disregarded on any later draw. In this case the population shrinks, but the names remaining still have an equal likelihood of being drawn on the next occasion. Researchers usually prefer to do sampling without replacement because they do not want to test the same person twice.

Suppose we chose the same two-digit number more than once, or chose a two-digit number not represented by any name in the population. We would go on to the next two-digit number in the row. What if we were forced to skip many numbers in the table because they were too large? That would be terribly inefficient. For example, what if there were 450 members in the population and we wanted to select 50 individually at random? Since the population is numbered from 001 to 450 we will have to skip approximately half the three-digit numbers our finger points to. One way to handle this problem (acceptable in terms of randomness) is mentally to subtract 500 from any number in the range from 501 to 999.

SYSTEMATIC SELECTION PLANS

An alternative to random choice is to use *systematic selection* of the sampling units in sequences separated on lists by the interval of selection (Kish, 1965). This method is often used when only manual procedures are available for sampling and the sample and population are both large. However, systematic samples may not be exactly random samples.

Suppose we are interested in selecting 1,000 households from the white pages of the telephone directory. Systematic selection starts randomly and is based on the selection of elements from the population at particular intervals (Sudman, 1983). Therefore, we need two things: the *sampling interval* and a *random start*. We can use a table of random digits to select the initial page and the name on that page. We then add to (or subtract from) the page selected a constant number and choose the name in the same place on that page. Afterward, we do the same thing again, and so forth. To illustrate: suppose we chose the number 48 by closing our eyes and pointing our finger to a particular row and column in our random digits table (i.e., a random start). We open the telephone book to page 48 and find the forty-eighth name on that page. Starting with that person we then choose the forty-eighth name on every tenth page (i.e., a sampling interval of 10 pages) from page 48 (e.g., pages 8, 18, 28, 38, 58, 68, etc.).

We said that systematic samples may not be exactly random samples, and in fact they are complex samples with unknown properties (Sudman, 1983). To illustrate, we will make a slight modification in our systematic selection procedure to help us deal more efficiently with refusals and unanswered calls. Whenever we encounter either problem, we will add 1 to the last digit in the telephone number of the person just called and try that number as an alternative. This is economical—and certainly it is systematic selection—but not all the numbers are independent. We may be dialing into a bank of numbers all from the same exchange. If so, that would necessarily introduce a nonrandom element into the final pool of respondents.

Another problem whenever we use lists is that not everyone is named on an available list. If we wanted the names of all members of the American Psychological Association (APA), the information would be readily available. But if we wanted the names of all experimental psychologists in the United States, the information would not be available. One reason is that not all experimental psychologists belong to the APA, or for that matter to any single scientific or professional organization. Similarly, if we wanted a list of everyone residing in Columbus, Ohio in 1989, we would find such information also to be unavailable. We could put together a partial list by meticulously combing through public records (e.g., tax records, voting lists, telephone directories), but still many names would elude us (e.g., names of children and perhaps elderly dependents, residents not registered to vote, people with unlisted telephones).

STRATIFICATION IN SAMPLING

In addition to simple random sampling, another approach to probability sampling is to select from several subpopulations, termed *strata* or *clusters*, into which the population is divided. The idea is to divide the population into subclasses and then sample in a way so as to ensure that each subclass is represented in proportion to its population.

For example, in what is called *stratified random sampling*, a separate sample is randomly selected within each homogeneous stratum (or "layer") of the population. The stratum means are then statistically weighted to form a combined estimate for the entire population. For instance, in a survey of political opinions, it might be useful to stratify the population according to party affiliation, sex, socioeconomic status, and other meaningful categories related to voting behavior. This ensures that one has enough men, women, Democrats, Republicans, etc., to draw inferences about each respective subgroup.

A popular variant of stratification in sampling is called *area probability sampling*. In this case the population is divided into selected units that have the same probability of being chosen as unselected units in the population cluster. Suppose we needed an area probability sample of 300 out of 6,000 estimated dwellings in a city. A good list of all the dwellings in the entire city does not exist (and would be too costly to prepare), but we can instead obtain a sample of dwellings by selecting a cluster of blocks using a city map. We might begin by dividing the entire area of the city's map into blocks and then selecting one of every 20 blocks into the sample. If we define the sample as the dwellings located within the boundaries of the sample blocks, the probability of selection for *any* dwelling is the selection of its block—which is set at 1/20 to correspond to the desired sampling rate of 300/6,000 (Kish, 1965).

One does not have to be a highly skilled statistician to draw up an area probability sampling plan. For example, one was developed by communication researcher Conrad Smith (1980) in his doctoral dissertation study to find out about television viewers' preferences in news telecasts in Salt Lake City, Utah. Smith developed his sampling plan using tract and block estimates that he obtained from census data found in the library. Except for a minor group of transients, people were thus identified with a place of residence, and that residence with a particular area. The neat thing about Smith's sampling plan—true of any area probability sampling plan—is that he could then reuse it repeatedly with minor modifications. To reuse his plan he had only to vary the random selection of the dwelling units within the sample areas (for further discussion, see, e.g., Babbie, 1975; Cornell and McLoone, 1963; Furno, 1966; Kish, 1965; Parten, 1950; and Warwick and Lininger, 1975).

POINT AND INTERVAL ESTIMATES IN SURVEY SAMPLING

Whatever technique is used, the survey researcher is usually interested in making point estimates and interval estimates regarding population values. *Point estimates* tell us about some particular characteristic of the population, e.g., the number of graduating seniors in a college class who want to go on to graduate school or the percentage of students who favor a particular candidate to become president of the student legislature. *Interval estimates* tell us how much the point estimates are likely to be in error, e.g., owing to variability in the composition of the population.

Suppose we used simple random sampling to survey 100 students out of a population of 2,500 graduating seniors. In response to the question "Do you hope to go on to graduate school?" we find that 25 of the students sampled replied in the affirmative. In order to make a point estimate, we extrapolate from this sample value to the population of graduating seniors. We multiply the sample proportion replying "yes" (.25) times the total number of students in the population (2,500), which tells us that approximately 625 seniors hope to do graduate work. How "approximate" is this estimate? The interval estimate gives the answer to this question: i.e., it tells us the probability that the estimated population value is correct within plus or minus some specified interval. Let us say we compute as "95 chances in 100" the probability that an interval of "25 percent, plus or minus 9 percent" contains the true frequency of graduating seniors who hope to go on to graduate school. In other words, our point estimate of 625 with its associated interval estimate enables us to feel fairly confident that the population value falls within the range of 400 to 850 graduating seniors (Cochran, 1963, pp. 57–58).

In this hypothetical case we randomly selected individual sampling units from the entire population as a single heterogeneous stratum. Would stratified sampling be more advantageous than simple random sampling for making unbiased estimates of population values if the population could be conveniently separated into more homogeneous strata? Remember that random sampling does not use any information that we have about the breakdown of the population, whereas stratified random sampling divides the population into subpopulations that are internally homogeneous (Snedecor and Cochran, 1980). For the answer to this question we turn to another illustration.

UTILITY OF STRATIFICATION

In 1980, after 97 years of trying, the Philadelphia Phillies baseball team won a World Series championship. There were six infielders on the roster that year, whose batting averages at the end of the season were as follows:

.277   Ramon Aviles
.267   Larry Bowa
.282   Pete Rose
.286   Mike Schmidt
.292   Manny Trillo
.161   John Vukovich

Batting averages are computed by dividing the number of official hits the player made by the number of official times that the player went to bat. Summing the six batting averages just above and dividing by 6 (the size of the population) we obtain the (unweighted) population mean (1.565/6 = .2608). We now ask, "How good an estimate of the population mean (rounded to .261) do we obtain by simple random sampling?"

To answer this question we must first decide on the size of sample we will use to estimate the population mean. For convenience we will define the sample size as any two members selected at random. For example, were we randomly to select Aviles and Rose, that would give us a point estimate of .280, i.e., (.277 + .282)/2 = .280 (rounded). How good is this estimate? The answer, called the *error of estimate*, is conveniently defined in this illustration as the closeness of .280 to the true value, i.e., .280 − .261 = +.019. Table 10.2 lists all possible combinations of two-member samples, the estimates derived from them, and the error of estimate for each sample. The average of the errors of estimate (taking account of their signs) gives the *bias* of the general sampling plan. Not surprisingly, we see (bottom of column 3) that the general sampling plan produced an

TABLE 10.2
Results for all possible simple random samples of size two

Sample	Estimate of population mean	Error of estimate
Aviles, Bowa	.272	+.011
Aviles, Rose	.280	+.019
Aviles, Schmidt	.282	+.021
Aviles, Trillo	.285	+.024
Aviles, Vukovich	.219	−.042
Bowa, Rose	.275	+.014
Bowa, Schmidt	.277	+.016
Bowa, Trillo	.280	+.019
Bowa, Vukovich	.214	−.047
Rose, Schmidt	.284	+.023
Rose, Trillo	.287	+.026
Rose, Vukovich	.222	−.039
Schmidt, Trillo	.289	+.028
Schmidt, Vukovich	.224	−.037
Trillo, Vukovich	.227	−.034
Total	3.917	.00
Mean	.261	

unbiased estimate—even though there is error associated with individual sample values.

In doing stratified random sampling, to which we turn next, we divide the population into a number of parts and then randomly sample independently in each part. Table 10.2 shows that every simple random sample containing Vukovich's name underestimated the population value but every sample without his name overestimated it. If we had reason to suspect this fact before the sampling, we could make use of that information to form strata so that a heterogeneous population is divided into two parts, each of which is fairly homogeneous (Snedecor and Cochran, 1980). Stratum 1 will consist of Vukovich, and stratum 2 will consist of the remaining five members (Aviles, Bowa, Rose, Schmidt, and Trillo).

For stratified random samples of size 2 we must be sure that Vukovich's name appears in every sample, and that we have randomly sampled independently in stratum 2. Suppose that Schmidt's name was randomly chosen. To obtain our point estimate using Vukovich's and Schmidt's scores, we weight Schmidt's score by $N = 5$ (the number of members in stratum 2), add Vukovich's score to this value, and then divide by $N = 6$ (the total number of members). To illustrate: we first weight Schmidt's score (.286 × 5 = 1.430), then add Vukovich's score to the product (1.430 + .161 = 1.591), and finally divide by the total N (1.591/6 = .265). The error of estimate of this sample is computed as .265 minus the true population value, or .265 − .261 = +.004. Table 10.3 shows the

TABLE 10.3
Results for all possible stratified random samples of size two

Sample	Stratum 1	Stratum 2	Estimate of population mean	Error of estimate
1	Vukovich	Aviles	.258	−.003
2	Vukovich	Bowa	.249	−.012
3	Vukovich	Rose	.262	+.001
4	Vukovich	Schmidt	.265	+.004
5	Vukovich	Trillo	.270	+.009
Total			1.304	.00
Mean			.261	

results for all possible stratified random samples of size 2. This particular plan would be better described as *stratified random sampling with unequal sampling fractions*, since stratum 1 is completely sampled and stratum 2 is sampled at a rate of 1 unit out of 5, or 20 percent (cf. Snedecor and Cochran, 1980). Again, we find (not surprisingly) that the general sampling plan is unbiased in that the average of the errors of estimate is zero.

Comparing the results in these two tables, we see the advantages of separating selections from strata of the population. In Table 10.2 the errors of estimate range from −.047 to +.028, a difference of .075. In Table 10.3 the errors of estimate range from −.012 to +.009, a difference of only .021. There are also fewer possible stratified samples of size 2 (Table 10.3) than there are simple random samples of the same size (Table 10.2). Not only is the actual error of an individual sample greater in simple random sampling than in stratified random sampling, but the potential for error is also greater when using simple random sampling than stratified random sampling. Some forethought (and, of course, information) is needed about possible mean differences for dividing the population into strata, which can then pay off handsomely in the utility of stratification.

NONRESPONSE BIAS AND ITS CONTROL

Previously, we referred to the fact that not everyone who is contacted by an opinion pollster—or for that matter by any type of researcher—will automatically agree to participate as a research subject. For example, marketing researchers Roger A. Kerin and Robert A. Peterson (1983) attempted to contact a substantial number of households in a nationwide consumer tracking study over a consecutive 12-month period in 1980–1981. Those called were obtained by means of a computerized telephone-number sampling system used to generate households with both listed and unlisted numbers within the continental United States. The outcomes were then coded as (1) no answer (after 5 rings), (2) busy signal, (3) out-of-service number, (4) ineligible respondent (e.g., underage respondent, or a business or similar organization), (5) refusal to be interviewed, and (6) actual completion of the interview. The independent variables coded were (1) period of the day, (2) geographical location of the household, (3) day of the week, and (4) month. Results of this study might serve as a general guide to help us anticipate the optimal conditions for telephone interviewing.

In all, 259,088 dialings were made, but only 8.4 percent resulted in actual completions of the interview. The remainder, the *nonrespondents*, included 1.4 percent who refused to participate even though eligible, 34.7 percent no answers, 2 percent busy signals, 20.3 percent out-of-service numbers, and 33.2 percent ineligible respondents. If these conditions are typical of computerized telephone-number sampling, one ought to select several times the number of completed interviews we actually want in order to compensate for high refusal rate and high rates of unanswered calls (cf. Downs, Smeyak, and Martin, 1980). Can we predict the optimal periods that would increase our ability to make successful contacts? The refusal rate was lower when the dialing period was 5–9 P.M. (14.0 percent) rather than 8 A.M. to 5 P.M. (15.7 percent). It was also lower in rural (10.2 percent refusals) as opposed to urban locations (16.7 percent refusals), and lowest on Sundays and Tuesdays (13.1 percent refusals for both days) while highest on Wednesdays (16.0 percent refusals) and Fridays (16.2 percent refusals). Potential interviewees were most likely to be at home during the months of December (11.3 percent at home) and January (12.0 percent at home) and less likely to be available during the other months of the year (ranging from 9.0 percent in September to 10.7 percent in February).

Can high rates of nonresponse impair the validity of survey studies, and if so, what can be done about it? Some answers to both parts of this question are contained in the results of a study by William Cochran (1963), which are summarized in Table 10.4. The results, based on three waves of questionnaires that were mailed out to fruit growers, also serve to operationalize the concept of *bias due to nonresponse*. One variable in this study dealt with the number of fruit trees owned, and data were available for the entire population of growers for just this variable. As a consequence, it is possible for us to calculate the degree of bias attributable to nonresponse present after the first, second, and third waves of questionnaires. Rows 1 to 3 provide the basic data in the form of (1) the number of respondents to each wave of questionnaires and the number of nonrespondents, (2) the percentage of the total population represented by each wave of respondents (and nonrespondents), and (3) the mean number of trees owned by respondents and nonrespondents at each wave. Examination of row 3 reveals the nature of the nonresponse bias, which is that the earlier respondents owned more trees on the average than did the later responders.

The remaining five rows of data are based on the cumulative number of respondents available after the first, second, and third waves. For each wave, five items of information are provided: (4) the mean number of trees owned by the respondents up to that point in the survey, (5) the mean number of trees owned by those who had not yet responded up to that point, (6) the difference between these two values, (7) the percentage of the population that had not yet responded, and (8) the magnitude of the bias up to that point in the survey. Examination of this last row shows that with each successive wave of respondents there was an appreciable decrease in the magnitude of the bias, which appears to be a fairly typical result of studies of this kind. That is, increasing the effort to recruit the nonrespondents decreases the bias of point estimates in the sample.

TABLE 10.4
Example of bias due to nonresponse in survey research

Basic data	Response to three mailings			Non-respondents	Total population
	First wave	Second wave	Third wave		
(1) Number of respondents	300	543	434	1839	3116
(2) Percent of population	10%	17%	14%	59%	100%
(3) Mean trees per respondent	456	382	340	290	329
Cumulative data					
(4) Mean trees per respondent ($\bar{Y}_1$)	456	408	385		
(5) Mean trees per nonrespondent ($\bar{Y}_2$)	315	300	290		
(6) Difference ($\bar{Y}_1 - \bar{Y}_2$)	141	108	95		
(7) Percent of nonrespondents (P)	90%	73%	59%		
(8) Bias = (P) × ($\bar{Y}_1 - \bar{Y}_2$)	127	79	56		

Source: W. G. Cochran, *Sampling Techniques,* 2d ed., Wiley, New York, 1963; table reprinted from R. Rosenthal and R. L. Rosnow, *The Volunteer Subject,* Wiley-Interscience, New York, 1975, by permission of the publisher.

Considerable theoretical attention continues to be paid to sample selection bias in all fields of behavioral science (e.g., Berk, 1983; Berk and Ray, 1982; Gniech, 1986; Heckman, 1980; Nederhof, 1981; Rosenthal and Rosnow, 1975; Rosnow and Rosenthal, 1970, 1976; Smith, 1984; Sudman, Sirken, and Cowan, 1988). In most circumstances of behavioral research we can compute the proportion of our population participants (P) and the statistic of interest (the point estimate) for these respondents ($\overline{Y}_1$), but we cannot compute the statistic of interest (the corresponding point estimate) for those who do not respond ($\overline{Y}_2$). Therefore, we are often in a position to suspect bias but are unable to give an estimate of its magnitude. In survey research conducted by telephone or questionnaire a further problem is that one is frequently unable to differentiate household refusals from potential respondent refusals. In the former case the nonrespondent was not the person who should be interviewed, but a "gatekeeper" within the household (Lavrakas, 1987).

Before we leave the topic of nonresponse bias, it would be of interest to ask what incentives may serve to increase the response rates in survey research. In a summary of the literature on stimulating responses to mailed questionnaires, sociologist Arnold S. Linsky (1975) concluded that five techniques had been proved most effective: (1) using one or more follow-ups or reminders such as telephone calls, postcards, and letters sent to initial nonresponders, (2) contacting potential respondents before they receive the questionnaire, (3) using "high-powered" mailings such as special delivery and airmail (as opposed to ordinary mail) and hand-stamped rather than postage-permit return envelopes, (4) offering cash rewards or premiums for participation, and (5) listing the name of the organization that sponsors the research and the title of the researcher signing the cover letter.

There is a point of diminishing returns with incentives, but in general they are effective means for increasing return rates in this type of research (Filion, 1975–1976; Goyder, 1982; Heberlein and Baumgartner, 1978; Mizes, Fleece, and Roos, 1984). In telephone survey research another option is to train the interviewers to handle difficult respondents and refusals. They are taught how to be politely persuasive without being overly aggressive and to tell the respondents how helpful their opinions are to the investigators. If there is resistance, the interviewer can offer to call back on another occasion: "I'm sorry we've bothered you at what apparently is a bad time for you" (Lavrakas, 1987).

FORTUITOUS SAMPLES IN EXPERIMENTAL RESEARCH

In fields such as experimental, personality, and social psychology, most behavioral scientists do not usually concern themselves with the particulars of a probability sampling plan when choosing subjects for research participation. One reason is that frequently it is simply impossible to work within the confines of such a plan. Another reason, even when such a plan is feasible, is that many researchers feel that "people are people" in terms of the principles that regulate behavior, and it should make no difference whether the research participants constitute a random sample of the population as a whole. However, it could be a problematic assumption if, say, the results found with volunteer subjects formed the basis of conclusions that did not generalize in the same way to a population of nonvolunteers.

If we are interested in making estimates regarding true population values, as in public opinion polling, we really have no option but to use probability sampling procedures. However, if we are interested in studying causal effects in the relationships between variables, we will frequently find it impossible to use survey sampling procedures. In this case we would resort to a quite different approach. After making a decision as to the kinds of research participants needed, the researcher decides on the number needed to reach the level of statistical power desired (discussed in Chapter 19) and then attempts to obtain appropriate subjects based on his or her own expert judgment.

VOLUNTEER BIAS EFFECTS?

Previously, we alluded to the possibility that, in some cases, the use of self-selected (i.e., volunteer) subjects could have a biasing effect on the results. It will be instructive if we consider some of the ways in which the volunteer status of the respondents or subjects might lead to spurious conclusions. We begin with an everyday example: the do-it-yourself "research" polls conducted by some radio and TV stations, magazines, and newspapers.

The typical procedure involves posing a yes-or-no question about some current controversial issue and inviting the public to call in to express an opinion. Sometimes the technique is falsely given a mystique of "scientific" respectability through the use of electronic equipment to tabulate respondents' opinions. The audience is instructed to dial one number to record a "yes" vote and another number to record a "no" vote. However, the validity of such results is so low as to render almost any generalization useless. In the first place, the majority of people who would volunteer their opinions in this way are in all likelihood nonrepresentative of the population in general, and also nonrepresentative of the particular audience of that program. In one case, WABC-TV in New York suspected organized groups of jamming their telephone lines. In another instance, KOB-TV skipped its polling one night and still received 20 calls voting "yes" and 38 voting "no" (Rosnow and Rosenthal, 1970). Furthermore, even if one could eliminate pranksters' responses and line jamming by groups with vested interests, one would still be left with a nonrepresentative sample. Some people would call in just to be able to disclose information about themselves, a pattern of behavior that is found to be more common among certain volunteers than nonvolunteers (Back, Hood, and Brehm, 1963).

A second way in which the volunteer status of the participants might affect the results is in the case of "test standardization" research. A standardized test is one in which the procedure for administering and scoring the instrument, and the various materials used, has been fixed to assure that one competent tester will obtain essentially the same "unbiased" results as any other. Many standardized tests are accompanied by *norms*—these are tables of values signifying the average, or normative, scores of other subjects who have taken the same test.

The purpose of the norms is to provide a "ruler" with which to measure and to interpret an individual's score. For example, a high school student's score on the Scholastic Aptitude Test (SAT) of the College Entrance Examination Board might be compared with the average SAT scores of other high school students throughout the country in order to provide a relative index against which to gauge the individual's proficiency. An obviously crucial assumption in establishing such norms is that the resulting values are truly representative of the specified population.

However, if one relied solely on samples of volunteer subjects in the test standardization research to establish norms, the resulting values could be seriously distorted. If one were standardizing an IQ test, for instance, the sample mean might be artificially inflated if one relied on a sample of volunteers for the standardization group, because volunteers generally score higher on intelligence tests than nonvolunteers (Rosenthal and Rosnow, 1975). This notion is illustrated in Figure 10-2, which depicts roughly the positive bias that could result from using other than random sampling to estimate IQ values in the general population. Merely increasing the size of the sample would not eliminate or reduce

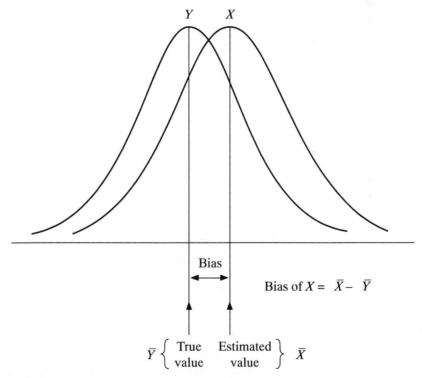

FIGURE 10-2
The curve symbolized by Y represents a theoretical normal distribution of IQs in the general population, and the curve labeled X represents a theoretical normal distribution of IQs among volunteers. To the extent that the mean of the X is different from the mean of the Y (as shown), the resultant bias constitutes a threat to the generalizability of the data.

this bias, but improving the representativeness of the sampling procedures obviously should.

A third example pertains to the results of experimental studies in which the investigator is not just interested in ascertaining population values, but is interested in determining the magnitude of the differences between such values when experimental groups are compared with control groups. The possibility that volunteers differ from nonvolunteers in their responses on an IQ test or on the SAT is interesting, but it is irrelevant to the question of whether volunteers respond any differently than nonvolunteers to a particular experimental manipulation. In other words, the experimenter is more interested in knowing whether or not the use of volunteers might bias the outcome of the investigation and, if so, in what direction it would tend to distort the differences between the behavior of those subjects placed in the experimental groups and those placed in the control groups.

In Chapter 4 we indicated some of the sources of internal invalidity in various experimental designs, and in discussing the Solomon design alluded to the particular threat to validity posed by the subjects' volunteer status. We now explore the external and internal validity questions in more detail, in terms of other relevant results and the theoretical implications of the characteristics of the volunteer subject. Before we turn to these questions, it will be instructive to summarize some of the evidence for the reliability of the act of volunteering for research participation. If it were a purely random event (i.e., completely unreliable), we could not expect to find any stable relationships between volunteering and various personal characteristics of subjects. But the research in this area suggests that there are a number of characteristics that relate predictably to the act of volunteering.

In a group of studies the reliability of volunteering for research participation ranged from a correlation of .97 down to .22 (Barefoot, 1969; Dohrenwend and Dohrenwend, 1968; Laming, 1967; Martin and Marcuse, 1958; Rosen, 1951; Wallace, 1954). The median reliability of volunteering for laboratory studies was .56, and for field studies it was .41. For studies requesting volunteers for the same task, the median reliability was .80, and for studies requesting volunteering for different tasks, it was .42. All the reliability coefficients are significantly different from zero. It also appears to be true that the act of volunteering for research participation has both general and specific predictors. That is, some people volunteer reliably more than others for a variety of tasks, and these reliable individual differences may be further stabilized when the particular task for which the volunteering was requested is specifically considered.

MEASURING THE NONVOLUNTEER

A basic question, of course, is, How does one find out the characteristics of those who do *not* volunteer to participate in psychological experiments, those who do *not* answer their mail or their telephone or their doorbell in survey research? The answer to this intriguing question is that a number of procedures have been found useful in comparing the characteristics of those more or less likely to find their way into the role of data producer for the behavioral scientist. For illustrative purpose we might group the procedures into one of two types, the "exhaustive" and the "nonexhaustive" approaches.

In the exhaustive approach all the potential subjects or respondents are identified by their status on all the variables on which volunteers and nonvolunteers are to be compared. The investigator might begin with an archive containing for each person listed all the information desired for the comparison. Requests for volunteers are then made some time later—sometimes years later—and those who volunteered are compared with those who did not volunteer on all the items of information in the archive in which the investigator is interested. For instance, most colleges administer psychological tests and questionnaires to all the incoming students during an orientation period. Such data, if they are obtainable by researchers, can be used not only to compare those who volunteer with those who do not volunteer for a psychological experiment later that same year, but also to compare the respondents with the nonrespondents to an alumni-organization questionnaire sent out years later.

In the nonexhaustive approach the data are not available for all the potential subjects or respondents, but information *is* available for subjects or respondents differing in the likelihood of finding their way into a final sample. For example, we might begin with a pool of volunteers and from this sample ask for volunteers for additional research, i.e., recruit "second-level" volunteers. These second-level volunteers are then compared with the second-level nonvolunteers on the data available. Differences between the second-level volunteers and nonvolunteers, however, are likely to underestimate the differences between the volunteers and the "true" nonvolunteers, because even the second-level nonvolunteers had at least been first-level volunteers. This problem is handled by extrapolation on a gradient of volunteering, as illustrated in Figure 10-3. The underlying assumption (not unreasonable, but no doubt often wrong) is that those who volunteer repeatedly, those who volunteer with less incentive, or those who volunteer more quickly are further up the curve from those who volunteer less often, with more incentive, or more slowly, and still further up the curve from those who do not volunteer at all. In this way, two or more levels of volunteering eagerness are employed to extrapolate to the zero level of volunteering. The hypothetical situation illustrated in this figure is based on the repeat volunteers' being higher in the need for social approval than the one-time volunteers are; it then requires extrapolation in which one guesses that the nonvolunteers would be lower still in the need for social approval.

VOLUNTEER CHARACTERISTICS AND THEIR IMPLICATIONS

A substantial amount of research has employed these techniques and other variants to identify the characteristics of volunteering versus not volunteering for research participation. Table 10.5 presents a summary of the particular characteristics that appear to warrant some confidence in their stability, roughly in order of the degree of confidence we can have in each (Rosenthal and Rosnow,

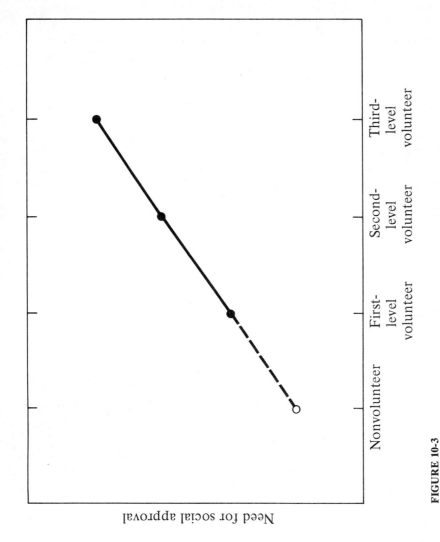

FIGURE 10-3
Hypothetical illustration of extrapolating probable characteristics of nonvolunteers from characteristics of volunteers found at various levels of volunteering.

TABLE 10.5
Volunteer characteristics
grouped by degree of confidence
of conclusion

I. *Maximum confidence*
1. Educated
2. Higher social class
3. Intelligent
4. Approval-motivated
5. Sociable

II. *Considerable confidence*
6. Arousal-seeking
7. Unconventional
8. Female
9. Nonauthoritarian
10. Jewish > Protestant > Catholic
11. Nonconforming

III. *Some confidence*
12. From smaller town
13. Interested in religion
14. Altruistic
15. Self-disclosing
16. Maladjusted
17. Young

1975). We see that five characteristics deserved "maximum" confidence, and that was because they were based on the results of the largest number of relevant studies (no fewer than 19) and the highest percentage of consistent results (no less than 86 percent of the statistically significant results were consistent). Other characteristics in this table are indicated as deserving somewhat less confidence because there were fewer relevant studies available or a lower percentage of supportive results. The specific conclusions to which the more succinct summaries in this table refer are as follows (after Rosenthal and Rosnow, 1975):

1. Volunteers tend to be better educated than nonvolunteers, especially when personal contact between investigator and respondent is not required.
2. Volunteers tend to have higher social class status than nonvolunteers do, especially when social class is defined by respondents' own status rather than by parental status.
3. Volunteers tend to be more intelligent than nonvolunteers when volunteering is for research in general, but not when volunteering is for somewhat less typical types of research such as hypnosis, sensory isolation, sex research, and small-group and personality research.
4. Volunteers tend to be higher in need for social approval than nonvolunteers.
5. Volunteers tend to be more sociable than nonvolunteers.

6. Volunteers tend to be more arousal-seeking than nonvolunteers, especially when volunteering is for studies of stress, sensory isolation, and hypnosis.

7. Volunteers tend to be more unconventional than nonvolunteers, especially when volunteering is for studies of sex behavior.

8. Females are more likely than males to volunteer for research in general, but less likely than males to volunteer for physically and emotionally stressful research (e.g., electric shock, high temperature, sensory deprivation, interviews about sex behavior).

9. Volunteers tend to be less authoritarian than nonvolunteers.

10. Jews are more likely to volunteer than Protestants, and Protestants are more likely to volunteer than Catholics.

11. Volunteers tend to be less conforming than nonvolunteers when volunteering is for research in general, but not when subjects are female and the task is relatively "clinical" in nature (e.g., hypnosis, sleep, or counseling research).

12. Volunteers tend to be from smaller towns than nonvolunteers, especially when volunteering is for questionnaire studies.

13. Volunteers tend to be more interested in religion than nonvolunteers, especially when volunteering is for questionnaire studies.

14. Volunteers tend to be more altruistic than nonvolunteers.

15. Volunteers tend to be more self-disclosing than nonvolunteers.

16. Volunteers tend to be more maladjusted than nonvolunteers, especially when volunteering is for potentially unusual situations (e.g., drugs, hypnosis, high temperature, or vaguely described experiments) or for medical research employing clinical (rather than psychometric) definitions of psychopathology.

17. Volunteers tend to be younger than nonvolunteers, especially when volunteering is for laboratory research and if they are females.

However, what should it mean to experimentalists who may rely on the use of volunteer subjects for us to say that volunteers are likely to be brighter, more sociable, more approval- and arousal-seeking etc., than nonvolunteers? One answer is that these characteristics may be viewed as a potential problem to be considered by the researchers, inasmuch as they might be viewed as posing a threat to the validity of the research conclusions. That, of course, is a highly speculative answer, and we do not want to misleadingly characterize the volunteer status of the research participant as a potentially serious problem in experimental research if it is not. In fact, there is more direct evidence with which to address this question in the results of a number of quite different experimental studies (e.g., Black, Schumpert, and Welch, 1972; Brower, 1948; Cox and Sipprelle, 1971; Goldstein, Rosnow, Goodstadt, and Suls, 1972; Green, 1963; Horowitz, 1969; Kotses, Glaus, and Fisher, 1974; Remington and Strongman, 1972; Rosnow and Suls, 1970; Straits and Wuebben, 1973).

For example, Kotses, Glaus, and Fisher (1974) compared the autonomic reactions of volunteers and nonvolunteers to random bursts of white noise. The subjects were introductory psychology students who either (1) volunteered without an inducement, (2) volunteered with the promise of being paid a nominal sum, (3) were in a pool in which the inducement was course credit rather than cash, or (4) were a coerced group that received no reward but was penalized for not participating. On one dependent variable, basal skin conductance, the magnitude of the changes was consistently greater in the two volunteer groups; the coercion and pay groups were at opposite ends of the response continuum. On another dependent variable, basal heart rate, the coercion and pay groups were more alike, with the coerced subjects showing the strongest responses.

Granted that it is a problem, how might the characteristics in Table 10.5 lead us to a more cogent understanding of the generalizability (and limitations) of our experimental findings when they are based on the responses of volunteer subjects? The answer will become clear as we view this question in the light of two studies conducted by two leading behavioral researchers of the past, Alfred Kinsey and Abraham Maslow; they will help us to illustrate all the logic that is needed to address this question.

In the 1940s and 1950s, Kinsey and his associates conducted a series of intensive interviews of about 8,000 American men and 12,000 American women in order to uncover the predominant sexual customs in the United States (Kinsey, Pomeroy, and Martin, 1948; Kinsey, Pomeroy, Martin, and Gebhard, 1953). These landmark studies became a source of controversy in the 1950s, however, when critics questioned the external validity of the conclusions reached (Cochran, Mosteller, and Tukey, 1953; Dollard, 1953; Hyman and Sheatsley, 1954). Maslow examined the problem empirically in a study in which it was arranged that Kinsey set up an office near the Brooklyn College campus (where Maslow was teaching at the time) and that appeals be made in Maslow's classes for volunteers to be interviewed by the Kinsey team (Maslow and Sakoda, 1952). Earlier, Maslow had discovered that individuals high in self-esteem (as measured by a paper-and-pencil test) had a strong tendency to express unconventional sexual attitudes (Maslow, 1942). In the follow-up study he now observed that those students who volunteered for the Kinsey interview generally scored higher in self-esteem than others who refused to participate. It follows that Kinsey's survey results may have misestimated (in fact, overestimated) some of the population values because the interviewees were all volunteer subjects.

With the aid of Table 10.5 we can employ a similar logic as that used by Maslow to predict whether the use of volunteer subjects in experimental studies might lead us to overestimate or underestimate a true causal relationship. Suppose we want to assess the validity of a new educational procedure that is designed to make young children less rigid in their thinking. We design an experiment and then ask parents and teachers to volunteer their children as research participants. Suppose the children who are volunteered are, like adults who volunteer themselves, low in authoritarianism (characteristic 9). Because we know that people who are low in authoritarianism are usually less rigid thinkers, we believe that using these subjects will lead us to make a more conservative assessment of the experimental relationship when we compare the results in the experimental group with those in the control group. Knowing what we do, we have greater confidence in the causal relationship to which the visible evidence in this study points.

We can also imagine the opposite type of inferential effect in another situation. Suppose we wanted to find out how persuasive a propaganda appeal was before using it in the field. We find it convenient to use volunteer subjects, and our research design involves assigning them at random to a message treatment or a control group. We know that volunteer subjects tend to be higher in the need for social approval than nonvolunteer subjects (characteristic 4), and we also know that people who score higher in need for approval are more readily influenced by a persuasive message than are low scorers (Buckhout, 1965). Putting this information together, we feel that it would be prudent not to make too strong a claim for the causal relationship that is visible in this study, because we believe the volunteers may have been overreacting in the experimental condition.

IMPROVING GENERALIZABILITY OF INDUCTIVE INFERENCES

Previously, we mentioned some of the ways that are used to try to improve generalizability in survey research by trying to reduce the nonresponse bias. In a similar vein, there are things we can do to try to improve generalizability in experimental research by trying to reduce the volunteer bias. Many institutions deal with this problem by recruiting from courses in which the vast majority of the students will volunteer for research participation to satisfy a course requirement. How can more "nonvolunteer" subjects be enticed into the sampling urn when captive participation is not the norm? On the basis of our review of the literature we would offer the following recommendations (Rosenthal and Rosnow, 1975):

1. Make the appeal for volunteers as interesting as possible, keeping in mind the nature of the target population.
2. Make the appeal for volunteers as nonthreatening as possible so that potential volunteers will not be put off by unwarranted fears of unfavorable evaluation.
3. State the theoretical and practical importance of the research for which volunteering is requested.
4. State in what way the target population is particularly relevant to the research being conducted and emphasize the responsibility potential volunteers have to participate in research that may benefit others.
5. When possible, offer potential volunteers not only pay for participation but also small courtesy gifts simply for taking time to consider whether they will want to participate.
6. Have the request for volunteering made by a person of status as high as possible, preferably by a woman of perceived high status.
7. Whenever possible, avoid research tasks that may be psychologically or biologically stressful.
8. Communicate the fact that volunteering is not an unusual behavior but, rather, is the norm.

9. After a target population has been defined, try to have someone known to that population make the appeal for volunteers—this request should be even more successful if a personalized appeal is made.

10. In situations where volunteering is regarded by the target population as normative, establish opportunities for "public" commitment to volunteer (e.g., ask the potential participants to raise their hand to volunteer); where non-volunteering is regarded as normative, follow a procedure involving "private" commitment (e.g., ask them to sign their name on a piece of paper that only the researcher will see).

A hasty reading of these recommendations might give the impression that they are designed only to increase rates of volunteering and thus to decrease volunteer bias. A more careful reading will reveal that the recommendations should have other benefits as well. They may make us more careful and thoughtful not only in how we make our appeals for research participants, but also in how we plan the research. Our relations with our potential subjects may become more reciprocal and more human, and our procedures may in turn become more humane. If we are to tell our subjects as much as possible about the significance of our research—as though they were another granting agency (which in fact they are, granting us time instead of money)—then we may also have to give up trivial research. We have more to say about ethics and values in human behavioral research in the next chapter.

REPRESENTATIVE RESEARCH DESIGNS

In this discussion we have focused primarily on the subject side of the experimenter-subject equation, but in some research it is particularly important to consider the representativeness of the experimenter as stimulus. Suppose we wanted to test the hypothesis that men and women respond differently to an experimental treatment when the experimenter is a man as opposed to a woman. A convenient design might consist of randomly assigning subjects of both sexes to a male or female experimenter. The problem with this design is that it is only representative in the context of the selection of subjects. It is not representative as regards the stimulus, the experimenter himself or herself. Because the design does not sample from among populations of experimenters and situations, we would be hard-pressed to conclude whether there is, or is not, a general relationship of the type hypothesized. It is possible that using other male or female experimenters would produce quite different results.

The problem, then, is that our use of only one person of each sex as a stimulus does not preclude the possibility that some of the other characteristics of this person may have stimulus value that is unknown and uncontrolled. There are, in other words, two major limitations of this "single-stimulus" experimental design (Maher, 1978). First, it is possible that obtained differences between those subjects who were exposed to the male experimenter and those who were exposed to the female experimenter may be due to the effects of uncontrolled stimulus variables. On the basis only of the information furnished by our data, we cannot tell whether the obtained differences are due to the validity of the tested hypothesis or to the effects of the uncontrolled variables (another threat to internal validity). Second, a lack of obtained differences between those subjects who were exposed to the male experimenter and those exposed to the female experimenter may also be due to the presence of an uncontrolled stimulus variable operating either to counteract the effect of the intended independent variable or to increase that effect artificially to a *ceiling* value (i.e., a top limit) in the different groups. Again, we have no way of distinguishing between this explanation and the possibility that the lack of difference is due to the invalidity of the tested hypothesis.

To deal with these concerns, Egon Brunswik (1947) introduced the notion of a *representative research design*, by which he meant that one would sample from both subjects and stimuli. If the stimulus is a person, then no satisfactory alternative exists to adequate sampling of stimulus persons, despite the cost of increasing the number of experimenters. Of course, there could be tangential benefits of increasing the number of experimenters, such as the ability to randomize expectancies, to permit statistical correction of expectancy effects, and so forth (discussed in Chapter 6). To achieve such results one would have to plan the research in such a way as to take further advantage of the fact of having employed a representative research design. Interestingly, Brunswik also advocated this as a "standard" approach in laboratory experimental research, i.e., whenever the researcher wishes to generalize from the particular stimulus to a population of stimuli representing the independent variable of interest.

CHAPTER
11

ETHICS AND VALUES IN HUMAN SUBJECT RESEARCH

WRONGS AND RIGHTS OF BEHAVIOR

The concept of *values* refers to the standards or principles by which the worth of something is judged, and that of *ethics* to the system of moral values by which the wrongs and rights of behavior (including the scientist's behavior) are judged. For a long time it was argued that science is neutral with regard to morality. Some theorists sought to draw a distinction between the natural and the behavioral sciences. The subject matter of the behavioral sciences makes it more difficult to maintain moral detachment, whereas that of the natural sciences may be more easily viewed with moral neutrality because it does not have human beings at its core. This distinction crumbled with the development of atomic physics and other scientific triumphs, as unrest surfaced concerning the morality of some of the most basic research in natural science. In this chapter we discuss the ethical dilemmas faced by behavioral scientists who are engaged in empirical research with human participants. Today, we no longer think of science (natural, biological, biomedical, behavioral, etc.) as an endless frontier unbounded by moral constraints of any sort (e.g., Beecher, 1970; Bok, 1978; Delgado and Leskovac, 1986; Holton and Morison, 1978; Katz, 1972; Kimmel, 1981, 1988; Schuler, 1982; Sieber, 1982).

By the late 1970s, most researchers had become accustomed to having an institutional review board (IRB) peer over their shoulders. Assurances of informed consent and peer review had been mandated by the U.S. government under a provision of the National Health Research Act of 1974, and a university that had any type of federal contract or grant was held accountable to federal guidelines regarding human subject research (cf. Kimmel, 1979, 1988). Basic questions were raised, however, about the effectiveness of the IRB approach in enforcing informed consent guidelines (Gray, Cooke, and Tannenbaum, 1978). In a famous case, an electroshock experiment by social psychologists to test a "suffering leads to liking" hypothesis was roundly attacked when it was disclosed that the voluntary consent of the participants had not been obtained (Smith, 1977; Tedeschi and Gallup, 1977; Tedeschi and Rosenfeld, 1981). The university charged with this violation was threatened with a cutoff of all federal funds for research, even though the experiment in question had not been federally funded.

We note the ethical recommendations of the American Psychological Association (APA), which were promulgated as a means of bridging the gap between ethical thought and the treatment of human subjects. (Other APA ethical requirements deal with the treatment of animal subjects in psychological experimentation.) The codification idea goes back to 1947, when a code of biomedical research ethics was advanced at the Nuremberg War Tribunal after World War II (Sasson and Nelson, 1969). Some behavioral researchers question the appropriateness of the APA imperatives, which they characterize as "mounting a . . . cannon to shoot a mouse" (Gergen, 1973a). The context in which such criticisms first surfaced is elaborated in this chapter.

We shall also focus on the insufficiency of the decision process implicit in assessments of the ethical worth of empirical research (cf. Rosnow, 1990). Figure 11-1 shows a decision-plane model that exemplifies the way in which most re-

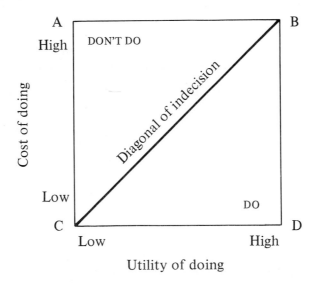

FIGURE 11-1
A decision-plane model of the costs and utilities of doing research. Studies falling at point *A* are *not* carried out, while studies at point *D* are carried out. Studies falling along the diagonal of indecision, *B-C*, are too hard to decide about.

searchers weigh the potential benefits from research against the risks to the human participants (Rosenthal and Rosnow, 1984). The "cost of doing" might include possible harm to subjects, time, expenditures of money, and effort, whereas the "utility of doing" might include benefits to people at this time and place, benefits to other people at other times and places, and benefits to the investigators. Risk-benefit analyses of this kind, because of inherent ambiguities, are difficult to justify when they fail to delineate the costs (and utilities) of *not* conducting a particular study.

Before we turn to these topics (as well as the problems of informed consent, the use of deception in research, and procedures for debriefing subjects), it is instructive to pose some ethical questions for readers to ponder. The dilemmas confronted by researchers are often complex, as the cases in the following two sections illustrate. We shall see that the dilemmas arise as much from the different philosophical views of people as from the nature of the research.

REACTION TO MILGRAM STUDIES

One set of studies in particular, those conducted by social psychologist Stanley Milgram (1963, 1965, 1975, 1977) beginning in the 1960s, has borne the brunt of much of the misgivings by behavioral researchers themselves (cf. Holden, 1979). To review, Milgram experimented on how far people would go in subjecting another person to pain at the order of an authority figure. Volunteer subjects, placed in the role of the "teacher," were deceived into believing that they would be giving varying degrees of painful electric shocks to another person (the "learner") each time he made a mistake in a learning task. Milgram also varied the physical proximity between the teacher and the learner, to see whether the teacher would be less ruthless in administering the electric shocks as he or she got closer to the learner. The results were that a great many subjects (the teachers) unhesitatingly obeyed the experimenter's command as they continued to increase the level of shocks administered to the learner. Even when there was feedback from the learner, who pretended to cry out in pain, many subjects were obedient to the authority of the experimenter's order to "please continue" or "you have no choice, you must go on."

The subjects were not told at the outset that the shock apparatus was a fake but were extensively debriefed once the experiment was over. Even though the learner was a confederate of Milgram's and there were no actual shocks transmitted, concerns about ethics and values have dogged these studies since they were first reported. For instance, psychologist Diana Baumrind (1964) quoted Milgram's own descriptions of the reactions of some of his participants:

> I observed a mature and initially poised businessman enter the laboratory smiling and confident. Within 20 minutes he was reduced to a twitching, stuttering wreck, who was rapidly approaching a point of nervous collapse. He constantly pulled on his earlobe, and twisted his hands. At one point he pushed his fist into his forehead and muttered: "Oh God, let's stop it." And yet he continued to respond to every word of the experimenter and obeyed to the end (Milgram, 1963, p. 377).

Baumrind posed the question of why Milgram had not terminated the investigation when he saw that it was so stressful to his subjects. She concluded that there could be no rational basis for doing this kind of research, unless the participants were previously informed of the dangers to themselves and effective steps were assured to restore their state of well-being afterward.

Milgram (1964) replied that it was not his intention to create stress, and, further, the extreme tension induced in some subjects had not been expected. Before carrying out the research he asked professional colleagues for their opinions, and none of the experts anticipated the behavior that subsequently resulted. He stated that he also thought the subjects would refuse to follow orders. In spite of the dramatic appearance of stress there was no real indication of injurious effects to the subjects, he added. In fact, the subjects and the learner had a friendly reconciliation after the study was completed, and the subjects were shown that the learner had not received dangerous electric shocks but had only pretended to receive them. Milgram also sent questionnaires to the subjects to elicit their reactions after they had read a full report of his investigation. Less than 1 percent regretted having participated, 15 percent were neutral or ambivalent, and over 80 percent responded that they were glad to have participated.

Another major criticism was that Milgram had instilled in his subjects a general distrust of authority, and this was unethical. He responded that the experimenter in this research was not just any authority, but someone who told the participants to act harshly and inhumanely toward another person. Milgram added that he "would consider it of the highest value if participation in the experiment could, indeed, inculcate a skepticism of this kind of authority" (Milgram, 1964).

Is morality in the eyes of the beholder? Ethical questions are often answered quite differently depending on whether the respondent implicitly subscribes to a consequentialist, a deontological, or a more pluralistic philosophy of morality (see Forsyth, 1980). The *consequentialist* view holds that an action is right or wrong depending on its consequences, whereas the *deontological* view insists that certain actions are "categorically" wrong no matter their consequences. Milgram deceived his subjects, and that was categorically wrong if we believe that lying in any form is immoral. Might it be argued that Baumrind's perception of Milgram's research was influenced by her knowledge of his results (the consequentialist approach), just as Milgram's perception was colored by his own, more *pluralistic* approach (i.e., containing elements of both the consequentialist and deontological points of view, but not a blanket condemnation of deception)?

Suppose that Milgram had *not* deceived his subjects, i.e., that he really had them shock the learner. Would the studies be *more* ethically objectionable? Or did Milgram wrong his subjects simply by virtue of the fact that he exposed them to a possibility of unwanted and unasked-for self-knowledge (cf. Cassell, 1982). How we reply to such questions reveals our own implicit values as consequentialist, deontological, or pluralistic (cf. Forsyth and Pope, 1984; Smith, 1983; Waterman, 1988).

CASES INVOLVING DECEPTION, UNFAIRNESS, AND INVASION OF PRIVACY

Another famous case, the "tearoom trade" study of Laud Humphreys done in the 1960s, raised ethical questions involving deception and the invasion of privacy in participant-observer studies. Humphreys, working on his doctoral dissertation research, conducted a study designed to learn about the motives and lifestyles of men who ostensibly led normal heterosexual lives in the community but then frequented public restrooms ("tearooms") to engage in homosexual activities (Humphreys, 1975).

Humphreys set himself up as a "watchqueen" (i.e., a lookout with the responsibility of warning the men who were engaged in homosexual activity) in a public lavatory in St. Louis, Missouri. After gaining the confidence of some of the men, he disclosed his role and the purpose of this pretense and encouraged their assistance in his research. Suspecting, however, that those with whom he had shared confidences may have been a nonrepresentative sample of tearoom participants, he asked them to help in locating others in the community who participated in the tearoom trade. To widen his sample of participants he also surreptitiously recorded the license numbers of the cars driven by the homosexual subjects. Afterward, he represented himself as a "market researcher" in order to find out the names and addresses of the owners from the Department of Motor Vehicles. A year later, he joined a public health survey team, changed his hairstyle, and approached the men for interviews in the guise of a public health researcher (Holden, 1979).

This research has been subject to several misgivings similar to those of Milgram's studies. The critics have argued that Humphreys lied to his subjects and to the Department of Motor Vehicles and also invaded the privacy of his subjects without their informed consent. Some faculty members at the institution at which Humphreys had done his doctoral work were so outraged that they demanded (unsuccessfully) that he be stripped of his Ph.D. degree (Kimmel, 1988). Humphreys, in his own defense, responded that he was scrupulous in protecting the confidentiality of the replies of his subjects, and that to get valid scientific results he had to do what he did. Does the utility of the research (i.e., its knowledge value) serve to outweigh the costs incurred by the deception and invasion of privacy experienced by the subjects? Was lying justified in this case?

Another famous case involved a 1973 field experiment designed in part to improve the quality of work life at the Rushton Mining Company in Pennsylvania (Blumberg, 1980; Susman, 1976). The Rushton project, developed on the basis of earlier research in the United Kingdom (Trist and Bamforth, 1951; Trist, Higgin, Murray, and Pollock, 1963), had as its specific aims to improve employee skills, safety, and job satisfaction while raising the level of performance and company earnings (Blumberg and Pringle, 1983).

After months of preparation by the researchers and the mining company, a call was issued for volunteers for a work group that would have direct responsibility for the production in one section of the mining operations. The volunteers were instructed to abandon their traditional roles and, after extensive training in safety laws, good mining practices, and job safety analysis, were then left to co-ordinate their own activities. Paid at the top rate, that of the highest-skilled job classification on that section, not surprisingly they became enthusiastic propo-nents of "our way of working."

All was not so rosy in the rest of the mine, however. Other workers, those in the control condition, expressed resentment and anger at the "haughtiness" of the volunteers. Why, they had even been treated to a steak and lobster dinner by the president of the company, the others complained! Why should these "inexpe-rienced" volunteers receive special treatment and higher pay than other miners with many more years on the job? Rumors circulated through the mine that the volunteers were "riding the gravy train," being "spoon-fed," and that autonomy was a "communist plot" because all the volunteers received the same rate yet the company was "making out" at their expense. The researchers were rumored to be "pinko" college people who wanted to "bust the union" (Blumberg and Pringle, 1983). The seeds of conflict were planted, and after a while the experiment had to be terminated.

In this case we see that action research can have its own set of problems, quite apart from those encountered by Milgram and by Humphreys. There was no deception or invasion of privacy in this experiment, but there was the prob-lem of "fairness" because a sizable number of workers (nonvolunteers, to be sure) did not receive the benefits enjoyed by those in the experimental group.

Still other ethical risks may be incurred in studies of this kind, and also in participant-observer studies. For example, there may be a moral cost involved simply in the publication of the results. That is, the report might (1) upset some persons who are able to identify themselves in the publication, (2) subject the community to possible embarrassment or to unwanted publicity, (3) make those who are identifiable vulnerable to others who have power over them, and (4) pos-sibly even weaken the scientific enterprise by communicating to people that sci-ence is exploitative (Johnson, 1982).

On the other hand, what would be the social and scientific costs of *not* dis-seminating research findings? In Chapter 1 we listed the ability to communicate, and by extension the written record itself, as one of the essentials of good scien-tific practice. The written record of the search for truth is the official archive that tells us about the observations that were made, the hypotheses that were tested (and those that were ignored), the ideas that were found wanting and those that withstood the test of further observations. As Barrass stated, "Scientists must write, therefore, so that their discoveries may be known to others" (1978, p. 25).

Deception, unfairness, invasion of privacy—these and other issues are not strictly limited to research situations. One author (Broome, 1984) discussed the ethical issue of fairness in selecting people for chronic hemodialysis (a medical procedure that can save the life of a person whose kidneys have failed). It is ex-pensive, and in many countries there are just not enough facilities available to treat everyone who could benefit. Because without treatment a patient quickly dies, how should a candidate for hemodialysis be selected? First come, first serve is one way that some hospitals pick candidates. The inventor of hemodialysis, B. H. Scribner in Seattle, is said to have selected people on the basis of their being under 40 years old, free from cardiovascular disease, pillars of the community, and contributors to the community's economics. He is also said to have taken into account whether they were married and whether they went to church.

Still another procedure is randomness. Broome points out that selecting people randomly—such as using a lottery to choose conscripts to fight in a war— is often justified as the "fairest" procedure because everyone has an equal shot at being selected for life or death. But suppose conscripts for the military are instead selected not randomly but on the grounds of who is the biggest and strongest? Which procedure is fairer—randomness or selection on the grounds of who is more likely to survive? Some hospitals choose candidates for hemodialysis on the basis of a lottery. In one variant (reminiscent of stratified random sampling) the patients are sorted into medically suitable and unsuitable groups (based on other health factors) and a random mechanism first applied to the suitables is then used to make the final judgment.

DECEPTION VERSUS OPENNESS IN BEHAVIORAL RESEARCH

In biomedical practice it may be fairness that is at issue, but in behavioral science it is more often "openness in research" that is in question. Imagine an experiment in which the experimenter greeted the subjects by saying, "Hello, today we are going to investigate the effects of physical distance from the victim on willingness to inflict pain on him. You will be in the 'close' condition, which means that you are expected to be somewhat less ruthless. In addition, you will be asked to fill out a test of fascist tendencies because we believe there is a positive relation between scores on our fascism test and obedience to an authority who requests that we hurt others. Any questions?"

A completely open statement to a research subject of what he or she is doing in an experiment might involve a briefing of this kind. Such a briefing would be manifestly absurd in this case if we were serious in our efforts to learn about human behavior. In other cases as well, if the subjects had full information about the scientists' experimental plans, procedures, and hypotheses, we might very well develop a science based on what the subjects thought the world was like or what the subjects believed the experimenters thought the world was like. Subjects' awareness of demand characteristics, coupled with their tendency to want to be "good subjects" or to "look good" in the eyes of the experimenter, could lead to a collision between ethics and artifacts (Suls and Rosnow, 1981, 1988).

Many researchers view the problem of the subjects' knowledge of the true intent of the experiment as sufficiently threatening to the validity (internal, external, construct) of the research that in many cases they have routinely employed one form or another of deception in their investigations (see Adair, Dushenko, and Lindsay, 1984; Arellano-Galdames, 1972; Gross and Fleming, 1982; Menges, 1973). One kind, deception by commission (i.e., *active deception*), might include (1) misrepresentation of the purpose of the investigation, (2) untrue statements about the identity of the researcher, (3) false promises, (4) violation of the promise of anonymity, (5) incorrect explanations of equipment and procedures, (6) use of confederates (pseudosubjects), and (7) use of placebos and secret application of medications and drugs (Arellano-Galdames, 1972). Another kind, deception by omission (i.e., *passive deception*), might include (1) concealed observation, (2) provocation and secret recording of negatively evaluated behavior, (3) unrecognized participant observation, (4) use of projective techniques and other personality tests, and (5) unrecognized conditioning of subjects' behaviors (Arellano-Galdames, 1972).

There are very few behavioral scientists who would advocate the use of deception for its own sake. Indeed, some take the position that deceptions are often counterproductive both methodologically and ethically. Psychologist Herbert C. Kelman (1968) comments:

> From a long-range point of view, there is obviously something self-defeating about the use of deception. As we continue to carry out research of this kind, our potential subjects become more and more sophisticated, and we become less and less able to meet the conditions that our experimental procedures require. Moreover, as we continue to carry out research of this kind, our potential subjects become increasingly distrustful of us, and our future relations with them are likely to be undermined. Thus, we are confronted with the anomalous circumstance that the more research we do, the more difficult and questionable it becomes (p. 220).

At the same time, there are perhaps few researchers who feel that behavioral science can do entirely without some of the deception practices noted above. No behavioral scientist would seriously advocate giving up the study of prejudice and discrimination. Yet, if all measures of prejudice and discrimination had to be openly labeled as such, it is questionable that it would be worth the effort to continue this research.

Were we to adopt a rigid moral orientation that decries deception as categorically wrong, then all forms of deception would need to be banished or ruled out. However, most people—behavioral scientists included—are willing to weigh and measure their sins, judging some to be larger than others. In the case of deception, fairly good agreement could probably be obtained on the proposition that refraining from telling a subject that an "experiment in the learning of verbal materials is designed to show whether earlier, later, or intermediate material is better remembered" is not a particularly serious breach of ethical moral values. The reason most behavioral scientists would probably not view this deception with alarm seems, on first glance, due to its involving an *omission* (passive deception) rather than a *commission* (active deception). A truth is left unspoken; a lie is not told. But what if the same experiment were presented as a "study of the effects of meaningfulness of verbal material on retention or recall"? That is a direct lie, designed to mislead the subject's attention from the temporal order of the material to some other factor in which the scientist is really not interested. Nevertheless, that change does not seem to make the deception so much more heinous even though now the "sin" is one of commission and the scientist has not withheld information from, but actively lied to, the subject.

It does not seem, then, that the active or passive style of a deception is its measure. Instead, its probable effect on the subject is what is significant, which brings us back to the consequentialist approach to ethics. That is, very few people would care whether subjects focused on the meaningfulness of verbal material rather than on the temporal order, because there seems to be no consequence (positive or negative) of this deception. It appears that it is not deception so much as it is *harmful* deception that we would like to minimize, and that it is the degree of harmfulness on which researchers may be able to agree fairly well.

On the one hand, most researchers would probably agree that it is not very harmful to subjects to be told that a test they are taking anonymously as part of the research is one of "personal reactions" (which it is) rather than a test of need for social approval, schizophrenic tendencies, or authoritarianism (which it may also be). On the other hand, most researchers would also probably agree that it could be harmful to college-aged students to be falsely told that a test shows them to be "abnormal" even if they are later told that they had been misled. Some of the potentially most harmful deceptions ought never to be employed, but then in behavioral science they are quite rare in any case. For the great bulk of deceptions for which there may be a range of potentially negative consequences, the investigator, colleagues, and to some extent, ultimately, the general community must decide whether the particular deception is worth the potential increase in knowledge.

FEDERAL AND SCIENTIFIC OVERSIGHT PROCEDURES

In the late 1960s and early 1970s, dramatic cases in biomedical research came to light that had resulted in serious damage or even death to the subjects (Beecher, 1966, 1970; Katz, 1972). The matter of human subject research, whether in biomedicine or behavioral science, became a public issue. It was discussed in journals and in magazines and newspapers, and became the topic of congressional hearings and professional conferences. In 1974, federal guidelines in the United States for protecting the rights and welfare of human research subjects were formulated. They have now been amended several times and appear in their latest form (in Titles 21 and 45 of the Code of Federal Regulations) as a "common core" of federal governance for all research conducted, supported, or regulated by the federal government. As a condition of receiving federal funding, an institution is legally required to file an "assurance" that any research will meet prescribed standards and requirements for informed consent, and that an IRB composed of a cross section of the scientific and lay communities will be established to review proposed and ongoing research projects (Delgado and Leskovac, 1986).

Previously, we alluded to the Nuremberg Code, which was developed to deal with the harms of medical research conducted by Nazi physicians on civilian prisoners in concentration camps during World War II. Most modern codes of ethics referring to human subject research can be understood as deriving from the principles of the Nuremberg Code, which stated that (1) voluntary consent of the human subject is required, (2) the subject must be fully informed of the nature and risks of experimentation, (3) any such risks should be avoided whenever possible in the design of the experiment, (4) the subject should be protected against even remote hazards, (5) the experiment should be conducted only by scientifically qualified persons, (6) the subject must be at liberty to terminate the experiment at any time, and (7) the scientist must also be prepared to terminate the experiment if at any time he or she has probable cause to believe that a continuation is likely to result in injury, disability, or death to the subject.

Proceeding along similar lines, various professional and scientific organizations in the United States and abroad have formulated their own general guidelines to help researchers reach a reasoned decision about the protection of their research participants. In the United States, a committee formed by the American Psychological Association drafted a code of ethics that was then adopted by APA and published in 1973. A decade later, the code was revised, with the 10 ethical guidelines shown below representing the core of the requirements insisted on by APA:

> The decision to undertake research rests upon a considered judgment by the individual psychologist about how best to contribute to psychological science and human welfare. Having made the decision to conduct research, the psychologist considers alternative directions in which research energies and resources might be invested. On the basis of this consideration, the psychologist carries out the investigation with respect and concern for the dignity and welfare of the people who participate and with cognizance of federal and state regulations and professional standards governing the conduct of research with human participants.
>
> A. In planning a study, the investigator has the responsibility to make a careful evaluation of its ethical acceptability. To the extent that the weighing of scientific and human values suggests a compromise of any principle, the investigator incurs a correspondingly serious obligation to seek ethical advice and to observe stringent safeguards to protect the rights of human participants.
>
> B. Considering whether a participant in a planned study will be a "subject at risk" or a "subject at minimal risk," according to recognized standards, is of primary ethical concern to the investigator.
>
> C. The investigator always retains the responsibility for ensuring ethical practice in research. The investigator is also responsible for the ethical treatment of research participants by collaborators, assistants, students, and employees, all of whom, however, incur similar obligations.
>
> D. Except in minimal-risk research, the investigator establishes a clear and fair agreement with research participants prior to their participation, that clarifies the obligations and responsibilities of each. The investigator has the obligation to honor all promises and commitments included in that agreement. The investigator informs the participants of all aspects of the research that might reasonably be expected to influence willingness to participate and explains all other aspects of the research about which the participants inquire. Failure to make full disclosure prior to obtaining informed consent requires additional safeguards to protect the welfare and dignity of the research participants. Research with children or with participants who have impairments that would limit understanding and/or communication requires special safeguarding procedures.
>
> E. Methodological requirements of a study may make the use of concealment or deception necessary. Before conducting such a study, the investigator has a spe-

cial responsibility to (1) determine whether the use of such techniques is justified by the study's prospective scientific, educational, or applied value; (2) determine whether alternative procedures are available that do not use concealment or deception; and (3) ensure that the participants are provided with sufficient explanation as soon as possible.

F. The investigator respects the individual's freedom to decline to participate in or to withdraw from the research at any time. The obligation to protect this freedom requires careful thought and consideration when the investigator is in a position of authority or influence over the participant. Such positions of authority include, but are not limited to, situations in which research participation is required as part of employment or in which the participant is a student, client, or employee of the investigator.

G. The investigator protects the participant from physical and mental discomfort, harm, and danger that may arise from research procedures. If risks of such consequences exist, the investigator informs the participant of that fact. Research procedures likely to cause serious or lasting harm to a participant are not used unless the failure to use these procedures might expose the participant to risk of greater harm or unless the research has great potential benefit and fully informed and voluntary consent is obtained from each participant. The participant should be informed of procedures for contacting the investigator within a reasonable time period following participation should stress, potential harm, or related questions or concerns arise.

H. After the data are collected, the investigator provides the participant with information about the nature of the study and attempts to remove any misconceptions that may have arisen. Where scientific or humane values justify delaying or withholding this information, the investigator incurs a special responsibility to monitor the research and to ensure that there are no damaging consequences for the participant.

I. Where research procedures result in undesirable consequences for the individual participant, the investigator has the responsibility to detect and remove or correct these consequences, including long-term effects.

J. Information obtained about a research participant during the course of an investigation is confidential unless otherwise agreed upon in advance. When the possibility exists that others may obtain access to such information, this possibility, together with the plans for protecting confidentiality, is explained to the participant as part of the procedure for obtaining informed consent.[1]

Drawing from philosophy, law, and the American experience, European psychologists had by the early 1980s formulated their own codes of ethical principles to help them meet their responsibilities to subjects (Schuler, 1981). Three principles that appear without exception in all European and American codes are (1) avoid physical harm, (2) avoid psychological harm, and (3) keep the data confidential (Schuler, 1982). The third requirement, which evolved to safeguard the information divulged by clients in clinical situations, is commonly justified on the basis of three claims: (1) that fairness requires respect for the research participant's privacy, (2) that psychological researchers have the professional right to keep such disclosures secret, and (3) that more honest responding by subjects

---

[1]Copyrighted in 1983 by the American Psychological Association and reprinted with permission.

should result when the investigator has promised to keep disclosures confidential (cf. Bok, 1978).

In spite of these ethical safeguards, critics see certain deficiencies in the current approach to protecting the rights of research participants. Except for federal regulations, very few codes have incorporated much in the way of penalties for noncompliance. The negative sanction for violating the requirements listed above are censure or expulsion from APA—by no means considered a severe penalty, because many psychologists engaged in productive, rewarding research careers do not belong to APA. As to the federal requirement of informed consent, the critics argue that it is weakened by a conflict of values between the researcher and the subject (Delgado and Leskovac, 1986). Presumably, the researcher is under pressures to produce publishable results, and these pressures may, consciously or subconsciously, disincline him or her to give full weight to the nuances of informed consent.

WHEN ETHICS AND ARTIFACTS COLLIDE

Earlier, we alluded to another side of this issue, which is that compliance with human subjects regulations presents a dilemma for behavioral researchers who are also concerned about minimizing subject-experimenter artifacts (Chapter 6). Providing the subjects with an explanation of the true purposes and procedures of the experiment may in some cases exacerbate the problem of demand characteristics and subject role behavior. To reveal to subjects the exact nature of the research in which they are participating might distort their reactions and severely jeopardize the tenability of the inferred causal relationships (Suls and Rosnow, 1981). These problems were dramatically demonstrated in two recent investigations.

Gerald T. Gardner (1978) performed a series of studies to examine the effects of noise on task performance. The purpose of the research was to replicate a widely cited phenomenon first reported by David Glass and Jerome Singer (1972), indicating that exposure to uncontrollable, unpredictable noise has negative aftereffects on task performance. Although Gardner's initial experiments duplicated Glass and Singer's findings, his two subsequent experiments did not, resulting in null effects. Bewildered by this outcome he searched for an explanation of the discrepancy. The only difference in procedure between the early and later studies in the series was that the first studies had been performed before the implementation of federal guidelines requiring informed consent, while the later studies were carried out using informed consent. To assess the possibility that openness in the research was responsible for the different results, Gardner conducted a final study in which two groups were exposed to uncontrollable noise, except that in one group there was informed consent while in the other there was not. Results of this study indicated that the procedure using openness prevented the emergence of negative aftereffects of the noise.

Gardner theorized that significant effects did not emerge because the openness created a perception in the subjects of control over the noise. Specifically, perceived control "could result from references . . . in the consent form to subjects' ability to withdraw from the experiment without penalty, to their freedom to choose an alternative to [subject] pool participation" (Gardner, 1978, p. 633). Apparently, conforming to the new ethical guidelines in this instance seriously impaired the emergence of the effects of laboratory stressors. Had federal guidelines been instituted when Glass and Singer initiated their research in the late 1960s, is it at least possible that some significant facts about environmental noise pollution would never have come to light?

A second study implies that very strict adherence to informed consent guidelines can sometimes result in findings opposite to those usually obtained. Clinical researchers Jerome H. Resnick and Thomas Schwartz (1973) used different ethical codes as the independent variable and assessed the effects of these codes on their experimental data. The experiment employed a widely used verbal conditioning task in which the experimenter says "good" or "okay" each time the subject begins a sentence with the pronoun *I* or *we* (called the *Taffel task*). However, half of the subjects were forewarned of the exact nature of the task in strict adherence with informed consent guidelines, while the remaining subjects were not fully informed of the exact nature of the study or its purpose. Resnick and Schwartz found that the latter group of subjects was conditioned as would be expected from previous research, but subjects in the former group (the "ethical" condition) showed a surprising reversal in conditioning rate. Had the classical research employing the Taffel task been carried out under maximally ethical conditions as defined by the APA ethics code, it seems at least possible that our scientific principles of verbal learning would all be reversed. Thus it appears that the behavioral scientist is caught between the Scylla of methodological precision and the Charybdis of ethical concerns.

STRATEGIES OF COMPROMISE AND RESOLUTION

While the problem may be clear, there are no easy solutions to it. Some theorists believe that a solution can be found in some middle ground (see Suls and Rosnow, 1981). To begin with the ethics side, it should be acknowledged that while there have been some dramatic cases in which subject safety has been risked, those cases are clearly in the minority. Social psychologist Kenneth Gergen (1973a) commented:

> Most of us have encountered studies that arouse moral indignation. We do not wish to see such research carried out in the profession. However, the important question is whether the principles we establish to prevent these few experiments from being conducted may not obviate the vast majority of contemporary research. We may be mounting a very dangerous cannon to shoot a mouse (p. 908).

One issue is whether the psychologists and other professionals who sit on review boards really have accurate perceptions about the degree of stress that experimental manipulations impose on the research subjects. In a questionnaire study, undergraduate students and psychologists were presented with a hypothetical experiment from a group of experiments that differed in the stress, physical pain, or threat to self-esteem that was inflicted on the subjects (Sullivan and Deiker, 1973). The students were asked whether they would have volunteered for the experiment had they known its exact nature and whether they felt that the procedures were unethical. The psychologists were asked about the propriety of using deception in each instance and whether the subjects would volunteer had they known the stress they would have to endure. Interestingly, a high percentage of the students indicated that they would have volunteered even if they had known about the aversive aspects of the studies, but the psychologists were far more negative toward present practices than the students.

The disclosure of information constitutes a separate issue. Are there instances when the disclosure of information would be more stressful than its nondisclosure? Resnick and Schwartz (1973), in their research described above, also posed the intriguing theoretical question: "Does being ethical trigger paranoid ideation in otherwise nonsuspicious subjects?" Is it possible in some cases that informed consent information could put the subject in a kind of "double bind," i.e., one producing more stress than if he or she had been left in the dark about the nature and intent of the study?

The possibility must also be considered that, even if powerful deceptions are used, the investigators may relieve the subject of any problems or concerns provoked by the experimental situation through careful debriefing. Kelman rightfully admonishes, "A good rule is that the subject ought not leave the laboratory with greater anxiety or lower self-esteem than he came in with" (1968, p. 222). It could be difficult to determine that this goal had been met, but there are procedures (discussed in a moment) that are designed to reduce the effects of stressful and deceptive instructions and experimental manipulations. Three steps seem necessary: (1) a careful debriefing immediately after the subject's participation, (2) a clear explanation of why deception was necessary (if it was deemed vital), and (3) an expression by the experimenter of regret for the necessity of the use of deception (see Carlsmith, Ellsworth, and Aronson, 1976; Tesch, 1977).

The presence of artifacts and the need for deception also require reexamination. Researchers might consider the possibility that the techniques employed to detect demand characteristics (discussed in Chapter 6) can also be used to minimize the level of deception in some studies. The quasi-control group is employed as a check for demand characteristics, and if none are uncovered, the investigator proceeds with the experiment. In the interests of both ethics and the control of artifacts the experimenter could then consider whether it may be possible to reduce the level of deception. To do so, the experimenter would develop a less deceptive manipulation and then run the quasi-control subjects again. If the subjects remained unaware of the demands, then the experimenter would use this lower level of deception and presumably still achieve the same purpose. In this way, concerns about artifacts and ethics can strengthen rather than work against each other. Such procedures are obviously time-consuming (and perhaps more costly), but given recent regulations, researchers may be forced to use additional techniques to keep deception at a minimum and to ensure that demand cues are not operating (e.g., Atwell, 1981; Smith, 1983; Suls and Rosnow, 1981).

HAMLET'S QUESTION APPLIED TO ETHICAL CONDUCT

It is also possible that a reciprocal resolution of the artifacts-ethics dilemma could be found if both investigators and review boards would adopt a wider decision-making process that considered the costs of harmful deception, the utility of possible research findings, and the costs of not conducting the study. This last consideration is sometimes overlooked. As John Darley (1980) has written, there is an ethical imperative to do sound research, for if we do not, then "we leave those who are attempting social change the prey of hucksters who are willing to put forth undocumented claims based on inadequate evidence" (p. 15). *To be or not to be* concerned with the moral and practical implications of research—Hamlet's question applied to the values and conduct of human subject research—needs to be applied to the costs and utilities of doing and not doing research (Rosenthal and Rosnow, 1984).

In this case the model in Figure 11-1 will prove to be insufficient, because it fails to consider the costs (and utilities) of *not* conducting a particular study. The failure to conduct a study that would be conducted is as much an act to be evaluated on ethical grounds as is the conducting of a study. The psychologist whose study might reduce violence or prejudice or mental illness, but who refuses to do the study because it involves an invasion of privacy, is making a decision that is to be evaluated on ethical grounds as surely as the decision of a researcher to investigate psychological problems with a procedure that carries a certain cost. The psychologist has not solved an ethical problem but only traded one problem for another. It would seem the conventional model requires a balancing of considerations based on a more complete analysis of the costs and utilities of *doing* and *not doing* a study.

This more complete analysis can be represented by the two decision squares shown in Figure 11-2 or by the two-dimensional model shown in Figure 11-3 (Rosenthal and Rosnow, 1984). Figure 11-2 is self-explanatory. Suppose, however, we added a new diagonal *A-D* (not shown) to these two squares and called it the "decision diagonal" (in contrast to *B-C* and *B'-C'*, the diagonals of indecision). For any point in the square of *doing* there would be a location on the cost axis and on the utility axis. Any such point can then be translated to an equivalent position on the decision diagonal. For example, if a point were twice as far from *A* as from *D*, we would see the translated point as located two-thirds of the way on the decision diagonal *A-D* (i.e., closer to *D* than to *A*). The same thing would apply to *not doing*, except now closeness to *A'* would mean "do" rather than "not do."

Putting these decision diagonals together gives Figure 11-3, and we are now back to two dimensions. In this composite plane, points near *D* tell us to do the study. Points near *D'* tell us not to do the study. Points on the indecision diagonal leave us unsure. Points on the *D'-D* decision diagonal (not shown) tell us whether we are closer to "don't do" or "do."

The purpose of Figure 11-3 is to get us to think about issues of cost and utility in terms of a more complete analysis. In recent years we have witnessed the results of methodological imperialism in those instances where the safety of

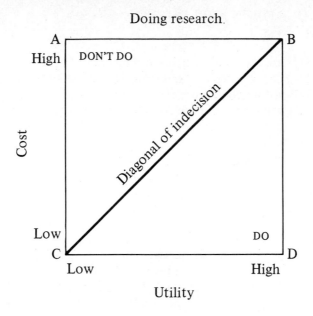

FIGURE 11-2
Decision planes representing the costs and utilities of doing (top plane) and not doing (bottom plane) research.

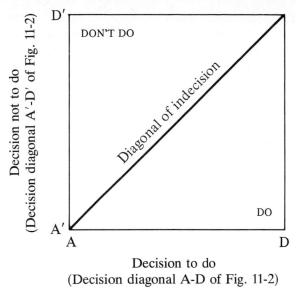

FIGURE 11-3
Composite plane representing both cases of Figure 11-2.

human subjects has been ignored or endangered (Beecher, 1970; Bok, 1978; Katz, 1972), but ethical imperialism can also have serious consequences. As West and Gunn (1978) have noted, if ethical guidelines are imposed absolutely, then "researchers may simply turn their attention to other topic areas that ethics committees and review boards find less objectionable" (p. 36). The result could be that research that needs to be done, to answer both scientific and important societal questions, would cease.

Considerations such as those encompassed by Figure 11-2, if adopted by a review board, may make it more difficult in the future to give simple absolute answers to questions of whether particular studies should be carried out. Those who argue that a given study is unethical and should be prohibited must be prepared to answer in ethical and moral terms for the consequences of *their* decision no less than those who recommend that the study be done. Of course, we recognize that in some instances a compromise will not be struck between the aims of the experimenters and the final decisions of the review panels. In such cases, nonexperimental methodologies may have to be relied on. However, we expect that in the vast majority of cases a bargain will be struck, given flexibility on both sides of the issue.

GUIDELINES FOR DEBRIEFING RESEARCH PARTICIPANTS

A careful debriefing interview of all research participants is ordinarily desirable as the final step in the data collection process, particularly in experimental studies because certain conditions have been manipulated by the researcher. This may not be possible in some instances, however, such as when the debriefing may produce stress or would be ineffective given the nature of the participants (e.g., children, the mentally ill or retarded). Nevertheless, in most cases it is ethically essential.

We mentioned the criticisms of Milgram's research as a result of his having duped the participants into believing that they were administering painful electric shocks to another person. Deception procedures such as those used in this research are inherently disquieting. Milgram viewed it of the utmost importance that all his subjects be assured that their "victim" had not received electric shocks at all. The debriefing techniques he employed remain a model of what can be done to alleviate possible stresses and anxieties in the subjects. To ensure that each subject knew exactly what the reality of the situation was, he carefully administered a postexperimental treatment to all subjects, then sent them a follow-up report and questionnaire. A year later, he conducted a psychiatric interview with a subsample of his group of subjects.

More specifically, during the postexperimental debriefing session each of the subjects had a friendly reconciliation with the learner and an extended discussion with the experimenter about the purpose of the study and why it was thought necessary to deceive the subject. Those subjects who had obeyed the experimenter when he told them to keep administering the electric shocks were assured that their behavior was normal and the feelings of conflict or tension that they had experienced were shared by other participants. The subjects were told that they would receive a comprehensive written report at the conclusion of the research. The report they received detailed the experimental procedures and findings, and the subject's own part in the research was treated with dignity. They also received a questionnaire that asked them once again to express their thoughts and feelings about their behavior. One year after the experiment was completed there was an additional follow-up study of 40 of the experimental subjects, who were intensively interviewed by a psychiatrist to identify any possible injurious effects resulting from the experiment.

Milgram's follow-up treatments were unusually extensive, far more so than are characteristic of most debriefing procedures. Most studies will not require debriefing covering so wide an area or span of time; social psychologists Eliot Aronson and J. Merrill Carlsmith (1968) have suggested some helpful guidelines, which are paraphrased below:

1. The most essential requirement is that the researcher communicate his or her own sincerity as a scientist. If the research involved any sort of deception, then it is important to tell the subject why it was necessary to resort to it and how the use of deception was carefully considered by the researcher. Science is the search for truth, and sometimes it may be necessary to resort to deception in order to uncover the truth. Responsible researchers will not view this matter lightly, and their sincere concern should be apparent.

2. In spite of the researcher's sincere wish to treat the subject responsibly, it is nevertheless possible that the subject will leave the experiment feeling gull-

ible, as if he or she has been "had." The researcher must assure the subject that being "taken in" does not reflect in any way on the subject's intelligence or character. Rather, it simply reflects on the effectiveness of the study's design, which the researcher has no doubt gone to some pains to achieve.

3. The debriefing session should proceed gradually. Researchers should have as their chief aim a gentle unfolding of the details of any deceptions used. Together, in a dialogue led by the researcher, the subject and the experimenter should examine the entire research process. If done patiently, the dialogue may go far in assuaging any negative feelings the subject could be harboring. Instead of thinking of themselves as "victims" of the researcher, the subjects begin to think of themselves as "coinvestigators" in the search for truth.

4. The researcher should reiterate assurances of confidentiality, and anonymity if possible. Presumably, the data will be coded and statistically analyzed without reference to any respondent's name.

5. For reasons known only to themselves, some subjects may give false assurances as to the effect of the study on how they feel. The researcher has a responsibility to alleviate the subjects' discomfort and restore a sense of well-being as much as possible. This may necessitate the questioning of remarks or reactions in detail, if they appear to mask hidden feelings of apprehension or residual anxiety on the part of the participant.

6. There are no reliable shortcuts to debriefing the subject as soon after the research as possible. Promising to mail the subject a report of the research in lieu of a personal debriefing may be expedient, but it is a weak substitute if there is residual anxiety. However, if it is possible that a personal interview may alert other subjects who have not yet participated in the research as to the nature of the study, then it may be reasonable to delay the debriefing, but only for as short a time as is practicable.

SCIENTIFIC AND SOCIETAL IMPERATIVES

In this chapter we have discussed the major questions concerning ethics and values that constantly confront behavioral scientists. Each researcher must weigh his or her responsibilities to science and to society very carefully. However, values enter into science not only in the ethics of the profession, but also in the selection of problems for scientific investigation (see Reynolds, 1975). Even when the research is not directly funded by some agency of society, it is at least countenanced and indirectly supported, because our society places a high value on science and gives the scientist a relatively free hand to study whatever he or she wants to study. There are, to be sure, limits on how far the scientist can go in the quest for knowledge, and we discussed these limits earlier. The point is that our society provides the circumstances and a psychological environment that are conducive to good scientific practices. The question, then, is what does the scientist owe society in return for that privilege?

Some would argue that the behavioral scientist owes society the assurance that the research will lead to betterment of the community. This position is widely heralded particularly during periods of social stress, when the clarion call is sounded for researchers to get out of their ivory towers and to formulate hypotheses that will be relevant to social problems. However, no scientist can guarantee the outcome of his or her work. Even the best of motives can produce results that do not further the state of well-being for which we strive.

The very nature of behavioral science is that it also challenges or questions societies' values and often elicits emotional responses. When we describe certain behaviors as being "normative" (i.e., usual or typical), the implication to the layperson is that we are saying that such behaviors are to be expected and therefore desirable. When we study prejudice or mental illness we are touching on highly charged social problems. Even when we study topics that may appear to us to be neutral (marriage and the family, the genetics of intelligence, learning behavior, etc.), we must realize that to others they may be supercharged with values and conflicts. The point is that our science must be conducted with a sense of responsibility and an awareness that research is not done in isolation from the surrounding community (see Melton, Levine, Koocher, Rosenthal, and Thompson, 1988).

As a consequence, it has been suggested that behavioral researchers should openly acknowledge that their work forces them to "tread on thin moral ice" (Atwell, 1981, p. 89). In studying human behavior we are constantly in jeopardy of violating someone's basic right—if only the right of privacy—and it is prudent that we study and discuss the moral dimensions of our research. In the end, the behavioral scientist's ethical responsibilities are twofold. On the one hand, the researcher must protect the integrity of his or her work, in order to ensure that the work measures up to the standards of good scientific practice. On the other hand, the researcher must also respect the dignity of those he or she studies and the values that allow the pursuit of scientific knowledge in a free society.

CHAPTER

12

SYSTEMATIC PLURALISM AND STATISTICAL DATA ANALYSIS

A TRANSITIONAL CHAPTER

This short chapter has several purposes, but its main objective is to serve as a transition between the first half and the second half of this book. Two other objectives involve more specific aims: (1) to give a flavor of the philosophical approach known as "contextualism" (with its Latin root *contextus*, "a joining together") inasmuch as it helps us to join together the epistemological suppositions (i.e., assumptions about the nature and limits of explanation) underlying the diversity of methods presented in this book and (2) to introduce a number of matters of methodological spirit and substance that will serve as focal points in the remaining chapters on statistical data analysis (see Rosnow and Rosenthal, 1989b). Let us take each of these more specific aims one at a time.

First, contextualism, like honey to bees, has been a "sweet" idea to behavioral scientists with diverse research and theoretical interests. One reason for its attractiveness is that it has been interpreted as advocating methodological and theoretical pluralism because of its implicit acceptance of "fallibilistic indeterminacy" (Rosnow and Georgoudi, 1986). This tongue twister simply means that, because each method or theory is limited (or "fallible") in some way (e.g., Fiske and Shweder, 1986; Rosnow, 1981), we *need* to resort to multiple methods and theories to get a fix on the infinite variety of complexities in the world. The argument for theoretical diversity is also explained by an analogy to physics: Newton developed mathematical theoretical laws that, because of their elegance and precision, became the accepted standards of exact science. However, later theoretical work by physicists such as Einstein, Heisenberg, and others (see Chapter 1) revealed the limits of Newtonian physics. It was not to say that Newton's laws were "false," only that their application was viewed as restricted to a particular level of analysis. Thus Newton's analysis was "closed off" in the same sense that Einstein's special theory of relativity or Heisenberg's atomic physics was also closed off (or "particularistic"). Contextualists argue that in order to build a solid body of knowledge about human cognition and behavior, theoretical diversity is absolutely essential inasmuch as each theory or hypothesis is particularistic in some way. Because there is no *single* proper or complete or unlimited perspective on reality, we are obliged to search for multiple routes, each at a different level of analysis (Lana, 1986; Rosnow, 1978, 1983).

Second, after we have finished with contextualism, we shall turn to the context of the statistical analysis of research data. In Chapter 1 we used the expression "think Yiddish, write British" to characterize the dominant discursive pattern of the intuitions and inductive inferences that have defined the scientific outlook in this century. One way of viewing our discussion of statistical data analysis is that it presents an in-depth examination of an essential aspect of the rhetoric of justification in behavioral science, i.e., the tightly logical outcome of this "thinking Yiddish." It will be recalled that "justification," in the vernacular language of philosophy of science, refers to the evaluation, defense, and confirmation of claims of truth. We shall be examining the traditional ways in which behavioral researchers draw on the strict logical consequences of statistical data analysis to shore up facts and inductive inferences, which is part of the "rhetoric" of justification.

WHAT IS CONTEXTUALISM?

Contextualism, as it was originally formulated, was conceived as one of several metaphysical creeds (or "world hypotheses") underlying the particular explanations by which human beings attempt to make sense of the world. It was identified and named by Stephen C. Pepper (1942, 1967), an American philosopher, based on his logical analysis of a wide variety of philosophical systems. The central assumption on which it was predicated, according to Pepper, is that human events are active, dynamic, developmental moments of a continuously changing reality. From this perspective, knowledge is best viewed as "embedded" in a changing or an evolving context of time, space, culture, and the local tacit rules of conduct, e.g., the rules of the scientific community. As reinterpreted by behavioral scientists, inasmuch as the context of explanation is an integral part of both *what* is explained and *how* it is explained, the meaning of events is like a message that makes sense only in terms of the total context in which it is embedded. This is not a trivial idea, because it reminds us that the scientific enterprise is part and parcel of an evolving sociohistorical context. In modern philosophy a nautical analogy compares the corpus of scientific facts and theories, as much as the scientific method, to a boat that must be reconstructed not in dry dock but at sea, one plank at a time (Howard, 1987). The point is that the scientific method ought not to be viewed as permanently fixed, but instead as constantly evolving.

We get a clearer fix on contextualism as it has been reinterpreted by behavioral scientists when we view it also as part of an evolving sociohistorical context. In the late nineteenth century, spurred on by earlier successes in physics that developed out of the classical work on mechanics, a number of leading behavioral theorists argued for a conception of human beings as complex machines (the "man as machine" notion). They endorsed such a conception as a way of tidying up what they regarded as the "clutter" of the subjective study of human behavior. In particular, eminent researchers in experimental psychology were inspired by the theoretical idea that the human system (like the physical systems described by Newton) operated in a world of events running in a predictable mechanism of causes and effects. No one asks *why* a machine works, only *how* it works. It followed (as noted in Chapter 4) that such a "machine" ought to be subject to causal laws so that, under rigorous experimental conditions, it should be possible to figure out *how* it works.

It was also believed that the study of human behavior could proceed with the same "detached curiosity" with which physicists, presumably, had been engaged in the study of mechanics. Dismissing as irrelevant (or at least underestimating) the fact that humans, unlike machines, are active, sensate creatures, theorists felt that value judgments, the distinction between "good" and "bad," and personal feelings had no place in a scientific enterprise gleaned from what was perceived as the *true* model of science. Coming along as it did in the heyday of the industrial revolution, this conception with its emphasis on mechanistic science as objective and value free was an intoxicating idea. Pioneering behavioral researchers, who were seeking credible "scientific" ways of addressing questions that had puzzled armchair theoreticians since antiquity, argued that human phenomena are subject to mechanical laws in such a way that, under tightly controlled experimental conditions, certain determinate relationships of a generalizable nature might be specifically isolated.

It was later realized that classical mechanics is neither the *only* true model of science nor even the *only* true model of physics itself (which has proved much more complex and abstract). In the 1960s and 1970s, the behavioral scientists (as much as philosophers and others) were confronted with further doubts about assumptions that had gone unchallenged for decades (see Rosnow, 1981). In social psychology, for instance, researchers went through a period of uncertainty and upheaval punctuated by questions about the methodological and philosophical underpinnings of their discipline. A major fatality in the ferment during this period was, in the words of British social psychologist John Shotter (1986), the "loss of a great hope: that of certainty." In previous discussions we referred to the experimental work of the artifact researchers, one of several developments that changed the face of much of behavioral science (Morawski, 1988). This work suggested to social psychologists and others that some of their controls used to increase experimental precision could distort the phenomena under investigation. It was not to say, however, that the experimental method was wrong and should be discarded, because that would be like throwing the baby out with the bathwater—nor was it suggested that all mechanists were experimentalists. Instead it was an attempt to establish the proper place of the experimental approach in a methodologically pluralistic science of human behavior (Rosnow, 1981).

The notion of a value-free human science, necessary to preserve the ideal of objectivity of researchers' operational methodology, was also thrown in doubt (Chapter 11). Still another threat to certainty erupted in the doubts voiced by European and American psychologists and sociologists, who protested against the idea of absolute laws ("universals") in a discipline devoted to the study of human behavior (e.g., Armistead, 1974; Gergen, 1973b, 1978; Harré and Secord, 1972; Israel and Tajfel, 1972; Pepitone, 1976)—the laws of human behavior are socioculturally and temporally particularistic, it was widely proclaimed.

Out of that crisis of confidence there emerged a number of nonmechanistic ideas concerned both with the nature of human activity and with the means by which we might explore and explain it (e.g., Buss, 1979; Farr and Moscovici, 1984; Georgoudi, 1981; Gergen, 1985; Harré, 1980; Jenkins, 1974; McGuire, 1983; Manicas and Secord, 1983; Margolis, Manicas, Harré, and Secord, 1986; Rosnow, 1981, 1983; Shotter, 1984). In spite of some differences (both real and apparent), all have usually emphasized (1) the active, intentional nature of much of human behavior, (2) the view of individuals as continuously engaged in the reconstruction of knowledge, (3) the researcher as an active participant rather than as a detached observer, (4) the deployment of multiple methods to uncover the processlike and intentional nature of cognition and behavior, and (5) the notion that human phenomena acquire meaning as part of a wider sociohistorical context. Researchers who regarded themselves as unified by philosophical contextualism, while they might disagree on specific points, nevertheless concurred that these common themes—explored in fields as diverse as linguistics, mass communication, behavioral analysis, life-span development, environmental psychology, cognitive psychology, personality and abnormal psychology, clinical psychology, and social psychology—could be easily subsumed within this philosophical framework (cf. Georgoudi and Rosnow, 1985a, 1985b; Hayes, 1987; Hayes and Brownstein, 1986; Hoffman and Nead, 1983; Jaeger and Rosnow, 1988; McGuire, 1983; Mishler, 1979; Morris, 1988; Rosnow and Georgoudi, 1986; Sarbin, 1977; Smith, 1988; Veroff, 1983).

Contextualists in behavioral science (like modern physicists looking in retrospect at classical mechanics) tend to regard the man as machine theory not as totally wrong or discardable, but instead as an oversimplification in terms of its explanatory claims. They note that, in the hands of some psychological theorists, it was used in an attempt to "explain away" change by various specific facts and theories. The contextualists argue that change is a *given*, not something to be explained away but instead a reflection of the inherent complexity and open-ended nature of ongoing, active events and their contexts. Another way of saying this is that contextualism promotes the idea of change ("turbulence") as a categorical feature of the world of everyday events, which are in constant flux (Mead, 1927). But we do not usually perceive the world as turbulent or temporary, because there has forever been a "persistent flight from the temporal to the eternal, the quest of an object on which the reason or the imagination might fix itself with the sense of having attained to something that is not merely perduring but immutable" (Lovejoy, 1936). The scientific method is one means by which we *impose* a sense of stability and immutability, inasmuch as that, in turn, enables us to navigate the deeper straits of turbulence.

Having said this, can we now make the leap to statistical data analysis—which is what the following chapters are all about—within the framework of contextualism? That question can be answered in the affirmative, because imposing a sense of order and lawfulness would seem to be what justification in science is all about. It is the content and context of justification to which the rest of this discussion is addressed in one way or another. Just as the meaning attributed to an event or situation is mediated in large part by the set of circumstances surrounding it, the content of justification is influenced by the rational and emotional context in which it exists. In the following chapters, all the while we describe and illustrate data-analytic procedures, we shall also be examining some ways of clearing away a number of obstacles in the content and context of justification. Previously we referred to the philosophical analogy that compares the corpus of scientific facts and theories to a boat that is being reconstructed at sea, one plank at a time. The aspects of statistical data analysis that we shall be discussing might be thought of as the connecting tools that help us to hold our facts and inductive inferences fast. In our reliance on statistical data-analytic tools used to reinforce the empirical foundation of behavioral science we want to choose the right tools for the job and to use them properly.

MATTERS OF METHODOLOGICAL SPIRIT

To set the stage further for the following chapters, we turn first to four problems pertaining to the methodological spirit, or essence, of statistical data analysis: (1) the overreliance on dichotomous significance-testing decisions, (2) the tendency to do many research studies in situations of low power, (3) the habit of defining the results of research in terms of significance levels alone, and (4) the overemphasis on single studies at the expense of cumulating results.

First, far more than is good for us, many behavioral researchers have for too long operated as if the only "proper" significance-testing decision is a dichotomous one, in which the evidence is interpreted as "anti-null" if p is not greater than .05 and "pro-null" if p is greater than .05. It may not be an exaggeration to say that many Ph.D. students have come to perceive the .05 alpha as axiomatic (i.e., a universal rule), and that if their dissertation p is less than .05, it can lead to joy, a doctoral degree, and a tenure-track position at a major university. However, if the p is greater than .05, it can mean ruin, despair, and a fear that their adviser will suddenly think of a new control condition that should be run.

The conventional wisdom behind this approach was alluded to in Chapter 2: The logic begins, more or less, with the proposition that one does not want to accept a hypothesis that stands a fairly good chance of being false, i.e., we ought to avoid type I errors. The logic goes on to state that either we accept hypotheses as probably true (not false) or we reject them, concluding that the null is too likely to regard it as rejectable. The .05 alpha is a good "fail-safe" standard because it is both convenient and stringent enough to safeguard against accepting an insignificant result as significant. The argument, while not beyond cavil, provides a systematic approach that most researchers would insist has served behavioral science well. We are not arguing for replacing the .05 alpha with another level of alpha, but we are saying that dichotomous significance testing is not axiomatic. It may seem obvious to many readers, but it is nevertheless important to underscore that the *strength of evidence for or against the null is a fairly continuous function of the magnitude of p.*

The second problem (previously noted in Chapter 2) is that researchers frequently have a tendency to work with low power as a consequence of ignoring the extent to which, in employing a particular size of sample, they are stacking the odds against reaching a given p value for some particular size of effect. Maybe this is because the mechanics of power analysis, even though its important implications for practice were recognized long ago by psychological statisticians, was dismissed in some leading textbooks for a time as too complicated to discuss. However, we will see in Chapter 19 that it is *not* a complicated problem. As a consequence of a series of seminal works by Jacob Cohen beginning in the 1960s (e.g., Cohen, 1962, 1965, 1969, 1977, 1988), the concept of power has resurfaced with a vengeance in behavioral science, and it behooves researchers to familarize themselves with the simple mechanics involved.

The third problem of methodological spirit concerns the tendency many researchers have to define the results of research in terms of significance levels alone. We will be taking a very close look at significance testing but also at effect-size estimation procedures. We shall see again that it is a good idea to calculate the effect size not only when the p value is "significant" but also when it is "nonsignificant." One reason for this is that computing effect sizes guides our judgment about the sample size needed in the next study we might conduct. Another reason, also discussed in detail, is that effect size tells us something very different from the p level. A result that is statistically significant is not necessarily practically significant as judged by the magnitude of the effect. Thus significant p values should not be interpreted as automatically reflecting large effects.

The final problem of methodological spirit to be discussed concerns the importance of cumulating research results whenever possible, in order to give a running account of the state of knowledge. The operationalization of this view involves evaluating the impact of a study not strictly on the basis of the particular p level. It instead involves evaluating this impact more on the basis of multiple criteria, including its own effect size as well as the revised effect size and combined probability that results from the addition of the new study to any earlier studies investigating the same or a similar relationship. This amounts to a call for a more meta-analytic view of doing science, an approach that has come up frequently in our previous discussions and is described in detail in Chapter 22.

Incidentally, an extra benefit of this approach is that the meta-analyst becomes more engrossed in the sum and substance of the research literature. We cannot do a meta-analysis just by reading abstracts and discussion summaries. Instead we have to look at the numbers and, very often, compute the correct ones ourselves. Meta-analysis requires that we cumulate *data*, not merely *conclusions*.

Reading a research report is quite a different matter when one needs to compute an effect size and a fairly precise significance level—often from a results section that never heard of effect sizes or precise significance levels.

MATTERS OF METHODOLOGICAL SUBSTANCE

There are also matters of methodological substance that provide focal points in the following chapters, primarily problems in the usage of data-analytic procedures. The most prominent issues concern (1) problems in the use of omnibus tests, (2) the need for contrasts, (3) the nearly universal misinterpretation of interaction effects, and (4) the problem of "hidden nesting."

First, suppose you reached a fork in the road and were not sure which path, A or B, to take to reach your destination Z. If you could ask one question of someone who knew the paths but who could respond only "yes" or "no," which would it be: (1) does A lead to Z or (2) does it make any difference which path I take? The answer, of course, is that you would ask question 1 because it addresses the information you need in a focused or precise way, which question 2 does not. No behavioral researcher would make the mistake of asking an unfocused question in this situation, but many do follow the common practice of employing unfocused ("omnibus") tests of hypotheses in their research when a focused test would be more appropriate (see Rosnow and Rosenthal, 1988). This is not the place to go into detail, but in later discussions we shall illustrate how focused statistical tests tell us the answers to specific questions. Common as omnibus tests are, the diffuse hypotheses they test are usually of dubious practical or theoretical significance. And the effect-size estimates they yield are almost always of doubtful utility.

Second, *contrasts*—i.e., tests of focused questions in which specific predictions can be analyzed by comparing ("contrasting") them to the obtained data—are particularly useful in this regard. For example, suppose counseling researchers interested in communication skill have children at five grade levels perform communication exercises on which expert judges rate the children on a 10-point scale. The researchers find that the mean scores of 10 children per grade in grades 7, 8, 9, 10, and 11, respectively, are 2.5, 3.0, 4.0, 5.0, and 5.5. Whereas the scores suggest a developmental progression, the standard omnibus test computed for grade levels could well turn out to be nonsignificant. The problem with the test is that it was diffuse and unfocused; it addressed the question of whether there were any differences among the five grade levels, disregarding entirely their temporal arrangement. Contrasts avoid this problem, and in this case would be much more likely to show the statistical significance of the progression in the obtained means.

This hypothetical case also correctly implies that there is an increase in statistical power that derives from employing contrasts, i.e., an increase in the probability of not making a type II error. Because behavioral scientists want to use statistical tests that will lead to rejection of the null hypothesis when it is false, contrasts are usually more "useful" or "successful" than is the standard omnibus significance test. Although most textbooks of statistics describe the logic and the procedures of contrast analysis, one still sees contrasts employed all too rarely. That is a real pity given the precision of thought and theory they encourage and (especially relevant to these times of publication pressure) given the boost in power conferred with the resulting increase in .05 asterisks. In later discussions we show that this kind of significance testing is easy to do with a pocket calculator and can be used for performing secondary analyses of published data.

Third, another problem discussed later concerns what may be the universally most misinterpreted empirical results in behavioral science—*interaction effects*. The mathematical meaning of interaction effects is unambiguous, and textbooks of mathematical and psychological statistics routinely include proper definitions of interaction effects. Despite this, a recent review of studies published in primary psychological journals reported that only a tiny percentage interpreted interactions in an unequivocally correct manner (Rosnow and Rosenthal, 1989a). The origin of the problem, as Dawes (1969, p. 57) suggested, may in part be a consequence of the "lack of perfect correspondence between the meaning of 'interaction' in the analysis of variance model and its meaning in other discourse." Chapter 17 is devoted entirely to this subject.

Fourth, the final problem is that of *hidden nesting*. It has to do with the concealed nonindependence of observations brought about by sampling without regard to sources of similarity in the persons sampled. For example, when the subjects are drawn from several classrooms, schools, business departments, wards, families, couples, etc., but *without attention* to that fact, both our significance testing and our effect-size estimation become problematic. The reason is that people in the same classrooms, wards, families, etc., are likely to be more similar to each other than they are to people in different classrooms, wards, families, etc., so that the usual assumptions underlying data analyses will not apply. The typical effect of this problem is that the actual *degrees of freedom* (i.e., the number of observations minus the number of restrictions limiting the observations' freedom to vary) of the study will fall somewhere between the number of people in the study and the number of "groups" of people in the study.

A FINAL NOTE

Before we turn to the second half of this book, it is worth repeating another underlying theme: *There will almost always be two kinds of information we want to have for each of our research questions, the size of the effect and its statistical significance*. This theme is well expressed by a fundamental conceptual equation to which we shall refer frequently in the following discussions:

$$\text{Magnitude of significance test} = \text{size of effect} \times \text{size of study}$$

The equation tells us that for any given (nonzero) effect size, the test of significance (e.g., t, F, chi-square, Z) will increase as the number of sampling units (size of study) increases. It also tells us that for any given size of effect (e.g., correlation coefficient) and for any given size of study (e.g., number of subjects) there will be a corresponding test of significance (as illustrated on the inside covers of this book). Much of the data-analytic work of the behavioral researcher consists of deciding how to determine these three elements of the conceptual equation in any particular study.

PART
V

FUNDAMENTALS OF DATA ANALYSIS

CHAPTER
13

DESCRIBING
AND DISPLAYING
DATA

DISPLAYS

Much of the fundamental work in behavioral science involves the description of a group of *sampling units*, that is, the people or things being studied. Sampling units are most often people or other animals, but they can be things like countries, states, cities, precincts, school districts, schools, classrooms, businesses, hospitals, wards, or clinics. Some type of number is assigned to each sampling unit on any particular variable, and the task of describing our data is that of summarizing the numbers representing the sampling units on that variable.

Suppose that we had measured nine people on a scale of anxiety and obtained the following numbers:

$$5, 8, 7, 6, 4, 6, 7, 5, 6$$

We might begin by ordering these numbers from lowest to highest to get a better view of their beginning and ending points and where they clump or bunch:

$$4, 5, 5, 6, 6, 6, 7, 7, 8$$

We can further clarify the nature of our observations by arranging them to reduce the number of categories to just the number of different score values, as in Figure 13-1.

This kind of arrangement is called a *distribution*, with score values increasing from left to right and the height of the curve reflecting the frequency of occurrence of the scores. Note that one axis is labeled X and the other Y; when describing research findings, we *usually* plot the independent variable on the X axis and the dependent variable on the Y axis. Thus, distributions of research

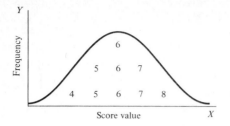

FIGURE 13-1
A distribution of score values.

data show the rise and fall of frequencies as we move over varying values of our independent variable. Another name for the horizontal axis, or X axis, is the *abscissa*; another name for the vertical axis, or Y axis, is the *ordinate*.

There is, however, no hard-and-fast rule that displays must resemble Figure 13-1. Data may also be plotted sideways, as in Figure 13-2.

It often happens that we have a set of scores we want to record, display, and summarize, and two developments have conspired to make the theory and technology of graphical displays of data an area of intense attention. These developments have been (a) the rapid growth of computer technology and (b) the scholarly impact of the work of John W. Tukey, one of the most influential statisticians of the present generation (Cleveland, 1985). The periodical literature on graphical displays of data has grown rapidly (e.g., Cleveland and McGill, 1985; Gross, 1983; Wainer, 1984; Wainer and Thissen, 1981), and several valuable textbooks have already appeared (e.g., Chambers, Cleveland, Kleiner, and Tukey, 1983; Cleveland, 1985; Tufte, 1983). For our present purposes it will be sufficient to show the use of two display techniques developed by Tukey (1977): the stem-and-leaf display and the box plot.

STEM-AND-LEAF DISPLAYS

In their review of graphical data analysis Wainer and Thissen (1981) state that "the stem-and-leaf display is the most important device for the analysis of small

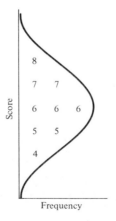

FIGURE 13-2
The distribution in Figure 13-1, with the variables interchanged on the two axes.

batches of numbers to appear since the *t*-test" (p. 199). Among the purposes served by employing this procedure are (a) storing data for current and later usage, (b) plotting data as a distribution from high to low scores, and (c) making it easier for research consumers to examine the patterning of the data. It has been said that pictures of the numbers are often more instructive than the numbers themselves (Tufte, 1983). The beauty of Tukey's stem-and-leaf procedure is that it is at the same time both the numbers and the picture of the numbers.

In Chapter 10 we referred to our research on volunteer characteristics and their implications (Rosenthal and Rosnow, 1975). As part of that program of research we were also interested in the nature of the volunteers who become *no-shows*, i.e., who fail to show up for their scheduled appointments to participate as research subjects. In our investigations we uncovered 20 studies that reported the proportion of research participants who failed to show up when scheduled. Those proportions of no-shows were as follows (not in any particular order): .41, .30, .14, .36, .19, .38, .12, .31, .24, .37, .10, .37, .40, .16, .30, .36, .42, .32, .03, .37. To help us make sense of these data, we begin by recording the values economically. Because these are two-digit numbers, we can list the leading digits (called *stems* by Tukey) just once and record for each leading digit (or stem) the second digits (or *leaves*) attached to it:

Leading digit (stems)	Second digit (leaves)
.4	1 0 2
.3	0 6 8 1 7 7 0 6 2 7
.2	4
.1	4 9 2 0 6
.0	3

We now have a frequency distribution that is at the same time a listing of all the original data. We read the top row, which has a stem of .4, and three leaves of 1, 0, 2, as representing the three values of .41, .40, .42; the 1st, the 13th, and the 17th entries in our original listing of results. We can make even more sense of the data if we now rearrange the leaves from smallest to largest on each stem. In our example of 20 rates of failing to show up we find:

Stems	Leaves
.4	0 1 2
.3	0 0 1 2 6 6 7 7 7 8
.2	4
.1	0 2 4 6 9
.0	3

And finally, we can summarize the stem-and-leaf display with certain key values of the distribution, such as the median, the scores found at the 25th and

75th percentiles, and the lowest and highest scores. For the present data these five summary values are:

Maximum	.42
75th percentile	.37
Median (50th percentile)	.32 (.315 rounded to nearest even digit)
25th percentile	.17
Minimum	.03

We see that the 50 percent of the studies that were midmost (25 to 75 percent) had values between .17 and .37 with a median no-show rate of .32. The practical implication? If we are counting on 40 volunteer participants to show up for our research, we had better schedule about 60.

Computations of our five summary values are easy enough for maximum and minimum scores. An easy way to compute the median is to multiply $n + 1$ (where n is the number of scores in the set) by .50 to get the *location* of the score we need. In this example $n = 20$, so the median value is $(20 + 1).50 = 10.5$, or halfway between the 10th score (.31) and the 11th score (.32), or .315 (rounded to the nearest even value). In a similar fashion, the 25th and 75th percentile scores can be located, respectively, by $(n + 1).25$ and $(n + 1).75$. For our example, these locate the $(21).25 = 5.25$th score (i.e., adding to the 5th score 25 percent of the distance between it and the 6th score) and the $(21).75 = 15.75$th score (i.e., adding to the 15th score 75 percent of the distance between it and the 16th score). Stem-and-leaf displays and their numerical summaries should be flexibly, not rigidly, employed, so it is not surprising that some investigators prefer other means of locating the 25th and 75th percentile values (e.g., the nearest whole number).

BOX PLOTS

Especially when the stem-and-leaf is of a large amount of data, and especially when there are several stem-and-leaf displays to be compared, it is useful to turn the five-value summary into another graphic. Called by Tukey (1977), its originator, a "box-and-whisker" plot, most others now call it a *box plot* or *box graph*. For our five-number summary (Figure 13-3) we plot the graphic on the left (A) such that the top and bottom dots represent the maximum and minimum scores, the top and bottom of the rectangle represent the 75th and 25th percentiles, and the line dividing the rectangle represents the median.

The box plot, like the full stem-and-leaf, shows that our data are not symmetrically distributed about the median. Instead, the data are skewed, with values furthest from the median heavily concentrated below rather than above the median.

Variations of the box plot abound. Some investigators prefer to graph the 10th and 90th percentile scores instead of the highest and lowest scores while making a dot mark for every value more extreme than the 10th or the 90th percentile (Cleveland, 1985), as shown in Figure 13-3 on the right (B).

COMPARING DISTRIBUTIONS BACK TO BACK

Another aspect of our investigation of volunteer subjects (discussed in Chapter 10) involved comparing females with males for their rates of volunteering for psychological research (Rosenthal and Rosnow, 1975). We found 63 studies that had reported the volunteering rates for both females and males. For each of these studies we subtracted the percentage of males volunteering from the percentage of females volunteering. We did this separately for general psychological studies and for studies involving stress. The results are shown below, in which positive values of the differences in percentages indicate that females volunteered more than males did (and negative values, that females volunteered less than males did):

Stress studies (N = 12) Leaves	Stems	*General Studies* Leaves (N = 51)
	+3	5
	+3	
	+2	5 9
	+2	0 1 1 1 1 2 2 2 4
	+1	6 6 7 8 8 8
	+1	0 1 1 1 2 2 2 3 3 3 4
9	+0	5 5 5 6 8 8 9
	+0	1 1 1 2 3 4 4
	0	0
2 1	−0	2 4
8 6	−0	
4 0	−1	1 3
6	−1	
0	−2	0 3
8 5	−2	6
	−3	
	−3	
	−4	
6	−4	

For obvious reasons this type of comparison is called a *back-to-back stem-and-leaf*. It shows immediately that females were much more likely to volunteer than males for general studies but that for studies involving stress, males were much more likely to volunteer. Another way to view these results is in terms of the back-to-back box plots shown in Figure 13-4.

We immediately see that both distributions are fairly symmetrical and unremarkable. However, the one for general studies is substantially higher than the one for stress studies. At a glance, these back-to-back box plots inform us in still another way that females were much more likely to volunteer than males for general studies and that the reverse occurred for studies involving stress. Thus we have a number of ways to group data, each providing a somewhat different perspective on the pattern of results.

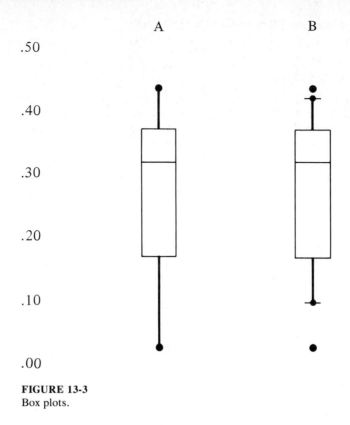

FIGURE 13-3
Box plots.

MEASURES OF CENTRAL TENDENCY

As the graphics we have discussed would suggest, one characteristic of distributions that we almost always want to describe is the location of their bulk or the central or typical values. Several measures are available for this purpose.

The *mode* is the score that occurs with the greatest frequency. In the series of scores 3, 4, 4, 4, 5, 5, 6, 6, 7, the modal score is 4. The series 3, 4, 4, 4, 5, 5, 6, 7, 7, 7, has two modes (at the values 4 and 7) and is called *bimodal*.

The *median*, already discussed above, is the midmost score in a series of *n* scores when *n* is an odd number. When *n* is an even number, the median is half the distance between the two midmost numbers. In the series 2, 3, 3, 4, 4, 5, 6, 7, 7, 8, 8, the median value is 5; in the series 2, 3, 3, 4, 4, 7, the median value is 3.5, halfway between the 3 and 4 at the center of the set of scores. Ties create a problem. The series 3, 4, 4, 4, 5, 6, 7 has one score below 4 and three above, four scores below 5 and two above, four scores below 4.5 and three above. What shall we regard as our median? A useful procedure is to view our series as perfectly ranked, so that a series 1, 2, 3, 3, 3, is seen as made up of a 1, a 2, a small 3, a larger 3, and a still larger 3 on the assumption that more precise measurement procedures would have allowed us to break the ties. Thus, in the series 1, 2, 3, 3, 3 we would regard 3, the "smallest" 3, as our median. There are two scores below

Stress studies   General studies

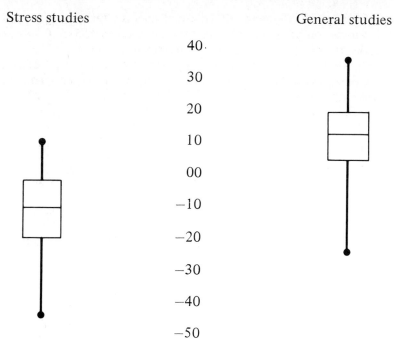

FIGURE 13-4
Back-to-back box plots.

this particular 3 and two above it. In reporting this median we can simply specify the median's value as 3, or we could further specify that it was the "smallest" 3.

The *mean* is the arithmetic average of our scores written symbolically as

$$\frac{\Sigma X}{N}$$

and read as "the sum of the scores divided by the number of scores."

Trimmed means are sometimes useful. We trim by dropping a particular percentage of the scores from both ends of the distribution and computing the mean of the remaining scores. A mean trimming 10 percent of the scores from each end of the following series, −20, 2, 3, 6, 7, 9, 9, 10, 10, 10, is 7.0, the untrimmed mean is 4.6. (In this case, trimming 10 percent from each end drops the −20 and the 10.) The median is unaffected by trimming, so the median of the data just presented is 8 with or without trimming. The mode, which may be affected by trimming, is 10 before trimming but bimodal at 9 and 10 after trimming. In general, we prefer medians and trimmed means to ordinary means when the distribution of scores is strongly asymmetric. Their use protects us from possibly misleading interpretations based on very unusual scores. For example, if we listed the family income for 10 families and found 9 of them with zero income and 1 with a $10 million income, the mean income of $1 million would be highly unrepresentative compared with the trimmed mean, median, or (in this case) even the mode. Medians and trimmed means also protect us somewhat against the intrusion of "wild" scores. Consider a series 4, 5, 5, 6, 6, 6, 7, 7, 8, of which the mean, median, mode, and trimmed mean are all 6. However, suppose that we erred and entered the data as 4, 5, 5, 6, 6, 6, 7, 7, 80. Our new (erroneous) mean would now be 14, but our median or trimmed mean would remain unaffected.

MEASURES OF SPREAD

In addition to knowing the central tendency (or roughly the typical value of a set of scores), we almost always also want to know about the degree to which scores deviate from these measures of central tendency (or how spread out the scores are). Several measures of spread, dispersion, or variability are available.

The *range* is the distance between the highest and lowest scores. In the series 2, 3, 4, 4, 6, 7, 9, we can define the *crude range* as the highest score (9) minus the lowest score (2), i.e., $9 - 2 = 7$. A refinement is often introduced that takes into account the fact that a score of 9 might, under conditions of more accurate measurement, fall somewhere between 8.5 and 9.5, while a score of 2 might, under conditions of more accurate measurement, fall somewhere between 1.5 and 2.5. Therefore, we can view the *extended range*, or corrected range, as running from a high of 9.5 to a low of 1.5, i.e., $9.5 - 1.5 = 8$. The use of the extended, or corrected, range, therefore, adds a half unit at the top of the distribution and a half unit at the bottom of the distribution, or a total of one full unit. The extended range is, therefore, defined as the highest score (H) minus the lowest score (L) plus one unit, or $(H - L) + 1$ unit. If the units are integers we have $(H - L) + 1$ as the definition of the extended range. However, if the units are tenths of integers we have $(H - L) + .1$ as the definition of the extended range. Consider the series 8.4, 8.7, 8.8, 9.0, 9.1. The crude range is $9.1 - 8.4 = 0.7$. The extended range runs from 9.15 to 8.35, and is thus $9.15 - 8.35 = 0.8$, or $(H - L) + .1$.

For most practical purposes we can use either the crude or the extended range. When measurement is not very accurate and when the crude range is small, however, we obtain a more accurate picture of the actual range when we employ the extended range. We illustrate with an extreme example. Suppose we have employed a three-point rating scale in our research and all our judges made ratings at the midpoint value, say 2 on a scale of 1 to 3. Then our crude range would be zero $(2 - 2)$, but our extended range would be 1 $(2.5 - 1.5)$, since some of our judges might have rated nearly as high as 2.5 and some nearly as low as 1.5 had those ratings been possible. If a crude but quantitative index is desired to help us decide between the crude and extended range, we can divide the former by the latter. This index (CR/ER) yields zero in the extreme example just given and .90 if the crude range were 9 and the extended range were 10. With CR/ER as high as .90 it seems reasonable to report either of the ranges. With CR/ER much lower, it might be more informative to report the extended range.

The range is very convenient to compute and quite informative for describing the spread of certain well-balanced distributions. It suffers badly, however, from being very much affected by even a single very deviant score. (Such "wild" scores are sometimes due to recording errors, such as recording a 10 as 100.)

Trimmed ranges refer to a type of range designed to make the index of spread less affected by a small number of extreme scores. The general principle is to drop some proportion of the data from both ends of the distribution and then report the range, usually the crude range, for the data that remain. Suppose we decide to drop the extreme 10 percent of the data from each end; that would leave as the highest remaining score $X_{.90}$ (i.e., the score falling at the 90th percentile) and would leave $X_{.10}$ (i.e., the score falling at the 10th percentile) as the lowest remaining score. The trimmed range of the middle 80 percent of the scores then would be $X_{.90} - X_{.10}$. However, before we can compute this range we must find $X_{.90}$ and $X_{.10}$. We find $X_{.90}$ by computing the location of the $X_{.90}$ score as $(N + 1).90$ and the location of the $X_{.10}$ score as $(N + 1).10$. Given the scores 10, 11, 12, 13, 14, 15, 16, 17, 18, 28, we have $N = 10$, so $(N + 1).90 = 11(.90) = 9.9$ and $(N + 1).10 = 1.1$. We must keep in mind that 9.9 and 1.1 are *not* the scores we want but the *locations* of the scores we want. The 9.9th score is nine-tenths of the way between the 9th and 10th scores, which for our example is nine-tenths of the way between 18 and 28, or 27. The 1.1th score is one-tenth of the way between the first and second scores, which for our example, is one-tenth of the way between 10 and 11, or 10.1. Then the trimmed range $X_{.90} - X_{.10} = 27 - 10.1 = 16.9$.

A particular trimmed range that is frequently used is $X_{.75} - X_{.25}$, the quartile range, which we encountered earlier in our discussion of box plots and related summaries of stem-and-leaf displays. We recall that we find the required endpoints by $(N + 1).75$ and $(N + 1).25$, respectively. Thus for scores of 4, 6, 9, 11, 15, $N = 5$, $(N + 1).75 = 6(.75) = 4.5$, and $(N + 1).25 = 6(.25) = 1.5$. The locations we want, therefore, are the 4.5th score and 1.5th score, or 13 and 5, respectively. The quartile range $X_{.75} - X_{.25}$, then, is $13 - 5 = 8$. In the normal distribution (to be reviewed below) the quartile range is roughly equivalent to $1\frac{1}{3}$ standard deviations. There is one particular point in the distribution we have encountered earlier, $X_{.50}$, which is the median, and it is located by $(N + 1).50$.

The *average deviation* tells the average distance from the mean of all the scores in our series. To compute the average deviation $(\bar{D})$ we subtract the mean $(\bar{X})$ from each score (X) in turn, add these differences (D) disregarding signs, and divide by the number of scores (N) in the series:

$$\bar{D} = \frac{\Sigma|X - \bar{X}|}{N} = \frac{\Sigma|D|}{N}$$

Given a series of scores 4, 5, 5, 6, 10, we find the mean to be $30/5 = 6$. The signed deviations D are found to be $-2, -1, -1, 0, +4$ for the values 4, 5, 5, 6, 10, respectively. The sum of the signed or *algebraic* deviations about the mean is always zero, but the sum of the unsigned or *absolute values* is not. For example, this sum is 8 for the present scores $(2 + 1 + 1 + 0 + 4)$ which, when divided by N, or 5 for this series, yields an average deviation of $8/5 = 1.6$. The average deviation uses more of the information in a series of scores than does the range (which uses only the largest and smallest scores), but it is less convenient to compute or estimate than the range.

The *variance* of a set of scores is the mean of the squared deviations of the scores from their mean. Symbolically, the variance, or σ^2 (read as sigma-squared), is written as

$$\sigma^2 = \frac{\Sigma(X - \bar{X})^2}{N}$$

The square root of the variance, $\sqrt{\sigma^2} = \sigma$, is called the *standard deviation*, perhaps the most widely used of all measures of dispersion, spread, or variability. Both the variance σ^2 and the standard deviation σ are often computed for our samples of scores. If our aim is to estimate the σ^2 of the population from which our sample has been randomly drawn, we can estimate it more accurately by a slightly different statistic, S^2, which is defined as

$$S^2 = \frac{\Sigma(X - \bar{X})^2}{N - 1}$$

and is the *unbiased estimator of the population value of σ^2*. Unbiased estimators of population values such as σ^2 are estimators that, in the long run, under repeated sampling, give the most accurate estimates. Interestingly, it turns out that S is not an unbiased estimator of the population value of σ, but that fact rarely works a hardship on us.

We illustrate the computation of σ^2, σ, S^2, and S for the following set of scores: 2, 4, 4, 5, 7, 8. The mean of these scores

$$\bar{X} = \frac{\Sigma X}{N} = \frac{2 + 4 + 4 + 5 + 7 + 8}{6} = \frac{30}{6} = 5$$

where X refers to each score and N refers to the number of scores. Therefore,

$$\sigma^2 = \frac{\Sigma(X - \bar{X})^2}{N}$$

$$= \frac{(2 - 5)^2 + (4 - 5)^2 + (4 - 5)^2 + (5 - 5)^2 + (7 - 5)^2 + (8 - 5)^2}{6}$$

$$= \frac{24}{6} = 4$$

and

$$\sigma = \sqrt{\sigma^2} = \sqrt{4} = 2$$

while

$$S^2 = \frac{\Sigma(X - \bar{X})^2}{N - 1}$$

$$= \frac{(2 - 5)^2 + (4 - 5)^2 + (4 - 5)^2 + (5 - 5)^2 + (7 - 5)^2 + (8 - 5)^2}{(6 - 1)}$$

$$= \frac{24}{5} = 4.8$$

and

$$S = \sqrt{S^2} = \sqrt{4.8} = 2.19$$

In most situations in which we want to *generalize* to some population we employ S^2 (or S); in most situations in which we want only to *describe* a particular set of scores (as in a classroom test) we employ σ^2 (or σ).

THE NORMAL DISTRIBUTION

The *normal distribution* is that special bell-shaped distribution that can be completely described from just our knowledge of the mean and the standard deviation. It is very useful in a wide variety of statistical procedures; descriptively it is especially useful (as we shall see shortly) because we can specify what proportion of the area is to be found in any region of the curve. In addition, many biological, psychological, and sociological attributes are actually distributed in a normal or nearly normal manner or can be transformed so that they will be distributed normally or nearly normally.

In a normal distribution, as shown in Figure 13-5, about two-thirds of the scores fall between -1σ and $+1\sigma$, and about 95 percent of the scores fall between -2σ and $+2\sigma$. Over 99 percent of the scores fall between -3σ and $+3\sigma$, but the tails of the normal curve never do quite touch down.

A normal curve with mean set equal to zero and σ set equal to one is called a *standard normal curve*. Any score obtained on any normally distributed measure can be transformed into a score corresponding to a location on the abscissa of a standard normal curve by subtracting from the obtained score the mean obtained score and dividing this difference by the standard deviation of the original distribution. For example, assuming a mean ($\bar{X}$) and standard deviation (σ) of 500 and 100, respectively, for the SAT tests (a standard assumption), an obtained SAT score of 625 is equivalent to a standard deviation score (or *standard score*, or *Z score*) of 1.25. That is,

$$Z \text{ score} = \frac{X - \bar{X}}{\sigma} = \frac{625 - 500}{100} = 1.25$$

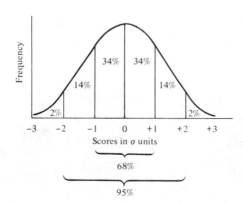

FIGURE 13-5
Areas in various segments of the normal distribution.

Employing a table of such Z values (see Appendix B, Table B.1) shows that only about 10.6 percent of those tested score as high as 625 or higher, while about 89.4 percent score lower.

A positive Z score is above the mean; a negative Z score is below the mean. An important use of Z scores is to permit the comparison (and the averaging) of scores from distributions of widely differing means and standard deviations. For example, by computing Z scores for height and weight we can tell whether a person is taller than he or she is heavy, relative to others in the distribution of height and weight. Or suppose we had two measures of course grades, one based on a midterm multiple-choice exam of 100 points with $\bar{X} = 70$ and $\sigma = 12$, another on a final essay exam of 10 points with $\bar{X} = 6$ and $\sigma = 1$. It would make no sense to sum or average a person's scores on the two exams. For instance, consider three students earning a total of 76 points:

	Raw scores			
Student	Exam I	Exam II	Total	Average
1	70	6	76	38
2	73	3	76	38
3	67	9	76	38

However, if we convert each raw score to a standard score (Z score), we find:

	Standard scores			
Student	Exam I*	Exam II[†]	Total	Average
1	0.00	0.00	0.00	0.00
2	0.25	-3.00	-2.75	-1.38
3	-0.25	3.00	2.75	1.38

*$\bar{X} = 70$, $\sigma = 12$ for the class as a whole.
[†]$\bar{X} = 6$, $\sigma = 1$ for the class as a whole.

Our first student scored at the mean both times. Our second student was slightly above-average on the first test but far below-average on the second. Our third student was slightly below-average on the first test but far above-average on the second test. The sums and averages of the Z scores take these facts into account, while the sums and averages of the raw scores are quite misleading as indices of students' course performance. Finally, Z scores can be weighted if we want them to be. In our example we weighted the Z scores for midterm and final equally (Z scores come equally weighted because their σ's are all alike, i.e., unity); if we want to weight the final exams double, we need only multiply the exam II Z scores by 2 before adding. If we did that, our three students would now have sums of weighted Z scores equal to 0.00, -5.75, and $+5.75$, respectively. Note that the sums of Z scores are *not* themselves Z scores of the distribution of summed Z scores. If we want these sums Z–scored, we must compute their mean and standard deviation and convert each sum of Z scores to a new Z by

$$Z = \frac{X - \bar{X}}{\sigma}$$

which, for the three students of the table above, yields Z scores of 0.00, -1.22, and $+1.22$, respectively. As a check, we can compute the mean and σ of this set of Z scores; as with any distribution of Z scores they should yield a mean of zero and σ of 1. Happily, they do.

DATA NOT DISTRIBUTED NORMALLY

Before leaving the topic of Z scores, we should note that when the Z scores are based on data that are approximately normally distributed, they tell us quite a lot about the proportion of scores likely to be found above and below the level of the Z score, as shown in Figure 13-5 and in Appendix B, Table B.1. That is a bonus of the Z score. However, it is not essential for Z scores to be based on a normal distribution to use them to put variables employing widely differing metrics onto a common scale, as we did in the example of exam I and exam II above.

We can illustrate that Z scores of not normally distributed data, though useful, do not tell us what we might expect based on Figure 13-5 and Appendix B, Table B.1. Consider the set of scores -3, -3, $+1$, $+1$. Their mean is -1 and $\sigma = 2$, and they become Z scores of -1, -1, $+1$, $+1$. While Z scores of $+1$ from a normal distribution exceed about 84 percent of the distribution, these Z scores of $+1$ exceed only 50 percent of the distribution.

CHAPTER
14

CORRELATION

PEARSON r

One of the major purposes of all the sciences is to describe relationships, and there is no more widely employed index of relationship than the *Pearson r*, short for *Karl Pearson's product-moment correlation coefficient*. The Pearson r can take on values between −1.00 and +1.00. A value of .00 means that there is no linear relationship between the two variables we are examining. (A linear relationship is one in which a fixed change in one variable is always associated with a fixed change in the other variable.) A value of +1.00 means that there is a perfect positive linear relationship between the variables (X and Y) such that as scores on one variable (X) increase, there are perfectly predictable *increases* in the scores on the other variable (Y). A value of −1.00 means that there is a perfect negative linear relationship between the variables such that as scores on X increase there are perfectly predictable *decreases* in the scores on Y. Correlations (r's) of +1.00, .00, and −1.00 are illustrated in Table 14.1 for three sets of four subjects, each of whom has been measured on two tests of personality, X and Y. (Also see Figure 14-1.)

Illustration A in Table 14.1 shows that the two variables may be perfectly correlated in the sense of Pearson's r even though the scores on X and Y never agree. Thus, if we are computing the degree of correlation between two judges of classroom behavior, such as degree of teacher warmth, we can achieve a high degree of correlation even though one judge rates systematically higher than the other. Inspection of illustration A shows also that the values of Y were chosen to be exactly twice the values of X. If the values of Y had been identical with the corresponding values of X, the Pearson r would also have been 1.00. Somewhat surprisingly to many students, doubling the values of one of the variables has no effect on the Pearson r. Thus, even when Y is chosen to be equal to $2X$, the Pearson r is still 1.00. In general, it is the case that multiplying the values of either or

TABLE 14.1
Illustrations of three correlation coefficients (r's)

	A r = 1.00		B r = .00		C r = −1.00	
	X	Y	X	Y	X	Y
Subject 1	8	16	8	6	8	−4
Subject 2	6	12	6	4	6	−3
Subject 3	4	8	4	4	4	−2
Subject 4	2	4	2	6	2	−1
Σ	20	40	20	20	20	−10

Note: In order to compute any correlation coefficient, each sampling unit (e.g., subject) must have two scores, one on variable X and one on variable Y.

both variables by any (nonzero) constant, or adding any constant to either or both variables, does not affect the value of the Pearson r. Such behavior is what we might expect if each set of scores (X and Y) were standard-scored (Z-scored) before we computed r. Indeed, that is exactly what is done since r can be defined as:

$$r_{xy} = \frac{\Sigma Z_x Z_y}{N}$$

That is, the correlation r_{xy} between X and Y is equal to the sum of the products of the Z scores of X and Y divided by the number (N) of pairs of X and Y scores. Now we can see why r is called a "product-moment" correlation: the Z's are distances from the mean (also called *moments*) that are multiplied by each other to form *products*.

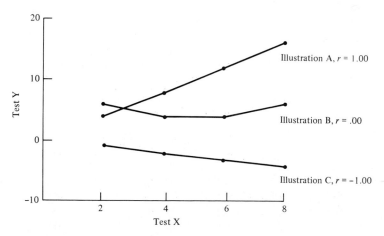

FIGURE 14-1
Plots of illustrations A, B, and C in Table 14.1.

To employ the formula above for computation, we begin by transforming our X and Y scores to Z scores. Returning to illustration A in Table 14.1, we find $(X - \bar{X})/\sigma_x = Z_x$ and $(Y - \bar{Y})/\sigma_y = Z_y$ for each person and then compute the products $Z_x Z_y$ as shown in Table 14.2.

It should be noted that the Z scores for $Y(Z_y)$ are identical with those for X although $Y = 2X$. That is because multiplying a set of scores by a constant also multiplies the standard deviation of that set of scores by the same constant, so that constancy of scale is preserved when Z scores are employed. The last column above shows the products of the Z scores and their mean, $(\Sigma Z_x Z_y)/N$, which equals r; in this case $4/4 = 1.00$.

Examining the formula for r shows that larger positive r's will be found when Z scores far above the mean of X are found alongside Z scores far above the mean of Y. Larger positive r's will also be found when Z scores far below the mean of X are found alongside Z scores far below the mean of Y (a large negative Z score multiplied by a large negative Z score yields an even larger *positive* Z score). The formula defining r is very clear conceptually but is not necessarily the most convenient formula for computing r. If a calculator is available that does not automatically compute r from the raw data of X and Y but does cumulate scores and squares of scores, the following formula is more convenient:

$$r_{xy} = \frac{N\Sigma XY - (\Sigma X)(\Sigma Y)}{\sqrt{[N\Sigma X^2 - (\Sigma X)^2][N\Sigma Y^2 - (\Sigma Y)^2]}}$$

Using the data of illustration A, we get the results shown in Table 14.3, and we find

$$r_{xy} = \frac{4(240) - (20)(40)}{\sqrt{[4(120) - (20)^2][4(480) - (40)^2]}} = \frac{160}{\sqrt{(80)(320)}} = \frac{160}{160} = 1.00$$

PROPORTION OF VARIANCE
INTERPRETATION OF CORRELATION

Although it is very useful to think of r simply as an index number such that a larger positive r represents a higher degree of linear relationship than does a smaller positive r, a number of other useful interpretations are possible.

TABLE 14.2
Computation of r

	X	Z_x	Y	Z_y	$Z_x Z_y$
Subject 1	8	1.34	16	1.34	1.80
Subject 2	6	0.45	12	0.45	0.20
Subject 3	4	−0.45	8	−0.45	0.20
Subject 4	2	−1.34	4	−1.34	1.80
Σ	20	0	40	0	4.00
$\bar{X}$	5	0	10	0	1.00*
σ	2.24	1.00	4.47	1.00	—

*This is the value of r.

TABLE 14.3
Alternative computation of r

	X	X^2	Y	Y^2	XY
Subject 1	8	64	16	256	128
Subject 2	6	36	12	144	72
Subject 3	4	16	8	64	32
Subject 4	2	4	4	16	8
Σ	20	120	40	480	240

Perhaps the most commonly employed interpretation involves r^2 rather than r; r^2 is interpreted as the proportion of the variance shared by X and Y, that is, the proportion of the variance among the Y scores that is attributable to variation in the X scores, and the proportion of the variance among the X scores that is attributable to variation in the Y scores. It is sometimes expressed as

$$r^2 + k^2 = 1.00$$

where r^2 is called the *coefficient of determination* (proportion of variance "accounted for") and k^2 is called the *coefficient of nondetermination* (the proportion of variance "not accounted for"). Although useful in some statistical applications (e.g., multiple regression and analysis of variance), the r^2 interpretation of correlation is only a poor reflection of the practical value of any given correlation coefficient (Rosenthal and Rubin, 1982a). We shall return to that idea later in this chapter.

As an illustration of the r^2 interpretation of r, consider two predictor variables X_1 and X_2 that have been employed to predict or explain the dependent variable Y, as shown in Table 14.4.

The correlation between the two predictor variables is .00, and the correlation (r) between either X_1 or X_2 and Y is .707. Squaring r yields $r^2 = (.707)^2 = .500$, the proportion of variance among the Y scores predictable from *either* the X_1

TABLE 14.4
Two predictors of a dependent variable

	Predictor variables		Dependent variable
	X_1	X_2	Y
Subject 1	3	3	6
Subject 2	3	1	4
Subject 3	1	3	4
Subject 4	1	1	2
Σ	8	8	16
$\overline{X}$	2	2	4
σ	1	1	1.41
σ^2	1	1	2

or the X_2 scores. That this proportion of variance of .500 should be found seems appropriate, since we actually created variable Y by adding up variables X_1 and X_2 and seeing to it that they would be weighted equally by ensuring that they had equal variances or standard deviations. If they did not have equal variances, the predictor with larger variance would correlate more highly with their sum, as shown in Table 14.5, in which we have left the values of X_1 intact but changed the values of X_2 for the sake of illustration.

Increasing the standard deviation of X_2 from 1 to 2 does not affect the correlation between X_1 and X_2 (still zero), but now the correlation between X_2 and Y has increased to .894 ($r^2 = .80$), and the correlation between X_1 and Y has decreased to .447 ($r^2 = .20$). This example shows that the ratio of the two values of r^2, .80/.20, is proportional to the ratio of the variances of the two predictor variables 4/1. For either example given (i.e., equal or unequal r^2 values), it is useful to note that the proportions of variance in the dependent variable (Y) predictable from X_1 and X_2 are additive and, when added, yield what is called the *multiple R^2*. In this case $R^2 = 1.00$ because $.50 + .50 = 1.00$ and $.80 + .20 = 1.00$. Whenever we are given predictor variables that are uncorrelated ($r = .00$) with each other, the multiple R^2 (which can take any value between .00 and 1.00) between the entire battery of predictor variables and the dependent variable is simply the sum of the individual r^2's. It is not common in practice, however, for predictor variables to show a zero correlation with each other. We shall have more to say about multiple correlation and its close relative, multiple regression, in Chapter 24. We refer to regression in those contexts in which we want to relate changes in level of one or more predictor variables to changes in level of the outcome variable. We refer to correlation as a more global index of closeness of relationship.

BINOMIAL EFFECT-SIZE DISPLAY

Another interpretation of r involves a method of displaying the practical importance of r. The procedure is called the *binomial effect-size display* (BESD) and

TABLE 14.5
Predictor variables with unequal variances

	Predictor variables		Dependent variable
	X_1	X_2	$Y(X_1 + X_2)$
Subject 1	3	4	7
Subject 2	3	0	3
Subject 3	1	4	5
Subject 4	1	0	1
Σ	8	8	16
$\overline{X}$	2	2	4
σ	1	2	2.24
σ^2	1	4	5

has been described in detail elsewhere (Rosenthal and Rubin, 1979b, 1982a). (The term *binomial* refers to the fact that in the BESD the research results are cast into dichotomous outcomes, such as success versus failure, improved versus not improved, or survived versus died.) Rosenthal and Rubin found that neither experienced behavioral researchers nor experienced statisticians had a good intuitive sense of the practical meaning of such indices of *effect size* (See Chapter 2) as r^2 or such near relatives of r^2 as omega-squared (Hays, 1981) and epsilon-squared (Welkowitz, Ewen, and Cohen, 1982). The BESD was introduced because (a) its interpretation was quite transparent to researchers, students, and laypersons, (b) it was applicable whenever r was employed, and (c) it was very conveniently computed.

The specific question addressed by BESD is, What is the effect on the *success rate* (e.g., survival rate, cure rate, improvement rate, selection rate, etc.) of the institution of a new treatment procedure? It therefore displays the change in success rate attributable to the new treatment procedure. A meta-analytic example shows the appeal of the display.

Earlier we described a type of research procedure known as "meta-analysis," meaning the "analysis of analyses," a procedure we describe in detail in Chapter 22. One such study has been reported by Mary Lee Smith and Gene Glass (1977), who coded and systematically integrated the results of nearly 400 controlled evaluations of psychotherapy and counseling. On the average, they found, the typical psychotherapy client is better off than 75 percent of untreated "control" individuals, which would seem to provide evidence of the efficacy of psychotherapy. Smith and Glass reported their observations in terms of effect sizes, that is, the degree to which the null hypothesis is false—the overall effect was calculated to be equivalent to an r of .32. Instead of agreeing with Smith and Glass's conclusion, some critics argued that the results of this meta-analysis sounded the "death knell" for psychotherapy because of the "modest" size of the effect, which accounted for "only 10 percent of the variance." To resolve this inconsistency in interpretation, it might be well to examine the BESD corresponding to an r of .32. For our illustration we choose a dependent variable of extreme importance—life or death. While most dependent variables are less important than life or death, we want to emphasize that the interpretation of the BESD is not affected by the choice of dependent variable.

Table 14.6 is the BESD corresponding to an r of .32 or an r^2 of .10. For convenience and consistency we set the row and column totals of the display to 100; however, the data yielding the r's we want to display in the BESD do *not* require equal or fixed totals.

Clearly it is absurd to label as "modest" an effect size equivalent to increasing the survival rate from 34 percent to 66 percent. Even so small an r as .20, accounting for "only" 4 percent of the variance, is associated with a decrease in death rate from 60 percent to 40 percent, hardly a trivial decrease. The same statistical interpretation would apply no matter what the treatment outcome measure was, whether it was survival rate, cure rate, selection rate, and so on.

A great convenience of the BESD is how easily we can convert it to r (or r^2) and how easily we can go from r (or r^2) to the display. Table 14.7 shows systematically the increase in *success rates* associated with various values of r^2 and r. Thus

TABLE 14.6
The BESD for an example accounting for "only" 10 percent of the variance

	Treatment outcome		
	Alive	Dead	Total
Treatment condition	66	34	100
Control condition	34	66	100
Total	100	100	200

an r of .30, accounting for 9 percent of the variance, is associated with an increase in success rate from 35 percent to 65 percent. The last column of the table shows that the difference in success rates is identical with r. Consequently the experimental group success rate in the BESD is computed as .50 + $r/2$, whereas the control group success rate is computed as .50 − $r/2$.

TABLE 14.7
Increases in success rate corresponding to various values of r^2 and r

r^2	r	Success rate increased		Difference in success rates (r)
		From	To	
.00	.02	.49	.51	.02
.00	.04	.48	.52	.04
.00	.06	.47	.53	.06
.01	.08	.46	.54	.08
.01	.10	.45	.55	.10
.01	.12	.44	.56	.12
.03	.16	.42	.58	.16
.04	.20	.40	.60	.20
.06	.24	.38	.62	.24
.09	.30	.35	.65	.30
.16	.40	.30	.70	.40
.25	.50	.25	.75	.50
.36	.60	.20	.80	.60
.49	.70	.15	.85	.70
.64	.80	.10	.90	.80
.81	.90	.05	.95	.90
1.00	1.00	.00	1.00	1.00

Note: For purposes of comparability across different studies, the two success rates (experimental and control) of the BESD always add to 1.00. It is *not* necessary, however, for the actual data to be displayed as a BESD to show success rates that add to any special value.

The use of the BESD to display the increase in success rate due to treatment or to selection more clearly communicates the real-world importance of treatment or selection effects than do the commonly used effect-size estimators based on the proportion of variance accounted for (Rosenthal and Rubin, 1982a).

It might appear that the BESD can be employed only when the outcome variable is dichotomous, but that is not the case. It can be shown that for many distributions, there is quite good agreement between (a) the correlation r between the treatment variable and the continuously distributed outcome variable and (b) the correlation ϕ (phi) between the treatment variable and the dichotomized outcome variable (Rosenthal and Rubin, 1982a).

One effect of the routine employment of a display procedure such as the 2×2 table of the BESD to index the *practical validity* of our research results would be to give us more useful and realistic assessments of how well we are doing in behavioral science.

Appropriate usage of the BESD requires that for any significance test computed, the effect-size estimate (r) associated with that test be reported as well. The interpretation of that r then is in terms of improvement in success rates as shown in Table 14.7. If we want to state this as a percentage, then we simply multiply $r \times 100$. Thus, $r = .40$ is equivalent to a difference in success rates of 40 percent.

SMALL CORRELATIONS, IMPORTANT EFFECTS

In the meta-analysis of psychotherapy outcome studies described above, the average size of effect was $r = .32$. The BESD shows this to be a very large effect indeed, from a practical point of view. Correlations much smaller than .32, however, can also reflect very important social, psychological, or biological effects.

As part of a massive study conducted by the Centers for Disease Control, 4,462 Army veterans of the Vietnamese war era (1965–1971) were examined. Of these, 2,490 had served in Vietnam, and 1,972 had served elsewhere. At the time of this study, approximately 13.7 percent of Vietnam veterans were identified as having suffered from alcohol abuse or dependence compared with about 9.2 percent of non-Vietnam veterans (Centers for Disease Control, 1988; Roberts, 1988). Thus, Vietnam veterans were about half again more likely to suffer from alcohol abuse or dependence as were non-Vietnam veterans (13.7 percent/9.2 percent = 1.49). How does this result translate into a correlation coefficient and a BESD?

Veteran status	Outcome		
	Alcohol problem	No alcohol problem	Total
Vietnam	341	2,149	2,490
Non-Vietnam	181	1,791	1,972
Total	522	3,940	4,462

The correlation between the variable of being versus not being a Vietnam veteran and the variable of having versus not having an alcohol problem can be computed in several different ways to be described in the section on the *phi coefficient* presented later in this chapter. For now we note that the correlation r or, equivalently, phi can be obtained from

$$r = \frac{\text{difference between cross products}}{\sqrt{\text{product of all four marginal totals}}}$$

$$= \frac{(341 \times 1{,}791) - (181 \times 2{,}149)}{\sqrt{(2{,}490)(1{,}972)(522)(3{,}940)}} = \frac{221{,}762}{3{,}177{,}872.7} = .0698$$

Thus, the Pearson r (or phi) associated with the difference between 13.7 percent and 9.2 percent is about .07 and is displayed in the following BESD:

	Problem	No Problem	Total
Vietnam	53.5*	46.5	100
Non-Vietnam	46.5	53.5	100
Total	100	100	200

*From $50 + 100r/2 = 50 + 7/2 = 53.5$; since rows and columns must add to 100, the remaining three values can be obtained by subtraction.

In the same research, about 4.5 percent of Vietnam veterans suffered from clinical depression compared with only about 2.3 percent of the non-Vietnam veterans. Thus, Vietnam veterans were approximately twice as likely to suffer depression as were the control veterans (4.5 percent/2.3 percent = 1.96). To obtain r (or phi) and the BESD we follow the above procedure.

	Depression	No depression	Total
Vietnam	112	2,378	2,490
Non-Vietnam	45	1,927	1,972
Total	157	4,305	4,462

$$r = \frac{(112 \times 1{,}927) - (45 \times 2{,}378)}{\sqrt{(2{,}490)(1{,}972)(157)(4{,}305)}} = \frac{108{,}814}{1{,}821{,}753.2} = .0597$$

The obtained correlation of approximately .06 is similar to that obtained for the variable of alcohol abuse or dependence, and the BESD therefore will be quite similar. It should be noted that the same difference in raw percentages or proportions translates into a larger r the further the two proportions are from .50. Thus, a 53 percent − 47 percent split (the BESD for the depression data) translates back into an r of .06. However, a 6 percent difference as far from .50 as possible:

	Symptom		Σ
	Present	**Absent**	
Illustrative condition 1	6	94	100
Illustrative condition 2	0	100	100
Σ	6	194	200

translates to an r of .18, since

$$r = \frac{(6 \times 100) - (0 \times 94)}{\sqrt{(100)\,(100)\,(6)\,(194)}} = \frac{600}{3,411.74} = .1759$$

A Cautionary note. In discussing the Vietnam veterans research we have been speaking of "effects." We want to emphasize here that we are using the term loosely. That is, this research was observational, nonexperimental research, so that we cannot conclude that it was serving in Vietnam that *caused* the additional problems of alcohol use or depression. All we can conclude is that having served in Vietnam is associated with a greater likelihood of developing problems of alcohol use or depression.

Note that for the results of the Vietnam veterans research, we are talking about major social problems that are indexed by effect sizes of $r =$ "only" about .07 and .06. Yet even smaller effect sizes, when based on large-scale, well-done studies (or on meta-analyses of many studies) can reflect effects of enormous consequence. To illustrate we return to the example of aspirin's effect on heart attack, which we discussed in Chapter 2. The results of that study were shown in Table 2.5.

At a special meeting held on December 18, 1987, it was decided to end this randomized, double-blind experiment (Steering Committee of the Physicians' Health Study Research Group, 1988). The reason for this unusual termination was that it had become so clear that aspirin prevented heart attacks (and deaths from heart attacks) that it would have been unethical to continue to give half the research subjects (physicians) a placebo. And what was the magnitude of this experimental effect that led to the early termination of the research? The correlation was .0337 as previously noted, with the calculation (based on the data in Table 2.5) shown below:

$$r = \frac{(189 \times 10,933) - (104 \times 10,845)}{\sqrt{(11,037)\,(11,034)\,(293)\,(21,778)}} = \frac{938,457}{27,876,280} = .0337$$

The r is small, to be sure, but the raw data above and the BESD below show that such a small r translates into a substantial number of lives saved when generalized to the population represented by these 22,071 physicians.

	Heart attack, %	No heart attack, %	Total
Aspirin	48.3	51.7	100.0
Placebo	51.7*	48.3	100.0
Total	100.0	100.0	200.0

*From $50 + \dfrac{100r}{2} = 50 + \dfrac{3.4}{2} = 51.7.$

This type of result is not at all unusual in biomedical research. Some years earlier, the National Heart, Lung, and Blood Institute discontinued its experiment on propranolol because its results in reducing death rates of patients who had suffered heart attacks were so dramatic as to make it unethical to continue giving half the subjects a placebo. The effect size in that experiment was approximately $r = .04$ (Kolata, 1981; see also Rosenthal 1990a).

SPEARMAN RANK CORRELATION

Most of the useful correlation coefficients are product-moment correlations, and they are generally special cases of the Pearson r we have been discussing. When the data are in ranked form, we apply the *Spearman rho*, but that is nothing more than a Pearson r computed on numbers that happen to be ranks. However, because ranked numbers are more predictable [in the sense that knowing only the number of pairs of scores (N) tells us both the mean and the standard deviation of the scores obtained], we have a simpler computational formula for scores that have been ranked. The only new ingredient in the definitional formula is D, the difference between the ranks assigned to the two members of each pair of sampling units. The Spearman rho (ρ), then, is computed as

$$\rho = 1 - \frac{6\Sigma D^2}{N^3 - N}$$

In the example shown in Table 14.8, four schools have been ranked by two observers on the warmth of the psychological climate created by the school's principal. The column headed D shows the difference between the ranks assigned by observers A and B, and the column headed D^2 shows these differences squared. The sum of these D^2 values (ΣD^2) is required for the computation of ρ. The columns headed Z_A and Z_B show the Z scores of the ranks assigned by observers A and B, respectively. The last column $Z_A Z_B$ shows the products of the Z-scored ranks assigned by observers A and B. Ordinarily we would need no Z scores to compute ρ, but here we wanted to illustrate the fact that ρ is equivalent to the Pearson r computed on the ranks.

Ranks as a Transformation

The Spearman rank correlation coefficient is employed when the scores to be correlated are already in ranked form, as when raters have been asked to rank a

TABLE 14.8
Two observers' rankings of four schools

	Observers A	B	D	D^2	Z_A	Z_B	$Z_A Z_B$
School 1	2	1	1	1	−0.45	−1.34	0.60
School 2	1	2	−1	1	−1.34	−0.45	0.60
School 3	3	3	0	0	0.45	0.45	0.20
School 4	4	4	0	0	1.34	1.34	1.80
Σ	10	10	0	2	0	0	3.20
$\overline{X}$	2.5	2.5	—	—	0	0	0.80
σ	1.12	1.12	—	—	1.00	1.00	—

$$\rho = 1 - \frac{6(2)}{4^3 - 4} = 1 - \frac{12}{60} = .80$$

$$r = \frac{\Sigma Z_A Z_B}{N} = \frac{3.20}{4} = .80$$

set of sampling units. In addition, however, ρ is sometimes employed as a very quick index of correlation when ρ is easy and painless to compute and r is hard and slow. Consider computing r between the pairs of scores as shown in Table 14.9 when no calculator is available.

Computing r would be painful, but computing ρ was easy because ranks are so easy to work with. Had we computed r, we would have obtained a value of .627. In this case, in which r = .627 and ρ = .800, which is the better estimate of "true" correlation? That question cannot be answered readily. If, for some reason, we regarded the obtained scores as being on just the scale of measurement required, we might prefer r to ρ. However, if there is nothing sacrosanct about the particular scale employed, and usually there is not, we might in any case choose to transform our scores to achieve greater symmetry (or lack of skewness) of distribution. Such transformations tend to increase the accuracy of statistical analyses, and ranking the scores is one form of transforming the data to reduce skewness. In this case we might have decided that the data should have been

TABLE 14.9
Computation of ρ

	X	Y	Rank X	Rank Y	D	D^2
Pair 1	6.8	79.713	2	1	1	1
Pair 2	12.2	47.691	1	2	−1	1
Pair 3	1.7	28.002	3	3	0	0
Pair 4	0.3	11.778	4	4	0	0

$$\rho = 1 - \frac{6(2)}{4^3 - 4} = 1 - \frac{12}{60} = .80$$

transformed to improve the symmetry of our distributions, since, in general, symmetrical distributions are preferable to skewed distributions for subsequent statistical analyses (Tukey, 1977). We might, for example, have decided to take the square roots of the data obtained. Had we done so, as Table 14.10 shows, the r between our square root–transformed scores would have become .799, in this case essentially the same value we obtained from the rank correlation ρ.

In this example, transforming the data to improve symmetry led to a higher r. Sometimes transforming the data leads to a lower r, however. Consider the data in Table 14.11 and their plots in Figure 14-2.

The correlation between X and Y is .9999, but the correlation between the more symmetrical transformed data (logs to the base 10 of X and Y) is only .80, precisely the value obtained by employing the rank correlation ρ. In this case ranking the data was a better transformation than the original data, i.e., better from the point of view of achieving symmetry; ranking the data had the same effect as taking the logs of the original data.

POINT BISERIAL CORRELATION

Another special case of the product-moment correlation r is the point biserial correlation, r_{pb}. In this case one of the variables is continuous (as are the variables employed for the usual case of r) while the other variable is dichotomous with arbitrarily applied numerical values, such as 0 and 1 or −1 and +1. (Such quantification of the two levels of a dichotomous variable is often called *dummy coding* when the numerical values 0 and 1 are employed.) A typical illustration

TABLE 14.10
Square root transformations

	X	Y	$\sqrt{X}$	$\sqrt{Y}$
Pair 1	6.8	79.713	2.61	8.93
Pair 2	12.2	47.691	3.49	6.91
Pair 3	1.7	28.002	1.30	5.29
Pair 4	0.3	11.778	0.55	3.43

$$r_{xy} = .627 \qquad r_{\sqrt{x}\,\sqrt{y}} = .799$$
$$\rho_{xy} = .800 \qquad \rho_{\sqrt{x}\,\sqrt{y}} = .800$$

TABLE 14.11
Logarithmic transformations

	X	Y	log X	log Y
Pair 1	100	10	2	1
Pair 2	10	100	1	2
Pair 3	1000	1000	3	3
Pair 4	10000	10000	4	4

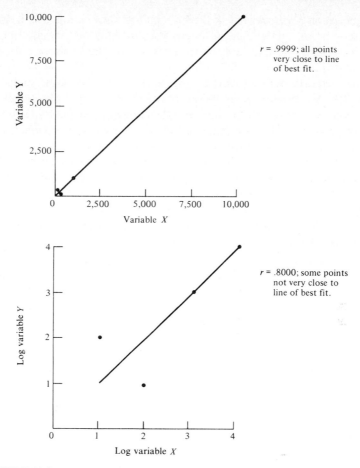

r = .9999; all points very close to line of best fit.

r = .8000; some points not very close to line of best fit.

FIGURE 14-2
Plots of the relationship between variables X and Y and variables log X and log Y.

might have us compare females with males on some measure of verbal skill with results as follows:

Males	Females
2	4
3	5
3	5
4	6

Here we have two groups of scores. But the situation does not look like the typical situation for correlation coefficients where we would expect to see *pairs* of scores (i.e., X and Y) for each subject, not just one score (Y) as above. In this example, scores on Y (the verbal skill measure) are shown, but X is hidden. The reason, of course, is that the group identification, male vs. female, implies the X scores. Rewriting the data array into a form that "looks more correlational" yields Table 14.12.

The correlation between verbal skill and gender for these eight pairs of scores was .816. Although we shall be reviewing the t test in a subsequent chapter, we may note here, in anticipation, the special relationship between t and the point biserial correlation r_{pb}. The t statistic enables us to assess the probability that the means of two samples could differ by the obtained amount if in nature, i.e., the population, there were a zero difference between the means, or if the null hypothesis of no relationship between the independent variable and the dependent variable were true. The independent variable in the case of the t test is membership in one of the two groups being compared (usually scored as 0 and 1 or -1 and $+1$), while the dependent variable is the score earned on the measures we want to compare for the two groups. As shown in Table 14.13, computing the t test for the sex-difference data yields $t = 3.46$. Computationally,

$$ t = \frac{\bar{X}_1 - \bar{X}_2}{\sqrt{\left(\frac{1}{n_1} + \frac{1}{n_2}\right)S^2 \text{ pooled}}} = \frac{5 - 3}{\sqrt{\left(\frac{1}{4} + \frac{1}{4}\right)0.6667}} = 3.46 $$

which with 6 df is significant at $p < .01$, one-tailed test.[1] This result tells us that a t this large would be obtained less than 1 percent of the time if we were drawing random samples from the populations of females and males (from which our subjects were randomly sampled), if those parent populations of females and males showed zero difference between the means *or* a zero correlation between the obtained scores (Y) and the dichotomously scored (e.g., 0, 1 or -1, $+1$) variable (X) of group membership.

For the data above we now have both a correlation r_{pb} of .816 and a t value of 3.46. If it was so easy to obtain either r or t for the same data, it must be possible to obtain t directly from r or r directly from t, and so it is. Indeed, there is a very important general relationship between r's of any form (or any other measure of the size of an effect or a relationship) and a test of significance. This general relationship, which we introduced at the conclusion of Chapter 12, can be expressed as a fundamental equation of data analysis as follows:

Significance test = size of effect × size of study

Thus, for any given (nonzero) effect size (such as r) t, or any other test of significance, will increase as the size of the study (i.e., the number of sampling

---

[1] Degrees of freedom (df) refer to the number of observations diminished by the number of restrictions limiting the observations' freedom to vary. Thus the df for a single sample of size n is equal to $n - 1$ because once the mean of the sample has been determined, only $n - 1$ of the observations are still free to vary. Analogously, when two samples are involved, as in the case of the t test, one df is lost or "used up" for each of the two samples so $df = (n_1 - 1) + (n_2 - 1) = n_1 + n_2 - 2 = N - 2$.

TABLE 14.12
Correlation between gender and verbal skill

	Verbal skill	Gender (0 = male; 1 = female)	Z_x	Z_y	$Z_x Z_y$
Subject 1	2	0	−1.64	−1	1.64
Subject 2	3	0	−0.82	−1	0.82
Subject 3	3	0	−0.82	−1	0.82
Subject 4	4	0	0.00	−1	0.00
Subject 5	4	1	0.00	1	0.00
Subject 6	5	1	0.82	1	0.82
Sugject 7	5	1	0.82	1	0.82
Subject 8	6	1	1.64	1	1.64
Σ	32	4	0	0	6.56
N	8	8	8	8	
$\overline{X}$	4.0	0.5	0	0	
σ	1.22	0.5	1	1	

units) increases. The particular index of the size of the study, e.g., N, df, $\sqrt{N}$, $\sqrt{df}$, varies with the particular index of effect size employed, which might be r, r^2, or $r/\sqrt{1 - r^2}$, depending on the test of significance involved. In the case of t and r the appropriate equation is

$$t = \frac{r}{\sqrt{1 - r^2}} \times \sqrt{df}$$

In this equation the size of the effect is defined as $r/\sqrt{1 - r^2}$ and the size of the study is defined as $\sqrt{df}$ (or, in this application, as $N - 2$). The quantity $r/\sqrt{1 - r^2}$ may be seen as the square root of $r^2/(1 - r^2)$, which is the ratio of the proportion of variance explained by r to the proportion of variance not explained by r, or a kind of signal-to-noise ratio. For our example, r was .816, so $r/\sqrt{1 - r^2} = 1.41$; the df (the number of pairs of scores minus 2) for r was $8 - 2 = 6$, so $t = 1.41 \times \sqrt{6} = 3.46$.

The general formula we gave for computing a significance test follows the scientific logic of first estimating the size of the relationship, and from that, by

TABLE 14.13
Basic data for a t test

	Males	Females
	2	4
	3	5
	3	5
	4	6
Σ	12	20
$\overline{X}$	3	5
n	4	4

employing an index of the size of the study, computing the test of significance that provides information about the probability that the null hypothesis of no relationship between X and Y is true. In practice, however, researchers have traditionally computed the significance test before they have computed the size of the effect (e.g., the correlation coefficient) because of the primacy of significance testing (Chapter 2). In such cases it is easy to obtain the effect-size estimate r from the obtained t by means of the following relationship:

$$r = \sqrt{\frac{t^2}{t^2 + (n_1 + n_2 - 2)}}$$

where n_1 and n_2 represent the sizes of the samples on which each of the means being compared was based.

The t test for the significance of a correlation coefficient applies not only to the point biserial correlation r_{pb}, but to the Pearson r and to the rank-correlation coefficient ρ as well (although in the case of ρ we would want to have at least seven pairs of scores to obtain a good approximation; a rule of thumb suggested by a comparison of Tables A11[i] and A11[ii] in Snedecor and Cochran, 1980).

Exact Tests for ρ

More exact tests of significance of the rank-correlation coefficient are also readily available for sample sizes of from 4 to 16 pairs of scores (Nijsse, 1988; Zar, 1984). The logic of these exact tests can be readily illustrated by considering this small example. Suppose two executives have ranked three managers as to their suitability for promotion. Executive 1 has ranked them as A, B, C. What is the exact probability that the correlation between the executives' rankings is 1.00? Executive 2 can rank the managers only 6 ways (not allowing ties): ABC, ACB, BAC, BCA, CAB, CBA. Only one of these rankings (ABC) results in a correlation of 1.00, and under the null hypothesis of zero correlation, all six rankings are equally likely. Therefore, the probability of a perfect correlation is 1/6, or .167. The probability of a perfect correlation for four ranked stimuli is 1 divided by the total number of ways 4 stimuli can be ranked, or $1/4! = 1/(4 \times 3 \times 2 \times 1) = 1/24 = .042$. (The term 4! is read as "four factorial" and interpreted as $4 \times 3 \times 2 \times 1$ or, more generally, as $N(N - 1)(N - 2) \ldots (2)(1)$. Simply listing all possible rankings of N stimuli allows the ready calculation of the probabilities of any outcome or of any set of outcomes, e.g., correlations exceeding any given value. Table B.10 of Appendix B shows, for various sample sizes, the magnitude of ρ required to reach various levels of significance.

PHI COEFFICIENT

Another special case of the product-moment correlation r is the phi coefficient ϕ. In this case both of the variables are dichotomous with arbitrarily applied numerical values such as 0 and 1 or -1 and $+1$. A typical illustration might have us compare Democrats with Republicans on their answer (yes or no) to a survey question, with results as follows:

	Democrats	Republicans	Σ
Yes	1	4	5
No	4	1	5
Σ	5	5	10

The 2 × 2 table of counts, also called a *contingency table*, shows that one Democrat and four Republicans answered yes while four Democrats and one Republican answered no. At first glance this contingency table does not resemble the typical situation for correlation coefficients, where we would expect to see pairs of scores (i.e., X and Y) for each subject. Closer evaluation shows, however, that the independent variable of party membership can be given numerical values, e.g., 0 and 1, and that the dependent variable of response to the question can be given similar numerical values. We noted earlier that this procedure of giving arbitrary numerical values to the two levels of a dichotomous variable is sometimes called "dummy coding" (especially when the numerical values assigned are 0 and 1) and was employed in our discussion of the point biserial correlation. Rewriting the data of our 2 × 2 table yields the arrangement shown in Table 14.14.

In our rewriting of the data, respondent 1 is drawn from the upper-left cell of the 2 × 2 table (the Democrat who said "yes"), respondents 2, 3, 4, and 5 represent the upper-right cell (the Republicans who said "yes"), respondents 6, 7, 8, and 9 represent the lower-left cell (the Democrats who said "no"), and respondent 10 is from the lower-right cell (the Republican who said "no").

TABLE 14.14
Correlation between response and party membership

	Party (X) (Rep. = 1; Dem. = 0)	Response (Y) (Yes = 1; No = 0)	Z_x	Z_y	Z_xZ_y
Respondent 1	0	1	−1	1	−1
Respondent 2	1	1	1	1	1
Respondent 3	1	1	1	1	1
Respondent 4	1	1	1	1	1
Respondent 5	1	1	1	1	1
Respondent 6	0	0	−1	−1	1
Respondent 7	0	0	−1	−1	1
Respondent 8	0	0	−1	−1	1
Respondent 9	0	0	−1	−1	1
Respondent 10	1	0	1	−1	−1
Σ	5	5	0	0	6
N	10	10	10	10	
$\overline{X}$	.5	.5	0	0	
σ	.5	.5	1	1	

Standard scores for variables X and Y

The Pearson r between party membership and response was .60 $(\Sigma Z_x Z_y / N = 6/10 = .60)$ for these data, suggesting that Republicans were more likely to say yes to this particular question. In this example, because both variables were dichotomous, we call the obtained r a phi (ϕ) to remind us of the dichotomous nature of both variables. If our sample size (N) is not too small (that is, $N > 20$), and if both variables are not too far from a 50/50 split of zeros and ones (that is, no greater than 75/25), we can test the significance of phi coefficients by t tests. Since

$$t = \frac{r}{\sqrt{1 - r^2}} \times \sqrt{df}$$

for our data,

$$t = \frac{.60}{\sqrt{1 - (.60)^2}} \times \sqrt{8} = 2.12$$

which is significant at the .034 level, one-tailed (see Table B.3 in Appendix B). This application of the t test for testing the significance of the phi coefficient is not well known but is well-documented (Cochran, 1950; Lunney, 1970; Snedecor and Cochran, 1967). The more common test of significance of the phi coefficient is the χ^2 test, which will be reviewed below. It comes as a surprise to many to learn that the χ^2 test does not necessarily yield more accurate tests of the significance of phi than does the t test computed as above (Cochran, 1950; Lunney, 1970).

So far in our discussion of phi we have treated it no differently from any other product-moment correlation. For two reasons, however, it will be useful to adopt an alternative approach to the phi coefficient. The first of these is computational convenience; the second is the availability of additional approaches to testing the significance of phi. Our alternative approach takes advantage of the fact that the data come to us in a 2 × 2 contingency table. In the table below we display again the data on the relationship between political party affiliation and response to a survey question. This time, however, we add one of four labels to each of the four cells: A, B, C, D.

	Democrats	Republicans	Σ
Yes	A 1	4 B	(A + B) = 5
No	C 4	1 D	(C + D) = 5
Σ	(A + C) = 5	(B + D) = 5	(A + B + C + D) = 10

We can compute phi from

$$\phi = \frac{BC - AD}{\sqrt{(A + B)(C + D)(A + C)(B + D)}} = \frac{(4)(4) - (1)(1)}{\sqrt{(5)(5)(5)(5)}} = \frac{15}{25} = .60$$

the identical value obtained employing $r = \Sigma Z_x Z_y / N$.

Earlier we noted the general relationship between tests of significance and measures of effect size and size of experiment

$$\text{Significance test} = \text{size of effect} \times \text{size of study}$$

For the phi coefficient another test of significance is χ^2 with one *df* [written as $\chi^2(1)$], which can be employed whenever N is not too small (that is, $N > 20$) and the two variables are not too far from a 50/50 split of zeros and ones. It is computed as

$$\chi^2(1) = \phi^2 \times N$$

in which ϕ^2 represents the size of the effect and N represents the size of the study.

For the data we have been examining, then,

$$\chi^2(1) = (.60)^2 \times 10 = 3.60$$

which is significant at the .058 level from a table of critical values of χ^2 such as Table B.5 in Appendix B. For χ^2 with one *df*, i.e., based on a 2×2 (or a 1×2) table, the tabled values of χ^2 are two-tailed with respect to the direction of the correlation (plus or minus), so that we divide the tabled p value by two if a one-tailed test is desired.

Sometimes χ^2 is computed before ϕ, and then two formulas are available:

$$\chi^2(1) = \frac{N(BC - AD)^2}{(A + B)(C + D)(A + C)(B + D)}$$

which for the data above yields:

$$\chi^2(1) = \frac{10[(4)(4) - (1)(1)]^2}{(5)(5)(5)(5)} = \frac{2250}{625} = 3.60$$

Alternatively,

$$\chi^2(1) = \sum \frac{(O - E)^2}{E}$$

which is read as the sum of the squared differences between the observed frequencies (O) and the expected frequencies (E) with each squared difference first divided by the expected frequency. The null hypothesis of no correlation (that is, that $\phi = 0$) leads to our computation of the expected frequencies. If the observed frequencies are nearly the same as those expected under the null hypothesis of no correlation, then $O - E$ will be small and $\chi^2(1)$ will be small, and it will not strongly suggest that the null hypothesis is false.

We compute the expected frequency (E) for any cell by multiplying the total of the row in which we find the cell by the total of the column in which we find the cell and dividing this product by the total number of observations (N). For the data we have been examining, the expected frequencies are all alike because $(5 \times 5)/10 = 2.5$ for all four cells. In the following display we show O and E for all four cells:

	Democrats	**Republicans**	
Yes	$O = 1$ $E = 2.5$	$O = 4$ $E = 2.5$	$\Sigma O = 5$ $\Sigma E = 5$
No	$O = 4$ $E = 2.5$	$O = 1$ $E = 2.5$	$\Sigma O = 5$ $\Sigma E = 5$
	$\Sigma O = 5$ $\Sigma E = 5$	$\Sigma O = 5$ $\Sigma E = 5$	$\Sigma\Sigma O = 10$ $\Sigma\Sigma E = 10$

Then,

$$\chi^2(1) = \Sigma \frac{(O - E)^2}{E} = \frac{(1 - 2.5)^2}{2.5} + \frac{(4 - 2.5)^2}{2.5} + \frac{(4 - 2.5)^2}{2.5} + \frac{(1 - 2.5)^2}{2.5}$$

$$= 3.60$$

If we compute $\chi^2(1)$ before computing phi, we can obtain ϕ as follows:

$$\phi = \sqrt{\frac{\chi^2(1)}{N}}$$

The sign we give our phi depends on how we want to dummy-code our variables. In the present example there is a positive correlation between being Republican and saying "yes" if we score being Republican as 1 and being a Democrat as 0, while scoring a "yes" response as 1 and a "no" response as 0. If the balance of the observed over the expected frequencies favors the cells agreeing in value of the dummy coding (1, 1 or 0, 0), we call phi "positive"; if the balance favors the cells disagreeing in value of the dummy coding (0, 1 or 1, 0), we call phi "negative."

Before leaving the topic of $\chi^2(1)$ as a test of significance for ϕ, we should mention that *corrections for continuity* are suggested in many textbooks for χ^2 computed from 2×2 tables. The effect of these corrections is to reduce the size of the $\chi^2(1)$ obtained, by diminishing the absolute difference between O and E by .5 (before squaring), to adjust for the difference between discrete and continuous distributions. More recent work suggests, however, that this correction sometimes does more harm than good in terms of yielding accurate p values (Camilli and Hopkins, 1978; Conover, 1974). In any case the correction described should definitely *not* be employed if our object is to compute phi as in the equation just above. That computation of phi requires that $\chi^2(1)$ be defined in the standard (not "corrected") manner.

Related to the $\chi^2(1)$ approach to the testing of the significance of a phi coefficient is the approach via the standard normal deviate Z. In this case the relationship between the test of significance and (1) the size of the effect and (2) the size of the study is given by

$$Z = \phi \times \sqrt{N}$$

For the data we have been using for illustration, $\phi = .60$ and $N = 10$, so

$$Z = .60 \times \sqrt{10} = 1.90$$

which is significant at the .029 level, one-tailed test, from a table of p values associated with standard normal deviates, Z's, such as Table B.1 of Appendix B. That value agrees perfectly with the one-tailed p value based on the $\chi^2(1)$ approach to testing the significance of phi. It *should*, since $\sqrt{\chi^2(1)}$ is identical with Z.

It is also useful to keep in mind the relationship

$$\phi = \frac{Z}{\sqrt{N}}$$

because we sometimes want to compute someone else's phi from their reported p value. Suppose a research report gives a $p = .005$ but neglects to give us any effect-size estimate. So long as we can find N, the total size of the study, in the report, it is a simple matter to estimate phi. Employing a table of standard normal deviates, i.e., a table of areas in the tails of the normal curve, we can find the Z associated with a p level of .005, one-tailed, to be 2.58. If we found N to be 36, we would be able to compute phi as follows:

$$\phi = \frac{2.58}{\sqrt{36}} = .43$$

CURVILINEAR (QUADRATIC) CORRELATION

So far our discussion has been only of linear correlation, in which the dependent variable (Y) can be seen to increase regularly as a function of regular increases (or decreases) in the independent variable (X). Sometimes, however, our predictions are not linear but *curvilinear*, as when we predict that performance (Y) will be better for medium levels of arousal (X) than for either high or low levels of arousal. The data below show the Pearson r between performance level (Y) and arousal level (X) for six subjects (see Table 14.15). The correlation is quite modest $(r = .13)$, and the plot of the level of performance as a function of arousal level shows why. The relationship between X and Y is not very linear; it seems instead to be substantially curvilinear; more specifically, it seems to be substantially *quadratic* (i.e., shaped like a U or an inverted U; see, for example, Figure 14-3). How can we compute a coefficient of curvilinear (quadratic) correlation between X and Y?

A number of procedures are available, and one of the simplest requires us only to redefine the variable X from "amount of X" (low to high) to "extremeness of X" (distance from the mean of X). Table 14.16 shows this redefinition. Each value of X is replaced by the absolute (unsigned) value of that score's difference

TABLE 14.15
Correlation between performance and arousal

	Arousal level (X)	Performance level (Y)	Z_x	Z_y	$Z_x Z_y$
Subject 1	4	1	−1.24	−1.58	+1.96
Subject 2	5	6	−1.04	0.00	0.00
Subject 3	8	9	−0.41	+0.95	−0.39
Subject 4	11	10	+0.21	+1.27	+0.27
Subject 5	15	7	+1.04	+0.32	+0.33
Subject 6	17	3	+1.45	−0.95	−1.38
Σ	60	36	0.00	0.00	+0.79
N	6	6			
$\overline{X}$	10	6			
σ	4.83	3.16			

$$ r = \frac{\Sigma Z_x Z_y}{N} = \frac{+0.79}{6} = .13 $$

from the mean score. Therefore, a positive correlation between the extremeness of X and the original score of Y will mean that more extreme levels of arousal are associated with higher levels of performance, while a negative correlation will mean that more extreme levels of arousal are associated with lower levels of performance.

In their original form, the scores on the X variable (arousal level) showed little correlation with the Y variable (performance level). In their redefined form ($|X - \overline{X}|$), however, the scores indicating absolute distance from the mean were very substantially correlated with performance level, $r = -.89$, showing that more extreme levels of arousal were associated with poorer performance (see Table 14.16). Later chapters will deal with the topic of curvilinear relationships in more detail.

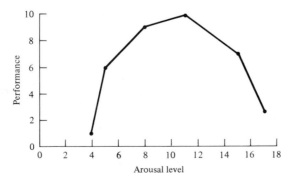

FIGURE 14-3
Curvilinear relationship between arousal level and performance.

TABLE 14.16
Correlation between performance and extremeness of arousal

	Extremeness of arousal level ($\|X - \bar{X}\|$)	Performance level (Y)	Z_x	Z_y	Z_xZ_y
Subject 1	6	1	+0.78	−1.58	−1.23
Subject 2	5	6	+0.31	0.00	0.00
Subject 3	2	9	−1.09	+0.95	−1.04
Subject 4	1	10	−1.56	+1.27	−1.98
Subject 5	5	7	+0.31	+0.32	+0.10
Subject 6	7	3	+1.25	−0.95	−1.19
Σ	26	36	0.00	0.00	−5.34
N	6	6			
$\bar{X}$	4.33	6			
σ	2.13	3.16			

$$r = \frac{\Sigma Z_x Z_y}{N} = \frac{-5.34}{6} = -.89$$

FIVE PRODUCT-MOMENT CORRELATIONS

In this chapter we have described five different product-moment correlations. Table 14.17 summarizes the chief characteristics of each.

Comparing Correlations

It often happens in behavioral research that the primary question is not so much about the relationship between two variables but about the *difference* in such relationships between two groups of subjects or between the same subjects measured under two conditions. For example, the superiority of females over males

TABLE 14.17
Product-moment correlations

Correlation	Characteristics of variables	Tests of significance*
Pearson r	Both continuous	t
Spearman rho (ρ)	Both ranked	t (or exact probability test if N is small especially if $N < 7$)
Point biserial (r_{pb})	One continuous, one dichotomous	t
Phi (ϕ)	Both dichotomous	χ^2, Z, t
Curvilinear r	Both continuous	t

*Table B.6 of Appendix B shows critical values of p associated with correlations based on varying df, where df = number of pairs of observations minus 2.

in the decoding of nonverbal cues is well established (Hall, 1984b). Such superiority can be indexed by the correlation between sex (coded as 0, 1) and skill at decoding nonverbal cues (a continuous measure; see, for example, Rosenthal, Hall, DiMatteo, Rogers, and Archer, 1979). If we were interested in whether this superiority is greater among high school students than among college students, we would have to compare the sex-skill correlations found in high school and college samples. Because the two correlations being compared are based on different independent subjects, comparisons of this type are called *comparisons of independent correlation coefficients*. If the two correlations being compared are based on the *same* subjects, the procedures are called *comparisons of nonindependent* (or *correlated*) *correlation coefficients*. An example is the comparison of the correlation between sex and sensitivity to nonverbal cues in the video versus the audio channels of nonverbal communication. It turns out, for example, that the correlation between sex and skill is higher, on the average, for decoding facial expressions than it is for decoding tone of voice (Rosenthal and De Paulo, 1979a, 1979b). Procedures for computing tests of significance of the difference between independent or correlated correlation coefficients are given in Chapter 22 (on meta-analytic procedures). In that chapter we describe procedures for combining as well as comparing correlation coefficients and other estimates of the magnitude of effects.

CHAPTER 15

COMPARING
MEANS

t TESTS, r, AND d

One of the most common situations in behavioral science is that in which we want to compare the means of two groups, e.g., an experimental versus a control group, one diagnostic category versus another, or one school system versus another. Perhaps the most common method of "comparing two means" is to employ the t test of the hypothesis that there is in the populations from which we have drawn our samples either (a) no difference between the two means or, equivalently, (b) no relationship between the independent variable of membership in one of the groups and the dependent variable of score on the response variable. The t test is a test of significance and as such is made up of two components, the size of the effect and the size of the study:

$$\text{Significance test} = \text{size of effect} \times \text{size of study}$$

In the preceding chapter on correlation we saw that when the size of the effect of the independent variable is indexed by r, the general relationship above can be rewritten more specifically as

$$t = \frac{r}{\sqrt{1 - r^2}} \times \sqrt{df}$$

Thus, we can compute the point biserial r between membership in one of the two groups (coded, for example, as 0, 1 or -1, $+1$) and the dependent variable and find t from this equation, which requires only that we also know the df for r. For this application df = the number of pairs of scores less two ($N - 2$).

An alternative to indexing the size of the effect by means of r is to index it by the standardized difference between the group means, $(M_1 - M_2)/S$, in which the difference between the group means is divided by the square root of the unbiased estimate of the population variance (S^2) pooled from the two groups:

$$t = \frac{M_1 - M_2}{S} \times \frac{1}{\sqrt{\dfrac{1}{n_1} + \dfrac{1}{n_2}}}$$

or, alternatively,

$$t = \frac{M_1 - M_2}{S} \times \sqrt{\frac{n_1 n_2}{n_1 + n_2}}$$

It should be noted that in these alternative formulas we have changed not only the size-of-effect component but the size-of-study component as well. That is, just as $(M_1 - M_2)/S$ does not equal $r/\sqrt{1 - r^2}$, neither does $\sqrt{n_1 n_2/(n_1 + n_2)} = \sqrt{df}$. Ordinarily, whenever we change the size-of-effect index, we also change the size-of-study index.

Sometimes we prefer to view the size of the effect as measured in standard score units (Z's) derived from the samples themselves. In these cases our interest is usually fixed on the effect size in the sample per se rather than on the effect size of the sample as an estimate of the effect size in the population. Therefore, our index of effect size changes from $(M_1 - M_2)/S$ to $(M_1 - M_2)/\sigma$, which is sometimes called *Cohen's d* (after Cohen, 1977, 1988), where S is based on pooling the quantities $\sqrt{\Sigma(X - \bar{X})^2/(N - 1)}$ and σ is based on pooling the quantities $\sqrt{\Sigma(X - \bar{X})^2/N}$. When we employ pooled σ rather than pooled S, the relationship between the test of significance t, the effect size $(M_1 - M_2)/\sigma = d$, and the size of the study becomes

$$t = \frac{M_1 - M_2}{\sigma} \times \left[\frac{\sqrt{n_1 n_2}}{(n_1 + n_2)} + \sqrt{df} \right]$$

When $n_1 = n_2$, the first term in the brackets simplifies to ½ and we can write

$$t = d \times \frac{\sqrt{df}}{2}$$

Sometimes, as part of a quantitative summary of a research domain, we would like to estimate d from other investigators' reports. We can do so readily if they have given us the results of their t test and their sample sizes n_1 and n_2, since

$$d = \frac{t(n_1 + n_2)}{\sqrt{df} \sqrt{n_1 n_2}}$$

When $n_1 = n_2$, this simplifies to

$$d = \frac{2t}{\sqrt{df}}$$

TABLE 15.1
Underestimation of *d* by "equal *n*" formula

Study	n_1	n_2	Estimated *d**	Accurate *d*[†]	Difference
1	50	50	.61	.61	.00
2	60	40	.61	.62	−.01
3	70	30	.61	.66	−.05
4	80	20	.61	.76	−.15
5	90	10	.61	1.01	−.40
6	95	5	.61	1.39	−.78
7	98	2	.61	2.16	−1.55
8	99	1	.61	3.05	−2.44

$$*d = \frac{2t}{\sqrt{df}} = \text{"equal } n\text{" formula.}$$

$$†d = \frac{t(n_1 + n_2)}{\sqrt{df}\,\sqrt{n_1 n_2}} = \text{general formula.}$$

If other investigators report their *t*'s and *df*'s but not their sample sizes, we can get a conservative estimate of *d* from using $d = 2t/\sqrt{df}$. When the investigator's sample sizes were equal, *d* will be accurate, but as n_1 and n_2 become more and more different, *d* will be progressively underestimated. Table 15.1 shows for eight studies, all with $t = 3.00$ and $df = n_1 + n_2 - 2 = 98$, the increasing underestimation of *d* when we employ the "equal *n*" formula. When the split is no more extreme than 70/30, however, the underestimation is still less than 10 percent.

MAXIMIZING *t*

Examination of the last four equations for computing *t* shows that *t* is maximized in three ways:

1. Driving the means further apart
2. Decreasing *S* or *σ*, the variability within groups
3. Increasing the effective size of the study

In planning our research we can maximize *t* by doing what we can to achieve the three goals above. For example, strong treatment effects will drive the means further apart. If our hypothesis were that longer treatment sessions were more beneficial than shorter treatment sessions, we would be more apt to find a significant difference if we compared sessions lasting 15 minutes with sessions lasting 45 minutes than if we compared sessions lasting 30 minutes with sessions lasting 35 minutes.

S or *σ*, the variability of response within groups, is decreased by maximizing the standardization of our procedures and employing subject samples that are fairly homogeneous in those characteristics that are substantially correlated with the dependent variable.

Finally, when the sample sizes (n_1 and n_2) are increased, the size of t will be increased. And, for any given total N (i.e., $n_1 + n_2$), we can try to make n_1 and n_2 as nearly equal as possible, since t tests thrive more when sample sizes are not too different for any fixed total N. Table 15.2 shows for various values of n_1 and n_2 (when $n_1 + n_2$ is fixed, e.g., $N = 100$) (1) the difference between n_1 and n_2, which serves as an index of sample-size inequality, (2) the arithmetic mean of the two sample sizes, (3) the harmonic mean of the two sample sizes, (4) an index of the effective size of the study, (5) the reduction in t as we have increasing inequality of n_1 and n_2, and (6) the effective loss of total sample size (N) as we have increasing inequality of n_1 and n_2. Compared with a study with $n_1 = n_2 = 50$, a study with $n_1 = 99$ and $n_2 = 1$ will show a decrease in t of 80 percent, the same effect we would have if we had lost 96 of our 100 subjects! Put another way, for any given effect size $(M_1 - M_2)/S$, t would be about the same size if we had 99 subjects in one group and 1 subject in the other group as it would if we had 2 subjects in each group.

INTERPRETING t

Behavioral and social researchers ordinarily like large t values from their investigations because larger t values are rarer events, i.e., events unlikely to occur if the null hypothesis were true. The two major ways of thinking about the null hypothesis for the t test situation are (1) the means do not differ in the populations from which we have randomly sampled our subjects, and (2) there is no relationship between the independent variable of group membership (X) and the dependent, or response, variable (Y). We illustrate each of these two ways of thinking about the null hypothesis with the following example: Imagine two populations of patients requiring treatment for some problem. These populations are identical in all ways except that one population received treatment procedure A while the other population received treatment procedure B. The null hypothesis would be true in our first way of thinking if the mean benefit score of the population receiving treatment A was identical with that of the population receiving treatment B. The null hypothesis would be true in our second way of thinking if the correlation between treatment condition (coded, e.g., A $= 1$, B $= 0$) and benefit score were exactly zero for the members of populations A and B combined.

We think of the t test as a single test of statistical significance, and so it is in terms of the formulas we have seen above. In some ways, however, we might better think of the t test as a family of tests of significance, a family of infinite size. There is a different distribution of t values for every possible value of $n_1 + n_2 - 2$, or df. The two most extreme t distributions are those when $df = 1$ and $df = \infty$. When $df = \infty$, the t distribution is the normal distribution. When $df = 1$, the t distribution is lower in frequency in the center and higher in frequency in the tails, so that it takes a larger t value to reach the same level of significance than it does when df is larger. Figure 15-1 shows the two most extreme t distributions.

The vast majority of all t distributions look much more like the normal distribution than like the t distribution when $df = 1$, and it is only when df is quite small that the divergence from normality is marked. All t distributions, however,

TABLE 15.2
Effects on t of unequal sample sizes

n_1	n_2	$n_1 - n_2$	Arithmetic mean $(\bar{n})$*	Harmonic mean $(\bar{n}_h)$†	$\sqrt{\dfrac{n_1 n_2}{n_1 + n_2}}$‡	Proportion reduction in t §	Loss of N ¶
50	50	0	50	50	5.00	.00	0
60	40	20	50	48	4.90	.02	4
70	30	40	50	42	4.58	.08	16
80	20	60	50	32	4.00	.20	36
90	10	80	50	18	3.00	.40	64
95	5	90	50	9.50	2.18	.56	81
98	2	96	50	3.92	1.40	.72	92.16
99	1	98	50	1.98	0.99	.80	96.04

*$(n_1 + n_2)/2$.

†$1 \Big/ \dfrac{1}{2}\left(\dfrac{1}{n_1} + \dfrac{1}{n_2}\right)$.

‡Index of effective size of study (I).

§$(5 - I)/5$ (for any nonzero t).

¶$2(\bar{n} - \bar{n}_h)$.

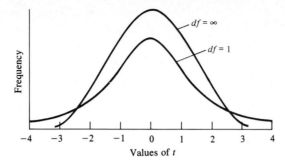

FIGURE 15-1
The two most extreme t distributions.

resemble the standard normal distribution in being symmetrical, in being centered at zero so that half the values are positive and half are negative, in having their greatest frequency near the center of the distribution, and in having tails that never do touch down, i.e., the upper and lower limits are $+\infty$ and $-\infty$. Table 15.3 illustrates the differences in t distributions by giving the areas found in the right-hand tail of selected t distributions. A more complete table of t values is in Appendix B, Table B.3.

TABLE 15.3
t values required for significance at various p levels

df	One-tailed p					
	.25	.10	.05	.025	.005	.001
1	1.00	3.08	6.31	12.71	63.66	318.31
2	.82	1.89	2.92	4.30	9.92	22.33
3	.76	1.64	2.35	3.18	5.84	10.21
4	.74	1.53	2.13	2.78	4.60	7.17
5	.73	1.48	2.02	2.57	4.03	5.89
6	.72	1.44	1.94	2.45	3.71	5.21
8	.71	1.40	1.86	2.31	3.36	4.50
10	.70	1.37	1.81	2.23	3.17	4.14
15	.69	1.34	1.75	2.13	2.95	3.73
20	.69	1.32	1.72	2.09	2.84	3.55
25	.68	1.32	1.71	2.06	2.79	3.45
30	.68	1.31	1.70	2.04	2.75	3.38
40	.68	1.30	1.68	2.02	2.70	3.31
60	.68	1.30	1.67	2.00	2.66	3.23
80	.68	1.29	1.66	1.99	2.64	3.20
100	.68	1.29	1.66	1.98	2.63	3.17
1,000	.68	1.28	1.65	1.96	2.58	3.10
10,000	.68	1.28	1.64	1.96	2.58	3.09
∞	.67	1.28	1.64	1.96	2.58	3.09

Studying Table 15.3 shows that for any level of significance p, the t value required to reach that level is smaller and smaller as df increases. In addition, of course, for any df a higher t value is required to reach more extreme (smaller) p levels. The most surprising fact about this table is the difference in t values required to reach the .001 level; when df is very large, a t of only about 3 is required, when $df = 1$, however, a t of about 318 is required!

One way to think about t is that if the null hypothesis were true—i.e., that the means in the population did not differ or that there were an r of zero between group membership (X) and scores on the dependent variable (Y)—the most likely value of t would be zero. However, even if the population mean difference were truly zero, we would often find nonzero t values by sheer chance alone. For example, with $df = 8$ we would obtain a t value of $+1.40$ or greater about 10 percent of the time, or of 1.86 or greater about 5 percent of the time, or of 4.50 or greater about one tenth of one percent of the time.

We must decide for ourselves whether we will regard any given t as an event rare enough to make us doubt that the null hypothesis is true. The larger the t and the smaller the p (more significant p's are *smaller*), the less likely it is that the null hypothesis is true. American behavioral researchers have an informal agreement to regard as "statistically significant" t values (and other tests of significance) with associated p levels of .05 or less, i.e., $p \leq .05$. There is evidence that decisions to believe or not believe (accept or reject) the null hypothesis are made in a binary manner based simply on whether p does or does not reach the .05 level (Nelson, Rosenthal, and Rosnow, 1986; Rosenthal and Gaito, 1963, 1964; Minturn, Lansky, and Dember, 1972).

The most experienced data-analytic statisticians do not share this view of a fixed critical level of significance and regard it as far wiser to report the actual p level obtained along with a statement of the size of the effect obtained (e.g., Snedecor and Cochran, 1967). There is something absurd in regarding as a "real" effect one that is supported by a $p = .05$ and as a zero effect one that is supported by a $p = .06$, yet this binary decision process does occur (Rosenthal and Gaito, 1964). It is helpful to keep in mind the general relationship

$$\text{Significance test} = \text{size of effect} \times \text{size of study}$$

which shows that for any size of effect that is not precisely zero we can achieve any level of significance desired simply by adding to the size of the study (N).

COMPUTING t

We have already given several formulas for computing t, as summarized below:

$$\text{Significance test} = \text{size of effect} \times \text{size of study}$$

(1) $\qquad t \qquad = \dfrac{r}{\sqrt{1 - r^2}} \quad \times \sqrt{df}$

(2) $\qquad t \qquad = \dfrac{M_1 - M_2}{S} \quad \times \dfrac{1}{\sqrt{\dfrac{1}{n_1} + \dfrac{1}{n_2}}}$

$$(3) \qquad t \qquad = \frac{M_1 - M_2}{S} \times \sqrt{\frac{n_1 n_2}{n_1 + n_2}}$$

$$(4) \qquad t \qquad = \frac{M_1 - M_2}{\sigma} \times \left(\frac{\sqrt{n_1 n_2}}{(n_1 + n_2)} + \sqrt{df} \right)$$

$$(5) \qquad t \qquad = d \qquad \times \frac{\sqrt{df}}{2}$$

While all of these formulas are useful conceptually and often useful computationally, they are not as compact as we might like for a primary computational formula. Perhaps the most generally useful computational formula for a t test designed to compare the means of two independent groups is based on equation (2) above, which is rewritten more compactly as follows:

$$t = \frac{M_1 - M_2}{\sqrt{\left(\frac{1}{n_1} + \frac{1}{n_2}\right) S^2}}$$

where M_1 and M_2 (or $\bar{X}_1$ and $\bar{X}_2$) are the means of the two groups, n_1 and n_2 are the number of sampling units in each of the two groups, and S^2 is the pooled estimate of the population variance computed as

$$S^2 = \frac{\Sigma(X_1 - \bar{X}_1)^2 + \Sigma(X_2 - \bar{X}_2)^2}{n_1 + n_2 - 2}$$

Suppose we had obtained the following scores from two groups of subjects with $n_1 = n_2 = 4$:

	Group 1	Group 2
	2	1
	3	2
	4	1
	5	2
Σ	14	6
n	4	4
$M = \bar{X}$	3.5	1.5

For each group, we compute the sum of the squares of the deviations of the scores from their mean:

	Group 1			Group 2		
(X_1)	$(X_1 - \bar{X}_1)$	$(X_1 - \bar{X}_1)^2$	(X_2)	$(X_2 - \bar{X}_2)$	$(X_2 - \bar{X}_2)^2$	
2	−1.5	2.25	1	−0.5	0.25	
3	−0.5	0.25	2	0.5	0.25	
4	0.5	0.25	1	−0.5	0.25	
5	1.5	2.25	2	0.5	0.25	
Σ 14	0	5.00	6	0	1.00	
$\bar{X}$ 3.5	0		1.5	0		

Then

$$S^2 = \frac{\Sigma(X_1 - \bar{X}_1)^2 + \Sigma(X_2 - \bar{X}_2)^2}{n_1 + n_2 - 2} = \frac{5 + 1}{4 + 4 - 2} = 1.00$$

so

$$t = \frac{3.5 - 1.5}{\sqrt{(\frac{1}{4} + \frac{1}{4})1.00}} = \frac{2}{\sqrt{.5}} = 2.83$$

with 6 df, a t of 2.83 is significant at about the .02 level, one-tailed test.

There is an alternative to the computation of S^2 that is more convenient when a hand-held calculator for obtaining sums of squared scores is available:

$$S^2 = \frac{\left(\Sigma X_1^2 - \frac{(\Sigma X_1)^2}{n_1}\right) + \left(\Sigma X_2^2 - \frac{(\Sigma X_2)^2}{n_2}\right)}{n_1 + n_2 - 2}$$

For the data given above

	Group 1		Group 2	
	(X_1)	$(X_1)^2$	(X_2)	$(X_2)^2$
	2	4	1	1
	3	9	2	4
	4	16	1	1
	5	25	2	4
Σ	14	54	6	10
$\bar{X}$	3.5	—	1.5	—

Then

$$S^2 = \frac{\left(54 - \frac{(14)^2}{4}\right) + \left(10 - \frac{(6)^2}{4}\right)}{4 + 4 - 2} = \frac{5 + 1}{6} = 1.00$$

Sometimes we want to compute t but do not have access to the original data. Instead, we may have access to certain summary statistics of the original data (our own or others') such as r, means, S, σ, d, n's, or df. Depending on which of these summary statistics we have available, different formulas for t will be useful. In Table 15.4 t is computed from the five formulas presented earlier. Had r and df been given, we would have employed the first formula listed to obtain t. Had $(M_1 - M_2)/S$ been given, we would have employed the second or third formula listed. Finally, had $(M_1 - M_2)/\sigma$ (or d) been given, we would have employed the fourth or fifth formula listed; the fourth formula if n_1 and n_2 were different, the fifth formula if n_1 and n_2 were equal or nearly so.

TABLE 15.4
Alternative computations of t

Significance test	=	Size of effect	×	Size of study	Example *	=	t
t	=	$\dfrac{r}{\sqrt{1-r^2}}$	×	$\sqrt{df}$	$\dfrac{.756}{\sqrt{1-(.756)^2}} \times \sqrt{6}$	=	2.83
t	=	$\dfrac{M_1 - M_2}{S}$	×	$\dfrac{1}{\sqrt{\dfrac{1}{n_1}+\dfrac{1}{n_2}}}$	$2.00 \times \dfrac{1}{\sqrt{\frac{1}{4}+\frac{1}{4}}}$	=	2.83
t	=	$\dfrac{M_1 - M_2}{S}$	×	$\sqrt{\dfrac{n_1 n_2}{n_1 + n_2}}$	$2.00 \times \sqrt{\dfrac{(4)(4)}{4+4}}$	=	2.83
t	=	$\dfrac{M_1 - M_2}{\sigma}$	×	$\left(\dfrac{\sqrt{n_1 n_2}}{(n_1 + n_2)} \times \sqrt{df}\right)$	$2.31 \times \left[\dfrac{\sqrt{(4)(4)}}{4+4} \times \sqrt{6}\right]$	=	2.83
t	=	d	×	$\dfrac{\sqrt{df}}{2}$	$2.31 \times \dfrac{\sqrt{6}}{2}$	=	2.83

*The data are from the example given on pp. 308 and 309.

t TESTS FOR NONINDEPENDENT SAMPLES

So far in our discussion of t tests employed to compare the means of two groups we have assumed the two groups of scores to be independent. That is, we thought of the scores in one group as having no relationship to the scores in the other group. Suppose, for example, that the two groups we have been comparing were two groups of children aged 10 to 11 who had been rated by judges on a 5-point scale of sociability. If group 1 had been the girls and group 2 had been the boys, might we not conclude that the children of groups 1 and 2 were independent of each other? Not necessarily. It might be the case, for example, that the four boys and four girls all came from just four families, as in Table 15.5.

When we examine the girls' and boys' scores over the four families, we find that a family member's sociability score is to some degree predictable from a knowledge of family membership. For example, Table 15.5 shows that the Smith children are judged to be most sociable while the Brown children are judged to be least sociable. For these data, then, common family membership has introduced a degree of relatedness between the observations of group 1 and group 2. Other ways in which a degree of correlation might have been introduced include membership in the same dyad, as when female and male couple members are to be compared with each other. Perhaps the most common example is the so-called repeated-measures design in which the same subjects are each measured twice—perhaps once after a treatment condition and once after a control condition, or once before and once after having been exposed to a learning experience.

Whenever pairs of observations *could* have been lined up next to each other because they were from the same family, the same dyad, or the same person, but were *not* lined up next to each other, we typically obtain t tests that are too small. That is because in these situations there is usually a positive correlation between scores earned by the two paired observations. In the example above, this correlation was .45. More rarely this type of correlation between pairmates is negative, and in those cases the resulting t will be too large if the t is computed ignoring this negative correlation (Kenny and Judd, 1986).

In these t tests for correlated data (or repeated measurements, or matched pairs) we perform our calculations not on the original $n_1 + n_2$ scores but on the *differences* between the n_1 and n_2 scores. For example, given the family data above we compute the difference score $(X_1 - X_2 = D)$ for each pair of lined-up scores as shown in Table 15.6.

TABLE 15.5
Sociability scores

Family	Girls: group 1	Boys: group 2	Mean
Brown	2	1	1.5
Clark	3	2	2.5
Jones	4	1	2.5
Smith	5	2	3.5
$\bar{X}$	3.5	1.5	2.5

TABLE 15.6
Sociability differences

Family	Girls	Boys	D
Brown	2	1	1
Clark	3	2	1
Jones	4	1	3
Smith	5	2	3
Σ	14	6	8
$\bar{X}$	3.5	1.5	2

We then make the following calculation of t:[1]

$$t = \frac{\bar{D}}{\sqrt{\left(\frac{1}{n}\right) S_D^2}} = \frac{2}{\sqrt{(\frac{1}{4})1.333}} = 3.46$$

where

$$S_D^2 = \frac{\Sigma(D - \bar{D})^2}{n - 1} = \frac{4}{3} = 1.333$$

Earlier, when we computed t for the two groups of scores above, forgetting about the fact that they were not independent, we obtained a t of 2.83, which with 6 df was significant at about the .02 level, one-tailed test. In the case of the matched pair t of 3.46 for the same data, our df are not 6 (i.e., $n_1 + n_2 - 2$) but only 3, because we operated on only a single sample of four difference scores, and so $df = n - 1 = 3$. For a t of 3.46 and $df = 3$, our p value is still about .02, because our larger t was offset by the loss of 3 df. Ordinarily sample sizes are larger than in this illustration, and when the data of the two groups are substantially correlated, we find substantial increases in t accompanied by substantially lower (more significant) p levels.

For the matched pair t we can show the relationship to effect size and to size of the study as in Table 15.7.

The relationships of t for correlated observations to size of effect and size of study are analogous to the situation of the t for independent observations, keeping in mind that for matched pairs there are only n pairs to operate on

TABLE 15.7
Alternative computations of t (nonindependent)

Significance test	=	Size of effect	×	Size of study	Example*		t
t	=	$\dfrac{r}{\sqrt{1 - r^2}}$	×	$\sqrt{df}$	$\dfrac{.894}{\sqrt{1 - (.894)^2}} \times \sqrt{3}$	=	3.46
t	=	$\dfrac{\bar{D}}{S_D}$	×	$\sqrt{n}$	$\dfrac{2}{1.155} \times \sqrt{4}$	=	3.46
t	=	d	×	$\sqrt{df}$	$\dfrac{2}{1.000} \times \sqrt{3}$	=	3.46

*The data are from the example given on pp. 311–313.

---

[1]The same formula can be employed when a single set of scores is to be compared with some specific theoretical value. Then we can form a D score for each person by subtracting the specific theoretical value from each person's obtained score. That is, D would equal X obtained minus X hypothesized from theory.

rather than $n_1 + n_2$ observations. In the third equation, d is defined as $\bar{D}/\sigma_D$, or the mean of the difference scores divided by the σ of the difference scores; df refers to $n - 1$ *pairs* of scores or $n - 1$ difference scores. In the second equation, S_D refers to S computed on the n difference scores, and n refers to the number of difference scores. In the first equation, r refers to the correlation between membership in group (girls versus boys) and observed score *corrected for family membership*. It does *not* refer to the correlation between the first and second measurement made within families, dyads, or individuals. It also does not refer to the correlation of the eight scores uncorrected for family membership with membership in the groups (girls versus boys). If we compute this r (scoring, e.g., girls $= 1$, boys $= 0$), we would obtain the point biserial r corresponding to the t test for uncorrelated observations, with $r = .756$ rather than .894.

There are two ways to understand where we get the r for the size of the treatment or group effect for matched-pair t tests. One way is via the analysis of variance, which will be reviewed and discussed later in this chapter. In this approach we compute the "sums of squares" for the group or condition effect and for the "error term" for the group or condition effect, and then find r as

$$r = \sqrt{\frac{SS_{\text{groups}}}{SS_{\text{groups}} + SS_{\text{error}}}}$$

For the present data our table of variance is

Source	SS	df	MS	F	t	r
Pairs	4	3	1.333			
Gender groups	8	1	8.000	12.00	3.46	.894
Residual or error	2	3	0.667			

and, therefore

$$r = \sqrt{\frac{8}{8 + 2}} = \sqrt{.80} = .894$$

Another approach to understanding where we get the r for the size of the treatment or group effect for matched pairs is by "correcting" the original data for the systematic effects of membership in a particular pair (e.g., the family, dyad, or individual that generated the two scores). This is accomplished by subtracting for each member of a pair the mean of the two pair members. This procedure has the effect of eliminating differences between the means of families, dyads, or individuals. Having thus removed statistically (or "partialed out") the effect of belonging to a particular pair, we can then compute the point biserial correlation between group membership (coded as 0, 1 or as -1, 1, for example) and the corrected observed score. However, in the process of correcting for pair membership we lose all the df for pairs. Since in our example there were four pairs, we lose $4 - 1 = 3$ df in the process of computing r from our pair-corrected or residual scores, as shown in Table 15.8.

TABLE 15.8
Correlation after correction for family membership

Family	Girls (X_1)	Boys (X_2)	Mean $(\bar{X})$	Mean-corrected $X_1 - \bar{X}$	$X_2 - \bar{X}$
Brown	2	1	1.5	+0.5	−0.5
Clark	3	2	2.5	+0.5	−0.5
Jones	4	1	2.5	+1.5	−1.5
Smith	5	2	3.5	+1.5	−1.5
Σ	14	6	10.00	4.0	−4.0
$\bar{X}$	3.5	1.5	2.5	1.0	−1.0

Child	Gender (1 = female; 0 = male)	Score (corrected)	Gender Z_x	Score Z_y	$Z_x Z_y$
1	1	0.5	1	0.45	0.45
2	1	0.5	1	0.45	0.45
3	1	1.5	1	1.34	1.34
4	1	1.5	1	1.34	1.34
5	0	−0.5	−1	−0.45	0.45
6	0	−0.5	−1	−0.45	0.45
7	0	−1.5	−1	−1.34	1.34
8	0	−1.5	−1	−1.34	1.34
Sum	4	0	0	0	7.16

$$r = \frac{\Sigma Z_x Z_y}{N} = \frac{7.16}{8} = .895$$

Therefore, our r based on computations from residuals (i.e., differences between scores and family means) agrees within rounding error with our r based on the analysis of variance. This process of correcting for pair membership will be described further in subsequent chapters dealing with two-way analysis of variance.

ASSUMPTIONS UNDERLYING THE USE OF t TESTS

Several assumptions are made in our use of t tests, and to the extent that these assumptions are not met, we may make incorrect inferences from our t tests. The basic assumptions are sometimes summarized by the statement that errors are IID normal, where "errors" refers to the deviation of each score from the mean of its group or condition, and IID normal is read as "independently and identically distributed in a normal distribution" (Box, Hunter, and Hunter, 1978, p. 78). The shorthand format of IID normal translates into three assumptions about the distribution of observations within conditions ("errors").

1. The Errors Are Independent (Independence)

If the errors are not independent of one another, the t we obtain may be very much in error. For example, if observations are strongly positively correlated, the obtained t may be several times larger than the accurate t (Snedecor and Cochran, 1980). Correlations among errors can be introduced in many ways. Suppose that we want to compare two types of group therapy. We assign 30 patients to each of the two types and within each type assign 10 patients to each of three groups. It might turn out that being in the same therapy group has made the patients in each group "too much alike," so that they are no longer independent or uncorrelated. If that were so, thinking that we had 30 independent sampling units in each condition could be quite misleading. In such a situation we might have to regard *groups* rather than persons as our sampling units, and we would thereby suffer a loss of *df* from 58, or $(30 + 30 - 2)$, to 4, or $(3 + 3 - 2)$. In this example each person within a group would be seen as a "repeated measurement" of each group. The analysis of such data is considered in Chapter 18. A valuable discussion of problems of independence can be found in the volume by Charles Judd and David Kenny (1981) and in a more recent paper by the same workers (Kenny and Judd, 1986).

2. The Errors Are Identically Distributed (Homogeneity of Variance)

For the t test situation in which two groups are being compared, the t obtained will be more accurate if the variances of the populations from which our data were drawn are more nearly equal. Only if the two population variances are very different *and* if the two sample sizes are very different is the violation of this assumption likely to lead to serious consequences. If just this situation has occurred, we can often transform the data to make the variances more nearly equal and then perform the t test on the transformed data. The most commonly used transformations involve taking the (a) square root, (b) logs, (c) reciprocal square root, or (d) reciprocals of the original data. George Box, William Hunter, and Stuart Hunter (1978) and John Tukey (1977) give more detailed guidance on when to use which transformation or reexpression of the data. The goal in this case, however, is clear. We want the one that makes our transformed data most nearly homogeneous in its variances.

3. The Errors Are Normally Distributed (Normality)

If the errors are very nonnormally distributed, some inaccuracy may be introduced into the t test. However, if the distributions are not *too* skewed or not *too* biomodal, there seems to be little cause for concern unless sample sizes are tiny (Hays, 1981).

The assumptions we have discussed as underlying the use of the t test are also important to keep in mind during the reading of the following material that deals with the use of the F test. *The very same assumptions described above as underlying the appropriate use of* t *also underlie the appropriate use of* F.

NONPARAMETRIC PROCEDURES

Nonparametric, or distribution-free, or, more generally, "sturdy" statistics make fewer assumptions than do such parametric procedures as t and F tests (Mosteller and Rourke, 1973).[2] These assumptions have to do with the shape of the underlying distributions from which we have drawn our samples, and so they refer to assumptions 2 and 3 of the preceding section. Thus, all nonparametric procedures make the independence assumption (assumption 1), and some make further assumptions of identity of shapes of distributions or of the symmetry of the population distribution (Siegel, 1956; Siegel and Castellan, 1988). Nonparametric procedures, therefore, are not at all assumption-free, but they can be useful adjunct procedures when, for example, homogeneity of variance (assumption 2) or crude normality [e.g., absence of serious skewness (assumption 3)] cannot be achieved with appropriate transformation. Ordinarily, nonparametric procedures are equivalent to parametric procedures applied to appropriately transformed data (Judd and McClelland, 1989).

Sometimes, when sample sizes are very small, there is no alternative to some form of nonparametric test of significance. That was exactly the situation we encountered in our discussion of Spearman's rank-correlation coefficient. When the number of pairs of scores being correlated is very small, we are forced to go to nonparametric procedures for computing the exact probabilities of various outcomes of rankings. We shall encounter an analogous situation when we discuss tables of counts in which the expected frequencies in a 2×2 table fall critically low (Chapter 23).

There is now such a rich profusion of nonparametric procedures that even a brief discussion of the major ones would require at least a small textbook of its own. Fortunately, there is a growing list of texts that can be recommended, beginning with the classic by Sidney Siegel (1956) and its recent revision (Siegel and Castellan, 1988) and including Bradley (1968), Conover (1980), Fraser (1957), Gibbons (1985), Hollander and Wolfe (1973), Lehmann (1975), Marascuilo and McSweeney (1977), Mosteller and Rourke (1973), Noether (1967), and Pratt and Gibbons (1981).

THE F TEST AND THE ANALYSIS OF VARIANCE

Earlier we discussed the comparison of two means by employing the t test. In the present section we discuss the comparison of two or more means by employing the F test. The F test can be used to test the hypothesis that there is in the population from which we have drawn our two or more samples (a) no difference between the two or more means or, equivalently, (b) no relationship between

---

[2]Although rigorous distinctions can be made between such terms as "nonparametric" and "distribution-free" (e.g., Huber, 1981; Marascuilo and McSweeney, 1977), for our present purpose that is not necessary.

membership in any particular group and score on the response variable. The F test, like the t test, is a test of significance and is, therefore, made up of two components, the size of the effect and the size of the study.

$$\text{Significance test} = \text{size of effect} \times \text{size of study}$$

When there are only two means to be compared and when we index the size of the effect by r^2, the general relationship above can be rewritten more specifically as

$$F = \frac{r^2}{1 - r^2} \times df$$

We can, therefore, compute the point biserial r between membership in one of the two groups (coded, for example, as 0, 1 or -1, $+1$) and the dependent variable and find F from this equation, which requires only that we also know the df for r; for this application df = the number of pairs of scores less two, or $N - 2$. If we take the square root of both sides of the equation above we have

$$\sqrt{F} = \frac{r}{\sqrt{1 - r^2}} \times \sqrt{df}$$

The right-hand side of this equation equals not only $\sqrt{F}$ but t as well, as we saw in the beginning of the discussion of the t test. For the special case of the comparison of two groups, then, $F = t^2$ or $\sqrt{F} = t$, and we could use either test to investigate the plausibility of the hypothesis that in the population from which we have drawn our samples there is no relationship between the independent and dependent variable, i.e., that $r = 0$. Just as is the case for t, the distribution of F is readily available in tables for the case of $r = 0$, so we can easily look up the probability that an F as large or larger than the one we obtained could have occurred if r were, in fact, zero. How, then, shall we decide whether to use t or F?

The advantage of t is that it is a signed statistic; i.e., it can be positive or negative in value, so that we can tell whether r is positive or negative or, put another way, whether the mean of the first group is greater than or less than the mean of the second group; F operates on r^2 or on the squared difference between the means, so F is the same whether the obtained r is positive or negative or whether group A is smaller or larger by the obtained amount than group B.

The limitation of t is that it can be employed only when there are just two means to be compared; the advantage of F is that it operates just as well for three groups, or four, or *any* number of groups as it does for just two groups. When more than two means are being compared, the relationship between F and the size of the effect and the size of the study is generalized to

$$F = \frac{\text{eta}^2}{1 - \text{eta}^2} \times \frac{df \text{ error}}{df \text{ means}}$$

where eta^2 is a correlation index defined as the proportion of variance in the dependent variable attributable to group membership, df error is analogous to the term df when we were discussing the t test, and df means is the number (k) of means being compared less one, or $k - 1$. Later in this chapter we shall be more precise about the definition of eta and df error.

When we were discussing t earlier in this chapter, we noted that the size of the effect could be indexed by r or by an index of standardized distance between the group means $(M_1 - M_2)/S$. In this latter index the difference between means is divided by the square root of the unbiased estimate of the population variance (S^2) pooled from the two groups. How might we incorporate the idea of standardized distances among means for the situation in which more than two means are to be compared? We might take all possible pairs of distances between means and take their average. This average distance between means, when divided by S computed from all the groups' data, would yield an *average* $(M - M)/S$ with signs disregarded. Such an index *would* be fairly informative, but it turns out to be less useful for *subsequent* statistical procedures than an index that focused on squared differences among means, or S^2_{means} defined as

$$S^2_{means} = \frac{\Sigma(M_k - \overline{M})^2}{k - 1}$$

where M_k is any of the k means being compared, $\overline{M}$ is the mean of these k means, and k is the number of means being compared.

A large S^2_{means} indicates that the means are far apart in the sense of squared distances from the grand mean. However, the actual meaning of "far" depends on the particular metric employed in the particular research, and we shall want to standardize the distance index S^2_{means} by the particular unit of measurement employed. We can accomplish this by dividing S^2_{means} by S^2, the variance computed separately within each group and averaged from all groups. For the situation in which we want to compare the means of any number of independent groups we can also define F in terms of this new effect-size estimate and n, the number of sampling units in each of the groups when all groups have the same n:

$$F = \frac{S^2_{means}}{S^2} \times n$$

When the n's of the groups are not equal, n may be replaced (for a conservative estimate of F) by the harmonic mean of the sample sizes. The estimate of F based on the harmonic mean of the sample sizes is conservative in the sense that the harmonic mean of unequal sample sizes is always smaller than the arithmetic mean of these sample sizes. The harmonic mean of the sample sizes $(\overline{n}_h)$ is found by

$$\overline{n}_h = 1 \left/ \frac{1}{k} \left(\frac{1}{n_1} + \frac{1}{n_2} + \cdots + \frac{1}{n_k} \right) = k \left/ \left(\frac{1}{n_1} + \frac{1}{n_2} + \cdots + \frac{1}{n_k} \right) \right.\right.$$

where k is the number of means being compared and n_1 to n_k are the sizes of the samples on which the various means are based.

Studying closely the definition of F in terms of $(S^2_{means}/S^2) \times n$ will solve a mystery that plagues students beginning their study of the analysis of variance. The mystery is, Why do we call it analysis of *variance* when what we are "really" doing is comparing *means*? Of course we're doing both. We are comparing variances—the variance among means is compared with the variance within conditions—(the basic level of variation or noise in the system) in order to find out how far apart the means are on average. For any given size of sample n, F will be larger if the S^2_{means} grows larger relative to the S^2 (the denominator value). It should also be pointed out that the analysis of variance is employed in situations other than the comparisons of means (e.g., in regression analysis discussed in Chapter 24) and that F tests are sometimes employed actually to compare variabilities of groups rather than their means. This latter use of F will be discussed later in this chapter.

AN ILLUSTRATION

Suppose we had 12 patients available for an experiment comparing four different treatment conditions or groups. We allocate three patients at random to each of the four conditions and obtain the improvement scores shown in Table 15.9.
On the basis of these scores,

$$\overline{M} = (8 + 4 + 4 + 2)/4 = 4.5$$

Since

$$F = \frac{S^2_{means}}{S^2} \times n$$

we begin by computing S^2_{means}:

$$S^2_{means} = \frac{\Sigma(M_k - \overline{M})^2}{k - 1} = \frac{(8 - 4.5)^2 + (4 - 4.5)^2 + (4 - 4.5)^2 + (2 - 4.5)^2}{4 - 1}$$

$$= \frac{(3.5)^2 + (-0.5)^2 + (-0.5)^2 + (-2.5)^2}{3} = \frac{19}{3} = 6.33$$

TABLE 15.9
Improvement scores in four conditions

	Psychotherapy plus drug treatment	Psychotherapy plus no drug treatment	No psychotherapy plus drug treatment	No psychotherapy plus no drug treatment
	9	6	5	4
	8	4	4	2
	7	2	3	0
Σ	24	12	12	6
M_k or $\overline{X}$	8	4	4	2
S^2_k	1.0	4.0	1.0	4.0

Next we want S^2, the pooled within-group variance collected over all groups:

$$S^2 = \frac{\Sigma(n_k - 1)S_k^2}{\Sigma(n_k - 1)} = \frac{(2)(1.0) + (2)(4.0) + (2)(1.0) + (2)(4.0)}{2 + 2 + 2 + 2} = \frac{20}{8} = 2.50$$

So

$$F = \frac{S_{means}^2}{S^2} \times n = \frac{6.33}{2.50} \times 3 = \frac{19.00}{2.50} = 7.60$$

Once we have computed F, we refer it to a table of the F distribution to learn the p level associated with an F value of that magnitude or greater. We shall return shortly to the use of F tables.

The formula we employed for computing F was useful for showing F to be a product of the size of the effect (S_{means}^2/S^2) and the size of the study (n), as is the case for all tests of significance. Although that formula is conceptually instructive, it is less computationally convenient for a variety of purposes.

The analysis of variance has the computation of F tests as only one of its purposes. The major general purpose of the analysis of variance is to divide up the total variance of all the observations into a number of separate sources of variance that can be compared with one another for purposes of both effect-size estimation and significance testing. In our present illustration of comparing the means of four groups, the total variation among the 12 scores is divided into two sources of variation: (a) variation between groups or conditions and (b) variation within groups or conditions. It will be useful here to look again at the basic idea of variance

$$S^2 = \frac{\Sigma(X - \bar{X})^2}{N - 1}$$

where S^2 is the unbiased estimate of the population value σ^2, and σ^2 for a sample differs from S^2 only in that the denominator $N - 1$ is replaced by N. The quantity S^2 is sometimes referred to as a "mean square" because the sum of the squares of the deviations [i.e., the $\Sigma(X - \bar{X})^2$] is divided by $N - 1$ (or df) yielding the squared deviation per df, a kind of average.

In the analysis of variance we are especially interested in the numerators of our various S^2's, e.g., for between conditions and for within conditions. The reason for that is the additive property of the numerators or "sums of squares of deviations about the mean." That is, these sums of squares add up to the total sums of squares in the following fashion:

Total sum of squares = between-conditions sum of squares

+ within-conditions sum of squares

The standard abbreviation for sum of squares is *SS*, so we have

Total *SS* = between-conditions *SS* + within-conditions *SS*

or

Total *SS* = between *SS* + within *SS*

The analysis of variance generally begins with the computation of these three sums of squares. Their definitions are as follows:

$$\text{Total } SS = \Sigma(X - \overline{M})^2$$

where X is each observation and $\overline{M}$ is the mean of the condition means. Here we add up as many squared deviations as there are scores altogether.

$$\text{Between-conditions } SS = \Sigma[n_k(M_k - \overline{M})^2]$$

where n_k is the number of observations in the kth condition; M_k is the mean of the kth condition, and $\overline{M}$ is the mean of the condition means. Here we add up as many quantities as there are conditions.

$$\text{Within-conditions } SS = \Sigma(X - M_k)^2$$

where X is each observation and M_k is the mean of the condition to which X belongs. Here we add up as many quantities as there are scores altogether.

Then, for the data of this illustration:

$$\begin{aligned}
\text{Total } SS = {}& (9 - 4.5)^2 + (8 - 4.5)^2 + (7 - 4.5)^2 + (6 - 4.5)^2 \\
& + (4 - 4.5)^2 + (2 - 4.5)^2 + (5 - 4.5)^2 + (4 - 4.5)^2 \\
& + (3 - 4.5)^2 + (4 - 4.5)^2 + (2 - 4.5)^2 + (0 - 4.5)^2 = 77
\end{aligned}$$

$$\begin{aligned}
\text{Between-conditions } SS = {}& 3(8 - 4.5)^2 + 3(4 - 4.5)^2 \\
& + 3(4 - 4.5)^2 + 3(2 - 4.5)^2 = 57
\end{aligned}$$

$$\begin{aligned}
\text{Within-conditions } SS = {}& (9 - 8)^2 + (8 - 8)^2 + (7 - 8)^2 + (6 - 4)^2 \\
& + (4 - 4)^2 + (2 - 4)^2 + (5 - 4)^2 + (4 - 4)^2 \\
& + (3 - 4)^2 + (4 - 2)^2 + (2 - 2)^2 + (0 - 2)^2 = 20
\end{aligned}$$

As a check on our arithmetic we add the sum of squares between conditions to the sum of squares within conditions to see whether their sum equals the total sum of squares. In this case they do, since

$$\text{Total } SS = \text{between-conditions } SS + \text{within-conditions } SS$$

$$77 = 57 + 20$$

A final comment about sums of squares: because they are sums of *squared* deviations, they can take on only values of zero or above. Sums of squares are never negative. Therefore, F's also are never negative.

THE TABLE OF VARIANCE

The results of an analysis of variance are displayed in the form shown in Table 15.10. The first column labels the source of variance, in this case simply the between-conditions and within-conditions sources. The second column lists the SS, and the third column lists the degrees of freedom for each source of variance. Since there were four conditions being compared, or four means, three of those means were free to vary once the mean of the means was determined. Thus if

TABLE 15.10
Table of variance

Source	SS	df	MS	F	eta	p
Between conditions	57	3	19.0	7.60	.86	.01
Within conditions	20	8	2.5			
Total	77	11	7.0			

there are k conditions, the degrees of freedom (df) for conditions are $k - 1$, or 3 in this case. The degrees of freedom within conditions are best obtained by determining the df within each condition and then adding. Within each condition we have $n - 1$ degrees of freedom, since within each condition of n scores only $n - 1$ of them are free to vary once we determine the mean of that condition. Thus the df within conditions are found by $\Sigma(n_k - 1)$, which in our present illustration is

$$\Sigma(n_k - 1) = (3 - 1) + (3 - 1) + (3 - 1) + (3 - 1) = 8$$

When we compute the df for between and within conditions as shown, we can check our computations by adding these df to see whether they agree with the df for the total computed directly as $N - 1$, the total number of observations less one. In the present case we have

$$df \text{ total} = df \text{ between} + df \text{ within}$$
$$11 = 3 + 8$$

The fourth column of the table of variance shows the mean squares obtained simply by dividing the sums of squares by the corresponding df. These quantities, the mean squares (or MS), can be viewed as the amounts of the total variation (measured in SS) attributable per df. The larger the MS for the between-condition source of variance relative to the within-condition source of variance, the less likely the null hypothesis of no difference between the condition means becomes. If the null hypothesis were true, then variation per df should be roughly the same for the df between groups and the df within groups.

The fifth column of our table of variance shows F, which is obtained by dividing the mean square between conditions by the mean square within conditions in applications of this type. F tests are also called "F ratios," since they are generally obtained by forming a ratio of two mean squares. The denominator mean square, often referred to as the *mean square for error,* serves as a kind of base rate for "noise level," or typical variation, while the numerator serves to inform us simultaneously about the size of the effect and the size of the study. Thus a numerator MS can be large relative to a denominator MS because the effect size (defined, for example, as eta^2 or as S^2_{means}/S^2) is large or the n per condition is large, or both are large. Large F's, therefore, should not be interpreted as reflecting large effects. Any conclusions about the size of the effect must be based on the direct calculation of an effect-size estimator. In the case of F, perhaps the most generally useful such effect-size estimate is eta, defined as

$$\text{eta} = \sqrt{\frac{SS \text{ between}}{SS \text{ between} + SS \text{ within}}}$$

Eta, then, is the square root of the proportion of the sums of squares (between + within) associated with the between-conditions source of variation. An equivalent computational formula that is convenient when we have access to an F but not to the original sums of squares is

$$\text{eta} = \sqrt{\frac{F(df \text{ between})}{F(df \text{ between}) + df \text{ within}}}$$

For the present illustration the sixth column in Table 15.10 shows eta computed as

$$\text{eta} = \sqrt{\frac{57}{57 + 20}} = \sqrt{.7403} = .86$$

or, as

$$\text{eta} = \sqrt{\frac{7.6(3)}{7.6(3) + 8}} = \sqrt{\frac{22.8}{22.8 + 8}} = .86$$

Eta^2 is interpreted as a proportion of variance accounted for, and the range, therefore, is like that for r^2, i.e., 0 to 1. However, r represents an index of linear relationship, and eta can serve as an index of any type of relationship. When there is only a single df between conditions, as when there are only two conditions being compared, eta and r are identical and may both be regarded as indices of linear relationships. As we shall see in our subsequent discussions of contrasts, we shall only rarely be interested in eta's based on more than a single df. Such eta's are difficult if not impossible to interpret in a substantively meaningful way. In addition, such eta's tend to be overestimates of the population values of eta, sometimes very gross overestimates. This overestimation is most severe when the number of df of the numerator of F is large relative to the number of df of the denominator of F (Guilford and Fruchter, 1978).

The final column of our table of variance gives the probability p that an F of the size obtained or larger could have been obtained if the null hypothesis were true and there were really no differences in the population between the means of the conditions of our research investigation. An alternative interpretation is that the p expresses the probability that an eta of the size obtained or larger could have occurred if the relationship between the independent variable of condition membership and the dependent variable of score on the response variable were actually zero in the population.

DISTRIBUTIONS OF *F*

In our discussion of the interpretation of t we noted that there was a different distribution of t values for every possible value of $n_1 + n_2 - 2$ (i.e., df). The situation for F is similar but more complicated because for every F ratio there are *two* relevant df to take into account: the df between conditions and the df within conditions. For every combination of df between and df within there is a different F distribution. While t distributions are centered at zero, with negative values running to negative infinity and positive values running to positive infinity, F distributions all begin at zero and range upward to positive infinity. The expected value of t is zero when the null hypothesis is true; the expected value of F, however, is $df/(df - 2)$, where the df are for within conditions. For most values of df, then, the expected value of F is a little more than 1.0. Just as was the case for t, values of F closer to zero are likely when the null hypothesis of no difference between groups is true, but values further from zero are unlikely and are used as evidence to suggest that the null hypothesis is probably false.

Inspection of a large number of F distributions shows that critical values of F required to reach the .05, .01, and .001 levels decrease as df within increases for any given df between. Similarly, critical values of F decrease as df between increase for any given df within, except for the special cases of df within = 1 or 2. For df within = 1 there is a substantial increase in the F's required to reach various critical levels as the df between increase from 1 to infinity. For df within = 2 there is only a very small increase in the F's required to reach various critical levels as the df between increase from 1 to infinity. In practice, however, there are very few studies with large df between and only 1 or 2 df within. A sample F distribution is shown in Figure 15-2 with df between and within = 3 and 16, respectively.

Table 15.11 illustrates the differences in various F distributions by giving the areas found in the right-hand tail of selected distributions. For each combination of df between and df within, two values are given, the F values required to reach the .05 and .01 levels, respectively. A much more detailed table of F values is found in Table B.4 of Appendix B.

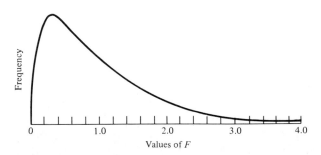

FIGURE 15-2
The F distribution for df of 3 and 16.

TABLE 15.11

F values required for significance at the .05 (upper entry) and .01 levels

Degrees of freedom within conditions (denominator)	Degrees of freedom between conditions (numerator)						Expected value of F when H_0 true
	1	**2**	**3**	**4**	**6**	**∞**	
1	161	200	216	225	234	254	—
	4052	4999	5403	5625	5859	6366	
2	18.5	19.0	19.2	19.2	19.3	19.5	—
	98.5	99.0	99.2	99.2	99.3	99.5	
3	10.1	9.55	9.28	9.12	8.94	8.53	3.00
	34.1	30.8	29.5	28.7	27.9	26.1	
4	7.71	6.94	6.59	6.39	6.16	5.63	2.00
	21.2	18.0	16.7	16.0	15.2	13.5	
5	6.61	5.79	5.41	5.19	4.95	4.36	1.67
	16.3	13.3	12.1	11.4	10.7	9.02	
6	5.99	5.14	4.76	4.53	4.28	3.67	1.50
	13.7	10.9	9.78	9.15	8.47	6.88	
8	5.32	4.46	4.07	3.84	3.58	2.93	1.33
	11.3	8.65	7.59	7.01	6.37	4.86	
10	4.96	4.10	3.71	3.48	3.22	2.54	1.25
	10.0	7.56	6.55	5.99	5.39	3.91	
15	4.54	3.68	3.29	3.06	2.79	2.07	1.15
	8.68	6.36	5.42	4.89	4.32	2.87	
20	4.35	3.49	3.10	2.87	2.60	1.84	1.11
	8.10	5.85	4.94	4.43	3.87	2.42	
25	4.24	3.38	2.99	2.76	2.49	1.71	1.09
	7.77	5.57	4.68	4.18	3.63	2.17	
30	4.17	3.32	2.92	2.69	2.42	1.62	1.07
	7.56	5.39	4.51	4.02	3.47	2.01	
40	4.08	3.23	2.84	2.61	2.34	1.51	1.05
	7.31	5.18	4.31	3.83	3.29	1.81	
60	4.00	3.15	2.76	2.52	2.25	1.39	1.03
	7.08	4.98	4.13	3.65	3.12	1.60	
120	3.92	3.07	2.68	2.45	2.17	1.25	1.02
	6.85	4.79	3.95	3.48	2.96	1.38	
∞	3.84	2.99	2.60	2.37	2.09	1.00	1.00
	6.63	4.60	3.78	3.32	2.80	1.00	

In the example of an analysis of variance we have been discussing, we obtained an F of 7.60 with 3 df in the numerator (between) and 8 df in the denominator (within or error), a result we write as $F(3,8) = 7.60$. When we refer this value to Table 15.11, we find at the intersection of 3 df for between and 8 df for within the values 4.07 and 7.59. Our obtained F, therefore, is substantially larger than an F required to be significant at $p = .05$ and almost exactly the size required to be significant at $p = .01$. How shall we interpret this result? The p value of .01 means that we would obtain an F of this size or larger (for numerator $df = 3$, denominator $df = 8$) only once in 100 times if we repeatedly conducted a study of four groups of size 3 each if there were, in the population, no differences among the four means or if there were no relationship between group membership and the response variable.

Before leaving our discussion of the distributions of F, we should note that the F's we compute in actual research situations will usually be distributed only approximately as F. The assumptions to be met before we can regard computed F's to be actually distributed as F were given near the end of our discussion of the t test (IID normal, that is, independently and identically distributed in a normal distribution). Of the three assumptions, the assumption of independence of errors (or sampling units) is most important, because if it is badly violated, our interpretation of F can go very wrong. Violations of the other two assumptions (homogeneity of variance and normality) are less serious in that F tends to be robust in the face of even some fairly serious violations of these assumptions.

AFTER THE F

Now we know that for the data of our example the group means would not likely be so far apart if the null hypothesis were true. What does that tell us about the results of our experiment? By itself, not very much. After all, we conducted our research to learn about the effects of psychotherapy and drug therapy separately and together. Knowing that the four groups of our study probably differ does not tell us whether psychotherapy helps, whether drugs help, whether both together help, whether one helps more than the other, etc. At the very least we need now to examine the means of the four groups:

Psychotherapy		No psychotherapy	
Drug	No drug	Drug	No drug
8	4	4	2

If the overall difference among the means is significant, then the greatest difference between the means is significant as well. In this case the greatest difference is that between the group receiving both psychotherapy and drug therapy and the group receiving neither psychotherapy nor drug therapy. To check the more exact significance of that difference we can compute t as described earlier:

$$t = \frac{M_1 - M_2}{\sqrt{\left(\frac{1}{n_1} + \frac{1}{n_2}\right)S^2}}$$

In this application of t, i.e., as a follow-up to an analysis of variance, we compute S^2 based on all the groups of the experiment, not just those directly involved in the t test. If we return to the definition of our mean square within (SS_{within}/df_{within})

$$MS_{within} = \frac{\Sigma(X - M_k)^2}{N - k}$$

where N is the total number of sampling units in the study and k is the number of conditions, we see that the MS_{within} is actually the S^2 pooled over, or collected from, all the conditions of the analysis. Then for the means of interest

$$t = \frac{M_1 - M_2}{\sqrt{\left(\frac{1}{n_1} + \frac{1}{n_2}\right)S^2}} = \frac{8 - 2}{\sqrt{\left(\frac{1}{3} + \frac{1}{3}\right)2.5}} = \frac{6}{1.29} = 4.65$$

which is significant at $p < .001$, one-tailed, or .002, two-tailed, when referred to a table of the t distribution with $df = 8$. Because we have based our computation of S^2 (or MS within, or MS error) on all the data of the experiment, not just on the data of the two groups being compared, our t test is made on the t distribution with df equal to that of the S^2, *not*, in this case, on $n_1 + n_2 - 2$. For many applications of the analysis of variance we assume homogeneity or similarity of variance from condition to condition, so that an S^2 or MS within based on more groups is more likely to be a better estimate of the population value of σ^2. The number of df available to estimate σ^2, therefore, defines the t distribution to which we refer our obtained t. The n_1 and n_2 of the denominator of the t test still reflect the actual number of cases per group on which the t is based. Thus, it is not our sample sizes that are increased by our using a more stable estimate of σ^2, only the df used for referring to t tables.

We might also want to compare the benefits of receiving both psychotherapy *and* the drug (mean $= 8$) with the benefits of receiving *either* psychotherapy (mean $= 4$) *or* the drug (mean $= 4$). In both cases

$$t = \frac{8 - 4}{\sqrt{\left(\frac{1}{3} + \frac{1}{3}\right)2.5}} = \frac{4}{1.29} = 3.10$$

which is significant at $p < .01$, one-tailed, when referred to the $t(8)$ distribution.

We might want to compare the benefits of receiving either psychotherapy or the drug with the no-treatment control condition. Both comparisons yield

$$t = \frac{4 - 2}{\sqrt{\left(\dfrac{1}{3} + \dfrac{1}{3}\right)2.5}} = \frac{2}{1.29} = 1.55$$

which is significant at about the .08 level, one-tailed. We have now compared each group with every other except for psychotherapy alone versus the drug alone, which by inspection yields a $t = 0$. Other comparisons are possible, taking more than one group at a time. Identifying the four groups as PD, P, D, and O, we could also make the following comparisons:

(PD + P)	versus	(D + O)
(PD + D)	versus	(P + O)
(PD + O)	versus	(P + D)
(PD + P + D)	versus	(O)
(PD + P + O)	versus	(D)
(PD + D + O)	versus	(P)
(P + D + O)	versus	(PD)

PROTECTING AGAINST "TOO MANY t TESTS"

So far, then, 13 fairly obvious comparisons are possible. If we were to make them all, we might expect some of those 13 t tests to yield significant results even if the null hypothesis were true. Generally, the more tests of significance computed on data for which the null hypothesis is true, the more significant results will be obtained, i.e., the more type I errors will be made. In Chapter 21, on contrasts, we shall deal with the issue in more detail. Here it is enough to offer only some brief and preliminary advice.

1. Plan the t tests of interest before the data are collected and conduct those t tests whether or not the overall F is significant. To perform these t tests only, no F need be computed; indeed our only reason for computing an analysis of variance is to reap the benefit of a more stable estimate of the σ^2 required for the denominator of our t tests. That is, each of our t tests is now based on the n_1 and n_2 of the two groups being compared, but the t distribution referred to in the tables is the one with the df of our error term (MS within), usually $N - k$.
2. If there are unexpected but interesting results for which t tests are computed, compute the overall F. If that F is significant, the t's computed are said to be "protected" against the problem of "capitalizing on chance," since some of the t's *must* be "legitimately" significant if the overall F is significant. For most practical purposes, the use of these protected t's is at least an adequate solu-

tion and, quite possibly, an optimal one (Balaam, 1963; Carmer and Swanson, 1973; Snedecor and Cochran, 1967, 1980).

3. Either for the case of planned t tests or for the case of unexpected results if many t tests are computed and (a) the overall F is not significant *and* (b) the investigators are worried lest they are capitalizing on chance, a simple and quite conservative procedure can be employed to adjust the interpretation of the p values obtained. The basic idea of this procedure, the *Bonferroni proce-dure,* is to divide the alpha level selected by the number of tests performed explicitly or implicitly (Harris, 1975; Hays, 1981; Morrison, 1976; Myers, 1979; Rosenthal and Rubin, 1983; 1984; Snedecor and Cochran, 1980). It makes no difference whether the tests performed are independent or not.

BONFERRONI PROCEDURES

Suppose, for example, that we plan to perform four t tests on our data but want to keep our overall alpha at the .05 level. If we divide .05 by 4, the number of tests planned, we find .0125 to be the adjusted level we would want to obtain to declare any of the four t's to be significant. If we have not planned our t tests and include only the largest obtained t's, we must divide the usual alpha level we prefer (most commonly, $p = .05$) by the number of *implicit* t tests. For example, if we have five groups to compare in our study and we test the three largest dif-ferences, we divide the .05 level not by 3 but by $(5 \times 4)/2 = 10$, the number of possible pairwise comparisons of five means; in this case we would require a p of $.05/10 = .005$ before we would declare a t test significant at an adjusted .05 level.

The Bonferroni approach does not require us to set the same alpha level for each t test, so we can allocate the total alpha (say .05) unequally. For example, suppose we plan to do eight t tests, but we want greater power for four of them because they are the major questions of the research project. We could set our alphas for these four t tests at .01 and set our alphas for the remaining four t tests at $[.05 - 4(.01)]/4 = .0025$. Our eight t tests are now tested at .01, .01, .01, .01, .0025, .0025, .0025, .0025, respectively, which, when added up, yield .05, our over-all alpha level (Harris, 1975; Myers, 1979; Rosenthal and Rubin, 1983, 1984). Or suppose we plan 11 t tests but have an overwhelming interest in only 1 of them. We could set our alpha level at .04 for that t test and divide the remaining .01 by 10, so that our alphas become .04 for the prime t test and .001 for each of the remaining 10 t tests.

Basically, then, we have been adjusting the p values obtained from each t test for the number of t tests carried out with the option of weighting the t tests unequally. We can assign a weight to each t test reflecting the importance of that test. Then the general procedure for adjusting alpha for the various weighted-for-importance t tests is

$$\alpha_j = \frac{\alpha W_j}{\Sigma W}$$

where α_j is the adjusted α level for the jth t test (i.e., the one in question), α is the overall probability of type I error (usually .05), W_j is the weight reflecting the importance of the jth t test, and ΣW is the sum of the weights of all our t tests (Rosenthal and Rubin, 1983). Suppose we planned to examine six t tests, which we weighted in importance as follows: 12, 6, 3, 2, 1, 1. The adjusted α levels for each would be

t test	W_j	Adjusted α levels
1	12	$\dfrac{.05(12)}{25} = .024$
2	6	$\dfrac{.05(6)}{25} = .012$
3	3	$\dfrac{.05(3)}{25} = .006$
4	2	$\dfrac{.05(2)}{25} = .004$
5	1	$\dfrac{.05(1)}{25} = .002$
6	1	$\dfrac{.05(1)}{25} = .002$
Total	25 (= ΣW)	$= .050$ (= $\Sigma\alpha_j$)

which add up to .05, our overall α level.

   Although we know how to adjust our alpha levels, it is usually much more informative to report the actual p level (adjusted for the number of t tests and their weights) than simply to report whether they did or did not reach the adjusted alpha level. The adjusted p value achieved (the ensemble-adjusted p value) is readily obtained from the following (Rosenthal and Rubin, 1983):

$$p \text{ adjusted} = \frac{p_j \Sigma W}{W_j}$$

where p_j is the actual (i.e., unadjusted) p obtained for the jth t test (the one in question), ΣW is the sum of all the weights, and W_j is the weight of the specific t test in question.

   Suppose we had obtained the following unadjusted p values for our six t tests: .005, .07, .08, .11, .001, .004. Then our corresponding ensemble-adjusted p values would be

t test	Ensemble-adjusted p value	
1	$\dfrac{.005(25)}{12}$	$=$ .010
2	$\dfrac{.07(25)}{6}$	$=$ .292
3	$\dfrac{.08(25)}{3}$	$=$ .667
4	$\dfrac{.11(25)}{2}$	$=$ 1.00*
5	$\dfrac{.001(25)}{1}$	$=$ .025
6	$\dfrac{.004(25)}{1}$	$=$ 1.00

*Values exceeding 1.00 are interpreted as 1.00

The values of these ensemble-adjusted p's reflect the conservative nature of the Bonferroni adjustment. Whereas three of the original six t tests showed $p \leq$ .005, none of the adjusted p values are that low and only two remain at $p <$ .05.

Although it will often be useful to weight our t tests by their importance, it is not necessary to do so. If we should prefer no weighting, which is equivalent to equal weighting, all our W_j's become 1 and ΣW becomes the sum of the k weights of 1 each, where k is the number of t tests. Therefore, in the unweighted case

$$p \text{ adjusted} = \frac{p_j \Sigma W}{W_j} = \frac{p_j k(1)}{1} = p_j k$$

For the set of six t tests we have been discussing, therefore, their unweighted ensemble-adjusted p values would simply be the unadjusted p multiplied by 6, or .03, .42, .48, .66, .006, .024, respectively. Note again that the particular weighting chosen to reflect the importance of each t of a set of t tests must be decided *before* the results of the t tests are known so that we cannot inadvertently assign importance weightings as a function of the results obtained. In all our applications of Bonferroni procedures it is of greatest value to our readers if we routinely report both the adjusted and the original p values.

Bonferroni Tolerance Value

We have assumed all along that either we planned all our t tests or that if we did not, we were at least able to calculate the number of implicit t tests computed. In large and complex data sets, that is sometimes difficult to do. In such cases it is useful to compute an accurate p value for the most significant result of any interest in the data set (p max) and then to divide this p into α (usually .05) to yield a tolerance value (k_t) for the number of t tests computed:

$$k_t = \frac{\alpha}{p \text{ max}}$$

The quantity k_t gives the number of t tests that could have been computed to keep the most significant result still properly adjusted within the α level chosen—usually .05.

For example, suppose a very complex study in which perhaps dozens or even scores of sensible t tests were possible. The most significant result was significant at .00015. Then

$$k_t = \frac{\alpha}{p \text{ max}} = \frac{.05}{.00015} = 333.3$$

This result tells us that more than 333 implicit t tests would have had to have been carried out in order for us to decide that the p max of .00015 was perhaps not significant after all. Whether such a number seems too high to be plausible depends on the actual research design employed. In this application of the Bonferroni procedure, as in all others, it makes no difference whether the tests being considered are independent of one another or not.

COMPARING TWO
INDEPENDENT VARIABILITIES

There are both methodological and substantive reasons to compare the variabilities or dispersions of two groups we may be comparing. The methodological reasons have to do with the assumption of homogeneity of variance underlying the use of t and F tests. Although we discussed this assumption earlier, we did not provide a formal procedure for comparing two independent variances to determine the degree to which our assumption had indeed been met. In this section we shall do so.

Before providing the procedure, we want to emphasize that there are often strong substantive grounds for comparing variances as well (Bryk and Raudenbush, 1988). We may have a specific hypothesis that a certain treatment will lead to greater variance than will a control condition regardless of whether we also predict a difference in means. For example, we might expect a moderate degree of stress to increase the variability of performance of an experimental group relative to the control group, because moderate stress may energize some subjects to perform better while it may upset and demoralize others. The net effect would be to increase the variability of the experimental group. Similarly, we might be interested in checking the variability of a new psychological treatment procedure to be sure that it is not simply helping a few patients quite a lot while also harming a few patients quite a lot, a state of affairs that cannot be examined simply by comparing the mean performance of the two conditions. Whatever our reason for wanting to compare the variabilities of two groups, the procedure is the same. We divide the larger of the two variances (S^2 larger) by the smaller of the two variances (S^2 smaller) and refer the quotient to an F table, i.e.,

$$F = \frac{S^2 \text{ larger}}{S^2 \text{ smaller}}$$

There are some subtleties to the use of the standard F tables (e.g., Table B.4 of Appendix B) for this purpose of comparing variabilities. First, we determine the df associated with the S^2 that is larger ($n_l = 1$) and find the column of our F table corresponding to that df. Next we determine the df associated with the smaller S^2 ($n_s - 1$) and find the row of our F table corresponding to that df. Now we use the F table in the usual way *except that we must first double the p levels shown*. Thus, p's of .001, .005, .01, .025, .05, .10, and .20 become p's of .002, .01, .02, .05, .10, .20, and .40, respectively. The reason is that standard F tables are set up assuming we will always put a particular S^2 in the numerator, e.g., the S^2 (or MS) between conditions, while putting a particular S^2 in the denominator, e.g., the S^2 (or MS) within conditions. When we use F tables for the purpose of comparing variabilities, however, we usually do not decide beforehand which S^2 or MS will be the numerator; instead, we put the larger S^2 over the smaller one. Doubling the p values shown in standard tables merely takes into account this unspecified direction of difference, or "two-tailed," feature of the F test used in this way. Of course, if we have specifically predicted which particular variability will be larger, we *can* make a one-tailed test using the p values as shown without doubling them first.

The F Test to Compare Independent Variabilities: An Illustration

Suppose we had conducted an experiment to learn whether our experimental group would show greater or less variability than our controls. The scores we obtained were as follows:

	Experimental	Control
	4	1
	16	4
	9	1
	25	4
Σ	54	10
n	4	4
M	13.5	2.5
S^2	83	3

Therefore, since S^2 larger/S^2 smaller $= F$, we find

$$F = \frac{S^2 \text{ larger}}{S^2 \text{ smaller}} = \frac{83}{3} = 27.67$$

with 3 df ($n_{exp} - 1 = 3$) for the numerator S^2 and 3 df ($n_{control} - 1 = 3$) for the denominator. We turn to Table B.4 of Appendix B to find the p value. At the intersection of column $df = 3$ and row $df = 3$ we find that an F of 29.46 is required for significance at the .01 level, while an F of 15.44 is required for significance at the .025 level. For the present application, however, in which we did not specifically test the one-tailed hypothesis that the experimentals would be more variable, we must *double* the tabled values of p. Therefore, our F is significant between the .02 and .05 levels, two-tailed.

Suppose that we were also interested in comparing the means of our two groups and, in doing so, find

$$t = \frac{M_1 - M_2}{\sqrt{\left(\frac{1}{n_1} + \frac{1}{n_2}\right)S^2}} = \frac{11}{\sqrt{\left(\frac{1}{4} + \frac{1}{4}\right)43}} = 2.37$$

with 6 df, $p = .03$ one-tailed, and a t associated with an effect size $r = .70$ or $d = 1.94$. Now we have learned that our experimentals have scored higher (from t) and more variably (from F) than our controls. But we may have a problem here.

Our F test comparing variabilities was quite large and, even with a very small sample size, significant. We computed a t to compare means, a t that depends for its proper use on the assumption of equal variances for our two groups. Yet we know the variances to be unequal. It seems wise here to transform our data in hopes that our transformation will make our variances more nearly equal. For data of this kind a square root transformation often helps because it tends to pull the large outlying values in closer to the bulk of the scores, and we shall try it here. The square roots of the original scores are as follows:

	Experimental	Control
	$2 (= \sqrt{4})$	$1 (= \sqrt{1})$
	$4 (= \sqrt{16})$	$2 (= \sqrt{4})$
	$3 (= \sqrt{9})$	$1 (= \sqrt{1})$
	$5 (= \sqrt{25})$	$2 (= \sqrt{4})$
Σ	14	6
n	4	4
M	3.5	1.5
S^2	1.6667	.3333

Therefore, for testing the difference between these variances,

$$F = \frac{S^2 \text{ larger}}{S^2 \text{ smaller}} = \frac{1.6667}{.3333} = 5.00$$

with 3 df for the numerator and for the denominator. Table B.4 of Appendix B shows F's of 5.39 and 2.94 required to reach the .10 and .20 levels, respectively, which is equivalent to p's of .20 and .40 in our present application. Our p now is not very small, and we may be satisfied that our transformation has worked quite well. We now compute our t test to compare means using these transformed scores and find

$$t = \frac{M_1 - M_2}{\sqrt{\left(\dfrac{1}{n_1} + \dfrac{1}{n_2}\right)S^2}} = \frac{2}{\sqrt{\left(\dfrac{1}{4} + \dfrac{1}{4}\right)1.00}} = 2.83$$

with 6 df, $p = .02$ one-tailed, and $r = .76$, $d = 2.31$. Our t test based on the square roots of our original scores is somewhat larger and more significant than was the t test based on the original scores, and the effect sizes are somewhat larger. These results are probably more accurate than those based on the original results, because we have better met the assumption of homogeneity of variance on which the use of the t tables depends to some extent.

When our original scores were transformed to their square roots, the F for comparing the two variabilities (i.e., S^2 larger/S^2 smaller) was not significant. However, the F was 5.00, perhaps a bit larger than we might like. Perhaps a different transformation would shrink that F even closer to the value of 1.00 we would obtain if the variabilities were the same. We will try a $\log_{10}$ transformation, a transformation made as easily as a square root transformation by pushing a single key of an inexpensive hand-held calculator, and a transformation that pulls large outlying values in more sharply than does the square root transformation. The $\log_{10}$ values of the original scores are as follows:

	Experimental	Control
	.60 (= log 4)	.00 (= log 1)
	1.20 (= log 16)	.60 (= log 4)
	.95 (= log 9)	.00 (= log 1)
	1.40 (= log 25)	.60 (= log 4)
Σ	4.15	1.20
n	4	4
M	1.04	.30
S^2	.12	.12

Therefore,

$$F = \frac{S^2 \text{ larger}}{S^2 \text{ smaller}} = \frac{.12}{.12} = 1.00$$

with 3 df for the numerator and for the denominator. Table B.4 of Appendix B shows that an F of 2.94 is required to reach the .20 level, which is equivalent to the .40 level for the present application of comparing variabilities without having made a specific prediction as to which variability will be larger. Our $\log_{10}$ transformation has worked very well indeed in achieving homogeneity of variabilities.

We now compute our t test to compare means using these transformed scores and find

$$t = \frac{M_1 - M_2}{\sqrt{\left(\dfrac{1}{n_1} + \dfrac{1}{n_2}\right)S^2}} = \frac{.74}{\sqrt{\left(\dfrac{1}{4} + \dfrac{1}{4}\right).12}} = 3.02$$

with 6 df, $p = .015$ one-tailed, and $r = .78$, $d = 2.47$. The t test based on the logs of the original scores is somewhat larger and more significant than was the t test based on the square root–transformed scores, and the effect sizes are some-what larger. Of the three sets of results based on the original scores (X), the square roots of these scores ($\sqrt{X}$), and the logs of these scores ($\log_{10} X$), these last are probably most accurate, since they best meet the assumption of homogeneity of variance. For the present example, however, all three expressions of the data—the original scores, the square root of the scores, and the logs of the scores—yield quite comparable results, as shown below:

Transformation	$F(3, 3)$	$t(6)$	p	r	d
X	27.67	2.37	.03	.70	1.94
$\sqrt{X}$	5.00	2.83	.02	.76	2.31
$\log X$	1.00	3.02	.015	.78	2.47

This illustrates the general finding that t tests and F tests to compare means are not too badly affected by even fairly substantial heterogeneities of variance, a finding that holds especially when sample sizes are equal (Hays, 1981; Scheffé, 1959).

COMPARING TWO CORRELATED VARIABILITIES

Our reasons for wanting to compare correlated variabilities are the same as for wanting to compare uncorrelated, or independent, variabilities. Our methodological reason is to check the reasonableness of our assumption of homogeneity of variance. Our substantive reason is to learn whether variabilities of the same sampling units (e.g., subjects) differ under different conditions. For example, we may measure subjects before and after a treatment condition to learn whether the variability of the subjects has increased over time. (Note that we cannot ascribe such a change to the treatment unless we also have a randomized control.) We may want to learn whether two raters of patients' nonverbal behavior differ with respect to the variability of the scale points used. Or we may want to compare the variability of the boys and girls in a collection of pairs of fraternal twins. In all these cases our procedure is the same. We compute S^2 for each of the two variabilities to be compared, *and* we compute the correlation between the pairs of measurements made for our sample of N persons or other sampling units measured twice. If our sampling units are the N subjects measured twice, we correlate their first and second measurements. If our sampling units are the N patients each measured (rated) by two raters, we correlate the N pairs of ratings generated by the first and second raters. If our sampling units are the N pairs of twins, we correlate the scores obtained by the girl and the boy members of the N pairs.

Our test for the comparison of correlated variabilities is a t test obtained as follows:

$$t = \frac{(S_1^2 - S_2^2)\sqrt{N - 2}}{2S_1S_2\sqrt{1 - r^2}}$$

where S_1 and S_2 are the two variabilities to be compared (S_1 referring to the larger value), N is the number of pairs of scores, and r is the correlation between the N pairs of scores described in the preceding paragraph (McNemar, 1969; Walker and Lev, 1953). The obtained value of t is entered into a t table with $df = N - 2$.

The t Test to Compare Correlated Variabilities: An Illustration

Suppose we had measured the same 18 sampling units twice (e.g., the same 18 persons pre and post or the brothers and sisters of 18 pairs of siblings) and had found the values of S^2 to be 64 and 36 for the two sets of scores and a correlation of .90 between the 18 pairs of scores.

Then t would be

$$t(16) = \frac{(64 - 36)\sqrt{18 - 2}}{2(8)(6)\sqrt{1 - (.90)^2}} = \frac{112}{96\sqrt{.19}} = 2.68$$

which with 16 df is significant at the .02 level, two-tailed test. Inspection of the equation yielding t shows that for any two different, nonzero values of S^2 and for $N > 2$, the larger r grows the larger also will t be; i.e., r is an index of the sensitivity to differences between values of S^2. For the present illustration, r's from zero to .95 yield t values from 1.17 to 3.74 with associated p levels from >.20 to <.002 as shown:

r	t	p (two-tailed)
.00	1.17	>.20
.20	1.19	>.20
.40	1.27	>.20
.60	1.46	<.20
.80	1.94	<.10
.90	2.68	<.02
.95	3.74	<.002

COMPARING THREE OR MORE INDEPENDENT VARIABILITIES

Just as was the case for the comparison of two variabilities, there are methodo-logical and substantive reasons for comparing three or more variabilities. The methodological reasons again have to do with checking on the reasonableness of the assumption of homogeneity of variance. The substantive reasons again have to do with conditions that might increase or decrease the variabilities of some groups relative to others. The tests described here permit us to evaluate the homogeneity of variance by means of procedures that take into account the number of implicit comparisons among variabilities that have been made.

For example, suppose we had two variabilities, or values of S^2, of 64 and 4, each based on $n = 5$, or $df = 4$. Employing the procedure of comparing two in-dependent variabilities, we find F to be $64/4 = 16$. Reference to Table B.4 of Appendix B for $df = 4$ for both the numerator and denominator S^2 shows F to be significant at $p = .02$, two-tailed. (Note that we doubled the p value from the tabled value of .01 to the .02 shown here, as explained earlier.) However, if the S^2 values 64 and 4 had been the largest and smallest of several (say, k) condi-tions, then there would have been a total of $k(k - 1)/2$ possible comparisons of variabilities. The larger the k, for any given sample size n or df (i.e., $n - 1$), the larger we would expect the largest obtained F to be, even if the null hypothesis of no differences among variances were true. The following methods adjust for this problem (Snedecor and Cochran, 1980; Walker and Lev, 1953; Winer, 1971).

Hartley's F_{max}

Hartley's F_{max} procedure is elegantly simple; we merely divide the largest vari-ability (S_{max}^2) by the smallest variability (S_{min}^2). The resulting F, called F_{max}, is then looked up in a special table that takes into account the number of groups being compared and the df of each of the groups. (If the n's are unequal but not *too* unequal, the harmonic mean of the df can be used as a reasonable approxi-mation.) Suppose we had six conditions to compare, each with the following n, df, and S^2.

Condition	n	df	S^2
1	5	4	25
2	5	4	36
3	5	4	9
4	5	4	49
5	5	4	4
6	5	4	64
Total	30	24	187

Then,

$$S_{max}^2 = 64 \quad \text{and} \quad S_{min}^2 = 4$$

so

$$F_{max} = \frac{S^2_{max}}{S^2_{min}} = \frac{64}{4} = 16$$

The obtained value of F_{max} is referred to Table B.11 of Appendix B. The columns show the number of conditions being compared (six in our case), while the rows show the df for each condition (four in our case). The two entries at the intersection of the column headed "6" and the row labeled "4" are 29.5 and 69, respectively. Thus if F_{max} had reached 29.5, it would have been significant at $p = .05$; if it had reached 69, it would have been significant at $p = .01$. Our F of 16, therefore, was not even close to being significant at the .05 level. Looking again at the row labeled "4", we see that if the number of conditions (k) had been only two or three, our F would have been significant at the .05 level.

Cochran's g Test

An alternative to Hartley's F_{max} test exists that is especially useful when we do not have access to the individual S^2 values of each group but we do have the pooled S^2 for all the groups in the form of the MS within. Under those conditions, if we know the largest of the S^2 values, we can test for its size relative to the sum of all the S^2 values—a sum that is equivalent to the MS within multiplied by k, the number of conditions. Thus,

$$\text{Cochran's } g = \frac{S^2_{max}}{\Sigma S^2} = \frac{S^2_{max}}{k(MS \text{ within})}$$

Tables have been constructed that allow us to determine the significance of the obtained g (Eisenhart, Hastay, and Wallis, 1947; Winer, 1971).

For the example of six groups given just above,

$$\text{Cochran's } g = \frac{S^2_{max}}{\Sigma S^2} = \frac{64}{187} = .3422$$

which Table B.12 of Appendix B shows is not large enough to reach the .05 level. With six groups and 4 df per group, a g of .4803 is required to reach the .05 level.

Bartlett's Test

Bartlett's test is a procedure that can be employed even when sample sizes for the various groups are very unequal. It is not, however, recommended as a test for checking the reasonableness of the assumption of homogeneity of variance; it is likely to yield more significant results than it should, relative to the substantial robustness of the F test that relies on the assumption of homogeneity of variance (Snedecor and Cochran, 1980). For that reason we omit the computational details, which are readily available in Snedecor and Cochran (1980, 1989), McNemar (1969), Walker and Lev (1953), Winer (1971), and elsewhere.

Levene's Test

When we have access to the raw data, Levene's test can be very useful no matter how unequal the group sizes. For each observation in each group we compute the *absolute* difference between the obtained score and the mean score of that condition. These absolute differences will be large when variabilities are large, but because no squaring is employed, this procedure is robust if the observations come from distributions with long tails (i.e., extreme values). Levene's test is simply the F test of the analysis of variance of the absolute deviation scores. If F is significant, the variances are judged as significantly heterogeneous (Snedecor and Cochran, 1980, 1989).

COMPARING THREE OR MORE CORRELATED VARIABILITIES

There is little discussion in textbooks of the situation in which three or more variabilities to be compared are not independent, e.g., when a sample is measured under three or more conditions. If such a test is needed, we recommend a natural extension of the Levene test, in which, for each sampling unit, we create a new score—the absolute difference between the original score and the mean of the condition. The resulting analysis of variance of the new scores will then provide an F test of the null hypothesis of homogeneity of variances of the original scores. Computational procedures for the required repeated-measures analysis of variance are described in Chapter 18.

SUMMARY OF PROCEDURES FOR COMPARING VARIABILITIES

Table 15.12 provides an overview of the various procedures for comparing two or more independent or correlated variabilities.

TABLE 15.12
Four types of tests for comparing variabilities

Number of Variabilities	Independence of Variabilities	
	Independent	Correlated
Two	F test	t test
Three or more	Hartley's F_{max} test* Cochran's g test* Bartlett's test Levene's test	Extension of Levene's test

*Sample sizes of the groups should not be too different.

PART
VI

BEYOND
ONE-WAY
ANALYSIS
OF VARIANCE

CHAPTER
16

FACTORIAL
DESIGN
OF EXPERIMENTS

AN ECONOMY OF DESIGN

Suppose that for the example we discussed in the last chapter a major question was whether psychotherapy was effective. Given the means of our four conditions

PD	P	D	O
8	4	4	2

we could test the difference between the psychotherapy-only group (P) and the no-treatment control group (O). We have already made this test and found $t(8) = 1.55$, with $p = .08$, one-tailed. However, inspection of the four means shows another comparison that could be made to test the effect of psychotherapy: PD versus D. This comparison [with $t(8) = 3.10, p < .01$, as reported earlier] is parallel to the earlier comparison of P versus O, except that now both the psychotherapy and the no-psychotherapy conditions are receiving drug therapy.

　　Rather than conduct two t tests, P versus O and PD versus D, we could conduct one simultaneous t test of (PD + P)/2 versus (D + O)/2 so that the conditions including psychotherapy could be compared with those not including psychotherapy. The advantage of thus combining our tests is that it increases the n_1 and n_2 of the denominator of the t test so that t will have greater power to reject the null hypothesis if the null hypothesis is false. An equally sensible and quite analogous test might ask whether drug therapy is beneficial, i.e., (PD + D)/2 versus (P + O)/2. The t test for psychotherapy would be computed as

$$t = \frac{[(8 + 4)/2] - [(4 + 2)/2]}{\sqrt{\left(\frac{1}{6} + \frac{1}{6}\right)2.5}} = \frac{6 - 3}{0.913} = 3.29$$

which is significant at $p = .006$, one-tailed, when referred to the $t(8)$ distribution. The results for the drug effect turn out in this example to be identical.

Ronald Fisher, for whom the F test was named, and who was responsible for so much of the development of the analysis of variance, noticed that in many cases a one-way analysis of variance could be rearrayed to form a two-dimensional (or higher-order) design of much greater power to reject the null hypothesis. Such experimental designs are called *factorial,* and they require that the two or more levels of each factor (variable) be administered in combination with the two or more levels of every other factor. For example, to rearrange the four means of the one-way analysis of variance that has served as our illustration into a factorial design, we rearray from

PD	**P**	**D**	**O**
$8^{\lfloor 3}$	$4^{\lfloor 3}$	$4^{\lfloor 3}$	$2^{\lfloor 3}$

Note: The number within the "L" symbol represents the number of units on which each mean is based.

to

	Psychotherapy		
	Present	**Absent**	**Mean**
Drug therapy:			
Present	$8^{\lfloor 3}$	$4^{\lfloor 3}$	$6^{\lfloor 6}$
Absent	$4^{\lfloor 3}$	$2^{\lfloor 3}$	$3^{\lfloor 6}$
Mean	$6^{\lfloor 6}$	$3^{\lfloor 6}$	$4.5^{\lfloor 12}$

Now the comparison of the two column means is the test of the effect of psychotherapy, and the comparison of the two row means is the test of the effect of drug therapy. The number of observations on which each mean is based has been doubled, from 3 to 6, as we moved from a comparison of one group with another group to a comparison of a column (or row) comprising two groups with another column (or row) also comprising two groups. Here then is the great economy of the factorial design; each condition or group contributes data to several comparisons. In the present example of a two-way analysis, the upper-left condition contributes its $n = 3$ to the comparison between columns and to the comparison between rows simultaneously.

EFFECTS AND THE STRUCTURE OF ANALYSIS OF VARIANCE

We can better understand our particular data, and we can better understand the nature of analysis of variance in general, by thinking of our obtained scores or means as being made up of two or more components that can be added to construct our obtained scores or means. Let us consider only the four means of our example:

	Psychotherapy	
	Present	Absent
Drug therapy:		
Present	8	4
Absent	4	2

We can decompose these four means into two components, one due to the grand mean and one due to the *effect* of being in a particular group. If we compute the grand mean of our four condition means we find $(8 + 4 + 4 + 2)/4 = 4.5$. We subtract this value from each of our four means to obtain:

	Psychotherapy	
	Present	Absent
Drug therapy:		
Present	3.5	−0.5
Absent	−0.5	−2.5

The differences between the cell means we started with and the grand mean are displayed above; they are called *residuals* (or leftovers) or *effects* of group or condition membership. We can write:

Residual (condition) effects	=	Group means	−	Grand mean
3.5	=	8	−	4.5
−0.5	=	4	−	4.5
−0.5	=	4	−	4.5
−2.5	=	2	−	4.5
Σ 0.0	=	18	−	18.0

or

Group means	=	Grand mean	+	Residual (condition) effects
8	=	4.5	+	3.5
4	=	4.5	+	(−0.5)
4	=	4.5	+	(−0.5)
2	=	4.5	+	(−2.5)
Σ 18	=	18.0	+	0.0

The sum of the condition effects or residuals is always equal to zero, so that examining them highlights which groups score the most above average (i.e., have the most positively signed mean) and which score the most below average (i.e., have the most negatively signed mean). The grand mean plus the condition residual or effect for each group mean is equal to the group mean.

When we move from a one-way analysis of variance to a two-way analysis of variance, such as in the case of a two-way factorial design, the condition effects or residuals are subdivided into *row effects, column effects,* and *residual,* or *interaction, effects.* So

$$\text{Group mean} = \text{grand mean} + \text{residual (condition) effect}$$

becomes

$$\text{Group mean} = \text{grand mean} + \text{row effect} + \text{column effect} + \text{interaction effect}$$

In order to decompose the group means into their four components we must compute the grand mean, the row effect, the column effect, and the interaction effect. The grand mean is the mean of all cell means. The row effect for each row is the mean of that row minus the grand mean; the column effect for each column is the mean of that column minus the grand mean. For our example:

	Psychotherapy		Row	Row
	Present	Absent	means	effects
Drug therapy:				
Present	8	4	6	1.5
Absent	4	2	3	−1.5
Column means	6	3	4.5 (grand mean)	
Column effects	1.5	−1.5		

The row effects are $6 - 4.5$ and $3 - 4.5$ for drug present and absent, respectively; the column effects are $6 - 4.5$ and $3 - 4.5$ for psychotherapy present and absent, respectively. The interaction effect is computed from

$$\text{Interaction effect} = \text{group mean} - \text{grand mean} - \text{row effect} - \text{column effect}$$

so, for our example, the four interaction effects are:

Group mean		Grand mean		Row effect		Column effect		Interaction effect
	−		−		−		=	
PD 8	−	4.5	−	1.5	−	1.5	=	0.5
D 4	−	4.5	−	1.5	−	(−1.5)	=	(−0.5)
P 4	−	4.5	−	(−1.5)	−	1.5	=	(−0.5)
O 2	−	4.5	−	(−1.5)	−	(−1.5)	=	0.5
Σ 18	−	18.0	−	0	−	0	=	0

For the time being we think of interaction effects simply as the "leftover effects," but we shall have a great deal more to say about them in the next chapter. To show how the group means are composed of additive pieces, we can rewrite the above as follows, noting that all effects (row, column, and interaction) add up to zero when added over all four conditions PD, D, P, and O, a characteristic of all residuals from a mean:

Group mean		Grand mean		Row effect		Column effect		Interaction effect
	=		+		+		+	
PD 8	=	4.5	+	1.5	+	1.5	+	0.5
D 4	=	4.5	+	1.5	+	(−1.5)	+	(−0.5)
P 4	=	4.5	+	(−1.5)	+	1.5	+	(−0.5)
O 2	=	4.5	+	(−1.5)	+	(−1.5)	+	0.5
Σ 18	=	18.0	+	0	+	0	+	0

What can be learned about the results of our experiment from studying the table of effects just above? The grand mean tells us the general "level" of our measurements and is usually not of great intrinsic interest. The row effect shows us that the groups receiving drugs do better than those not receiving drugs. The column effect shows us that the groups receiving psychotherapy do better than those not receiving psychotherapy. The interaction effect shows us that the group receiving *both* psychotherapy and the drug and the group receiving *neither* psychotherapy nor the drug both benefit more than do the groups receiving *either* psychotherapy or the drug. That is not to say, of course, that for the present study it is better overall to receive neither psychotherapy nor the drug than to receive either psychotherapy or the drug. Although it is slightly better from the point of view of the *interaction effect alone* to receive neither treatment, this advantage in the interaction effect (i.e., 0.5) is more than offset by the disadvantage in the row effect (i.e., −1.5) and in the column effect (i.e., −1.5) to be receiving neither treatment.

INDIVIDUAL DIFFERENCES AS ERROR

We have seen how the mean of each group or condition can be decomposed into elements made up of the grand mean, the row effect, the column effect, and the interaction effect in the case of a two-dimensional design, such as a two-way factorial design. That does not quite tell the whole story, however, because it does not take into account that the various *scores* found in each condition show variability from the *mean* of that condition. That is, each score can be rewritten as a deviation or residual from the mean of that condition. The magnitude of these deviations reflects how poorly we have done in predicting individual scores from a knowledge of condition or group membership; these deviations or residuals are accordingly called *error*. A particular score shows a "large" error if it falls far from the mean of its condition but only a "small" error if it falls close to the mean of its condition. We can write error as

$$\text{Error} = \text{score} - \text{group mean}$$

so that

$$\text{Score} = \text{group mean} + \text{error}$$

but

$$\text{Group mean} = \text{grand mean} + \text{row effect}$$
$$+ \text{column effect} + \text{interaction effect}$$

so

$$\text{Score} = \text{grand mean} + \text{row effect} + \text{column effect}$$
$$+ \text{interaction effect} + \text{error}$$

From this we can show the makeup of each of the original 12 scores of the study we have been using as our illustration (see Table 16.1). We can employ the decomposition of the individual scores to understand better the computation of the various terms of the analysis of variance. Beneath each column of the display we show the sum of the 12 values (ΣX) and the sum of the squares of the 12 values (ΣX^2). Earlier, when we analyzed the results of the present study as a one-way analysis of variance, we computed three sources of variance:

$$\text{Total } SS = \Sigma(X - \overline{M})^2 = 77$$
$$\text{Between-conditions } SS = \Sigma[n_k(M_k - \overline{M})^2] = 57$$
$$\text{Within-conditions } SS = \Sigma(X - M_k)^2 = 20$$

The total SS is defined as the sum of the squared differences between every single score and the grand mean, i.e., $(9 - 4.5)^2 + \cdots + (0 - 4.5)^2 = 77$. Alternatively, we can subtract the sum of the squared grand means, shown in Table 16.1 as 243 (and expressed symbolically as $N\overline{M}^2$ or as $(\Sigma X)^2/N$), from the sum of the squared scores, shown as 320 (and expressed symbolically as ΣX^2), to obtain the same value, 77. In the one-way analysis of variance this total SS is allocated to two sources of variance, a between-conditions and a within-conditions source.

TABLE 16.1
Table of effects

Condition	Patient	Score	=	Grand mean	+	Row effect	+	Column effect	+	Interaction effect	+	Error
PD	1	9	=	4.5	+	1.5	+	1.5	+	0.5	+	1
PD	2	8	=	4.5	+	1.5	+	1.5	+	0.5	+	0
PD	3	7	=	4.5	+	1.5	+	1.5	+	0.5	+	(−1)
D	4	5	=	4.5	+	1.5	+	(−1.5)	+	(−0.5)	+	1
D	5	4	=	4.5	+	1.5	+	(−1.5)	+	(−0.5)	+	0
D	6	3	=	4.5	+	1.5	+	(−1.5)	+	(−0.5)	+	(−1)
P	7	6	=	4.5	+	(−1.5)	+	1.5	+	(−0.5)	+	2
P	8	4	=	4.5	+	(−1.5)	+	1.5	+	(−0.5)	+	0
P	9	2	=	4.5	+	(−1.5)	+	1.5	+	(−0.5)	+	(−2)
O	10	4	=	4.5	+	(−1.5)	+	(−1.5)	+	0.5	+	2
O	11	2	=	4.5	+	(−1.5)	+	(−1.5)	+	0.5	+	0
O	12	0	=	4.5	+	(−1.5)	+	(−1.5)	+	0.5	+	(−2)
ΣX		54	=	54		0		0		0		0
ΣX^2		320	=	243		27		27		3		20

In moving from a one-way to a two-way analysis of variance, the *within-conditions* source of variance, the source attributable to error, remains unchanged. Table 16.1, showing the contributions of various sources to each score, shows that the sum of the squared effects due to error is 20, as before. However, the *between-conditions* source of variance has now been further broken down into three components as follows:

Between-conditions SS	=	Row-effect SS	+	Column-effect SS	+	Interaction-effect SS
57	=	27	+	27	+	3

where 57 is the between-conditions SS computed earlier showing the overall variation among the four treatment conditions, and the row, column, and interaction effects of 27, 27, and 3, respectively, are as shown in the bottom row of Table 16.1. The table of variance for the two-way analysis differs from the table of variance for the one-way analysis in reflecting the further subdivision of the between-conditions SS.

THE TABLE OF VARIANCE

Examination of the table of variance (Table 16.2) shows a large eta (.76) and significant ($p = .012$) effect of the drug and a large eta (.76) and significant ($p = .012$) effect of psychotherapy. The table of effects (Table 16.1) indicates that it was more beneficial to have the drug than not to have it, and more beneficial to have the psychotherapy than not to have it. The interaction effect, the residual between-conditions variation after the row and column effects were removed, was not close to statistical significance, though the size of the effect (eta = .36) was not trivial in magnitude. Because of the importance of interaction effects in two-way and higher-order analyses of variance, and because of the frequency with which they are misinterpreted by even very experienced investigators, we shall return later to discuss interaction effects in some detail.

TABLE 16.2
The table of variance for a two-way analysis

Source	SS	df	MS	F	eta	p
Between conditions	57	3	19.0	7.60	.86	.01
Drug (row)	27	1	27.0	10.80	.76	.012
Psychotherapy (column)	27	1	27.0	10.80	.76	.012
Interaction	3	1	3.0	1.20	.36	.30
Within conditions	20	8	2.5			
Total	77	11	7.0			

The table of variance shown as Table 16.2 employs eta as its estimate of effect size. Earlier in our discussion of the one-way analysis of variance we defined eta as

$$eta = \sqrt{\frac{SS \text{ between}}{SS \text{ between} + SS \text{ within}}}$$

Eta, therefore, is similar to r in representing the square root of the proportion of variance accounted for. However, eta is a very nonspecific index of effect size when it is based on a source of variance with $df > 1$ and is, therefore, much less informative than r, which tells us about linear relationship. For example, in Table 16.2, the eta of .86 based on 3 df for the between-conditions effect is large, but we cannot say much about what makes it large. The three eta's listed below that eta, however, are each based on just a single df, and as noted earlier, when eta is of this special type ($df = 1$) it is identical with r and may be interpreted as r. That helps quite a bit, as we can now say that the size of the effect of drug is $r = .76$ with all the different ways we have of interpreting that, including the BESD described in our discussion of correlations in Chapter 14. For the table of variance shown as Table 16.2, the size of the effect of psychotherapy is also $r = .76$, and the size of the effect of interaction is $r = .36$, which, while not significant with such a small-sized study, is of at least promising magnitude. Our use of eta or r as an effect-size estimate in the context of the analysis of variance regards each effect of the analysis (e.g., row, column, and interaction effects) as though it were the only one investigated in that study. We mention this fact so that it will not seem strange that the sum of the values of r^2 or of eta^2 may exceed 1.00. Table 16.3 illustrates this.

In looking at the column for proportion of total SS, we see what proportion of all the SS of the study is associated with each source of variation including the error term. The definition, therefore, is

$$\frac{\text{Proportion of}}{\text{Total } SS} = \frac{SS \text{ effect of interest}}{SS \text{ effect of interest} + SS \text{ all other between effects} + SS \text{ within}}$$

In this definition, therefore, we keep increasing the size of the denominator as we keep increasing the number of variables investigated. Ordinarily, however,

TABLE 16.3
Summing values of eta^2 in a study

Source	SS	Proportion of total SS	r^2 or eta^2
Drug	27	.35	.574
Psychotherapy	27	.35	.574
Interaction	3	.04	.130
Within conditions	20	.26	
Total	77	1.00	1.278

when we define proportion of variance as r^2 or eta^2, we disregard all between effects except for the one whose magnitude we are estimating. Therefore, in our more usual usage we define r^2 or eta^2 as follows:

$$r^2 \text{ or } eta^2 = \frac{SS \text{ effect of interest}}{SS \text{ effect of interest} + SS \text{ within}}$$

TESTING THE GRAND MEAN

Earlier in our discussion of the grand mean we noted that we were ordinarily not interested in any intrinsic way in the magnitude of the grand mean. This lack of interest is due in part to the arbitrary units of measurement often employed in behavioral research. Scores on ability tests, for example, might be equally well expressed as IQ scores with $M = 100$ and $\sigma = 20$, or as T scores with $M = 50$ and $\sigma = 10$, or as Z scores with $M = 0$ and $\sigma = 1$. The constant of measurement, then (e.g., 100, 50, 0), would be of little interest.

Sometimes, however, the constant of measurement may be of interest. For example, we may want to compare our sample of subjects with an earlier sample just to see whether the overall means are similar. This might be the case if we had failed to replicate a relationship obtained by an earlier investigator and wondered if our sample differed so much from the earlier one on the dependent variable that differences in sample characteristics might account for our failure to replicate the earlier result.

A second reason we might be interested in our grand mean is that our dependent variable might estimate some skill that might or might not be better than chance. For example, in various measures of sensitivity to nonverbal communication, it would be of interest to know whether, on the average, a particular skill, such as understanding tone of voice, was better than a chance level of accuracy (Rosenthal, 1979b; Rosenthal, Hall, DiMatteo, Rogers, and Archer, 1979).

A third reason we might be interested in our grand mean is that our dependent variable might already be a difference score, such as the difference between a pre- and a posttest measurement. In that case a test of the grand mean is equivalent to a *matched-pair t test* and tells us whether the two measurements, pre- and posttest, differ systematically. Related closely to the assessment of change is the assessment of experimental difference, as when a sample of teachers or of experimenters is led to expect superior performance from some students or subjects. Then the dependent variable per teacher or experimenter sometimes is defined as the difference between (a) the performance obtained from the student or subject for whom the higher expectation had been created and (b) the performance obtained from the student or subject of the control condition. In that case a test of the grand mean tells us whether, overall, teachers or experimenters tended to obtain the results they had been led to expect (Rosenthal, 1966, 1976; Rosenthal and Jacobson, 1968; Rosenthal and Rubin, 1978).

The t Test

The general formula for the t test on the grand mean is

$$t = \frac{\overline{M} - C}{\sqrt{\left(\frac{1}{N}\right)} MS \text{ error}}$$

where $\overline{M}$ is the grand mean, C is the comparison score established on theoretical grounds, N is the total number of subjects or other sampling units, and MS error is the estimate of the variation of the scores of the sampling units within their experimental conditions, i.e., the MS within. For the illustration we have been considering, if we wanted to know whether the grand mean of 4.5 was significantly greater than zero, we would find

$$t = \frac{4.5 - 0}{\sqrt{\left(\frac{1}{12}\right)} 2.5} = 9.86$$

which, with 8 df (the df for the MS error or MS within), is significant at $p <$ .000005, one-tailed.

Suppose that we were interested also in comparing our grand mean with the comparison score based on the grand mean of a large norm group of patients. In that case C would not be zero but, rather, the grand mean of the norm group. Suppose that value were 5.0. Then,

$$t = \frac{4.5 - 5.0}{\sqrt{\left(\frac{1}{12}\right)} 2.5} = -1.10$$

which, with 8 df, has an associated p value of about .30, two-tailed. We might conclude that there is not a very significant difference between the average score of our 12 patients and the average score of the patients of the norm group. Of course, with a sample of only 12 patients our power to reject the null hypothesis is quite low unless the true effect size is quite large, and we are likely to make many type II errors (see Chapter 19).

In our examples employing the t test we have so far assumed that our comparison score was a theoretical score that was known exactly rather than a score that was itself only an estimate of a population value. Suppose, for example, that we wanted to compare our grand mean of 4.5 to the grand mean of 3.0 we obtained in an earlier study employing six patients. If we employed the same t test described so far, we would obtain

$$t = \frac{4.5 - 3.0}{\sqrt{\left(\frac{1}{12}\right)} 2.5} = 3.29$$

which, with 8 df, is significant at about the .01 level, two-tailed. This p level is accurate if we assume the comparison score of 3.0 to be a theoretical value, but is not accurate if we want to take into account the fact that the comparison level is only an estimate based on six patients. Assuming the same MS error for both studies, we compute this type of t by employing both sample sizes in the denominator:

$$t = \frac{\overline{M} - C}{\sqrt{\left(\dfrac{1}{N_{\overline{M}}} + \dfrac{1}{N_C}\right) MS \text{ error}}}$$

For our data,

$$t = \frac{4.5 - 3.0}{\sqrt{\left(\dfrac{1}{12} + \dfrac{1}{6}\right) 2.5}} = 1.90$$

which, with 8 df, is significant at about the .10 level, two-tailed. Employing the actual sample size on which the comparison score is based will generally tend to decrease the obtained t from what it would have been had we employed a theoretical comparison score, and this decrease is greater when the actual sample size is smaller.

In this example we assumed that the MS error for the two studies was equivalent but that we did not actually know the MS error for the comparison score. Therefore, we employed as the MS error for our t test only the MS error for our new study. The df for our t test was, therefore, only 8, since that was the number of df on which our MS error was based. If we had known the MS error for the earlier study, we could have pooled the MS error for the two studies as follows:

$$MS \text{ error pooled} = \frac{df_1 \, MS \text{ error}_1 + df_2 \, MS \text{ error}_2}{df_1 + df_2}$$

then we could compute t from

$$t = \frac{\overline{M} - C}{\sqrt{\left(\dfrac{1}{N_{\overline{M}}} + \dfrac{1}{N_C}\right) MS \text{ error pooled}}}$$

The df for this t would be the sum of the df of the two pooled MS errors, i.e., $df_1 + df_2$.

The F Test

Early in our discussion of the analysis of variance we saw that $t^2 = F$ for the situation of only a single df for the numerator of F. F tests on the grand mean of any one study involve only a single df for the numerator of F, so that all the t test procedures we have been discussing can be employed as F test procedures simply by squaring the computational formulas for t.

If we happen to be working with totals rather than means, the direct F test of the hypothesis that the grand mean differs from zero is obtained by

$$F = \frac{(\Sigma X)^2/N}{MS\ \text{error}}$$

where $(\Sigma X)^2$ is the square of the sum of all scores and N is the number of all such scores. For the example we have been using, the grand sum was 54 (i.e., the grand mean of 4.5 multiplied by the N of 12) so that

$$F = \frac{(54)^2/12}{2.5} = \frac{243}{2.5} = 97.20$$

which, with df of 1 for numerator and 8 for denominator, is significant at $p <$ .00001. The square root of the obtained F is 9.86, precisely the value of t we obtained earlier when we tested the difference between the grand mean of 4.5 and zero.

We can relate the result of the preceding F test to our earlier discussion of individual differences as error (see Table 16.1). There we showed the decomposition of each of the 12 individual scores and the sum of the squared entries for each source of variance as follows:

	Score	=	Grand mean	+	Row effect	+	Column effect	+	Interaction effect	+	Error
ΣX^2	320	=	243	+	27	+	27	+	3	+	20

The entry for the grand mean, the sum of the 12 values of 4.5, each of which had been squared [i.e., $12(4.5)^2$], is identical with the numerator of the F test above, which tested the hypothesis that the grand mean differs from zero. If we subtract that value from the sum of the raw scores squared, we find $320 - 243 = 77$, the total sum of squares of deviations about the grand mean.

COMPUTATIONAL PROCEDURES: EQUAL AND UNEQUAL SAMPLE SIZES

In the case of a one-way overall or omnibus analysis of variance it did not matter for the computational procedure whether we had the same number of units per condition or not. In a two-way or higher-order analysis, however, special care must be taken when the number of sampling units varies from condition to condition. Several procedures are available for dealing with this situation, of which the most wasteful is discarding a random subset of the units of each condition until the sample sizes of all conditions are equal. That procedure is almost never justified.

Several multiple-regression procedures are also available for handling the computations of a two-way analysis of variance with unequal sample sizes per condition (Overall and Spiegel, 1969; Overall, Spiegel, and Cohen, 1975). All these procedures yield identical results when sample sizes are equal, but can differ fairly substantially as sample sizes become increasingly unequal. The procedure we present here can be employed when sample sizes are equal *or* unequal; it is intuitively appealing, and it is computationally convenient. Furthermore, it yields results closer to the "fully simultaneous multiple-regression method" (FSMR) recommended by Overall, Spiegel, and Cohen (1975) than do the competing methods described by Overall and Spiegel (1969). Indeed, for factorial designs of any size, having always two levels per factor, i.e., a 2^k factorial, it yields results that are identical with those obtained by the FSMR method (Horst and Edwards, 1982). In general, the multiple-regression approaches to the analysis of variance proceed by converting the independent variables of the analysis of variance to dummy variables, all of which can then be used as predictors of the dependent variable.

Employing Unweighted Means

The procedure we present is called the *unweighted means analysis,* a procedure that is especially natural for those studies in which we would have preferred equal sample sizes had they been possible. It can be used for situations of equal *or* unequal sample sizes, and it requires only three simple steps (Walker and Lev, 1953; Winer, 1971).

1. Compute a *one-way* analysis of variance on the k groups or conditions.
2. Compute a two-way (or higher) analysis of variance on the *means* of all conditions just as though each condition had yielded only a single score (i.e., the mean).
3. Compute the error term required for the analysis in step 2 by multiplying the *MS* error from step 1 by $1/\bar{n}_h$, where $\bar{n}_h$ is the harmonic mean of the various sample sizes of the different conditions. The quantity $1/\bar{n}_h$, the factor by which we scale down the *MS* error from step 1 to make it the "right size" for the analysis of step 2, is computed by

$$\frac{1}{\bar{n}_h} = \frac{1}{k}\left(\frac{1}{n_1} + \frac{1}{n_2} + \cdots + \frac{1}{n_k}\right)$$

where $\bar{n}_h$ is the harmonic mean of the sample sizes, k is the number of conditions, and the various n's (n_1 to n_k) are the number of sampling units per condition.

We now apply these steps to the set of data that has been serving as our illustration. As it happens, this set of data does have equal sample sizes, but the computational procedures are identical whether sample sizes are equal or unequal.

1. ONE-WAY ANALYSIS OF VARIANCE. The one-way analysis of variance of our data

	PD	P	D	O
	9	6	5	4
	8	4	4	2
	7	2	3	0
Mean	8	4	4	2

yields the following table of variance, as reported earlier:

Source	SS	df	MS	F	eta	p
Between conditions	57	3	19.0	7.60	.86	.01
Within conditions	20	8	2.5			

Recall from Chapter 15 that equal sample sizes are *not* required for a one-way analysis of variance.

2. TWO-WAY ANALYSIS OF VARIANCE. The two-way analysis of variance on the *means* of all conditions is computed as follows:

$$\text{Total } SS = \Sigma (M - \overline{M})^2$$

where M is the mean of each condition and $\overline{M}$ is the grand mean. Here we add up as many squared deviations as there are conditions altogether.

$$\text{Row } SS = \Sigma [c(M_R - \overline{M})^2]$$

where c is the number of columns contributing to the computation of M_R, the mean of each row, and $\overline{M}$ is the grand mean. Here we add up as many quantities as there are rows.

$$\text{Column } SS = \Sigma [r(M_C - \overline{M})^2]$$

where r is the number of rows contributing to the computation of M_C, the mean of each column, and $\overline{M}$ is the grand mean. Here we add up as many quantities as there are columns.

$$\text{Interaction } SS = \text{total } SS - \text{row } SS - \text{column } SS$$

For the data of our present illustration we have:

	Psychotherapy		
	Present	**Absent**	**Mean**
Drug therapy:			
Present	8	4	6
Absent	4	2	3
Mean	6	3	4.5

$$\text{Total } SS = (8 - 4.5)^2 + (4 - 4.5)^2 + (4 - 4.5)^2 + (2 - 4.5)^2 = 19$$

$$\text{Row } SS = 2(6 - 4.5)^2 + 2(3 - 4.5)^2 = 9$$

$$\text{Column } SS = 2(6 - 4.5)^2 + 2(3 - 4.5)^2 = 9$$

$$\text{Interaction } SS = 19 - 9 - 9 = 1$$

Note that in working only with condition means we have set all our "sample sizes" equal; i.e., they all equal 1, the one mean of the condition.

3. ERROR TERM. The error term (MS error) required for the sources of variance just computed from the means of conditions is obtained by multiplying the MS error from step 1 (found to be 2.5) by $1/\bar{n}_h$, the reciprocal of the harmonic mean of the sample sizes, here found to be

$$\frac{1}{\bar{n}_h} = \frac{1}{4}\left(\frac{1}{3} + \frac{1}{3} + \frac{1}{3} + \frac{1}{3}\right) = \frac{1}{3}$$

Therefore, our new error term, appropriately scaled down, is found to be $\frac{1}{3} \times 2.5 = 0.833$. Our table of variance, based on this set of computational procedures, is then displayed as shown in Table 16.4

Earlier, we showed the table of variance for the same study but with computations based on the original 12 scores rather than on the means of the four different conditions. The results of F tests and the magnitudes of eta and of p are identical with those obtained by the method of unweighted means shown in Table 16.4. However, the magnitudes of all SS and MS are smaller in the present

TABLE 16.4
Unweighted means analysis

Source	SS	df	MS	F	eta	p
Drug (row)	9	1	9	10.80	.76	.012
Psychotherapy (column)	9	1	9	10.80	.76	.012
Interaction	1	1	1	1.20	.36	.30
Error term ($MS_E \times 1/\bar{n}_h$)	—	8	0.833			

table by a factor of $1/\bar{n}_h$, the reciprocal of the harmonic mean sample size per condition. The effect of employing the unweighted means analysis, then, is to shrink the SS and MS in a uniform way that has no effect whatever on either significance tests or effect-size estimates. This example illustrates that when sample sizes are equal, the unweighted means analysis yields results identical with those obtained from an ordinary analysis employing all the original scores.

Effects on F of Unequal Sample Sizes

Earlier, in our discussion of increasing the size of t, we saw that for any given total N, and given that the effect size was not zero, t would increase as the sizes of each sample became more nearly equal. The same situation holds for F, that for any given total N, F will increase as the sizes of the two or more samples or conditions become more nearly equal. We can demonstrate this for the data we have been employing for our illustration. The four groups were of equal size (3, 3, 3, 3) with a total N of 12 patients. Table 16.5 shows the effects on F, eta, and p when the sample sizes are made increasingly heterogeneous. For our example we show the F, eta, and p only for the drug (row) effect, but that is sufficient to illustrate the point.

Table 16.5 shows that as the sample sizes become more heterogeneous, where *heterogeneity* is defined by the relative magnitude of the σ of the sample sizes, F and eta both decrease and p becomes larger, i.e., less significant. F decreases by as much as 57 percent, eta decreases by as much as 20 percent, and the quite significant p of .012 goes to "nonsignificance" ($p = .064$), a result that would cause greatest pain to researchers endorsing dichotomous decisions about whether to believe or not believe the null hypothesis—a view we do not encourage.

The results shown in Table 16.5 are by no means extreme. When the total N increases, much more extreme effects are possible. For example, for the four conditions of the experiment that has been serving as our example, if the N had been 100, equal-sized samples of 25 each would have yielded an $F(1, 96)$ of 131.58, keeping the effect size of eta $= .76$ constant. However, if the N of 100 had been allocated as heterogeneously as possible (1, 1, 1, 97), $F(1, 96)$ would

TABLE 16.5
Effects on F, eta, and p of heterogeneity of sample sizes

Sample sizes	σ*	$\bar{n}_h$	$1/\bar{n}_h$	MS error $(2.5 \times 1/n_h)$	$F(1, 8)$	eta[†]	p
3, 3, 3, 3	0	3.00	.333	0.833	10.80	.76	.012
2, 2, 4, 4	1.00	2.67	.375	0.938	9.59	.74	.015
1, 1, 5, 5	2.00	1.67	.600	1.500	6.00	.65	.040
1, 1, 1, 9	3.46	1.29	.778	1.944	4.63	.61	.064

*Of the four sample sizes.

[†]$\text{eta} = \sqrt{\dfrac{(F)(df \text{ numerator})}{(F)(df \text{ numerator}) + (df \text{ denominator})}}$.

have been 7.00 and eta would have been .26, a reduction in F of 95 percent and a reduction in eta of 66 percent!

HIGHER-ORDER FACTORIAL DESIGNS

So far in our discussion of factorial designs we have dealt only with two-way, or two-dimensional, designs, but there are many occasions to employ higher-order designs. For example, suppose that the experiment we have been describing had been carried out twice, once for female patients and once for male patients. We could reap the general benefit of factorial designs of using subjects for more comparisons and building up the sample sizes per comparison by analyzing these two experiments as a single, higher-order factorial experiment with design and results as shown in Table 16.6. This design is referred to as a *2 × 2 × 2 factorial design* or as a *2^3 factorial*, because there are three factors each with two levels: drug (present versus absent), psychotherapy (present versus absent), and sex of patient (female versus male). Assume that there were three patients in each condition, so that $N = 2 \times 2 \times 2 \times 3 = 24$. Assume further that our preliminary one-way analysis of variance (step 1 of the unweighted means procedure) happened to yield an MS error of 2.5, exactly what we found in our earlier one-way analysis of the original 12 scores. Step 3 of the unweighted means procedure requires us to multiply this MS error of 2.5 by $1/\bar{n}_h$, which for this study is

$$\frac{1}{\bar{n}_h} = \frac{1}{8}\left(\frac{1}{3} + \frac{1}{3} + \frac{1}{3} + \frac{1}{3} + \frac{1}{3} + \frac{1}{3} + \frac{1}{3} + \frac{1}{3}\right) = \frac{1}{3}$$

so that our error term will be $2.5 \times \frac{1}{3} = 0.833$, exactly the same error term we found before. It remains now only to compute the three-way analysis of variance on the eight means shown in the table.

Computations via Subtables

In a three-way analysis of variance we will compute three main effects, one for each factor, three two-way interactions of all factors taken two at a time, and one three-way interaction. Computations require us to construct the three two-way tables by averaging the two means (in this example) that contribute to the mean of each of the 2×2 tables (see Table 16.7).

TABLE 16.6
Improvement scores in eight conditions

	Female patients		Male patients	
	Psychotherapy	No psychotherapy	Psychotherapy	No psychotherapy
Drug	10	5	6	3
No drug	4	1	4	3

TABLE 16.7
Two-way tables of a three-way design

Subtable 1: sex of patient × drug			
	Female	Male	Mean
Drug	$7.5^{\lfloor 2 *}$	$4.5^{\lfloor 2}$	$6.0^{\lfloor 4}$
No drug	$2.5^{\lfloor 2}$	$3.5^{\lfloor 2}$	$3.0^{\lfloor 4}$
Mean	$5.0^{\lfloor 4}$	$4.0^{\lfloor 4}$	$4.5^{\lfloor 8}$

Subtable 2: sex of patient × psychotherapy			
	Female	Male	Mean
Psychotherapy	$7.0^{\lfloor 2}$	$5.0^{\lfloor 2}$	$6.0^{\lfloor 4}$
No psychotherapy	$3.0^{\lfloor 2}$	$3.0^{\lfloor 2}$	$3.0^{\lfloor 4}$
Mean	$5.0^{\lfloor 4}$	$4.0^{\lfloor 4}$	$4.5^{\lfloor 8}$

Subtable 3: drug × psychotherapy			
	Psychotherapy	No psychotherapy	Mean
Drug	$8.0^{\lfloor 2}$	$4.0^{\lfloor 2}$	$6.0^{\lfloor 4}$
No drug	$4.0^{\lfloor 2}$	$2.0^{\lfloor 2}$	$3.0^{\lfloor 4}$
Mean	$6.0^{\lfloor 4}$	$3.0^{\lfloor 4}$	$4.5^{\lfloor 8}$

Note: The number within the "⌊" symbol represents the number of means on which this mean is based.

The entries of our three 2 × 2 tables are found as follows: The mean for females given drugs, the top-left condition of subtable 1, is found by averaging the two conditions in which there are females given drugs, namely, females given drugs who are also given psychotherapy ($M = 10$) and females given drugs who are not given psychotherapy ($M = 5$). The row and column means can be checked readily because each factor produces row or column means in two different 2 × 2 tables. Thus the female and male mean improvement scores can be compared in subtables 1 and 2, the drug and no-drug mean scores can be compared in subtables 1 and 3, and the psychotherapy and no-psychotherapy mean scores can be compared in subtables 2 and 3.

The general strategy is to compute the main effects first, then the two-way interactions which are residuals when the two contributing main effects are subtracted from the variation in the two-way tables, and the three-way interaction which is a residual when the three main effects and three two-way interactions are subtracted from the total variation among the eight condition means. The computational formulas follow:

$$\text{"Total" } SS = \Sigma(M - \overline{M})^2$$

where M is the mean of each condition and $\overline{M}$ is the grand mean of all conditions. Here we add up as many squared deviations as there are conditions altogether. (We have put quotation marks around "Total" as a reminder that this is a "total" SS only when we are considering the data of the analysis to consist only of the condition means.)

$$\text{Sex of patient } SS = \Sigma[dp(M_S - \overline{M})^2]$$

where d is the number of levels of the drug factor, p is the number of levels of the psychotherapy factor, M_S is the mean of all conditions of a given sex, and $\overline{M}$ is the grand mean. Here we add up as many quantities as there are levels of the factor "sex of patient." Note that we have given up the row and column designations because with higher-order designs we run out of things to call factors, e.g., in a five-way design. Accordingly, in higher-order designs we simply employ the names of the factors as the names of the dimensions.

$$\text{Drug } SS = \Sigma[sp(M_D - \overline{M})^2]$$

where s is the number of levels of the sex of patient factor, p and $\overline{M}$ are as before, and M_D is the mean of all the conditions contributing observations to each level of the drug factor. Here we add up as many quantities as there are levels of the drug factor.

$$\text{Psychotherapy } SS = \Sigma[sd(M_P - \overline{M})^2]$$

where s, d, and $\overline{M}$ are defined as above and M_P is the mean of all the conditions contributing observations to each level of the psychotherapy factor. Here we add up as many quantities as there are levels of the psychotherapy factor.

$$\text{Sex} \times \text{drug interaction } SS = \Sigma[p(M_{SD} - \overline{M})^2] - \text{sex } SS - \text{drug } SS$$

where M_{SD} is the mean of all conditions contributing observations to each mean of subtable 1 of Table 16.7 and other terms are as defined above. Here we add up as many quantities as there are entries in that subtable.

$$\text{Sex} \times \text{psychotherapy interaction } SS = \Sigma[d(M_{SP} - \overline{M})^2]$$
$$- \text{sex } SS - \text{psychotherapy } SS$$

where M_{SP} is the mean of all conditions contributing observations to each mean of subtable 2 and other terms are as defined above. Here we add up as many quantities as there are entries in that subtable.

$$\text{Drug} \times \text{psychotherapy interaction } SS = \Sigma[s(M_{DP} - \overline{M})^2]$$
$$- \text{drug } SS - \text{psychotherapy } SS$$

where M_{DP} is the mean of all conditions contributing observations to each mean of subtable 3 and other terms are as defined above. Here we add up as many quantities as there are entries in that subtable.

$$\text{Sex} \times \text{drug} \times \text{psychotherapy interaction } SS = \text{total } SS$$
$$- \text{sex } SS - \text{drug } SS - \text{psychotherapy } SS - \text{sex} \times \text{drug } SS$$
$$- \text{sex} \times \text{psychotherapy } SS - \text{drug} \times \text{psychotherapy } SS$$

For the data of our $2 \times 2 \times 2$ factorial design we find

$$\text{Total } SS = (10 - 4.5)^2 + (5 - 4.5)^2 + (6 - 4.5)^2 + (3 - 4.5)^2$$
$$+ (4 - 4.5)^2 + (1 - 4.5)^2 + (4 - 4.5)^2 + (3 - 4.5)^2 = 50$$

$$\text{Sex of patient } SS = [2 \times 2(5 - 4.5)^2] + [2 \times 2(4 - 4.5)^2] = 2$$

$$\text{Drug } SS = [2 \times 2(6 - 4.5)^2] + [2 \times 2(3 - 4.5)^2] = 18$$

$$\text{Psychotherapy } SS = [2 \times 2(6 - 4.5)^2] + [2 \times 2(3 - 4.5)^2] = 18$$

$$\text{Sex} \times \text{drug } SS = 2(7.5 - 4.5)^2 + 2(4.5 - 4.5)^2 + 2(2.5 - 4.5)^2$$
$$+ 2(3.5 - 4.5)^2 - \text{sex } SS - \text{drug } SS = 8$$

$$\text{Sex} \times \text{psychotherapy } SS = 2(7 - 4.5)^2 + 2(5 - 4.5)^2$$
$$+ 2(3 - 4.5)^2 + 2(3 - 4.5)^2$$
$$- \text{sex } SS - \text{psychotherapy } SS = 2$$

$$\text{Drug} \times \text{psychotherapy } SS = 2(8 - 4.5)^2 + 2(4 - 4.5)^2$$
$$+ 2(4 - 4.5)^2 + 2(2 - 4.5)^2$$
$$- \text{drug } SS - \text{psychotherapy } SS = 2$$

$$\text{Sex} \times \text{drug} \times \text{psychotherapy } SS = \text{total } SS - SS_S$$
$$- SS_D - SS_P - SS_{SD} - SS_{SP} - SS_{DP} = 0$$

Table of Variance

These computations are summarized in the table of variance shown as Table 16.8. When we examine the effects of drug, psychotherapy, and the interaction of drug and psychotherapy, we find that the effect sizes (eta's) of .76, .76, and .36, respectively, are identical with the effect sizes obtained in our earlier two-way

TABLE 16.8
Unweighted means analysis

Source	SS	df	MS	F(1, 16)	eta*	p
Sex of patient	2	1	2	2.40	.36	.14
Drug	18	1	18	21.61	.76	.0003
Psychotherapy	18	1	18	21.61	.76	.0003
Sex $\times$ drug	8	1	8	9.60	.61	.007
Sex $\times$ psychotherapy	2	1	2	2.40	.36	.14
Drug $\times$ psychotherapy	2	1	2	2.40	.36	.14
Sex $\times$ drug $\times$ psychotherapy	0	1	0	0.00	.00	1.00
Error term ($MS_E \times 1/\bar{n}_h$)	—	16	0.833[†]			

$$\text{*eta} = \sqrt{\frac{F(df \text{ numerator})}{F(df \text{ numerator}) + (df \text{ denominator})}}.$$

[†]Based on our finding that $MS_E = 2.5$.

analysis of variance. That is as it should be, of course, since the subtable of the drug × psychotherapy combination (Table 16.7, subtable 3) shows exactly the same four means as were shown by the two-way table of our earlier 2 × 2 factorial analysis of variance, and, in addition, our error term has remained the same. Although our eta's have not changed, our F's have all increased and our p levels are much smaller in the present analysis relative to our earlier two-way analysis. That too is what we would expect since the *size* of our study has increased. In fact, as discussed in the last chapter, our F tests have doubled because the size of our experiment (*df* for error) has doubled, since

$$F = \frac{r^2}{1 - r^2} \times df$$

Inspection of the table of variance shown in Table 16.8 suggests a tendency (eta = .36) for the sex of the patient to make some difference, and subtables 1 and 2 of Table 16.7 show that females earned higher improvement scores than did males. We will postpone discussion of the remaining interaction effects of this table of variance until the next chapt   The topic of interaction is so important and so widely misunderstood, not pei.   s in theory but in practice, that we want to highlight the topic in a chapter of its own.

Generalizing Computational Procedures

It is not at all unusual for behavorial researchers to employ factorial designs of more than three dimensions. For example, it is easy to imagine repeating the three-way factorial just described for two or more levels of age, e.g., patients between 20 and 40 and patients between 40 and 60. The computations for this 2^4 factorial design (or 2 × 2 × 2 × 2) are quite analogous to those described for the 2^3 design. We proceed by constructing all possible two-way tables (AB, AC, AD, BC, BD, CD) and all possible three-way tables (ABC, ABD, ACD, BCD), and then compute the required four main effects, six two-way interactions, four three-way interactions, and one four-way interaction.

CHAPTER 17

INTERACTION
EFFECTS

SEPARATION OF INTERACTION FROM
MAIN EFFECTS

In the last chapter we introduced the idea of interaction effects briefly but post-poned detailed discussion to the present chapter. We did that to give the topic of interaction effects the status of an independent chapter, which it deserves for three reasons: (1) the *frequency* with which interactions occur and are discussed in the behavioral sciences, (2) the *importance* of interactions in so many substantive areas of the behavioral sciences, and (3) the widespread *misunderstanding* surrounding the concept of interaction (Rosnow and Rosenthal, 1989a).

Referees and advisory editors for various journals in the behavioral sciences, and consultants in research methods, find the misinterpretation of interaction effects to be one of the most common methodological errors made. The nature of the error is almost always the same: the effects of the interaction are not separated from the main effects.

An Illustration

Suppose we are comparing a new method of teaching reading with an old method and have employed both female and male pupils as our subjects. The tables of means and of variance are as shown, respectively, in Table 17.1 and Table 17.2. In the published report an investigator might accurately state that there was a significant effect of method such that pupils taught by the new method performed better than those taught by the old method. The investigator might also

TABLE 17.1
Table of means

	Females	Males	Mean
Experimental (new method)	4	10	7
Control (old method)	4	2	3
Mean	4	6	5

TABLE 17.2
Table of variance

Source	SS	df	MS	F	eta	p
Method	16	1	16	4.00	.25	.05
Sex of pupil	4	1	4	1.00	.13	—
Interaction	16	1	16	4.00	.25	.05
Error term (MS error $\times \frac{1}{16}$)	240	60	4			

state correctly that there was no significant effect of sex of pupil on performance. Finally, the investigator might say, *but it would be wrong*, that the significant interaction effect shown in Figure 17-1 demonstrated that males but not females benefited from the new teaching method.

In what way has the investigator erred in referring the reader to this figure? The figure is a perfectly accurate display of the *overall* results of the study including *both* main effects *plus* an interaction, but it is *not* an accurate display of the interaction the investigator believed was being displayed. An accurate display of the interaction might appear as shown in Figure 17-2. Here we see that the *interaction* shows that males benefit from the new method precisely to the same degree that females are harmed by it. The diagram of the interaction is X-shaped; indeed, it is true *in general* that in any 2 × 2 analysis of variance the display of any nonzero interaction will be X-shaped. This will become clearer as we proceed.

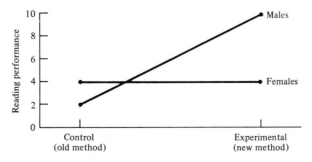

FIGURE 17-1
Figure showing two main effects as well as interaction.

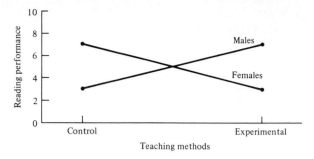

FIGURE 17-2
Figure showing interaction effect.

DEFINING INTERACTION

Interaction effects are residual effects, or effects remaining in any analysis after lower-order effects have been removed, as explained in Chapter 16. In a two-way design (A × B), the interaction effects are the effects remaining after the row and column effects (the effects of A and B) have been removed. In a three-way design (A × B × C), and in higher-order designs, there are four or more different interactions. In an A × B × C design there are three two-way interactions (A × B; A × C; B × C), each of which is the residual set of effects remaining after the removal of the two main effects designated by the letters naming the interaction; there is also a three-way interaction (A × B × C), which is the residual set of effects remaining after the removal of the three main effects and the three two-way interactions. In an A × B × C × D, or four-way, design, there are six two-way interactions (A × B; A × C; A × D; B × C; B × D; C × D), four three-way interactions (A × B × C; A × B × D; A × C × D; B × C × D), and one four-way interaction. In general, a *higher-order interaction* is defined as the residual set of effects remaining after the main effects and all lower-order interactions relevant to the higher-order interaction have been removed. Thus the A × B × C × D interaction is defined as the set of effects remaining after the four main effects, the six two-way interactions, and the four three-way interactions have been subtracted from the total of all between-conditions effects.

DISPLAYING THE RESIDUALS

Before an interaction effect can be understood, it must be identified and examined; i.e., the residuals defining the interaction must be displayed. The logic is straightforward, but in a very high-order interaction the computation can become burdensome, and regrettably there are very few social science data-analytic packages that routinely provide the residuals in a useful tabular format. In a two-dimensional design, however, the computations are simple. Consider the results of our experiment on the effects of a new method of teaching reading on reading performance scores, as shown in Table 17.3.

TABLE 17.3
Reading scores in four conditions

| Teaching method: | Sex of pupils | | Mean | Row effect |
	Females	Males		
New (experimental)	4	10	7	2
Old (control)	4	2	3	-2
Mean	4	6	5	
Column effect	-1	1		

To find the interaction effects we must subtract the row and column effects from each condition of the experiment. *Row effects* are defined for each row as the mean of that row minus the grand mean. The row effects are $7 - 5 = 2$ for the new teaching method and $3 - 5 = -2$ for the old teaching method. To remove the row effect we subtract the row effect from every condition within that row. Subtracting 2 from the top row in Table 17.3 yields means of 2 and 8; subtracting -2 from the bottom row yields means of 6 and 4 (recall that subtracting a negative value is equivalent to adding a positive value). The table of means we started with, now with row effects removed (or "corrected for" row effects), has been amended as shown in Table 17.4.

We must still remove the effects of columns. *Column effects* are defined for each column as the mean of that column minus the grand mean. The column effects are $4 - 5 = -1$ for the females and $6 - 5 = 1$ for the males. To remove the column effect we subtract it from every condition within that column. Subtracting -1 from the first column of the row-corrected table shown as Table 17.4 yields means of 3 and 7; subtracting 1 from the second column yields means of 7 and 3. The table of means we started with, now with both row and column effects removed, has been amended as shown in Table 17.5. Once the row and column effects are all zero, we can be sure that what is left is only the set of residuals defining the interaction effect, sometimes with, and sometimes without, the grand mean added.

It is these means that were shown in Figure 17-2 displaying the correct interaction effects. However, these interaction effects are inflated by the presence

TABLE 17.4
Reading scores corrected for row effects

| Teaching method: | Sex of pupils | | Mean | Row effect |
	Females	Males		
New	2	8	5	0
Old	6	4	5	0
Mean	4	6	5	
Column effect	-1	1		

TABLE 17.5
Reading scores corrected for row and column effects

| Teaching method: | Sex of pupils | | Mean | Row effect |
	Females	Males		
New	3	7	5	0
Old	7	3	5	0
Mean	5	5	5	
Column effect	0	0		

of the grand mean, an inflation useful for display purposes earlier when we wanted to compare the results of the experiment, defined as the condition means, with the interaction effect alone. In most situations, however, we prefer to display the interaction effects freed of the effect of the grand mean. To remove the grand mean from Table 17.5, simply subtract it from every condition of the experiment. For our example that yields the results shown in Table 17.6.

It should be noted that all four conditions show the same absolute value of the interaction effects, only the signs differ. That is always the case in a 2×2 analysis, and the signs on one of the diagonals are always different from the signs on the other diagonal if the interaction is not precisely zero. It is thus convenient to think of an interaction in a 2×2 table as the difference between the means of the two diagonals, just as it is convenient to think of the row or column effects as the differences between the row means or the column means.

Returning now to Figure 17-1, we can see that it is an accurate display of the results of the experiment. It does show that females did not benefit from the new teaching method but that males did. That statement, however, is not a statement about the interaction effect per se but a statement made up in part of (1) a method effect (the new method is better), (2) a sex effect (males score higher, though not significantly so), and (3) an interaction effect, which we interpret as showing that females are hurt by the new method as much as males are helped by it.

TABLE 17.6
Reading scores corrected for row and column effects and for the grand mean

| Teaching method: | Sex of pupils | | Mean | Row effect |
	Females	Males		
New	−2	2	0	0
Old	2	−2	0	0
Mean	0	0	0	
Column effect	0	0		

CONSTRUCTING TABLES OF MEANS:
A CHECK ON UNDERSTANDING

It is useful as a check on our understanding of interaction effects and the additive nature of the analysis of variance to construct tables of means to our specifications. We list a series of 2 × 2 tables with no entries in them and fill in the four means to match the following specifications, one for each 2 × 2 table; by "effects" we mean any nonzero effect.

1. Column effect only
2. Row effect only
3. Row effect and column effect only, with row effect larger
4. Interaction effect only
5. Interaction effect and row effect, with interaction effect larger
6. Interaction effect and column effect, with column effect larger
7. Row effect, column effect, and interaction effect, with row effect largest and column effect smallest

As an illustration of how to approach such practice problems, begin with an empty A × B table:

	A_1	A_2	Mean	Row effect
B_1				
B_2				
Mean				
Column effect				

Beginning with the grand mean, choose any value—positive, zero, or negative—but keep to a single-digit integer for simplicity. If a grand mean of 2 were chosen, we would have:

	A_1	A_2	Mean	Row effect
B_1	2	2	2	0
B_2	2	2	2	0
Mean	2	2	2	
Column effect	0	0		

Since we want the column effect to be smallest, choose the smallest possible integers (+1 and −1) to add to each condition within each of the two columns, yielding:

	A_1	A_2	Mean	Row effect
B_1	3	1	2	0
B_2	3	1	2	0
Mean	3	1	2	
Column effect	+1	−1		

In order that the interaction effect be larger than the column effect, we might choose the values of +2 and −2, adding the former value to the conditions on one diagonal and the latter to the conditions on the other diagonal, yielding:

	A_1	A_2	Mean	Row effect
B_1	5	−1	2	0
B_2	1	3	2	0
Mean	3	1	2	
Column effect	+1	−1		

Finally, in order that the row effect be larger than the interaction, we might choose the values of +3 and −3, to add to each condition within each of the two rows, yielding:

	A_1	A_2	Mean	Row effect
B_1	8	2	5	+3
B_2	−2	0	−1	−3
Mean	3	1	2	
Column effect	+1	−1		

As a check on the construction of the 2 × 2 table, we can decompose it, as in the last chapter, into its various additive components.

	Group mean	=	Grand mean	+	Row effect	+	Column effect	+	Interaction effect
A_1B_1	8	=	2	+	3	+	1	+	2
A_2B_1	2	=	2	+	3	+	(−1)	+	(−2)
A_1B_2	−2	=	2	+	(−3)	+	1	+	(−2)
A_2B_2	0	=	2	+	(−3)	+	(−1)	+	2
ΣX	8	=	8	+	0	+	0	+	0
ΣX^2	72	=	16	+	36	+	4	+	16

Examination of the four group means above and their additive components shows that row effects were larger than interaction effects, which in turn were larger than column effects, as required by our specifications. In a 2 × 2 table the absolute values of the two row effects are identical, with one of the signs positive and the other sign negative. Exactly the same situation holds for the column effects. For the interaction, all four effects are identical in absolute value, but the two effects on one diagonal are opposite in sign to the two effects on the other diagonal. In this case, therefore, we can rank-order the sizes of effects by rank-ordering the absolute values of the three effects contributing to any one of our four means.

MORE COMPLEX TWO-WAY DESIGNS

So far we have considered only the simple case of interaction in a 2 × 2 design. In such a design we have seen that the residuals defining the interaction are all identical in absolute value, with positive signs on one diagonal and negative signs on the other diagonal. In larger designs the situation is more complex. Because this is a chapter on interaction, our focus in the following example will be on the study of the interaction effects. This emphasis is not due to our regarding interaction effects as in any way more important than main effects. Rather, it is because interaction effects are so much more often misinterpreted than are main effects.

For our example we consider an experiment in which four different treatment procedures are administered to three different types of patients, with results as shown in Table 17.7.

Patients of each of the three types were assigned at random to one of four treatment conditions: (1) a course of 10 electroconvulsive treatments, or ECTs, (2) a course of 3 electroconvulsive treatments, (3) a combination of supportive psychotherapy and chemotherapy, and (4) supportive psychotherapy alone. In order to see the interaction of treatment × patient type, both the row and col-

TABLE 17.7
Improvement scores in 12 conditions

Patient type	Treatment conditions				
	A_1 ECT(10)*	A_2 ECT(3)	A_3 Supp.† + drug	A_4 Supp. only	Mean
B_1 Psychotic depression	8	6	4	2	5
B_2 Neurotic depression	11	8	5	8	8
B_3 Paranoid reaction	2	4	6	8	5
Mean	7	6	5	6	6

*Ten electroconvulsive treatments.
†Supportive psychotherapy.

umn effects must be subtracted off. Usually it is desirable also to subtract off the grand mean, and we begin by doing that. Since the grand mean is 6, simply subtract 6 from every one of the 3 × 4, or 12, condition means, yielding:

	A_1	A_2	A_3	A_4	Mean
B_1	2	0	−2	−4	−1
B_2	5	2	−1	2	2
B_3	−4	−2	0	2	−1
Mean	1	0	−1	0	0

Once the grand mean has been subtracted, the new row means are the row effects, and the new column means are the column effects. To remove the row effects, simply subtract the effect of each row (row mean minus grand mean) from every condition within that row. Doing that for the present data yields:

	A_1	A_2	A_3	A_4	Mean
B_1	3	1	−1	−3	0
B_2	3	0	−3	0	0
B_3	−3	−1	1	3	0
Mean	1	0	−1	0	0

Subtracting the column effect from every condition mean within that column then yields:

	A_1	A_2	A_3	A_4	Mean
B_1	2	1	0	-3	0
B_2	2	0	-2	0	0
B_3	-4	-1	2	3	0
Mean	0	0	0	0	0

Now that the grand mean, row effects, and column effects have been removed, we are left with the interaction effect shown just above. The effects contributing most to the interaction are the effects furthest from zero, and one way to approach the interpretation of the interaction is one residual at a time, starting with the largest absolute value. In this case the A_1B_3 condition shows the greatest residual (-4), suggesting that least improvement is shown by paranoid patients given a course of 10 ECT treatments, disregarding row and column effects. The next two largest residuals are the A_4B_1 and A_4B_3 conditions. The former suggests that support alone offered to psychotic depressive patients is relatively damaging (-3), while the latter suggests that support alone offered to paranoid patients is *relatively* quite beneficial (3). The term "relatively" is used here to emphasize that the effects shown by certain combinations of treatments and patients are large or small only in relation to other effects shown here *after the removal of the main effects of treatments and patients*.

We can be more systematic in our examination of the residuals by listing them in order of magnitude as shown in Table 17.8. Examining first the positive residuals suggests that paranoid patients may do better given support, while depressive patients may do better given ECT. Examining the negative residuals suggests that paranoid patients may do worse given ECT, while depressive patients may do worse given support. It may be of value to simplify our design from four treatments to two by combining the two conditions receiving ECT and the two conditions receiving support. We can further simplify our design from three patient types to two by combining the two depressed groups. That yields a 2×2 table, in each quarter of which we can record the sum of the residuals contributing to that quarter, as shown below:

	ECT $(A_1 + A_2)$	Support $(A_3 + A_4)$	Mean
Depressives $(B_1 + B_2)$	5	-5	0
Paranoids (B_3)	-5	5	0
Mean	0	0	0

TABLE 17.8
Systematic ordering of residuals

Residual	Patient	Treatment
3	Paranoid	Support only
2	Psychotic depression	ECT 10
2	Neurotic depression	ECT 10
2	Paranoid	Support + drug
1	Psychotic depression	ECT 3
0	Psychotic depression	Support + drug
0	Neurotic depression	ECT 3
0	Neurotic depression	Support only
−1	Paranoid	ECT 3
−2	Neurotic depression	Support + drug
−3	Psychotic depression	Support only
−4	Paranoid	ECT 10

This simplification of the interaction to a 2×2 table represents one reasonable attempt to understand the patterning of the residuals defining the interaction. In subsequent chapters dealing with contrasts we shall give more details about the simplification of complex interaction effects.

The complexity of an interaction depends in part on the *df* associated with the interaction, with *df* computed as the product of the *df* associated with each of its constituent elements. In the study we have just been discussing, there were four treatment conditions, so $df = 3$ for treatments, and three types of patients, so $df = 2$ for patient type; therefore *df* for the treatment $\times$ patient type interaction $= 3 \times 2 = 6$. Finding a pattern in these 6 *df*, such as the one shown on page 374 as a 2×2 table, represents simplifying the 6-*df* interaction to a 1-*df* portion of that interaction. Elsewhere we provide procedures for assessing how well we have done in simplifying the interpretation of an interaction with multiple *df* in the numerator of its *F* test and, more generally, how well we have done in the interpretation of any effect, interaction or main effect, with multiple *df* in the numerator of the *F* test when we impose a simplifying structure (Rosenthal and Rosnow, 1985).

An accurate description of the simplified structure of our interaction might be that depressed patients are benefited by ECT to the same degree that they are harmed by support, while paranoid patients benefit from support to the same degree that they are harmed by ECT. Note that we are describing the *interaction* effects or residuals and not necessarily the original condition means, which are a reflection *not* merely of the interaction but of the row and column effects as well.

An alternative simplification of the 6-*df* interaction might involve keeping in mind the number of ECTs administered as well as whether ECT was administered at all. Thus we might have three levels of ECT:

	(A_1) High ECT (10)	(A_2) Low ECT (3)	($A_3 + A_4$) No ECT	Mean
Depressives ($B_1 + B_2$)	4	1	−5	0
Paranoids (B_3)	−4	−1	5	0
Mean	0	0	0	0

Interpretation of this simplification might be that in going from none to some to more ECTs depressives are increasingly benefited, while paranoids are decreasingly benefited.

Constructing Tables of Means

Earlier in this chapter we noted that it was useful to construct 2 × 2 tables of means to our specifications. We have also found it useful to do so with larger tables. For example, one can list a series of empty tables ranging in dimension from 2 × 3 to 4 × 5 and, for each one, fill in means such that row effects will be largest, interaction effects intermediate, and column effects smallest, etc., with different specifications for each empty table.

THREE-WAY DESIGNS

Near the end of Chapter 16 we presented a table of variance for a 2 × 2 × 2 design (see Table 16.8), but we postponed discussion of the interaction effects until the present chapter. In that study there were 3 two-way interactions, and for the purpose of computation of the three-way analysis of variance, we constructed three subtables of means, one for each two-way combination of the three factors of the study (see Table 16.7). The three factors were sex of patient, drug, and psychotherapy. Since we have already given several illustrations of how to go from a table of means to a table of effects, we will here simply show the table of effects corresponding to each table of means. In the tables of effects shown as Tables 17.9a to 17.9c the row and column "means" are the row and column effects, respectively, and the four entries in the 2 × 2 table are the residuals defining the interaction.

The interaction of sex of patient × drug (Table 17.9a) was found to be significant ($p = .007$) and large (eta = .61). Now our examination of the residuals tells us that females did as much better with the drug as they did worse without it, while males did as much better without the drug as they did worse with it. Does this mean that males are better off without the drug? No, in this study there is a large main effect of drug, and it is better to have the drug than not

TABLE 17.9a
Sex of patient × drug combination

	Table of means			Table of effects		
	Female	Male	Mean	Female	Male	Mean
Drug	7.5	4.5	6.0	1.0	−1.0	1.5
No drug	2.5	3.5	3.0	−1.0	1.0	−1.5
Mean	5.0	4.0	4.5	0.5	−0.5	0

TABLE 17.9b
Sex of patient × psychotherapy combination

	Table of means			Table of effects		
	Female	Male	Mean	Female	Male	Mean
Psychotherapy	7.0	5.0	6.0	0.5	−0.5	1.5
No psychotherapy	3.0	3.0	3.0	−0.5	0.5	−1.5
Mean	5.0	4.0	4.5	0.5	−0.5	0

have it for males as well as females. The interaction tells us only that the benefits of the drug are less for males than they are for females, not that the drug is disadvantageous to males in any *absolute* sense.

The interaction of sex of patient × psychotherapy (Table 17.9b) was found to be "significant" at only the .14 level, though the effect size was not trivial (eta = .36). Examination of the residuals shows that females did better with psychotherapy, while males did better without psychotherapy relative, respectively, to females receiving no psychotherapy and males receiving psychotherapy. Phrased another way, we could say that psychotherapy benefited females [(0.5) − (−0.5) = 1.0] more than it benefited males [(−0.5) − (0.5) = −1.0].

The interaction of drug × psychotherapy (Table 17.9c) also did not reach the conventional level of significance (p = .14), but its effect size was substantial (eta = .36). The residuals defining this interaction show that psychotherapy is more beneficial to those receiving the drug, and that the absence of psychotherapy is more beneficial to those not receiving the drug relative to the remaining two combinations (disregarding the main effects, as interactions always do). Phrased another way, we could say that the interaction shows that receiving *both* drug and psychotherapy and receiving *neither* drug nor psychotherapy were more beneficial than receiving *either* one of the treatments alone. Once again we must emphasize that this does not mean that patients are better off receiving no treatment than receiving either treatment alone. On the contrary, the table of means in Table 17-9c shows that either drug or psychotherapy alone is more beneficial than neither treatment. However, considering *only* the interaction component of the variation among the means, it *is* true that neither treatment is better than either treatment.

TABLE 17.9c
Drug × psychotherapy combination

	Table of means			Table of effects		
	Psychotherapy	No psychotherapy	Mean	Psychotherapy	No psychotherapy	Mean
Drug	8	4	6	0.5	−0.5	1.5
No drug	4	2	3	−0.5	0.5	−1.5
Mean	6	3	4.5	1.5	−1.5	0

TABLE 17.10
Table of means

	Female patients		Male patients	
	Psychotherapy	No psychotherapy	Psychotherapy	No psychotherapy
Drug	10	5	6	3
No drug	4	1	4	3

Defining Three-Way Interactions

Interactions are defined by residuals, and we have now had some experience in computing these residuals for two-way interactions. In the case of three-way interactions we subtract off all 3 main effects and all 3 two-way interactions in order to find the residuals defining the three-way interaction. From the three subtables we have been examining we can find all the effects needed to calculate the residuals for the three-way interactions. The original table of means was as shown in Table 17.10.

For illustration we focus on the top-left condition, with a mean of 10. We begin by subtracting off the grand mean, which Tables 17.9*a*, 17.9*b*, and 17.9*c* all show to be 4.5, yielding the mean as a residual from the grand mean as 10 − 4.5 = 5.5. From this condition effect we will in turn subtract the 3 main effects and the 3 two-way interactions.

The mean of 10 is for the condition of female patients who do receive the drug and the psychotherapy. The table of effects of Table 17.9*a* shows at the bottom of column 1 the effect of being female at 0.5 and at the end of the top row the effect of receiving the drug at 1.5. The table of effects of Table 17.9*b* shows at the end of the top row the effect of receiving psychotherapy at 1.5. Each of these effects could also have been found in an alternative location: the effect of being female at the bottom of column 1 of the table of effects of Table 17.9*b*, the effect of receiving the drug at the end of the top row of the table of effects of Table 17.9*c*, and the effect of receiving psychotherapy at the bottom of column 1 of the table of effects of Table 17.9*c*. Now we subtract each of these three main effects from the residual defining the condition effect of 5.5, yielding:

Condition effect		Sex effect		Drug effect		Psychotherapy effect		Combined interaction effect
5.5	−	0.5	−	1.5	−	1.5	=	2.0

The value of 2.0 is now made up of all the contributions to the condition effect made up of all 3 two-way interactions plus the three-way interaction. To find the three-way interaction residual, therefore, we will want only to subtract the 3 two-way interaction residuals from this value of 2.0. The 3 two-way interaction residuals are found in Tables 17.9*a*, 17.9*b*, and 17.9*c*. The upper-left condition of the table of effects of Table 17.9*a* shows the sex of patient × drug interaction effect to be 1.0 for females receiving drugs. The upper-left condition of the table of effects of Table 17.9*b* shows the sex of patient × psychotherapy interaction effect to be 0.5 for females receiving psychotherapy. The upper-left condition of the table of effects of Table 17.9*c* shows the drug × psychotherapy interaction effect to be 0.5 for those receiving both drug and psychotherapy.

In finding the interaction effect relevant to the condition mean or residual that we are trying to decompose into its elements, great care must be taken to select the particular residual that applies to the mean we are working with. In a three-way design, when we are working with the mean of condition $A_1B_1C_1$, the AB residual we need is A_1B_1, the AC residual we need is A_1C_1, and the BC residual we need is B_1C_1. For the present case the combined interaction effect had a residual value of 2.0, from which we subtract the residuals of the 3 two-way interactions to find the residual defining the three-way interaction:

Combined interaction effect	—	Sex × drug interaction	—	Sex × psychotherapy interaction	—	Drug × psychotherapy interaction	=	Three-way interaction
2.0	—	1.0	—	0.5	—	0.5	=	0

If we repeated this procedure for each of the eight condition means of the present experiment, we would find all the three-way interaction effects to be zero; i.e., there was no three-way interaction effect whatever in the present study. Table 17.11 summarizes the main effects and interactions that add up to yield each of the eight means for the present experiment. It is analogous to, and an extension of, an earlier example of how condition means may be viewed as made up of additive pieces (see page 347).

We can employ the decomposition of the condition means in Table 17.11 to understand better the computation of the various terms of the analysis of variance. Beneath each column of the display in the table we show the sum of the eight values (ΣX) and the sum of the squares of the eight values (ΣX^2). For all 3 main effects, for all 3 two-way interactions, and for the three-way interaction, these sums of squared residuals are identical to the SS computed near the end of the last chapter from the seven computational formulas provided there (see Table 16.8).

Computing the residuals that define the three-way interaction was not especially difficult, but it did take some time. Defining a four-way, five-way, or higher-order interaction is also not especially difficult, but it takes more and more time to do the arithmetic required. As suggested earlier, some behavioral science computer packages automatically provide the residuals defining all interactions tested.

FURTHER NOTES ON INTERPRETATION

Organismic Interactions

Although interactions are defined by, and therefore completely described by, a table of residuals, such a table is not usually of interest to the investigator without some additional interpretation. In an abstract discussion of interaction we can view a 2 × 3 table of residuals without labeling the rows and columns and without thinking about the scientific meaning of the interaction. Investigators of a

TABLE 17.11
Table of effects

	Grand mean	+ Sex	+ Drug	+ Psycho-therapy	+ S×D	+ S×P	+ D×P	+ S×D×P
10 =	4.5	+ 0.5	+ 1.5	+ 1.5	+ 1.0	+ 0.5	+ 0.5	+ 0
5 =	4.5	+ 0.5	+ 1.5	+ (−1.5)	+ 1.0	+ (−0.5)	+ (−0.5)	+ 0
4 =	4.5	+ 0.5	+ (−1.5)	+ 1.5	+ (−1.0)	+ 0.5	+ (−0.5)	+ 0
1 =	4.5	+ 0.5	+ (−1.5)	+ (−1.5)	+ (−1.0)	+ (−0.5)	+ 0.5	+ 0
6 =	4.5	+ (−0.5)	+ 1.5	+ 1.5	+ (−1.0)	+ (−0.5)	+ 0.5	+ 0
3 =	4.5	+ (−0.5)	+ 1.5	+ (−1.5)	+ (−1.0)	+ 0.5	+ (−0.5)	+ 0
4 =	4.5	+ (−0.5)	+ (−1.5)	+ 1.5	+ 1.0	+ (−0.5)	+ (−0.5)	+ 0
3 =	4.5	+ (−0.5)	+ (−1.5)	+ (−1.5)	+ 1.0	+ 0.5	+ 0.5	+ 0
ΣX 36 =	36.0	+ 0	+ 0	+ 0	+ 0	+ 0	+ 0	+ 0
ΣX^2 212 =	162	+ 2	+ 18	+ 18	+ 8	+ 2	+ 2	+ 0

381

substantive problem, however, must go further. They must try to make sense of the phenomenon. Consider the simple interaction:

	Drug A	Drug B
Male	+1	−1
Female	−1	+1

If our entries are effectiveness scores, we conclude that, at least for the interaction component of our results, drug A is relatively better for males while drug B is relatively better for females. The term "relatively" is used here to emphasize that the effects shown by certain combinations of drug and gender are large or small only in relation to other effects shown *after the removal of the main effects of drug and gender*.

It often happens in behavioral research that different treatment techniques are differentially effective for different subgroups. Such interactions, known as *organismic interactions*, reflect the fact that some types of interventions are especially effective for some but not other types of persons.

Synergistic Effects Are Not Interactions

Sometimes two or more treatments are applied simultaneously, and synergistic effects occur such that receiving both treatments leads to better results than would have been predicted from a knowledge of the effects of each treatment taken alone. For example, in the following instance it appears that treatment A alone or treatment B alone has no beneficial value, but that the combination of treatments A and B is very beneficial:

		Treatment A	
		Present	Absent
Treatment B	Present	4	0
	Absent	0	0

Such a *positive synergistic* effect is probably best described in just that way, i.e., that both treatments are required for any benefits to result. Note, however, that such a description is of the four means and not of the residuals. If we subtract the grand mean, row effects, and column effects, we will find an interaction effect that tells quite a different story and that is identical in magnitude with the row effects and with the column effects. The interaction, taken by itself, will tell us that both treatments or neither treatment is superior to either one treatment or the other.

It is often the case, when row, column, and interaction effects are all of comparable magnitudes, that we would do well to interpret the results by examining the means apart from the row, column, and interaction effects preplanned by our design. In a later chapter on contrasts (Chapter 21), we shall see that if we had planned a study expecting the results shown just above, it would have been poor data-analytic procedure to cast the data into a 2 × 2 factorial design and analyze it without the use of a planned contrast.

Negative synergistic effects are also possible, as shown here:

		Treatment A	
		Present	Absent
Treatment B	Present	0	4
	Absent	4	4

These results suggest that the treatments are harmful when taken together and not helpful when taken in isolation, since neither does better than the control group of no treatment. The results of this study, like those of the preceding one, are made up of row effects, column effects, and interaction effects that are all identical in size. The residual defining the interaction would suggest that receiving either treatment in isolation is better than receiving both treatments or neither treatment. As in the example of positive synergism, if we had anticipated results of this type, a 2 × 2 factorial design would not have been optimal; discussion of this is to be found in the later chapter on contrasts. Before leaving the topic of negative synergism, we should note that a possible basis for negative synergism is a ceiling effect, as when the measuring instrument is simply unable to record benefits above a certain level (e.g., 4 in this case). In such an instance, the results might appear as follows:

		Treatment A	
		Present	Absent
Treatment B	Present	4	4
	Absent	4	0

Crossed-Line Interactions

Crossed-line interactions are interactions in which residuals for one group of subjects or sampling units show a relatively linear increase while residuals for another group of subjects show a relatively linear decrease. Actually, all 2 × 2 interactions are of this type, since they are all characterized by an X shape, e.g., one group improves in going from control to experimental condition, and the other group gets worse in going from control to experimental condition. However, we usually consider interactions to be of the crossed-line type only when there are three or more levels for each of the groups being compared.

As an illustration, consider three measures of sensitivity to nonverbal communication that have been administered to female and male students. The three measures are designed to measure sensitivity to the face, to the body, and to tone of voice, respectively. Of these three channels, the face is thought to be most easily controlled, and tone is thought to be least easily controlled (Rosenthal and DePaulo, 1979a, 1979b). A fairly typical result in research of this type might yield the following accuracy scores:

| | Channel | | | |
	Face	Body	Tone	Mean
Female	6	4	2	4.0
Male	3	2	1	2.0
Mean	4.5	3.0	1.5	3.0

The corresponding table of effects would be as follows:

| | Channel | | | |
	Face	Body	Tone	Mean
Female	0.5	0.0	−0.5	1.0
Male	−0.5	0.0	0.5	−1.0
Mean	1.5	0.0	−1.5	0.0

The row effects show that females are better decoders of nonverbal cues than are males, a well-known result (Hall, 1979, 1984b). The column effects show that face cues are easiest to decode and tone of voice cues are hardest to decode of these three types of cues, also a well-known result (Rosenthal, Hall, Di Matteo, Rogers, and Archer, 1979). The interaction effects show that as the type of cue becomes more controllable by the encoder, the females' advantage over the males increases, a frequently obtained result (Rosenthal and DePaulo, 1979a, 1979b). A plot of these results would show an X-shaped figure (such as that shown in Figure 17-2 near the beginning of this chaper), with one group increasing as the other group is decreasing. A convenient way to display crossed-line interactions is to plot the *difference* between the residuals for the two groups. In this case such a plot would show a linear increase in the superiority of women over men as the channels became more controllable:

	Channel		
	Face	**Body**	**Tone**
Female	0.5	0.0	−0.5
Male	−0.5	0.0	0.5
Difference (female advantage)	1.0	0.0	−1.0

Crossed-Quadratic Interactions

Sometimes the residuals of one group are U-shaped, while the residuals of the other group are shaped like an inverted U, or ∩. This type of nonlinear shape, where the line changes direction once (going up and then down, or vice versa), is called a *quadratic curve*. Curves changing direction twice (going up, down, and up again, or vice versa) are called *cubic curves*. With each additional change in direction, cubic curves become *quartic curves*, quartic curves become *quintic curves*, and so on. (Chapter 21 provides illustrations of some of these curves.)

As an illustration of a crossed-quadratic interaction, consider two groups of children tested under three conditions of arousal. Inspecting the cell means (but not the interaction residuals), the younger group of children seems less affected by arousal level than the older group, as shown in the following results:

	Arousal level			
	Low	**Medium**	**High**	**Mean**
Age:				
Younger	3	6	3	4
Older	5	11	5	7
Mean	4.0	8.5	4.0	5.5

The corresponding table of effects (i.e., interaction residuals, row effects, and column effects) would be as follows:

	Arousal level			
	Low	**Medium**	**High**	**Mean**
Age:				
Younger	0.5	−1.0	0.5	−1.5
Older	−0.5	1.0	−0.5	1.5
Mean	−1.5	3.0	−1.5	0.0

The row effects show that the older children perform better than the younger children, and the column effects show that medium arousal level is associated with better performance than is either low or high arousal level. The residuals show crossed-quadratic curves, with younger children showing a U-shaped performance curve relative to the older children, who show an inverted-U-shaped performance curve. Once again we must emphasize that these residuals refer exclusively to the interaction component of the results. Inspection of the condition means shows both groups of children producing an inverted-U-shaped function. The older children simply show more of one relative to the younger children.

Constructing Tables of Interaction Residuals

Earlier in this chapter we noted that it was useful to construct tables of means to our specifications. Here we add that we have also found it useful to construct tables of interaction residuals to our specifications. We employ a range of table dimensions from 2×2 to 2×5 and place residual values into a series of empty tables to illustrate such types of interaction as organismic, crossed-line, and crossed-quadratic interactions. We also suggest labeling each level of each row and column in a plausible way. We will know that our tables are exclusively made up of interaction effects when our row and column means are all equal to zero.

SIMPLIFYING COMPLEX TABLES OF RESIDUALS

A general principle for the simplification of tables of residuals is to subtract one level of a factor from the other level of that factor for any two-level factor for which the difference between levels can be regarded as substantively meaningful. Following this procedure, a two-way interaction may be viewed as a change in a main effect due to the introduction of a second independent variable; a three-way interaction may be viewed as a change in a main effect due to the introduction of a two-way interaction, or as a change in a two-way interaction due to the introduction of a third independent variable.

Another general principle for the simplification of tables of residuals involves a process of concept formation for the diagonals of a table of residuals, usually a 2×2 table. If a suitable concept can be found to describe each diagonal of a 2×2 table of residuals, the interpretation of the interaction will be simplified to the interpretation of a main effect of diagonals. We will illustrate each of these two methods.

The Method of Meaningful Differences

We have already had a brief exposure to this method in our discussion of crossed-line interactions. In that example we subtracted the residuals for males from the residuals for females to create difference scores that represented the advantage of being female over male in the decoding of nonverbal cues. We then compared these female advantage scores for three types of measures of sensitivity to nonverbal cues and were thus able to interpret an interaction of test × sex as simply the main effect of test on the differences between the sexes. An even simpler example might be:

	A	B	A − B
Subjects:			
Type X	+1	−1	2
Type Y	−1	+1	−2

In this case two treatments, A and B, are each administered to two types of people, types X and Y. By taking the difference between treatments A and B we form a new measure, the advantage of treatment A over B. These advantage scores (A − B) can then be compared for persons of type X and Y. In this example the advantage of treatment A over B is greater for type X than for type Y people because 2 is greater than −2. By subtracting B from A we have reduced a two-dimensional display of residuals to a one-dimensional display.

The Method of Meaningful Diagonals

In this method we simplify the table of residuals by imposing substantive meaning on the residuals located on the diagonals, usually of a 2 × 2 table. For example we might be studying the outcome of psychotherapy as a function of the sex of the therapists and the sex of the patients with interaction effects as follows:

	Sex of therapist	
	Female	Male
Sex of patient:		
Female	+1	−1
Male	−1	+1

The diagonal going from upper left to lower right might be conceptualized as the *same-sex dyad* diagonal, while the diagonal going from lower left to upper right might be conceptualized as the *opposite-sex dyad* diagonal. We could then state that the mean residual for same-sex dyads is greater (+1) than that for opposite-sex dyads (−1). By employing a construct to describe the diagonals, we have reduced a two-dimensional display of residuals to a one-dimensional display as shown:

	Same-sex dyad	Opposite sex dyad
	+1	−1
	+1	−1
Mean	+1	−1

Combined Methods

It is often possible to combine the two methods we have described to achieve a greater simplification of a fairly complex interaction. Consider the following three-way interaction in which male and female experimenters administered a task to male and female subjects, with the experimenters sometimes having been led to expect high achievement, sometimes having been led to expect low achievement from their subjects:

	Low expectations		High expectations	
	Female *E*	**Male *E***	**Female *E***	**Male *E***
Female *S*	−1	+1	+1	−1
Male *S*	+1	−1	−1	+1

We begin the simplification process by applying the *method of meaningful differences*. In this case it makes the most substantive sense to subtract the residuals for low expectations from the residuals for high expectations. These differences then represent expectancy effects, positive in sign when they are in the predicted direction (high > low) and negative in sign when they are in the opposite direction (high < low). The results of this first step are as shown:

	Table of differences (High − Low)	
	Female *E*	**Male *E***
Female *S*	+2	−2
Male *S*	−2	+2

Now the three-way interaction of sex of experimenter, sex of subject, and expectancy has been simplified to a two-way interaction of sex of experimenter and sex of subject with the dependent variable of difference scores or expectancy effect scores. We can now apply the *method of meaningful diagonals* to this two-way table and interpret the originally complex three-way interaction as showing that same-sex dyads show greater expectancy effects than do opposite-sex dyads.

A Five-Way Interaction

The same general procedures can often be applied to an even more complicated situation, a five-way interaction, as shown in the following case. This time we have female and male experimenters who are either black or white, administering a task to male and female subjects who are either black or white, sometimes having been led to expect high, and sometimes low, performance. The design, then, is a race of E × sex of E × race of S × sex of S × expectancy of E factorial, each with two levels of each factor: a $2 \times 2 \times 2 \times 2 \times 2$, or 2^5, factorial design. The effects for the five-way interaction are as shown in Table 17.12.

Our first step again is to eliminate one dimension of the design by subtracting the low expectancy residuals from the high expectancy residuals, yielding the results shown in Table 17.13.

The entries of this table of difference scores can be viewed as a 2×2 interaction (race of E × race of S) of 2×2 interactions (sex of E × sex of S). The upper-left and lower-right 2×2 tables are identical with each other and opposite in signs to the 2×2 tables of the upper right and lower left. The first-named diagonal describes the same-race dyads, the second-named diagonal describes the opposite-race dyads. Within each of the four quadrants of the larger 2×2 table there are smaller 2×2 tables in which one diagonal describes same-sex dyads and in which the other diagonal describes opposite-sex dyads. Keeping that in mind leads us to our interpretation of the five-way interaction. Expectancy effects are greater for same-sex dyads that are also same-race dyads or different-sex dyads that are also different-race dyads than for dyads differing only on sex or only on race. We can redisplay this five-way interaction (or four-way interaction of difference scores) as a two-way interaction of two-way interactions of difference scores (see Table 17.14).

Employing the principle illustrated in our earlier example, we made a single factor (same versus different) of the race of E × race of S interaction, and a single factor (same versus different) of the sex of E × sex of S interaction.

Such simplification of complex interactions is not always possible, though it is more likely when there is conceptual meaning to the diagonal cells of any 2×2 contained within a 2^n factorial design. In general, too, such simplification is more likely when there are fewer levels to the factors of the experiment and thus fewer *df* associated with the higher-order interaction that we are trying to understand. Some higher-order interactions will prove more intractable than others, but by carefully examining the residuals, by employing the methods of meaningful differences and meaningful diagonals, and by employing the contrast procedures discussed in detail in later chapters, we can often make some progress.

TABLE 17.12
Residuals defining a five-way interaction

	Black E				White E			
	Male E		Female E		Male E		Female E	
	High expect.	Low expect.	High expect.	Low expect.	High expect.	Low expect.	High expect.	Low expect.
Black S:								
Male S	+1	−1	−1	+1	−1	+1	+1	−1
Female S	−1	+1	+1	−1	+1	−1	−1	+1
White S:								
Male S	−1	+1	+1	−1	+1	−1	−1	+1
Female S	+1	−1	−1	+1	−1	+1	+1	−1

390

TABLE 17.13
Table of expectancy effects (high-low)

	Black *E*		White *E*	
	Male *E*	Female *E*	Male *E*	Female *E*
Black *S*:				
Male *S*	+2	−2	−2	+2
Female *S*	−2	+2	+2	−2
White *S*:				
Male *S*	−2	+2	+2	−2
Female *S*	+2	−2	−2	+2

TABLE 17.14
Table of mean expectancy effects

	Race of dyad	
	Same	Different
Sex of dyad:		
Same	+2	−2
Different	−2	+2

A Note on Complexity

Sometimes our research questions are complex, and complex designs and analyses may be required. However, just because we know how to deal with complexity is no reason to value it for its own sake. If our questions are simple, simpler designs and simpler analyses are possible. Especially for the beginning researcher, there is considerable practical benefit to be derived from keeping the designs and analyses as simple as possible, in the same way that we use Occam's razor for developing parsimonious hypotheses.

CHAPTER
18

REPEATED-MEASURES DESIGNS

USE OF REPEATED MEASURES

So far in our discussion of analysis of variance, each of our sampling units was observed only once. Thus, for example, each subject, patient, school, city, or other sampling unit contributed only one observation to the total number of observations. In Chapter 4 we noted that such arrangements are called "between-subjects designs" because all of the variation among the obtained scores is based on individual differences between subjects. In these designs subjects are said to be *nested* within their treatment conditions. By "nested" we mean that subjects are observed under only a single condition of the study. Often, however, it is very efficient to administer two or more treatment conditions to the same sampling units, thereby permitting sampling units to serve as their "own control." In these designs, subjects are said to be *crossed* by treatment conditions rather than nested within them. By "crossed" we mean that subjects are observed under two or more conditions of the study. The more the scores of the sampling units under one condition of the experiment are correlated with the scores of the sampling units under another condition of the experiment, the more advantageous it is to employ the sampling units under more than one condition, i.e., to employ them for repeated measures. Previously we also referred to such arrangements as "within-subject designs" to acknowledge that there were repeated measures on each individual subject.

Sometimes, too, the very nature of the research question seems to call for a repeated-measures-type design. For example, if we are interested in examining the effects of practice on the performance of a learning task, or the effects of age in a longitudinal study of development, it seems natural to employ the same sampling units repeatedly over time. Another very common research situation in which it is natural and advantageous to employ a repeated-measures design is that in which a series of tests or subtests is to be administered to a group of subjects. For example, we might want to administer the 11 subtests of a standardized test of intelligence, or the 15 subtests of a standardized test of personality, or the 4 subtests of a measure of sensitivity to nonverbal cues. Similarly, of course, we might want to administer two or more different types of tests, such as a test of intelligence and a test of personality.

The simplest type of repeated-measures (or within-subjects) design is one in which each of several sampling units is measured twice. In situations of this type we have a choice of procedures for comparing the scores obtained under each condition of measurement. We can employ the analysis of variance procedures to be detailed in the pages that lie ahead, or we can compute a special t test for repeated measures. As it turns out, we have already described this special case situation for comparing two means generated by the same sampling units — in Chapter 15 in the section on t tests for nonindependent samples (see page 311).

COMPUTATIONS

Suppose we want to examine the effects on performance scores of repeated practice sessions. Four subjects are administered the same task on three occasions, with results as shown in Table 18.1.

The layout is called a 4×3 arrangement, since there are four levels of the between-subjects factor and three levels of the within-subjects factor (i.e., each subject is measured on three occasions). The analysis begins just like that of any two-way analysis of variance, yielding a row effect (subjects in this case), a column effect (sessions in this case), and a row $\times$ column interaction effect (subjects $\times$ sessions in this case). The analysis differs from other two-way designs we have seen earlier in that there is only a single observation in each combination of row and column. The required sums of squares are obtained as follows:

$$\text{Total } SS = \Sigma(X - \overline{M})^2$$

where X is each individual score and $\overline{M}$ is the grand mean. Here we add up as many squared deviations as there are scores altogether.

$$\text{Row } SS = \Sigma[c(M_R - \overline{M})^2]$$

TABLE 18.1
Performance scores on three occasions

	Session 1	Session 2	Session 3	Mean
Subject 1	0	7	3	3.33
Subject 2	1	7	4	4.00
Subject 3	3	8	5	5.33
Subject 4	4	8	6	6.00
Mean	2.0	7.5	4.5	4.67

where c is the number of columns contributing to the computation of M_R, the mean of each row, and $\overline{M}$ is the grand mean. Here we add up as many quantities as there are rows.

$$\text{Column } SS = \Sigma[r(M_C - \overline{M})^2]$$

where r is the number of rows contributing to the computation of M_C, the mean of each column, and $\overline{M}$ is the grand mean. Here we add up as many quantities as there are columns. Finally,

$$\text{Interaction } SS = \text{total } SS - \text{row } SS - \text{column } SS$$

For the data of our illustration we have

$$\begin{aligned}
\text{Total } SS = &(0 - 4.67)^2 + (7 - 4.67)^2 + (3 - 4.67)^2 + (1 - 4.67)^2 \\
&+ (7 - 4.67)^2 + (4 - 4.67)^2 + (3 - 4.67)^2 + (8 - 4.67)^2 \\
&+ (5 - 4.67)^2 + (4 - 4.67)^2 + (8 - 4.67)^2 + (6 - 4.67)^2 = 76.67
\end{aligned}$$

$$\begin{aligned}
\text{Row } SS = &3(3.33 - 4.67)^2 + 3(4.00 - 4.67)^2 \\
&+ 3(5.33 - 4.67)^2 + 3(6.00 - 4.67)^2 = 13.35
\end{aligned}$$

$$\text{Column } SS = 4(2.0 - 4.67)^2 + 4(7.5 - 4.67)^2 + 4(4.5 - 4.67)^2 = 60.67$$

$$\text{Interaction } SS = 76.67 - 13.35 - 60.67 = 2.65$$

The table of variance is best set up so that the distinction between the within-subjects and the between-subjects sources of variance is highlighted. Earlier we saw that between-subjects sources of variance were those associated with individual differences between subjects. Within-subjects sources of variance are those associated with differences in individual subjects' scores from condition to condition.

In the table of variance shown as Table 18.2 we have distinguished sharply between the sources of variance that are due to within- versus between-subject variation. Such sharp distinctions are useful when there are several sources of variation due to between-subject sources and several due to within-subject sources. The distinctions simplify our bookkeeping and, as we shall see, help us employ the appropriate error term for tests of significance.

TABLE 18.2
Table of variance: repeated measures

Source	SS	df	MS	F	eta	p
Between subjects*	13.35	3	4.45			
Within subjects:[†]						
Sessions	60.67	2	30.33	68.93	.98	<.001
Sessions × subjects[‡]	2.65	6	0.44			

*This term, the subjects effect, would not normally be tested for significance as discussed in the following pages.

[†]Note that in earlier chapters when we referred to *within* sources of variance, we were referring to variation that was within *conditions* but *between* subjects.

[‡]Error term for sessions effect.

FIXED AND RANDOM EFFECTS

There is another distinction that will help us employ the appropriate error term: the distinction between fixed and random factors. *Fixed* factors are those in which we have selected particular levels of the factor in question not by random sampling but on the basis of our interest in those particular effects. We are not entitled to view these levels as representative of any other levels of the factor in question, i.e., we cannot generalize to other levels of the fixed factor. Most factors involving experimental manipulations, or such organismic variables as gender, race, and social class, and such repeated-measures factors as time, sessions, subtests, etc., are fixed factors.

Random factors are those in which we view the levels of the factor as having been randomly sampled from a larger population of such levels. The most common random factor in behavioral research is that of sampling units, especially persons or other organisms. In Table 18.2, if we regard the between-subjects factor as a random factor, we can test its significance only very conservatively. If we regard it as a fixed factor, so that we restrict any inferences only to these four subjects, we can test the significance of the subjects factor against the sessions $\times$ subjects interaction, though the test will be conservative when sessions are also regarded as fixed effects. To clarify these issues we will consider all combinations of fixed and random effects for between- and within-subject factors.

Imagine that we want to study four countries as our between sampling units factor. If we are interested only in these four countries and do not choose to view them as a sample from a larger population of countries, we regard them as fixed. Alternatively, we can view them as a sample from which we want to generalize, and we must then regard them as random.

Imagine further a diachronic (longitudinal) design in which we have a summary score for each country for each of three decades. These three scores are our repeated-measures, or within sampling units, factor. We regard these scores as fixed if we have chosen them specifically as critical decades of the century in question. We regard the scores as random, however, if we view them as a sample of the decades to which we want to generalize. Thus we can have four combinations of between (e.g., countries) and within (e.g., decades) sampling units factors and fixed and random effects. The four combinations are shown in Table 18.3, in the next section, and each combination is then discussed in turn. Our discussion is intended as a kind of reference manual rather than as an exposition of the underlying mathematical models that would be required for a more theoretically based discussion. See, for example, Green and Tukey (1960), Snedecor and Cochran (1967, 1980, 1989), and Winer (1971).

There is a general principle that helps in determining the appropriateness of an error term: the effects (fixed or random) we want to test are properly tested by dividing the *MS* for that effect by the *MS* for a random source of variation. The random source may be nested within the various levels of the factor of interest, or it may be crossed with the various levels of the factor of interest. Thus, the source of variance that would be a proper error term for factor A might be the independent observations made under each level of factor A. These nested observations always served as the proper error term in the analyses of variance we discussed in earlier chapters. They remain as the proper error terms for the between-subjects factors in analyses that include repeated-measures factors as well. When we want to test most repeated-measures factors, we normally employ an error term that is an interaction of a random factor (e.g., subjects nested within levels of a between-subjects factor) and the factor we want to test. When we examine the four types of design of Table 18.3, we shall see that where there is no random factor available, either for nesting within or crossing with the factor we want to test, there will be no proper test of significance available. Sometimes, however, a useful but conservative test *is* available. That is the situation, for example, in the type A design.

ERROR TERMS IN FOUR DESIGNS

Table 18.3 shows various combinations of fixed and random effects for within and between sampling units.

Type A (Between Fixed, Within Fixed)

The interaction MS can be employed as the error term for the MS between and the MS within subjects, but it is likely to lead to F's that are too conservative. Only if there is *in nature* a zero interaction effect will the F tests be accurate. The only way to test whether the interaction effect really is likely to be zero is to make multiple observations for each combination of row and column effects. Such multiple observations might be made by randomly sampling several years from each decade in our example of four countries studied for three decades. This within combination MS, computed as any other within-condition source of variance, is the appropriate error term for the between effect, the repeated-measures effect, and the interaction effect. When the interaction MS is used as the error term for the row or column effect, a large F can be trusted to be at least that large, but a small F may or may not reflect the absence of a row or column effect. The table of variance shown as Table 18.4 illustrates the type A situation. The abbreviations employed in Table 18.4 and in the following three tables are as follows:

  B = Between-subjects MS
  W = Within-subjects MS
BW = Between $\times$ within subjects interaction MS
  O = Ordinary error; i.e., MS for replications within combinations of B $\times$ W

Type B (Between Fixed, Within Random)

The interaction MS is the appropriate error term for the between sampling units effect, but is the appropriate error term for the within or repeated-measures effect only if the interaction effect is really zero. The appropriate error term for the within-subjects effect (and for the interaction) is the variation of the multiple observations made for each combination of row and column, as shown in Table 18.5.

TABLE 18.3
Four types of design

		Within sampling units	
		Fixed	**Random**
Between sampling units	**Fixed**	Type A	Type B
	Random	Type C	Type D

TABLE 18.4
Illustration of type A design
(Both factors fixed)

Source	Abbreviations	Error term, "proper"	Error term, "conservative"*
Between countries[†]	B	O	BW
Within countries:			
Decades[‡]	W	O	BW
Decades × countries[§]	BW	O	
Years within decade × country combinations[¶]	O		

*Used when O is not available, as when only a single observation has been made for every B × W combination.
[†]Computed as is the row effect of any two-way factorial design.
[‡]Computed as is the column effect of any two-way factorial design.
[§]Computed as is the interaction effect of any two-way factorial design.
[¶]Computed as is the within-cell error of any two-way factorial design.

TABLE 18.5
Illustration of type B design
(Between factor fixed, within factor random)

Source	Abbreviations	Error term, "proper"	Error term, "conservative"*
Between countries	B	BW[†]	
Within countries:			
Decades	W	O	BW
Decades × countries	BW	O	
Years within BW	O		

*Used when O is not available.
[†]Use of O as error term can lead to F's that are seriously inflated.

Type C (Between Random, Within Fixed)

The interaction *MS* is the appropriate error term for the within sampling units effect, but is the appropriate error term for the between sampling units effect only if the interaction effect is really zero. The appropriate error term for the between-subjects effect (and for the interaction) is the variation of the multiple observations made for each combination of row and column, as shown in Table 18.6.

Type D (Between Random, Within Random)

The interaction *MS* is the appropriate error term for both the between- and within-subject effects. The interaction effect could be tested against the variation of the multiple observations made for each combination of row and column as shown in Table 18.7. More detailed information about the consequences for significance testing of various combinations of fixed and random factors can be found in Green and Tukey (1960), Snedecor and Cochran (1967, 1980, 1989), and Winer (1971).

TABLE 18.6
Illustration of type C design
(Between factor random, within factor fixed)

Source	Abbreviations	Error term, "proper"	Error term, "conservative"*
Between countries	B	O	BW
Within countries:			
Decades	W	BW[†]	
Decades × countries	BW	O	
Years within BW	O		

*Used when O is not available.
[†]Use of O as error term can lead to *F*'s that are seriously inflated.

TABLE 18.7
Illustration of type D design
(Both factors random)

Source	Abbreviations	Error term, "proper"	Error term, "conservative"*
Between countries	B	BW[†]	
Within countries:			
Decades	W	BW[†]	
Decades × countries	BW	O	
Years within BW	O		

*Not applicable to this design.
[†]Use of O as error term can lead to *F*'s that are seriously inflated.

LATIN SQUARES

In the example we gave of four subjects, each measured three times, there was no alternative to administering the three sessions of testing in the sequence 1, 2, 3. However, suppose that we were administering three drugs, A, B, and C, to four patients. If we employed the design:

	Drug A	Drug B	Drug C
Subject 1			
Subject 2			
Subject 3			
Subject 4			

such that each subject were given the three drugs in the same sequence A, then B, then C (or ABC), we would have entangled, or confounded, two different variables. The variable of drug (A versus B versus C) and the variable of order or position in the sequence (first drug versus second drug versus third drug) would be confounded.

Suppose our hypothesis had been that drug A would be best and we found from our study that drug A was indeed best. It would not be appropriate to conclude that drug A actually was better than drugs B and C. A plausible rival hypothesis is that the first-administered drug is best. To avoid this type of confounding, we employ a technique called *counterbalancing* (a *counterbalance* is a weight balancing another weight). In counterbalancing, the sequence of administration of treatments is balanced (or varied systematically) so that, on the average, there is no longer a relationship between, or confounding of, the variables that had been entangled, such as order (first-presented) and drug type (drug A) in the present example.

Counterbalancing is essential when we are interested in studying matters of organization and sequencing in the presentation of stimuli. For example, an important research question for social psychologists is to determine the circumstances under which it is advantageous to present a message before the opposition has a chance to reach the audience and when it is better to present the message afterward, in order to have the last word. Those researchers who investigate this question use the term *primacy* to refer to the case where opinions or actions are influenced more by the arguments presented first, and *recency* where they are influenced more by the arguments presented last. To test for primacy and recency, it is necessary to use a counterbalanced design. Half of the subjects, at random, receive a pro and then a con argument; the remaining subjects receive a con and then a pro argument. In this way, it is possible to avoid the problem of confounding primacy versus recency effects with the specific effects of the pro versus con arguments (Rosnow, 1968).

A commonly employed design that has counterbalancing built in is called the *latin square,* a design in which the number of rows equals the number of columns. A latin square requires a square array of letters (or numbers) in which each letter (or number) appears once and only once in each row and in each column. Frequently the rows represent sequences of administration of the treatments, the columns represent the order of administration of the treatments, and the letters represent specific treatments administered in particular orders as part of particular sequences, as in the accompanying table.

	Order of administration		
	1	2	3
Sequence 1 (ABC)	A	B	C
Sequence 2 (BCA)	B	C	A
Sequence 3 (CAB)	C	A	B

In sequence 1 treatments are administered in the sequence A, then B, then C. In sequences 2 and 3 the treatments are administered in different sequences, BCA and CAB, respectively. The requirement of a latin square is satisfied so long as each row and each column contains each treatment condition once and only once. If sequences are found to differ, the difference must be due to differences in sequence of treatment, not to differences in treatments administered, since all treatments are administered in each sequence. The difference also cannot be due to differences in order or position (e.g., first, second, third), since all sequences are composed of the same set of orders or positions. If orders differ, the variability must be due to differences in order, not to differences in treatments administered, since all treatments are administered in each order. It also cannot be due to differences in sequence (e.g., ABC, BCA, CAB), since all orders comprise equal parts of each sequence. If treatments (e.g., A versus B versus C) differ, it must be due to differences in treatment not to differences in sequence, since all sequences contain all treatments. It also cannot be due to differences in order, since all treatments occur equally often in each order. It is in these senses, then, that latin squares avoid confounding by systematic counterbalancing.

The Analysis of Latin Squares

In a latin square the sequence effect tells how sequences differ, the order effect tells how orders differ. But neither of these effects is usually the reason for the research. We usually want to know how treatments differ; but where is the treatment effect in a latin square? It turns out that in the smallest possible latin square, the 2×2, the treatment effect is identical with, or an "alias" of, the sequence $\times$ order interaction:

	Order	
	1	2
Sequence 1 (AB)	A	B
Sequence 2 (BA)	B	A

The interaction of this 2×2 design compares the diagonal of A's with the diagonal of B's and is, therefore, equivalent to the test of the treatment effect. The sources of variance are as follows:

Source	df
Sequences	1
Orders	1
Treatments (sequences $\times$ orders)	1

In this analysis significance testing is a problem, since there are no *df* available for error terms for the three sources of variance shown. Very conservative *F*'s can be computed by employing as the error term for each effect the mean of the *MS*'s of the remaining two.

As the size of the latin square increases, the *df* available for a suitable error term increase and *F*'s become less conservative. The sequence $\times$ order interaction continues to provide the treatment effect, but the remainder of that interaction not associated with the treatment effect becomes the error term for all other effects.

Although larger latin squares yield more accurate *F*'s, accurate in the sense of fewer type II errors, it remains a characteristic of latin squares that *F*'s will be too small, on the average. The reason is that the denominator of the *F* tests is always some type of effect (row, column, or interaction) that could itself be nonzero. When these effects are nonzero but are used as denominators of *F* tests, those *F*'s will be too small. When these effects are zero, the *F*'s obtained will tend to be more accurate and less conservative.

Larger Squares

Some larger latin squares with their sources of variance and associated *df* are shown in Table 18.8. In general, if the latin square has *a* sequences, *a* orders, and *a* treatments, the *df* for each source of variance are as follows:

Source	df
Sequences	$a - 1$
Orders	$a - 1$
(Sequences $\times$ orders)	$((a - 1)^2)$
Treatments	$a - 1$
Residual sequences $\times$ orders	$(a - 1)(a - 2)$

Computations

With *a* sequences, orders, and treatments and with M_S, M_O, M_T and $\overline{M}$ representing the means of sequences, orders, treatments, and the grand mean, respectively,

TABLE 18.8
Some latin squares and their sources of variance

3 × 3 latin square				Sources of variance	
Order				**Source**	**df**
1	**2**	**3**		Sequences	2
				Orders	2
Sequence 1: A	B	C		(Sequences × orders)	(4)
Sequence 2: B	C	A		Treatments	2
Sequence 3: C	A	B		Residual sequences × orders	2

4 × 4 latin square					Sources of variance	
Order					**Source**	**df**
1	**2**	**3**	**4**		Sequences	3
					Orders	3
Sequence 1: A	B	C	D		(Sequences × orders)	(9)
Sequence 2: B	C	D	A		Treatments	3
Sequence 3: C	D	A	B		Residual sequences × orders	6
Sequence 4: D	A	B	C			

5 × 5 latin square						Sources of variance*	
Order						**Source**	**df**
1	**2**	**3**	**4**	**5**		Sequences	4
						Orders	4
Sequence 1: A	B	C	D	E		(Sequences × orders)	(16)
Sequence 2: B	C	D	E	A		Treatments	4
Sequence 3: C	D	E	A	B		Residual sequences × orders	12
Sequence 4: D	E	A	B	C			
Sequence 5: E	A	B	C	D			

*In any of these latin squares we could also think of the sequences effect as part of the treatment × order interaction effect and the orders effect as part of the treatment × sequences interaction effect. These are only conceptual alternatives and do not yield different statistical results.

we obtain the *SS* as follows:

$$\text{Total } SS = \Sigma(X - \overline{M})^2$$

$$\text{Sequences } SS = \Sigma[a(M_s - \overline{M})^2]$$

$$\text{Orders } SS = \Sigma[a(M_O - \overline{M})^2]$$

$$\text{Sequences} \times \text{orders } SS = \text{total } SS - \text{sequences } SS - \text{orders } SS$$

$$\text{Treatment } SS = \Sigma[a(M_T - \overline{M})^2]$$

$$\text{Residual } SS = \text{sequences} \times \text{orders } SS - \text{treatment } SS$$

For an example of the computations, assume that four patients have been administered four treatments in counterbalanced order with results shown in

TABLE 18.9
Effects of four treatments

	Order				
	1	2	3	4	Mean
Sequence 1 (ABCD)	4	3	8	5	5
Sequence 2 (BCDA)	0	6	7	7	5
Sequence 3 (CDAB)	2	2	10	10	6
Sequence 4 (DABC)	6	5	7	14	8
Mean	3	4	8	9	6

Table 18.9. Note that sequences are completely confounded with patients, i.e., we could label sequences as subjects if we preferred.

$$\text{Total } SS = (4 - 6)^2 + (3 - 6)^2 + (8 - 6)^2 + (5 - 6)^2 + (0 - 6)^2 + (6 - 6)^2$$
$$+ (7 - 6)^2 + (7 - 6)^2 + (2 - 6)^2 + (2 - 6)^2 + (10 - 6)^2$$
$$+ (10 - 6)^2 + (6 - 6)^2 + (5 - 6)^2 + (7 - 6)^2 + (14 - 6)^2 = 186$$

$$\text{Sequences } SS = 4(5 - 6)^2 + 4(5 - 6)^2 + 4(6 - 6)^2 + 4(8 - 6)^2 = 24$$

$$\text{Orders } SS = 4(3 - 6)^2 + 4(4 - 6)^2 + 4(8 - 6)^2 + 4(9 - 6)^2 = 104$$

$$\text{Sequences} \times \text{orders } SS = 186 - 24 - 104 = 58$$

To compute the treatment SS we will have to collect the scores associated with each of the four treatments, A, B, C, and D. To minimize clerical errors, we can rearrange the data obtained from a sequence $\times$ order to a sequence $\times$ treatments data display as follows:

	Treatments				
	A	B	C	D	Mean
Sequence 1	4	3	8	5	5
Sequence 2	7	0	6	7	5
Sequence 3	10	10	2	2	6
Sequence 4	5	7	14	6	8
Mean	6.5	5.0	7.5	5.0	6

Then,

$$\text{Treatment } SS = 4(6.5 - 6)^2 + 4(5.0 - 6)^2 + 4(7.5 - 6)^2 + 4(5.0 - 6)^2 = 18$$

and

$$\text{Residual } SS = 58 - 18 = 40$$

The resulting table of variance then is

Source	SS	df	MS	F	eta	p
Sequences	24	3	8.00	1.20	.61	.39
Orders	104	3	34.67	5.20	.85	.042
(Sequences × orders)	(58)	(9)				
Treatments	18	3	6.00	0.90	.56	.49
Residual sequences × orders	40	6	6.67			

OTHER COUNTERBALANCING DESIGNS

Latin squares are employed when the number of subjects or other sampling units equals the number of treatments we wish to administer to each subject. But suppose that we have more sampling units than we have treatments, what is to be done? Two general strategies are useful: *multiple squares* and *rectangular arrays.*

Rectangular Arrays

If we had three treatments to administer to six subjects, we could randomly assign half the subjects to each of two squares of size 3 × 3 and treat each square as a different experiment or as a replication of the same experiment. Alternatively, however, we could assign each of the six subjects a unique sequence of the three treatments. Since the number of unique sequences of treatments is $t!$ (where t is the number of treatments) and $3! = 6$, we have just the right number of subjects for this study.[1] If we had four treatments to administer to each subject and we wanted each subject to have a unique sequence, we would need $4! = 24$ subjects, etc. Such designs may be called $t \times t!$ designs, and their analysis is analogous to that of the latin square. Examples of $t \times t!$ designs are given in Table 18.10 for $t = 3$ and $t = 4$. When $t = 2$ we have our familiar 2 × 2 latin square once again.

    If we have fewer sampling units available than the $t!$ required by our design, we can form a series of latin squares instead, or sample randomly from the $t!$ sequences, but with the constraint that each treatment must occur in each order as nearly equally often as possible. The employment of this constraint tends to maximize the degree of counterbalancing that *is* possible even though complete counterbalancing may *not* be possible.

    If we have more sampling units available than the $t!$ required by our design, two general strategies are useful: *multiple rectangular arrays* and *subjects-within-sequences designs.*

---

[1] Recall that $N! = N$ factorial $= N(N - 1)(N - 2)\cdots(2)(1)$ so that $3! = (3)(2)(1) = 6$.

Subjects-within-Sequences Designs

If we had $2 \times t!$ subjects available, we could randomly assign half the subjects to each of two rectangular arrays of size $t \times t!$ We then treat each array as a different experiment or as a replication of the same experiment. The same type of procedure can be employed for any multiple of $t!$ subjects, of course. Alternatively, we could assign several subjects at random to each of the $t!$ sequences in such a way as to keep the number of subjects per sequence as nearly equal as possible.

As an example, suppose we had 18 subjects available for a study of three treatment procedures. The six possible sequences of three treatments ($3! = 6$) are as displayed in the $t \times t!$ ($t = 3$) design of Table 18.10, and we assign three subjects at random to each of these six sequences. In this design subjects are *not* confounded with sequences as they are in latin squares or rectangular arrays lacking replications for each sequence. Instead, subjects are *nested* within sequences so that the differences between sequences can be tested. The sources of variance for this example are as shown in Table 18.11.

There are a number of noteworthy features of this design and analysis. First, there is more than a single error term in the design. In the earlier chapters on analysis of variance, there had always been only a single error term, and it had always been associated with the individual differences among subjects (or other sampling units) collected from within each of the conditions of the study. In the present design there is also such an error term (subjects within sequences), and it is used to test whether the sequences of the experiment differ from one another. We want to note especially that this error term is within *conditions* but *between* subjects. The other error term in this design is the orders × subjects within-sequences interaction. This error term is used to test all the within-subjects sources of variation, and it is itself a *within-subjects* source of variation. It is typical for error terms employed to test within-subjects sources of variation that they are formed by crossing the repeated-measures factors by the random factor of sampling units, usually subjects or subjects within conditions.

There is another feature of this design that is common to latin square and rectangular array repeated-measures designs. It is the fact that to test for treatments we must reach into the order × sequence interaction and pull out the variation of the treatment means around the grand mean. That represents only a minor complication for the analysis.

The computation of this analysis is a simple extension of the computational procedures we have seen so far in this chapter. It is easiest to begin with a 3×18 design in mind, 3 levels of order and 18 levels of subjects. The between-subjects SS is then broken down into a sequences SS and a subjects-within-sequences SS. The latter can be obtained as the difference between the between-subjects SS and the sequences SS. The order SS is computed in the usual manner, and the order × subjects interaction is broken down into an order × sequences SS and an order × subjects-within-sequences SS. The latter can be obtained as the difference between the order × subjects SS and the order × sequences SS.

TABLE 18.10
Examples of $t \times t!$ designs

$t \times t!$ design: $t = 3$					Sources of variance	
	Order				**Source**	**df**
	1	**2**	**3**			
					Sequences	5
Sequence 1	A	B	C		Orders	2
Sequence 2	A	C	B		(Sequences × orders)	(10)
Sequence 3	B	A	C		Treatments	2
Sequence 4	B	C	A		Residual sequences × orders	8
Sequence 5	C	A	B			
Sequence 6	C	B	A			

$t \times t!$ design: $t = 4$					Sources of variance	
	Order				**Source**	**df**
	1	**2**	**3**	**4**		
					Sequences	23
Sequence 1	A	B	C	D	Orders	3
Sequence 2	A	B	D	C	(Sequences × orders)	(69)
Sequence 3	A	C	B	D	Treatments	3
Sequence 4	A	C	D	B	Residual sequences × orders	66
Sequence 5	A	D	B	C		
Sequence 6	A	D	C	B		
Sequence 7	B	A	C	D		
Sequence 8	B	A	D	C		
Sequence 9	B	C	A	D		
Sequence 10	B	C	D	A		
Sequence 11	B	D	A	C		
Sequence 12	B	D	C	A		
Sequence 13	C	A	B	D		
Sequence 14	C	A	D	B		
Sequence 15	C	B	A	D		
Sequence 16	C	B	D	A		
Sequence 17	C	D	A	B		
Sequence 18	C	D	B	A		
Sequence 19	D	A	B	C		
Sequence 20	D	A	C	B		
Sequence 21	D	B	A	C		
Sequence 22	D	B	C	A		
Sequence 23	D	C	A	B		
Sequence 24	D	C	B	A		

THREE OR MORE FACTORS

So far in our discussion of repeated-measures designs we have examined only two-factor designs, one factor as a between-subjects factor and one factor as a within-subjects or repeated-measures factor. Repeated-measures designs, how-

TABLE 18.11
Sources of variance: subjects within sequences

Source	df	Comments
Between subjects:	(17)	
Sequences	5	Tested against subjects
Subjects within sequences	12	
Within subjects:	(36)*	
Orders	2	Tested against orders × subjects
Orders × sequences†	10	Usually not tested
Treatments	2	Tested against orders × subjects
Residual orders × sequences	8	Tested against orders × subjects
Orders × subjects within sequences	24	

*Computed as (N of subjects) × (df for levels of repeated measures); in this study there are 18 subjects (N) and three levels of the repeated-measures factor ($df = 3 - 1 = 2$), so there are $N \times df$ (levels) $= 18 \times 2 = 36$ df for within subjects. Put another way, df for within subjects is 1 less than the number of observations per subject multiplied by the number of subjects.
†This term is subdivided into the following two terms.

ever, are frequently more complex in having two or more between-subjects factors, two or more within-subjects factors, or both.

Two or More Between-Subjects Factors

Increasing the number of between-subjects factors does not increase the complexity of the design as much as increasing the number of within-subjects factors. Suppose, for example, that we wanted to examine the effects on four subtests of a personality test of three age levels and two genders. Our design might appear as in Table 18.12.

TABLE 18.12
Design comprising two between factors and one within factor

Between factors		Repeated measures			
		Subtests			
Age	Sex	1	2	3	4
12	Female				
	Male				
14	Female				
	Male				
16	Female				
	Male				

408   BEYOND ONE-WAY ANALYSIS OF VARIANCE

If we assume two subjects for each of the $3 \times 2 = 6$ between-subjects conditions, the sources of variance and *df* would be as follows:

Source	df
Between subjects:	(11)
Age	2
Sex	1
Age × sex	2
Subjects (within conditions)	6
Within subjects:	(36)*
Subtests	3
Subtests × age	6 ⎤
Subtests × sex	3 ⎥
Subtests × age × sex	6 ⎬ Subtests × between subjects
Subtests × subjects (within conditions)	18 ⎦

*Computed as (*N* of subjects) × (*df* for levels of repeated measures); in this study there are 12 subjects (*N*) and four levels of the repeated-measures factor (*df* = 4 − 1 = 3), so there are *N* × *df* (levels) = 12 × 3 = 36 *df* for within subjects.

The computation of the *SS* involves nothing new. It is easiest to think of the design, for computational purposes, as a 12-subject × 4-measurements array. We compute first all the between-subjects *SS*'s, beginning with the total between-subjects *SS*. We then compute the age *SS*, the sex *SS*, the age × sex *SS*, and subtract these three *SS*'s from the total between-subjects *SS*. This gives us the subjects-within-conditions *SS*. As designs become more complicated, computing the *df* for each source of variance becomes increasingly useful as a check on whether we have left out any sources of variance. For example, since there are 12 subjects in this design, we know there are 12 − 1 = 11 *df* available between subjects. We also know the *df* for age (3 − 1 = 2), sex (2 − 1 = 1), age × sex [(3 − 1 = 2) × (2 − 1 = 1) = 2], and subjects-within conditions [(2 − 1) × 6 = 6]. These four sources of variance are a decomposition of the total between-subjects source of variance, and the sum of their *df* should equal the *df* for the total between-subjects variance. In this case we find this requirement to be satisfied.

The within-subjects sources of variation are made up of the main effect of subtests (*df* = 3) and the subtests × between-subjects interaction (*df* = 3 × 11 = 33). This latter interaction is further decomposed into a series of interactions: subtests × age; subtests × sex; subtests × age × sex; and subtests × subjects (within conditions). The *df* of these four interactions add up (6 + 3 + 6 + 18) to 33, the total *df* for the subtests × between-subjects interaction.

Computations for 2 (between) × 3 (between) × 4 (within) Design

We illustrate the required computations for the 2 × 3 × 4 design with the data given in Table 18.13. We begin by regarding the design as a simple 12-subject ×

TABLE 18.13
Results of a repeated-measures study with two between-subjects factors and one within-subjects factor

Between factors			Repeated measures				
			Subtests				
Age	Sex	Subject	1	2	3	4	Mean
12	Female	1	2	3	7	8	5.0
12	Female	2	1	2	3	6	3.0
12	Male	3	1	1	3	3	2.0
12	Male	4	1	2	1	4	2.0
14	Female	5	5	4	7	8	6.0
14	Female	6	4	5	8	7	6.0
14	Male	7	1	2	4	5	3.0
14	Male	8	1	4	6	9	5.0
16	Female	9	5	9	9	9	8.0
16	Female	10	6	5	8	9	7.0
16	Male	11	5	6	9	8	7.0
16	Male	12	4	5	7	8	6.0
	Mean		3.0	4.0	6.0	7.0	5.0

4-subtests array for which we will first compute the row (subjects) and column (subtests) sums of squares as shown at the beginning of this chapter.

$$\text{Total } SS = \Sigma(X - \overline{M})^2 = (2 - 5)^2 + (3 - 5)^2 + (7 - 5)^2$$
$$+ \cdots + (5 - 5)^2 + (7 - 5)^2 + (8 - 5)^2 = 340$$

$$\text{Row (subject) } SS = \Sigma[c(M_R - \overline{M})^2] = 4(5.0 - 5)^2 + 4(3.0 - 5)^2 + 4(2.0 - 5)^2$$
$$+ \cdots + 4(7.0 - 5)^2 + 4(7.0 - 5)^2 + 4(6.0 - 5)^2 = 184$$

$$\text{Column (repeated-measures) } SS = \Sigma[r(M_c - \overline{M})^2]$$
$$= 12(3.0 - 5)^2 + 12(4.0 - 5)^2 + 12(6.0 - 5)^2$$
$$+ 12(7.0 - 5)^2 = 120$$

$$\text{Row} \times \text{column interaction } SS = \text{total } SS - \text{row } SS - \text{column } SS$$
$$= 340 - 184 - 120 = 36$$

Of the sums of squares computed above only the column SS (or subtest SS) is one we will use directly in our final table of variance. The remaining sums of squares above will be used in the computation of other sums of squares required for our final table of variance.

Our next step is to decompose the row (or subject) SS into its components of subject age SS, subject sex SS, subject age $\times$ sex SS, and subjects-within-conditions SS, by means of the following formulas:

$$\text{Subject age } SS = \Sigma[nst(M_A - \overline{M})^2]$$

where n is the number of subjects in each of the conditions formed by the crossing of the two between-subjects factors (or the harmonic mean of the numbers of subjects in each of these conditions when n's are not equal), s is the number of levels of the sex factor, t is the number of levels of the subtests (column) factor, M_A is the mean of all conditions of a given age, and $\overline{M}$ is the grand mean, i.e., the mean of all condition means.

$$\text{Subject sex } SS = \Sigma[nat(M_S - \overline{M})^2]$$

where a is the number of levels of the age factor; n, t, and $\overline{M}$ are as above; and M_S is the mean of all conditions of a given sex.

$$\text{Subject age } \times \text{ sex } SS = \Sigma[nt(M_{AS} - \overline{M})^2]$$
$$- \text{ subject age } SS - \text{ subject sex } SS$$

where M_{AS} is the mean of all observations contributing to each of the combinations of the two between-subjects factors, and n, t, and $\overline{M}$ are as above.

Subjects-within-conditions SS = row (subject) SS
$$- \text{ subject age } SS - \text{ subject sex } SS$$
$$- \text{ subject age } \times \text{ sex } SS$$

where the row (subject) SS was computed from our initial 12-subject $\times$ 4-subtest array.

Our arithmetic is simplified if we construct the table of means formed by the crossing of the two between-subjects factors as shown in Table 18.14.

For the data of the present study we find

$$\text{Age } SS = [2 \times 2 \times 4(3.0 - 5)^2] + [2 \times 2 \times 4(5.0 - 5)^2]$$
$$+ [2 \times 2 \times 4(7.0 - 5)^2] = 128$$

$$\text{Sex } SS = [2 \times 3 \times 4(5.83 - 5)^2] + [2 \times 3 \times 4(4.17 - 5)^2] = 33$$

$$\text{Age } \times \text{ sex } SS = [2 \times 4(4.0 - 5)^2] + [2 \times 4(2.0 - 5)^2$$
$$+ [2 \times 4(6.0 - 5)^2]$$
$$+ [2 \times 4(4.0 - 5)^2] + [2 \times 4(7.5 - 5)^2$$
$$+ [2 \times 4(6.5 - 5)^2] - \text{ age } SS - \text{ sex } SS$$
$$= 164 - 128 - 33 = 3$$

$$\text{Subjects-within-conditions } SS = 184 - 128 - 33 - 3 = 20$$

Now that we have computed all the needed between-subject sources of variance, we turn our attention to the within-subjects sources of variance that are

TABLE 18.14
Table of means: age × sex of subject

Age	Sex of subject		Mean
	Female	Male	
12	4.0[8]	2.0[8]	3.0[16]
14	6.0[8]	4.0[8]	5.0[16]
16	7.5[8]	6.5[8]	7.0[16]
Mean	5.83[24]	4.17[24]	5.0[48]

Note: The figures within the "⌐" symbols indicate the number of observations on which each type of mean is based.

made up of the main effect of subtests (the already computed column effect) and the crossing of this main effect with age, sex, age × sex, and subjects (within conditions) to form four interactions. The interaction sums of squares are computed as follows:

$$\text{Subtests} \times \text{age } SS = \Sigma[ns(M_{TA} - \overline{M})^2] - \text{subtests } SS - \text{age } SS$$

where M_{TA} is the mean of all observations contributing to each combination of subtest (T) and age (A), and all other terms are as above.

$$\text{Subtests} \times \text{sex } SS = \Sigma[na(M_{TS} - \overline{M})^2] - \text{subtests } SS - \text{sex } SS$$

where M_{TS} is the mean of all observations contributing to each combination of subtest and sex, and all other terms are as above.

$$\text{Subtests} \times \text{age} \times \text{sex } SS = \Sigma[n(M_{TAS} - \overline{M})^2] - \text{subtests } SS$$
$$- \text{age } SS - \text{sex } SS - \text{subtests} \times \text{age } SS$$
$$- \text{subtests} \times \text{sex } SS - \text{age} \times \text{sex } SS$$

where M_{TAS} is the mean of all observations contributing to each combination of subtest, age, and sex, and all other terms are as above.

$$\text{Subtests} \times \text{subjects-within-conditions } SS = \text{row} \times \text{column interaction } SS$$
$$- \text{subtests} \times \text{age } SS$$
$$- \text{subtests} \times \text{sex } SS$$
$$- \text{subtests} \times \text{age} \times \text{sex } SS$$

where the row × column interaction SS was computed earlier from our initial 12-subject × 4-subtest array.

Again, our arithmetic will be simplified if, for each of the next three interactions to be computed, we construct the appropriate tables of means (see Tables 18.15 to 18.17). Then, from Table 18.15 we find

$$\text{Subtests} \times \text{age } SS = [2 \times 2(1.25 - 5)^2] + [2 \times 2(2.00 - 5)^2]$$
$$+ [2 \times 2(3.50 - 5)^2 + \cdots + [2 \times 2(6.25 - 5)^2]$$
$$+ [2 \times 2(8.25 - 5)^2] + [2 \times 2(8.50 - 5)^2]$$
$$- \text{subtests } SS - \text{age } SS$$
$$= 252 - 120 - 128 = 4$$

From Table 18.16 we find

$$\text{Subtests} \times \text{sex } SS = [2 \times 3(3.83 - 5)^2] + [2 \times 3(4.67 - 5)^2]$$
$$+ \cdots + [2 \times 3(5.00 - 5)^2] + [2 \times 3(6.17 - 5)^2]$$
$$- \text{subtests } SS - \text{sex } SS$$
$$= 154 - 120 - 33 = 1$$

From Table 18.17 we find

$$\text{Subtests} \times \text{age} \times \text{sex } SS = 2(1.5 - 5)^2 + 2(2.5 - 5)^2 + \cdots + 2(8.0 - 5)^2$$
$$+ 2(8.0 - 5)^2 - \text{subtests } SS - \text{age } SS$$
$$- \text{sex } SS - \text{subtests} \times \text{age } SS$$
$$- \text{subtests} \times \text{sex } SS - \text{age} \times \text{sex } SS$$
$$= 300 - 120 - 128 - 33 - 4 - 1 - 3 = 11$$

$$\text{Subtests} \times \text{subjects-within-conditions } SS = 36 - 4 - 1 - 11 = 20$$

We have now computed all the ingredients required to complete our table of variance (see Table 18.18). The analysis of variance of these data shows that all three main effects were significant. Although none of the interactions were

TABLE 18.15
Table of means: subtests × age

	Subtests				
Age	1	2	3	4	Mean
12	1.25[4]	2.00	3.50	5.25	3.00[16]
14	2.75	3.75	6.25	7.25	5.00
16	5.00	6.25	8.25	8.50	7.00
Mean	3.00[12]	4.00	6.00	7.00	5.00[48]

Note: The figures within the "L" symbols indicate the number of observations on which each type of mean is based.

TABLE 18.16
Table of means: subtests × sex

Sex	1	2	3	4	Mean
	Subtests				
Female	3.83[6]	4.67	7.00	7.83	5.83[24]
Male	2.17	3.33	5.00	6.17	4.17
Mean	3.00[12]	4.00	6.00	7.00	5.00[48]

Note: The figures within the "└" symbols indicate the number of observations on which each type of mean is based.

TABLE 18.17
Table of means: subtests × age × sex

Age	Sex	1	2	3	4	Mean
		Subtests				
12	Female	1.5[2]	2.5	5.0	7.0	4.0[8]
12	Male	1.0	1.5	2.0	3.5	2.0
14	Female	4.5	4.5	7.5	7.5	6.0
14	Male	1.0	3.0	5.0	7.0	4.0
16	Female	5.5	7.0	8.5	9.0	7.5
16	Male	4.5	5.5	8.0	8.0	6.5
	Mean	3.0[12]	4.0	6.0	7.0	5.0[48]

Note: The figures within the "└" symbols indicate the number of observations on which each type of mean is based.

significant, we note that the effect sizes (eta's) were quite substantial for several of these interactions, suggesting that replications with larger sample sizes might reach statistical significance.

The example we have been following employed an equal number of subjects ($n = 2$) within each combination of the between-subjects factor. Had these numbers not been equal, we could still have employed the same computational procedures with only one small modification. We would simply have replaced n, wherever it occurred, by $\bar{n}_h$, the harmonic mean of the sample sizes. We recall from the discussion of the factorial design of experiments in Chapter 16 that the harmonic mean of the sample sizes is defined as

$$\bar{n}_h = \frac{1}{\frac{1}{k}\left(\frac{1}{n_1} + \frac{1}{n_2} + \cdots + \frac{1}{n_k}\right)}$$

Returning to the table of variance, Table 18.18, we can see that the four interactions involving subtests are formed readily by crossing the subtests factor with each of the between-subjects effects in turn. We can illustrate this by adding an additional between-subjects factor to the present design, say, diagnosis. We

TABLE 18.18
Table of variance: two between-subjects factors and one within-subjects factor

Source	SS	df	MS	F	eta*	p
Between subjects:	(184)	(11)				
Age	128	2	64.00	19.22	.93	.003
Sex	33	1	33.00	9.91	.79	.02
Age × sex	3	2	1.50	0.45	.36	.66
Subjects (within conditions)	20	6	3.33			
Within subjects:	(156)	(36)				
Subtests	120	3	40.00	36.04	.93	.0001
Subtests × age	4	6	.67	0.60	.41	.73
Subtests × sex	1	3	.33	0.30	.22	.82
Subtests × age × sex	11	6	1.83	1.65	.60	.19
Subtests × subjects (within conditions)	20	18	1.11			

$$*\text{eta} = \sqrt{\frac{F \ (df \ \text{numerator})}{F \ (df \ \text{numerator}) + (df \ \text{denominator})}}.$$

assume that half the children in each of the six conditions are hyperactive and half are not, so that our design becomes

Between factors			Repeated measures			
			Subtests			
Age	Sex	Diagnosis	1	2	3	4
12	Female	Hyperactive Normal				
	Male	Hyperactive Normal				
14	Female	Hyperactive Normal				
	Male	Hyperactive Normal				
16	Female	Hyperactive Normal				
	Male	Hyperactive Normal				

Assuming for the present example that we had five subjects in each of our 12 between-subjects conditions, our new listing of sources of variance is

Source	df
Between subjects:	(59)
Age	2
Sex	1
Diagnosis	1
Age × sex	2
Age × diagnosis	2
Sex × diagnosis	1
Age × sex × diagnosis	2
Subjects (within conditions)	48
Within subjects:	(180)*
Subtests	3
Subtests × age	6
Subtests × sex	3
Subtests × diagnosis	3
Subtests × age × sex	6
Subtests × age × diagnosis	6
Subtests × sex × diagnosis	3
Subtests × age × sex × diagnosis	6
Subtests × subjects	144

*Computed as (N of subjects) × (df for levels of repeated measures); in this study there are 60 subjects (N) and four levels of the repeated-measures factor ($df = 4 - 1 = 3$), so there are $N \times df$ (levels) = $60 \times 3 = 180$ df for within subjects.

Once again, all interactions involving the within-subjects factor, subtests in this case, are formed simply by prefixing the within-subjects factor to each of the between-subjects factors in turn. Even with this four-factor design (three between and one within) computations are not difficult. They may be tedious, however, if the number of subjects per condition is large and a calculator rather than a computer is to be employed. Again it is easiest to think of the design as a subjects × subtests design, with all between-subjects main effect and interaction SS's subtracted from the total between-subjects SS to yield the subjects-within-conditions SS.

No matter how many between-subjects sources of variance there are, all of them are tested against the MS for subjects within conditions.[2] It is essential to keep in mind, however, that the various between-subjects sources of variance have meaning only if the *sum* of the repeated-measures scores is meaningful. For example, if the four subtests of the personality test we have been using as our illustration were all scored such that a high number were reflective of "good adjustment" (or "poor adjustment"), then the sum of these scores would be meaningful, and all the between-subjects effects would be interpretable. However, if some of the subtests reflected good adjustment and some reflected poor adjustment, the sum (and the mean) of the four scores would be meaningless, and all between-subjects effects would be essentially meaningless. (In situations of this sort we could readily transform the one or two scores coded in the opposite direction so that their direction of scoring would be consistent with the other scores.)

It should also be noted that when we decide that the sum of the repeated-measures scores is meaningful, the components of this sum have not necessarily contributed equally to the sum. Those components that are more variable (in the sense of S^2) contribute more heavily to the variation in the sum of the components. Thus, if the values of S^2 differ appreciably from each other, and if we want all components to contribute equally to the variation in the sum, we first transform each component to its standard score with mean $= 0$ and $\sigma^2 = 1$.

Even if the between-subjects sources of variance were meaningless because the sum of the repeated measures was not a meaningful variable, the within-subjects sources of variance might be quite informative. The interactions of the within-subjects factor and the between-subjects factors indicate the extent to which the main effect of the repeated measure (subtest in our present example) is affected by the various between-subjects sources of variance.

When there is only a single within-subjects factor, as in the present illustrations, there is only a single error term for all the within-subjects sources of variation, the repeated-measures factor × subjects-within-conditions interaction, or the subtests × subjects-within-conditions interaction in our present example. However, as we add within-subjects factors, the number of error terms grows

---

[2]This assumes that all between-subjects sources of variance are regarded as fixed effects, the most frequent situation. A little later we discuss the situation in which these effects are not all regarded as fixed.

very quickly, such that every main effect within subjects and every interaction between two or more within-subjects factors has its own error term. These error terms are generally formed by the crossing of each source of variance by the subjects-within-conditions source of variance. Table 18.19 shows how quickly the number of error terms for the within-subjects sources of variance grows as the number of within-subjects factors grows. Table 18.19 shows that for each additional within-subjects factor, the number of error terms more than doubles. We shall illustrate only for three and for seven error terms.

TWO WITHIN-SUBJECTS FACTORS

Suppose our subjects were five female and five male teachers, each of whom was assigned a different set of four pupils to teach in a brief teaching situation. Of each of these 10 sets of four pupils, two were female and two were male. Furthermore, one of the female and one of the male pupils was designated (at random) to her or his teacher as showing special intellectual promise (high expectancy) while nothing was said of the remaining pupils (low expectancy). The main conditions of our design might be displayed as follows:

		Repeated measures			
		Female		Male	
Between subjects*		Low	High	Low	High
Sex of teacher	Female				
	Male				

*Note that in this study teachers are serving as subjects.

TABLE 18.19
Number of within-subjects error terms required as a function of number of within-subjects factors

Number of factors	Number of error terms
1	1
2	3
3	7
4	15
5	31
6	63
7	127
8	255
9	511
10	1023

Special note should be taken of the fact that the four *different* pupils can still be regarded as providing repeated measures. That is because we decided that we would employ teachers as our sampling units (a random factor) and each child's score would be viewed as a repeated measurement of the teacher who taught that child. Further note should be taken of the fact that the four repeated measurements can, in this study, be viewed as a 2 × 2 design: two levels of expectancy × two levels of pupil sex. The sources of variance, *df*, and error terms would be as shown in Table 18.20.

It should be noted that each of the three repeated-measures error terms was formed by crossing the relevant repeated-measures factor by the random factor of sampling units—in this case, teachers (within sex).

Computations for 2 (between) × 2 (within) × 2 (within) Design

We illustrate the required computations with the data of Table 18.21. We begin by regarding the design as a simple 10-teacher × 4-levels of repeated measurement array for which we will compute first the row (teachers) and column (repeated-measures) sums of squares as shown in the preceding section on computing a two between-factors and one within-factor study.

$$\text{Total } SS = \Sigma(X - \overline{M})^2 = (3 - 5)^2 + (7 - 5)^2 + (2 - 5)^2$$
$$+ \cdots + (8 - 5)^2 + (4 - 5)^2 + (3 - 5)^2 = 260$$

$$\text{Row (teacher) } SS = \Sigma[c(M_R - \overline{M})^2] = 4(5.0 - 5)^2 + 4(5.0 - 5)^2$$
$$+ 4(6.0 - 5)^2 + \cdots + 4(4.0 - 5)^2$$
$$+ 4(5.0 - 5)^2 + 4(5.0 - 5)^2 = 72$$

$$\text{Column (repeated-measures) } SS = \Sigma[r(M_c - \overline{M})^2] = 10(4.0 - 5)^2$$
$$+ 10(8.0 - 5)^2 + 10(3.0 - 5)^2$$
$$+ 10(5.0 - 5)^2 = 140$$

$$\text{Row} \times \text{column-interaction } SS = \text{total } SS - \text{row } SS - \text{column } SS$$
$$= 260 - 72 - 140 = 48$$

Our next step is to decompose the row (or teacher) *SS* into its components of sex-of-teacher *SS* and teachers-within-sex *SS* by means of the following formulas:

$$\text{Sex-of-teacher } SS = \Sigma[npe(M_S - \overline{M})^2]$$

where n is the number of teachers within each sex of teacher (or $\bar{n}_h$ if these n's are not equal), p is the number of levels of the pupil sex factor, e is the number of levels of the expectancy factor, M_S is the mean of all conditions of a given teacher sex, and $\overline{M}$ is the grand mean, i.e., the mean of all condition means.

$$\text{Teachers-within-sex } SS = \text{row (teacher) } SS - \text{sex-of-teacher } SS$$

TABLE 18.20
Error terms for two within-subjects factors

Source	df	Error terms
Between subjects:	(9)	
Sex of teacher	1	
Teachers (within sex)	8	Error term for preceding line
Within subjects:	(30*)	
Expectancy	1	
Expectancy × sex of teacher	1	
Expectancy × teachers (within sex)	8	Error term for preceding two lines
Pupil sex	1	
Pupil sex × sex of teacher	1	
Pupil sex × teachers (within sex)	8	Error term for preceding two lines
Expectancy × pupil sex	1	
Expect. × pupil sex × sex of teacher	1	
Expect. × pupil sex × teachers (within sex)	8	Error term for preceding two lines

*Computed as (N of subjects) × (df for levels of repeated measures); this design has four levels of repeated measures, two levels of expectancy for each of two genders, so df (levels) = $4 - 1 = 3$, and, since $N = 10$ subjects, df for within subjects = $10 \times 3 = 30$.

TABLE 18.21
Results of a repeated-measures study with one between-subjects factor and two within-subjects factors

	Teacher	Repeated measures				Mean
		Female pupil		Male pupil		
		Low	High	Low	High	
Female teachers	1	3	7	2	8	5.0
	2	3	9	3	5	5.0
	3	5	8	5	6	6.0
	4	7	10	4	7	7.0
	5	7	11	6	4	7.0
Male teachers	6	2	6	0	4	3.0
	7	1	5	1	5	3.0
	8	3	7	3	3	4.0
	9	4	9	2	5	5.0
	10	5	8	4	3	5.0
	Mean	4.0	8.0	3.0	5.0	5.0

For the present study the mean scores obtained by female teachers and male teachers were 6.0 and 4.0, respectively. Therefore,

Sex-of-teacher $SS = [5 \times 2 \times 2(6.0 - 5)^2] + [5 \times 2 \times 2(4.0 - 5)^2] = 40$

and

$$\text{Teachers-within-sex } SS = 72 - 40 = 32$$

We now turn our attention to the various within-teachers sources of variance. We consider first the SS for expectancy, expectancy × sex of teacher, and expectancy × teachers (within sex):

$$\text{Expectancy } SS = \Sigma[nsp(M_E - \overline{M})^2]$$

where s is the number of levels of the sex-of-teacher factor, M_E is the mean of all conditions of a given level of expectancy, and the other terms are as above.

Expectancy × sex-of-teacher $SS = \Sigma[np(M_{ES} - \overline{M})^2]$
$$- \text{ expectancy } SS - \text{ sex-of-teacher } SS$$

where M_{ES} is the mean of all observations contributing to each combination of expectancy and teacher sex, and the other terms are as above.

Expectancy × teachers-within-sex $SS = \Sigma[p(M_{ET} - \overline{M})^2]$
$$- \text{ expectancy } SS - \text{ row (teacher) } SS$$
$$- \text{ expectancy } \times \text{ sex-of-teacher } SS$$

where M_{ET} is the mean of all observations contributing to each combination of expectancy and individual teacher, and the other terms are as above. Note that the row SS term is identical with sex-of-teacher SS + teachers-within-sex SS.

To help our arithmetic we construct a table of the appropriate means (see Table 18.22). From this table we find

$$\text{Expectancy } SS = [5 \times 2 \times 2(3.5 - 5)^2] + [5 \times 2 \times 2(6.5 - 5)^2] = 90$$

Condensing the table to obtain the means of the expectancy $\times$ sex-of-teacher combinations (M_{ES}) gives

	Expectancy	
Teacher sex	Low	High
Female	4.5[10]*	7.5
Male	2.5	5.5

*The number of observations per condition.

$$\begin{aligned}
\text{Expectancy} \times \text{sex-of-teacher } SS &= [5 \times 2(4.5 - 5)^2] \\
&+ [5 \times 2(7.5 - 5)^2] + [5 \times 2(2.5 - 5)^2] \\
&+ [5 \times 2(5.5 - 5)^2] \\
&- \text{expectancy } SS - \text{sex-of-teacher } SS \\
&= 130 - 90 - 40 = 0
\end{aligned}$$

TABLE 18.22
Table of means: expectancy × teachers

	Teachers	Expectancy		
		Low	High	Mean
Female teachers	1	2.5[2]	7.5	5.0[4]
	2	3.0	7.0	5.0
	3	5.0	7.0	6.0
	4	5.5	8.5	7.0
	5	6.5	7.5	7.0
Male teachers	6	1.0	5.0	3.0
	7	1.0	5.0	3.0
	8	3.0	5.0	4.0
	9	3.0	7.0	5.0
	10	4.5	5.5	5.0
	Mean	3.5[20]	6.5	5.0[40]

Note: The figures within the "⌐" symbols indicate the number of observations on which each type of mean is based.

Expectancy × teachers-within-sex $SS = 2(2.5 - 5)^2 + 2(7.5 - 5)^2$
$$+ \cdots + 2(4.5 - 5)^2 + 2(5.5 - 5)^2$$
$$- \text{expectancy } SS - \text{row (teacher) } SS$$
$$- \text{expectancy} \times \text{sex-of-teacher } SS$$
$$= 180 - 90 - 72 - 0 = 18$$

Again note that the row (teacher) SS is identical with sex-of-teacher SS + teachers-within-sex SS.

We consider next the SS for pupil sex, pupil sex × sex of teacher, and pupil sex × teachers (within sex).

$$\text{Pupil-sex } SS = \Sigma[nse(M_P - \bar{M})^2]$$

where M_P is the mean of all conditions of a given level of pupil sex, and the other terms are as above.

$$\text{Pupil-sex} \times \text{sex-of-teacher } SS = \Sigma[ne(M_{PS} - \bar{M})^2] - \text{pupil-sex } SS$$
$$- \text{sex-of-teacher } SS$$

where M_{PS} is the mean of all observations contributing to each combination of pupil sex and teacher sex, and the other terms are as above.

$$\text{Pupil-sex} \times \text{teachers-within-sex } SS = \Sigma[e(M_{PT} - \bar{M})^2] - \text{pupil-sex } SS$$
$$- \text{row (teacher) } SS - \text{pupil sex}$$
$$\times \text{sex-of-teacher } SS$$

where M_{PT} is the mean of all observations contributing to each combination of pupil sex and individual teacher, and the other terms are as above. The row SS is identical with sex-of-teacher SS + teachers-within-sex SS.

Again we construct a table of the appropriate means (see Table 18.23). From this table we find

$$\text{Pupil-sex } SS = [5 \times 2 \times 2(6.0 - 5)^2] + [5 \times 2 \times 2(4.0 - 5)^2] = 40$$

Condensing the table to obtain the means of the pupil-sex × sex-of-teacher combinations (M_{PS}) gives

Teacher sex	Pupil sex	
	Female	Male
Female	7.0[10]*	5.0
Male	5.0	3.0

*The number of observations per condition.

TABLE 18.23
Table of means: pupil sex × teachers

	Teachers	Pupil sex		Mean
		Female	Male	
	1	$5.0^{\lfloor 2}$	5.0	$5.0^{\lfloor 4}$
Female	2	6.0	4.0	5.0
teachers	3	6.5	5.5	6.0
	4	8.5	5.5	7.0
	5	9.0	5.0	7.0
	6	4.0	2.0	3.0
	7	3.0	3.0	3.0
Male	8	5.0	3.0	4.0
teachers	9	6.5	3.5	5.0
	10	6.5	3.5	5.0
	Mean	$6.0^{\lfloor 20}$	4.0	$5.0^{\lfloor 40}$

Note: The figures within the "∟" symbols indicate the number of observations on which each type of mean is based.

Pupil-sex × sex-of-teacher $SS = [5 \times 2(7.0 - 5)^2]$
$$+[\, 5 \times 2(5.0 - 5)^2] + [5 \times 2(5.0 - 5)^2]$$
$$+ [5 \times 2(3.0 - 5)^2]$$
$$- \text{pupil-sex } SS - \text{sex-of-teacher } SS$$
$$= 80 - 40 - 40 = 0$$

Pupil-sex × teachers-within-sex $SS = 2(5.0 - 5)^2 + 2(5.0 - 5)^2$
$$+ \cdots + 2(6.5 - 5)^2 + 2(3.5 - 5)^2$$
$$- \text{pupil-sex } SS - \text{row (teacher) } SS$$
$$- \text{pupil-sex } \times \text{sex-of-teacher } SS$$
$$= 128 - 40 - 72 - 0 = 16$$

The row SS is identical with sex-of-teacher SS + teachers-within-sex SS.

Finally, we consider the SS for expectancy × pupil sex, expectancy × pupil sex × sex of teacher, and expectancy × pupil sex × teachers (within sex).

Expectancy × pupil-sex SS
$$= \Sigma[ns(M_{EP} - \bar{M})^2 - \text{expectancy } SS - \text{pupil-sex } SS$$

where M_{EP} is the mean of all observations contributing to each combination of expectancy and pupil sex, and the other terms are as above.

Expectancy $\times$ pupil-sex $\times$ sex-of-teacher $SS = \Sigma[n(M_{EPS} - \overline{M})^2]$
$\quad\quad\quad$ − expectancy SS − pupil-sex SS − sex-of-teacher SS
$\quad\quad\quad$ − expectancy $\times$ pupil-sex SS − expectancy $\times$ sex-of-teacher SS
$\quad\quad\quad$ − pupil-sex $\times$ sex-of-teacher SS

where M_{EPS} is the mean of all observations contributing to each combination of expectancy, pupil sex, and sex of teacher, and where the other terms are as above.

Expectancy $\times$ pupil-sex $\times$ teachers-within-sex $SS = \Sigma[(M_{EPT} - \overline{M})^2]$
$\quad\quad\quad$ − expectancy SS − pupil-sex SS − row (teacher) SS
$\quad\quad\quad$ − expectancy $\times$ pupil-sex SS − expectancy $\times$ sex-of-teacher SS
$\quad\quad\quad$ − pupil-sex $\times$ sex-of-teacher SS − expectancy $\times$ pupil-sex
$\quad\quad\quad$ $\times$ sex-of-teacher SS − expectancy $\times$ teachers-within-sex SS
$\quad\quad\quad$ − pupil-sex $\times$ teachers-within-sex SS (or, more compactly,
$\quad\quad\quad\quad$ total SS
$\quad\quad\quad$ − all other sums of squares)[3]

where M_{EPT} is the mean of all observations contributing to each combination of expectancy, pupil sex, and individual teacher. In this example, there is only one such observation for each combination of these three factors, and the original 10 teachers $\times$ 4 repeated measures table shows these observations.

$\quad$ We begin with a condensed version of the original table of the results of the present study to show the means of the expectancy $\times$ pupil-sex combinations (M_{EP}):

	Pupil sex	
Expectancy	Female	Male
Low	4.0[10]*	3.0
High	8.0	5.0

*The number of observations per condition.

Expectancy $\times$ pupil-sex $SS = [5 \times 2(4.0 - 5)^2] + [5 \times 2(3.0 - 5)^2]$
$\quad\quad\quad\quad\quad\quad + [5 \times 2(8.0 - 5)^2] + [5 \times 2(5.0 - 5)^2]$
$\quad\quad\quad\quad\quad\quad$ − expectancy SS − pupil-sex SS
$\quad\quad\quad\quad\quad\quad\quad = 140 - 90 - 40 = 10$

---

[3]Note that in this case, $\Sigma[(M_{EPT} - \overline{M})^2]$ is identical with $\Sigma(X - \overline{M})^2 = $ total SS.

Next we show the table of eight means (M_{EPS}) required for the three-way interaction of expectancy $\times$ pupil sex $\times$ sex of teacher:

Teacher sex	Female		Male	
	Low	High	Low	High
Female	5.0$^{|5*}$	9.0	4.0	6.0
Male	3.0	7.0	2.0	4.0

*The number of observations per condition.

Expectancy $\times$ pupil-sex $\times$ sex-of-teacher SS

$$= 5(5.0 - 5)^2 + 5(9.0 - 5)^2 + \cdots + 5(2.0 - 5)^2 + 5(4.0 - 5)^2$$
$$- 90 - 40 - 40 - 10 - 0 - 0 = 180 - 180 = 0$$

Expectancy $\times$ pupil-sex $\times$ teachers-within-sex SS

$$= 260 \text{ (total } SS) - 90 - 40 - 72 - 10 - 0 - 0 - 0 - 18 - 16 = 14$$

We have now computed all the SS required to complete our table of variance (see Table 18.24). The analysis of variance of these data shows all three main effects and one 2-way interaction to be significant.

The present example employed an equal number of teachers ($n = 5$) in each condition of teacher sex. Had these numbers not been equal, we could still have employed the same computational procedures with just one modification. We would simply have replaced the quantity n by $\bar{n}_h$ wherever n was called for. Recall that $\bar{n}_h$ is the harmonic mean of the sample sizes found in each between-subjects condition of the study, i.e.,

$$\bar{n}_h = \frac{1}{\dfrac{1}{k}\left(\dfrac{1}{n_1} + \dfrac{1}{n_2} + \cdots + \dfrac{1}{n_k}\right)}$$

Aggregating Error Terms

When the number of df per error term is small, as it is in this example, we want to consider aggregating the three within-subjects error terms in order to obtain a more stable single estimate (in this example, based on 24 df). This averaging together of error terms (each weighted by its df) is usually recommended only if the ratio of the largest to the smallest error term is about 2.0 or less (Green and Tukey, 1960). *Aggregation* is often referred to as *pooling*, especially when the decision to pool is based on tests of significance of differences among error variances.

In the analysis of variance we have just completed, the three within-subjects error terms range from 1.75 to 2.25, with the ratio of the largest mean square to the smallest mean square only $2.25/1.75 = 1.29$. Therefore, these three

TABLE 18.24
Table of variance: one between-subjects factor and two within-subjects factors

Source	SS	df	MS	F	eta*	p
Between subjects:	(72)	(9)				
Sex of teacher	40	1	40.00	10.00	.75	.013
Teachers (within sex)	32	8	4.00			
Within subjects:	(188)	(30)				
Expectancy	90	1	90.00	40.00	.91	.0002
Expectancy × sex of teacher	0	1	0.00	0.00	.00	1.00
Expectancy × teachers (within sex)	18	8	2.25			
Pupil sex	40	1	40.00	20.00	.85	.002
Pupil sex × sex of teacher	0	1	0.00	0.00	.00	1.00
Pupil sex × teachers (within sex)	16	8	2.00			
Expectancy × pupil sex	10	1	10.00	5.71	.65	.043
Expectancy × pupil sex × sex of teacher	0	1	0.00	0.00	.00	1.00
Expectancy × pupil sex × teachers (within sex)	14	8	1.75			

*eta $= \sqrt{\dfrac{F(df \text{ numerator})}{F(df \text{ numerator}) + (df \text{ denominator})}}$.

error terms are good candidates for aggregation. The general formula for the aggregation of k error terms is

$$MS \text{ aggregated} = \frac{MS_1(df_1) + MS_2(df_2) + \cdots + MS_k(df_k)}{df_1 + df_2 + \cdots + df_k}$$

where MS_1 to MS_k are the k error terms to be aggregated, and df_1 to df_k are the k df associated with the k MS's for error. For the data of Table 18.24 we have

$$MS \text{ aggregated} = \frac{2.25(8) + 2.00(8) + 1.75(8)}{8 + 8 + 8} = 2.00$$

When it is more convenient to work with sums of squares, the general formula is written as

$$MS \text{ aggregated} = \frac{SS_1 + SS_2 + \cdots + SS_k}{df_1 + df_2 + \cdots + df_k}$$

where SS_1 to SS_k are the k sums of squares of the k error sources of variance and df_1 to df_k are their associated df. For the data of Table 18.24 we have

$$MS \text{ aggregated} = \frac{18 + 16 + 14}{8 + 8 + 8} = 2.00$$

Once we have computed an aggregated error term, it replaces all the individual error terms that contributed to its computation. Some of the F's computed using the new error term will be larger (those in which the original MS error was larger) and some will be smaller (those in which the original MS error was smaller).

THREE WITHIN-SUBJECTS FACTORS

In our example of three within-subjects factors, we retain the basic plan of the preceding example but assume that each teacher teaches eight pupils instead of four. In addition, we assume that for each combination of expectancy and pupil sex, there is one hyperactive child and one normal child:

	Repeated measures							
	Female				Male			
	Hyperactive		Normal		Hyperactive		Normal	
Between subjects	Low*	High	Low	High	Low	High	Low	High
Sex of teacher:								
Female								
Male								

*Level of expectancy.

The sources of variance, df, and error terms of this design would be as shown in Table 18.25. Note how easily we could generate all new sources of vari-

TABLE 18.25
Error terms for three within-subjects factors

Source	df	Error terms
Between subjects:	(9)	
Sex of teacher	1	
Teachers (within sex)	8	Error term for preceding line
Within subjects:	(70*)	
Expectancy	1	
Expectancy × sex of teacher	1	
Expectancy × teachers (within sex)	8	Error term for preceding two lines
Pupil sex	1	
Pupil sex × sex of teacher	1	
Pupil sex × teachers (within sex)	8	Error term for preceding two lines
Expectancy × pupil sex	1	
Expectancy × pupil sex × sex of teacher	1	
Expectancy × pupil sex × teachers (within sex)	8	Error term for preceding two lines
Diagnosis	1	
Diagnosis × sex of teacher	1	
Diagnosis × teachers (within sex)	8	Error term for preceding two lines
Diagnosis × expectancy	1	
Diagnosis × expectancy × sex of teacher	1	
Diagnosis × expectancy × teachers (within sex)	8	Error term for preceding two lines
Diagnosis × pupil sex	1	
Diagnosis × pupil sex × sex of teacher	1	
Diagnosis × pupil sex × teachers (within sex)	8	Error term for preceding two lines
Diagnosis × expectancy × pupil sex	1	
Diagnosis × expectancy × sex (P) × sex (T)	1	
Diagnosis × expectancy × sex (P) × teachers (within sex)	8	Error term for preceding two lines

*Computed as (N of subjects) × (df for levels of repeated measures); this design has eight levels arranged as a $2 \times 2 \times 2$ format, so df for levels of repeated measures = $8 - 1 = 7$, N of subjects = 10, and df for within subjects = $10 \times 7 = 70$.

ance simply by adding the new within-subjects factor of diagnosis and then crossing that term systematically with all preceding sources of variance. Just as in the previous example, we want to consider aggregating the various error terms to form a more stable overall error term. In this example we have one error term that is a four-way interaction, three error terms that are three-way interactions, and three error terms that are two-way interactions. In this situation it is useful to begin with the higher-order interactions and aggregate them first. For example, we might begin by aggregating (if $F < 2$) the three-way interactions (along with the four-way, since there is just one) to form the new error term for all terms tested by any of these error terms. We might then aggregate the two-way interaction error terms (if $F < 2$) to form the new error term for all terms tested by any of these error terms. Finally, if the two new error terms are themselves aggregable ($F < 2$), we can use this new super-error term to test all within-subjects sources of variation. In any of the aggregations described, the error terms should be weighted by their *df*.

FIXED OR RANDOM FACTORS

So far in our discussion of three or more factors in designs employing repeated measures, we have assumed that all factors other than subjects within conditions have been fixed factors rather than random factors. This is, in fact, the most common situation. We should, however, note the consequences for significance testing of having other factors in the design that are random rather than fixed. For our illustration, assume we have chosen five female and five male teachers for each of four schools to teach a brief lesson to two pupils, one of whom has been designated at random as a pupil of high intellectual potential. Our design can be displayed as follows:

Between subjects		Repeated measures	
School	Sex	Control	High expectancy
1	Female		
	Male		
2	Female		
	Male		
3	Female		
	Male		
4	Female		
	Male		

The sources of variance, *df*, and error terms are

Source	*df*	Error terms*
Between subjects:	(*39*)	
Sex of teacher	1	
School	3	
Sex of teacher × school	3	Error term for sex of teacher
Teachers (within conditions)	32	Error term for preceding two lines
Within subjects:	(*40*[†])	
Expectancy	1	
Expectancy × sex of teacher	1	
Expectancy × school	3	Error term for expectancy
Expectancy × sex of teacher × school	3	Error term for expectancy × sex of teacher
Expectancy × teachers	32	Error term for preceding two lines

*Assuming school to be a random rather than a fixed factor.
[†]Computed as (*N* of subjects) × (*df* for levels of repeated measures); in this study there are 40 subjects (*N*) and two levels of the repeated-measures factor (*df* = 2 − 1 = 1), so there are *N* × *df* (levels) = 40 × 1 = 40 *df* for within subjects.

If all our factors, including school, had been fixed, there would have been only two error terms. Teachers (within conditions) would have served as the error term for all three between-subjects effects, and expectancy × teachers would have served as the error term for all four within-subjects effects. However, with schools considered a random factor, we find there to be five error terms rather than two. Now the sex-of-teacher effect is tested against the sex-of-teacher × school interaction, an error term that has only 3 *df*. This is in contrast to the 32 *df* associated with the error term we would employ if schools were a fixed rather than random factor. The advantage of considering schools as a random factor is that we can then generalize to the population of schools represented by those four schools. The disadvantage of considering schools as a random factor is the low power to reject the null hypothesis associated with our having only four schools in our study.

In practice, it sometimes happens that we can have the best of both worlds. This happens when the mean square error considering the effect random is about the same size as the mean square error considering the effect fixed. In our example, that would occur if the mean square for sex of teacher × school were about the same size as the mean square for teachers within conditions. If that *were* the case, we could aggregate the two error terms. We would weight each by its *df* and use the new pooled error term instead of either of the two components.

Let us turn now to the within-subjects factors. We find that expectancy is tested against the expectancy × school interaction, and the expectancy × sex-of-teacher interaction is tested against the expectancy × sex-of-teacher × school interaction. The comments made above in the discussion of the sex-of-teacher effect apply here also. Note that both of the fixed effects (sex of teacher, expectancy) and their interaction (sex of teacher × expectancy) are tested against error terms formed by crossing the effect to be tested by the random effect (schools, in this example). More detailed discussions of forming error terms in repeated-measures designs are available in Winer (1971).

When we have three or more factors, two or more of which are random effects, there will be one or more effects that cannot be tested "properly" by any error term. Nevertheless, useful approximate procedures employing "quasi *F*'s" are available and are discussed, for example, by Snedecor and Cochran (1980, 1989), Wickens and Keppel (1983), and Winer (1971).

DID REPEATED MEASURES HELP?

Our basic reason for employing repeated-measures designs, in which the effects of greatest interest are the main effects of the repeated-measures factors or interactions involving the repeated-measures factors, is to use subjects as their "own control" in hopes of increasing the precision of our experiment. As we said at the beginning of this chapter, the more the scores of the subjects (or other sampling units) under one condition of the experiment are correlated with the scores of the subjects under another condition of the experiment, the more advantage accrues to us when we employ repeated-measures designs. Very low correlations between scores earned under one condition and scores earned under other conditions of the experiment suggest that there was little statistical advantage to our having employed a repeated-measures design.[4] Consider a very simple repeated-measures design in which five subjects are each tested on three subtests:

	Subtests		
	1	2	3
Subject 1	5	6	7
Subject 2	3	6	4
Subject 3	3	4	6
Subject 4	2	2	3
Subject 5	1	4	4

For these five subjects we can compute the correlation (r) between their performance on subtests 1 and 2, 1 and 3, and 2 and 3. These three r's were .64, .80, and .58, respectively, with a mean r of .67. This very substantial average correlation suggests that a repeated-measures design would be very efficient compared with a between-subjects design. Computing the mean of three r's was not arduous. Suppose, however, that there were 10 subtests instead of 3. Then there would be $(10 \times 9)/2 = 45$ correlations to compute and to average. A much easier approach is available via the analysis of variance; it involves computation of the intraclass r, an index that was described briefly in Chapter 3.

The Intraclass r

The intraclass r is an index of the degree of similarity of observations made on a given sampling unit, such as a subject. If there is a high correlation between pairs of observations made on subjects (e.g., subtest 1 and subtest 2), then the intraclass r will tend to be high. In fact, the intraclass r tends to be a good estimate of the mean correlation obtained by correlating all possible pairs of observations made on subjects (e.g., subtest 1 with 2, 1 with 3, 2 with 3, etc.). To compute the intraclass r we begin with the mean squares of the analysis of variance. For our example we have

Source	SS	df	MS
Between subjects	24.0	4	6.00
Within subjects:			
Subtests	11.2	2	5.60
Subtests × subjects	6.8	8	0.85

---

[4] There may still be a logistical advantage, however, since it is usually more efficient to measure n subjects k times each than to measure $n \times k$ subjects once each.

The intraclass r is computed by

$$r_I = \frac{MS_S - MS_{S \times K}}{MS_S + (k - 1)MS_{S \times K}}$$

where MS_S = mean square for subjects, $MS_{S \times K}$ = mean square for subjects $\times$ repeated-measures factor, and k = number of levels of the repeated-measures factor. For our example,

$$r_I = \frac{6.00 - 0.85}{6.00 + (3 - 1)0.85} = .67$$

a value that agrees with the mean r of .67 reported earlier.

The Intraclass r in a More Complex Design

As an illustration of the use of the intraclass r in a more complex design consider an experiment in which the effects of two treatments are measured in three successive weeks. Our purpose is to assess the typical correlation among the three occasions of measurement but with the correlation computed separately within each treatment condition. Note that if we computed the correlation among the occasions for all subjects, our correlations would be inflated by the magnitude of the treatment effect. The data were as follows:

	Occasions		
	1	2	3
Treatment A:			
Subject 1	2	2	4
Subject 2	2	0	3
Subject 3	1	1	3
Subject 4	3	1	2
Treatment B:			
Subject 5	3	3	5
Subject 6	3	2	3
Subject 7	4	2	4
Subject 8	2	1	4

The analysis of variance of these data yielded the following sources of variance:

Source	SS	df	MS
Between subjects:			
1. Treatments	6.00	1	6.00
2. Subjects within treatments	5.33	6	0.89
Within subjects:		(16)	
3. Occasions	16.00	2	8.00
4. Occasions × treatments	0.00	2	0.00
5. Occasions × subjects	6.66	12	0.56
6. Aggregated terms 2 and 5	11.99	18	0.67
7. Aggregated terms 2, 4, and 5	11.99	20	0.60

The intraclass r is computed by

$$r_I = \frac{MS_S - MS_{S \times K}}{MS_S + (k-1)MS_{S \times K}} = \frac{.89 - .56}{.89 + (3-1).56} = .16$$

If we had computed the correlations among the three occasions separately within each treatment condition, our r's would have been .00, $-.50$, $+.50$, $+.50$, .00, $+.50$, with a mean r of .17, a value agreeing well with the intraclass r of .16.

Lines 6 and 7 of the table of variance show two ways we might have aggregated sources of variance. Had we employed the aggregated terms, our intraclass r's would have been .10 and .14 for aggregated terms 6 and 7, respectively—values not dramatically different from the unaggregated value of .16. In the present example the use of any of the three error terms would have been very reasonable. In general, the fewer the df for the original error term, and the less dramatic the difference between the terms considered for aggregation, the better we will do in the long run to aggregate our terms.

One thing we usually should *not* do to find out the correlations among the three occasions of measurement is to correlate the scores for all subjects, disregarding their treatment conditions. In the present example, this would yield r's of .50, .17, and .67, with a mean r of .44. The difference between this mean r of .44 and the mean r of .17 when r's were computed within the two treatment conditions is due entirely to the effects of the treatment. The equivalent intraclass r is one in which the treatment effect is aggregated with the subjects-within-treatment effect and is then regarded as the MS_S, e.g., $(SS$ treatments $+ SS$ subjects$)/(df$ treatments $+ df$ subjects$) = (6 + 5.33)/(1 + 6) = 11.33/7 = 1.62$. Hence,

$$r_I = \frac{1.62 - .56}{1.62 + (3-1).56} = .39$$

a value greatly inflated by the addition of the treatment variation to the subject variation.

REPEATED MEASURES AND THE
FORMATION OF COMPOSITE VARIABLES

In many repeated-measures designs each of the repeated measures can be viewed as a replication of the measurement of some underlying construct. For example, if the repeated measurements are the 11 subtests of a standard test of intelligence, or the 4 subtests of a test of social adjustment, or the 3 psychophysiological indices of stress reaction, the sum of the 11, or 4, or 3 subtests constitutes a meaningful composite index of intelligence, social adjustment, or stress reaction.

The between-subjects sources of variance are essentially analyses of the repeated measures considered as a composite variable. Where the sum of the repeated measures is sensibly interpretable as an index of some construct, repeated-measures analyses have special advantages in terms of statistical power and in terms of testing for homogeneity of effects.

The advantages of statistical power accrue to us because as we add more measurements of an underlying construct, we are better able to observe the effects of experimental conditions on the composite measure of the construct than on randomly chosen subsets of the composite. The principle at work here is that we have a better chance to show effects with better-measured constructs, and, all else equal, more repeatedly measured constructs *are* better measured (Guilford, 1954; Rosenthal and Rubin, 1986).

The advantages of the repeated-measures analysis of the components over analysis of the results only for the sum of the measures (i.e., the composite) are that we can thereby learn whether the experimental treatments, or other factors of the design, are affecting different components or subtests differentially. That is exactly what the treatment $\times$ subtests interaction will tell us.

In applications of this kind the repeated measurements tend to be positively correlated, often between .20 and .80. It turns out that the advantages of repeated-measures designs, in the sense of using more rather than fewer repeated measures of a construct, tend to increase when the intercorrelations among the repeated measurements are lower. This can be seen to be reasonable when we note that each measure can contribute more that is unique to the composite when that measure is not too highly correlated with other measures. If the correlations among the measures were 1.00, after all, any one measure would be as good as the total.

When we discussed the assumptions underlying the use of t and F tests for comparing means in Chapter 15, we noted the assumption of homogeneity of variance. In the next section we shall summarize those assumptions and add two more that are relevant to repeated-measures F tests. Here we want to note a special implication of heterogeneity of variance of the repeated-measures variables for the interpretation of the sum of the repeated measures, i.e., the composite index of the construct. This implication is that individual variables contribute to the composite in proportion to their variance. Thus those measures with large variances may contribute much more to the formation of the composite than the investigator may intend. One way of dealing with this problem and ensuring that all variables contribute equally to the composite is to transform each variable to Z scores, i.e., scores having a mean of zero and a standard deviation of 1.00. A fuller discussion of the formation of composite variables is found in Chapter 24 and especially in Rosenthal (1987a).

A NOTE ON ASSUMPTIONS

Before leaving our discussion of repeated-measures analyses of variance, we should note that the F's we compute in actual research situations will usually be distributed only approximately as F. Three of the assumptions to be met before we can regard computed F's to be actually distributed as F were given when we discussed the comparison of means by the use of t tests, and again in our discussion of the distributions of F. These assumptions were (1) independence of errors (or sampling units), (2) homogeneity of variance, and (3) normality (with all three summarized as IID normal).

In the case of repeated-measures analyses, there is an *additional* assumption having to do with the relative magnitudes of the intercorrelations among the various levels of the repeated-measures factors. For practical purposes, we regard this assumption as met to the degree that we have homogeneity of correlation coefficients among the various levels of the repeated-measures factors (Hays, 1981; Snedecor and Cochran, 1980, 1989; Winer, 1971). In those repeated-measures designs in which there are two or more levels of between-subjects factors (e.g., treatments, sex, age, ability, etc.), there is the further assumption that the pattern of intercorrelations among the various levels of the repeated-measures factors is consistent from level to level of the between-subjects factors (Winer, 1971). These assumptions apply only to F tests on repeated measures with more than a single df in the numerator. Therefore, any F test in which there are only two levels of the repeated-measures factor does not need to meet these assumptions. Indeed, when there are only two levels, only one correlation is possible! Even when there are more than two levels of the repeated-measures factor, however, these assumptions are not needed when we have tested some focused hypothesis about the results by means of a contrast, since contrasts also have only a single df for the numerator of the F used to test them. We shall consider the topic of contrasts in Chapter 21.

PART
VII

POWER
AND FOCUSED
ANALYSES

ASSESSING
AND INCREASING
POWER

POWER ANALYSIS

It is often the case that we can improve the design of our research studies by giving careful consideration to an analysis of the *power* of the research. To introduce the procedures of power analysis we will want to review the basic types of
errors referred to in Chapter 2. The type I error (or "error of the first kind") involves rejecting the null hypothesis when it is in fact true. In its usual application
in the behavioral sciences the type I error represents an error of gullibility or of
overeagerness. It claims an effect or a relationship where none exists. The type
II error (or "error of the second kind") involves failing to reject the null hypothesis when it is in fact false. In its usual application in the behavioral sciences the
type II error represents an error of conservatism or blindness to a relationship. It
denies the existence of an effect or a relationship that does exist. By convention,
the probability of a type I error is called alpha (α), and the probability of a type
II error is called beta (β).

    Power is defined as the probability of rejecting the null hypothesis when
the null hypothesis is false and, therefore, in need of rejecting. Power increases
as the probability of a type II error (β) decreases or, more specifically:

$$\text{Power} = 1 - \beta$$

Put another way, power is the probability of *not* making a type II error, i.e., of
not overlooking an effect or a relationship that is really there.

Two major purposes of power analysis include (1) the planning of research and (2) the evaluation of research already completed. In the planning of research, a power analysis is conducted to determine the size of the sample needed to reach a given alpha (α) level for any particular size of effect that might be expected. In the evaluation of completed research and its accompanying inferences, we employ a power analysis to help us decide whether a given failure to detect an effect at a given alpha was likely to have been due primarily to the employment of too small a sample. Let us consider an example.

Smith conducts an experiment on the effects of her new treatment of learning disabilities by randomly assigning 40 children to the experimental condition and 40 children to the control condition. Smith reports that the treatment-condition children improved significantly more than the control-condition children at $t(78) = 2.21$, $p < .05$. Jones is skeptical and decides to check on Smith's results by assigning children at random to the same two conditions. Jones has 20 children available for the research, and he assigns 10 to each condition. His results show $t(18) = 1.06$, p not even close to .05 (actually greater than .30). Jones publishes his findings, claiming Smith's results were unreplicable, or were the results of an artifact, or were otherwise not to be believed.

Readers relying on p levels to tell them whether the research had been replicated or not might be seriously misled by Jones's conclusions of nonreplication (Rosenthal, 1990b). A closer look at Jones's data showed not only that Jones's results were in the same direction as Smith's but, more importantly, that Jones's effect size of $\frac{1}{2}\sigma$ (computed as $2t/\sqrt{df}$) was exactly the same as Smith's effect size of $\frac{1}{2}\sigma$ (computed as $2t/\sqrt{df}$). In short, the two studies showed the same result, but Smith's sample size was large enough to show an effect at $p < .05$ (actual power for her t test was about .6), while Jones's sample size was not large enough to show the effect at $p < .05$ (actual power for his t test was only about .2, or one-third as great as Smith's).

In a given study the determination of the level of power at which we would be operating depends on (1) the particular statistic we employ to determine the level of significance, (2) the level of alpha (α) we select, (3) the size of the sample we employ, and (4) the size of the effect we are studying.

EFFECT SIZE

There are a great many different ways in which to represent the size of the effects under investigation. We shall consider a number of these in due course, but for now we focus our attention on two of the most common, most serviceable, and most easily understood: eta and d.

Eta, which was described earlier in Chapter 15, can be defined as the square root of the proportion of variance accounted for. It can also be defined as the square root of the ratio of the sum of squares of the effect to the sum of squares of the effect plus the sum of squares of the error, or

$$\text{eta} = \sqrt{\frac{SS \text{ effect}}{SS \text{ effect} + SS \text{ error}}} \tag{1}$$

If the sums of squares are not available, only a little rearrangement of terms is required to show that we can give eta in terms of F instead:

$$\text{eta} = \sqrt{\frac{(F)(df \text{ effect})}{(F)(df \text{ effect}) + (df \text{ error})}} \qquad (2)$$

The interpretation of eta is analogous to the interpretation of the Pearson product-moment correlation coefficient (r), but with the understanding that eta may refer to nonlinear as well as to linear relationships. Eta may be seen as the general case of which r is a special instance.

Particularly when the research involves the comparison of two groups, it is common to index the size of the effect by examining the difference between the means. Such differences, however, have little meaning apart from the (often arbitrary) scale of measurement employed. It is useful, therefore, to divide the difference between the means by the common within-group σ so that the effect size will be represented in σ units. Jacob Cohen (1969, 1977, 1988), in his extensive treatment of this topic, refers to such standardized differences as units of $d-$ units that were described earlier in our chapter on the t test (Chapter 15).

$$d = \frac{\text{mean 1} - \text{mean 2}}{\sigma} \qquad (3)$$

In experimental research we often try to maximize d. We do this by increasing the numerator and by decreasing the denominator of the expression above. We try to increase the mean difference (the numerator) by selecting treatment conditions we believe to be as powerful as possible, and we try to decrease the within-groups σ (the denominator) by increasing the standardization of our procedures, by increasing the reliability of our measurements, by selecting more homogeneous sampling units for our study, and by using related methods for increasing precision, i.e., decreasing uncontrolled variation.

Often we find that d or σ has not been reported in published studies. In addition, it may happen that the MS for error has not been reported, so that we cannot calculate σ ourselves ($\sigma \cong \sqrt{MS}$ error). In those cases we can get a good approximation of d by doubling the associated t value and dividing by the $\sqrt{df}$ (or $N - 2$) on which the t test was based (Friedman, 1968; a procedure we discussed in Chapter 15)

$$d = \frac{2t}{\sqrt{df}} \qquad (4)$$

Table 19.1 helps us review the use of the indices of effect size discussed so far. The results of the study shown are in the form of dichotomous (0, 1) scores for both conditions of the study. Dichotomous data work well and are easy to work with computationally.

First we compute eta according to Equation 1, which gives

$$\text{eta} = \sqrt{\frac{1.80}{1.80 + 3.20}} = .60$$

TABLE 19.1
Experimental results and the table of variance

Experimental results		Table of variance					
Control	Experimental	Source	SS	df	MS	F	t*
1	1	Between conditions	1.80	1	1.800	10.11	3.18
1	1	Within conditions	3.20	18	0.178		
0	1						
0	1						
0	1						
0	1						
0	1						
0	1						
0	0						
0	0						
Σ 2	8						
$\overline{X}$ 0.2	0.8						
σ 0.4	0.4						

*$t = \sqrt{F}$ when F is based only on a single df in the numerator.

Then we compute eta according to Equation 2, which gives

$$eta = \sqrt{\frac{(10.11)(1)}{(10.11)(1) + 18}} = .60$$

Next we compute d according to Equation 3, which gives

$$d = \frac{0.8 - 0.2}{.4} = 1.50$$

Finally, we compute d according to Equation 4, which gives

$$d = \frac{2(3.18)}{\sqrt{18}} = 1.50$$

For the situation in which F has only a single df in the numerator, eta can be seen as simply r. We can show the relationship between r and d so that, given one, we can easily find the other. Given r we can find d by

$$d = \frac{2r}{\sqrt{1 - r^2}}$$

and, given d we can find r by

$$r = \frac{d}{\sqrt{d^2 + 4}}$$

The experimental results we reported above were chosen not only to be very easy to work with computationally, but also to show a simple generalization of our procedures to the case of a 2×2 contingency table. We can redisplay the data above as follows:

Score	Control	Experimental	Σ
1	2	8	10
0	8	2	10
Σ	10	10	20

Recalling from our chapter on correlation that

$$\chi^2(1) = \Sigma \frac{(O - E)^2}{E}$$

we find for these data that $\chi^2(1) = 7.2$. This value, when divided by our total N of 20, equals .36, of which the square root is .60. That turns out to be both the phi (ϕ) coefficient summarizing the data of the contingency table and also the eta we computed earlier on the same data. In general, for a 2×2 contingency table, we compute phi, a product-moment correlation, as follows:

$$\phi = \sqrt{\frac{\chi^2}{N}}$$

By convention, whether our effect size is indexed by d or r or ϕ, we employ a positive sign when the effect is in the predicted direction and a negative sign when the effect is in the unpredicted direction.

POWER TABLES

The most comprehensive, elegant, and useful discussion of power analysis in behavioral research is that by Cohen (1969, 1977, 1988). He has provided a large number of tables that are indispensable to behavioral researchers, and Table 19.2 is a composite based on many of those tables. For each of seven statistics ranging from t to F, the effect-size index suggested by Cohen is given, along with his definitions of "small," "medium," and "large" effect sizes. The rest of the table allows us to read the sample sizes required to operate at each power level from .15 to .90 or to read the power at which we were operating for any given sample size. In section A the power and sample size equivalences are given for an alpha level of .05, two-tailed, and for medium-effect sizes as defined by Cohen. Section B gives the equivalences for medium effects tested at .01, two-tailed, Section C gives the equivalences for small effects at .05, two-tailed.

Whenever the table involves the comparison of two or more samples (e.g., t, F, $r_1 - r_2$, $P_1 - P_2$), the sample sizes are assumed equal. When sample sizes

TABLE 19.2
Multipurpose power tables

	Statistic						
	t	r	$r_1 - r_2$	$P - .50$	$P_1 - P_2$	χ^2	F
Effect-size index	d	r	q	g	h	w	f
Effect size:							
Small	.20	.10	.10	.05	.20	.10	.10
Medium	.50	.30	.30	.15	.50	.30	.25
Large	.80	.50	.50	.25	.80	.50	.40

A. Sample size (rounded) required to detect "medium" effect at .05, two-tailed

Power	t	r	$r_1 - r_2$	$P - .50$	$P_1 - P_2$	χ^2 ($df = 1$)	F ($df = 1$ for numerator)
.15	10	10	20	<10	<10	<25	10
.20	10	15	30	10	10	<25	10
.30	20	25	50	20	20	25	20
.40	25	35	70	35	25	30	25
.50	30	40	90	45	30	45	30
.60	40	55	115	55	40	55	40
.70	50	65	140	70	50	70	50
.80	65	85	175	90	65	90	65
.90	85	115	235	110	85	120	85
Definition of n^*	a	b	c	d	c	d	a

B. Sample size (rounded) required to detect "medium" effect at .01, two-tailed

Power	t	r	$r_1 - r_2$	$P - .50$	$P_1 - P_2$	χ^2 $(df = 1)$	F $(df = 1)$
.15	20	30	55	30	20	25	20
.20	25	35	70	40	25	35	25
.30	35	45	95	50	35	45	35
.40	45	60	125	60	45	60	45
.50	55	70	150	70	55	75	55
.60	65	85	180	85	65	90	65
.70	80	100	220	100	75	110	80
.80	95	125	260	130	95	130	95
.90	120	160	330	160	120	160	120

C. Sample size (rounded) required to detect "small" effect at .05, two-tailed

Power	t	r	$r_1 - r_2$	$P - .50$	$P_1 - P_2$	χ^2 $(df = 1)$	F $(df = 1)$
.15	45	85	170	90	40	80	45
.20	65	125	250	120	65	125	65
.30	105	200	400	200	105	200	105
.40	150	300	600	300	140	300	150
.50	200	400	800	400	200	400	200
.60	250	500	1000	500	250	500	250
.70	300	600	1250	650	300	600	300
.80	400	800	1600	800	400	800	400
.90	550	1000	2100	1000	500	1000	550

*a = Each group or condition; b = *n* of score pairs; c = *n* of each sample; d = total *N*.

Source: Based on J. Cohen, *Statistical Power Analysis for the Behavioral Sciences*, Academic Press, New York, 1977.

are not equal, we employ the harmonic mean ($\bar{n}_h$) of the sample sizes as our approximation.

INDICES OF EFFECT SIZE

We turn now to a consideration of each of the seven statistics of Table 19.2 and the index of effect size associated with each.

t Statistic

The effect size associated with t is called d, already defined as

$$d = \frac{(M_1 - M_2)}{\sigma}$$

We note in our inspection of the entries under t in sections A, B, and C in Table 19.2 that to achieve even the modest power level of .50 we require respective sample sizes of 30, 55, and 200, *in each group* for the three combinations of expected effect size and alpha. It should be noted here that there are several variants of the effect size d, in particular Glass's delta (Δ) and Hedges's g (Rosenthal, 1984). Glass's Δ is defined as the difference between the group means divided by the S of the control group—recall that S is $\sqrt{\Sigma(X - \bar{X})^2/(N - 1)}$ while σ is $\sqrt{\Sigma(X - \bar{X})^2/N}$— and Hedges's g is defined as the difference between the group means divided by the S of both groups pooled. (Note that Hedges's g is different from the g in Table 19.2.) While the use of any of these three effect-size indices can be well justified, we shall emphasize Cohen's d in particular, because of the great utility of Cohen's power tables, which were set up for use specifically with d.

r Statistic

The effect size associated with r is, of course, r itself. The definitions of small, medium, and large effects are not quite consistent between r and t. The table below shows in the third column the levels of r that are equivalent to each level of d. Thus Cohen requires a somewhat larger effect when examining r than when examining t when medium and, especially, large effects are under discussion:

	d	Cohen's r	r equivalent to d*
Small	.20	.10	.10
Medium	.50	.30	.24
Large	.80	.50	.37

*Where r is obtained from d by $r = \dfrac{d}{\sqrt{d^2 + 4}}$.

To achieve the moderate power level of .50 we will require sample sizes of 40, 70, and 400 sampling units, respectively, for the three combinations of expected effect size and alpha shown in sections A, B, and C of Table 19.2. Comparison of sample sizes listed for t and for r show the sample sizes required for r to be uniformly higher. It should be noted, however, that the entries under t are the n's for each of two groups, while the entries for r are the total sample size. In fact, for most power levels and for most effect sizes and alpha levels, the total sample sizes required by r are smaller than those required by t. This difference appears to be due partly to the fact that "medium" and "large" effects are actually larger for r than for d, and partly to the fact that t cannot take advantage of both between-group and within-group linearity of regression. The table below shows t for the comparison between two sets of two scores each:

		t		
Subject	Treatment condition	Within-condition specific prediction	Score	$\overline{X}$
1	Control	None	2	3.0
2	Control	None	4	
3	Experimental	None	6	7.0
4	Experimental	None	8	

$t(2) = 2.83, p < .11, r = .89$

		r	
Subject	Treatment condition	Within condition specific prediction*	Score
1	Control	−3	2
2	Control	−1	4
3	Experimental	1	6
4	Experimental	3	8

$r(2) = 1.00, t \to \infty, p \to 0$

*Based, for example, on subjects' test scores.

There is no effect on t if the scores within each group are rearranged. There is an effect on r, however, of having accurately predicted on the basis of some theory which of the scores in each group should be higher; the correlation over all four scores is perfect. If even one of the pairs of numbers of the experimental or control group had been interchanged in the bottom section of the table above, however, r would have dropped from 1.00 to .80 ($t = 1.89$, $df = 2$, $p < .20$). In short, where there really is more nearly perfect linear regression between the predicted and obtained results, r is likely to be more powerful than t, that is because t has lost some of the information in the independent variable (or predictor variable) by dichotomizing the four discriminable predictor values (-3, -1, $+1$, $+3$) to just two levels of -1 and $+1$.

$r_1 - r_2$ Statistic

The difference between two independent correlation coefficients is indexed by q, the difference between the Fisher z transformations[1] associated with each r. Fisher's z is defined as $\frac{1}{2}\ln[(1 + r)/(1 - r)]$. To achieve a power level of .50, we need, respectively, 90, 150, and 800 sampling units for *each r* for the three combinations of expected effect size and alpha shown in sections A, B, and C of Table 19.2.

It is worth noting that the testing of differences between correlation coefficients is a more "difficult" enterprise than is usually realized, often requiring enormous sample sizes to detect differences. Why should it be so difficult to detect the differences between the value of one r and another r when it is so much easier to detect the difference between the value of one r and zero? The answer lies in the difference between the confidence interval around a second observed r and that around a theoretical value of zero. The latter, of course, has no confidence interval, while the former has a real confidence interval "to be overcome." Consider an r of .30 based on an N of 45. The t associated with this r is 2.01 and $p = .05$. The 95 percent confidence interval around the obtained r is between .01 and .54. There is no overlap with zero. Now imagine that we wanted to compare this obtained r with another obtained r of 0.0 based on the same sample size of 45. The confidence interval of this latter r runs from $-.29$ to $+.29$ and overlaps very considerably with the confidence interval of our r of .30 as shown in Figure 19-1. It is this overlap that keeps the r's from being found to differ significantly.

$P - .50$ Statistic

The difference between an obtained proportion (P) and .50 is referred to as g. To achieve a power level of .50, we need 45, 70, and 400 sampling units for the three combinations of expected effect size and alpha shown in sections A, B, and C of Table 19.2.

---

[1] This transformation makes equal differences (between z's) equally detectable, whereas equal differences between r's are not equally detectable, e.g., .90–.70 in units of r is much more detectable than .40–.20 (Cohen, 1988). In addition, significance tests of differences among r's are more accurate when this transformation is employed (Alexander, Scozzaro, and Borodkin, 1989).

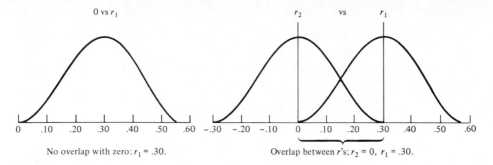

FIGURE 19-1
Comparison of a correlation coefficient with (*a*) a theoretical value of zero and with (*b*) a correlation coefficient of zero.

$P_1 - P_2$ Statistic

The difference between two obtained proportions is indexed by the difference *h* between the arcsin transformations of the two proportions. This transformation, like that employed for *r*, makes equal differences in the transformed scale equally detectable (Cohen, 1977, 1988). To achieve a power level of .50 requires 30, 55, and 200 sampling units *for each sample* for the three combinations of expected effect size and alpha shown in sections A, B, and C of Table 19.2. To employ the arcsin transformation, simply replace each of the proportions to be compared (*X*) by the arcsin equivalent (*a*) from Table B.13 of Appendix B. Then, Cohen's *h* is simply the difference between the two arcsin equivalents: $h = a_1 - a_2$. An additional effect-size indicator (π), called *pi*, has recently been proposed that allows us to evaluate more readily the practical significance of the effect in which an obtained proportion (*P*) is compared with the proportion expected under the null hypothesis (Rosenthal and Rubin, 1989, in press). The proportion index (π) shows the proportion of hits on a scale on which .50 is always the null value. It is obtained from the following:

$$\pi = \frac{P(k - 1)}{1 + P(k - 2)}$$

where *P* is the raw proportion of hits and *k* is the number of alternative choices available. For example, if there were four choices, choosing the correct alternative .60 of the time would be equivalent to choosing the correct alternative .82 of the time given only two choices. Power analyses for π can be carried out on Cohen's *h* (i.e., $a_1 - a_2$) where one of the values of *a* is a constant, but, in this case, use of Cohen's power tables of *h* (or Table 19.2) requires us to multiply *h* by $\sqrt{2}$ to adjust for the fact that one of our proportions is a constant with no sampling variation (Cohen, 1977, p. 203, or 1988, p. 203).

χ^2 Statistic

The effect size associated with χ^2 is called w. It is defined as the square root of the sum over all cells (of any size table of frequencies) of the square of the difference between the proportion expected and the proportion obtained in each cell divided by the proportion expected in that cell, or

$$w = \sqrt{\Sigma \frac{(P \text{ expected} - P \text{ obtained})^2}{P \text{ expected}}}$$

The definition of w, then, looks like the square root of the definition of χ^2 except that the raw frequencies employed in the computation of χ^2 have been replaced by the proportions of total N found in each cell or expected in each cell. For a 2×2 table w is equivalent to phi (ϕ), so $\phi = w = \sqrt{\chi^2/N}$. In terms of the contingency coefficient C (where $C = \sqrt{\chi^2/(\chi^2 + N)}$), $w = \sqrt{C^2/(1 - C^2)}$. To achieve a power level of .50, we will require 45, 75, and 400 sampling units, respectively, for the three combinations of expected effect size and alpha shown in sections A, B, and C of Table 19.2.

F Statistic

The effect size associated with F is called f and is defined as the σ of the means divided by the σ within conditions. In the case of just two groups, f is related to d by $f = d/2$. More generally f is related to the correlation ratio, eta, by

$$f = \sqrt{\frac{\text{eta}^2}{1 - \text{eta}^2}}$$

Achieving a power level of .50 (or any other given power level) when only two groups are involved requires sample sizes identical with those required for t. When F is based on more than two groups, we should note that power decreases in tests of main effects as the number of df of the between-group factors increases for a given fixed total N. In addition, power for an interaction decreases as the number of df of the interaction increases for a given fixed total N.

In using Cohen's power tables (1977, 1988), we redefine n to n' before entering the tables, where

$$n' = \frac{df \text{ error} + df \text{ effect} + 1}{df \text{ effect} + 1}$$

Thus, given the sample sizes (n's) shown below:

	A_1	A_2	A_3	Σ
B_1	10	10	10	30
B_2	10	10	10	30
B_3	10	10	10	30
B_4	10	10	10	30
Σ	40	40	40	120

we would find df to be as follows:

$$df \text{ error} = 120 - 12 = 12(10 - 1) = 108$$
$$df \text{ effect A} = 3 - 1 = 2$$
$$df \text{ effect B} = 4 - 1 = 3$$
$$df \text{ effect AB} = (3 - 1) \times (4 - 1) = 6$$

Therefore,

$$n^1 \text{ for the A effect} = \frac{108 + 2 + 1}{2 + 1} = 37$$

and

$$n^1 \text{ for the B effect} = \frac{108 + 3 + 1}{3 + 1} = 28$$

and

$$n^1 \text{ for the AB effect} = \frac{108 + 6 + 1}{6 + 1} = 16.4$$

Using the required power tables provided by Cohen (1977, 1988) we would find the power levels for alpha $= .05$ and a medium effect size of $f = .25$ to be .65, .58, and .46 for the A, B, and AB effects, respectively. These results illustrate the loss of power involved when, for a fixed total N, the df for various effects show an increase. Here, then, is a major reason to organize our scientific questions into focused questions such as are addressed by t tests, F tests with a single df in the numerator, and χ^2's with 1 df, and more generally, by contrasts of any type.

The details of the use of contrasts will be given in Chapter 21, but here we can illustrate one possible contrast among the four means of the B effect. Suppose our contrast had been to compare the mean of groups B_1 and B_2 with the mean of groups B_3 and B_4. We could compute such a contrast by the procedures of Chapter 21 or by a t test of the sort described in Chapter 15. Then n^1 for this contrast would be

$$n^1 = \frac{df \text{ error} + df \text{ effect} + 1}{df \text{ effect} + 1} = \frac{108 + 1 + 1}{1 + 1} = 55$$

since the df for the effect is always 1 for any contrast. The power level for this contrast would be .75, noticeably greater than for any of the three effects involving multiple df in the numerator of the F test. For χ^2 tests of $df > 1$ and for F tests of $df > 1$ in the numerator, we recommend doing power calculations on the contrasts that address specific scientific questions whenever possible. If the power calculations must be made on χ^2 tests of $df > 1$ and F tests with $df > 1$ in the numerator, Cohen's tables (1977, 1988) provide all the information required.

EXPANDED POWER TABLES FOR
r AND $r_1 - r_2$

To keep our multipurpose power table (Table 19.2) compact, we were not able to give a variety of effect sizes postulated to exist in the population. Because of the widespread utility of the effect-size index r and because other effect-size indices can so frequently be converted to r, we provide a more detailed table of postulated effect sizes for r with values from .10 to .70. Careful study of Table 19.3 shows clearly how, for any given level of power, larger effect sizes are more detectable. To operate at a probability of rejecting the null hypothesis 90 percent of the time at the .05 level, two-tailed, requires an N (i.e., a total number of sampling units) of about 1,000 if the population r is .10 but only an N of about 15 if the population r is .70.

One purpose for which we definitely cannot use Table 19.3 is to compare two independent correlation coefficients. We have already seen how much more difficult it is to reject the null hypothesis of no difference between independent correlation coefficients than it is to reject the null hypothesis that a single r does not differ from zero. Accordingly, we also provide a more detailed table of postulated effect sizes for q (i.e., $z_{r_1} - z_{r_2}$) with values from .10 to .70 (Table 19.4). Comparing Tables 19.3 and 19.4 shows that, much of the time, it takes sample sizes twice as large to achieve similar levels of power when we want to compare r's to each other rather than to a theoretical value of zero.

USING POWER TABLES

In this section we give some concrete examples of the use of power tables to plan the conduct of our research and to help us better interpret the meaning of research results already obtained. The effect-size indicators that we employ here

TABLE 19.3
Rounded sample sizes (total N) required to detect various effects (r) at .05, two-tailed

Power	Effect sizes (r)						
	.10	.20	.30	.40	.50	.60	.70
.15	85	25	10	10	10	10	10
.20	125	35	15	10	10	10	10
.30	200	55	25	15	10	10	10
.40	300	75	35	20	15	10	10
.50	400	100	40	25	15	10	10
.60	500	125	55	30	20	15	10
.70	600	155	65	40	25	15	10
.80	800	195	85	45	30	20	15
.90	1000	260	115	60	40	25	15

Source: Based on J. Cohen, *Statistical Power Analysis for the Behavioral Sciences,* Academic Press, New York, 1977, pp. 92–93.

TABLE 19.4
Rounded sample sizes (*N* for *each* of two samples)
required to detect various effects (*q*) at .05, two-tailed

Power	.10	.20	.30	.40	.50	.60	.70
			Effect sizes ($q = z_{r_1} - z_{r_2}$)*				
.15	170	45	20	15	10	10	10
.20	250	65	30	20	15	10	10
.30	400	105	50	30	20	15	15
.40	600	150	70	40	30	20	15
.50	800	195	90	50	35	25	20
.60	1000	240	115	65	45	30	25
.70	1250	315	140	80	55	40	30
.80	1600	400	175	100	65	50	35
.90	2100	540	235	135	90	65	45

Source: Based on J. Cohen, *Statistical Power Analysis for the Behavioral Sciences,* Academic Press, New York, 1977, pp. 125–126.

*Note that *q* is the difference between two Fisher *z* transformations of *r* and not the difference between two *r*'s.

are *d*, *r*, and *q* (i.e., $z_{r_1} - z_{r_2}$). Many more detailed examples are available in Cohen's comprehensive coverage of the topic (1977, 1988).

Effect-Size Indicator *d*

Suppose we are planning an experiment on a new treatment procedure that we believe will have quite subtle effects but that, because of its low cost, might have considerable social benefits per dollar expended. We believe the effect to be of a magnitude between .15 and .25 of a standard deviation. Table 19.2 shows that for small effects (section C) equivalent to a *d* of .20 we will need 200 subjects in *each* of our two groups to be able to detect a difference at $p \leq .05$, two-tailed, even half the time. If that power level of .50 seems too risky, we may want to consider the power level Cohen recommmends, which is .80. To reach that power level will cost us 800 subjects altogether, 400 in each of our two groups.

Now suppose we have just read an article in which some other investigator has evaluated the same new treatment procedure that was of interest to us. That investigator reports that he could not find any effect of the new treatment and that $t = 1.41$ for his sample of 200 subjects (100 in each condition). Our first step in trying to understand these results is to compute the effect-size estimate, say, *d*. Since $d = 2t/\sqrt{df}$, his *d* was $2(1.41)/\sqrt{200 - 2} = 198 = .20$, exactly the effect size we expected to find, on the average. His results, therefore, provide good support for the idea of an effect of that magnitude. Turning to the issue of significance testing, we enter Table 19.2, section C (because we expected, and this investigator found, only a small effect size of $d = .20$). There we find that for a study of 100 subjects for each condition there was less than a .30 chance of finding the effect significant at $p \leq .05$, two-tailed. The investigator should not have been surprised to find a nonsignificant result (at .05) given the postulated (and obtained) effect size and the size of the sample employed in his research.

Effect-Size Indicator r

Suppose we are planning a study of the relationship between two measures of sensitivity to nonverbal communication. We believe the correlation to fall somewhere between .30 and .60 and want to be quite sure of being able to reject the null hypothesis at .05, two-tailed. We may, therefore, decide to plan our data collection such that we will be operating at a power level of .90. Table 19.3 shows that to achieve a 90 percent probability of rejecting the null hypothesis if it is false, we will need total sample sizes of about 115, 60, 40, or 25 if the actual effect sizes are .30, .40, .50, or .60, respectively.

Now suppose another investigator has also examined the relationship between our two tests and has found no significant relationship, concluding that "there is no evidence for such a relationship." The investigator obtained a t of 1.59 for her N of 20 pairs of scores, which corresponds to an r of .35, since $r = \sqrt{t^2/(t^2 + df)}$. This value falls within the range of r's we believed likely for the relationship investigated and closer to the lower end. Now considering the issue of significance testing, we note that if the true effect size were, in fact, about .35 (the obtained value), an investigator employing 20 subjects would have only about a .30 chance of rejecting the null at $p \leq .05$, two-tailed (interpolating between the columns headed .30 and .40). If the true effect size were an r of .40, the investigator's power would have been about .40; if the true effect size were an r of .50, the investigator's N of 20 would have "bought" a power level of .60, and if r were actually .60 in the population, the power level would have been .80.

Effect-Size Indicator q to Test $r_1 - r_2$

Suppose we now hypothesize that the correlation between our two tests should be higher for younger than for older children, since younger children seem to show less cognitive differentiation (DePaulo and Rosenthal, 1979). For our first study we have available 30 younger children and 50 older children. We are aware that much larger sample sizes are necessary to show significant differences between two r's than to show a single r to differ from zero, but these 80 children are all we have. What we want to know, however, is the level of power at which we will be operating assuming various differences between our r's (measured in units of Z_r).

To employ Table 19.4 we need the harmonic mean of the two sample sizes, which in this case will be

$$\bar{n}_h = \frac{1}{\frac{1}{2}\left(\frac{1}{n_1} + \frac{1}{n_2}\right)} = \frac{2}{\left(\frac{1}{n_1} + \frac{1}{n_2}\right)} = \frac{2}{\frac{1}{30} + \frac{1}{50}} = 37.5$$

If we assume a small to medium q of .20, Table 19.4 shows we will be operating at a level of power below .15. Assuming a medium to large q of .40, we will be operating at a level of power over .35, and, assuming a very large q of .60, our power level will be about .67.

Now suppose another investigator had also investigated our hypothesis of different correlations for different age groups. By now we know not to take too seriously the finding of "no significant difference" apart from the actual effect size obtained. Therefore, when we learn of the other investigator's research, we go directly to the effect size he or she obtained and assess the power level at which the investigator was operating given his or her effect size as the best guess of the population value of the effect size (or given some other postulated population effect size). For this example let us assume sample sizes of 30 and 50 and obtained correlations of .60 and .37 differing in the predicted direction but not significantly so, since

$$ Z = \frac{z_{r_1} - z_{r_2}}{\sqrt{\dfrac{1}{n_1 - 3} + \dfrac{1}{n_2 - 3}}} = \frac{.69 - .39}{\sqrt{\dfrac{1}{27} + \dfrac{1}{47}}} = 1.24 $$

$p = .11$, one-tailed. For a population or true effect size of $q = .69 - .39 = .30$, n's of 30 and 50 with the harmonic mean $\bar{n}$ of 37.5 are associated in Table 19.4 with a power level between .20 and .30.

THE NEGLECT OF POWER

Jacob Cohen has not only provided us with the most comprehensive, elegant, and useful discussion of power analysis in behavioral research (Cohen, 1969, 1977, 1988), he has also pioneered in the empirical work demonstrating that the business of the behavioral researcher is conducted with a remarkably high risk of committing type II errors (Cohen, 1962). In fact, for medium effect sizes and $\alpha = .05$ the odds were better than 50:50 that the null hypothesis would not be rejected when it was false and, therefore, in need of rejection. In their recent update on this line of work Sedlmeier and Gigerenzer (1989) report that in the intervening quarter of a century, the situation has, if anything, gotten worse. We continue to operate at low levels of power and perhaps even worse, we continue to neglect the very concept of power and the consequences of the neglect of power.

Cohen (e.g., 1977, 1988) has pointed out that we can get some operational idea of investigators' conceptions of the relative seriousness of type I (α) versus type II (β) errors by forming the ratio of β/α. For example, if an investigator has decided to set α at .05 and is conducting a test of significance with power $= .40$, β will be 1–.40, or .60. Then the ratio of β/α will be .60/.05 $= 12$ implying a conception of type I errors (α) as 12 times more serious than type II errors (β) (Rosnow and Rosenthal, 1988).

Table 19.5 shows the ratios of β/α for varying sample sizes, under three conditions of assumed effect size (r), and for two levels of α. As we would expect, our index of relative seriousness of α and β errors shows that we weight α errors more seriously relative to β errors as sample sizes, effect sizes, and significance levels decrease. In our planning of our own research we can use Table 19.5

TABLE 19.5
Ratios of type II/type I error rates for various sample sizes, effect sizes, and significance levels (two-tailed)

| | Effect sizes (r) and significance levels (.05 and .10) | | | | | |
| | $r = .10$ | | $r = .30$ | | $r = .50$ | |
N	.05	.10	.05	.10	.05	.10
10	19	9	17	8	13*	5†
20	19	9	15	6	7*	2†
30	18	8	13	5	3	1
40	18	8	10	4	2	
50	18	8	9	3		
60	18	8	7	2		
70	17	8	6	2		
80	17	8	4	1		
90	17	8	4	1		
100	17	7	3			
120	16	7	2			
140	16	7	1			
160	15	6				
180	15	6				
200	14	6				
300	12	5				
400	10	4				
500	8	3				
600	6	2				
700	5	2				
800	4	1				
900	3					
1000	2					

Note: Entries are to nearest integer; blanks indicate values < 1.
*For $r = .70$ these ratios would drop to 6 and < 1, respectively.
†For $r = .70$ these ratios would drop to 2 and < 1, respectively.

to remind us of how we have operationalized the relative seriousness of α and β errors for any given level of effect size postulated, α level selected, and size of sample planned. In our evaluation of research already completed in which the results were declared nonsignificant, we can assess the investigator's operationalization of the relative seriousness of errors of the first or second kind.

CHAPTER
20

BLOCKING
AND
THE INCREASE
OF POWER

THE NATURE OF BLOCKING

In the last chapter we saw that one way to increase power is to increase the size of the effect under investigation. One way to increase the size of the effect is to decrease the size of the within-group or error variation. Blocking helps us to achieve this goal of increased precision and, as we shall see later, can serve other ends as well. *Blocking* refers to the stratification or subdividing of subjects or other sampling units in such a way that persons (or other units) within a common block (or level of stratification) are more similar to each other on the dependent variable than they are to persons (or other units) within a different block. We begin our discussion of blocking by considering the following illustration.

Ten psychiatric patients suffering from different levels of chronic anxiety are available for a study of a new type of treatment. Half the patients are to receive the new treatment and half are to receive the placebo control. The dependent variable is the patients' subsequent anxiety level. Because the patients' anxiety level (after the treatment condition or control condition has been administered) is very likely to correlate substantially with the patients' anxiety level before the experiment, this preexperimental level of anxiety is a natural candidate for the role of blocking variable. In order to employ a blocking procedure in this experiment while still maintaining random assignment of subjects to treatment, we find the two subjects highest in preexperimental anxiety and assign one of them at random to each of our two conditions. We then find the two subjects

457

with the next highest levels of anxiety and assign them at random to our treatment and control conditions. We continue in this way until all our subjects have been assigned.

Table 20.1 shows the results of this hypothetical experiment and the table of variance. The treatment effect is found to be large and significant at $p < .05$, and the blocking variable of preexperimental anxiety level is found to be even larger and more significant.

The magnitude of the treatment effect is

$$\text{eta} = \sqrt{\frac{3.60}{3.60 + 1.40}} \quad \text{or} \quad \sqrt{\frac{10.29(1)}{10.29(1) + 4}} = .85$$

while the magnitude of the blocking variable effect is

$$\text{eta} = \sqrt{\frac{77.40}{77.40 + 1.40}} \quad \text{or} \quad \sqrt{\frac{55.29(4)}{55.29(4) + 4}} = .99$$

TABLE 20.1
Results illustrating blocking

Anxiety blocking levels	Treatment	Control	Σ
Highest	8	9	17
High	6	7	13
Medium	3	5	8
Low	1	3	4
Lowest	1	1	2
Σ	19	25	44
$\overline{X}$	3.8	5.0	4.4

Source	SS	df	MS	F*	p	eta
Treatments	3.60	1	3.60	10.29	.04	.85
Anxiety blocks	77.40[†]	4	19.35	55.29	.002	.99
Residual	1.40	4	0.35			

*Distributed as F assuming treatments and blocks to be fixed factors and assuming no true interaction. If there *is* a true interaction, F will be too small.

†After we have studied Chapter 21 dealing with contrasts, we will be able to decompose this effect into a single-*df* contrast for linear trend ($SS = 76.05$) and a 3-*df* leftover component ($SS = 1.35$). This leftover component can be aggregated with the residual error term to yield a more stable estimate of error based on 7 *df* instead of only 4 *df*.

TABLE 20.2
Results from Table 20.1, omitting blocking

	Treatment	Control
	8	9
	6	7
	3	5
	1	3
	1	1
Σ	19	25
$\overline{X}$	3.8	5.0

Source	SS	df	MS	F	p	eta
Treatments	3.60	1	3.60	0.37	.56	.21
Residual	78.80	8	9.85			

What would have been the results of the experiment just described if we had not bothered to block? Table 20.2 shows the unblocked results and the analysis of variance. The results of the analysis of variance not employing blocking show that the effects of treatments were not significant. Comparison of the tables of variance based on blocking and no blocking shows no difference between the mean squares for treatment. However, the residual (error) variance of the unblocked analysis has been decomposed into a large between-blocks component and a small residual variance in the blocked analysis. This decomposition illustrates the essence of blocking, which is that it removes from the unblocked error variance large sources of variation known to be associated with systematic pre-experimental differences among subjects or other sampling units. The same difference between means can, therefore, be interpreted as not at all significant in the unblocked case, while it can be interpreted as clearly significant in the case employing blocking. The data of Tables 20.1 and 20.2 could also have been analyzed by means of t tests, of course: a matched-pair t test and a t test for independent samples, respectively.

ASSESSING THE BENEFITS OF BLOCKING

The advantage of blocking can be viewed in another way—in terms of the size of the sample required to achieve the same F ratio for blocked and unblocked analyses (Snedecor and Cochran, 1967, p. 311; 1980, p. 264; 1989, p. 263). The number (reps) of replications (blocks) required to achieve a given F ratio for unblocked compared with blocked designs is computed as follows:

$$\text{reps} = \frac{MS \text{ error}_{\text{unblocked}} \text{ (no. of blocks)}}{MS \text{ error}_{\text{blocked}}} \tag{1}$$

For the example we have been examining

$$\text{reps} = \frac{(9.85)\,(5)}{0.35} = 140.7$$

This unusually large value tells us that we would have to employ over 140 "pairs" of subjects in our unblocked experiment to reach the same F we obtained with 5 pairs of subjects in our blocked experiment. The tables below provide an illustration based on the data we have been examining comparing a treatment with a control group.

	Treatment	Control	Mean
Mean	3.8	5.0	4.4
N	140.7	140.7	140.7

We compute the SS between conditions by

$$\Sigma[n_k(M_k - \overline{M})^2] = 140.7(3.8 - 4.4)^2 + 140.7(5.0 - 4.4)^2 = 101.30$$

and we obtain the SS for residual from the unblocked table of variance (Table 20.2) to yield

Source	SS	df	MS	F
Treatments	101.30	1	101.30	10.28
Residual	78.80	8	9.85	

      The F of 10.28 of the table above agrees (within rounding error) with the F of 10.29 of the table of variance with blocking shown above. Equation 1 above tells us the number of replications, subjects, or blocks needed for the F of an unblocked design to match the F of a blocked design, but it makes no allowance for the change in df brought about by increasing N and eliminating the blocking variable. In this example, the df for the blocked error term was 4 (the df for the original unblocked error term was 8), and the df for the unblocked error term based on the new N required to match the blocked design F would be $2(140.7) - 2 = 279.4$. Therefore, while the old F of 10.29 with 4 df for the error term is significant at .04, the same F with 279.4 df for the error term would be significant at $p < .002$, a noticeable difference in level of significance.

      If it were desired to match the p level of the unblocked to the blocked design rather than to match the F's, we could get an approximate value with the help of some algebra. In this example with only two treatments, the number of cases required in *each* unblocked condition to match the p level of the blocked conditions is given by

$$\text{reps} = \frac{2(F_\alpha)\,(MS\text{ error})}{(M_1 - M_2)^2} \tag{2}$$

where F_α is the approximate F required for the alpha we are trying to match, MS error is the unblocked error variance, and M_1 and M_2 are the treatment condition means. For our example

$$\text{reps} = \frac{(2)\,(4.41)\,(9.85)}{(1.2)^2} = 60.33$$

Thus when we were trying to match F's, the ratio of unblocked to blocked sampling units was 140.7/5 (or about 28/1). When we tried to match p levels, the ratio of unblocked to blocked sampling units was 60.3/5 (or about 12/1). In general, it is only when the blocked experiment is very small that we find such a large difference between the matching of F's and the matching of p's.

This example was designed to illustrate a dramatic effect of blocking. We ensured this effect by choosing our results to reflect a very large correlation between the blocking variable and the dependent variable. The larger this correlation, the greater the benefits of blocking in increasing the precision of the experiment. For our example of just two treatment conditions the intraclass correlation is

$$r_{\text{I}} = \frac{MS_{\text{S}} - MS_{\text{error}}}{MS_{\text{S}} + (k - 1)MS_{\text{error}}} = \frac{MS_{\text{blocks}} - MS_{\text{error}}}{MS_{\text{blocks}} + MS_{\text{error}}} = .96$$

In this example, the correlation of the five treatment scores with their associated control scores was also .96.

BLOCKING AND THE ANALYSIS OF COVARIANCE

The *analysis of covariance* may be viewed roughly as a special case of analysis of variance, in which the observed scores have been adjusted for individual differences within conditions on some predictor variable or covariate known to correlate with the dependent variable. A typical covariate is simply the pretest administration of the same (or similar) test that is to be employed as the dependent variable.

Increasing Precision

It may have occurred to those familiar with the analysis of covariance (see the chapter on multivariate procedures) that we might profitably have employed that technique instead of the blocking method. Sometimes analysis of covariance turns out to be even better than blocking at increasing the precision of our experiments, and that is especially likely when pretest and posttest scores are most highly correlated. When pretest and posttest scores are perfectly correlated and have equal variances, analysis of covariance becomes the special case of the analysis of variance of the pre-post change scores. With respect to the magnitude of the correlation between the pretest and posttest variables, D. R. Cox (1957) has developed useful rules of thumb suggesting that:

1. Blocking may be superior to analysis of covariance in increasing precision when the correlation between the blocking variable and the dependent variable is .6 or less.
2. Analysis of covariance may be superior to blocking when the correlation reaches or exceeds .8.
3. In the region between .6 and .8 neither method seems clearly superior.

A very special advantage of blocking over the analysis of covariance must be noted, however. Blocking is equally as efficient for curvilinear as for linear relationships between independent and dependent variables. Analysis of covariance, as it is ordinarily applied, benefits us only to the extent that the relationship between independent and dependent variables is linear.[1]

To illustrate, let us return to the original data table of our example (Table 20.1). Suppose we began to interchange the labels on the rows indicating the patients' level of anxiety. Leaving the scores in their present locations, we would bring toward zero the linear correlation between the independent variable of anxiety level and the dependent variable of subsequent anxiety level, thus rendering analysis of covariance useless as it is ordinarily applied. However, interchanging labels without moving the obtained scores would have no effect on the intraclass correlation; it would remain unchanged as would the advantage of blocking. To put it another way, when analysis of covariance would work well, blocking, especially if enough levels are employed, would also work well. When blocking would work well, however, analysis of covariance (as ordinarily applied) might or might not work well.

Another advantage of blocking over analysis of covariance is that blocking can be employed even when the blocks differ in qualitative rather than quantitative ways. Thus our blocks could be pairs of twins on whom no pretests are available; groups of countries, states, businesses, adjacent plots of land; or any other partitioning of our sampling units that stratifies them such that units within blocks are thought to be more similar to one another than to units in different blocks. Blocking always imposes some cost in terms of loss of df for error, but that cost is usually small in relation to decreased MS error. At any rate, if there were little reduction in MS error associated with blocking, we could always unblock the blocking to regain our lost df.

Detecting Interactions

Most of our discussion so far has dealt with the relative benefits of blocking in increasing precision. There is another benefit to be had from blocking: the detec-

---

[1] Modern multiple regression approaches to analysis of covariance would permit us to control for quadratic, cubic, etc., relationships as well as linear relationships between the independent and dependent variables (Cohen and Cohen, 1983).

TABLE 20.3
Table of means and residuals

Age	Means		Residuals	
	Treatment	**Control**	**Treatment**	**Control**
Above 60	6	7	.33	−.33
40–59	3	6	−.67	.67
Below 40	6	7	.33	−.33

tion of interactions between the experimental and the blocking variable. In most cases when we examine such interactions, it is in designs in which each block has a number of replications for each treatment condition. Table 20.3 gives an example of blocking with replications in a study of treatment effects on the anxiety level of people of three age groups. The table of variance for these data would show mean squares for treatment, blocks, treatment × blocks interaction, and a residual (within-cell) term to serve as the denominator for F tests on the preceding terms assuming treatments and blocks to be fixed effects. The direction of the interaction is such that middle-aged persons appear to benefit more from treatment than do either older or younger persons to a greater degree than is true for the control group subjects.

When there are no replications within each combination of conditions of the treatments-by-blocks design, certain components of interactions are still testable, but only by means of conservative F tests. Such testing involves the extraction of contrasts from the overall treatments × blocks interaction (see the next chapter dealing with contrasts). The significance of such contrasts is then tested against the residual.

A NOTE ON r^2 OR eta^2

For our basic illustration of blocking we compared a treatment to a control group, once with blocking on anxiety level and once without blocking. Blocking increased the F for treatments from 0.37 to 10.29, reduced the p from .56 to .04, and increased eta (the effect size) from .21 to .85. These eta's were computed as

$$\text{eta} = \sqrt{\frac{SS \text{ treatment}}{SS \text{ treatment} + SS \text{ error}}}$$

We want to emphasize here, as we did in the chapter on the factorial design of experiments, that in this definition of r or eta we have disregarded all other sources of variance except the treatment SS (or other effect for which we are computing r or eta) and the error SS. This definition makes it possible for the sum of the values of r^2 or eta^2 to exceed 1.00, but it is a more useful definition in most instances than

$$\text{eta} = \sqrt{\frac{SS \text{ treatment}}{SS \text{ total}}}$$

That is because it reflects our growing ability to predict behavior as we successively decrease our error term by learning to specify other important sources of variance that are subtracted from the error term by means of blocking.

If we employed this latter definition of eta or r (employing SS total), we would find eta to be .21 with or without blocking. If we employed the former definition of eta or r, we would find the eta for treatments to be .85 (and .99 for anxiety blocks).

BLOCKING AND REPEATED MEASURES

Although this chapter deals specifically with blocking, we have actually encountered the idea of blocking much earlier in this book. In Chapter 15, for example, we introduced the t test for nonindependent samples, or "matched-pair t test." That t test was an example of blocking because each pair of observations came from a single block or sampling unit. Such a t test is the simplest form of a repeated-measures design, and all repeated-measures designs are examples of designs employing blocking. The more highly (positively, not negatively) correlated with each other the successive observations made on the same sampling units, the more we benefit in increased precision from having employed repeated-measures designs versus between-subjects designs.

Some of the between-subjects designs we have seen earlier, e.g., in the chapters on factorial designs and interaction effects (Chapters 16 and 17), also employed blocking on variables likely to be correlated with the dependent variable such as the sex of the patient and the diagnostic category of the patient. Typically, however, we tend to get the greatest increase of precision when we block on the sampling unit itself.

BLOCKING WITHIN BLOCKS

Imagine that we wanted to learn whether nonverbal cues from the face, the body, or tone of voice were decoded with differing degrees of accuracy. And suppose we had 30 students available to serve as decoders. Because we know that there are important individual differences in decoding accuracy, we decide to employ blocking on individual subjects, i.e., a repeated-measures design. We have 60 stimulus clips (each lasting 2 seconds) to be decoded: 20 each to test accuracy at decoding face, body, and tone of voice. The design appears to be as shown in Table 20.4.

TABLE 20.4
Channels × subjects design

	Face	Body	Tone
Subject 1			
Subject 2			
·········			
Subject 30			

But how shall we present the 60 clips or items to our decoders? If we arrange the 60 items at random, it might turn out that, by chance, face items (for example) might be overrepresented in the last half of the set of 60 stimuli. Then, if face cues turned out to be most accurately decoded, we could not be sure whether it was really the case that face cues were best decoded or only that later items were better decoded (perhaps due to practice), since the face channel was confounded with later occurrence. There are many ways to deal with this type of problem, and we describe one of these procedures here (see Rosenthal, 1987a, for further details). We divide our 60 items into 20 blocks of 3 items each. To each of our 20 blocks we assign at random one clip of the face, one of the body, and one of the tone. The design then changes to that of Table 20.5.

The original analysis of variance would have been as shown in Table 20.6. The analysis of variance with blocking to control for confounding of channels with order of presentation would be as shown in Table 20.7.

In this example blocking by order of presentation does not necessarily increase the precision of the experiment but does eliminate the potential confounding effects of order of presentation. In addition, it allows us to learn from the blocks × channels interaction the extent to which the differences between channels change over time. By the use of contrasts in the blocks × channels in-

TABLE 20.5
Channels × subjects × blocks design

		Blocks							
		1	2	3	4	.	.	.	20
Subject 1	Face Body Tone								
. . .									
Subject 30	Face Body Tone								

TABLE 20.6
Analysis of variance for Table 20.4

Source	df	Error terms
Decoders	29	
Channels	2	
Channels × decoders	58	Error term for preceding line
Items	1710	Error term for preceding line
Total	1799	

TABLE 20.7
Analysis of variance for Table 20.5

Source	df	Error terms
Decoders	29	
Channels	2	
Channels × decoders	58	Error term for preceding line
Blocks	19	
Blocks × decoders	551	Error term for preceding line
Blocks × channels	38	
Blocks × channels × decoders	1102	Error term for preceding line
Total	1799	

Note: Further details on this type of analysis are found in Chapter 18.

teraction we could learn the extent to which the superiority of one or two channels increases or decreases linearly over time. It is to the topic of contrasts that we turn in the next chapter.

CHAPTER 21

CONTRAST ANALYSIS: AN INTRODUCTION

FOCUSED VERSUS OMNIBUS F TESTS

We introduce the topic of *contrasts* (or comparisons) with a hypothetical example of a one-way analysis of variance. A developmental psychologist administered a cognitive task to a total of 50 children in a cross-sectional study. There were 10 children at each of the following age levels: 8, 9, 10, 11, 12. Tables 21.1 and 21.2, respectively, show the mean obtained at each level and the analysis of variance of these data.

The tables show us that F for age levels $= 1.03, p = .40$, i.e., that the differences among the five means are far from significant. Shall we conclude that for this study age was not an effective variable? If we did so, we would be making a very grave error, though unfortunately a fairly common one.

TABLE 21.1
Mean performance score at five age levels*

		Age levels		
8	**9**	**10**	**11**	**12**
2.0	3.0	5.0	7.0	8.0

*$n = 10$ at each age level.

TABLE 21.2
Analysis of variance of performance scores

Source	SS	df	MS	F	p
Age levels	260	4	65	1.03	.40
Within	2835	45	63		

Figure 21-1 shows the performance means of the five age levels; we see clearly that the resulting plot does not appear consistent with the conclusion that age and performance are not related. Indeed, correlating levels of age and levels of performance yields $r(3) = .992, p < .001$ (two-tailed).

How can we reconcile such clear and obvious results (the plot, the r, the p) with the results of the analysis of variance telling us that age did not matter? The answer is that the F above addresses a question that may be of relatively little interest to us. The question is diffuse and unfocused; i.e., are there *any* differences among the five groups, disregarding entirely the arrangement of the ages that constitute the levels of the independent variable? Thus, arranging the ages 8, 9, 10, 11, 12, would yield the same F as arranging them 12, 11, 10, 9, 8, or 10, 9, 11, 12, 8. This diffuse question is unlikely to have been the one our developmental researcher wanted to address. Far more likely he or she wanted to know whether performance increased with age or whether there was a *quadratic* (U-shaped or ∩-shaped) trend.

The correlation we computed addressed the more focused question of whether performance increased linearly with age. In this example the r worked well, but note that we had only 3 *df* for testing the significance of that r. We shall want a more general, flexible, and powerful way of asking focused questions of our data. Once we learn how to do this, there will be relatively few circumstances under which we will want to use unfocused, diffuse, or omnibus F tests. That, then, is the purpose of contrasts—to permit us to ask more focused questions of our data. What we get in return for the small amount of computation

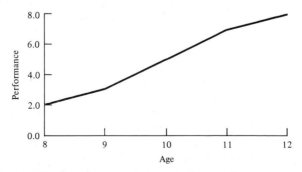

FIGURE 21-1
Mean performance score at five age levels.

required to employ contrasts is very much greater statistical power and very much greater clarity of substantive interpretation of research results.

DEFINITIONS AND AN EXAMPLE

Constrasts are comparisons, employing two or more groups, set up in such a way that the results obtained from the several conditions involved in the research are compared (or "contrasted") with the predictions based on theory, hypothesis, or hunch. These predictions are expressed as weights (called λ and pronounced "lambda"), and they can take on any convenient numerical value so long as the sum of the weights ($\Sigma\lambda$) is zero for any given contrast. Contrasts are quite easy to compute within the context of the analysis of variance. The following formula (Snedecor and Cochran, 1967, p. 308) shows the computation of a contrast in terms of a sum of squares for the single df test being made. Because contrasts are based on only one df, the sum of squares is identical with the mean square and needs only to be divided by the appropriate mean square for error to yield an F test for the contrast

$$MS \text{ contrast} = SS \text{ contrast} = \frac{L^2}{n\Sigma\lambda^2}$$

where L = sum of all condition totals (T), each of which has been multiplied by the weight (λ) called for by the hypothesis, or

$$L = \Sigma[T\lambda] = T_1\lambda_1 + T_2\lambda_2 + T_3\lambda_3 + \cdots + T_k\lambda_k$$

k = number of conditions; n = number of observations in each condition, given equal n per condition[1]; and, λ = weights required by the hypothesis such that the sum of the weights equals zero.

We can apply this formula directly to the data of our example. The means were given as 2.0, 3.0, 5.0, 7.0, and 8.0, each mean based on an n of 10. To obtain the required values of T, we multiply these means by n and get 20, 30, 50, 70, and 80. For each T we also need a λ based on our theory. If our prediction were that there would be a linear trend, i.e., that there would be a regular increment of performance for every regular increment of age, we might first think of using age levels as our λ's, and they would be 8, 9, 10, 11, 12. However, the sum of these λ's is not zero, as required, but 50. Fortunately, that is easy to correct. We simply subtract the mean age level of 10 (i.e., 50/5) from each of our λ's and thus obtain (8 − 10), (9 − 10), (10 − 10), (11 − 10), (12 − 10), or −2, −1, 0, +1, +2, a set of weights that does sum to zero. To save ourselves the effort of having to calculate these weights, Table 21.3 on page 475 provides them for linear, quadratic, and cubic orthogonal (i.e., independent) trends, curves, or polynomials (algebraic expressions of two or more terms) (after Snedecor and Cochran, 1967, p. 572). Later in this chapter these orthogonal polynomials will be described in more detail.

---

[1] Later in this chapter we discuss the situation of unequal n per condition.

For our present example we have

	Age Level					
	8	**9**	**10**	**11**	**12**	**Σ**
T	20	30	50	70	80	250
λ	-2	-1	0	$+1$	$+2$	0
$T\lambda$	-40	-30	0	70	160	160

In our formula for SS contrast, we need L^2, n, and $\Sigma\lambda^2$. $L = \Sigma[T\lambda] = 160$, so $L^2 = (160)^2$; $n = 10$ as given earlier, and $\Sigma\lambda^2 = (-2)^2 + (-1)^2 + (0)^2 + (+1)^2 + (+2)^2 = 10$. So,

$$\frac{L^2}{n\Sigma\lambda^2} = \frac{(160)^2}{10(10)} = 256 = SS \text{ contrast} = MS \text{ contrast}$$

To compute the F test for this contrast we need only divide it by the mean square for error of our analysis of variance to find $F(1, 45) = 256/63 = 4.06$, $p = .05$. Since all F's employed to test contrasts have only one df in the numerator, we can always take the square root of these F's to obtain the t test for the contrast, in case we want to make a one-tailed t test. In this example a one-tailed t test would be quite sensible, and $t(45) = 2.02$, $p = .025$, one-tailed.

It is characteristic of contrast sums of squares that they are identical whether we employ a given set of weights or their opposite, i.e., the weights multiplied by -1. Thus, had we used the weights $+2$, $+1$, 0, -1, -2 instead of the weights -2, -1, 0, $+1$, $+2$ in the preceding example, we would have obtained identical results, namely, SS contrast $= 256$, and $F(1, 45) = 4.06$, $p = .05$. This p value, though one-tailed in the F distribution (in that it refers only to the right-hand portion of the F distribution) is two-tailed with respect to the hypothesis that performance increases with age. If we take $\sqrt{F} = t$, we must be very careful in making one-tailed t tests to be sure that the results do in fact bear out our prediction and not its opposite. A convenient device is to give t a positive sign when the result is in the predicted direction (e.g., performance improves with age) and a negative sign when the result is in the opposite direction (e.g., performance worsens with age).

To estimate the size of the effect of the linear relationship between performance and age, we can employ the information that

$$r = \sqrt{\frac{(df \text{ numerator})F}{(df \text{ numerator})F + df \text{ denominator}}} = \sqrt{\frac{t^2}{t^2 + df}}$$

$$= \sqrt{\frac{4.06}{4.06 + 45}} = .29$$

Thus, the correlation (r) between age level and average performance level is of moderate size. An alternative computational formula for the effect size r is

$$r = \sqrt{\frac{SS \text{ contrast}}{SS \text{ contrast} + SS \text{ error}}} = \sqrt{\frac{256}{256 + 2835}} = .29$$

What if we had divided the SS contrast by the total SS between age groups and taken the square root? We would have found $\sqrt{256/260} = .992$, exactly the r we obtained earlier by direct computation of the correlation between age level and mean performance level. This r, based on only 3 df, was valuable to us as an alerting device that we were about to make an error by forgetting to take account of the increasing nature of age. However, the r of .992 is a poor estimate of the relationship between individual children's age and performance, though it does a better job of estimating the correlation of age and performance for the mean age and mean performance of groups of children, with $n = 10$ per group. (Not only in this example but generally as well, it is often the case that correlations based on groups or other aggregated data are higher than those based on the original nonaggregated data.)

ADDITIONAL EXAMPLES

Testing for linear trend in age is a natural procedure for developmental researchers, but other contrasts may be preferred under some conditions. Suppose our investigator were confident only that 12-year-olds would be superior to 8-year-olds. The investigator could have chosen weights (λ's) as follows:

	8	9	10	11	12	Σ
			Age Level			
T	20	30	50	70	80	250
λ	-1	0	0	0	$+1$	0
$T\lambda$	-20	0	0	0	$+80$	60

The SS contrast then would have been

$$\frac{L^2}{n\Sigma\lambda^2} = \frac{(60)^2}{10(2)} = 180 = MS \text{ contrast}$$

which, when divided by the mean square for error of our earlier analysis of variance, yields

$$F(1, 45) = \frac{180}{63} = 2.86$$

and therefore $t(45) = 1.69$, $p = .05$, one-tailed.

Comparing the 12-year-olds to the 8-year-olds is something we knew how to do even before we knew about contrasts (see Chapter 15). We could simply compute the t test to compare these groups. Had we done so we would have found

$$t = \frac{M_1 - M_2}{\sqrt{\left(\frac{1}{n_1} + \frac{1}{n_2}\right)MS \text{ error}}} = \frac{8.0 - 2.0}{\sqrt{\left(\frac{1}{10} + \frac{1}{10}\right)63}} = 1.69$$

$df = 45$ (the df associated with the mean square error), $p = .05$, one-tailed. Comparing the ordinary t test with the contrast t test shows them to be identical, as indeed they should be. Note that in both cases we employed the MS error based on all five groups, not just on the two groups being compared.

Suppose now that our hypothesis had been that both the 8- and 9-year-olds would score significantly lower than the 12-year-olds. We could then have chosen weights (λ's) as follows:

	Age Level					
	8	9	10	11	12	Σ
T	20	30	50	70	80	250
λ	-1	-1	0	0	$+2$	0
$T\lambda$	-20	-30	0	0	160	110

(Recall that our λ's must add to zero, so that the $\lambda = +2$ of the 12-year-olds is needed to balance the -1 and -1 of the 8- and 9-year-olds.)

The SS contrast would have been

$$\frac{L^2}{n\Sigma\lambda^2} = \frac{(110)^2}{10(6)} = 201.67 = MS \text{ contrast}$$

which, when divided by the mean square for error of our earlier analysis of variance, yields

$$F(1, 45) = \frac{201.67}{63} = 3.20$$

and $t(45) = 1.79$, $p = .04$, one-tailed.

Had we decided to compute a simple t test between the mean of the 8- and 9-year-olds and the mean of the 12-year-olds, we could have done so as follows:

$$t = \frac{M_1 - M_2}{\sqrt{\left(\frac{1}{n_1} + \frac{1}{n_2}\right)MS \text{ error}}} = \frac{8.0 - 2.5}{\sqrt{\left(\frac{1}{10} + \frac{1}{20}\right)63}} = 1.79$$

with $df = 45$ and $p = .04$, one-tailed. M_2 is found from $(2.0 + 3.0)/2 = 2.5$ and n_2 is given by n (8-year-olds) + n (9-year-olds) = 20.

Once again the two methods of computing t yield identical results.

UNEQUAL n PER CONDITION

So far in our discussion of contrasts we have assumed equal n per condition. When n's are not equal, we employ an unweighted means approach (see Chapter 16). Our basic formula for computing SS contrast is $L^2/n\Sigma\lambda^2$, which can be rewritten as $(\Sigma T\lambda)^2/n\Sigma\lambda^2$. To employ the unweighted means procedure we redefine the T and the n of the preceding formula, so that n becomes the harmonic mean of the n's, and T becomes the mean of the condition multiplied by the harmonic mean of the n's thus:

$$\text{Redefined } n = \frac{k}{\Sigma\,(1/n)} = \bar{n}_h \text{ (harmonic mean } n)$$

where k is the number of conditions and $\Sigma(1/n)$ is the sum of the reciprocals of the n's, and redefined $T = M\bar{n}_h$, where M is the mean of a condition and $\bar{n}_h$ is n as redefined above.

If we had a study of five conditions in which the n's were 10, 10, 10, 10, and 10, the arithmetic mean n and the harmonic mean n would both $= 10$. If the same 50 observations were allocated to conditions as 4, 6, 10, 14, 16, the arithmetic mean n would still be 10 but the harmonic mean n would only be 7.69, since

$$\frac{k}{\Sigma\dfrac{1}{n}} = \frac{5}{\left(\dfrac{1}{4} + \dfrac{1}{6} + \dfrac{1}{10} + \dfrac{1}{14} + \dfrac{1}{16}\right)} = 7.69$$

It would always be appropriate to employ the redefined n and redefined T, since they are required when n's are unequal and since they are identical with the original definitions of n and T when n's are equal. The equivalence of $\bar{n}_h$ to n when the n's are equal is shown by

$$\bar{n}_h = \frac{k}{\Sigma\dfrac{1}{n}} = \frac{k}{k\left(\dfrac{1}{n}\right)} = n \qquad \text{when } n\text{'s are equal}$$

The unweighted means procedure employing harmonic mean n's works very well when sample sizes are not greatly different from one another. An alternative procedure that is always appropriate but that may be preferred when n's are more different from one another is as follows:

$$SS \text{ contrast} = \frac{[\Sigma(T_i/n_i)\lambda_i]^2}{\Sigma(\lambda_i^2/n_i)}$$

where T_i/n_i is the mean of the ith condition, and λ_i and n_i are the contrast weight and sample size for the ith mean. If we prefer, we can also use the above relationship to compute directly a t test for any contrast as follows:

$$t = \frac{\Sigma M_i\lambda_i}{\sqrt{[\Sigma(\lambda_i^2/n_i)]S^2}}$$

where $M_i = T_i/n_i$, the mean of the ith condition or group, S^2 is the usual pooled error (MS error), and λ_i and n_i are as immediately above (Snedecor and Cochran, 1980, p. 228; 1989, p. 230).

ORTHOGONAL CONTRASTS

When we consider a set of research results based on k conditions, it is possible to compute up to $k - 1$ contrasts, each of which is uncorrelated with, or *orthogonal* to, every other contrast. Contrasts are orthogonal to each other when the correlation between them is zero, and the correlation between them will be zero when the sum of the products of the corresponding weights, or λ's, is zero. Thus the following two sets of contrast weights are orthogonal:

	Condition				
Contrast	A	B	C	D	Σ
λ_1 set	-3	-1	$+1$	$+3$	0
λ_2 set	$+1$	-1	-1	$+1$	0
Product $\lambda_1\lambda_2$	-3	$+1$	-1	$+3$	0

The set of contrast weights λ_1 can be seen to represent four points on a straight line, while the set λ_2 can be seen to represent four points on a U-shaped function. The third row, labeled $\lambda_1\lambda_2$, shows the products of these linear and quadratic weights, which add up to zero and are thus orthogonal.

A particularly useful set of orthogonal contrasts based on the coefficients of orthogonal polynomials (curves or trends) should be considered whenever the k conditions of the study can be arranged from the smallest to the largest levels of the independent variable, as is the case when age levels, dosage levels, learning trials, or other ordered levels constitute the independent variable. Table 21.3 shows us that when there are three levels or conditions (represented as $k = 3$), the weights defining a linear trend are -1, 0, $+1$, while the orthogonal weights defining the quadratic trend are $+1$, -2, $+1$. No matter how many levels of k there may be, the linear trend λ's always show a consistent gain (or loss), while the quadratic trend λ's always show a change in direction from down to up in a U curve (or up to down in a $\cap$ curve). Cubic trends, which can be assessed when there are four or more conditions, show two changes of direction, from up to down to up (or down to up to down).

Figure 21-2 shows the results of three hypothetical studies that were (a) perfectly linear, (b) perfectly quadratic, and (c) perfectly cubic. The three figures show idealized results. In most real-life applications we find combinations of linear and nonlinear results. For example, the results in Figure 21-3 show a curve that has both strong linear and strong quadratic components.

TABLE 21.3
Weights for orthogonal polynomial-based contrasts

		Ordered conditions									
k*	Polynomial†	1	2	3	4	5	6	7	8	9	10
2	Linear	−1	+1								
3	Linear	−1	0	+1							
	Quadratic	+1	−2	+1							
4	Linear	−3	−1	+1	+3						
	Quadratic	+1	−1	−1	+1						
	Cubic	−1	+3	−3	+1						
5	Linear	−2	−1	0	+1	+2					
	Quadratic	+2	−1	−2	−1	+2					
	Cubic	−1	+2	0	−2	+1					
6	Linear	−5	−3	−1	+1	+3	+5				
	Quadratic	+5	−1	−4	−4	−1	+5				
	Cubic	−5	+7	+4	−4	−7	+5				
7	Linear	−3	−2	−1	0	+1	+2	+3			
	Quadratic	+5	0	−3	−4	−3	0	+5			
	Cubic	−1	+1	+1	0	−1	−1	+1			
8	Linear	−7	−5	−3	−1	+1	+3	+5	+7		
	Quadratic	+7	+1	−3	−5	−5	−3	+1	+7		
	Cubic	−7	+5	+7	+3	−3	−7	−5	+7		
9	Linear	−4	−3	−2	−1	0	+1	+2	+3	+4	
	Quadratic	+28	+7	−8	−17	−20	−17	−8	+7	+28	
	Cubic	−14	+7	+13	+9	0	−9	−13	−7	+14	
10	Linear	−9	−7	−5	−3	−1	+1	+3	+5	+7	+9
	Quadratic	+6	+2	−1	−3	−4	−4	−3	−1	+2	+6
	Cubic	−42	+14	+35	+31	+12	−12	−31	−35	−14	+42

*Number of conditions.
†Shape of trend.

We have noted that it is possible to compute up to $k - 1$ orthogonal contrasts among a set of k means or totals. Thus if we had four conditions, we could compute three orthogonal contrasts, each based on a different polynomial or trend, the linear, quadratic, and cubic. The sums of squares of these three contrasts would add up to the total sum of squares among the four conditions. However, although there are only $k - 1$ orthogonal contrasts in a given set, such as those based on orthogonal polynomials, there is an infinite number of *sets* of contrasts that could be computed, each of which is made up of $k - 1$ orthogonal contrasts. The *sets* of contrasts, however, would not be orthogonal to one another. For example, in the following contrasts, set I comprises mutually orthogo-

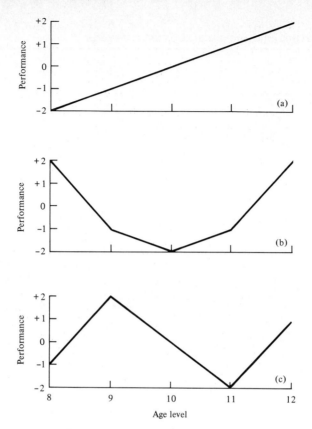

FIGURE 21-2
Illustrations of (*a*) linear, (*b*) quadratic, and (*c*) cubic trends.

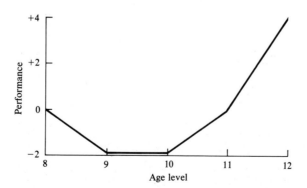

FIGURE 21-3
Curve showing linear and quadratic components.

nal contrasts, as does set II, but none of the three contrasts in set I is orthogonal to any of the contrasts of set II:

	Contrast set I					Contrast set II			
	A	B	C	D		A	B	C	D
λ_1	−3	−1	+1	+3	λ_1	−1	−1	−1	+3
λ_2	+1	−1	−1	+1	λ_2	−1	−1	+2	0
λ_3	−1	+3	−3	+1	λ_3	−1	+1	0	0

NONORTHOGONAL CONTRASTS

Although there is some advantage to employing orthogonal contrasts, in that each contrast addresses a fresh and nonoverlapping question, there is no a priori reason not to employ correlated (or nonorthogonal) contrasts. An especially valuable use of these contrasts is in the comparison of certain plausible competing hypotheses. Suppose we tested children at age levels 6, 8, 10, and 12. One plausible developmental prediction (which we call hypothesis I) is for a constant rate of improvement with age, while a rival hypothesis (II) predicts only that 12-year-olds will differ from all younger children. Table 21.4 shows the results of this research, the contrast weights used to test each hypothesis, the sums of squares associated with each contrast, and the sums of squares between all conditions ($df = 3$).

TABLE 21.4
Mean performance score at four age levels*

	Age levels				
	6	8	10	12	Σ
Means	4.0	4.0	5.0	7.0	20
Hypothesis I λ's	−3	−1	+1	+3	0
Hypothesis II λ's	−1	−1	−1	+3	0

$$SS_I = \frac{L^2}{n\Sigma\lambda^2} = \frac{(\Sigma T\lambda)^2}{n\Sigma\lambda^2} = \frac{[40(-3) + 40(-1) + 50(+1) + 70(+3)]^2}{10[(-3)^2 + (-1)^2 + (+1)^2 + (+3)^2]} = 50$$

$$SS_{II} = \frac{L^2}{n\Sigma\lambda^2} = \frac{(\Sigma T\lambda)^2}{n\Sigma\lambda^2} = \frac{[40(-1) + 40(-1) + 50(-1) + 70(+3)]^2}{10[(-1)^2 + (-1)^2 + (-1)^2 + (+3)^2]} = 53.3$$

$$SS \text{ between conditions} = \frac{(40)^2}{10} + \frac{(40)^2}{10} + \frac{(50)^2}{10} + \frac{(70)^2}{10} - \frac{(200)^2}{40} = 60$$

*$n = 10$ at each age level.

Both the contrasts do a good job of fitting the data, with SS_I taking up 50/60 (or 83 percent) of the between-conditions SS and SS_{II} taking up 53.3/60 (or 89 percent) of the between-conditions SS. Hypothesis II did a bit better than hypothesis I but probably not enough better to make us give up hypothesis I. That both hypotheses did well should not surprise us too much, since the correlation between the weights representing the two hypotheses was quite substantial ($r = .77$). There might even have been a third hypothesis that predicted that 6- and 12-year-olds would differ most but that 8- and 10-year-olds would not differ from one another. Such a prediction would have been expressed by hypothesis III λ's of $-1, 0, 0, +1$. Hypothesis III would have been correlated .95 with hypothesis I and .82 with hypothesis II. The SS contrast for this set of weights would be 45, accounting for 75 percent of the total variance among conditions. If we should want to assess the various hypotheses, controlling for or adjusting for the contribution of one or more correlated hypotheses, we can do so by means of partial correlations (see Chapter 24).

TWO-WAY ANALYSES OF VARIANCE

So far, our discussion has dealt only with contrasts taken among the means of the conditions of a one-way analysis of variance. We now consider the decomposition of the main effects and interactions of two-way analyses of variance into appropriate and informative contrasts. Table 21.5 shows the hypothetical results of an experiment on the treatment of depression. We see that there were four levels of the treatment factor and three levels of the age factor. There were 40 patients each in the older, middle-aged, and younger samples, and 10 of these patients were randomly assigned to each of the four treatment conditions. Two of the treatment groups were hospitalized and two were not. Within the former conditions, one group was treated traditionally while the other received milieu (environmental) therapy. Within the latter conditions, one group was given psychotherapy while the other was given a new companionship program. This table

TABLE 21.5
Hypothetical results of an experiment in treating depression

| Patient age | Nonhospitalization | | Hospitalization | | |
	Psychotherapy A	Companionship program B	Traditional treatment C	Milieu therapy D	Σ
Old	5 $^{\lfloor 10}$	7	2	2	16 $^{\lfloor 40}$
Middle-aged	9	7	4	8	28
Young	7	7	0	2	16
Σ	21 $^{\lfloor 30}$	21	6	12	60 $^{\lfloor 120}$

Note: Data are sums of benefit scores; $n = 10$. The figures within the "∟" symbols indicate the number of observations on which the total is based.

TABLE 21.6
Traditional analysis of variance of data in Table 21.5

Source	SS	df	MS	F	eta	p
Treatment	5.40	3	1.80	36.00	.71	$1/10^{15}$
Age	2.40	2	1.20	24.00	.55	$1/10^{8}$
Interaction	1.60	6	.27	5.34	.48	$1/10^{4}$
Within	5.40	108	.05			

shows the *sums* of the 10 observations for each of the 12 combinations of treatment and age. Table 21.6 gives the traditional two-way analysis of variance of these data, an analysis we regard as merely preliminary.

DECOMPOSITION OF MAIN EFFECTS

For our contrast analysis, we start by computing a set of orthogonal contrasts among the four levels of treatments. There are three questions we wish to address by means of these contrasts: (a) Does hospitalization make a difference? (b) Given nonhospitalization, does psychotherapy differ from the companionship program? (c) Given hospitalization, does traditional treatment differ from milieu therapy? Table 21.7 shows the treatment totals (taken from Table 21.5), the weights (λ) assigned for each of our three orthogonal contrasts, and $T\lambda$ the product of the totals T × the weights λ. Note that the weights are assigned according to the particular questions to be answered. For λ_1 the weights are consistent with question (a), which contrasts hospitalization (traditional and milieu) with nonhospitalization (psychotherapy and companionship). For λ_2 the weights

TABLE 21.7
Treatment totals and contrast weights

	Nonhospitalization		Hospitalization		
	Psychotherapy	Companionship	Traditional	Milieu	Σ
T (Totals)	$21^{\lfloor 30}$	$21^{\lfloor 30}$	$6^{\lfloor 30}$	$12^{\lfloor 30}$	$60^{\lfloor 120}$
λ_1 (nonhospital vs. hospital)	+1	+1	−1	−1	0
λ_2 (psychotherapy vs. companionship)	+1	−1	0	0	0
λ_3 (traditional vs. milieu)	0	0	−1	+1	0
$T\lambda_1$	21	21	−6	−12	24
$T\lambda_2$	21	−21	0	0	0
$T\lambda_3$	0	0	−6	+12	6

Note: The figures within the "⌐" symbols indicate the number of observations on which the total is based.

are consistent with question (b), which contrasts only the two nonhospitalization treatments, therefore assigning zero weights to the irrelevant treatments. For λ_3, which addresses question (c), this is reversed, with the zero weights now assigned to the nonhospitalization treatments.

The right-hand column of Table 21.7 provides the sums of the preceding four column entries. The first value (60) is the grand sum of all scores for the study. The next three values reassure us that we have met the requirement that contrast weights must sum to zero. The final three values (24, 0, and 6) are the sums of $T\lambda$ products, or the L's we require to compute contrasts. Since SS's are given by $L^2/n\Sigma\lambda^2$, our three contrast SS's are

$$\text{Contrast } SS_1 \text{ (nonhospital vs. hospital)} = \frac{(24)^2}{30(4)} = 4.8$$

$$\text{Contrast } SS_2 \text{ (psychotherapy vs. companionship)} = \frac{(0)^2}{30(2)} = 0.0$$

$$\text{Contrast } SS_3 \text{ (traditional vs. milieu)} = \frac{(6)^2}{30(2)} = 0.6$$

Summing these three SS's yields 5.4, which is equal to the total between-treatments SS based on 3 df, as shown in Table 21.6. Special note should be made of the fact that n is always the number of cases on which the total (T) is based. In the present contrasts, each T is based on 30 observations (10 at each of three age levels). Had the number of observations in the $4 \times 3 = 12$ conditions been unequal, we would have redefined T for each of the 12 conditions as the mean score for that condition multiplied by the harmonic mean of the n's of the 12 conditions. In that case the treatment sums would have become the sum of the three redefined values of T, because each treatment total is made up of three conditions, one at each age level. The n for that treatment total would then become three times the harmonic mean n. We postpone interpretation of our contrasts until we come to our final table of variance.

We turn next to the decomposition of the patients' age factor into two orthogonal contrasts. In this case, since age is an ordered variable (rather than categorical or nominal), we turn to the table of weights for orthogonal polynomial-based contrasts (Table 21.3) to find the weights for a linear and a quadratic trend. We see that for a three-level factor the weights for linear and quadratic trends are $-1, 0, +1$ and $+1, -2, +1$, respectively. The linear trend addresses the question of whether older patients benefit more (or less) from the average treatment than younger patients. The quadratic trend addresses the question of whether middle-aged patients benefit more (or less) from the average treatment than do (the average of) the older and younger patients. Table 21.8 shows the age-effect totals of our earlier table, the weights assigned for each of our two orthogonal polynomial contrasts, and the product of totals × weights ($T\lambda$).

We compute the contrast SS for the linear trend by

$$\frac{L^2}{n\Sigma\lambda^2} = \frac{[16(+1) + 28(0) + 16(-1)]^2}{40[(+1)^2 + (0)^2 + (-1)^2]} = \frac{(0)^2}{40(2)} = 0.0$$

TABLE 21.8
Age-effect totals and contrast weights

Patient age	Totals	Linear (λ_1)	Quadratic (λ_2)	Totals × λ_1	Totals × λ_2
Old	$16\underline{|40}$	+1	+1	16	16
Middle-aged	$28\underline{|40}$	0	−2	0	−56
Young	$16\underline{|40}$	−1	+1	−16	16
Σ	$60\underline{|120}$	0	0	0	−24

Note: The figures within the "∟" symbols indicate the number of observations on which the total is based.

and we compute the contrast SS for the quadratic trend by

$$\frac{L^2}{n\Sigma\lambda^2} = \frac{[16(+1) + 28(-2) + 16(+1)]^2}{40[(+1)^2 + (-2)^2 + (+1)^2]} = \frac{(-24)^2}{40(6)} = 2.4$$

Adding these two SS yields 2.4, which is equal to the total between-age SS based on 2 *df* and shown in our table of variance (Table 21.6). We postpone interpretation of our contrasts until we come to our final table of variance.

DECOMPOSITION OF INTERACTION EFFECTS

Having decomposed the main effects of treatments and of age, we turn our attention now to the decomposition of the interaction effects. Many kinds of contrasts could be employed to decompose the interaction. One that is frequently used in two-factor studies addresses the question of whether the contrasts of one main effect are altered by the contrasts of the other main effect. For example, we might ask whether the predicted effect of hospitalization varies as a function of linear trend in age, e.g., so that younger patients benefit more than older ones from nonhospitalization. Constructing the contrast weights for these crossed (interaction) contrasts is accomplished by multiplying the contrast weight (λ) defining the column-effect contrast (treatments, in this example) by the contrast weight (λ) defining the row-effect contrast (patient age, in this example), as is shown in Table 21.9.

To obtain the entries of column 1 under treatment contrast, we multiply the heading λ of column 1 (psychotherapy) by each of the three row λ's (patient age). In this case, multiplying +1 by +1, 0, −1 in turn yields +1, 0, −1. Results for column 2 (companionship) are identical. For column 3 (traditional), we multiply −1 by +1, 0, −1 and obtain −1, 0, +1; the same result is obtained for column 4 (milieu).

Interpretation of the Contrasts

Since we had three treatment-effect contrasts and two age-effect contrasts (as shown in Tables 21.7 and 21.8), we can obtain six crossed-interaction contrasts by

TABLE 21.9
Construction of crossed (interaction) contrast weights by multiplying column × row contrast weights

| | | Treatment contrast | | | | |
| | | Nonhospitalization | | Hospitalization | | |
Patient age	Age contrast	Psychotherapy +1	Companionship +1	Traditional −1	Milieu −1	Σ*
Old	+1	+1	+1	−1	−1	0
Middle-aged	0	0	0	0	0	0
Young	−1	−1	−1	+1	+1	0
Σ*		0	0	0	0	0

*Note that the row and column sums must be zero for contrast weights that are exclusively part of interaction effects.

crossing each treatment contrast by each age contrast. These six contrasts are:

1. Hospitalization vs. nonhospitalization × linear trend in age
2. Psychotherapy vs. companionship × linear trend in age
3. Traditional vs. milieu therapy × linear trend in age
4. Hospitalization vs. nonhospitalization × quadratic trend in age
5. Psychotherapy vs. companionship × quadratic trend in age
6. Traditional vs. milieu therapy × quadratic trend in age

Table 21.10 shows the construction of the weights for these crossed (interaction) contrasts, and Table 21.11 shows the computation of the sums of squares for two of these contrasts, numbers (1) and (4). The sums of squares of the remaining contrasts, which were similarly computed, are reported in Table 21.12.

Table 21.12 shows the two-factor analysis of variance (that was shown earlier in Table 21.6) now fully decomposed so that we have a contrast for each of the 3 *df* for treatment, for each of the 2 *df* for age level, and for each of the 6 *df* for the treatments × age levels interaction. The last column gives the magnitudes of each effect in terms of *r*, and we shall interpret our results in order of their effect size. It should be noted that to learn the direction of each of these effects we must examine the means or the residuals defining main effects and the residuals defining the interactions. The table of variance does not yield that information.

(H)   Hospitalization: Better outcomes accrue to the nonhospitalized than to the hospitalized; part of treatment effect.

(Q)   Quadratic trend: Better outcomes accrue to the middle-aged than to the average of the young and old; part of age effect.

TABLE 21.10
Construction of crossed (interaction) contrast weights by multiplying column × row contrast weights: six contrasts

Patient age	Age contrast	Interaction set	Nonhospitalization		Hospitalization		
			Psychotherapy	Companionship	Traditional	Milieu	
			+1	+1	−1	−1	*
Old	+1	1	+1†	+1	−1	−1	
Middle	0		0	0	0	0	
Young	−1		−1	−1	+1	+1	
			+1	−1	0	0	*
Old	+1	2	+1	−1	0	0	
Middle	0		0	0	0	0	
Young	−1		−1	+1	0	0	
			0	0	−1	+1	*
Old	+1	3	0	0	−1	+1	
Middle	0		0	0	0	0	
Young	−1		0	0	+1	−1	

483

TABLE 21.10 *(continued)*

Patient age	Age contrast	Interaction set	Nonhospitalization		Hospitalization		
			Psychotherapy	**Companionship**	**Traditional**	**Milieu**	
			+1	**+1**	**−1**	**−1**	*
Old	**+1**	**4**	+1	+1	−1	−1	
Middle	**−2**		−2	−2	+2	+2	
Young	**+1**		+1	+1	−1	−1	
			+1	**−1**	**0**	**0**	*
Old	**+1**	**5**	+1	−1	0	0	
Middle	**−2**		−2	+2	0	0	
Young	**+1**		+1	−1	0	0	
			0	**0**	**−1**	**+1**	*
Old	**+1**	**6**	0	0	−1	+1	
Middle	**−2**		0	0	+2	−2	
Young	**+1**		0	0	−1	+1	

*Treatment contrast weights.

†Such interaction contrast entries are the products of the contrast weights (λ) of the row and of the column into which the entry falls. In this example, since this entry falls into a row with $\lambda = +1$ and a column with $\lambda = +1$ it is equal to $(+1)(+1) = +1$.

TABLE 21.11
Computation of sums of squares for contrasts (1) and (4) of Table 21.10

Patient age	Nonhospitalization		Hospitalization	
	Psychotherapy	Companionship	Traditional	Milieu

a. Subtable of condition totals from Table 21.5 ($n = 10$ per condition)

Old	5	7	2	2
Middle	9	7	4	8
Young	7	7	0	2

b. Subtable of residuals defining interaction*

Old	−1	1	1	−1
Middle	0	−2	0	2
Young	1	1	−1	−1

c. Subtable of contrast computations

$$\text{Contrast } SS = \frac{L^2}{n\Sigma\lambda^2}$$

$$\text{Contrast } SS(1) = \frac{[-1(+1) + 1(+1) + 1(-1) + -1(-1) + 0(0) + -2(0) + 0(0) + 2(0) +}{10[(+1)^2 + (+1)^2 + (-1)^2 + (-1)^2 + (0)^2 + (0)^2 + (0)^2 + (0)^2 +}$$

$$\frac{1(-1) + 1(-1) + -1(+1) + -1(+1)]^2}{(-1)^2 + (-1)^2 + (+1)^2 + (+1)^2]} = \frac{(-4)^2}{10(8)} = 0.2$$

$$\text{Contrast } SS(4) = \frac{[-1(+1) + 1(+1) + 1(-1) + -1(-1) + 0(-2) + -2(-2) + 0(+2) +}{10[(+1)^2 + (+1)^2 + (-1)^2 + (-1)^2 + (-2)^2 + (-2)^2 + (+2)^2 + (+2)^2 +}$$

$$\frac{2(+2) + 1(+1) + 1(+1) + -1(-1) + -1(-1)]^2}{(+1)^2 + (+1)^2 + (-1)^2 + (-1)^2]} = \frac{(12)^2}{10(24)} = 0.6$$

*Computed from subtable (a) by subtracting the grand mean, column effects, and row effects from the original cell entries. See the discussion of interaction effects in Chapter 17. Each of the residuals is still a sum of 10 observations, but after subtraction of row, column, and grand mean (total) effects.

(T)   Traditional: For the hospitalized, better outcomes accrue to those receiving milieu therapy rather than traditional treatment; part of treatment effect.

(HQ)   Hospital × Quadratic: Hospitalization is relatively more effective for the middle-aged than for the young and old (averaged) but nonhospitalization is relatively more effective for the young and old (averaged); part of treatment × age interaction.

(PQ)   Psychotherapy × Quadratic: For the nonhospitalized, psychotherapy is more effective for the middle-aged than for the young and old (averaged), but the companionship program is relatively more effective for the young and old (averaged).

To serve as a practice exercise, interpretation of the remaining contrasts (including TQ, which is as large as PQ) is left to the reader.

TABLE 21.12
Two-factor analysis of variance decomposed such that all between-condition _df_ are specified

Source	SS	df	MS	F	p	r
Treatment:	_(5.4)_	_(3)_	_(1.8)_	_(36)_	_(.001)_	
Hospitalized vs. not (H)	4.8	1	4.8	96	.001	.69
Psychotherapy vs. companionship (P)	0.0	1	0.0	00	—	.00
Traditional vs. milieu (T)	0.6	1	0.6	12	.001	.32
Age:	_(2.4)_	_(2)_	_(1.2)_	_(24)_	_(.001)_	
Linear trend (L)	0.0	1	0.0	0	—	.00
Quadratic trend (Q)	2.4	1	2.4	48	.001	.55
Treatment × Age	_(1.6)_	_(6)_	_(0.267)_	_(5.34)_	_(.001)_	
HL	0.2	1	0.2	4	.05	.19
PL	0.1	1	0.1	2	.20	.13
TL	0.1	1	0.1	2	.20	.13
HQ	0.6	1	0.6	12	.001	.32
PQ	0.3	1	0.3	6	.02	.23
TQ	0.3	1	0.3	6	.02	.23
Within	5.4	108	.05			

IGNORING THE FACTORIAL STRUCTURE

We have shown how to decompose the main effects and interaction of a two-way analysis of variance into several sets of orthogonal contrasts. In this section we want to emphasize that just because an experiment has a two-way structure is not sufficient reason to analyze it as such. Our first responsibility is to answer our research question. Suppose that question, put to the data of Table 21.5, were whether the middle-aged patients given psychotherapy did better than all other groups combined. We would approach that question as though we were dealing with a one-way analysis, assigning a λ of 11 to the group of middle-aged patients receiving psychotherapy and a λ of -1 to each of the remaining 11 groups of patients. Then, employing the sums shown in Table 21.5, we would find

$$\text{Contrast } SS = \frac{L^2}{n\Sigma\lambda^2} = \frac{(48)^2}{10(132)} = 1.75$$

Since Table 21.6 or a one-way analysis of variance shows the MS within to be 0.05, the F for our contrast is $1.75/0.05 = 35.00$, p very small, and $r = .49$. Computing such planned contrasts that transcend particular main effects and interactions is quite often the first thing we do, but it does not preclude our subsequent computation of contrasts based on decomposing main effects and interactions, should those contrasts address scientifically important questions.

REPEATED MEASURES AND OTHER
ADVANCED TOPICS

In this chapter all our contrasts were computed in the context of between-subjects designs. Contrasts are just as useful (in some ways more useful) in the context of repeated-measures designs. A fundamental heuristic device in that context is to form a contrast score (L) for each subject (or other sampling unit), with L defined in the usual way as

$$L = \Sigma(T\lambda) = T_1\lambda_1 + T_2\lambda_2 + \cdots + T_k\lambda_k$$

where T_i is the subject's score in each of the k conditions or occasions of measurement and λ_i is the contrast weight assigned to that particular condition or occasion (Snedecor and Cochran, 1980, pp. 330–332; 1989, pp. 329–331). Hypotheses about the differences among the means of the conditions or occasions of measurement can then be tested by employing the following t test on the mean L score:

$$t = \frac{\bar{L}}{\sqrt{S^2/N}}$$

where $\bar{L}$ is the mean of the L scores, S^2 is computed from the L scores, and N is the number of L scores. A more detailed discussion of the computation of contrasts in repeated-measures designs than we can give here is readily available (Rosenthal and Rosnow, 1985).

Finally, when a *set* of research results is available and we want to compare these results, procedures for doing so by means of contrasts in significance levels and effect sizes are also available (Rosenthal, 1984; Rosenthal and Rubin, 1979a, 1982b, 1986). It is to this topic of comparing (and combining) the results of two or more studies that we turn in the next chapter.

PART
VIII

ADDITIONAL TOPICS IN DATA ANALYSIS

CHAPTER
22

META-ANALYSIS: COMPARING AND COMBINING RESULTS

BACKGROUND

It has become almost obligatory to end research reports with the clarion call for further research. Yet it seems fair to say that we have been better at issuing such calls than at knowing what to do with the answers. There are many areas of behavioral science for which we do in fact have available the results of numerous studies all addressing essentially the same question. The summaries of the results of these sets of studies, however, have not been nearly so informative as they might have been, either with respect to summarized significance levels or with respect to summarized effect sizes. Even the best reviews of research by the most sophisticated workers have rarely told us more about each study of a set of studies than that it did or did not reach a given p level and the direction of the relationship between the variables investigated. This state of affairs is beginning to change, however. More and more reviews of the literature are moving from the traditional, literary format to the quantitative format (e.g., Cooper and Rosenthal, 1980; Glass, McGaw, and Smith, 1981; Hall 1980, 1984b; Harris and Rosenthal, 1985; Powell, Thompson, Caspersen, and Kendrick, 1987; Rosenthal, 1980a, 1984, 1986, 1987b; Shoham-Salomon and Rosenthal, 1987.

If one were to trace historically (and ever so briefly) the development of the movement to quantify runs of studies, we might begin with Ronald Fisher (1938), for his thinking about the combination of the significance levels of independent studies; move through Frederick Mosteller and Robert Bush (1954), for their broadening of the Fisher perspective in both (a) introducing several new methods of combining independent probability levels to social and behavioral scientists and (b) showing that effect sizes as well as significance levels could be usefully combined; and end in the present day with an expanding number of investigators such as Gene V Glass (1976, 1980) and others (including Cooper, 1984, 1989; Hedges and Olkin, 1985; Hunter and Schmidt, 1990; Light and Pillemer, 1984; Light and Smith, 1971; Mullen, 1989; Mullen and Rosenthal, 1985; Pillemer and Light, 1980; Rosenthal, 1969, 1978a, 1980b, 1984; in press; Rosenthal and Rubin, 1978, 1980b, 1986, 1988; M. L. Smith, 1980; Smith and Glass, 1977; Smith, Glass, and Miller, 1980; Wachter, 1988; Wachter and Straf, in press).

COMPARING TWO STUDIES

Even when we have been quite rigorous and sophisticated in the interpretation of the results of a single study, we are often prone to err in the interpretation of two or more studies. Earlier we reported an example of such error involving a report by an investigator (say, Smith) of a significant relationship between X and Y followed by a rebuttal by another investigator (say, Jones) that there was no such relationship. A closer look at their data showed that Smith's results—$t(78) = 2.21$, $p < .05$, $d = .50$, $r = .24$—were more significant than Jones's results—$t(18) = 1.06$, $p > .30$, $d = .50$, $r = .24$—but that the studies were in perfect agreement as to their estimated sizes of effect defined by either d or r. A comparison of their respective significance levels by procedures to be described below reveals, furthermore, that these p's are not significantly different ($p = .42$). Clearly Jones was wrong in claiming that he had failed to replicate Smith's results. We shall begin this section by considering some procedures for comparing quantitatively the results of two independent studies, e.g., studies conducted with different research participants or other sampling units.

As a handy guide to the 20 examples that follow, Table 22.1 lists each example number and the meta-analytic procedure it illustrates.

TABLE 22.1
Guide to 20 examples of meta-analytic procedures

	Example numbers	
	Significance testing	Effect-size estimation
Comparing:		
Two studies	1, 2, 3	4, 5, 6
Three or more studies		
Diffuse tests	13	14
Focused tests	15	16
Combining:		
Two studies	7, 8, 9	10, 11, 12
Three or more studies	17, 18	19, 20

Significance Testing

Ordinarily when we compare the results of two studies, we are more interested in comparing their effect sizes than their p values. However, sometimes we cannot do any better than comparing their p values, and here is how we do it (Rosenthal and Rubin, 1979a): For each of the two test statistics we obtain an accurate p level, accurate, say, to two digits (not counting zeros before the first nonzero value), such as $p = .43$ or .024, or .0012. That is, if $t(30) = 3.03$, we give p as .0025, not as "$<.05$." Extended tables of the t distribution are helpful here (e.g., Federighi, 1959, which is reproduced in Table B.3, Appendix B) as are inexpensive calculators with built-in distributions of Z, t, F, and χ^2. For each p we find Z, the standard normal deviate corresponding to the p value. The last row of Table B.3 just cited and the table of Z's of Appendix B will both be useful in finding the accurate Z. Both p's should be one-tailed, and the corresponding Z's will have the same sign if both studies show effects in the same direction, but different signs if the results are in the opposite direction. It is customary to assign positive signs to Z's falling in the predicted direction and negative signs to Z's falling in the unpredicted direction. The difference between the two Z's when divided by $\sqrt{2}$ yields a new Z that corresponds to the p value that the difference between the Z's could be so large, or larger, if the two Z's did not really differ. Recapping,

$$\frac{Z_1 - Z_2}{\sqrt{2}}$$

is distributed as Z, so we can enter this newly calculated Z in a table of Z's (Appendix B, Table B.1) to find the p value associated with finding a Z of the size obtained or larger.

EXAMPLE 1. Studies A and B yield results in opposite directions, and neither is "significant." One p is .06, one-tailed, the other is .12, one-tailed, but in the opposite tail. The Z's corresponding to these p's are found in a table of the normal curve to be $+1.56$ and -1.18 (note the opposite signs to indicate results in opposite directions). Then, from the preceding equation we have

$$\frac{Z_1 - Z_2}{\sqrt{2}} = \frac{(1.56) - (-1.18)}{1.41} = 1.94$$

as the Z of the difference between the two p values or their corresponding Z's. The p value associated with a Z of 1.94 is .026, one-tailed, or .052, two-tailed. The two p values thus may be seen to differ significantly, or nearly so, suggesting that the results of the two studies are not consistent with respect to significance levels even allowing for normal sampling fluctuation.

EXAMPLE 2. Studies A and B yield results in the same direction, and both are significant. One p is .04, the other is .000025. The Z's corresponding to these p's are 1.75 and 4.06 (since both Z's are in the same tail, they have the same sign).

From the preceding equation we have

$$\frac{Z_1 - Z_2}{\sqrt{2}} = \frac{(4.06) - (1.75)}{1.41} = 1.64$$

as our obtained Z of the difference. The p associated with that Z is .05, one-tailed, or .10, two-tailed, so we may want to conclude that the two p values differ significantly, or nearly so. It should be emphasized, however, that finding one Z greater than another does not tell us whether that Z was greater because the size of the effect was greater, the size of the study was greater, or both.

EXAMPLE 3. Studies A and B yield results in the same direction, but one is "significant" ($p = .05$) and the other is not ($p = .06$). This illustrates the worst-case scenario for inferential errors where investigators might conclude that the two results are "inconsistent" because one is significant and the other is not. Re-grettably, this example is not merely theoretical. Just such errors have been made and documented (Nelson, Rosenthal, and Rosnow, 1986; Rosenthal and Gaito, 1963, 1964). The Z's corresponding to these p's are 1.64 and 1.55. Therefore,

$$\frac{Z_1 - Z_2}{\sqrt{2}} = \frac{(1.64) - (1.55)}{1.41} = .06$$

is our obtained Z of the difference between a p value of .05 and .06. The p value associated with this difference is .476, one-tailed, or .952, two-tailed. This example shows clearly just how trivial the difference between significant and non-significant results can be.

Effect-Size Estimation

When we ask whether two studies are telling the same story, what we usually mean is whether the results (in terms of the estimated effect size) are reasonably consistent with each other or whether they are significantly heterogeneous. For the purpose of the present chapter the discussion will be restricted to r as the effect-size indicator, but analogous procedures are available for comparing such other effect-size indicators as Cohen's d (1977, 1988) or differences between proportions (Hsu, 1980; Rosenthal and Rubin, 1982).

For each of the two studies to be compared we compute the effect-size r and find for each of these r's the associated Fisher z,[1] defined as $\frac{1}{2}\ln[(1 +$

---

[1]The advantage of the Fisher z transformation is that equal differences between any pair of Fisher z's are equally detectable, a situation that does not hold for untransformed r's. For raw r's, the difference between .00 and .86, for example (a difference of .86 units of r but a difference of 1.3 units of Fisher z), is no more detectable than the difference between .86 and .99 (a difference of .13 units of r but a difference of 1.3 units of Fisher z). In addition, significance tests of differences between r's are more accurate when this transformation is employed (Alexander, Scozzaro, and Borodkin, 1989). In this chapter we employ the lowercase z for the Fisher transformation and the capital Z for the standard normal deviate.

$r)/(1 - r)$]. A table to convert our obtained r's to Fisher z's is available in Appendix B (Table B.7). Then, when N_1 and N_2 represent the number of sampling units (e.g., subjects) in each of our two studies, the quantity

$$\frac{z_1 - z_2}{\sqrt{\dfrac{1}{N_1 - 3} + \dfrac{1}{N_2 - 3}}}$$

is distributed as Z (Snedecor and Cochran, 1967, 1980). The quantity $N - 3$ corresponds to the df for each of the z's.

EXAMPLE 4. Studies A and B yield results in opposite directions with effect sizes of $r = .60$ ($N = 15$) and $r = -.20$ ($N = 100$), respectively. The Fisher z's corresponding to these r's are .69 and $-.20$, respectively (note the opposite signs of the z's to correspond to the opposite signs of the r's). Then, from the preceding equation we have

$$\frac{(.69) - (-.20)}{\sqrt{\dfrac{1}{12} + \dfrac{1}{97}}} = 2.91$$

as the Z of the difference between the two effect sizes. The p value associated with a Z of 2.91 is .002, one-tailed, or .004, two-tailed. These two effect sizes, then, differ significantly.

EXAMPLE 5. Studies A and B yield results in the same direction with effect sizes of $r = .70$ ($N = 20$) and $r = .25$ ($N = 95$), respectively. The Fisher z's corresponding to these r's are .87 and .26, respectively. From the preceding equation we have

$$\frac{(.87) - (.26)}{\sqrt{\dfrac{1}{17} + \dfrac{1}{92}}} = 2.31$$

as our obtained Z of the difference. The p associated with that Z is .01, one-tailed, or .02, two-tailed. Here is an example of two studies that agree there is a significant positive relationship between variables X and Y, but disagree significantly in their estimates of the size of the relationship.

EXAMPLE 6. Studies A and B yield effect-size estimates of $r = .00$ ($N = 17$) and $r = .30$ ($N = 45$), respectively. The Fisher z's corresponding to these r's are .00 and .31, respectively. Therefore,

$$\frac{(.00) - (.31)}{\sqrt{\dfrac{1}{14} + \dfrac{1}{42}}} = -1.00$$

is our obtained Z of the difference between our two effect-size estimates. The p associated with that Z is .16, one-tailed, or .32, two-tailed. Here we have an example of two effect sizes, one zero ($r = .00$), the other ($r = .30$) significantly different from zero [$t(43 = 2.06, p < .025$, one-tailed], that do not differ significantly from one another. This illustrates well how careful we must be in concluding that results of two studies are heterogeneous just because one is significant and the other is not or because one has a zero estimated effect size and the other does not.

COMBINING TWO STUDIES

Significance Testing

After we compare the results of any two independent studies, it is an easy matter also to combine the p levels of the two studies. In this way we get an overall estimate of the probability that the two p levels might have been obtained if the null hypothesis of no relationship between X and Y were true. Many methods for combining the results of two or more studies are available and have been described elsewhere (Rosenthal, 1978a, 1983, 1984). Here it is necessary to give only the simplest and most versatile of the procedures, the method of adding Z's called the *Stouffer method* by Mosteller and Bush (1954).

This method, just like the method of comparing p values, asks us first to obtain accurate p levels for each of our two studies and then to find the Z corresponding to each of these p levels. Both p's must be given in one-tailed form, and the corresponding Z's will have the same sign if both studies show effects in the same direction. They will have different signs if the results are in the opposite direction. The sum of the two Z's when divided by $\sqrt{2}$ yields a new Z. This new Z corresponds to the p value that the results of the two studies combined, or results even further out in the same tail, could have occurred if the null hypothesis of no relationship between X and Y were true. Recapping,

$$\frac{Z_1 + Z_2}{\sqrt{2}}$$

is distributed as Z. Should we want to do so, we could weight each Z by its df, its estimated quality, or by any other desired weights (Mosteller and Bush, 1954; Rosenthal, 1978a, 1980, 1984).

The general procedure for weighting Z's is to (a) multiply each Z by any desired weight (symbolized by ω, the Greek letter omega, and assigned before inspection of the data), (b) add the weighted Z's, and (c) divide the sum of the weighted Z's by the square root of the sum of the squared weights as follows:

$$\text{Weighted } Z = \frac{\omega_1 Z_1 + \omega_2 Z_2}{\sqrt{\omega_1^2 + \omega_2^2}}$$

Example 9 will illustrate this procedure.

EXAMPLE 7. Studies A and B yield results in opposite directions, and both are significant. One p is .05, one-tailed; the other is .0000001, one-tailed, but in the opposite tail. The Z's corresponding to these p's are found in a table of normal deviates (see Appendix B, Table B.1) to be -1.64 and 5.20, respectively (note the opposite signs to indicate results in opposite directions). Then, we have

$$\frac{Z_1 + Z_2}{\sqrt{2}} = \frac{(-1.64) + (5.20)}{1.41} = 2.52$$

as the Z of the combined results of studies A and B. The p value associated with a Z of 2.52 is .006, one-tailed, or .012, two-tailed. Thus, the combined p supports the result of the more significant of the two results. If these were actual results, we would want to be very cautious in interpreting our combined p. This is because the two p's we combined were so very significantly different from each other. We would try to discover what differences between studies A and B might have led to results so significantly different.

EXAMPLE 8. Studies A and B yield results in the same direction, but neither is significant. One p is .11, the other is .09, and their associated Z's are 1.23 and 1.34, respectively. From the preceding equation we have

$$\frac{(1.23) + (1.34)}{1.41} = 1.82$$

as our combined Z. The p associated with that Z is .034, one-tailed, or .068, two-tailed.

EXAMPLE 9. Studies A and B are those of Example 7, but now we have found from a panel of experts that study A earns a weight (ω_1) of 3.4 on assessed internal validity while study B earns only a weight (ω_2) of .09. The Z's for studies A and B had been -1.64 and 5.20, respectively. Therefore, we find the weighted $Z(Z_\omega)$ as follows:

$$Z_\omega = \frac{(3.4)(-1.64) + (0.9)(5.20)}{\sqrt{(3.4)^2 + (0.9)^2}} = \frac{-0.896}{3.517} = -0.25$$

i.e., the Z of the weighted combined results of studies A and B. The p value associated with this Z is .40, one-tailed, or .80, two-tailed. Note that the weighting has led to a nonsignificant result in this example. In Example 7, where there was no weighting (or, more accurately, equal weighting with $\omega_1 = \omega_2 = 1$), the p value was significant at $p = .012$, two-tailed.

As a further illustration of weighting the combined Z, suppose we had wanted to weight not by quality of study but by df. If df for studies A and B had been 36 and 144, respectively, the weighted Z would have been

$$Z_\omega = \frac{(36)(-1.64) + (144)(5.20)}{\sqrt{(36)^2 + (144)^2}} = \frac{689.76}{148.43} = 4.65$$

This result shows the combined Z ($p < .000002$, one-tailed) to have been moved strongly in the direction of the Z with the larger df because of the substantial difference in df between the two studies. Note that when weighting Z's by df, we have decided to have the size of the study play a very large role in determining the combined p. The role is very large because the size of the study has already entered into the determination of each Z and is, therefore, entering a second time into the weighting process.

Effect-Size Estimation

When we want to combine the results of two studies, we are as interested in the combined estimate of the effect size as we are in the combined probability. Just as was the case when we compared two effect-size estimates, we shall consider r as our effect-size estimate in the combining of effect sizes. However, we note that many other estimates are possible (e.g., Cohen's d or differences between proportions).

For each of the two studies to be combined, we compute r and the associated Fisher z and have

$$\frac{z_1 + z_2}{2} = \bar{z}$$

as the Fisher z corresponding to our mean r. We use an r to z or z to r table (see Appendix B, Tables B.7 and B.8) to look up the r associated with our mean $\bar{z}$. Tables are preferable to finding r from z from the following: $r = (e^{2z} - 1)/(e^{2z} + 1)$ where $e \cong 2.71828$, the base of the system of natural logarithms. Should we want to do so, we could weight each Z by its df, its estimated quality, or any other desired weights assigned before inspection of the data.

The weighted mean z is obtained as follows:

$$\text{Weighted mean } z = \frac{\omega_1 z_1 + \omega_2 z_2}{\omega_1 + \omega_2}$$

Example 12 will illustrate this procedure.

EXAMPLE 10. Studies A and B yield results in opposite directions, one $r = .80$, the other $r = -.30$. The Fisher z's corresponding to these r's are 1.10 and -0.31, respectively. Therefore, we have

$$\frac{z_1 + z_2}{2} = \frac{(1.10) + (-0.31)}{2} = .395$$

as the mean Fisher z. From our z to r table we find a z of .395 associated with an r of .38.

EXAMPLE 11. Studies A and B yield results in the same direction, one $r = .95$, the other $r = .25$. The Fisher z's corresponding to these r's are 1.83 and .26, respectively. Therefore, we have

$$\frac{1.83 + .26}{2} = 1.045$$

as the mean Fisher z. From our z to r table we find a z of 1.045 to be associated with an r of .78. Note that if we had averaged the two r's without first transforming them to Fisher z's, we would have found the mean r to be $(.95 + .25)/2 = .60$, substantially smaller than .78. This illustrates that the use of Fisher's z gives heavier weight to r's that are further from zero in either direction.

EXAMPLE 12. Studies A and B are those of Example 6, but now we have decided to weight the studies by their df (i.e., $N - 3$ in this application; Snedecor and Cochran, 1967, 1980, 1989). Therefore, we replace the general weight indicators ω_1 and ω_2 by df_1 and df_2 to find the weighted mean z from

$$\text{Weighted } \bar{z} = \frac{df_1 z_1 + df_2 z_2}{df_1 + df_2}$$

In Example 6 we had r's of .00 and .30, based on N's of 17 and 45, respectively. The Fisher z's corresponding to our two r's are .00 and .31. Therefore, we find our weighted z to be

$$\frac{(17 - 3).00 + (45 - 3).31}{(17 - 3) + (45 - 3)} = \frac{13.02}{56} = .232$$

which corresponds to an r of .23.

Finally, it should be noted that before combining tests of significance, or effect-size estimates, it is very useful first to test the significance of the difference between the two p values or the two effect sizes. If the results of the studies *do* differ, we should be most cautious about combining their p values or effect sizes—especially when their results are in opposite directions.

COMPARING THREE OR MORE STUDIES: OVERALL TESTS

Although we can do quite a lot in the way of comparing and combining the results of sets of studies with just the procedures given so far, it does happen often that we have three or more studies of the same relationship that we want to compare or combine or both. The purpose of this section is to present generalizations of the procedures given in the last section so that we can compare and combine the results of any number of studies.

Significance Testing

Given three or more p levels to compare, we first find the standard normal deviate Z corresponding to each p level. All p levels must be one-tailed, and the corresponding Z's will have the same sign if all studies show effects in the same direction. They will have different signs if the results are not in the same direction. The statistical significance of the heterogeneity of the Z's can be obtained from a χ^2 computed as follows (Rosenthal and Rubin, 1979a):

$$\Sigma(Z_j - \bar{Z})^2$$

which is distributed as χ^2 with $K - 1$ df. In this equation Z_j is the Z for any one study, and $\bar{Z}$ is the mean of all the Z's obtained. A significant $\chi^2(K - 1)$ tells us that the Z's we have tested for heterogeneity (or the p's associated with those Z's) differ significantly among themselves.

EXAMPLE 13. Studies A, B, C, and D yield one-tailed p values of .15, .05, .01, and .001, respectively. Study C, however, shows results opposite in direction from those of studies A, B, and D. From our normal table we find the Z's corresponding to the four p levels to be 1.04, 1.64, -2.33, and 3.09. (Note the negative sign for the Z associated with the result in the opposite direction.) Then, from the preceding equation we have

$$\Sigma(Z_j - \bar{Z})^2 = [(1.04) - (0.86)]^2 + [(1.64) - (0.86)]^2$$
$$+ [(-2.33) - (0.86)]^2 + [(3.09) - (0.86)]^2 = 15.79$$

as our χ^2 value, which for $K - 1 = 4 - 1 = 3$ df is significant at $p = .0013$. The four p values we compared, then, are clearly significantly heterogeneous. Beyond the question of whether a set of p levels differ significantly among themselves, we sometimes want to test specific hypotheses about which studies will show the more significant p levels. This can be done by computing contrasts among the obtained p levels (Rosenthal and Rubin, 1979a); these computations will be presented soon in the section dealing with contrasts.

Effect-Size Estimation

Here we want to assess the statistical heterogeneity of three or more effect-size estimates. We again restrict our discussion to r as the effect-size estimator, though analogous procedures are available for comparing such other effect-size estimators as d or differences between proportions (Rosenthal and Rubin, 1982b).

For each of the three or more studies to be compared we compute the effect size r, its associated Fisher z, and $N - 3$, where N is the number of sampling units on which each r is based. Then the statistical significance of the heterogeneity of the r's can be obtained from a χ^2 computed as follows (Snedecor and Cochran, 1967, 1980, 1989):

$$\Sigma[(N_j - 3)(z_j - \bar{z})^2]$$

which is distributed as χ^2 with $K - 1$ df. In this equation z_j is the Fisher z corresponding to any r, and $\bar{z}$ is the weighted mean z, i.e.,

$$\frac{\Sigma[(N_j - 3)z_j]}{\Sigma(N_j - 3)}$$

EXAMPLE 14. Studies A, B, C, and D yield effect sizes of $r = .70$ $(N = 30)$, $r = .45$ $(N = 45)$, $r = .10$ $(N = 20)$, and $r = -.15$ $(N = 25)$, respectively. The Fisher z's corresponding to these r's are found from our table of Fisher z to be .87, .48, .10, and $-.15$, respectively. The weighted mean z is found from the equation just above to be

$$\frac{[27(.87) + 42(.48) + 17(.10) + 22(-.15)]}{[27 + 42 + 17 + 22]} = \frac{42.05}{108} = .39$$

Then, from the equation for χ^2 above, we have

$$\Sigma[(N_j - 3)(z_j - \bar{z})^2] = 27(.87 - .39)^2 + 42(.48 - .39)^2$$
$$+ 17(.10 - .39)^2 + 22(-.15 - .39)^2 = 14.41$$

as our χ^2 value, which for $K - 1 = 3$ df is significant at $p = .0024$. The four effect sizes we compared are clearly significantly heterogeneous. Just as was the case for a set of p values, procedures are also available for computing contrasts among the obtained effect-size estimates (Rosenthal and Rubin, 1982b); these computations will be presented in the following section.

COMPARING THREE OR MORE STUDIES: CONTRASTS

Significance Testing

Although we know how to answer the diffuse question of the significance of the differences among a collection of significance levels, we are often able to ask a more focused and more useful question. For example, given a set of p levels for studies of teacher-expectancy effects, we might want to know whether results from younger children are more statistically significant than are results from older children (Rosenthal and Rubin, 1978). Normally, our greater interest would be in the relationship between our weights derived from theory and our obtained effect sizes. Sometimes, however, the effect-size estimates, along with their sample sizes, are not available. More rarely, we may be intrinsically interested in the relationship between our weights and the obtained levels of significance.

As was the case for diffuse tests, we begin by finding the standard normal deviate Z corresponding to each p level. All p levels must be one-tailed, and the corresponding Z's will have the same sign if all studies show effects in the same direction, but different signs if the results are not in the same direction. The statistical significance of the contrast testing any specific hypothesis about the set of p levels can be obtained from a Z computed as follows (Rosenthal and Rubin, 1979a):

$$Z = \frac{\Sigma \lambda_j Z_j}{\sqrt{\Sigma \lambda_j^2}}$$

In this equation λ_j is the theoretically derived prediction or contrast weight for any one study, chosen such that the sum of the λ_j's will be zero, and Z_j is the Z for any one study.

EXAMPLE 15. Studies A, B, C, and D yield one-tailed p values of $1/10^7$, .0001, .21, and .007, respectively, all with results in the same direction. From a normal table we find the Z's corresponding to the four p levels to be 5.20, 3.72, .81, and 2.45. Suppose that studies A, B, C, and D had involved differing amounts of peer tutor contact of 8, 6, 4, and 2 hours of peer tutoring per month, respectively. We might, therefore, ask whether there was a linear relationship between the number of hours of contact and the statistical significance of the result favoring peer tutoring. The weights of a linear contrast involving four studies are 3, 1, −1, and −3. From the preceding equation we have

$$\frac{\Sigma \lambda_j Z_j}{\sqrt{\Sigma \lambda_j^2}} = \frac{(3)5.20 + (1)3.72 + (-1).81 + (-3)2.45}{\sqrt{(3)^2 + (1)^2 + (-1)^2 + (-3)^2}} = \frac{11.16}{\sqrt{20}} = 2.50$$

as our Z value, which is significant at $p = .006$, one-tailed. The four p values, then, tend to grow linearly more significant as the number of hours of contact time increases.

Effect-Size Estimation

Here we want to ask a more focused question of a set of effect sizes. For example, given a set of effect sizes for studies of peer tutoring, we might want to know whether these effects are increasing or decreasing linearly with the number of hours of contact per month. We again emphasize r as the effect-size estimator, but analogous procedures are available for comparing such other effect-size estimators as Cohen's d or differences between proportions (Rosenthal and Rubin, 1982a).

As was the case for diffuse tests, we begin by computing the effect size r, its associated Fisher z, and $N - 3$, where N is the number of sampling units on which each r is based. The statistical significance of the contrast, testing any specific hypothesis about the set of effect sizes, can be obtained from a Z computed as follows (Rosenthal and Rubin, 1982b):

$$\frac{\Sigma \lambda_j z_j}{\sqrt{\Sigma \dfrac{\lambda_j^2}{\omega_j}}}$$

which is distributed as Z. In this equation, λ_j is the contrast weight determined from some theory for any one study, chosen such that the sum of the λ_j's will be zero. The z_j is the Fisher z for any one study, and ω_j is the inverse of the variance of the effect size for each study. For Fisher z transformations of the effect size r, the variance is $1/(N_j - 3)$, so $\omega_j = N_j - 3$.

EXAMPLE 16. Studies A, B, C, and D yield effect sizes of $r = .89, .76, .23,$ and $.59$, respectively, all with $N = 12$. The Fisher z's corresponding to these r's are found from tables of Fisher z to be 1.42, 1.00, .23, and .68, respectively. Suppose that studies A, B, C, and D had involved differing amounts of peer tutor contact, say, 8, 6, 4, and 2 hours of contact per month, respectively. We might, therefore, ask whether there was a linear relationship between number of hours of contact and size of effect favoring peer tutoring. As in Example 15, the appropriate weights, or λ's, are 3, 1, -1, and -3. Therefore, from the preceding equation we have

$$\frac{\Sigma \lambda_j z_j}{\sqrt{\Sigma \dfrac{\lambda_j^2}{\omega_j}}} = \frac{(3)1.42 + (1)1.00 + (-1).23 + (-3).68}{\sqrt{\dfrac{(3)^2}{9} + \dfrac{(1)^2}{9} + \dfrac{(-1)^2}{9} + \dfrac{(-3)^2}{9}}} = \frac{2.99}{\sqrt{2.222}} = 2.01$$

as our Z value, which is significant at $p = .022$, one-tailed. The four effect sizes, therefore, tend to grow linearly larger as the number of hours of contact time increases. Interpretation of this relationship must be very cautious. After all, studies were not assigned at random to the four conditions of contact hours. It is generally the case that variables moderating the magnitude of effects found should not be interpreted as giving strong evidence for any causal relationships. Moderator relationships can, however, be very valuable in suggesting the possibility of causal relationships, possibilities that can then be studied experimentally or as nearly experimentally as possible.

COMBINING THREE OR MORE STUDIES

Significance Testing

After comparing the results of any set of three or more studies, it is an easy matter also to combine the p levels of the set of studies to get an overall estimate of the probability that the set of p levels might have been obtained if the null hypothesis of no relationship between X and Y were true. Of the various methods available, we present here only the generalized version of the method presented earlier in our discussion of combining the results of two groups.

This method requires only that we obtain Z for each of our p levels, all of which should be given as one-tailed. Z's disagreeing in direction from the bulk of the findings are given negative signs. Then, the sum of the Z's divided by the square root of the number (K) of studies yields a new statistic distributed as Z. Recapping

$$\frac{\Sigma Z_j}{\sqrt{K}}$$

is distributed as Z.

Should we want to do so, we could weight each of the Z's by its df, its estimated quality, or any other desired weights so long as they are assigned before inspection of the results (Mosteller and Bush, 1954; Rosenthal, 1978a, 1984).

The general procedure for weighting Z's is to (a) multiply each Z by any desired weight, (b) add the weighted Z's, and (c) divide the sum of the weighted Z's by the square root of the sum of the squared weights as follows:

$$\text{Weighted } Z = \frac{\Sigma \omega_j Z_j}{\sqrt{\Sigma \omega_j^2}}$$

Example 18 will illustrate the application of this procedure.

EXAMPLE 17. Studies A, B, C, and D yield one-tailed p values of .15, .05, .01, and .001, respectively. Study C, however, shows results opposite in direction from the results of the remaining studies. The four Z's associated with these four p's, then, are 1.04, 1.64, -2.33, and 3.09. Therefore, we have

$$\frac{\Sigma Z_j}{\sqrt{K}} = \frac{(1.04) + (1.64) + (-2.33) + (3.09)}{\sqrt{4}} = 1.72$$

as our new Z value, which has an associated p value of .043, one-tailed, or .086, two-tailed. We would normally employ the one-tailed p value if we had correctly predicted the net direction of the findings but would employ the two-tailed p value if we had not. The combined p that we obtained in this example supports the results of the majority of the individual studies. However, even if these p values (.043 and .086) were more significant, we would want to be very cautious about drawing any simple overall conclusion because of the very great heterogeneity of the four p values we were combining. Example 13, which employed the same p values, showed that this heterogeneity was significant at $p = .0013$. It should be emphasized again, however, that this great heterogeneity of p values could be due to heterogeneity of effect sizes, heterogeneity of sample sizes, or both. To find out about the sources of heterogeneity, we would have to look carefully at the effect sizes and sample sizes of each of the studies involved.

EXAMPLE 18. Studies A, B, C, and D are those of Example 17, but now we have decided to weight each study by the mean rating of internal validity assigned it by a panel of methodologists. These weights (ω) were 2.4, 2.2, 3.1, and 3.8 for studies A, B, C, and D, respectively. We find

$$\text{Weighted } Z = \frac{\Sigma \omega_j Z_j}{\sqrt{\Sigma \omega_j^2}} = \frac{(2.4)(1.04) + (2.2)(1.64) + (3.1)(-2.33) + (3.8)(3.09)}{\sqrt{(2.4)^2 + (2.2)^2 + (3.1)^2 + (3.8)^2}}$$

$$= \frac{10.623}{\sqrt{34.65}} = 1.80$$

as the Z of the weighted combined results of studies A, B, C, and D. The p value associated with this Z is .036, one-tailed, or .072, two-tailed. In this example weighting by quality of research did not lead to a very different result than was obtained when weighting was not employed (Example 17); in both cases $p \cong .04$, one-tailed. Actually, it might be more accurate to say for Example 17 that weighting was equal with all ω's $= 1$ than to say that no weighting was employed.

Effect-Size Estimation

When we combine the results of three or more studies, we are at least as interested (and in most instances, more interested) in the combined estimate of the effect size as we are in the combined probability. We follow here our earlier procedure of considering r as our primary effect-size estimator, while recognizing that many other estimates are possible. For each of the three or more studies to be combined we compute r and the associated Fisher z and have

$$\frac{\Sigma z}{K} = \bar{z}$$

as the Fisher $\bar{z}$ corresponding to our mean r (where K refers to the number of studies combined). We use a table of Fisher z to find the r associated with our mean z. Should we want to give greater weight to larger studies or to better studies, we could weight each z by its df, i.e., $N - 3$ (Snedecor and Cochran, 1967, 1980, 1989), by its estimated research quality, or by any other weights assigned before inspection of the data.

The weighted mean z is obtained as follows:

$$\text{Weighted } \bar{z} = \frac{\Sigma \omega_j z_j}{\Sigma \omega_j}$$

Example 20 will illustrate the application of this procedure.

EXAMPLE 19. Studies A, B, C, and D yield effect sizes of $r = .70, .45, .10,$ and $-.15$, respectively. The Fisher z values corresponding to these r's are .87, .48, .10, and $-.15$, respectively. Therefore, we have

$$\frac{\Sigma z}{K} = \frac{(.87) + (.48) + (.10) + (-.15)}{4} = .32$$

as our mean Fisher z. From our table of Fisher z values we find a z of .32 to correspond to an r of .31. Just as in our earlier example of combined p levels, however, we would want to be very cautious in our interpretation of this combined effect size. If the r's we have just averaged were based on substantial sample sizes, as was the case in Example 14, they would be significantly heterogeneous. Therefore, averaging without special thought and comment would be inappropriate.

EXAMPLE 20. Studies A, B, C, and D are those of Example 19, but now we have decided to weight each study by a mean rating of ecological validity assigned to it by several experts. These weights were 1.7, 1.6, 3.1, and 2.5, respectively.

Therefore, we find

$$\text{Weighted } z = \frac{\Sigma \omega_j z_j}{\Sigma \omega_j} = \frac{(1.7)(.87) + (1.6)(.48) + (3.1)(.10) + (2.5)(-.15)}{1.7 + 1.6 + 3.1 + 2.5}$$

$$= \frac{2.182}{8.90} = .24$$

as our mean Fisher z, which corresponds to an r of .24. In this example weighting by quality of research led to a somewhat smaller estimate of combined effect size than did equal weighting (.24 versus .31).

COMPARING AND COMBINING RESULTS THAT ARE NOT INDEPENDENT

In all the meta-analytic procedures we have discussed so far it has been assumed that the studies being compared or combined were separate, independent studies. That is, we have assumed that different subjects (or other sampling units) were found in the studies being compared or summarized. Sometimes, however, the same subjects (or other sampling units) contribute data to two or more studies or to two or more dependent variables within the same study. In such cases the results of the two or more studies or the results based on two or more dependent variables are not independent, and the meta-analytic procedures we have described so far cannot be applied without adjustment.

General procedures for comparing and combining nonindependent significance levels and effect sizes have been described elsewhere by Strube (1985) and by Rosenthal and Rubin (1986), respectively. We cannot give the details of all these procedures here, but because it is so frequently useful, we will give the procedure for comparing two nonindependent effect sizes, specifically correlation coefficients (r).

Comparing Two Nonindependent Correlation Coefficients

The situation we describe is one in which a single sample of persons is measured on three variables, X, Y, and Z, where X and Y are conceptualized as predictor variables and Z is conceptualized as an outcome variable. Three correlations are possible among these three variables; r_{xz}, r_{yz}, and r_{xy}. We want to compare the magnitude of two of these correlations, r_{xz} and r_{yz}. The standard procedure for this comparison is *Hotelling's t test*, which is distributed as t with $df = N - 3$ (Walker and Lev, 1953):

$$t_H = (r_{xz} - r_{yz}) \sqrt{\frac{(N-3)(1 + r_{xy})}{2(1 - r_{xy}^2 - r_{xz}^2 - r_{yz}^2 + 2r_{xy}r_{xz}r_{yz})}}$$

AN ILLUSTRATION. In a study of the classroom behavior of children, teachers' ratings of 347 children were available on three variables:

X: How curious the children were (a predictor variable)

Y: How affectionate the children were (a predictor variable)

Z: How likely the children were to be successful in the future (the outcome variable)

The three correlations among these variables were $r_{xz} = .63$, $r_{yz} = .23$, and $r_{xy} = .28$. We want to know whether ratings of curiosity predict ratings of future success $(r_{xz} = .63)$ significantly better than ratings of affectionateness predict ratings of future success $(r_{yz} = .23)$. Therefore,

$$t_H = (.63 - .23)\sqrt{\frac{344(1 + .28)}{2[1 - (.28)^2 - (.63)^2 - (.23)^2 + 2(.28)(.63)(.23)]}}$$

$$= (.40)\sqrt{\frac{440.32}{2[.552944]}} = 7.98$$

$p < 1/10^{13}$ and $df = 344$. Thus there is little question that the variable *curious* correlates more highly with the variable *future success* than does the variable *affectionate*.

Under most circumstances this t test for comparing nonindependent correlation coefficients works well, but there are special (and probably rare) circumstances when it will yield t's substantially too large. Steiger (1980) has recommended that a modification of Hotelling's test proposed by Williams (1959) be employed instead:

$$t_W = (r_{xz} - r_{yz})\sqrt{\frac{(N - 1)(1 + r_{xy})}{2A\left(\frac{N - 1}{N - 3}\right) + B}}$$

where

$$A = (1 - r_{xy}^2 - r_{xz}^2 - r_{yz}^2 + 2r_{xy}r_{xz}r_{yz})$$

$$B = \left(\frac{r_{xz} + r_{yz}}{2}\right)^2 (1 - r_{xy})^3$$

For the example above, $A = .552944$ and $B = .069014$, so

$$t_W = (.63 - .23)\sqrt{\frac{346(1.28)}{2(.552944)\left(\frac{346}{344}\right) + .069014}}$$

$$= (.40)\sqrt{\frac{442.88}{1.181332}} = 7.74$$

$p < 1/10^{13}$.

For this example, then, the more conservative t_W gave a value only 3 percent smaller than the value of t_H.

Recently, a still more accurate procedure, a Z test, has been proposed by Meng, Rosenthal, and Rubin (1990) in which

$$Z = (z_1 - z_2) \sqrt{\frac{N - 3}{2(1 - r_{xy})h}}$$

where z_1 and z_2 are the Fisher transformations of the r's being compared (r_{xz} and r_{yz}), N is the number of sampling units, r_{xy} is the correlation between the two predictor variables,

$$h = \frac{1 - f\bar{r}^2}{1 - \bar{r}^2}$$

$$f = \frac{1 - r_{xy}}{2(1 - \bar{r}^2)}$$

which must be ≤ 1 and $\bar{r}^2$ is the mean of r_{xz}^2 and r_{yz}^2. For the data we have been using as our illustration, then,

$$\bar{r}^2 = \frac{(.63)^2 + (.23)^2}{2} = .2249$$

$$f = \frac{1 - .28}{2(1 - .2249)} = .4645$$

$$h = \frac{1 - (.4645)(.2249)}{1 - .2249} = 1.1554$$

$$Z = (.741 - .234) \sqrt{\frac{347 - 3}{2(1 - .28)1.1554}}$$

$$= (.507) \sqrt{\frac{344}{2(.72)1.1554}} = 7.29$$

$p < 1/10^{12}$. A Z of 7.29 is equivalent[2] to a t of 7.59 so we can compare the results of the present t test to those obtained earlier (7.98 and 7.74). The present result, then, is about 5 percent smaller than the result of the Hotelling t and about 2 percent smaller than the result of the Williams t. In most cases these three tests will yield similar results, but it seems best generally to use the third of these, the Z test employing Fisher transformations of the r's to be compared.

THE FILE DRAWER PROBLEM

Both behavioral researchers and statisticians have long suspected that the studies published in the behavioral and social sciences are a biased sample of the studies that are actually carried out (Bakan, 1967; McNemar, 1960; Smart, 1966; Sterling, 1959). The extreme view of this problem, the *file drawer problem*, is that the jour-

---

[2]From the relationship (Wallace, 1959): $Z = [df \log_e(1 + t^2/df)]^{1/2}[1 - 1/(2df)]^{1/2}$.

nals are filled with the 5 percent of the studies that show type I errors, while the file drawers back at the lab are filled with the 95 percent of the studies that show nonsignificant (e.g., $p > .05$) results (Rosenthal, 1979a; Rosenthal and Rubin, 1988; Wachter, 1988).

In the past there was very little we could do to assess the net effect of studies tucked away in file drawers that did not make the magic .05 level (Nelson, Rosenthal, and Rosnow, 1986; Rosenthal and Gaito, 1963, 1964). Now, however, although no definitive solution to the problem is available, we can establish reasonable boundaries on the problem and estimate the degree of damage to any research conclusion that could be done by the file drawer problem. The fundamental idea in coping with the file drawer problem is simply to calculate the number of studies averaging null results ($Z = 0.00$) that must be in the file drawers before the overall probability of a type I error can be just brought to any desired level of significance, say, $p = .05$. This number of filed studies, or the tolerance for future null results, is then evaluated for whether such a tolerance level is small enough to threaten the overall conclusion drawn by the reviewer. If the overall level of significance of the research review will be brought down to the level of *just significant* by the addition of just a few more null results, the finding is not resistant to the file drawer threat.

Computation

To find the number (X) of new, filed, or unretrieved studies averaging null results required to bring the new overall p to any desired level, say, just significant at $p = .05$ ($Z = 1.645$), one simply writes:

$$1.645 = k\bar{Z}_k / \sqrt{k + X}$$

where k is the number of studies combined, and $\bar{Z}_k$ is the mean Z obtained for the k studies.

Rearrangement shows that

$$X = (k/2.706)[k(\bar{Z}_k)^2 - 2.706]$$

An alternative formula that may be more convenient, when the sum of the Z's (ΣZ) is given rather than the mean Z, is as follows:

$$X = [(\Sigma Z)^2 / 2.706] - k$$

One method based on counting rather than adding Z's may be easier to compute and can be employed when exact p levels are not available; but it is probably less powerful. If X is the number of new studies required to bring the overall p to .50 (not to .05), s is the number of summarized studies significant at $p < .05$, and n is the number of summarized studies not significant at .05, then

$$X = 19s - n$$

Another conservative alternative (to be used when exact p levels are not available) is to set $Z = .00$ for any nonsignificant result and to set $Z = 1.645$ for any result significant at $p < .05$.

The equations above all assume that each of the k studies is independent of all other $k - 1$ studies, at least in the sense of employing different sampling units. There are other senses of independence, however. For example, we can think of two or more studies conducted in a given laboratory as less independent than two or more studies conducted in different laboratories. Such nonindependence can be assessed by such procedures as intraclass correlations. Whether nonindependence of this type serves to increase type I or type II errors appears to depend in part on the relative magnitude of the Z's obtained from the studies that are "correlated" or "too similar." If the correlated Z's are, on the average, as high (or higher) as the grand mean Z corrected for nonindependence, the combined Z we compute treating all studies as independent will be too large. If the correlated Z's are, on the average, clearly low relative to the grand mean Z corrected for nonindependence, the combined Z we compute treating all studies as independent will tend to be too small.

ILLUSTRATION. In 1969, ninety-four experiments examining the effects of interpersonal self-fulfilling prophecies, such as those discussed in Chapter 6, were summarized (Rosenthal, 1969). The mean Z of these studies was 1.014, k was 94, and Z for the studies combined was $9.83 = 94(1.014)/(94)^{1/2}$.

How many new, filed, or unretrieved studies (X) would be required to bring this very large Z down to a barely significant level ($Z = 1.645$)? From the second equation of the preceding section,

$$X = (94/2.706)[94(1.014)^2 - 2.706] = 3{,}263$$

One finds that 3,263 studies averaging null results ($\bar{Z} = .00$) must be crammed into file drawers before one would conclude that the overall results were due to sampling bias in the studies summarized by the reviewer. In a more recent summary of the same area of research (Rosenthal and Rubin, 1978), the mean Z of 345 studies was estimated to be 1.22, k was 345, and X was 65,123. In a still more recent summary of the same area of research, the mean Z was 1.30, k was 443, and X was 122,778. Thus, over 120,000 unreported studies averaging a null result would have to exist somewhere before the overall results could reasonably be ascribed to sampling bias.

The Tolerance Table

Table 22.2 is a table of tolerance values with five convenient mean Z values heading the columns and various numbers of available studies (k) indexing the rows. The intersection of any row and column yields the number of new studies (X) required to bring the combined p for all studies, old and new together, down to the level of being just significant at $p = .05$ ($Z = 1.645$).

There is both a sobering and a cheering lesson to be learned from this table and from the equations given above. The sobering lesson is that small numbers of studies, even when their combined p is significant, if they are not *very* significant, may well be misleading. That is because only a few studies filed away could change the combined significant results to a nonsignificant one. Thus, 15 studies

TABLE 22.2
Tolerances for future null results as a function of mean Z ($\bar{Z}$) and number of studies summarized (k)

k	$\bar{Z}$ +0.50	+1.00	+1.50	+2.00	+2.50
1	—	—	—	—	1
2	—	—	1	3	7
3	—	—	4	10	17
4	—	1	9	19	32
5	—	4	15	31	52
6	—	7	23	47	77
7	—	11	33	65	106
8	—	15	45	86	139
9	—	20	58	110	178
10	—	26	73	137	220
15	5	68	172	317	504
20	16	127	312	571	903
25	32	205	494	898	1,418
30	53	302	718	1,300	2,048
40	107	551	1,290	2,325	3,655
50	180	873	2,028	3,645	5,724
60	272	1,270	2,933	5,261	8,254
80	511	2,285	5,241	9,380	14,701
100	823	3,595	8,214	14,681	22,996
150	1,928	8,164	18,558	33,109	51,817
200	3,495	14,581	33,059	58,927	92,187
300	8,014	32,959	74,533	132,737	207,571
500	22,596	91,887	207,371	369,049	576,920

Note: The p values corresponding to the mean Z ($\bar{Z}$) values are .308, .159, .067, .023, and .006, respectively. Dashes in the table indicate that $X < 1$ (X is the number of new studies required to bring the combined p for all studies to the level of being just significant at $p = .05$).

averaging a Z of +0.50 have a combined p of .026. But if there were only six studies tucked away showing a mean Z of 0.00, the tolerance level for null results (five in this case) would be exceeded, and the significant result would become nonsignificant. Or, if there were two studies averaging a Z of +2.00, the combined p would be about .002. But uncovering four new studies averaging a Z of 0.00 would bring p into the "not significant" region, because four exceeded the tabled tolerance level of three shown in the tolerance table.

The cheering lesson is that when the number of studies available grows large, or the mean directional Z grows large, or both situations are present, the file drawer as a plausible rival hypothesis can be safely ruled out. If 300 studies are found averaging a Z of +1.00, it would take 32,959 + 1 studies to bring the new combined p to a nonsignificant level. That many file drawers full are simply too improbable.

At the present time no firm guidelines can be given as to what constitutes an unlikely number of unretrieved or unpublished studies. For some areas of research 100 or even 500 unpublished and unretrieved studies may be a plausible state of affairs, while for others even 10 or 20 seems unlikely. Probably any rough-and-ready guide should be based partly on k, so that as more studies are known, it becomes more plausible that other studies in that area may be in those file drawers. Perhaps we could regard as robust to the file drawer problem any combined results for which the tolerance level (X) reaches $5k + 10$. That seems a conservative but reasonable tolerance level; the $5k$ portion suggests that it is unlikely that the file drawers have more than five times as many studies as the reviewer, and the $+ 10$ sets the minimum number of studies that could be filed away at 15 (when $k = 1$).

It appears that more and more reviewers of research literature will be estimating average effect sizes and combined p's of the studies they summarize. It would be very helpful to readers if for each combined p they presented, reviewers also gave the tolerance for future null results associated with their overall significance level.

CHAPTER 23

CHI-SQUARE AND THE ANALYSIS OF TABLES

TABLE ANALYSIS AND CHI-SQUARE

There are so many data-analytic procedures useful to the student and practitioner of behavioral research that no one book can present them all in sufficient detail to be useful. In this chapter we present some material on the analysis of frequency counts cast into tabular form that we feel will be useful even though we can be only introductory in our exposition.

In previous chapters we repeatedly referred to the relationship between tests of significance and measures of effect size and size of study:

$$\text{Significance test} = \text{size of effect} \times \text{size of study}$$

For 2×2 tables of counts, one specific form of this general relationship is

$$\chi^2(1) = \phi^2 \times N$$

where $\chi^2(1)$ is the test statistic on $df = 1$. We determine df in any two-dimensional table of counts as (number of rows $- 1$) $\times$ (number of columns $- 1$). Thus, for a 2×2 table we have $(2 - 1) \times (2 - 1) = 1\ df$. The term ϕ^2 (phi squared) is the squared product-moment correlation between the variable defined by the two rows and the variable defined by the two columns. As usual, N is the total number of sampling units in our study. A χ^2, therefore, is a test of significance of the effect-size estimate ϕ^2. To be consistent with our preference for product-moment correlation coefficients, rather than their squares, as effect-size estimates, we might prefer to say that Z, the standard normal deviate and the square root of $\chi^2(1)$, is a test of significance of ϕ because

$$Z = \phi \times \sqrt{N}$$

In our computation of χ^2's from 2×2 tables of counts we must keep in mind that there must be N independent sampling units, each having contributed to only one of the four cells of the 2×2 table. It would not do, for example, to have $N/2$ sampling units, each having contributed two observations to the total number of observations (N).

We also would like the frequencies expected in each cell, if the null hypothesis of no relationship is true, not to be too small. At one time it was thought that the expected frequency should not fall below 5 for any cell. Evidence now indicates, however, that very usable χ^2 values can be obtained even with expected frequencies as low as 1, so long as the total number of independent observations (N) is not too small. We know from the work of Gregory Camilli and Kenneth Hopkins (1978) that an N of 20 is large enough, but small expected frequencies may work quite well in even smaller studies. The same workers have also shown that corrections for continuity may do more harm than good. One correction for continuity, the *Yates correction*, involves reducing each occurrence of the term $O - E$ by 0.5 before employing the computational formula for $\chi^2(1)$:

$$\chi^2(1) = \sum \frac{(O - E)^2}{E}$$

where O is the observed frequency in each cell, and E is the expected frequency in that cell (see the discussion of the phi coefficient in Chapter 14).

LARGER TABLES OF COUNTS

There is a large and growing literature on the analysis of tables of counts of any size, much of it emphasizing the "log-linear model." A definitive text is that by Yvonne Bishop, Stephen Fienberg, and Paul Holland (1975), an excellent brief introduction is provided by Hays (1981), and discussions of intermediate length are available in texts by Everitt (1977), Fienberg (1977), Kennedy (1983), and Upton (1978). The *log-linear model* approaches tables of counts in a manner analogous to the analysis of variance. Although we do not describe the log-linear model in this chapter, our approach to larger tables of counts is consistent with the use of log-linear contrasts as recently developed by John Kennedy and Andy Bush (1988) and with our own general preference for testing specific rather than omnibus, unfocused hypotheses. Just as in our approach to the F statistic, in which we want the numerator *df* to be no greater than unity, we will want the *df* for our χ^2 tests to be no greater than unity. (The denominator *df* for F is roughly analogous to N in the case of tables of counts, and given a choice, we like *those* quantities to be large rather than small.)

Quantifying Qualitative Data

In Chapter 14 we saw how we could quantify qualitative data in the case of a
2×2 table:

	Democrats	Republicans	Σ
Yes	1	4	5
No	4	1	5
Σ	5	5	10

The qualitative difference Republican versus Democrat can be quantified by assigning a 0 to one of these and a 1 to the other. If we give being a Republican a
1 and being a Democrat a 0, we have a scale of "Republicanness"; if we assign
the 1 to the Democrats, we have a scale of "Democraticness." Similarly, we assign a 0 or a 1 to the dependent variable of item response. If we assign a 1 to yes
and a 0 to no, we have a scale of agreement with the item, or "yesness"; if we
reverse the numbers assigned, we have a scale of disagreement, or "noness." In
this example, we find a phi coefficient of .60 when "Republicans" was coded 1
and "yes" was coded 1 while "Democrats" and "no" were coded 0. Suppose, however, that instead of a 2×2 table we had a 2×3 table:

		Independent variable			
		Democrats	Republicans	Others	Σ
Dependent variable	Yes	1	4	2	7
	No	4	1	2	7
	Σ	5	5	4	14

We could still "dummy code" the dependent variable of yes versus no as before, but what shall we do with the three levels of the independent variable? Assuming that we know very little about "Others," it would make no sense to call
Others .5. If we did, that would mean we had created a scale in which Others fall
halfway between the anchoring ends of our scale Democrat–Republican. That
might be a reasonable numerical assignment for some political group, but not for
one about which we knew nothing. Instead, we would create a series of dummy
variables as follows:

"*Democraticness*": Democrats = 1; Republicans = 0; Others = 0
"*Republicanness*": Republicans = 1; Democrats = 0; Others = 0
"*Otherness*": Others = 1; Democrats = 0; Republicans = 0

TABLE 23.1
Variables × respondent data matrix

	Dependent variable: Agreement	Independent variable		
		"Democraticness"	"Republicanness"	"Otherness"
Respondent 1	1	1	0	0
Respondent 2	1	0	1	0
Respondent 3	1	0	1	0
Respondent 4	1	0	1	0
Respondent 5	1	0	1	0
Respondent 6	1	0	0	1
Respondent 7	1	0	0	1
Respondent 8	0	1	0	0
Respondent 9	0	1	0	0
Respondent 10	0	1	0	0
Respondent 11	0	1	0	0
Respondent 12	0	0	1	0
Respondent 13	0	0	0	1
Respondent 14	0	0	0	1

Given the three dummy-coded independent variables, and the single dummy-coded dependent variable of "Yesness" (or agreement with the item presented), we can rewrite the data of the preceding table as shown in Table 23.1. The table of intercorrelations (phi coefficients) among the four variables in the table is

	Agreement	"Democraticness"	"Republicanness"	"Otherness"
Agreement	—	−.45	+.45	.00
"Democraticness"		—	−.56	−.47
"Republicanness"			—	−.47
"Otherness"				—

Inspecting the correlation matrix above shows that Republicans, compared with non-Republicans (Democrats plus Others), are more likely to agree with the item (answer it *yes*). Democrats, compared with non-Democrats (Republicans plus Others), are less likely to agree; and being in the category Other rather than non-Other (Democrats plus Republicans) is unrelated to agreement. The three correlations among the independent variables are all fairly strongly negative, as we would expect, since the more one belongs to group A the "less" one can belong to group B or group C. In the extreme case of just two variables (e.g., Democratic versus Republican) the intercorrelation would be −1.00, so no information would be added by using both variables.

Sometimes we can do better than dummy-coding the variables. Instead, if we can order the levels of a dimension on some underlying conceptual continuum, we can create a score based on each row's or column's position on that continuum. Suppose that we had obtained the following data:

| | Improvement scores | | | |
	None	Slight	Moderate	Σ
Mildly depressed	1	2	5	8
Moderately depressed	2	5	1	8
Severely depressed	5	2	1	8
Σ	8	9	7	24

Rather than forming a series of dummy variables, we could create a scaled independent variable of severity of depression such that

$$\text{Mildly depressed} = 1 \quad \begin{pmatrix} \text{or } 0 \\ \text{or } 1 \\ \text{or } 2 \end{pmatrix} \quad \begin{pmatrix} \text{or } -1 \\ \text{or } 0 \\ \text{or } +1 \end{pmatrix}$$
$$\text{Moderately depressed} = 2$$
$$\text{Severely depressed} = 3$$

Similarly, we could create a scaled dependent variable of degree of improvement after therapy such that

$$\text{No improvement} = 1 \quad \begin{pmatrix} \text{or } 0 \\ \text{or } 1 \\ \text{or } 2 \end{pmatrix} \quad \begin{pmatrix} \text{or } -1 \\ \text{or } 0 \\ \text{or } +1 \end{pmatrix}$$
$$\text{Slight improvement} = 2$$
$$\text{Moderate improvement} = 3$$

We could then simply compute the correlation r between degree of depression and degree of improvement. We would have one pair of scores 1, 1; two pairs of scores 1, 2; five pairs of scores 1, 3 for the first row, etc., and $r = -.52$, suggesting that more severe levels of depression are associated with lower levels of improvement. We could test the significance of that r by means of t. It would *not* do to test significance by means of the $x^2(4)$ test of the 3×3 table. The reason is not simply because the expected frequencies might be somewhat low for our taste. Rather it is because that overall x^2 with $(3 - 1) \times (3 - 1) = 4$ *df* tests a different and more diffuse hypothesis, namely, that there is some type of relationship between the rows and columns, instead of the more focused hypothesis of a linear relationship tested by the t test for r.

Distributions of Chi-Square

The computation of x^2 for a table of any size is most easily accomplished by

$$x^2 = \Sigma \frac{(O - E)^2}{E}$$

This quantity, when based on independent observations and expected frequencies not too small, tends to be distributed as chi-square on df = (number of rows − 1) × (number of columns − 1).

Just as was the case for F (see Chapter 15), there is a different chi-square distribution for every value of df. Also as for F, all chi-square distributions begin at zero and range upward to infinity. We recall that the expected value of t was zero when the null hypothesis was true, and that the expected value of F was $df/(df − 2)$, where df are for the denominator mean square. For chi-square distributions the expected value, when the null hypothesis of no relationship is true, is equal to the df defining that chi-square distribution. Thus for χ^2 based on 1, 4, or 10 df, the average value of the χ^2 obtained if the null hypothesis were true would be 1, 4, and 10, respectively. The median of a given distribution tends to be just less than the mean (df), and the mode for chi-square distributions of df = 2 or more is $df − 2$.

Just as was the case for F, values of χ^2 further and further into the right-hand tail are less and less likely if the null hypothesis were true and are used as evidence to suggest that the null hypothesis is probably false. Although in data-analytic work we use tables of χ^2 rather than pictured distributions, it is instructive to see some examples of χ^2 distributions, as in Figure 23-1 (after Lindquist, 1953).

Comparison of the three distributions in the figure shows that they move to the right with increases in df, and they tend to greater symmetry as well. Table 23.2 illustrates the differences in various chi-square distributions by giving

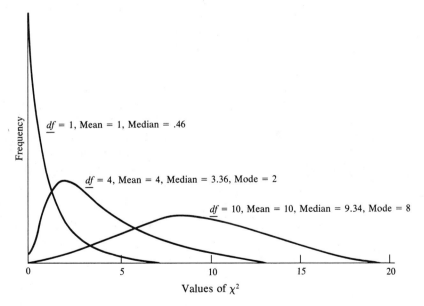

FIGURE 23-1
Three chi-square distributions: df = 1, 4, and 10.

TABLE 23.2
χ^2 values required for significance at various p levels

				p level					
df	.80	.50	.30	.20	.10	.05	.02	.01	.001
1	.06	.46	1.07	1.64	2.71	3.84	5.41	6.64	10.83
2	.45	1.39	2.41	3.22	4.60	5.99	7.82	9.21	13.82
3	1.00	2.37	3.66	4.64	6.25	7.82	9.84	11.34	16.27
4	1.65	3.36	4.88	5.99	7.78	9.49	11.67	13.28	18.46
5	2.34	4.35	6.06	7.29	9.24	11.07	13.39	15.09	20.52
6	3.07	5.35	7.23	8.56	10.64	12.59	15.03	16.81	22.46
8	4.59	7.34	9.52	11.03	13.36	15.51	18.17	20.09	26.12
10	6.18	9.34	11.78	13.44	15.99	18.31	21.16	23.21	29.59
15	10.31	14.34	17.32	19.31	22.31	25.00	28.26	30.58	37.70
20	14.58	19.34	22.78	25.04	28.41	31.41	35.02	37.57	45.32
25	18.94	24.34	28.17	30.68	34.38	37.65	41.57	44.31	52.62
30	23.36	29.34	33.53	36.25	40.26	43.77	47.96	50.89	59.70

Note: For $df > 30$ the p value for any χ^2 can be estimated by first finding the standard normal deviate Z associated with that p; e.g., a Z of 1.96 is associated with a p of .05 (two-tailed). We find Z from $Z = \sqrt{2\chi^2} - \sqrt{2\,df - 1}$.

the areas found to the right of the tabled values. Thus for 1 df the table shows that a χ^2 value of 3.84 or greater is found only .05 of the time if the null hypothesis of no relationship is true. A value of 10.83 or greater is found only .001 of the time.

An Illustration

For our illustration of the analysis of a table larger than 2×2, we present the results of a 3×3 study (Gilbert, McPeek, and Mosteller, 1977). In this study a set of 53 investigations was categorized (1) into three levels of experimental control achieved by the investigators while simultaneously being categorized (2) into three levels of enthusiasm shown by the investigators for their newly tested medical treatments. The results were as follows:

	Degree of enthusiasm			
Degree of control	High	Medium	Low	Σ
High	0	3	3	6
Medium	10	3	2	15
Low	24	7	1	32
Σ	34	13	6	53

As a preliminary step, and to illustrate the computation, we begin by applying the general formula for χ^2

$$\chi^2 = \sum \frac{(O - E)^2}{E}$$

The table above gives us our O's (observed values), and the table below our E's (expected values). If the null hypothesis of no relationship between the rows and columns were true, we would expect the O's and E's to be equal. That is, we would find the observed entry for each cell to be the product of the row total of the row to which the cell belongs and the column total of the column to which the cell belongs divided by the total number of observations, N. This, of course, is the formula for computing the expected frequencies, that is,

$$E = \frac{\text{row total} \times \text{column total}}{N}$$

In this case, the expected frequencies are as follows:

	Degree of enthusiasm			
Degree of control	**High**	**Medium**	**Low**	Σ
High	3.85	1.47	0.68	6.00
Medium	9.62	3.68	1.70	15.00
Low	20.53	7.85	3.62	32.00
Σ	34.00	13.00	6.00	53.00

Note that the row and column totals are identical in the two tables. To compute χ^2 we use only the cell data as follows:

$$\chi^2(4) = \sum \frac{(O - E)^2}{E} = \frac{(0 - 3.85)^2}{3.85} + \frac{(3 - 1.47)^2}{1.47} + \frac{(3 - 0.68)^2}{0.68}$$

$$+ \frac{(10 - 9.62)^2}{9.62} + \frac{(3 - 3.68)^2}{3.68} + \frac{(2 - 1.70)^2}{1.70}$$

$$+ \frac{(24 - 20.53)^2}{20.53} + \frac{(7 - 7.85)^2}{7.85} + \frac{(1 - 3.62)^2}{3.62} = 16.13$$

$p = .0028$.

A result this large or larger (occurring only .0028 of the time in repeated samplings if the null hypothesis of no relationship between the variables of experimental control and enthusiasm of the investigator were true) unfortunately tells us only that there is likely to be some sort of relationship, but it says nothing about what type of relationship there might be. This is analogous to the situation of an overall diffuse F test with more than 1 df in the numerator in which we must look at the condition means to see what the results actually show. More satisfactory approaches to the analysis of larger tables of counts are available than settling for unfocused, omnibus χ^2 tests of $df > 1$.

THE ANALYSIS OF VARIANCE OF QUALITATIVE DATA

One alternative to the χ^2 test of qualitative data involves the application of the analysis of variance. In this approach, suggested by William Cochran (1950), we begin by quantifying the qualitative data as shown earlier in this chapter. If the various rows or columns representing the dependent variable can be scaled or ordered, as in our earlier example of three levels of improvement (scored 1, 2, or 3), then each subject or other sampling unit can be assigned one of several numbers to serve as the dependent variable scores. Even if such scaling is not possible, we can still create a number of dependent variables, each one dummy-coded (0 or 1). Once we have scaled or dummy-coded (a special case of scaling) a score for each subject, we compute the analysis of variance in the usual way. However, now the subjects' scores will be only 0 or 1; 1, 2, or 3; or some other (usually small) set of possible values.

Except for very small studies (say, $df < 20$), and for very extreme splits of 0 versus 1 data,[1] the F tests obtained from the analysis of variance give quite accurate results (Edwards, 1972; Hsu and Feldt, 1969; Lunney, 1970; Snedecor and Cochran, 1967, 1980; Winer, 1971). Indeed, Cochran (1950) has suggested that such results based on F might, under some conditions, be more accurate than those based on χ^2. Ralph D'Agostino (1971; following Snedecor and Cochran, 1967) has shown that for even fairly extreme splits, transformations (e.g., arcsin, logit) can be employed to make the analysis of variance still work well.

An Illustration

We illustrate the use of the analysis of variance employing the same data we employed in the preceding example of χ^2 (Gilbert, McPeek, and Mosteller, 1977). In this example we can do better than dichotomize the dependent variable of degree of enthusiasm. We can assign the scores 1, 2, and 3 to the categories low, medium, and high levels of enthusiasm, respectively. We can now write the scores for each of the three levels of the independent variable of degree of experimental control as follows:

Degree of control	Listing of scores
High (6 observations)	2 2 2 1 1 1
Medium (15 observations)	3 3 3 3 3 3 3 3 3 2 2 2 1 1
Low (32 observations)	3 3 3 3 3 3 3 3 3 3 3 3 3 3 3 3 3 3 3 3 3 3 3 2 2 2 2 2 2 2 1

---

[1] We might regard as an extreme split one in which 90 percent of the observations were of one type (0 or 1) and 10 percent were of the other type.

The analysis of variance of these data is summarized as follows:

			Table of variance			
Source	**SS**	**df**	**MS**	**F**	**eta**	**p**
Between conditions	7.505	2	3.753	10.60	.55	.00015
Within conditions	17.702	50	0.354			

We note that the omnibus F is more significant than the omnibus χ^2 (.00015 versus .0028). We might have expected this if we felt that degree of enthusiasm would be affected by degree of control, since the scores employed in the analysis of variance were able to use the information that $3 > 2 > 1$. The χ^2 result would not have been any different even if our levels of enthusiasm (columns) had been interchanged. Although our F has used more information than our χ^2, it is still somewhat diffuse or omnibus ($df = 2$ for numerator rather than 1), though less diffuse or unfocused than the χ^2 ($df = 4$). What does the analysis of variance show us? The means of the three conditions were as follows:

Degree of control	**Condition means**
High	1.50
Medium	2.53
Low	2.72

These means indicate that studies showing a higher degree of control elicited less enthusiasm from their investigators than did studies showing a lower degree of control. The p value for that statement, however, has not been determined. Our omnibus F test tells only that the means differ somehow. Had we planned the appropriate comparison, we might simply have computed the t test between the high and low degree of control conditions but employing the MS error from the overall analysis of variance as shown:

$$t(50) = \frac{M_1 - M_2}{\sqrt{\left(\dfrac{1}{n_1} + \dfrac{1}{n_2}\right)MS\text{ error}}} = \frac{2.72 - 1.50}{\sqrt{\left(\dfrac{1}{32} + \dfrac{1}{6}\right)0.354}} = 4.61$$

$p = .000028$, two-tailed, $r = .61$.

A conceptually similar test could be made employing a linear contrast on the means of the three groups (Chapter 21 gives computational details). For these data the contrast $F(1,50) = 23.84$, $t = \sqrt{F} = 4.88$, $p = .000011$, two-tailed, $r = .57$. This contrast, based on an unweighted means analysis of variance, agrees well with the results of the ordinary (weighted means) t test with r's of .57 and .61, respectively. (Actually, both these r's are more accurately given as negative, since higher scores on the independent variable are associated with lower scores on the dependent variable.)

A third and quite direct estimate of the size of the relationship between degree of experimental control and degree of investigator enthusiasm is available. Since we can scale the independent variable of degree of experimental control (high $= 3$, medium $= 2$, low $= 1$), we can simply correlate for the 53 investigators their degree of enthusiasm scored 1, 2, or 3 with the degree of experimental control scored 1, 2, or 3. This correlation was $r(51) = -.49$, $t(51) = 3.97$, $p = .00023$, two-tailed, a result in fairly good agreement with those obtained by our two alternative methods; (a) the t on the extreme groups omitting the intermediate condition (which in this example is identical to the linear contrast taking differences in sample sizes into account, see page 473) and (b) the linear contrast following the unweighted means analysis of variance.

TESTING SPECIFIC HYPOTHESES BY SUBDIVIDING LARGER TABLES

By employing the analysis of variance approach to tables of counts, we were able to apply familiar methods (t tests, contrasts, and correlations) to the investigation of specific hypotheses rather than having to settle for an overall unfocused, diffuse χ^2. Methods are available for computing contrasts in the log-linear models, but we will not discuss those here. For a detailed discussion see *Discrete Multivariate Analysis* (Bishop, Fienberg, and Holland, 1975) and Kennedy and Bush's more recent treatment of the topic (1988). Here we shall describe only some simple, useful methods for subdividing tables of counts into one or more 2 × 2 tables, each of which is based on only a single *df*. That is, each table addresses only a single question. Although these are not contrasts in the usual sense, they are very much in the spirit of contrasts.

The Chi-Square Corner Cells Test

When the data in both the rows and columns can be arranged in some meaningful order from more to less of that variable, a very simple $\chi^2(1)$ test can be performed on the four corner cells of the contingency table. Because this test does not use as much of the information as does the analysis of variance with contrasts, we recommend it only as a quick preliminary test. Basically it examines the effects of the most extreme levels of the independent variable on the distribution of cases between the most extreme possible outcomes. A good example is our illustration of degree of experimental control and degree of enthusiasm. The table of counts was

	Degree of enthusiasm		
Degree of control	High	Medium	Low
High	0	3	3
Medium	10	3	2
Low	24	7	1

Because both the rows and columns are arranged in order of magnitude, (high, medium, low), our corner cells test is applicable. The corners are

	High	Low	Σ
High	0	3	3
Low	24	1	25
Σ	24	4	28

The expected frequencies computed from the marginals of the 2×2 table above are

	High	Low	Σ
High	2.57	0.43	3.00
Low	21.43	3.57	25.00
Σ	24.00	4.00	28.00

The resulting $\chi^2(1)$ is 20.16, $p = .000007$, phi $= .85$. The size of the effect is, of course, "inflated" by our having compared extreme groups rather than having used all, or nearly all, the scores. There is nothing wrong with this, since good research design often involves choosing extreme groups. However, it is important to keep in mind that the large χ^2 and phi are due in part to our having chosen extreme groups on both the independent and the dependent variable. There is another issue to be addressed for this χ^2; the expected frequency of 0.43 is probably too small for comfort. One way to get an "independent opinion" about the correct significance level is to compute the *Fisher exact probability test* (Siegel, 1956), which we consider in some detail in a moment. Another way to get a second opinion is to use the combined category chi-square test.

Combined Category Chi-Square Test

We employ the combined category chi-square test by combining adjacent rows or columns that have been meaningfully arranged from higher to lower levels of the variables that are defined by the rows and columns. Our corner cells test involved the four corners of the original data table:

	Degree of enthusiasm			
Degree of control	**High**	**Medium**	**Low**	Σ
High	0	3	3	6
Medium	10	3	2	15
Low	24	7	1	32
Σ	34	13	6	53

The expected frequencies for the four corner cells were

	High	Low
High	2.57	0.43
Low	21.43	3.57

where the upper-right corner, cell B, showed the very low expected frequency. Therefore, cell B is most in need of having its expected frequency increased. There are two ways to increase that expected frequency by combining categories: we can recruit (1) the row or (2) the column adjacent to cell B (or any other cell in need of augmented expected frequency). Recruiting the adjacent row yields the following tables of obtained and expected frequencies:

	Obtained frequencies				Expected frequencies		
	High	Low	Σ		High	Low	Σ
High	10	5	15	High	12.75	2.25	15.00
Low	24	1	25	Low	21.25	3.75	25.00
Σ	34	6	40	Σ	34.00	6.00	40.00

Recruiting the adjacent column yields the following tables of obtained and expected frequencies:

	Obtained frequencies				Expected frequencies		
	High	Low	Σ		High	Low	Σ
High	0	6	6	High	3.79	2.21	6.00
Low	24	8	32	Low	20.21	11.79	32.00
Σ	24	14	38	Σ	24.00	14.00	38.00

For the present example, recruiting the adjacent row yielded $\chi^2(1) = 6.32$, $p = .012$, phi $= .40$. Recruiting the adjacent column yielded $\chi^2(1) = 12.21$, $p = .0005$, phi $= .57$. It goes without saying that one does not compute both $\chi^2(1)$'s and present only the results of the more "favorable" $\chi^2(1)$. We either present both $\chi^2(1)$'s, p's, and phi's or adopt a set of rules beforehand telling us which $\chi^2(1)$ to compute. For example, rule 1 might be that we choose the table of which the smallest expected frequency is 5 or greater. If both tables (or neither table) give an expected frequency of 5 or greater, we go to rule 2, which might be that we choose the table with the more nearly equal (in percentage of total N) column totals, on the grounds that binomial data are better behaved when the splits are closer to 50/50.

Another rule, rule 3, if it were needed, might be that we choose the table with the more nearly equal (in percentage of total N) row totals, on the grounds that groups more nearly equal in size generally yield more powerful tests of significance. Note that in our terminology we have used "columns" to refer to the dependent variable and "rows" to refer to the independent variable. If we choose to set up our table differently, the rows and columns of rules 2 and 3 above become the columns and rows, respectively.

If we had applied our rules to the present situation, rule 1 would not have helped, since neither the recruitment of rows nor the recruitment of columns led to the smallest expected frequency reaching or exceeding 5. Rule 2, however, would have led us to choose the column recruitment method, since it yielded a column split of .63 − .37, whereas the row recruitment method yielded a column split of .85 − .15. In this example the column recruitment method yielded a phi of .57, a value that agreed well with the correlations obtained by the various other procedures described earlier.

Sometimes it happens that neither the recruitment of rows nor the recruitment of columns helps much to increase the expected frequency of the cell with the smallest expected frequency. In that case we simply continue to recruit columns or rows until we have achieved a satisfactory expected frequency.

THE FISHER EXACT PROBABILITY TEST

The Fisher exact test is another way to get a second opinion about the data in a 2×2 table of counts. A detailed discussion is available in Siegel (1956) and Siegel and Castellan (1988), and a shorter one in Hays (1981). Briefly, we find Fisher's exact test useful when we have a 2×2 table of independent observations, as in a 2×2 χ^2-type situation but when expected frequencies are very low. The test gives the one-tailed p that a particular table of counts or one reflecting a still stronger relationship between the two variables could have occurred if the null hypothesis of no relationship between the two variables were true and if the row and column totals were viewed as fixed. With cells labeled as

		Score		
		High	**Low**	
Group	**High**	A	B	$(A + B)$
	Low	C	D	$(C + D)$
		$(A + C)$	$(B + D)$	N

we find p for any one outcome (i.e., our obtained outcome, or one more extremely disconfirming of the null hypothesis of no relationship between the two variables) from the following relationship:

$$p = \frac{(A + B)!(C + D)!(A + C)!(B + D)!}{N!A!B!C!D!}$$

In using the Fisher exact test we compute p for our obtained table *and for each possible table showing a more extreme outcome than the one we obtained.* The p we want as a test for our hypothesis of no relationship is the sum of these p's.

The data for which we were seeking a second opinion were

Degree of control	Enthusiasm		
	High	Low	Σ
High	0	3	3
Low	24	1	25
Σ	24	4	28

In this case our result is the most extreme one (the most inconsistent with the null hypothesis of no relationship between the variables) we could obtain given our row and column totals. Therefore, we will need to obtain only a single p for our test. (When one of the cell entries is zero, we cannot have a more extreme result given fixed marginal totals.) For the table above we find

$$p = \frac{3!25!24!4!}{28!0!3!24!1!} = .0012$$

We interpret this to mean that there was only a 12-in-10,000 chance of obtaining cell entries as extreme as this if there were no relationship between the independent and dependent variables and given the row and column totals for our data. [Computing p was burdensome before the advent of inexpensive hand-held calculators, because factorials are unpleasant to compute by hand; e.g., $10! = 1 \times 2 \times 3 \times 4 \times 5 \times 6 \times 7 \times 8 \times 9 \times 10 = 3,628,800$; recall too that $0! = 1$. Siegel (1956), Siegel and Castellan (1988), and Zar (1984) provide useful tables for the Fisher exact test, but it is preferable to compute the actual p rather than to use only critical values of p.]

Our Fisher exact probability result of .0012, while quite significant, is not nearly so significant as the p based on our chi-square corner cells test. That difference appears to be primarily due to the unusually small expected frequency (0.43) in cell B of our χ^2 test, a frequency small enough to make us nervous about the accuracy of the χ^2 test.

What about an effect-size estimate? A serviceable approximation is obtained by finding the standard normal deviate Z that corresponds to our obtained p. Squaring Z and dividing by N gives us an estimate of the effect size analogous to that obtained by $\chi^2(1)/N = \phi^2$. Because we prefer the unsquared effect-size estimate, we employ

$$\phi \text{ estimated} = \sqrt{\frac{Z^2}{N}}$$

since

$$\phi = \sqrt{\frac{\chi^2(1)}{N}} \quad \text{and} \quad \chi^2(1) = Z^2$$

For our data, p was .0012, so Z was 3.04 and

$$\phi \text{ estimated} = \sqrt{\frac{(3.04)^2}{28}} = .57$$

an effect-size estimate that, though quite substantial, is much smaller than the ϕ of .85 obtained from our $\chi^2(1)$ test. That effect size [as well as the $\chi^2(1)$] was inflated primarily by the small expected frequency in cell B. The ϕ estimated at .57 agrees very well with the r's obtained earlier when we compared the high and low degree of control conditions following the analysis of variance. The r based on the unweighted means contrast was .57; that for the t test (weighted means) was .61.

In our example, the four cell entries were the most extreme that could have occurred as evidence against the hypothesis of no relationship between the variables given the four marginal totals. Earlier we noted that if the outcome obtained is not the most extreme possible, we must compute p for our result *and for every outcome more extreme.* The p we employ then is the sum of the p's obtained from all our tables, i.e., our own data-outcome p plus the p's of all outcomes more extreme. For example, suppose we had obtained these results:

	High	**Low**	Σ
High	1	2	3
Low	23	2	25
Σ	24	4	28

then

$$p = \frac{3!25!24!4!}{28!1!2!23!2!} = .044$$

The p of .044 is the p of this particular result, but the p we want is the p of our result and any more extreme. Therefore, we must also compute p for the more extreme result. In this case the only more extreme result possible is the one we really did obtain with $p = .0012$.[2] Now we add our p to those more extreme to get the value we need.

$$p = .044 + .0012 = .045$$

---

[2]One approach to finding all outcomes more extreme than a given outcome is to reduce by one the smallest cell frequency, a procedure that increases by one the two adjacent frequencies and decreases by one the diagonally opposite frequency. We continue this procedure until one of our cell frequencies is zero.

Note that the margins remain the same for the computation of each p. Only the cell counts change.

Before we leave this section of the Fisher exact test as a procedure for getting a second opinion on a χ^2 test, it will be useful to comment briefly on both these tests as examples of *nonparametric* statistical procedures. Nonparametric procedures are those in which it is less important to know the shape of the population distribution from which the research samples were drawn (Snedecor and Cochran, 1980). We know that t tests and F tests depend on the assumption of normal distributions, though both are fairly effective even when that assumption is not met. It is widely believed that χ^2 tests are nonparametric in the sense that no assumption about the population distribution is made. Cochran (1950), however, has pointed out that χ^2 tests may depend as much as do F tests on the assumption of normality, so χ^2 tests may not be so nonparametric after all. The Fisher exact test is far more truly nonparametric.

In this book generally we have not tried to cover nonparametric procedures, because data transformations often make the more flexible and powerful "parametric" procedures work about as well as do the nonparametric procedures.

Strengthening the Fisher Exact Test

We have seen that we are most likely to want to use the Fisher exact test when our sample sizes are small; i.e., when some of the expected frequencies are very small. However, it is just in such cases that the Fisher test is quite conservative (owing to the fact that counts cannot increase gradually but only in discontinuous jumps, e.g., 2 to 3 rather than 2 to 2.1 or 2.2), leading us too often to conclude that there is no significant effect. Fortunately, Overall (1980) and Overall, Rhoades, and Starbuck (1987) describe a procedure that strengthens the Fisher test appreciably. To employ this procedure we need only augment by 1 the frequencies of those cells of the 2×2 table in which the observed frequency is greater than the expected frequency and proceed with the usual computation of the Fisher test.

Suppose a small study in which 5 of 11 patients are randomly assigned to a new treatment procedure while the remaining 6 are assigned to the controls. If the null hypothesis of no difference between the treatment and control were true, what would be the probability of obtaining the following results?

Condition	Outcome		Σ
	Improved	**Not improved**	
Experimental	5	0	5
Control	3	3	6
Σ	8	3	11

We could begin to answer our question by computing the Fisher test, knowing that if we obtained a significant result (say, .05 or less), the true probability would be lower still. The Fisher test here yields

$$p = \frac{(A + B)!(C + D)!(A + C)!(B + D)!}{N!A!B!C!D!} = \frac{5!6!8!3!}{11!5!0!3!3!} = .12$$

Because one of the cell entries here is zero, there is no more extreme outcome possible, and so the one-tailed p above is that required for the Fisher test.

To employ the adjustment suggested by Overall, we begin by computing the expected frequencies for each cell. The expected frequency for cell A, for example, is $[(A + B)(A + C)]/N$, and all the resulting expected frequencies are

	Outcome		
Condition	**Improved**	**Not improved**	Σ
Experimental	3.64	1.36	5
Control	4.36	1.64	6
Σ	8	3	11

Because the cells in the upper-left to lower-right diagonal show larger obtained frequencies (5 and 3) than their expected frequencies (3.64 and 1.64), we augment those cells by 1 each and recompute the Fisher exact test. Augmenting these two cells yields the following table of "obtained" frequencies, and the accompanying recomputation of p:

	Outcome		
	Improved	**Not improved**	Σ
Experimental	6	0	6
Control	3	4	7
Σ	9	4	13

$$p = \frac{6!7!9!4!}{13!6!0!3!4!} = .049$$

We see that, when we employ Overall's correction, the one-tailed p of .12 of the uncorrected Fisher test has been reduced to a one-tailed p of $<.05$.

Adjustments for $\chi^2(1)$ Tests in 2 × 2 Tables

Suppose that for the original data just above we had employed not the Fisher exact test but the more common χ^2 test. We could use the general formula for χ^2 we have employed earlier, or for the 2 × 2 case we could use the raw score formula introduced in Chapter 14 in which the cells were labeled as for the Fisher table A, B, C, and D. Then

$$\chi^2(1) = \frac{N(AD - BC)^2}{(A + B)(C + D)(A + C)(B + D)} = \frac{11[(5)(3) - (0)(3)]^2}{(5 + 0)(3 + 3)(5 + 3)(0 + 3)}$$

$$= 3.44$$

To obtain the one-tailed p, we find Z from $\sqrt{\chi^2(1)}$ to be 1.85, $p = .032$, one-tailed. We note that this value is quite close to the adjusted Fisher test result of .049 even though all four cells have expected frequencies less than 5 and two cells have expected frequencies between 1 and 2. Suppose we had not done the strengthened Fisher test and were concerned about the small expected frequencies. The traditional adjustment is the Yates correction referred to in the beginning of this chapter. When applied to the present data, the Yates correction yields a $\chi^2(1)$ of 1.37 and a Z of 1.17, one-tailed $p = .12$, just as we found with the overly conservative unadjusted Fisher exact test.

Fortunately, much more accurate procedures than the Yates correction are available to guard against the increase in type I errors that may occur when some cells of the $\chi^2(1)$ test have very small expected frequencies. One of these is also attributable to Overall (1980): we employ the same augmentation procedure we used to strengthen the Fisher exact test and *then* employ the Yates correction. To illustrate, our original cell frequencies of 5, 0, 3, 3 were augmented to 6, 0, 3, 4, yielding a Fisher exact p of .049. The expected frequencies for these four augmented cell entries are

	Outcome		
	Improved	**Not improved**	Σ
Experimental	4.15	1.85	6
Control	4.85	2.15	7
Σ	9	4	13

We now compute χ^2 with the Yates correction as follows:

$$\chi^2(1) = \frac{N\left(|AD - BC| - \frac{N}{2}\right)^2}{(A + B)(C + D)(A + C)(B + D)} = \frac{13\left(|(6)(4) - (0)(3)| - \frac{13}{2}\right)^2}{(6 + 0)(3 + 4)(6 + 3)(0 + 4)}$$

$$= 2.63$$

To obtain the one-tailed p, we find Z from $\sqrt{\chi^2(1)}$, which is 1.62 with $p < .053$.

To recap our results, we can show the p values obtained by the $\sqrt{\chi^2(1)}$ test and the Fisher exact test with and without the Overall adjustment procedures:

	Fisher exact test	$\sqrt{\chi^2(1)}$ test
Unadjusted	.12*	.032
Overall-adjusted	.049	.053

*The Yates corrected $\sqrt{\chi^2(1)}$ yielded the same p of .12.

For these four tests it is clear that the Fisher exact test is appreciably different from the remaining three values, which differ relatively little among themselves. When the unadjusted $\chi^2(1)$ seems risky, either of the Overall adjustment procedures can be recommended [for still other procedures that can be employed, see Haber (1986) and Overall, Rhoades, and Starbuck (1987)].

COMPLETE PARTITIONING OF LARGER TABLES

The chapter on contrasts (Chapter 21) shows that for any diffuse, overall F test with k df in the numerator we can compute a set of k orthogonal contrasts, each of which addresses a focused, precise question. In an analogous way we can take a table of counts larger than 2×2 with df = (number of rows $-$ 1) $\times$ (number of columns $-$ 1) = k and subdivide or partition it into a set of k 2×2 tables that address focused, precise questions. A summary of procedures for partitioning, and a general method for computing $\chi^2(1)$ for any of the resulting 2×2 tables, is presented by Jean Bresnahan and Martin Shapiro (1966).

One procedure for the complete partitioning of a table is to begin in, e.g., the upper-left corner cell, so that for the top row the two new cells will contain the frequency of the upper-left cell and the remainder of the frequencies in that row, respectively. For the bottom row the two new cells will contain the frequency of the first column minus the frequency of the top-left cell and the balance of all frequencies not in either the top row or the leftmost column, respectively. We illustrate with the data of our example of degree of enthusiasm as a function of degree of experimental control:

		Enthusiasm		
Control	High	Medium	Low	Σ
High	0	3	3	6
Medium	10	3	2	15
Low	24	7	1	32
Σ	34	13	6	53

The midmost vertical and horizontal lines show where we made the partitions of the overall table to yield *subtable 1*:

	High	Lower	Σ
High	0	6	6
Lower	34	13	47
Σ	34	19	53

We obtain subtable 2 by omitting the first column completely and repeating the procedure shown for the remainder of the table.

	Medium	Low	Σ
High	3	3	6
Medium	3	2	5
Low	7	1	8
Σ	13	6	19

The midmost vertical and horizontal lines show where we made the partitions of the remainder table to yield *subtable 2*:

	Medium	Low	Σ
High	3	3	6
Lower	10	3	13
Σ	13	6	19

We have now run out of columns to drop, so we begin to drop rows. We return to our original table and drop the top row, leaving as our remainder table:

	High	Medium	Low	Σ
Medium	10	3	2	15
Low	24	7	1	32
Σ	34	10	3	47

The midmost vertical and horizontal lines show where we made the partitions of the remainder table to yield *subtable 3*:

	High	Lower	Σ
Medium	10	5	15
Lower	24	8	32
Σ	34	13	47

We have now run out of rows to drop, but we can return to dropping columns, i.e., the first column of the remainder table just above, leaving us the remainder table below, which turns out also to be the final subtable, *subtable 4*:

	Medium	**Low**	**Σ**
Medium	3	2	5
Low	7	1	8
Σ	10	3	13

Computing $\chi^2(1)$'s for Partitioned Tables

The general formula for computing $\chi^2(1)$'s for each table is

$$\chi^2(1) \text{ partitioned} = \text{``}\chi^2\text{'' cells} - \text{``}\chi^2\text{'' rows} - \text{``}\chi^2\text{'' columns} + \text{``}\chi^2\text{'' total}$$

where

$$\text{``}\chi^2\text{'' cells} = \sum^4 \frac{(O_c - E_c)^2}{E_c}$$

the sum (over the four cells of the subtable) of the standard χ^2 quantity $(O - E)^2/E$ but where the expected frequencies have been computed not from the subtable but from the full table; where

$$\text{``}\chi^2\text{'' rows} = \sum^2 \frac{(O_r - E_r)^2}{E_r}$$

the sum (over the two row totals of the subtable) of the standard χ^2 quantity $(O - E)^2/E$. Here, the observed row total is based on the subtable, but the expected row total is obtained from the full table-derived expected frequencies found in the subtable; where

$$\text{``}\chi^2\text{'' columns} = \sum^2 \frac{(O_k - E_k)^2}{E_k}$$

defined as for rows above, and where

$$\text{``}\chi^2\text{'' total} = \frac{(O_t - E_t)^2}{E_t}$$

the squared difference between the observed and expected total (N) for the subtable.

To illustrate the computations, we begin with the expected frequencies of the original table:

	Enthusiasm			
Control	**High**	**Medium**	**Low**	**Σ**
High	3.85	1.47	0.68	6.00
Medium	9.62	3.68	1.70	15.00
Low	20.53	7.85	3.62	32.00
Σ	34.00	13.00	6.00	53.00

Next we display (in Table 23.3) our four subtables each with its corresponding table of expected frequencies. These are based *not* on the subtable, but on the full table.

Finally we display the results of each step of our computation in a table designed to provide computational checks (see Table 23.4).

We illustrate the computational details only for subtable 4 of Table 23.3.

$$\text{``}\chi^2\text{'' cells} = \frac{(3 - 3.68)^2}{3.68} + \frac{(2 - 1.70)^2}{1.70} + \frac{(7 - 7.85)^2}{7.85} + \frac{(1 - 3.62)^2}{3.62} = 2.17$$

$$\text{``}\chi^2\text{'' rows} = \frac{(5 - 5.38)^2}{5.38} + \frac{(8 - 11.47)^2}{11.47} = 1.08$$

$$\text{``}\chi^2\text{'' columns} = \frac{(10 - 11.53)^2}{11.53} + \frac{(3 - 5.32)^2}{5.32} = 1.21$$

$$\text{``}\chi^2\text{'' total} = \frac{(13 - 16.85)^2}{16.85} = 0.88$$

The sum of the four partitioned $\chi^2(1)$'s is identical (within rounding error) with the overall $\chi^2(4)$ based on the original 3×3 table of frequencies. Now we can see which of the components of the overall χ^2 made the greatest contribution to the overall χ^2. This contribution is based in part on the strength of the

TABLE 23.3
Subtables of observed (and expected) frequencies

	Observed frequencies			Expected frequencies		
Subtable 1						
	0	6	6	3.85	2.15	6.00
	34	13	47	30.15	16.85	47.00
	34	19	53	34.00	19.00	53.00
Subtable 2						
	3	3	6	1.47	0.68	2.15
	10	3	13	11.53	5.32	16.85
	13	6	19	13.00	6.00	19.00
Subtable 3						
	10	5	15	9.62	5.38	15.00
	24	8	32	20.53	11.47	32.00
	34	13	47	30.15	16.85	47.00
Subtable 4						
	3	2	5	3.68	1.70	5.38
	7	1	8	7.85	3.62	11.47
	10	3	13	11.53	5.32	16.85

TABLE 23.4
Results of computations of partitioned $\chi^2(1)$'s

	Partitioned $\chi^2(1)$ =		"χ^2" cells	−	"χ^2" rows	−	"χ^2" columns	+	"χ^2" total
Subtable 1	12.12	=	12.12	−	0	−	0	+	0
Subtable 2	2.95	=	10.72	−	7.77	−	0	+	0
Subtable 3	0.31	=	1.68	−	0	−	1.37	+	0
Subtable 4	0.76	=	2.17	−	1.08	−	1.21	+	0.88
Σ	16.14	=	26.69	−	8.85	−	2.58	+	0.88

correlation ϕ found in each table and partly on the N for each table. Therefore, as usual, we want to compare phi's as much as we want to compare $\chi^2(1)$'s, as in the summary table below:

Subtable	$\chi^2(1)$	p	phi
1	12.12	.0005	.48
2	2.95	.09	.39
3	0.31	.58	.08
4	0.76	.38	.24

Subtable 1 showed both the largest and the most significant result. That subtable presented data showing higher levels of enthusiasm to be associated with lower levels of experimental control.

Subtable 2, while not significant at .05, showed nearly as large an effect as subtable 1, but the interpretation of the result should be cautious. Examining the expected frequencies for subtable 2 shows that most of the "χ^2" cells figure is due to the upper-right cell with expected frequency of only 0.68. Consequently, we may not want to put too much confidence in the result of subtable 2. Subtables 3 and 4 appear to require little comment.

A further word of caution is required. In interpretation of the individual 2×2 $\chi^2(1)$ results, there is a tendency to look only at the observed frequencies. Accurate interpretation of the computed χ^2's, however, requires that we examine the observed frequencies *in relation to the expected frequencies*.

The particular partitioning of the overall 3×3 table is not unique. Just as there are many sets of k orthogonal contrasts that can be computed for an F of k df in the numerator, so there are many alternative sets of k 2×2 tables that can be computed for a χ^2 with k df. For example, instead of beginning with the upper-left cell of the full table, we could have followed the exactly analogous procedure beginning with some other corner. When we begin with the lower-left cell, we obtain the four sets of observed and expected frequencies, $\chi^2(1)$'s, p's, and phi's shown in Table 23.5.

Each of the four subtables in Table 23.5 supports the same hypothesis that greater levels of enthusiasm are associated with lower levels of experimental control; but the size of the effect and its level of significance vary.

Just because it is possible to partition a table of frequencies completely is no reason to do so. It is a useful exploratory data-analytic procedure and is quite

TABLE 23.5
Analyses of four subtables

	Observed frequencies		Expected frequencies		χ^2	p	ϕ
Subtable 1							
	10	11	13.47	7.53	4.13	.042	.28
	24	8	20.53	11.47			
Subtable 2							
	6	5	5.15	2.38	2.36	.12	.35
	7	1	7.85	3.62			
Subtable 3							
	0	6	3.85	2.15	8.29	.004	.63
	10	5	9.62	5.38			
Subtable 4							
	3	3	1.47	0.68	1.34	.25	.35
	3	2	3.68	1.70			

valuable as a source of hypotheses for further investigation. Typically, however, we would approach the 2×2 $\chi^2(1)$ tests in the same spirit as we approach contrasts following an analysis of variance. We compute the $df = 1$ tests that we planned to make—those that address the questions of interest to us.

The Corner Cells Test Subtable

When the data are ordered from more to less in both the rows and columns (as is the case for the example we have been using), it is natural to employ the *corner cells test* we described earlier. The modification we make here is based on the idea of partitioning a table completely. It involves our using the expected frequencies computed from the full table, not just from the corner cells alone. Our computations are just as for any of the subtables of a partitioned table where

Partitioned $\chi^2(1)$ = "χ^2" cells − "χ^2" rows − "χ^2" columns + "χ^2" total

For the corner cells test of our example

	Obtained frequency				Expected frequency		
	High	**Low**	Σ		**High**	**Low**	Σ
High	0	3	3	**High**	3.85	0.68	4.53
Low	24	1	25	**Low**	20.53	3.62	24.15
Σ	24	4	28	Σ	24.38	4.30	28.68

$$\chi^2(1) = 14.25 - 0.55 - 0.03 + 0.02 = 13.69$$

with $p = .0001$ and $\phi = .70$.

This corner cells test with expected frequencies based on the entire table yielded a somewhat more conservative value of χ^2 and ϕ compared with the original corner cells test with expected frequencies based only on the data from the four corner cells. That $\chi^2(1)$ was 20.16, $\phi = .85$, probably inflated by an unusually low expected frequency of 0.43 in one of the cells.

CONTRASTS IN PROPORTIONS

Throughout our discussion of the subdividing of larger tables we have emphasized the conceptual relationship between the study of contrasts following the analysis of variance and the study of 2×2 tables following the analysis of larger tables. It sometimes happens for larger tables that one dimension can be ordered from more to less, and that information from the other dimension can be expressed as a proportion of the total frequency found in each level of the ordered dimension. In situations of that sort, contrasts can be computed directly, and we illustrate this method for the example we have been following.

Control		**Enthusiasm** High	Medium	Low	Σ
A {	High	0	3	3	6
	Medium	10	3	2	15
B	Low	24	7	1	32
$N = A + B$		34	13	6	53

Because it leads to a more nearly 50/50 split, we designate the bottom row rather than the top row as B; the two top rows together are designated A. For each of our three columns, we will also want the quantities $P = B/N$; $S_p^2 = P(1 - P)/N$, the squared standard error of the proportion; and λ, the contrast weights. From these ingredients we can compute a Z test of significance of the contrast by means of a formula suggested by Donald B. Rubin (1981).

	High	Medium	Low
$P = B/N$	.71	.54	.17
$S_p^2 = \dfrac{P(1 - P)}{N}$	.0061	.0191	.0232
λ	+1	0	−1

Since

$$Z = \frac{\Sigma P\lambda}{\sqrt{\Sigma S_p^2 \lambda^2}}$$

$$Z = \frac{.71(+1) + .54(0) + .17(-1)}{\sqrt{.0061(1) + .0191(0) + .0232(1)}} = \frac{.54}{\sqrt{.0293}} = 3.15$$

for which $p = .0016$, two-tailed, $Z^2 = \chi^2(1) = 9.92$, and $\phi = .43$.

    This result is somewhat more conservative than those of the various alternative analyses, e.g., the contrasts following the analysis of variance. The reason appears to be the loss of information involved in treating the top two rows of our data table as though they were homogeneous. Actually, those two rows provide additional evidence in support of the relationship between degree of experimental control and level of enthusiasm. We can demonstrate this by repeating our contrast in the proportions of just the top two rows.

		High	Medium	Low	Σ
A	High	0	3	3	6
B	Medium	10	3	2	15
N		10	6	5	21
P		1.0000	0.5000	0.4000	
S_p^2		0	.0417	.0480	
λ		+1	0	-1	

$$Z = \frac{1.0(+1) + .5(0) + .4(-1)}{\sqrt{0(1) + .0417(0) + .0480(1)}} = \frac{.60}{\sqrt{.0480}} = 2.74$$

for which $p = .0062$, two-tailed, $Z^2 = \chi^2(1) = 7.51$, and $\phi = .60$.

    Therefore, the data in the top two rows alone provide additional strong support for the relationship between degree of control and level of enthusiasm.

    An alternative procedure we might have employed would have performed the contrast in the proportions omitting the medium level of degree of experimental control. That would have yielded a Z of 3.46, $p = .00054$, $\phi = .56$, a value in good agreement with those obtained following the analysis of variance. The r based on the unweighted means contrast was .57; that for the t test (weighted means) was .61.

STANDARDIZING ROW AND COLUMN TOTALS

As tables of counts grow very large, it becomes almost impossible to determine by inspection just what is going on in the data. A major problem is that our eye is likely to be attracted to very large values. For example, in the following table, what stands out?

24	10	6
36	15	9
48	20	12
132	55	33

We are most likely to see the 132 as a standout cell. Actually, however, that value is just what we would expect if the null hypothesis of no relationship between the variables were true. It is a large value only because it falls in a large row and a large column. We could do better than inspecting the raw counts by making a table of partial χ^2 values, i.e., computing $(O - E)^2/E$ for each cell. At least that would tell us where the bulk of the χ^2 value is coming from. However, what shall we do about very small expected frequencies that yield perhaps exaggeratedly large values of partial χ^2?

Computing $(O - E)^2/E$ for each cell is one way of taking the size of the row and column into account. A very valuable alternative has been described by Frederick Mosteller (1968), who shows us how to take the size of the row and column totals into account. The method has been called *standardizing the margins,* and it proceeds by setting all row totals equal to each other and all column totals equal to each other. We illustrate the method with our continuing example.

| | **Enthusiasm** | | | |
Control	**High**	**Medium**	**Low**	Σ
High	0	3	3	6
Medium	10	3	2	15
Low	24	7	1	32
Σ	34	13	6	53

An Example

We begin by dividing each cell count by the sum of the column in which we find the count.

	High	**Medium**	**Low**	Σ
High	.00	.23	.50	.73
Medium	.29	.23	.33	.85
Low	.71	.54	.17	1.42
Σ	1.00	1.00	1.00	3.00

This first step has equalized (standardized to 1.00 in this case) the column totals, but the row totals are far from equal. To set them equal we now divide each entry of this new table by its row total, yielding:

	High	Medium	Low	Σ
High	.00	.32	.68	1.00
Medium	.34	.27	.39	1.00
Low	.50	.38	.12	1.00
Σ	.84	.97	1.19	3.00

For simplicity we are presenting only two decimal places, but it is usually wise to employ three or four decimal places while calculating. We now continue the process of dividing the counts of each new table by the column totals, which unequalizes the row totals. We then divide the counts of the following table by the row totals, and so on until the row totals are all equal and the column totals are all equal. The individual row totals will not equal the individual column totals except in cases where the number of rows and columns are equal. We continue the process of dividing by column totals, then by row totals. In the following table, the subtables on the right always follow the subtables immediately to their left; the results of a division in a right-hand subtable are displayed in the next left-hand subtable below, so that progress through the whole table is like reading sentences down a page.

	Dividing by column totals				Dividing by row totals			
	High	Medium	Low	Σ	High	Medium	Low	Σ
High	.00	.33	.58	0.91	.00	.36	.64	1.00
Medium	.41	.28	.32	1.01	.40	.28	.32	1.00
Low	.59	.39	.10	1.08	.55	.36	.09	1.00
Σ	1.00	1.00	1.00	3.00	.95	1.00	1.05	3.00
High	.00	.36	.61	0.97	.00	.37	.63	1.00
Medium	.42	.28	.30	1.00	.42	.27	.31	1.00
Low	.58	.36	.09	1.03	.56	.35	.09	1.00
Σ	1.00	1.00	1.00	3.00	.98	.99	1.03	3.00
High	.00	.37	.62	0.99	.00	.38	.62	1.00
Medium	.43	.27	.30	1.00	.43	.27	.30	1.00
Low	.57	.36	.08	1.01	.57	.35	.08	1.00
Σ	1.00	1.00	1.00	3.00	1.00	1.00	1.00	3.00

The row and column totals have now all converged to unity; we have finished standardizing the margins. There is one more step, however, that will throw our results into bolder relief, and that is to subtract from each entry of the final table the grand mean of all cells. In this case that value is $3.00/9 = .33$, yielding as our table of residuals the following:

Control	Enthusiasm		
	High	Medium	Low
High	−.33	.05	.29
Medium	.10	−.06	−.03
Low	.24	.02	−.25

The interpretation of this display is quite direct and, of course, quite consistent with the results we have been examining in our continuing analyses of these data. The greatest overrepresentation is in the upper-right and lower-left corners, while the greatest underrepresentation is in the upper-left and lower-right corners. Clearly, the higher the degree of control, the lower the level of enthusiasm. The entries from the middle row and middle column are all fairly small. It is the corners where the action is. The crossed linear contrast weights shown below fit these results very well.

	High	Medium	Low
High	−1	0	+1
Medium	0	0	0
Low	+1	0	−1

In fact, the correlation (r) (over the nine cells) of the relative frequencies and the contrast weights is .966, showing how good the fit of the data is to the crossed linear contrast weights.

A More Complex Example

In this more complex illustration, 1,264 college students were cross-classified by (a) the field of study (humanities or social, biological, or physical science) in which they intended to concentrate (the rows) and (b) the field of study in which they actually took their degree (the columns).

Intended field of study	Field in which degree was awarded				
	Humanities	Social science	Biological science	Physical science	Σ
Humanities	133	158	14	4	309
Social science	57	312	17	5	391
Biological science	16	72	94	10	192
Physical science	34	102	56	180	372
Σ	240	644	181	199	1264

After the first step in standardizing the margin we obtain the following table:

	Humanities	Social science	Biological science	Physical science	Σ
Humanities	.55	.25	.08	.02	.90
Social science	.24	.48	.09	.03	.84
Biological science	.07	.11	.52	.05	.75
Physical science	.14	.16	.31	.90	1.51
Σ	1.00	1.00	1.00	1.00	4.00

We omit the next 10 such tables and report the final table in which the margins have been successfully standardized.

	Humanities	Social science	Biological science	Physical science	Σ
Humanities	.60	.26	.09	.05	1.00
Social science	.27	.55	.12	.06	1.00
Biological science	.08	.13	.66	.13	1.00
Physical science	.05	.06	.13	.76	1.00
Σ	1.00	1.00	1.00	1.00	4.00

For our final table of residuals from the mean $(4.00/16 = .25)$ we then have

	Humanities	Social science	Biological science	Physical science
Humanities	.35	.01	−.16	−.20
Social science	.02	.30	−.13	−.19
Biological science	−.17	−.12	.41	−.12
Physical science	−.20	−.19	−.12	.51

The overwhelming result, of course, is that students are much more likely to graduate in their intended field than in any other. We could provide contrast weights to help us assess the extent to which that is the case. Our weights are given below:

	H	SS	BS	PS
H	3	−1	−1	−1
SS	−1	3	−1	−1
BS	−1	−1	3	−1
PS	−1	−1	−1	3

The correlation (r) (over the 16 cells) of the relative frequencies and the contrast weights is .951, showing a very good fit between the data and the contrast weights.

We can go a little further in understanding the data if we note that the four fields of study can be arrayed on a dimension of "soft" to "hard." That is, humanities are "softer" than the social sciences, which in turn are softer than the biological sciences, and these in turn are softer than the physical sciences. If that is a reasonable ordering, theoretically speaking, then we might suggest that when people do not graduate in their intended field they are more likely to graduate in a field more adjacent (rather than not adjacent) on the scale of soft-hard. The weights below are appropriate to this hypothesis and are orthogonal to the weights shown in the preceding table.

	H	SS	BS	PS
H	0	2	−1	−1
SS	1	0	1	−2
BS	−2	1	0	1
PS	−1	−1	2	0

The correlation (r) (over the 16 cells) of the relative frequencies and these contrast weights was .193, suggesting at least a moderate relationship between second choices of field for graduation and adjacency to original choice.

CHAPTER
24

MULTIVARIATE PROCEDURES

BACKGROUND

In the following pages we provide an overview of the statistical procedures generally called *multivariate*. However, as we shall see, some of the procedures described in detail in earlier sections of this book were in some senses also multivariate. Our intent here is to introduce the major multivariate procedures within the framework of a system of classification that will make it easier to think about the many different techniques.

Whereas in earlier sections we provided computational procedures for all the methods presented, we shall not do so here. First, there is not space enough left. Second, the computations are generally complex and unpleasant even with the help of an excellent hand-held calculator. Finally, the computations are almost always done by computer; happily, however, there are many packaged programs available to get the computations done.

Because we are only illustrative in this section, details must be found elsewhere. Of the many excellent sources on multivariate methods of analysis we have found especially useful the books by Jacob Cohen and Patricia Cohen (1983), William Cooley and Paul Lohnes (1971), Richard Harris, (1985), Charles Judd and Gary McClelland (1989), Donald Morrison (1976), and Norman Nie, C. Hadlai Hull, Jean Jenkins, Karin Steinbrenner, and Dale Bent (1975). Although we cannot describe even briefly all the various multivariate procedures, the classification and overview we provide should be sufficient that most omitted procedures may be viewed as (a) close relatives of those described, (b) special cases of those described, or (c) combinations of those described.

It simplifies our thinking about multivariate procedures if we conceive of one or more sets of independent or predictor variables and one or more sets of dependent or criterion variables. Then our first classificatory principle is simply whether the procedure is concerned with *either* the independent (predictor) *or* the dependent (criterion) variables or whether it is concerned with *both* the independent (predictor) *and* the dependent (criterion) variables. We begin our discussion with the former.

RELATIONSHIPS WITHIN SETS OF VARIABLES: REDESCRIPTORS

The first class of procedures has in common that a set of variables—either independent (predictor) variables or dependent (criterion) variables—is to be redescribed in such a way as to meet one or more of the following goals:

1. *Reduce the number of variables* required to describe, predict, or explain the phenomena of interest
2. *Assess the psychometric properties* of standardized measures or measures under construction
3. *Improve the psychometric properties* of measures under construction by suggesting (a) how test and subtest reliability might be improved by adding relatively homogeneous items or variables, (b) how subtests are related to each other, and (c) what new subtests might be usefully constructed
4. *Test hypotheses* derived from theories implying certain types of patterns of descriptors emerging from the analyses
5. *Generate hypotheses* in the spirit of exploratory data analysis on the basis of unexpected descriptors emerging from the analyses

Of the many specific procedures falling into this class we focus on one to give a flavor of the usage of that procedure. We also describe some others falling into this class, but only very briefly.

PRINCIPAL COMPONENTS ANALYSIS

Suppose that a number of variables, say, 11, have been administered to a large group of people and we want to know whether we could do an adequate job of describing the total variation in the data on all 11 variables with a much smaller number of "supervariables" or components. *Principal components analysis* rewrites the original set of 11 variables into a new set of 11 components (usually) that have the following properties. The first principal component rewrites the original variables into the linear combination that does the best job of discriminating among the subjects of our sample.[1] It is the single supervariable that accounts for the maximum possible variance in all the original variables.

---

[1] In a linear combination, each of the original values is multiplied by a mathematically determined weight, and the products of the original values and their weights are summed for each subject to form their new score on the component.

The second principal component is essentially the same *type* of supervariable, except that it operates on the variation in the data remaining after removal of the variation attributable to the first principal component. Thus the two components are orthogonal, since there is no overlap between the first and second principal components. That is, the second operates only on the leftovers of the first. After the second principal component has been extracted, the third is computed, and so on until as many components have been computed as there are variables. (If one or more of the original variables is completely predictable from the other original variables, the total number of components computed is reduced accordingly.)

How does it help us in our search for "supervariables" to rewrite 11 variables as 11 components? The logic of the method is such that the first few components computed tend to account for much more of the total variation among subjects on the full set of variables than would be the case for an equal number of the original variables, chosen at random. Thus, the first principal component alone might account for 30, 40, or 50 percent of the total variation among the subjects on the 11 variables. In contrast, only 9.1 percent would be expected if the early components were no more supervariables than any variable chosen randomly from the original set of 11.

We can illustrate with the small example below how just a few components can reexpress most of the information in several variables. As in principal components (and related) procedures we begin with the matrix of intercorrelations. Here we show only five variables intercorrelated; variables correlating most highly with one another have been listed closest to one another, i.e., A, B, and C and then D and E.

	Variables				
Variables	**A**	**B**	**C**	**D**	**E**
A	1.00	.80	.70	.10	.00
B	.80	1.00	.90	.20	.10
C	.70	.90	1.00	.10	.00
D	.10	.20	.10	1.00	.80
E	.00	.10	.00	.80	1.00

Since the lower-left and upper-right large triangles of this correlation matrix are mirror images, we can concentrate on just one of these, say, the lower-left. To call attention to the major features, we decompose the large triangle into three smaller geometric shapes, a triangle, a rectangle, and a square:

	A	B
B	.80	
C	.70	.90

	A	B	C
D	.10	.20	.10
E	.00	.10	.00

	D
E	.80

The triangle of three correlations represents all the intercorrelations of variables A, B, and C, which a more formal analysis would show to be important contributors to the first principal component. The median intercorrelation is .80. The square represents the correlation (.80) of variables D and E, which a more formal analysis would show to be important contributors to the second principal component. The rectangle shows the correlations between the variables A, B, and C and the variables D and E. The median correlation is .10. The diagram below gives the average intercorrelation *within* a group of variables constituting a supervariable and the average intercorrelation *between* the variables constituting a supervariable:

$$\text{I} \qquad\qquad\qquad\qquad\qquad\qquad\qquad\qquad \text{II}$$
$$.80 \text{——————} .10 \text{——————} .80$$

The difference between the median of all within and the median of all between correlations, .80 versus .10 in this case, provides information on the strength and "purity" of the supervariable. In this example the two supervariables are nearly independent of each other and highly consistent internally.

This example is not technically an example of principal components analysis, but it serves to convey the spirit of the enterprise. Actually the example is an illustration of one of the related procedures called "cluster analysis."

The process of principal components analysis also begins with the intercorrelation of all the variables. Then the components are computed, and the *loading* (or *component loading* or *factor loading*) of each variable on each component is computed. These loadings are the correlations between each variable (usually the rows) and the newly computed components (usually the columns). Each component is understood or interpreted in terms of the pattern of loadings. We illustrate this presently.

Typically, however, the components as first extracted from the correlations among the variables are not very interpretable (except perhaps the first component). They are typically made more interpretable by a process called *rotation*. We illustrate this process by showing a plot of the data of the following matrix of correlations of variables with components; just the first two components are shown (see Figure 24-1).

	Loadings before rotation	
	Component I	Component II
Variable 1	.60	.55
Variable 2	.50	.50
Variable 3	.70	.60
Variable 4	.50	−.50
Variable 5	.60	−.55
Variable 6	.70	−.60

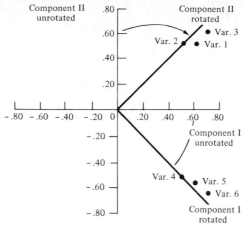

FIGURE 24-1
Loadings of six variables on two rotated and unrotated components (or factors).

With respect to the original unrotated components, I and II, all the variables loaded highly on component I, while half the variables showed a strong positive and half showed a strong negative loading on component II. When we rotate the axes, in this particular case 45 degrees clockwise, we find that three of the variables load highly only on one rotated component, while the other three load highly only on the other rotated component. The new *rotated component loadings* have now become

	Loadings after rotation	
	Component I	**Component II**
Variable 1	.04	.82
Variable 2	.00	.70
Variable 3	.06	.92
Variable 4	.70	.00
Variable 5	.82	.04
Variable 6	.92	.06

If we were now told that variables 1, 2, and 3 were alternative measures of sociability, and variables 4, 5, and 6 were alternative measures of intellectual ability, the rotated components would be far more useful than the unrotated. The unrotated would be very difficult to interpret; the rotated would suggest that our six variables could be reduced to two supervariables, or *composite variables* (sociability and intellectual ability), that were independent of each other (orthogonal). That is, when we rotated the axes of components I and II, we kept them orthogonal (at right angles to one another). Sometimes it is useful to allow the rotations to be nonorthogonal, as when the hypothesized underlying super-variables are thought to be somewhat correlated in the real world. Such nonorthogonal rotations are called *oblique*.

The most commonly used method of orthogonal rotation is called *varimax*; it tries to maximize the variation of the squared loadings for each component by making the loadings go to zero or to 1.00 to the extent possible. This method of rotation helps make components easier to interpret.

APPLICATIONS: CONSTRUCT VALIDITY

As part of the construct validation of a new measure of sensitivity to nonverbal cues, the *PONS* test, it was important to assess the independence of this measure from measures of intellectual functioning (Rosenthal, Hall, DiMatteo, Rogers, and Archer, 1979). For a sample of 110 high school students we had available their PONS subtest scores to items reflecting sensitivity to nonverbal cues that were positive and submissive in content, positive and dominant, negative and submissive, and negative and dominant.

In addition, we had available scores on the verbal SAT, the math SAT, and the Otis IQ test. If the PONS were really independent of intellectual ability, as hoped and hypothesized, we should obtain two principal components that, after varimax rotation, should yield an "intelligence component" and an orthogonal "nonverbal sensitivity component." Here is what was found:

| Variable | Loadings after rotation | |
	Component 1	Component 2
Otis IQ	.19	.64
Verbal SAT	−.02	.89
Math SAT	−.07	.84
PONS:		
Positive-submissive	.66	.02
Positive-dominant	.82	−.00
Negative-submissive	.77	.06
Negative-dominant	.78	.06

These results, then, were in good agreement with the predictions and the hopes. The first rotated component was essentially a PONS component; the second was an intellectual component. Just as had been the case for our simpler hypothetical example above, before rotation the first principal component had shown positive loadings by all the variables; the second principal component had shown positive loadings by some of the variables (the three intellectual variables) and negative loadings by some of the variables (the four variables of sensitivity to nonverbal cues).

APPLICATIONS: SUBTEST CONSTRUCTION

The preceding application of principal components analysis was to construct validation. The next application is to *subtest formation*. The PONS test of sensitivity to nonverbal cues was made up of 220 items, 20 in each of 11 channels. The channels were in either the visual or the auditory domain as follows:

	Visual channels			
Auditory channels	**None**	**Face**	**Body**	**Face + body**
None		1	2	3
Content-filtered	4	5	6	7
Random-spliced	8	9	10	11

Face-channel items showed only facial cues, body-channel items showed only body cues, while face + body–channel items showed both. Content-filtered items preserved tone but not content, by removing high frequencies. Random-spliced items preserved different aspects of tone but not content by random scrambling of speech.

After intercorrelating the 11 channels and channel combinations shown above, extracting four principal components and rotating orthogonally (varimax), we obtained the loadings shown in Table 24.1.

TABLE 24.1
Eleven PONS subtests' loadings on four components

	Loadings on components			
Variables	**1**	**2**	**3**	**4**
Face	.62	.12	.10	.15
Face + body	.68	.07	.11	.24
Face + random-spliced	.70	.02	.06	.22
Face + content-filtered	.65	−.03	.09	.20
Face + body + random-spliced	.67	.30	.09	.05
Face + body + content-filtered	.70	.06	.10	.32
Random-spliced	.14	.95	.03	.12
Content-filtered	.20	.04	.96	.14
Body	.47	−.04	.02	.59
Body + random-spliced	.33	.07	.12	.57
Body + content-filtered	.11	.13	.08	.82
Sum of squared loadings	3.11	1.04	1.01	1.66
Percentage of variance	28	9	9	15
Number of variables defining components	6	1	1	3
Number of items defining components	120	20	20	60

The first component was characterized by face presence, reflecting ability to decode nonverbal cues from any combination of channels so long as the face was included as a source of information. The second and third principal components each reflected a specific skill: decoding random-spliced and content-filtered cues, respectively, in the absence of any visual cues. The fourth principal component reflected ability to decode body cues in the absence of facial cues.

The first row at the bottom of the matrix of loadings shows the sum of the squared loadings, the amount of variance accounted for by that factor. (Alternative terms for the sum of the squared loadings, before rotation, are *eigenvalue*, *latent root, characteristic root*, or just *root*; Armor, 1974.) The second row at the bottom of Table 24.1 shows the percentage of variance accounted for by each component. It is computed by dividing the sum of the squared loadings for that component by the total number of variables, 11 in this illustration. For the present analysis these first two rows show that the first and fourth components are more important in the sense of accounting for more variance than are the second and third components. Note that this can occur only after rotation. Before rotation no succeeding component can be larger than a preceding component, because each succeeding component is extracted only from the residuals of the preceding component.

The third row at the bottom of Table 24.1 lists the number of variables serving to define each component. The last row lists the number of raw test items contributing to the variables defining each component.

A variety of procedures are available for forming scales from principal components analyses. Many of these generate scores for each subject for each component in such a way as to keep scores on the various components uncorrelated with each other. In our own work, however, we have used a simple procedure that often leads to psychologically more interpretable scales, subtests, or composite variables, although our composite variables may no longer be entirely uncorrelated with each other. We simply combine all the variables serving to define each component, giving equal weight to each variable, a procedure that is recommended for both theoretical and statistical reasons (Dawes and Corrigan, 1974). How we actually combine variables depends on their form. If they are all measured on similar scales and have similar standard deviations, we simply add or average the variables.[2] That was the situation for the analysis above. Since scores of each variable could range from 0 to 20 and standard deviations were similar, we simply added subjects' scores on the variables serving to define each component.

Thus, each subject could earn a score of 0 to 120 on the composite variable based on the first rotated component, scores of 0 to 20 on the second and third rotated components, and scores of 0 to 60 on the fourth rotated component.

---

[2]This assumes that all variables have loadings of the same sign or are positively correlated with each other. A variable negatively correlated with the others can be employed only after changing its scale into the proper direction, e.g., by multiplying each observation by −1.

When the variables are not all on the same scale or metric, we would transform all variables to standard scores before adding or averaging. When there are no missing data, it may not matter whether we add or average the scores on the variables defining each component. However, when there may be missing data, it is safer to use the mean of the variables rather than their sum as the new or super variable.

One rarely is very interested in seeing the loadings of as many principal components (either unrotated or rotated) as there are variables. A number of quantitative criteria are available to help decide how many to examine. For subtest or composite variable construction we recommend a step-up approach in which we examine in turn the rotated first two components, then the first three, then the first four, and so on. The solution we choose should be the one that makes the most substantive sense. Experience suggests that looking only at the rotated end result (i.e., the loadings of all variables on all the components extracted based on any of several quantitative rules for stopping the extraction process) typically yields more components than are needed to construct useful, meaningful subtests or composite variables and fewer components that are interpretable. It should be noted that at each step up, the definition of each component changes. Thus the first component after rotating two components will not be the same component as the first component after rotating three or four or more components.

APPLICATIONS: RELIABILITY ANALYSIS

Since the first unrotated principal component is the best single summarizer of the linear relationships among all the variables, it can be employed as the basis for an estimate of the internal-consistency reliability of a test. We would probably employ such an estimate only where it made substantive sense to think of an overall construct tapped by all the variables to some degree. Such might be the case for many measures of ability, adjustment, achievement, and the like.

It would make sense, for example, to think of an ability to decode nonverbal cues. We might, therefore, estimate the internal consistency of the PONS test from the first principal component *before rotation*. After rotation it would no longer be the best single summarizer, though it would probably give a far better structure to the data working in concert with other rotated components.

David Armor (1974) provides the computational formula for his index of reliability, theta, an index that gives a maximum possible reliability

$$\text{theta} = \frac{V}{V-1}\left(\frac{L-1}{L}\right)$$

where V is the number of variables and L is the latent root (eigenvalue or sum of squared loadings). For the 220 items of the PONS test with each item regarded as a variable, we found

$$\text{theta} = \frac{220}{219}\left(\frac{13.217-1}{13.217}\right) = .929$$

The analogous reliability based on the 11 channels rather than the 220 items was

$$\text{theta} = \frac{11}{10} \left(\frac{4.266 - 1}{4.266} \right) = .842$$

It should be noted that the latent root of 4.266 for the 11 variable analysis is substantially (37 percent) larger than the latent root of 3.113 obtained for the first principal component after rotation.

Armor's theta is a very convenient index of reliability that we employ routinely in our own work so long as we have other reasons to employ principal components analyses in any case. However, because it is an index of maximum possible reliability, we recommend using it along with the more conservative reliability estimation procedures, e.g., those based on analysis of variance or intercorrelations adjusted by the Spearman-Brown procedure (see, e.g., Chapter 3 and, for more detail, Rosenthal, 1987a).

Before we leave this brief discussion of reliability, it may be useful to ask how it is possible that a test (e.g., the PONS) could be made up of several orthogonal principal components and still have high internal-consistency reliability. By definition, we know that the orthogonal components cannot be making any contribution of correlation to each other. However, the way internal-consistency reliability for a total test score is defined, this reliability increases as the mean of the intercorrelations increases and as the number of items increases. Therefore, a mean intercorrelation lowered by the presence of orthogonal components can be compensated for by an increase in the number of items that correlate positively with some other items. Longer tests, therefore, can have high internal-consistency reliability even when they comprise orthogonal components or factors.

OTHER REDESCRIPTORS

The most commonly used alternative to the principal components method for the redescription of variables is actually an entire family of alternatives called *factor analysis*. Sometimes principal components analysis is viewed as a special type of factor analysis, but there are subtle differences between principal components and other forms of factor analysis. For example, some forms of factor analysis make more assumptions than are required for principal components analysis and introduce a greater series of options for viewing the data. As a result, different investigators exercising different options will obtain different factor structures from the same data. Beginners would do well to employ principal components with varimax rotation as their standard procedure. Stanley Mulaik (1972) and R. J. Rummel (1970) provide detailed comparisons of various types of factor analysis, and Jae-On Kim (1975) and Kim and Mueller (1978) provide briefer overviews.

Cluster analysis represents a family of methods for grouping variables ranging from some very simple to some very complicated procedures. A very simple form of cluster analysis was illustrated when we first introduced principal components analysis; there we used as a criterion of cluster tightness the difference between the average within-cluster intercorrelations and the average between-cluster correlations. Kenneth Bailey (1974) gives a detailed summary of the methods, and Ki Hang Kim and Fred Roush (1980) give a brief but quite mathematical discussion.

In clustering, it is not necessary that it be variables that are grouped together. We could instead cluster the subjects or other sampling units for whom measurements have been obtained. Then, instead of grouping variables together that correlate highly over a list of persons, we could group persons together that correlate highly over a list of variables. A typology of persons or other sampling units could thereby be constructed.

It should be noted, however, that factor analysis and principal components analysis can also be employed to the same end. We illustrate what is involved with a small example; these procedures involve what amounts to an exchange of rows with columns, assuming that we always intercorrelate columns with an eye to their redescription.

Data matrices

IA. Redescribing variables* Variable						IIA. Redescribing persons[†] Person						
	1	2	3	4	5		1	2	3	4	5	6
Person 1						Variable 1						
Person 2						Variable 2						
Person 3						Variable 3						
Person 4						Variable 4						
Person 5						Variable 5						
Person 6												

*To redescribe the variables as clusters, factors, or types.
[†]To redescribe the persons as clusters, factors, or types.

We call the two tables above *data matrices*; the one on the left has each person's scores on all variables in one row, while the one on the right has each variable's scores for each person in one row. From these data matrices we compute the correlation matrices shown below by correlating each column's scores with every other column's scores:

Correlation matrices

IB* Variable						IIB[†] Person						
	1	2	3	4	5		1	2	3	4	5	6
Variable 1						Person 1						
Variable 2						Person 2						
Variable 3						Person 3						
Variable 4						Person 4						
Variable 5						Person 5						
						Person 6						

*Matrix IB has each correlation based on six observations, i.e., the six persons.
[†]Matrix IIB has each correlation based on five observations, i.e., the five variables.

Clustering or factoring the correlation matrices above would lead to a re-description of the five variables in terms of some (usually smaller) number of groupings of variables in the case of the matrix on the left (IB), and to a re-description of the six persons in terms of some (usually smaller) number of group-ings of persons in the case of the matrix on the right (IIB). Our example of six persons measured on five variables was convenient as an illustration, but we should note that, in general, factors will be more reliable when the N on which each correlation is based is much larger than the number of variables or persons being intercorrelated and factor-analyzed.

Many other procedures have been developed to serve as redescriptors. They have in common that they examine the relationships among objects or stimuli in terms of some measure of similarity or dissimilarity, and then try to infer some number of dimensions that would meaningfully account for the ob-tained pattern of similarities or dissimilarities among the objects or stimuli. The methods have been called *dimensional analysis* (a term referring to distance anal-ysis), *multidimensional scaling, multidimensional unfolding, proximity analysis, similarity analysis, smallest-space analysis,* and other procedures summarized by various authors (see Coombs, Dawes, and Tversky, 1970; Rummel, 1970; and the more detailed discussions by Guttman, 1966; Lazarsfeld and Henry, 1968; Torg-erson, 1958; Young and Hamer, 1987; and especially by Shepard, Romney, and Nerlove, 1972).

RELATIONSHIPS AMONG SETS OF VARIABLES

The remaining multivariate procedures that will be summarized only briefly are those in which we are interested in the relationship between two or more sets of variables heuristically classified as independent (predictor) and dependent (crite-rion) variables. Table 24.2 provides a structure for the survey of these procedures.

The left half of the table lists the procedures in which a set of independent or predictor variables is assessed for its relationship to a single dependent or crite-rion variable. The right half of the table lists the analogous procedure but for which there is more than one dependent or criterion value. Thus each of the six method pairs of the table has one member of the pair based on a single depen-dent variable and one based on multiple dependent variables.

The first four method pairs are labeled "correlational," and the last two method pairs are labeled "analysis of variance." While this traditional distinc-tion is useful in helping us find our way to the various packaged computer pro-grams, it is also useful for conceptual purposes to view the analysis of variance procedures as special cases of the correlational procedures both subsumed under the same fundamental model for the analysis of data, the general linear model (Cohen and Cohen, 1983). In what follows we describe briefly each of the method pairs in turn.

Method Pair 1: Multiple (Canonical) Correlation

Multiple correlation (also briefly discussed in Chapter 14) is the correlation be-tween two or more predictor variables and a single dependent variable. The mul-

TABLE 24.2
Multivariate procedures for examining relationships among sets of variables

Traditionally labeled		Dependent-variable status	
		Single	Multiple*
Correlational	Method pair 1	Multiple correlation	Canonical correlation
	Method pair 2	Discriminant function	Multiple discriminant function
	Method pair 3	Path analysis	Multiple path analysis
	Method pair 4	Multiple partial correlation	Complex multiple partial correlation
Analysis of variance	Method pair 5	Multilevel analysis of variance	Multivariate multilevel analysis of variance
	Method pair 6	Analysis of covariance	Multivariate analysis of covariance

*Interpretation of the results of these procedures is almost always ambiguous, and special caution should be exercised before any of these are employed in any but the most exploratory spirit.

tiple correlation coefficient R is a Pearson product-moment correlation between the dependent variable and a composite independent variable. This composite variable is made up, to varying degrees, of the individual independent variables in proportion to their importance in helping to maximize the value of R. Thus we can learn from the procedures of multiple correlation and regression both the absolute value as a predictor of the entire set of predictors and the relative value as a predictor of each independent variable compared with the others. By dummy-coding the various factors of an analysis of variance and employing these as independent variables, many, but not all (i.e., fixed but not random factor designs), models of the analysis of variance can be approached readily by way of multiple correlation or regression. (It should be noted that we are using the terms "correlation" and "regression" interchangeably in this context. A more technical usage would have us refer to *regression* in contexts where we want to relate changes in level of X to changes in level of Y, whereas we would refer to *correlation* as a more global index of closeness of relationship.)

Because multiple correlation or multiple regression can be viewed as having a structure that is basic to all the multivariate procedures shown in Table 24.2, we will spend a little more time describing its virtues (well known) and its problems (too infrequently recognized). Our discussion draws heavily on the authoritative work of Lincoln E. Moses (1986).

In multiple regression the value of the predicted or outcome variable Y is viewed as depending on α, the intercept on the Y axis, and the values of the predictor variables, $X_1, X_2, X_3, \ldots, X_k$, each multiplied by a coefficient β chosen in practice so as to minimize the sum of the squared discrepancies between the predicted and obtained values of Y. A term e is added to describe the discrepancy between a particular value of Y and the predicted value for that Y. Thus, for two predictor variables, X_1 and X_2, the equation, formula, or model is

$$Y = \alpha + \beta_1 X_1 + \beta_2 X_2 + e$$

As the number of predictor variables increases, we become more and more grateful for computers to help us calculate the changing values of α and β. As the computer brings any new predictor variable into the equation, all the β's (and the α) change so that the magnitude, sign, and statistical significance of each regression coefficient *depend entirely on exactly which other predictor variables are in the regression equation.* Thus, in describing the results of a regression analysis, statements about which predictors are most, least, second-most, etc., important depend not only on the peculiarities of the particular sample being studied, but on the precise battery of predictors that has been employed as well.

A word of caution is also required about the interpretation of the significance levels printed out by multiple regression statistical packages. The p values printed for the overall R and for the regression coefficients of each predictor variable are the same whether the particular battery of predictors was planned as the only battery of predictors to be employed (almost never the case) or whether some algorithm was used to pick out the best set of k predictors from a larger set of possible predictors (almost always the case). The printed p values are accurate only in the former (unlikely) case; they are not accurate in the latter (common) case. Indeed, it is not a trivial matter as to how one would even go about obtaining an accurate p value (Moses, 1986).

There are particular problems of replicability in employing multiple regression. Especially when the k predictors of the first study were selected from a larger set of possible predictors, it is very likely that the multiple R^2 will decrease substantially in any replication study. Such predictable decreases in the cross validation of a battery of predictors is called *shrinkage* in the context of multiple regression.

A special problem of multiple regression is that of *collinearity*, or high correlations, among the predictor variables. Collinearity makes it hard to interpret the substantive meaning of regression coefficients. For example, how shall we think of the regression coefficient for the variable of having made Phi Beta Kappa in the context of a regression equation with college grades and SAT scores as fellow predictor variables? Moses (1986) points out that one consequence of collinearity is that we may have a large R^2 and yet find none of the regressors to be significant. Because of collinearity, the work of any one predictor is not very important to the overall prediction enterprise. The analogy given by Moses is that of 10 people carrying a load that could be carried by 8. The group is doing its job, but any one or two people could be omitted and never be missed.

In the preceding paragraphs we have tried to create a cautious attitude toward the use of multiple regression in its generic use as a procedure for predicting an outcome variable from a battery of predictor variables. For the special use of employing multiple regression procedures to draw causal inferences in the absence of randomized assignment of subjects we want to create an attitude of caution greater still! Donald Campbell and Robert Boruch (1975), Thomas Cook and Campbell (1979), and others, e.g., Director (1979), having argued convincingly that multiple regression approaches to inferring causality can yield results that are very misleading. In particular, evidence from multiple regression analyses about the effects of social programs often tends to underestimate the benefits of these programs. In fact, their effects are likely to be seen (erroneously) as actually harmful when the pretest differences favor the control group over the intervention group.

Canonical correlation is the correlation between two or more predictor variables and two or more dependent variables. The canonical correlation coefficient CR is a Pearson product-moment correlation between a composite independent and a composite dependent variable. These composite variables are constructed by weighting each constituent variable in proportion to the importance of its contribution to maximizing the value of CR. Multiple R can be seen as a special case of CR when there is only one dependent variable. When there are more dependent variables, we can compute more CR's, in fact as many CR's as there are dependent variables (or independent variables if there are fewer of them than of dependent variables). Each successively computed CR is again a correlation between a composite independent and a composite dependent variable, but with each computed so as to be independent of the preceding composites computed. Since each CR is operating on the residuals from the preceding CR, successive CR's grow smaller and smaller just as successive principal components do.

From a practical point of view, we would not often recommend the use of canonical correlation, since the results obtained are often difficult to interpret. In particular, the significance level associated with a canonical correlation is likely to have little substantive meaning. For the situation for which canonical correlations apply, we have found it more useful to generate several reasonably uncorrelated independent supervariables (with the help of principal components or cluster analysis) and several reasonably uncorrelated dependent supervariables (with the help of principal components or cluster analysis). We would then employ ordinary correlation, and sometimes multiple correlation, separately for each of the relatively orthogonal dependent variables. Although we do not recommend canonical correlation for hypothesis testing or confirmatory analyses, we have found the procedure useful from time to time as a hypothesis-generating procedure, i.e., in the spirit of exploratory data analysis (Rosenthal, Blanck, and Vannicelli, 1984).

Method Pair 2: (Multiple) Discriminant Function

The *discriminant function* is the set of optimal weights (given the predictor variables) that does the best job of discriminating whether subjects or other sampling units are members of one or another group. Since we can dummy-code group membership as 0 and 1, we can regard discriminant function analysis as a special case of multiple correlation or regression in which we have a dichotomous $(0,1)$ dependent variable.

The *multiple discriminant function* is the set of optimal weights given each predictor variable that does the best job of discriminating among subjects' memberships in three or more groups. Since multiple groups can be turned into multiple dependent variables by dummy coding (so that we have one less variable than we had groups), we can regard multiple discriminant function analysis as a special case of canonical correlation, in which the dependent variables are dichotomous. (It should be noted that we get the same result whether we regard the dummy-coded group membership variables as the dependent variables or as the independent variables.)

The same note of caution on practical usage we offered in the case of multiple and canonical correlation applies to these special cases.

Method Pair 3: (Multiple) Path Analysis

Path analysis is a special case of multiple regression in which the goal is usually the drawing of causal inference, and in which we have a strong basis for ordering causal priorities. For example, if our predictor variables included gender, social class, and education, we could order these three variables on a dimension of time, with gender being determined first, then social class (defined, say, as parental income and occupation when the subject began formal education), and finally education of subject (defined as number of years). We would then employ multiple regression in a repeated way with each variable contributing to the prediction of every other variable coming later in time. If the dependent variable were income, all three predictors would be relevant to income, with gender contributing directly to income but also by way of influencing social class and education, which in turn also affect the dependent variable. Social class, having been partially affected by gender, then can affect income directly but also by way of education. Education, having been affected by gender and social class, can then also affect income directly. The diagram in Figure 24-2 summarizes the lines of influence.

Multiple path analysis is a logically implied special case of canonical correlation again involving the repeated application of multiple correlational methods to time-ordered variables, but with two or more ultimate dependent variables. A composite dependent variable is constructed with weights maximizing the predictive relationships between the time-ordered predictor variables and the composite dependent variable. As many sets of predictive relationships can be computed as there are dependent variables. This procedure has been little employed to date but may prove useful in the future. The diagram in Figure 24-3 summarizes the procedure. All the cautions we have raised in connection with multiple regression and canonical correlation apply as well to path analytic procedures (also discussed in Chapter 5 on quasi-experimental designs). In fact,

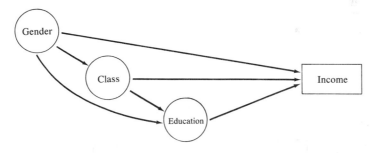

FIGURE 24-2
Path analysis showing the prediction of income from three time-ordered variables.

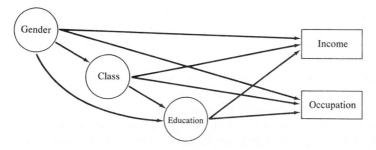

FIGURE 24-3
Multiple path analysis showing the prediction of income and occupation from three time-ordered variables.

since path analytic procedures are so often employed in the service of drawing causal inference, we urge special caution in their use. The short version of this caution is that there are no statistical procedures for drawing strong causal inference from nonexperimental research; not path analysis, not structural equation modeling, not anything. The longer version of this caution is found in part in Freedman's cautionary work (1987a, 1987b) and in that of his respondents, e.g., Bentler (1987), and Rogosa (1987), and other participants in a special issue of the *Journal of Educational Statistics,* summer, 1987, vol. 12, no. 2.

Method Pair 4: (Complex) Multiple Partial Correlation

Multiple partial correlation is ordinary multiple correlation or regression performed on a set of variables from which the effects of one or more other variables have been removed. The effects of these "third-party" variables (also called *covariates* or *control variables*) can be removed from either the independent or dependent variable set (*multiple part correlations*) or from both (*multiple partial correlations*); for details see Cooley and Lohnes (1971).

Complex multiple partial correlation is ordinary canonical correlation performed on a set of variables from which the effects of one or more other variables have been removed. The effects of the third-party variables can be removed from either the independent or the dependent variable set (complex multiple part correlation) or from both (complex multiple partial correlation). For details see Jacob Cohen's paper on *set correlation* (1982), and Jacob and Patricia Cohen's book (1983) on multiple regression/correlation.

Method Pair 5: (Multivariate) Multilevel Analysis of Variance

Multilevel analysis of variance has been discussed in detail in many of the earlier chapters of this book. We list it here only to be consistent, since the procedure does involve more than one independent variable. Even a one-way analysis of variance, if there are more than two levels, can be viewed as made up of a series of (dummy-coded) independent variables. Given a series of independent variables and a single dependent variable, we could approach many types of analysis very readily by means of multiple correlation or regression. Fixed-effects analyses could be handled very easily, for example, but random-effects analyses could be handled only with considerably greater difficulty.

Multivariate multilevel analysis of variance is the generalization of the analysis of variance to more than a single dependent variable. As such, it can be seen as closely akin to canonical correlation, especially the type of canonical correlation in which one set of variables is dichotomous (multiple discriminant function). Many types of multivariate analysis of variance problems can be approached readily through canonical correlation if the independent variables are fixed rather than random.

Method Pair 6: (Multivariate) Analysis of Covariance

Analysis of covariance is essentially an analysis of variance performed on a dependent variable that has been corrected or adjusted for a subject's score on some other variable (a covariate) that correlates (usually substantially) with the dependent variable. Analysis of covariance procedures are used successfully to increase the precision of the analysis and, with far more dubious success, to reduce bias in nonexperimental studies (Judd and Kenny, 1981). These procedures are closely related to those of the multiple partial correlation and other multiple regression procedures. Covariates are usually chosen for their high degree of correlation with the dependent variable within the various conditions of the design of the study. In a before-after (i.e., pretest-posttest) design, for example, one could employ a repeated-measures analysis, or several levels of blocking, or an analysis on the posttest-only but with the pretest employed as a covariate. Some comparisons among these procedures are given in Chapter 20 in the section on blocking and the analysis of covariance. When analysis of covariance is employed to reduce bias in nonexperimental studies, the same cautions apply as were offered in our discussion of the use of multiple regression to draw causal inference.

Multivariate analysis of covariance is analysis of covariance for the situation of multiple dependent variables. It is closely related to complex multiple partial correlation.

As a practical matter we would only rarely recommend the use of either the multivariate analysis of variance or covariance. With correlated dependent variables we have found it more useful to generate several fairly orthogonal supervariables (usually by means of principal component or clustering methods described earlier) to serve as our dependent variables, following this by analysis of variance or covariance separately for each dependent variable.

A final word about multivariate procedures. It is just about as easy to have the computer produce a multiple discriminant function analysis as a *t* test, and we have seen eager researchers call for them by the dozen. But as we have argued against the diffuse, unfocused *F* test (or effect-size estimators) based on more than a single *df* in the numerator, we want to argue against the diffuse, unfocused tests of significance and effect-size estimates that typically emerge from many of the multivariate procedures. We encourage their use, however, in exploratory contexts and as preliminary tests analogous to the omnibus *F* of the analysis of variance when they are to be followed up by focused and precise tests of significance and effect-size estimates.

PART
IX

APPENDIXES

A

WRITING LITERATURE REVIEWS AND ORIGINAL-STUDY PAPERS

COMMUNICATING IDEAS

The purpose of this appendix is to introduce readers to the rudiments of preparing two kinds of research reports: the literature review (or integrative research paper) and the original-study (or empirical research) paper. For behavioral scientists, whatever field they specialize in, there are stylistic techniques and tried-and-true mechanical rules that constitute almost recipes for terse, readable reports. We anticipate that there will be two types of readers of this discussion: (1) students and professional researchers who are submitting journal articles and (2) students who are writing papers to fulfill a course requirement.

The former group will find it helpful, if not essential, to be conversant with the *Publication Manual of the American Psychological Association* (APA). Another useful resource on scientific writing is Daryl Bem's (1987) recent chapter titled "Writing the Empirical Journal Article." Bem makes a special point of the importance of clarity of presentation, because an article's acceptance can hinge on whether it is written in a terse yet clear, informative style. It is also important that authors who are writing journal articles become acquainted with the standardization demanded by the particular journal to which their work is to be submitted. The page allocations of primary journals are limited, and editors look disapprovingly at manuscripts which are too wordy or imprecise, or which fail to conform to accepted rules of style and form.

567

The latter group of authors, students writing papers for a course requirement, may find some of the technical details insisted upon by scientific journals
and professional writing manuals to be cumbersome, or even superfluous. Such
authors may be more in need of a general writing manual that guides them step
by step through the process involved in writing effective reports and term papers. They will want to learn more about the steps involved in selecting a topic,
finding sources, and then writing and presenting the final manuscript, which a
general writing manual will tell students (e.g., Rosnow and Rosnow, 1986).

We begin by reviewing five steps in preparing a literature review, which
roughly parallel the stages of original-research studies. Two additional sources
that readers can turn to for guidance are Harris M. Cooper's *Integrating Research: A Guide for Literature Reviews* (2d ed.) (1989) and Richard J. Light and
David B. Pillemer's *Summing Up: The Science of Reviewing Research* (1984). Next,
we describe two major aspects of the process involved in writing an original-
study paper, its form and content. By its *form* we mean a group of stylistic elements that, taken together, constitute the way in which the paper is presented.
Its *content* refers to the formula for the presentation of the substantive work.
These two aspects are detailed in this discussion separately, but in the finished
paper they should blend to form a cohesive presentation.

This appendix concludes with the original manuscript of an empirical journal article that was prepared according to the rules specified in the APA publication manual (third edition). A number of basic stylistic elements required by
journals that subscribe to the APA format are highlighted by the use of anno-
tated comments. Whether for papers to be submitted for publication or to fulfill
a course requirement, the APA manual can usually be consulted as a final ar-
biter of mechanical and style rules.

WRITING EFFECTIVE
LITERATURE REVIEWS

Because the inferences made in an integrative research review are as central to
the progress of scientific knowledge as those made in the empirical studies cited,
both require that we pay the same careful attention to details of accepted methodology. Harris Cooper, cited just above, has proposed that a series of five steps
be followed so as to approach the preparation of an effective literature review
more systematically.

The first step, which is similar to the conceptualization of the research
problem in original-research studies, involves formulation of the aim of the review. At this stage the variables and concepts are defined and a rationale for why
certain variables are presumed to be related (in causal or noncausal ways) is developed. In this way, even if we start with a very broad conception, we can begin
to think about how to narrow the vast body of literature into a more manageable
entity. As we proceed, we may find that there are different operational definitions and levels of abstraction for the same or similar kinds of variables, but our
conception will help us to distinguish relevant from irrelevant studies. Occam's

razor is a good principle to keep in mind, for the more abstract the conception, the less able we are to discriminate among various studies. On the other hand, it is almost always better to be exhaustive in our coverage rather than to exclude a possibly relevant study because our conception was too narrow. Similarly, the more operational details examined, the more externally valid will be our review conclusions—because we present more information about contextual (e.g., situational and individual) variations.

The second step involves the collection of data, and we begin by deciding what procedures should be used to find relevant evidence. It is not unlike defining the population of subjects that will be relevant in an original-research study, in that we must consider both those elements that we hope to represent in the study and those that are actually accessible to us. Some evidence is inaccessible to reviewers simply because it is not in print. It has been observed that about half the researchers who produce a rejection of the null hypothesis will submit a report for publication, whereas only 6 percent who fail to reject the null hypothesis ever attempt to publish (Greenwald, 1975). This suggests a decided bias in favor of statistically significant published findings available to us for review.

There are several techniques for generating a data base of relevant empirical reports:

a. One approach for building a pool of key studies, unpublished as well as published papers, involves the "invisible college" of scientists working on similar problems. Major researchers are usually aware of one another's interests and frequently exchange published and unpublished ("preprints") reports of findings. Even though they are busy people, they may be willing to take the time to correspond with persons who are not published authors themselves.

b. A more practical approach to tracking down relevant published reports and some unpublished ones (e.g., presentations at professional meetings that happen to be cited in published reports) is called the "ancestry" technique. It calls for tracking relations from one study to another on the basis of the list of references or notes contained in each published report that we can find.

c. A third alternative, usually the most direct way to track down relevant published and (some) unpublished works (e.g., dissertation studies), is to employ abstracting services. Some major abstracting services are the *Psychological Abstracts,* the *Child Developmental Abstracts and Bibliography,* and the *Educational Resources Information Center Files.* Summaries of dissertations can be found in *Dissertation Abstracts International,* and there are numerous other archival references available in most research libraries. A speedy way of retrieving this information is to do an "on-line computer search," in which we supply a list of key words or phrases and the computer scans several abstracting services for us. No retrieval system is perfect, however. Authors who want to develop an exhaustive bibliography will need to use more than one retrieval system and approach to ensure that they have not omitted any important evidence. For a complete listing of bibliographic retrieval sources for the behavioral scientist, see an article written by Mary Lu Rosenthal (1985).

The third step involves the evaluation of the data. Having amassed a body of evidence, we must decide what results should be included in the review. Some workers in integrative research reviewing believe there should be only one criterion for discarding data, questionable internal validity. Other workers in this field believe that no data should be discarded; they argue that the quality of the research should be one of the factors examined to help future readers decide about the determinants of large versus small effects (e.g., Glass, McGaw, and Smith, 1981; Rosenthal, 1976, 1984; Rosenthal and Rosnow, 1975). Another option, useful when facing an enormous number of studies, is to select a stratified sample by dividing the population of studies by the kind of research design and then making a random selection of each kind—this is one way of reducing the labor in a review (Light and Pillemer, 1984; Rosenthal and Rubin, 1978).

The fourth step involves the analysis and interpretation of separate studies in order to lead to a set of unified statements about the research literature and the objective of the review. An example would be the set of conclusions about volunteer characteristics listed and discussed in Chapter 10. Recently developed statistical aids for helping us quantitatively synthesize or integrate data in order to tease out systematic patterns are discussed in Chapter 22 (on meta-analysis). We must be very careful, whatever method we use, that we do not misconstrue correlational evidence as supporting causality when it does not. Reviewers should also expect to have to reanalyze some of the previously published findings, such as when effect sizes are unreported or when a focused test is needed but is unreported (e.g., only omnibus significance tests are reported).

For authors who are writing articles for publication, the final step in the review process is the public presentation of the results to the scientific community. Published reviews can be found in the *Psychological Bulletin* and similar journals in other areas of behavioral science. Other places to look for models are research *monographs* (book-length research syntheses, and chapters in the *Annual Review* series (e.g., *Annual Review of Anthropology, Annual Review of Sociology, Annual Review of Public Health, Annual Review of Medicine, Annual Review of Psychology*) available in many research libraries. Examination of these sources will reveal that writing an effective literature review calls for many hours of hard work.

FORM OF ORIGINAL-STUDY PAPERS

The kinds of matters to be considered when we talk about the form of an original-study paper include the process of gathering information, formulation of an outline, and techniques for beginning, writing, and revising the manuscript. Within this aspect of report writing fall specific elements of style, such as spelling, punctuation, and the proper formats for presenting footnotes, graphics, and references.

It is assumed that the processes of formulating and researching a specific hypothesis have, as one of their outcomes, sufficiently narrowed the topic so that it need not be a consideration as we begin to plan the paper. At this point, while the research findings are fresh in mind, it is well to arrive at a working title. It should be succinct while at the same time adequately descriptive of the paper's objective. The title can be changed, but a good working title gives a direction and keeps the author's thoughts on course. The final title should contain key words that pinpoint what the research is about, so that readers leafing through the table of contents of a journal will be able to determine readily whether or not the article pertains to their field of interest. Many researchers make a habit of perusing *Current Contents: Social & Behavioral Sciences,* a weekly periodical that reprints tables of contents from journals in sociology, anthropology, linguistics, psychology, psychiatry, education, political science, law, economics and business, and so on. Each issue also contains an author index and address directory so that if journals are unavailable in the reference section of the local research library, readers can request reprints and related work by writing to the authors directly.

Formulating the title, just as writing the introduction, is not something we do before analyzing our data, however. In Chapters 2 and 12 we noted the distinction made between discovery and justification, and it enters in at this stage as well. We do not want to foreclose on the possibility of new insights that were not even imaginable when we developed our strategy and rationale for the investigation. It has been said that the greatest value of any data-analytic method accrues to us when it forces us to notice what we never expected to see (Tukey, 1977). As Bem put it, "If you see dim traces of interesting patterns, try to reorganize the data to bring them into bolder relief... In the confining content of an empirical study, there is only one strategy for discovery: exploring the data" (1987, p. 172). There is a danger, to be sure, and it is that "spurious findings can emerge by chance, and we need to be cautious about anything we discover in this way... But there are no statistical correctives for overlooking an important discovery because we were insufficiently attentive to the data. Let us err on the side of discovery" (p. 173).

Having thoroughly analyzed and thoughtfully digested the results, we are then ready to formulate our working title. It is also the time to return to the library to gather further information to ensure that we have covered our topic thoroughly. A good deal of work will have been done already, during the course of data collection and analysis and even before the research was undertaken. But there may be fresh insights and serendipitous discoveries, which should send us back to the literature. There is no adequate substitute for a thorough literature review, whenever possible in the primary materials rather than in secondary sources. In a famous case, Sigmund Freud rested an important interpretation in his psychoanalytic study of Leonardo da Vinci on the erroneous understanding that a bird mentioned in a secondary source (a translation of one of Leonardo's early memories) was a vulture. It turned out to be an inaccurate translation of the Italian word, which actually meant another kind of bird, a kite (Anderson, 1981). In making use of secondary sources, we are relying on the accuracy of a writer who is not the original author. Is the translation we are using a careful, accurate one that is as close to the original language as possible, or is it a "literary translation" that smooths over the rough spots in the original so as to make the material more palatable for casual readers?

No matter what material we use, it cannot be stressed too strongly that it is of prime importance to take accurate notes and to document them fully. Many experienced researchers have found that a convenient way to take notes is to use index cards and to alphabetize them by author. Begin by writing the author, title, publisher, and year of the work, using a separate card for each source. In making use of these sources we can either paraphrase or quote directly, but a careful record of the page numbers should be made in either case. When making a direct quote, we must also be sure to copy it exactly and enclose it within quotation marks. If the quotation contains more than 40 words, it will usually appear in the typewritten manuscript as a free-standing block (called a *block quotation*) set off by indenting each line five spaces from the left margin.

Like workers who build a scaffold for holding themselves and their materials during the erection of a building, experienced authors make an outline to serve as a structure for holding together their ideas and their source materials during the writing of a paper. A good outline should give shape and coherence to our ideas, as well as bring order to notes that we have taken and the raw data we have collected. If the outline is done properly, the paper will then practically write itself. The outline can take the form of sentence, topic, or paragraph, but in any case should proceed from the most general to the most specific. Think of the first outline as making a list—which is to say, a rough grouping—of the points we wish to include in the paper. The process of taking notes and ordering them will help us to reorganize the sections of the outline into a cohesive unit that will direct the writing of the paper. The important point is that the final outline will reflect each of the main ideas we have chosen to consider, and they will be fleshed out with specifics that illustrate or amplify these ideas.

Using the outline as a starting point, we are ready to begin to write. It is important to keep in mind the level of sophistication of the readers for whom the paper is intended and to fit the style to those expectations. Of course, it is just as important that one's writing not be pedantic, out of laziness, a feeling of insecurity, or a slavish concern with making it appear scientific. Kai Erikson (1987, pp. 95–96), a sociologist and editor, reminds us of George Orwell's critique of how some sociologists try to make a simple subject appear scientific. Admiring the familiar passage from Ecclesiastes:

> I returned and saw under the sun that the race is not to the swift nor the battle to the strong, neither yet bread to the wise nor yet riches to men of understanding, nor yet favor to men of skill, but time and chance happeneth to them all.

Orwell then translated it into sociologese:

> Objective consideration of contemporary phenomenon compels the conclusion that success or failure in competitive activities exhibits no tendency to be commensurate with innate capacity, but that a considerable element of the unpredictable must invariably be taken into account.

Erickson offers us a critical view of both passages. The poetry of the biblical language, he points out, distracts us from its message. He states, "The content is in fact nonsense: the race usually does go to the swift, the battle always does go to the strong, and the advantages almost always do go to people of skill" (1987, p. 96). On the other hand, Erickson argues, the "awkward, stilted, rough, and tedious prose" of the parody lacks not only grace and wit, but cogency.

Besides writing clearly and directing what we have to say to the level of sophistication of the readers, there are a number of other basic concerns. Another stylistic element to keep in mind is to avoid the use of sexist language. Accomplishing this means, among other things, that we must at times be specific in the use of personal pronouns (such as "he" and "she"), so as not to imply incorrectly similarities or generalizations where there are or could be sex differences. It is also well to define any terms that will be used in the paper. Some technical reports (but not journal articles) include a glossary at the back, especially useful if the writing involves unusual terms or expressions. Structure the paper around a topic sentence that states what was investigated. We use additional sentences to modify, specify, and build on these foundations. There are some words and phrases that can help readers to follow the thread of the writing more easily, e.g., "first," "in addition," "finally,""another important," "even more important." A phrase like "not only but also" can give direction to a sentence or a paragraph.

The APA manual is not the only accepted style manual, and if we are writing for a journal, there is always a specific prescribed style that the journal will insist on. Submitting a paper written in an inappropriate style conveys the idea that the author is lazy or careless, or that the paper submitted is an unrevised version of one that was previously rejected by another journal. It is vital that words be spelled correctly and used properly. Experienced authors have a good dictionary beside them as they begin to write. It will be invaluable not only as a spelling and definition reference but as a guide to the singulars and plurals, usages, and abbreviations of Latin words that commonly appear in scientific reports.

Some of the more common abbreviations used in footnotes and bibliographies of reports (not necessarily those using the APA style) are

> op. cit., from *opere citato* ("in the work cited")
> ibid., from *ibidem* ("in the same place")
> et al., from *et alii, -ae, -a* ("and others")
> i.e., from *id est* ("that is")
> cf., from *confer* ("compare")
> e.g., from *exempli gratia* ("for example")

Typical errors that careless or inexperienced authors make in using these abbreviations include mistakenly omitting the first period in "e.g." ("eg.") and incorrectly adding a period after "et" ("et. al.").

Without going into details of content, which will be considered in the next section, we proceed with the writing of the paper. When the paper has been completed, it is well to put it aside for a few days. It is then possible to begin the first revision, which is the next step, from a fresh point of view. To revise, it is necessary to read the paper carefully with a critical eye. Be on guard against lapses in logic, awkward or trite phrasing, run-on sentences, incomplete sentences, as well as faulty punctuation and spelling. We are now ready to rewrite the paper, section by section, cutting whatever is superfluous and rewording transitions between paragraphs so that the flow of the presentation is smooth and tight.

Once we are completely satisfied that we have done the best job we can, a clean typewritten copy of the manuscript should be made. If one is using a word processor, it is a good idea to "spell-check" the document before printing it. However, a maxim of computerese is "garbage in, garbage out"; it reminds us to proof the printed document carefully, because mistakes (e.g., weird spacings, accidental deletions, failures to delete) can, and often will, slip even into "corrected" documents. However, we are not through at this point! It is now time to get feedback from others. Choose one or two readers whose judgment is sound and who will give the work an objective critical analysis. We must be open-minded to all kinds of feedback, including suggestions for substantive as well as grammatical and stylistic changes. In each revision (and there may be many) the paper will be improved, our writing skills sharpened, and the odds of its being accepted for publication increased markedly.

CONTENT OF ORIGINAL-STUDY PAPERS

It is customary to begin the research report with an introduction. This section should contain a clear statement of the problem to be considered and a discussion of the way in which the paper builds on what others have said, so that there is a logical thread throughout. A brief literature review is usually included in order to show the development of the hypotheses and the reason the research was done, as well as to provide the rationale for the particular methods chosen to accomplish the research. One way of knowing that a poor transition has been made between the introductory section of an empirical research paper and the methods section is to be surprised by the methods described. One purpose of the introduction is to prepare the reader for the particular methods employed. The strongest introductions describe the questions or hypotheses posed in such a way as to make the methods section appear to be an inexorable consequence of those questions or hypotheses. The reader's reaction should be: "Well, of course, that's what the researchers had to do to get decent answers to their questions."

The second section of the report is the specification of methods and procedures, in which we spell out what method of inquiry we have chosen. It is important to give relevant information as to our choice of subjects: who they are, how they were recruited (Did they volunteer? Were they paid?), their age and sex, the number of subjects who dropped out (and why) or were dropped by the researcher (and why), and any other information that we think may be pertinent to the internal and external validity of the results. We must also detail the particular instruments and measurements used. If they are standardized tests, it is sufficient simply to name them. But if not, they should be treated at greater length, especially with regard to their reliability and validity.

The analysis of the results follows this section. To present the results in a manner that can be easily understood, it is often helpful to use tables, graphs, or charts. When these are used, be sure to label, title, and caption them completely. Indicate where they belong in the body of the text: "Insert Figure 1 about here." Follow standard practices as to format; here it is helpful if we refer to style manuals. It is important to reiterate findings shown in figures within the body of the text so that the information is presented in verbal as well as in pictorial form. In describing the figure, however, we may find that the verbal description will suffice, and we can then delete the figure because we want to be specific and detailed but not redundant. Raw data, even though unreported, should be saved. If a reader wants to reanalyze our findings, he or she then can obtain the necessary data by writing to us. At the same time, it is necessary to be selective about what is included in this section because journal space is precious to editors and publishers. We should strive to avoid "telling all we know" so as not to make the paper too discursive—which is a characteristic of the writing of neophyte authors.

The next major section of the paper is that in which we discuss the findings. To begin to pull the paper together it is well at this point to refer to the introductory section. If there was more than one hypothesis, discuss each of these in turn to show its relation to the findings. There may be serendipitous findings, and these too should be treated in depth. Consider specifically how various types of validity (see Chapters 3, 4, 5, 6, and 10) might be affected by the conditions of the investigation. It is always a good idea to try to anticipate criticisms and to deal with the imagined objections before they arise. The last section deals with the conclusions we have reached, but it is stylistically correct to include this section as the final part of the discussion. The conclusions should be given as specifically and succinctly as we can. We should try to derive implications based on the results and, if possible, to suggest areas of future research.

The summary (or abstract) is written once the main body of the paper has been completed. In a technical report it may appear at the beginning or end of the paper, but in a journal article that conforms to APA style it will always appear at the beginning. This summary should highlight and tie together the objectives, findings, and conclusions as succinctly as possible. It tells the readers briefly what the paper is about and provides key information that can help those using an abstracting service to determine whether the paper is pertinent to their scholarly interest.

PREPARING THE FINAL VERSION FOR JOURNAL SUBMISSION

The following pages show the typewritten manuscript of an original-research report that was accepted for publication by a scientific journal.[1] The format con-

---

[1]*Source: Aggressive Behavior,* 1988, vol. 14, pp. 105–112; reprinted by permission of the first author and the journal.

forms to the rules for the publication of manuscripts specified in the APA manual (third edition)—the side arrows note particular points of interest. Note that it is double-spaced, the purpose being to provide each person in the publication process (the journal editor, the referees, the copy editors, the printer) with space for handwritten marks and notes. The arrangement of pages in an original-research study typed according to APA specifications will be title page, abstract, text (introduction, methods, results, discussion), references, author identification notes, footnotes, tables, figure captions, and figures. The printed article will appear differently, but this arrangement is preferred for easier handling by the copy editor and the printer.

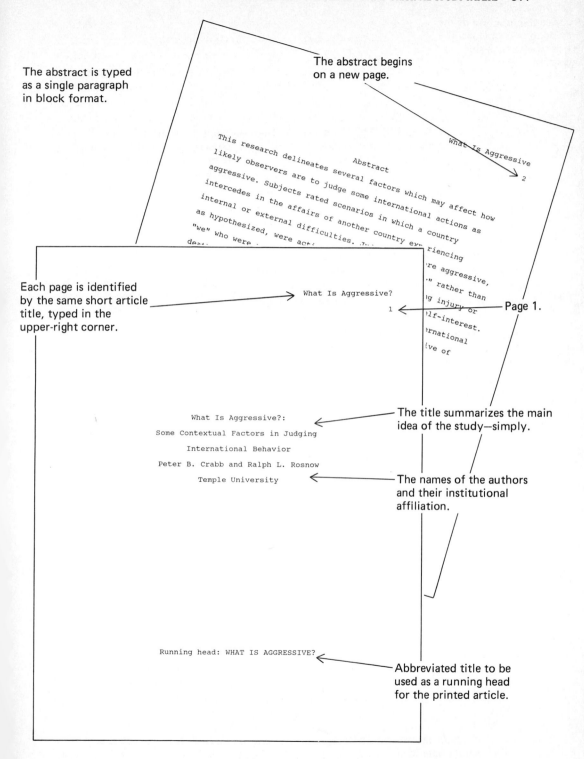

The abstract is typed as a single paragraph in block format.

The abstract begins on a new page.

What Is Aggressive

2

Abstract

This research delineates several factors which may affect how likely observers are to judge some international actions as aggressive. Subjects rated scenarios in which a country intercedes in the affairs of another country experiencing internal or external difficulties. ... as hypothesized, were act... "we" who were . dea..

re aggressive,
." rather than
ig injury or
lf-interest.
rnational
ive of

Each page is identified by the same short article title, typed in the upper-right corner.

What Is Aggressive?

1

Page 1.

What Is Aggressive?:

Some Contextual Factors in Judging

International Behavior

Peter B. Crabb and Ralph L. Rosnow

Temple University

The title summarizes the main idea of the study—simply.

The names of the authors and their institutional affiliation.

Running head: WHAT IS AGGRESSIVE?

Abbreviated title to be used as a running head for the printed article.

Because the function of the introduction is obvious, it is not labeled by a side heading.

What Is Aggressive?

3

The text begins on a new page.

What Is Aggressive?:

Some Contextual Factors in Judging

International Behavior

The title of the article is repeated so that if the editor removes page 1 for blind reviewing, the referees will still be apprised of the title.

World bodies--from the 1915 Congress of Vienna, The Hague and Versailles peace conferences, to the United Nations--have forever struggled with the definition of aggression. One French law expert, after exhaustive review, concluded that he was like the person told to define an elephant; he did not know how to do it, but he knew it was something big (Shenker, 1971). On the other hand, Goldstein (1986) argues that aggression be viewed as a continuum on which any behavior might fall depending on how much hostility the action and intention contain. The problem is that the same actions and intentions may be seen and judged differently depending on whether it is "we" or "they" who are responsible (e.g., Jervis, 1976; White, 1984).

Double quotation marks are used to introduce a word or phrase that is used in a special way.

Thus it is recognized that aggression, no less than any other behavior, does not occur in a social vacuum. Like a message that makes sense only in terms of the total context in which it occurs, actions and intentions are embedded in a context that gives meaning to how they are interpreted (Rosnow & Georgoudi, 1986). The purpose of this research was to delineate several contextual factors that may affect interpretations of international actions. Specifically, we were interested in specifying some of the conditions under which an action is judged

For example (e.g.).

that results in injury (e.g., U.S. economic and political alliance with the government of South Africa). The definition of aggression adopted in this study integrates all three criteria: "any form of behavior directed toward the goal of harming or injuring another living being who is motivated to avoid such treatment" (Baron, 1977, p. 12). At the level of international

Page number of quoted passage.

international behavior, as much as in everyday life, motives are not always concordant with actions (cf. Fung, Kipnis, & Rosnow,

The latin abbreviation (cf.) is not underlined.

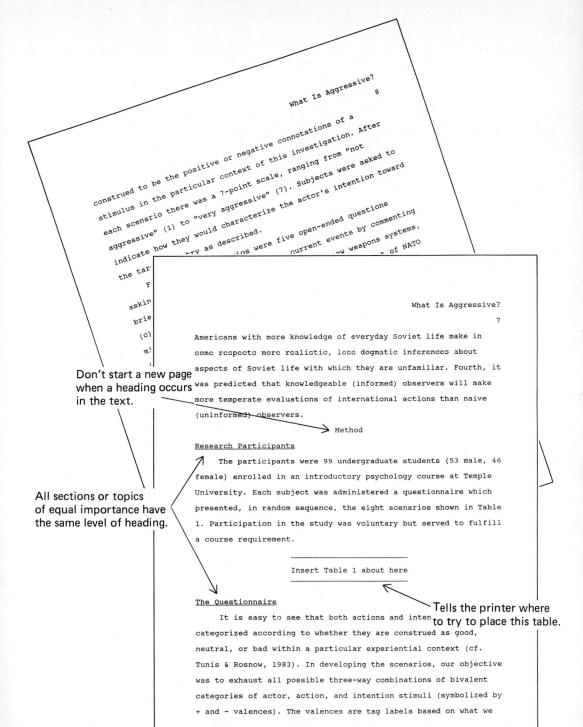

What Is Aggressive?   8

construed to be the positive or negative connotations of a stimulus in the particular context of this investigation. After each scenario there was a 7-point scale, ranging from "not aggressive" (1) to "very aggressive" (7). Subjects were asked to indicate how they would characterize the actor's intention toward the tar␣

F

askin

brie

(c)

m␣

␣os were five open-ended questions

␣ry as described.

current events by commenting

␣w weapons systems,

␣ of NATO

Don't start a new page when a heading occurs in the text.

What Is Aggressive?

7

Americans with more knowledge of everyday Soviet life make in some respects more realistic, less dogmatic inferences about aspects of Soviet life with which they are unfamiliar. Fourth, it was predicted that knowledgeable (informed) observers will make more temperate evaluations of international actions than naive (uninformed) observers.

Method

Research Participants

The participants were 99 undergraduate students (53 male, 46 female) enrolled in an introductory psychology course at Temple University. Each subject was administered a questionnaire which presented, in random sequence, the eight scenarios shown in Table 1. Participation in the study was voluntary but served to fulfill a course requirement.

Insert Table 1 about here

All sections or topics of equal importance have the same level of heading.

The Questionnaire

It is easy to see that both actions and inten categorized according to whether they are construed as good, neutral, or bad within a particular experiential context (cf. Tunis & Rosnow, 1983). In developing the scenarios, our objective was to exhaust all possible three-way combinations of bivalent categories of actor, action, and intention stimuli (symbolized by + and - valences). The valences are tag labels based on what we

Tells the printer where to try to place this table.

Statistical significance
level and effect size value.

What Is Aggressive?

10

actions carried out for the expressed benefit of the other

country (positive intentions). There was a highly significant and

substantial main effect of intention as predicted, $F(1,97)$ =

59.03, $p < .0001$, $r = .62$, with scenarios representing self-

serving motives judged as slightly aggressive (+0.84) and those

representing altruistic motives judged barely as nonaggressive

(-0.(

Tabl(

eval

"we"

and

25.9

more

expe

know

mean

were

aggr

effe

subt

for

is p

What Is Aggressive?

9

Results

Table 2 shows the mean aggressiveness ratings for each cell

in this 2 X 2 X 2 X 2 design: (a) actor, (b) action, (c)

intention, and (d) knowledge. Individual scores were analyzed by

analysis of variance (ANOVA), with repeated measures on the first

three factors. For convenience of interpretation, An acronym (ANOVA) for

subtracted from the 7-point scores to rescale them "analysis of variance."

continuum from most aggressive (+3) to most nonaggressive (-3),

with a score of 0.0 denoting a neutral judgment. Overall, the

mean response was +0.38, indicating a slight bias toward the

aggressive end of the continuum. Column means Underline the symbol (N) for

weighted for unequal N's of informed and uninf the number of subjects.

Aggressive?

11

for

his effect

on is

so

n

tors

aim

_____

Insert Table 2 about here

_____

The first prediction was that international actions capable

of injury or death will be judged more harshly than other

actions. Overall, the use of military action was judged as

moderately aggressive (weighted mean = +1.44) and the use of

economic action was judged as slightly nonaggressive (weighted

mean = -0.68). Consistent with the results in Table 2, there was

an impressive main effect of action, with $F(1,97)$ = 139.79,

$p < .0001$, effect size $r = .77$.

The second prediction was that actions carried out Underline statistical symbols

interest (negative intentions) will be judged more harsh expressed by italicized Latin

letters (e.g., p, F, r, t, Z).

...ion tended to be evaluated more harshly than ...o-way interaction. Scenarios

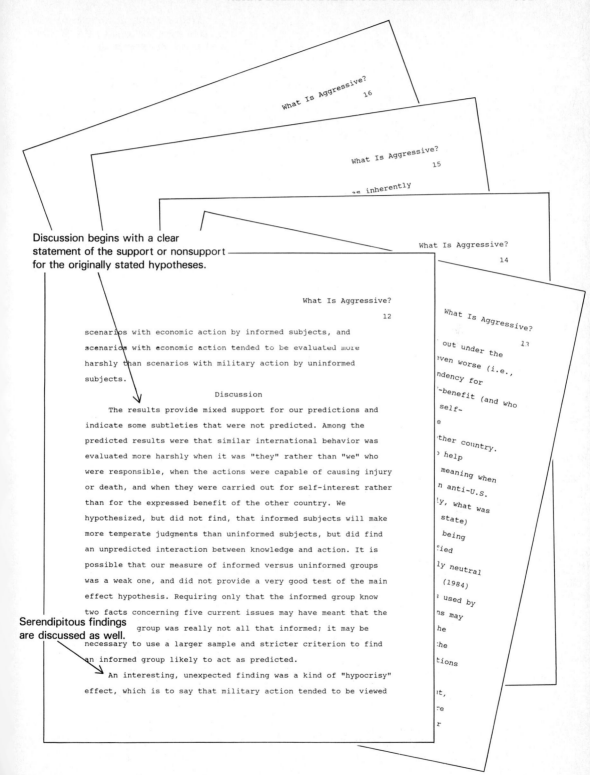

What Is Aggressive?

16

What Is Aggressive?

15

as inherently

Discussion begins with a clear statement of the support or nonsupport for the originally stated hypotheses.

What Is Aggressive?

14

What Is Aggressive?

12

scenarios with economic action by informed subjects, and

scenarios with economic action tended to be evaluated more

harshly than scenarios with military action by uninformed

subjects.

Discussion

The results provide mixed support for our predictions and

indicate some subtleties that were not predicted. Among the

predicted results were that similar international behavior was

evaluated more harshly when it was "they" rather than "we" who

were responsible, when the actions were capable of causing injury

or death, and when they were carried out for self-interest rather

than for the expressed benefit of the other country. We

hypothesized, but did not find, that informed subjects will make

more temperate judgments than uninformed subjects, but did find

an unpredicted interaction between knowledge and action. It is

possible that our measure of informed versus uninformed groups

was a weak one, and did not provide a very good test of the main

effect hypothesis. Requiring only that the informed group know

two facts concerning five current issues may have meant that the

group was really not all that informed; it may be

necessary to use a larger sample and stricter criterion to find

an informed group likely to act as predicted.

An interesting, unexpected finding was a kind of "hypocrisy"

effect, which is to say that military action tended to be viewed

Serendipitous findings are discussed as well.

What Is Aggressive?

13

out under the

even worse (i.e.,

ndency for

-benefit (and who

self-

e

ther country.

help

meaning when

n anti-U.S.

ly, what was

state)

being

ied

ly neutral

(1984)

used by

ns may

he

the

tions

it,

re

r

Choose references judiciously and
cite them accurately; this section
begins on a new page.

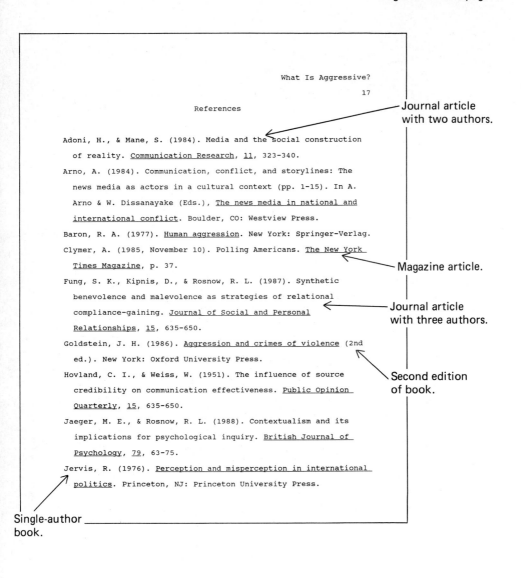

What Is Aggressive?

17

References

Adoni, H., & Mane, S. (1984). Media and the social construction
    of reality. Communication Research, 11, 323-340.

Arno, A. (1984). Communication, conflict, and storylines: The
    news media as actors in a cultural context (pp. 1-15). In A.
    Arno & W. Dissanayake (Eds.), The news media in national and
    international conflict. Boulder, CO: Westview Press.

Baron, R. A. (1977). Human aggression. New York: Springer-Verlag.

Clymer, A. (1985, November 10). Polling Americans. The New York
    Times Magazine, p. 37.

Fung, S. K., Kipnis, D., & Rosnow, R. L. (1987). Synthetic
    benevolence and malevolence as strategies of relational
    compliance-gaining. Journal of Social and Personal
    Relationships, 15, 635-650.

Goldstein, J. H. (1986). Aggression and crimes of violence (2nd
    ed.). New York: Oxford University Press.

Hovland, C. I., & Weiss, W. (1951). The influence of source
    credibility on communication effectiveness. Public Opinion
    Quarterly, 15, 635-650.

Jaeger, M. E., & Rosnow, R. L. (1988). Contextualism and its
    implications for psychological inquiry. British Journal of
    Psychology, 79, 63-75.

Jervis, R. (1976). Perception and misperception in international
    politics. Princeton, NJ: Princeton University Press.

Journal article
with two authors.

Magazine article.

Journal article
with three authors.

Second edition
of book.

Single-author
book.

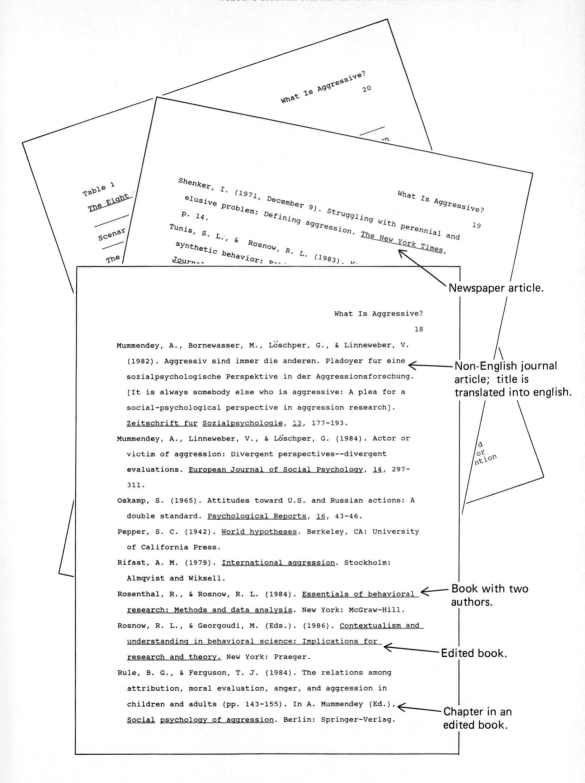

What Is Aggressive?

20

Table 1

The Eight

Scenar

The

Shenker, I. (1971, December 9). Struggling with perennial and
elusive problem: Defining aggression. *The New York Times*,
p. 14.

Tunis, S. L., & Rosnow, R. L. (1983). *P*.
synthetic behavior: *P*.
Journ

What Is Aggressive?

19

Newspaper article.

What Is Aggressive?

18

Mummendey, A., Bornewasser, M., Löschper, G., & Linneweber, V.
(1982). Aggressiv sind immer die anderen. Pladoyer fur eine
sozialpsychologische Perspektive in der Aggressionsforschung.
[It is always somebody else who is aggressive: A plea for a
social-psychological perspective in aggression research].
Zeitschrift fur Sozialpsychologie, *13*, 177-193.

Mummendey, A., Linneweber, V., & Löschper, G. (1984). Actor or
victim of aggression: Divergent perspectives--divergent
evaluations. *European Journal of Social Psychology*, *14*, 297-
311.

Oskamp, S. (1965). Attitudes toward U.S. and Russian actions: A
double standard. *Psychological Reports*, *16*, 43-46.

Pepper, S. C. (1942). *World hypotheses*. Berkeley, CA: University
of California Press.

Rifaat, A. M. (1979). *International aggression*. Stockholm:
Almqvist and Wiksell.

Rosenthal, R., & Rosnow, R. L. (1984). *Essentials of behavioral*
research: Methods and data analysis. New York: McGraw-Hill.

Rosnow, R. L., & Georgoudi, M. (Eds.). (1986). *Contextualism and*
understanding in behavioral science: Implications for
research and theory. New York: Praeger.

Rule, B. G., & Ferguson, T. J. (1984). The relations among
attribution, moral evaluation, anger, and aggression in
children and adults (pp. 143-155). In A. Mummendey (Ed.),
Social psychology of aggression. Berlin: Springer-Verlag.

Non-English journal article; title is translated into english.

Book with two authors.

Edited book.

Chapter in an edited book.

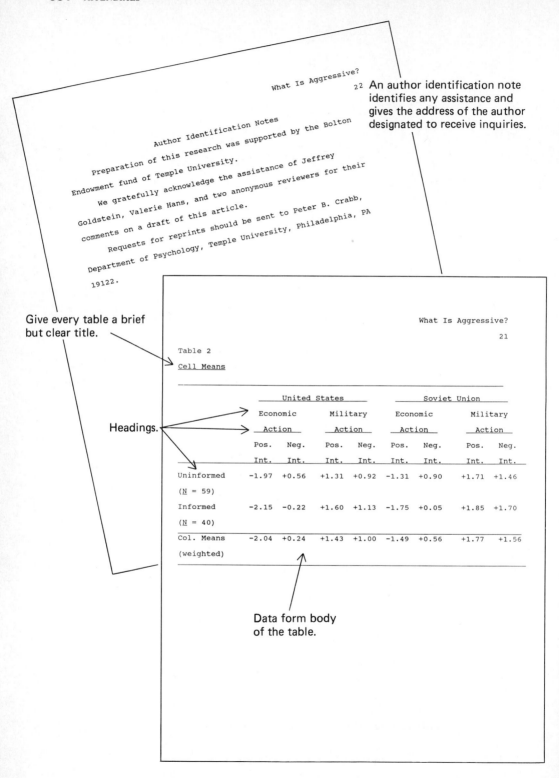

What Is Aggressive?

22

An author identification note identifies any assistance and gives the address of the author designated to receive inquiries.

Author Identification Notes

Preparation of this research was supported by the Bolton Endowment fund of Temple University.

We gratefully acknowledge the assistance of Jeffrey Goldstein, Valerie Hans, and two anonymous reviewers for their comments on a draft of this article.

Requests for reprints should be sent to Peter B. Crabb, Department of Psychology, Temple University, Philadelphia, PA 19122.

Give every table a brief but clear title.

What Is Aggressive?

21

Table 2

Cell Means

	United States				Soviet Union			
	Economic Action		Military Action		Economic Action		Military Action	
	Pos. Int.	Neg. Int.	Pos. Int.	Neg. Int.	Pos. Int.	Neg. Int.	Pos. Int.	Neg. Int.
Uninformed (N = 59)	-1.97	+0.56	+1.31	+0.92	-1.31	+0.90	+1.71	+1.46
Informed (N = 40)	-2.15	-0.22	+1.60	+1.13	-1.75	+0.05	+1.85	+1.70
Col. Means (weighted)	-2.04	+0.24	+1.43	+1.00	-1.49	+0.56	+1.77	+1.56

Headings.

Data form body of the table.

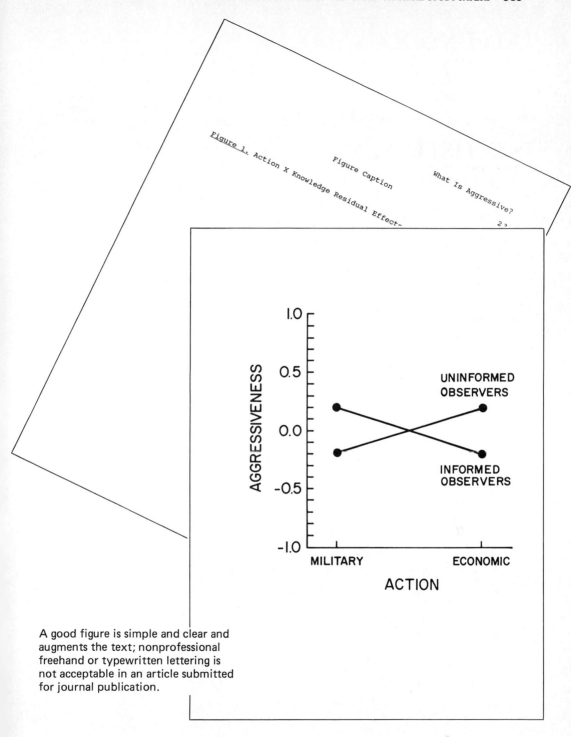

Figure 1. Action X Knowledge Residual Effects

Figure Caption

What Is Aggressive?

A good figure is simple and clear and augments the text; nonprofessional freehand or typewritten lettering is not acceptable in an article submitted for journal publication.

APPENDIX
B

STATISTICAL
TABLES

TABLE B.1
Table of standard normal deviates (Z)

					Second digit of Z					
Z	.00	.01	.02	.03	.04	.05	.06	.07	.08	.09
.0	.5000	.4960	.4920	.4880	.4840	.4801	.4761	.4721	.4681	.4641
.1	.4602	.4562	.4522	.4483	.4443	.4404	.4364	.4325	.4286	.4247
.2	.4207	.4168	.4129	.4090	.4052	.4013	.3974	.3936	.3897	.3859
.3	.3821	.3783	.3745	.3707	.3669	.3632	.3594	.3557	.3520	.3483
.4	.3446	.3409	.3372	.3336	.3300	.3264	.3228	.3192	.3156	.3121
.5	.3085	.3050	.3015	.2981	.2946	.2912	.2877	.2843	.2810	.2776
.6	.2743	.2709	.2676	.2643	.2611	.2578	.2546	.2514	.2483	.2451
.7	.2420	.2389	.2358	.2327	.2296	.2266	.2236	.2206	.2177	.2148
.8	.2119	.2090	.2061	.2033	.2005	.1977	.1949	.1922	.1894	.1867
.9	.1841	.1814	.1788	.1762	.1736	.1711	.1685	.1660	.1635	.1611
1.0	.1587	.1562	.1539	.1515	.1492	.1469	.1446	.1423	.1401	.1379
1.1	.1357	.1335	.1314	.1292	.1271	.1251	.1230	.1210	.1190	.1170
1.2	.1151	.1131	.1112	.1093	.1075	.1056	.1038	.1020	.1003	.0985
1.3	.0968	.0951	.0934	.0918	.0901	.0885	.0869	.0853	.0838	.0823
1.4	.0808	.0793	.0778	.0764	.0749	.0735	.0721	.0708	.0694	.0681
1.5	.0668	.0655	.0643	.0630	.0618	.0606	.0594	.0582	.0571	.0559
1.6	.0548	.0537	.0526	.0516	.0505	.0495	.0485	.0475	.0465	.0455
1.7	.0446	.0436	.0427	.0418	.0409	.0401	.0392	.0384	.0375	.0367
1.8	.0359	.0351	.0344	.0336	.0329	.0322	.0314	.0307	.0301	.0294
1.9	.0287	.0281	.0274	.0268	.0262	.0256	.0250	.0244	.0239	.0233
2.0	.0228	.0222	.0217	.0212	.0207	.0202	.0197	.0192	.0188	.0183
2.1	.0179	.0174	.0170	.0166	.0162	.0158	.0154	.0150	.0146	.0143
2.2	.0139	.0136	.0132	.0129	.0125	.0122	.0119	.0116	.0113	.0110
2.3	.0107	.0104	.0102	.0099	.0096	.0094	.0091	.0089	.0087	.0084
2.4	.0082	.0080	.0078	.0075	.0073	.0071	.0069	.0068	.0066	.0064
2.5	.0062	.0060	.0059	.0057	.0055	.0054	.0052	.0051	.0049	.0048
2.6	.0047	.0045	.0044	.0043	.0041	.0040	.0039	.0038	.0037	.0036
2.7	.0035	.0034	.0033	.0032	.0031	.0030	.0029	.0028	.0027	.0026
2.8	.0026	.0025	.0024	.0023	.0023	.0022	.0021	.0021	.0020	.0019
2.9	.0019	.0018	.0018	.0017	.0016	.0016	.0015	.0015	.0014	.0014
3.0	.0013	.0013	.0013	.0012	.0012	.0011	.0011	.0011	.0010	.0010
3.1	.0010	.0009	.0009	.0009	.0008	.0008	.0008	.0008	.0007	.0007
3.2	.0007									
3.3	.0005									
3.4	.0003									
3.5	.00023									
3.6	.00016									
3.7	.00011									
3.8	.00007									
3.9	.00005									
4.0*	.00003									

Note: All p values are one-tailed in this table.

*Additional values of Z are found in the bottom row of Table B.3, since t values for $df = \infty$ are also Z values.

Source: Reproduced from S. Siegel, *Nonparametric Statistics,* McGraw-Hill, New York, 1956, p. 247, with the permission of the publisher.

TABLE B.2
Summary table of t

df	p = .9	.8	.7	.6	.5	.4	.3	.2	.1	.05	.02	.01
1	.158	.325	.510	.727	1.000	1.376	1.963	3.078	6.314	12.706	31.821	63.657
2	.142	.289	.445	.617	.816	1.061	1.386	1.886	2.920	4.303	6.965	9.925
3	.137	.277	.424	.584	.765	.978	1.250	1.638	2.353	3.182	4.541	5.841
4	.134	.271	.414	.569	.741	.941	1.190	1.533	2.132	2.776	3.747	4.604
5	.132	.267	.408	.559	.727	.920	1.156	1.476	2.015	2.571	3.365	4.032
6	.131	.265	.404	.553	.718	.906	1.134	1.440	1.943	2.447	3.143	3.707
7	.130	.263	.402	.549	.711	.896	1.119	1.415	1.895	2.365	2.998	3.499
8	.130	.262	.399	.546	.706	.889	1.108	1.397	1.860	2.306	2.896	3.355
9	.129	.261	.398	.543	.703	.883	1.100	1.383	1.833	2.262	2.821	3.250
10	.129	.260	.397	.542	.700	.879	1.093	1.372	1.812	2.228	2.764	3.169
11	.129	.260	.396	.540	.697	.876	1.088	1.363	1.796	2.201	2.718	3.106
12	.128	.259	.395	.539	.695	.873	1.083	1.356	1.782	2.179	2.681	3.055
13	.128	.259	.394	.538	.694	.870	1.079	1.350	1.771	2.160	2.650	3.012
14	.128	.258	.393	.537	.692	.868	1.076	1.345	1.761	2.145	2.624	2.977
15	.128	.258	.393	.536	.691	.866	1.074	1.341	1.753	2.131	2.602	2.947
16	.128	.258	.392	.535	.690	.865	1.071	1.337	1.746	2.120	2.583	2.921
17	.128	.257	.392	.534	.689	.863	1.069	1.333	1.740	2.110	2.567	2.898
18	.127	.257	.392	.534	.688	.862	1.067	1.330	1.734	2.101	2.552	2.878
19	.127	.257	.391	.533	.688	.861	1.066	1.328	1.729	2.093	2.539	2.861
20	.127	.257	.391	.533	.687	.860	1.064	1.325	1.725	2.086	2.528	2.845
21	.127	.257	.391	.532	.686	.859	1.063	1.323	1.721	2.080	2.518	2.831
22	.127	.256	.390	.532	.686	.858	1.061	1.321	1.717	2.074	2.508	2.819
23	.127	.256	.390	.532	.685	.858	1.060	1.319	1.714	2.069	2.500	2.807
24	.127	.256	.390	.531	.685	.857	1.059	1.318	1.711	2.064	2.492	2.797
25	.127	.256	.390	.531	.684	.856	1.058	1.316	1.708	2.060	2.485	2.787
26	.127	.256	.390	.531	.684	.856	1.058	1.315	1.706	2.056	2.479	2.779
27	.127	.256	.389	.531	.684	.855	1.057	1.314	1.703	2.052	2.473	2.771
28	.127	.256	.389	.530	.683	.855	1.056	1.313	1.701	2.048	2.467	2.763
29	.127	.256	.389	.530	.683	.854	1.055	1.311	1.699	2.045	2.462	2.756
30	.127	.256	.389	.530	.683	.854	1.055	1.310	1.697	2.042	2.457	2.750
∞	.12566	.25335	.38532	.52440	.67449	.84162	1.03643	1.28155	1.64485	1.95996	2.32634	2.57582

Note: All p values are *two-tailed* in this table. Table B.3 presents a more detailed table of t values for *one-tailed* $p \leq .25$.

Source: Reproduced from E. F. Lindquist, *Design and Analysis of Experiments in Psychology and Education,* Houghton Mifflin, Boston, 1953, p. 38, with the permission of the publisher.

TABLE B.3
Extended table of t

df	.25	.10	.05	.025	.01	.005	.0025	.001
1	1.000	3.078	6.314	12.706	31.821	63.657	127.321	318.309
2	.816	1.886	2.920	4.303	6.965	9.925	14.089	22.327
3	.765	1.638	2.353	3.182	4.541	5.841	7.453	10.214
4	.741	1.533	2.132	2.776	3.747	4.604	5.598	7.173
5	.727	1.476	2.015	2.571	3.365	4.032	4.773	5.893
6	.718	1.440	1.943	2.447	3.143	3.707	4.317	5.208
7	.711	1.415	1.895	2.365	2.998	3.499	4.029	4.785
8	.706	1.397	1.860	2.306	2.896	3.355	3.833	4.501
9	.703	1.383	1.833	2.262	2.821	3.250	3.690	4.297
10	.700	1.372	1.812	2.228	2.764	3.169	3.581	4.144
11	.697	1.363	1.796	2.201	2.718	3.106	3.497	4.025
12	.695	1.356	1.782	2.179	2.681	3.055	3.428	3.930
13	.694	1.350	1.771	2.160	2.650	3.012	3.372	3.852
14	.692	1.345	1.761	2.145	2.624	2.977	3.326	3.787
15	.691	1.341	1.753	2.131	2.602	2.947	3.286	3.733
16	.690	1.337	1.746	2.120	2.583	2.921	3.252	3.686
17	.689	1.333	1.740	2.110	2.567	2.898	3.223	3.646
18	.688	1.330	1.734	2.101	2.552	2.878	3.197	3.610
19	.688	1.328	1.729	2.093	2.539	2.861	3.174	3.579
20	.687	1.325	1.725	2.086	2.528	2.845	3.153	3.552
21	.686	1.323	1.721	2.080	2.518	2.831	3.135	3.527
22	.686	1.321	1.717	2.074	2.508	2.819	3.119	3.505
23	.685	1.319	1.714	2.069	2.500	2.807	3.104	3.485
24	.685	1.318	1.711	2.064	2.492	2.797	3.090	3.467
25	.684	1.316	1.708	2.060	2.485	2.787	3.078	3.450
26	.684	1.315	1.706	2.056	2.479	2.779	3.067	3.435
27	.684	1.314	1.703	2.052	2.473	2.771	3.057	3.421
28	.683	1.313	1.701	2.048	2.467	2.763	3.047	3.408
29	.683	1.311	1.699	2.045	2.462	2.756	3.038	3.396
30	.683	1.310	1.697	2.042	2.457	2.750	3.030	3.385
35	.682	1.306	1.690	2.030	2.438	2.724	2.996	3.340
40	.681	1.303	1.684	2.021	2.423	2.704	2.971	3.307
45	.680	1.301	1.679	2.014	2.412	2.690	2.952	3.281
50	.679	1.299	1.676	2.009	2.403	2.678	2.937	3.261
55	.679	1.297	1.673	2.004	2.396	2.668	2.925	3.245
60	.679	1.296	1.671	2.000	2.390	2.660	2.915	3.232
70	.678	1.294	1.667	1.994	2.381	2.648	2.899	3.211
80	.678	1.292	1.664	1.990	2.374	2.639	2.887	3.195
90	.677	1.291	1.662	1.987	2.368	2.632	2.878	3.183
100	.677	1.290	1.660	1.984	2.364	2.626	2.871	3.174
200	.676	1.286	1.652	1.972	2.345	2.601	2.838	3.131
500	.675	1.283	1.648	1.965	2.334	2.586	2.820	3.107
1,000	.675	1.282	1.646	1.962	2.330	2.581	2.813	3.098
2,000	.675	1.282	1.645	1.961	2.328	2.578	2.810	3.094
10,000	.675	1.282	1.645	1.960	2.327	2.576	2.808	3.091
∞	.674	1.282	1.645	1.960	2.326	2.576	2.807	3.090

Note: All p values are one-tailed in this table. For p values > .25 see Table B.2.

TABLE B.3 (*Continued*)

df \ p	.0005	.00025	.0001	.00005	.000025	.00001
1	636.619	1,273.239	3,183.099	6,366.198	12,732.395	31,830.989
2	31.598	44.705	70.700	99.992	141.416	223.603
3	12.924	16.326	22.204	28.000	35.298	47.928
4	8.610	10.306	13.034	15.544	18.522	23.332
5	6.869	7.976	9.678	11.178	12.893	15.547
6	5.959	6.788	8.025	9.082	10.261	12.032
7	5.408	6.082	7.063	7.885	8.782	10.103
8	5.041	5.618	6.442	7.120	7.851	8.907
9	4.781	5.291	6.010	6.594	7.215	8.102
10	4.587	5.049	5.694	6.211	6.757	7.527
11	4.437	4.863	5.453	5.921	6.412	7.098
12	4.318	4.716	5.263	5.694	6.143	6.756
13	4.221	4.597	5.111	5.513	5.928	6.501
14	4.140	4.499	4.985	5.363	5.753	6.287
15	4.073	4.417	4.880	5.239	5.607	6.109
16	4.015	4.346	4.791	5.134	5.484	5.960
17	3.965	4.286	4.714	5.044	5.379	5.832
18	3.922	4.233	4.648	4.966	5.288	5.722
19	3.883	4.187	4.590	4.897	5.209	5.627
20	3.850	4.146	4.539	4.837	5.139	5.543
21	3.819	4.110	4.493	4.784	5.077	5.469
22	3.792	4.077	4.452	4.736	5.022	5.402
23	3.768	4.048	4.415	4.693	4.972	5.343
24	3.745	4.021	4.382	4.654	4.927	5.290
25	3.725	3.997	4.352	4.619	4.887	5.241
26	3.707	3.974	4.324	4.587	4.850	5.197
27	3.690	3.954	4.299	4.558	4.816	5.157
28	3.674	3.935	4.275	4.530	4.784	5.120
29	3.659	3.918	4.254	4.506	4.756	5.086
30	3.646	3.902	4.234	4.482	4.729	5.054
35	3.591	3.836	4.153	4.389	4.622	4.927
40	3.551	3.788	4.094	4.321	4.544	4.835
45	3.520	3.752	4.049	4.269	4.485	4.766
50	3.496	3.723	4.014	4.228	4.438	4.711
55	3.476	3.700	3.986	4.196	4.401	4.667
60	3.460	3.681	3.962	4.169	4.370	4.631
70	3.435	3.651	3.926	4.127	4.323	4.576
80	3.416	3.629	3.899	4.096	4.288	4.535
90	3.402	3.612	3.878	4.072	4.261	4.503
100	3.390	3.598	3.862	4.053	4.240	4.478
200	3.340	3.539	3.789	3.970	4.146	4.369
500	3.310	3.504	3.747	3.922	4.091	4.306
1,000	3.300	3.492	3.733	3.906	4.073	4.285
2,000	3.295	3.486	3.726	3.898	4.064	4.275
10,000	3.292	3.482	3.720	3.892	4.058	4.267
∞	3.291	3.481	3.719	3.891	4.056	4.265

Note: All *p* values are one-tailed in this table.

TABLE B.3 (*Continued*)

df	.000005	.0000025	.000001	.0000005	.00000025	.0000001
1	63,661.977	127,323.954	318,309.886	636,619.772	1,273,239.545	3,183,098.862
2	316.225	447.212	707.106	999.999	1,414.213	2,236.068
3	60.397	76.104	103.299	130.155	163.989	222.572
4	27.771	33.047	41.578	49.459	58.829	73.986
5	17.807	20.591	24.771	28.477	32.734	39.340
6	13.555	15.260	17.830	20.047	22.532	26.286
7	11.215	12.437	14.241	15.764	17.447	19.932
8	9.782	10.731	12.110	13.257	14.504	16.320
9	8.827	9.605	10.720	11.637	12.623	14.041
10	8.150	8.812	9.752	10.516	11.328	12.492
11	7.648	8.227	9.043	9.702	10.397	11.381
12	7.261	7.780	8.504	9.085	9.695	10.551
13	6.955	7.427	8.082	8.604	9.149	9.909
14	6.706	7.142	7.743	8.218	8.713	9.400
15	6.502	6.907	7.465	7.903	8.358	8.986
16	6.330	6.711	7.233	7.642	8.064	8.645
17	6.184	6.545	7.037	7.421	7.817	8.358
18	6.059	6.402	6.869	7.232	7.605	8.115
19	5.949	6.278	6.723	7.069	7.423	7.905
20	5.854	6.170	6.597	6.927	7.265	7.723
21	5.769	6.074	6.485	6.802	7.126	7.564
22	5.694	5.989	6.386	6.692	7.003	7.423
23	5.627	5.913	6.297	6.593	6.893	7.298
24	5.566	5.845	6.218	6.504	6.795	7.185
25	5.511	5.783	6.146	6.424	6.706	7.085
26	5.461	5.726	6.081	6.352	6.626	6.993
27	5.415	5.675	6.021	6.286	6.553	6.910
28	5.373	5.628	5.967	6.225	6.486	6.835
29	5.335	5.585	5.917	6.170	6.426	6.765
30	5.299	5.545	5.871	6.119	6.369	6.701
35	5.156	5.385	5.687	5.915	6.143	6.447
40	5.053	5.269	5.554	5.768	5.983	6.266
45	4.975	5.182	5.454	5.659	5.862	6.130
50	4.914	5.115	5.377	5.573	5.769	6.025
55	4.865	5.060	5.315	5.505	5.694	5.942
60	4.825	5.015	5.264	5.449	5.633	5.873
70	4.763	4.946	5.185	5.363	5.539	5.768
80	4.717	4.896	5.128	5.300	5.470	5.691
90	4.682	4.857	5.084	5.252	5.417	5.633
100	4.654	4.826	5.049	5.214	5.376	5.587
200	4.533	4.692	4.897	5.048	5.196	5.387
500	4.463	4.615	4.810	4.953	5.094	5.273
1,000	4.440	4.590	4.781	4.922	5.060	5.236
2,000	4.428	4.578	4.767	4.907	5.043	5.218
10,000	4.419	4.567	4.756	4.895	5.029	5.203
∞	4.417	4.565	4.753	4.892	5.026	5.199

Note: All p values are one-tailed in this table.

Standard normal deviates (Z) corresponding to t can be estimated quite accurately from

$$Z = \left[df \, \log_e\left(1 + \frac{t^2}{df}\right) \right]^{1/2} \left[1 - \frac{1}{2df}\right]^{1/2}$$

Source: Reproduced from E.T. Federighi, Extended tables of the percentage points of Student's *t*-distribution, *Journal of the American Statistical Association*, 1959, *54*, 683–688, with the permission of the publisher.

TABLE B.4
Table of F

df_2	df_1 / p	1	2	3	4	5	6	8	12	24	∞
1	.001	405284	500000	540379	562500	576405	585937	598144	610667	623497	636619
	.005	16211	20000	21615	22500	23056	23437	23925	24426	24940	25465
	.01	4052	4999	5403	5625	5764	5859	5981	6106	6234	6366
	.025	647.79	799.50	864.16	899.58	921.85	937.11	956.66	976.71	997.25	1018.30
	.05	161.45	199.50	215.71	224.58	230.16	233.99	238.88	243.91	249.05	254.32
	.10	39.86	49.50	53.59	55.83	57.24	58.20	59.44	60.70	62.00	63.33
	.20	9.47	12.00	13.06	13.73	14.01	14.26	14.59	14.90	15.24	15.58
2	.001	998.5	999.0	999.2	999.2	999.3	999.3	999.4	999.4	999.5	999.5
	.005	198.50	199.00	199.17	199.25	199.30	199.33	199.37	199.42	199.46	199.51
	.01	98.49	99.00	99.17	99.25	99.30	99.33	99.36	99.42	99.46	99.50
	.025	38.51	39.00	39.17	39.25	39.30	39.33	39.37	39.42	39.46	39.50
	.05	18.51	19.00	19.16	19.25	19.30	19.33	19.37	19.41	19.45	19.50
	.10	8.53	9.00	9.16	9.24	9.29	9.33	9.37	9.41	9.45	9.49
	.20	3.56	4.00	4.16	4.24	4.28	4.32	4.36	4.40	4.44	4.48
3	.001	167.5	148.5	141.1	137.1	134.6	132.8	130.6	128.3	125.9	123.5
	.005	55.55	49.80	47.47	46.20	45.39	44.84	44.13	43.39	42.62	41.83
	.01	34.12	30.81	29.46	28.71	28.24	27.91	27.49	27.05	26.60	26.12
	.025	17.44	16.04	15.44	15.10	14.89	14.74	14.54	14.34	14.12	13.90
	.05	10.13	9.55	9.28	9.12	9.01	8.94	8.84	8.74	8.64	8.53
	.10	5.54	5.46	5.39	5.34	5.31	5.28	5.25	5.22	5.18	5.13
	.20	2.68	2.89	2.94	2.96	2.97	2.97	2.98	2.98	2.98	2.98
4	.001	74.14	61.25	56.18	53.44	51.71	50.53	49.00	47.41	45.77	44.05
	.005	31.33	26.28	24.26	23.16	22.46	21.98	21.35	20.71	20.03	19.33
	.01	21.20	18.00	16.69	15.98	15.52	15.21	14.80	14.37	13.93	13.46
	.025	12.22	10.65	9.98	9.60	9.36	9.20	8.98	8.75	8.51	8.26
	.05	7.71	6.94	6.59	6.39	6.26	6.16	6.04	5.91	5.77	5.63
	.10	4.54	4.32	4.19	4.11	4.05	4.01	3.95	3.90	3.83	3.76
	.20	2.35	2.47	2.48	2.48	2.48	2.47	2.47	2.46	2.44	2.43
5	.001	47.04	36.61	33.20	31.09	29.75	28.84	27.64	26.42	25.14	23.78
	.005	22.79	18.31	16.53	15.56	14.94	14.51	13.96	13.38	12.78	12.14
	.01	16.26	13.27	12.06	11.39	10.97	10.67	10.29	9.89	9.47	9.02
	.025	10.01	8.43	7.76	7.39	7.15	6.98	6.76	6.52	6.28	6.02
	.05	6.61	5.79	5.41	5.19	5.05	4.95	4.82	4.68	4.53	4.36
	.10	4.06	3.78	3.62	3.52	3.45	3.40	3.34	3.27	3.19	3.10
	.20	2.18	2.26	2.25	2.24	2.23	2.22	2.20	2.18	2.16	2.13
6	.001	35.51	27.00	23.70	21.90	20.81	20.03	19.03	17.99	16.89	15.75
	.005	18.64	14.54	12.92	12.03	11.46	11.07	10.57	10.03	9.47	8.88
	.01	13.74	10.92	9.78	9.15	8.75	8.47	8.10	7.72	7.31	6.88
	.025	8.81	7.26	6.60	6.23	5.99	5.82	5.60	5.37	5.12	4.85
	.05	5.99	5.14	4.76	4.53	4.39	4.28	4.15	4.00	3.84	3.67
	.10	3.78	3.46	3.29	3.18	3.11	3.05	2.98	2.90	2.82	2.72
	.20	2.07	2.13	2.11	2.09	2.08	2.06	2.04	2.02	1.99	1.95
7	.001	29.22	21.69	18.77	17.19	16.21	15.52	14.63	13.71	12.73	11.69
	.005	16.24	12.40	10.88	10.05	9.52	9.16	8.68	8.18	7.65	7.08
	.01	12.25	9.55	8.45	7.85	7.46	7.19	6.84	6.47	6.07	5.65
	.025	8.07	6.54	5.89	5.52	5.29	5.12	4.90	4.67	4.42	4.14
	.05	5.59	4.74	4.35	4.12	3.97	3.87	3.73	3.57	3.41	3.23
	.10	3.59	3.26	3.07	2.96	2.88	2.83	2.75	2.67	2.58	2.47
	.20	2.00	2.04	2.02	1.99	1.97	1.96	1.93	1.91	1.87	1.83
8	.001	25.42	18.49	15.83	14.39	13.49	12.86	12.04	11.19	10.30	9.34
	.005	14.69	11.04	9.60	8.81	8.30	7.95	7.50	7.01	6.50	5.95
	.01	11.26	8.65	7.59	7.01	6.63	6.37	6.03	5.67	5.28	4.86
	.025	7.57	6.06	5.42	5.05	4.82	4.65	4.43	4.20	3.95	3.67
	.05	5.32	4.46	4.07	3.84	3.69	3.58	3.44	3.28	3.12	2.93
	.10	3.46	3.11	2.92	2.81	2.73	2.67	2.59	2.50	2.40	2.29
	.20	1.95	1.98	1.95	1.92	1.90	1.88	1.86	1.83	1.79	1.74
9	.001	22.86	16.39	13.90	12.56	11.71	11.13	10.37	9.57	8.72	7.81
	.005	13.61	10.11	8.72	7.96	7.47	7.13	6.69	6.23	5.73	5.19
	.01	10.56	8.02	6.99	6.42	6.06	5.80	5.47	5.11	4.73	4.31
	.025	7.21	5.71	5.08	4.72	4.48	4.32	4.10	3.87	3.61	3.33
	.05	5.12	4.26	3.86	3.63	3.48	3.37	3.23	3.07	2.90	2.71
	.10	3.36	3.01	2.81	2.69	2.61	2.55	2.47	2.38	2.28	2.16
	.20	1.91	1.94	1.90	1.87	1.85	1.83	1.80	1.76	1.72	1.67

df_2 \ df_1	p	1	2	3	4	5	6	8	12	24	∞
10	.001	21.04	14.91	12.55	11.28	10.48	9.92	9.20	8.45	7.64	6.76
	.005	12.83	9.43	8.08	7.34	6.87	6.54	6.12	5.66	5.17	4.64
	.01	10.04	7.56	6.55	5.99	5.64	5.39	5.06	4.71	4.33	3.91
	.025	6.94	5.46	4.83	4.47	4.24	4.07	3.85	3.62	3.37	3.08
	.05	4.96	4.10	3.71	3.48	3.33	3.22	3.07	2.91	2.74	2.54
	.10	3.28	2.92	2.73	2.61	2.52	2.46	2.38	2.28	2.18	2.06
	.20	1.88	1.90	1.86	1.83	1.80	1.78	1.75	1.72	1.67	1.62
11	.001	19.69	13.81	11.56	10.35	9.58	9.05	8.35	7.63	6.85	6.00
	.005	12.23	8.91	7.60	6.88	6.42	6.10	5.68	5.24	4.76	4.23
	.01	9.65	7.20	6.22	5.67	5.32	5.07	4.74	4.40	4.02	3.60
	.025	6.72	5.26	4.63	4.28	4.04	3.88	3.66	3.43	3.17	2.88
	.05	4.84	3.98	3.59	3.36	3.20	3.09	2.95	2.79	2.61	2.40
	.10	3.23	2.86	2.66	2.54	2.45	2.39	2.30	2.21	2.10	1.97
	.20	1.86	1.87	1.83	1.80	1.77	1.75	1.72	1.68	1.63	1.57
12	.001	18.64	12.97	10.80	9.63	8.89	8.38	7.71	7.00	6.25	5.42
	.005	11.75	8.51	7.23	6.52	6.07	5.76	5.35	4.91	4.43	3.90
	.01	9.33	6.93	5.95	5.41	5.06	4.82	4.50	4.16	3.78	3.36
	.025	6.55	5.10	4.47	4.12	3.89	3.73	3.51	3.28	3.02	2.72
	.05	4.75	3.88	3.49	3.26	3.11	3.00	2.85	2.69	2.50	2.30
	.10	3.18	2.81	2.61	2.48	2.39	2.33	2.24	2.15	2.04	1.90
	.20	1.84	1.85	1.80	1.77	1.74	1.72	1.69	1.65	1.60	1.54
13	.001	17.81	12.31	10.21	9.07	8.35	7.86	7.21	6.52	5.78	4.97
	.005	11.37	8.19	6.93	6.23	5.79	5.48	5.08	4.64	4.17	3.65
	.01	9.07	6.70	5.74	5.20	4.86	4.62	4.30	3.96	3.59	3.16
	.025	6.41	4.97	4.35	4.00	3.77	3.60	3.39	3.15	2.89	2.60
	.05	4.67	3.80	3.41	3.18	3.02	2.92	2.77	2.60	2.42	2.21
	.10	3.14	2.76	2.56	2.43	2.35	2.28	2.20	2.10	1.98	1.85
	.20	1.82	1.83	1.78	1.75	1.72	1.69	1.66	1.62	1.57	1.51
14	.001	17.14	11.78	9.73	8.62	7.92	7.43	6.80	6.13	5.41	4.60
	.005	11.06	7.92	6.68	6.00	5.56	5.26	4.86	4.43	3.96	3.44
	.01	8.86	6.51	5.56	5.03	4.69	4.46	4.14	3.80	3.43	3.00
	.025	6.30	4.86	4.24	3.89	3.66	3.50	3.29	3.05	2.79	2.49
	.05	4.60	3.74	3.34	3.11	2.96	2.85	2.70	2.53	2.35	2.13
	.10	3.10	2.73	2.52	2.39	2.31	2.24	2.15	2.05	1.94	1.80
	.20	1.81	1.81	1.76	1.73	1.70	1.67	1.64	1.60	1.55	1.48
15	.001	16.59	11.34	9.34	8.25	7.57	7.09	6.47	5.81	5.10	4.31
	.005	10.80	7.70	6.48	5.80	5.37	5.07	4.67	4.25	3.79	3.26
	.01	8.68	6.36	5.42	4.89	4.56	4.32	4.00	3.67	3.29	2.87
	.025	6.20	4.77	4.15	3.80	3.58	3.41	3.20	2.96	2.70	2.40
	.05	4.54	3.68	3.29	3.06	2.90	2.79	2.64	2.48	2.29	2.07
	.10	3.07	2.70	2.49	2.36	2.27	2.21	2.12	2.02	1.90	1.76
	.20	1.80	1.79	1.75	1.71	1.68	1.66	1.62	1.58	1.53	1.46
16	.001	16.12	10.97	9.00	7.94	7.27	6.81	6.19	5.55	4.85	4.06
	.005	10.58	7.51	6.30	5.64	5.21	4.91	4.52	4.10	3.64	3.11
	.01	8.53	6.23	5.29	4.77	4.44	4.20	3.89	3.55	3.18	2.75
	.025	6.12	4.69	4.08	3.73	3.50	3.34	3.12	2.89	2.63	2.32
	.05	4.49	3.63	3.24	3.01	2.85	2.74	2.59	2.42	2.24	2.01
	.10	3.05	2.67	2.46	2.33	2.24	2.18	2.09	1.99	1.87	1.72
	.20	1.79	1.78	1.74	1.70	1.67	1.64	1.61	1.56	1.51	1.43
17	.001	15.72	10.66	8.73	7.68	7.02	6.56	5.96	5.32	4.63	3.85
	.005	10.38	7.35	6.16	5.50	5.07	4.78	4.39	3.97	3.51	2.98
	.01	8.40	6.11	5.18	4.67	4.34	4.10	3.79	3.45	3.08	2.65
	.025	6.04	4.62	4.01	3.66	3.44	3.28	3.06	2.82	2.56	2.25
	.05	4.45	3.59	3.20	2.96	2.81	2.70	2.55	2.38	2.19	1.96
	.10	3.03	2.64	2.44	2.31	2.22	2.15	2.06	1.96	1.84	1.69
	.20	1.78	1.77	1.72	1.68	1.65	1.63	1.59	1.55	1.49	1.42
18	.001	15.38	10.39	8.49	7.46	6.81	6.35	5.76	5.13	4.45	3.67
	.005	10.22	7.21	6.03	5.37	4.96	4.66	4.28	3.86	3.40	2.87
	.01	8.28	6.01	5.09	4.58	4.25	4.01	3.71	3.37	3.00	2.57
	.025	5.98	4.56	3.95	3.61	3.38	3.22	3.01	2.77	2.50	2.19
	.05	4.41	3.55	3.16	2.93	2.77	2.66	2.51	2.34	2.15	1.92
	.10	3.01	2.62	2.42	2.29	2.20	2.13	2.04	1.93	1.81	1.66
	.20	1.77	1.76	1.71	1.67	1.64	1.62	1.58	1.53	1.48	1.40

df_2	df_1 p	1	2	3	4	5	6	8	12	24	∞
19	.001	15.08	10.16	8.28	7.26	6.61	6.18	5.59	4.97	4.29	3.52
	.005	10.07	7.09	5.92	5.27	4.85	4.56	4.18	3.76	3.31	2.78
	.01	8.18	5.93	5.01	4.50	4.17	3.94	3.63	3.30	2.92	2.49
	.025	5.92	4.51	3.90	3.56	3.33	3.17	2.96	2.72	2.45	2.13
	.05	4.38	3.52	3.13	2.90	2.74	2.63	2.48	2.31	2.11	1.88
	.10	2.99	2.61	2.40	2.27	2.18	2.11	2.02	1.91	1.79	1.63
	.20	1.76	1.75	1.70	1.66	1.63	1.61	1.57	1.52	1.46	1.39
20	.001	14.82	9.95	8.10	7.10	6.46	6.02	5.44	4.82	4.15	3.38
	.005	9.94	6.99	5.82	5.17	4.76	4.47	4.09	3.68	3.22	2.69
	.01	8.10	5.85	4.94	4.43	4.10	3.87	3.56	3.23	2.86	2.42
	.025	5.87	4.46	3.86	3.51	3.29	3.13	2.91	2.68	2.41	2.09
	.05	4.35	3.49	3.10	2.87	2.71	2.60	2.45	2.28	2.08	1.84
	.10	2.97	2.59	2.38	2.25	2.16	2.09	2.00	1.89	1.77	1.61
	.20	1.76	1.75	1.70	1.65	1.62	1.60	1.56	1.51	1.45	1.37
21	.001	14.59	9.77	7.94	6.95	6.32	5.88	5.31	4.70	4.03	3.26
	.005	9.83	6.89	5.73	5.09	4.68	4.39	4.01	3.60	3.15	2.61
	.01	8.02	5.78	4.87	4.37	4.04	3.81	3.51	3.17	2.80	2.36
	.025	5.83	4.42	3.82	3.48	3.25	3.09	2.87	2.64	2.37	2.04
	.05	4.32	3.47	3.07	2.84	2.68	2.57	2.42	2.25	2.05	1.81
	.10	2.96	2.57	2.36	2.23	2.14	2.08	1.98	1.88	1.75	1.59
	.20	1.75	1.74	1.69	1.65	1.61	1.59	1.55	1.50	1.44	1.36
22	.001	14.38	9.61	7.80	6.81	6.19	5.76	5.19	4.58	3.92	3.15
	.005	9.73	6.81	5.65	5.02	4.61	4.32	3.94	3.54	3.08	2.55
	.01	7.94	5.72	4.82	4.31	3.99	3.76	3.45	3.12	2.75	2.31
	.025	5.79	4.38	3.78	3.44	3.22	3.05	2.84	2.60	2.33	2.00
	.05	4.30	3.44	3.05	2.82	2.66	2.55	2.40	2.23	2.03	1.78
	.10	2.95	2.56	2.35	2.22	2.13	2.06	1.97	1.86	1.73	1.57
	.20	1.75	1.73	1.68	1.64	1.61	1.58	1.54	1.49	1.43	1.35
23	.001	14.19	9.47	7.67	6.69	6.08	5.65	5.09	4.48	3.82	3.05
	.005	9.63	6.73	5.58	4.95	4.54	4.26	3.88	3.47	3.02	2.48
	.01	7.88	5.66	4.76	4.26	3.94	3.71	3.41	3.07	2.70	2.26
	.025	5.75	4.35	3.75	3.41	3.18	3.02	2.81	2.57	2.30	1.97
	.05	4.28	3.42	3.03	2.80	2.64	2.53	2.38	2.20	2.00	1.76
	.10	2.94	2.55	2.34	2.21	2.11	2.05	1.95	1.84	1.72	1.55
	.20	1.74	1.73	1.68	1.63	1.60	1.57	1.53	1.49	1.42	1.34
24	.001	14.03	9.34	7.55	6.59	5.98	5.55	4.99	4.39	3.74	2.97
	.005	9.55	6.66	5.52	4.89	4.49	4.20	3.83	3.42	2.97	2.43
	.01	7.82	5.61	4.72	4.22	3.90	3.67	3.36	3.03	2.66	2.21
	.025	5.72	4.32	3.72	3.38	3.15	2.99	2.78	2.54	2.27	1.94
	.05	4.26	3.40	3.01	2.78	2.62	2.51	2.36	2.18	1.98	1.73
	.10	2.93	2.54	2.33	2.19	2.10	2.04	1.94	1.83	1.70	1.53
	.20	1.74	1.72	1.67	1.63	1.59	1.57	1.53	1.48	1.42	1.33
25	.001	13.88	9.22	7.45	6.49	5.88	5.46	4.91	4.31	3.66	2.89
	.005	9.48	6.60	5.46	4.84	4.43	4.15	3.78	3.37	2.92	2.38
	.01	7.77	5.57	4.68	4.18	3.86	3.63	3.32	2.99	2.62	2.17
	.025	5.69	4.29	3.69	3.35	3.13	2.97	2.75	2.51	2.24	1.91
	.05	4.24	3.38	2.99	2.76	2.60	2.49	2.34	2.16	1.96	1.71
	.10	2.92	2.53	2.32	2.18	2.09	2.02	1.93	1.82	1.69	1.52
	.20	1.73	1.72	1.66	1.62	1.59	1.56	1.52	1.47	1.41	1.32
26	.001	13.74	9.12	7.36	6.41	5.80	5.38	4.83	4.24	3.59	2.82
	.005	9.41	6.54	5.41	4.79	4.38	4.10	3.73	3.33	2.87	2.33
	.01	7.72	5.53	4.64	4.14	3.82	3.59	3.29	2.96	2.58	2.13
	.025	5.66	4.27	3.67	3.33	3.10	2.94	2.73	2.49	2.22	1.88
	.05	4.22	3.37	2.98	2.74	2.59	2.47	2.32	2.15	1.95	1.69
	.10	2.91	2.52	2.31	2.17	2.08	2.01	1.92	1.81	1.68	1.50
	.20	1.73	1.71	1.66	1.62	1.58	1.56	1.52	1.47	1.40	1.31
27	.001	13.61	9.02	7.27	6.33	5.73	5.31	4.76	4.17	3.52	2.75
	.005	9.34	6.49	5.36	4.74	4.34	4.06	3.69	3.28	2.83	2.29
	.01	7.68	5.49	4.60	4.11	3.78	3.56	3.26	2.93	2.55	2.10
	.025	5.63	4.24	3.65	3.31	3.08	2.92	2.71	2.47	2.19	1.85
	.05	4.21	3.35	2.96	2.73	2.57	2.46	2.30	2.13	1.93	1.67
	.10	2.90	2.51	2.30	2.17	2.07	2.00	1.91	1.80	1.67	1.49
	.20	1.73	1.71	1.66	1.61	1.58	1.55	1.51	1.46	1.40	1.30

TABLE B.4 *(Continued)*

df₂	df₁ / p	1	2	3	4	5	6	8	12	24	∞
28	.001	13.50	8.93	7.19	6.25	5.66	5.24	4.69	4.11	3.46	2.70
	.005	9.28	6.44	5.32	4.70	4.30	4.02	3.65	3.25	2.79	2.25
	.01	7.64	5.45	4.57	4.07	3.75	3.53	3.23	2.90	2.52	2.06
	.025	5.61	4.22	3.63	3.29	3.06	2.90	2.69	2.45	2.17	1.83
	.05	4.20	3.34	2.95	2.71	2.56	2.44	2.29	2.12	1.91	1.65
	.10	2.89	2.50	2.29	2.16	2.06	2.00	1.90	1.79	1.66	1.48
	.20	1.72	1.71	1.65	1.61	1.57	1.55	1.51	1.46	1.39	1.30
29	.001	13.39	8.85	7.12	6.19	5.59	5.18	4.64	4.05	3.41	2.64
	.005	9.23	6.40	5.28	4.66	4.26	3.98	3.61	3.21	2.76	2.21
	.01	7.60	5.42	4.54	4.04	3.73	3.50	3.20	2.87	2.49	2.03
	.025	5.59	4.20	3.61	3.27	3.04	2.88	2.67	2.43	2.15	1.81
	.05	4.18	3.33	2.93	2.70	2.54	2.43	2.28	2.10	1.90	1.64
	.10	2.89	2.50	2.28	2.15	2.06	1.99	1.89	1.78	1.65	1.47
	.20	1.72	1.70	1.65	1.60	1.57	1.54	1.50	1.45	1.39	1.29
30	.001	13.29	8.77	7.05	6.12	5.53	5.12	4.58	4.00	3.36	2.59
	.005	9.18	6.35	5.24	4.62	4.23	3.95	3.58	3.18	2.73	2.18
	.01	7.56	5.39	4.51	4.02	3.70	3.47	3.17	2.84	2.47	2.01
	.025	5.57	4.18	3.59	3.25	3.03	2.87	2.65	2.41	2.14	1.79
	.05	4.17	3.32	2.92	2.69	2.53	2.42	2.27	2.09	1.89	1.62
	.10	2.88	2.49	2.28	2.14	2.05	1.98	1.88	1.77	1.64	1.46
	.20	1.72	1.70	1.64	1.60	1.57	1.54	1.50	1.45	1.38	1.28
40	.001	12.61	8.25	6.60	5.70	5.13	4.73	4.21	3.64	3.01	2.23
	.005	8.83	6.07	4.98	4.37	3.99	3.71	3.35	2.95	2.50	1.93
	.01	7.31	5.18	4.31	3.83	3.51	3.29	2.99	2.66	2.29	1.80
	.025	5.42	4.05	3.46	3.13	2.90	2.74	2.53	2.29	2.01	1.64
	.05	4.08	3.23	2.84	2.61	2.45	2.34	2.18	2.00	1.79	1.51
	.10	2.84	2.44	2.23	2.09	2.00	1.93	1.83	1.71	1.57	1.38
	.20	1.70	1.68	1.62	1.57	1.54	1.51	1.47	1.41	1.34	1.24
60	.001	11.97	7.76	6.17	5.31	4.76	4.37	3.87	3.31	2.69	1.90
	.005	8.49	5.80	4.73	4.14	3.76	3.49	3.13	2.74	2.29	1.69
	.01	7.08	4.98	4.13	3.65	3.34	3.12	2.82	2.50	2.12	1.60
	.025	5.29	3.93	3.34	3.01	2.79	2.63	2.41	2.17	1.88	1.48
	.05	4.00	3.15	2.76	2.52	2.37	2.25	2.10	1.92	1.70	1.39
	.10	2.79	2.39	2.18	2.04	1.95	1.87	1.77	1.66	1.51	1.29
	.20	1.68	1.65	1.59	1.55	1.51	1.48	1.44	1.38	1.31	1.18
120	.001	11.38	7.31	5.79	4.95	4.42	4.04	3.55	3.02	2.40	1.56
	.005	8.18	5.54	4.50	3.92	3.55	3.28	2.93	2.54	2.09	1.43
	.01	6.85	4.79	3.95	3.48	3.17	2.96	2.66	2.34	1.95	1.38
	.025	5.15	3.80	3.23	2.89	2.67	2.52	2.30	2.05	1.76	1.31
	.05	3.92	3.07	2.68	2.45	2.29	2.17	2.02	1.83	1.61	1.25
	.10	2.75	2.35	2.13	1.99	1.90	1.82	1.72	1.60	1.45	1.19
	.20	1.66	1.63	1.57	1.52	1.48	1.45	1.41	1.35	1.27	1.12
∞	.001	10.83	6.91	5.42	4.62	4.10	3.74	3.27	2.74	2.13	1.00
	.005	7.88	5.30	4.28	3.72	3.35	3.09	2.74	2.36	1.90	1.00
	.01	6.64	4.60	3.78	3.32	3.02	2.80	2.51	2.18	1.79	1.00
	.025	5.02	3.69	3.12	2.79	2.57	2.41	2.19	1.94	1.64	1.00
	.05	3.84	2.99	2.60	2.37	2.21	2.09	1.94	1.75	1.52	1.00
	.10	2.71	2.30	2.08	1.94	1.85	1.77	1.67	1.55	1.38	1.00
	.20	1.64	1.61	1.55	1.50	1.46	1.43	1.38	1.32	1.23	1.00

Source: Reproduced from E. F. Lindquist, *Design and Analysis of Experiments in Psychology and Education,* Houghton Mifflin, Boston, 1953, pp. 41–44, with the permission of the publisher.

TABLE B.5
Table of χ^2

df	Probability													
	.99	.98	.95	.90	.80	.70	.50	.30	.20	.10	.05	.02	.01	.001
1	.00016	.00063	.00393	.0158	.0642	.148	.455	1.074	1.642	2.706	3.841	5.412	6.635	10.827
2	.0201	.0404	.103	.211	.446	.713	1.386	2.408	3.219	4.605	5.991	7.824	9.210	13.815
3	.115	.185	.352	.584	1.005	1.424	2.366	3.665	4.642	6.251	7.815	9.837	11.345	16.268
4	.297	.429	.711	1.064	1.649	2.195	3.357	4.878	5.989	7.779	9.488	11.668	13.277	18.465
5	.554	.752	1.145	1.610	2.343	3.000	4.351	6.064	7.289	9.236	11.070	13.388	15.086	20.517
6	.872	1.134	1.635	2.204	3.070	3.828	5.348	7.231	8.558	10.645	12.592	15.033	16.812	22.457
7	1.239	1.564	2.167	2.833	3.822	4.671	6.346	8.383	9.803	12.017	14.067	16.622	18.475	24.322
8	1.646	2.032	2.733	3.490	4.594	5.527	7.344	9.524	11.030	13.362	15.507	18.168	20.090	26.125
9	2.088	2.532	3.325	4.168	5.380	6.393	8.343	10.656	12.242	14.684	16.919	19.679	21.666	27.877
10	2.558	3.059	3.940	4.865	6.179	7.267	9.342	11.781	13.442	15.987	18.307	21.161	23.209	29.588
11	3.053	3.609	4.575	5.578	6.989	8.148	10.341	12.899	14.631	17.275	19.675	22.618	24.725	31.264
12	3.571	4.178	5.226	6.304	7.807	9.034	11.340	14.011	15.812	18.549	21.026	24.054	26.217	32.909
13	4.107	4.765	5.892	7.042	8.634	9.926	12.340	15.119	16.985	19.812	22.362	25.472	27.688	34.528
14	4.660	5.368	6.571	7.790	9.467	10.821	13.339	16.222	18.151	21.064	23.685	26.873	29.141	36.123
15	5.229	5.985	7.261	8.547	10.307	11.721	14.339	17.322	19.311	22.307	24.996	28.259	30.578	37.697
16	5.812	6.614	7.962	9.312	11.152	12.624	15.338	18.418	20.465	23.542	26.296	29.633	32.000	39.252
17	6.408	7.255	8.672	10.085	12.002	13.531	16.338	19.511	21.615	24.769	27.587	30.995	33.409	40.790
18	7.015	7.906	9.390	10.865	12.857	14.440	17.338	20.601	22.760	25.989	28.869	32.346	34.805	42.312
19	7.633	8.567	10.117	11.651	13.716	15.352	18.338	21.689	23.900	27.204	30.144	33.687	36.191	43.820
20	8.260	9.237	10.851	12.443	14.578	16.266	19.337	22.775	25.038	28.412	31.410	35.020	37.566	45.315
21	8.897	9.915	11.591	13.240	15.445	17.182	20.337	23.858	26.171	29.615	32.671	36.343	38.932	46.797
22	9.542	10.600	12.338	14.041	16.314	18.101	21.337	24.939	27.301	30.813	33.924	37.659	40.289	48.268
23	10.196	11.293	13.091	14.848	17.187	19.021	22.337	26.018	28.429	32.007	35.172	38.968	41.638	49.728
24	10.856	11.992	13.848	15.659	18.062	19.943	23.337	27.096	29.553	33.196	36.415	40.270	42.980	51.179
25	11.524	12.697	14.611	16.473	18.940	20.867	24.337	28.172	30.675	34.382	37.652	41.566	44.314	52.620
26	12.198	13.409	15.379	17.292	19.820	21.792	25.336	29.246	31.795	35.563	38.885	42.856	45.642	54.052
27	12.879	14.125	16.151	18.114	20.703	22.719	26.336	30.319	32.912	36.741	40.113	44.140	46.963	55.476
28	13.565	14.847	16.928	18.939	21.588	23.647	27.336	31.391	34.027	37.916	41.337	45.419	48.278	56.893
29	14.256	15.574	17.708	19.768	22.475	24.577	28.336	32.461	35.139	39.087	42.557	46.693	49.588	58.302
30	14.953	16.306	18.493	20.599	23.364	25.508	29.336	33.530	36.250	40.256	43.773	47.962	50.892	59.703

Note: For larger values of *df*, the expression $\sqrt{2\chi^2} - \sqrt{2df - 1}$ may be used as a normal deviate with unit variance, remembering that the probability for χ^2 corresponds with that of a single tail of the normal curve.

Source: Reproduced from E. F. Lindquist, *Design and Analysis of Experiments in Psychology and Education,* Houghton Mifflin, Boston, 1953, p. 29, with the permission of the publisher.

TABLE B.6
Significance levels of r (from $t = r\sqrt{(N - 2)/(1 - r^2)}$)

				Probability level			
$(N - 2)$	.20	.10	.05	.02	.01	.001	.0001
1	.951	.988	.997	.9995	.9999	1.000	1.0000
2	.800	.900	.950	.980	.990	.999	.9999
3	.687	.805	.878	.934	.959	.991	.998
4	.608	.729	.811	.882	.917	.974	.992
5	.551	.669	.754	.833	.874	.951	.981
6	.507	.622	.707	.789	.834	.925	.966
7	.472	.582	.666	.750	.798	.898	.948
8	.443	.550	.632	.716	.765	.872	.929
9	.419	.521	.602	.685	.735	.847	.910
10	.398	.497	.576	.658	.708	.823	.891
11	.380	.476	.553	.634	.684	.801	.873
12	.365	.458	.532	.612	.661	.780	.854
13	.351	.441	.514	.592	.641	.760	.837
14	.338	.426	.497	.574	.623	.742	.820
15	.327	.412	.482	.558	.606	.725	.804
16	.317	.400	.468	.542	.590	.708	.789
17	.308	.389	.456	.528	.575	.693	.774
18	.299	.378	.444	.516	.561	.679	.760
19	.291	.369	.433	.503	.549	.665	.747
20	.284	.360	.423	.492	.537	.652	.734
22	.271	.344	.404	.472	.515	.629	.711
24	.260	.330	.388	.453	.496	.607	.689
25	.255	.323	.381	.445	.487	.597	.679
30	.233	.296	.349	.409	.449	.554	.633
35	.216	.275	.325	.381	.418	.519	.596
40	.202	.257	.304	.358	.393	.490	.564
45	.190	.243	.288	.338	.372	.465	.537
50	.181	.231	.273	.322	.354	.443	.513
55	.172	.220	.261	.307	.338	.424	.492
60	.165	.211	.250	.295	.325	.408	.474
65	.159	.203	.240	.284	.312	.393	.457
70	.153	.195	.232	.274	.302	.380	.442
75	.148	.189	.224	.264	.292	.368	.429
80	.143	.183	.217	.256	.283	.357	.416
85	.139	.178	.211	.249	.275	.347	.405
90	.135	.173	.205	.242	.267	.338	.395
95	.131	.168	.200	.236	.260	.329	.385
100	.128	.164	.195	.230	.254	.321	.376
125	.115	.147	.174	.206	.228	.288	.338
150	.105	.134	.159	.189	.208	.264	.310
175	.097	.124	.148	.174	.194	.248	.288
200	.091	.116	.138	.164	.181	.235	.270
300	.074	.095	.113	.134	.148	.188	.222
500	.057	.074	.088	.104	.115	.148	.173
1000	.041	.052	.062	.073	.081	.104	.123
2000	.029	.037	.044	.052	.058	.074	.087
5000	.018	.023	.028	.033	.037	.047	.055

Note: All p values are two-tailed in this table.

Source: Reproduced, in part, from H. M. Walker and J. Lev, *Statistical Inference,* Holt, New York, 1953, p. 470, with the permission of the author and publisher; and from A. L. Sockloff and J. N. Edney, *Some Extension of Student's t and Pearson's r Central Distributions.* Temple University Measurement and Research Center, Technical Report 72-5, May 1972, with the permission of the first author.

TABLE B.7
Table of Fisher's z transformation of r

					Second digit of r					
r	.00	.01	.02	.03	.04	.05	.06	.07	.08	.09
.0	.000	.010	.020	.030	.040	.050	.060	.070	.080	.090
.1	.100	.110	.121	.131	.141	.151	.161	.172	.182	.192
.2	.203	.213	.224	.234	.245	.255	.266	.277	.288	.299
.3	.310	.321	.332	.343	.354	.365	.377	.388	.400	.412
.4	.424	.436	.448	.460	.472	.485	.497	.510	.523	.536
.5	.549	.563	.576	.590	.604	.618	.633	.648	.662	.678
.6	.693	.709	.725	.741	.758	.775	.793	.811	.829	.848
.7	.867	.887	.908	.929	.950	.973	.996	1.020	1.045	1.071
.8	1.099	1.127	1.157	1.188	1.221	1.256	1.293	1.333	1.376	1.422

					Third digit of r					
r	.000	.001	.002	.003	.004	.005	.006	.007	.008	.009
.90	1.472	1.478	1.483	1.488	1.494	1.499	1.505	1.510	1.516	1.522
.91	1.528	1.533	1.539	1.545	1.551	1.557	1.564	1.570	1.576	1.583
.92	1.589	1.596	1.602	1.609	1.616	1.623	1.630	1.637	1.644	1.651
.93	1.658	1.666	1.673	1.681	1.689	1.697	1.705	1.713	1.721	1.730
.94	1.738	1.747	1.756	1.764	1.774	1.783	1.792	1.802	1.812	1.822
.95	1.832	1.842	1.853	1.863	1.874	1.886	1.897	1.909	1.921	1.933
.96	1.946	1.959	1.972	1.986	2.000	2.014	2.029	2.044	2.060	2.076
.97	2.092	2.109	2.127	2.146	2.165	2.185	2.205	2.227	2.249	2.273
.98	2.298	2.323	2.351	2.380	2.410	2.443	2.477	2.515	2.555	2.599
.99	2.646	2.700	2.759	2.826	2.903	2.994	3.106	3.250	3.453	3.800

Note: z is obtained as $\frac{1}{2} \log_e \frac{(1 + r)}{(1 - r)}$.

Source: Reprinted by permission from *Statistical Methods* by George W. Snedecor and William G. Cochran, 7th ed., (c) 1980, by the Iowa State University Press, Ames, Iowa 50010.

TABLE B.8
Table of *r* equivalents of Fisher's *z*

z	.00	.01	.02	.03	.04	.05	.06	.07	.08	.09
.0	.000	.010	.020	.030	.040	.050	.060	.070	.080	.090
.1	.100	.110	.119	.129	.139	.149	.159	.168	.178	.187
.2	.197	.207	.216	.226	.236	.245	.254	.264	.273	.282
.3	.291	.300	.310	.319	.327	.336	.345	.354	.363	.371
.4	.380	.389	.397	.405	.414	.422	.430	.438	.446	.454
.5	.462	.470	.478	.485	.493	.500	.508	.515	.523	.530
.6	.537	.544	.551	.558	.565	.572	.578	.585	.592	.598
.7	.604	.611	.617	.623	.629	.635	.641	.647	.653	.658
.8	.664	.670	.675	.680	.686	.691	.696	.701	.706	.711
.9	.716	.721	.726	.731	.735	.740	.744	.749	.753	.757
1.0	.762	.766	.770	.774	.778	.782	.786	.790	.793	.797
1.1	.800	.804	.808	.811	.814	.818	.821	.824	.828	.831
1.2	.834	.837	.840	.843	.846	.848	.851	.854	.856	.859
1.3	.862	.864	.867	.869	.872	.874	.876	.879	.881	.883
1.4	.885	.888	.890	.892	.894	.896	.898	.900	.902	.903
1.5	.905	.907	.909	.910	.912	.914	.915	.917	.919	.920
1.6	.922	.923	.925	.926	.928	.929	.930	.932	.933	.934
1.7	.935	.937	.938	.939	.940	.941	.942	.944	.945	.946
1.8	.947	.948	.949	.950	.951	.952	.953	.954	.954	.955
1.9	.956	.957	.958	.959	.960	.960	.961	.962	.963	.963
2.0	.964	.965	.965	.966	.967	.967	.968	.969	.969	.970
2.1	.970	.971	.972	.972	.973	.973	.974	.974	.975	.975
2.2	.976	.976	.977	.977	.978	.978	.978	.979	.979	.980
2.3	.980	.980	.981	.981	.982	.982	.982	.983	.983	.983
2.4	.984	.984	.984	.985	.985	.985	.986	.986	.986	.986
2.5	.987	.987	.987	.987	.988	.988	.988	.988	.989	.989
2.6	.989	.989	.989	.990	.990	.990	.990	.990	.991	.991
2.7	.991	.991	.991	.992	.992	.992	.992	.992	.992	.992
2.8	.993	.993	.993	.993	.993	.993	.993	.994	.994	.994
2.9	.994	.994	.994	.994	.994	.995	.995	.995	.995	.995

Note: r is obtained as $\dfrac{e^{2z} - 1}{e^{2z} + 1}$.

Source: Reprinted by permission from *Statistical Methods* by George W. Snedecor and William G. Cochran, 7th ed., (c) 1980, by the Iowa State University Press, Ames, Iowa 50010.

TABLE B.9
Table of random digits

000	10097	32533	76520	13586	34673	54876	80959	09117	39292	74945
001	37542	04805	64894	74296	24805	24037	20636	10402	00822	91665
002	08422	68953	19645	09303	23209	02560	15953	34764	35080	33605
003	99019	02529	09376	70715	38311	31165	88676	74397	04436	27659
004	12807	99970	80157	36147	64032	36653	98951	16877	12171	76833
005	66065	74717	34072	76850	36697	36170	65813	39885	11199	29170
006	31060	10805	45571	82406	35303	42614	86799	07439	23403	09732
007	85269	77602	02051	65692	68665	74818	73053	85247	18623	88579
008	63573	32135	05325	47048	90553	57548	28468	28709	83491	25624
009	73796	45753	03529	64778	35808	34282	60935	20344	35273	88435
010	98520	17767	14905	68607	22109	40558	60970	93433	50500	73998
011	11805	05431	39808	27732	50725	68248	29405	24201	52775	67851
012	83452	99634	06288	98083	13746	70078	18475	40610	68711	77817
013	88685	40200	86507	58401	36766	67951	90364	76493	29609	11062
014	99594	67348	87517	64969	91826	08928	93785	61368	23478	34113
015	65481	17674	17468	50950	58047	76974	73039	57186	40218	16544
016	80124	35635	17727	08015	45318	22374	21115	78253	14385	53763
017	74350	99817	77402	77214	43236	00210	45521	64237	96286	02655
018	69916	26803	66252	29148	36936	87203	76621	13990	94400	56418
019	09893	20505	14225	68514	46427	56788	96297	78822	54382	14598
020	91499	14523	68479	27686	46162	83554	94750	89923	37089	20048
021	80336	94598	26940	36858	70297	34135	53140	33340	42050	82341
022	44104	81949	85157	47954	32979	26575	57600	40881	22222	06413
023	12550	73742	11100	02040	12860	74697	96644	89439	28707	25815
024	63606	49329	16505	34484	40219	52563	43651	77082	07207	31790
025	61196	90446	26457	47774	51924	33729	65394	59593	42582	60527
026	15474	45266	95270	79953	59367	83848	82396	10118	33211	59466
027	94557	28573	67897	54387	54622	44431	91190	42592	92927	45973
028	42481	16213	97344	08721	16868	48767	03071	12059	25701	46670
029	23523	78317	73208	89837	68935	91416	26252	29663	05522	82562
030	04493	52494	75246	33824	45862	51025	61962	79335	65337	12472
031	00549	97654	64051	88159	96119	63896	54692	82391	23287	29529
032	35963	15307	26898	09354	33351	35462	77974	50024	90103	39333
033	59808	08391	45427	26842	83609	49700	13021	24892	78565	20106
034	46058	85236	01390	92286	77281	44077	93910	83647	70617	42941
035	32179	00597	87379	25241	05567	07007	86743	17157	85394	11838
036	69234	61406	20117	45204	15956	60000	18743	92423	97118	96338
037	19565	41430	01758	75379	40419	21585	66674	36806	84962	85207
038	45155	14938	19476	07246	43667	94543	59047	90033	20826	69541
039	94864	31994	36168	10851	34888	81553	01540	35456	05014	51176
040	98086	24826	45240	28404	44999	08896	39094	73407	35441	31880
041	33185	16232	41941	50949	89435	48581	88695	41994	37548	73043
042	80951	00406	96382	70774	20151	23387	25016	25298	94624	61171
043	79752	49140	71961	28296	69861	02591	74852	20539	00387	59579
044	18633	32537	98145	06571	31010	24674	05455	61427	77938	91936

TABLE B.9   (*Continued*)

045	74029	43902	77557	32270	97790	17119	52527	58021	80814	51748
046	54178	45611	80993	37143	05335	12969	56127	19255	36040	90324
047	11664	49883	52079	84827	59381	71539	09973	33440	88461	23356
048	48324	77928	31249	64710	02295	36870	32307	57546	15020	09994
049	69074	94138	87637	91976	35584	04401	10518	21615	01848	76938
050	09188	20097	32825	39527	04220	86304	83389	87374	64278	58044
051	90045	85497	51981	50654	94938	81997	91870	76150	68476	64659
052	73189	50207	47677	26269	62290	64464	27124	67018	41361	82760
053	75768	76490	20971	87749	90429	12272	95375	05871	93823	43178
054	54016	44056	66281	31003	00682	27398	20714	53295	07706	17813
055	08358	69910	78542	42785	13661	58873	04618	97553	31223	08420
056	28306	03264	81333	10591	40510	07893	32604	60475	94119	01840
057	53840	86233	81594	13628	51215	90290	28466	68795	77762	20791
058	91757	53741	61613	62269	50263	90212	55781	76514	83483	47055
059	89415	92684	00397	58391	12607	17646	48949	72306	94541	37408
060	77513	03820	86864	29901	68414	82774	51908	13980	72893	55507
061	19502	37174	69979	20288	55210	29773	74287	75251	65344	67415
062	21818	59313	93278	81757	05686	73156	07082	85046	31853	38452
063	51474	66499	68107	23621	94049	91345	42836	09191	08007	45449
064	99559	68331	62535	24170	69777	12830	74819	78142	43860	72834
065	33713	48007	93584	72869	51926	64721	58303	29822	93174	93972
066	85274	86893	11303	22970	28834	34137	73515	90400	71148	43643
067	84133	89640	44035	52166	73852	70091	61222	60561	62327	18423
068	56732	16234	17395	96131	10123	91622	85496	57560	81604	18880
069	65138	56806	87648	85261	34313	65861	45875	21069	85644	47277
070	38001	02176	81719	11711	71602	92937	74219	64049	65584	49698
071	37402	96397	01304	77586	56271	10086	47324	62605	40030	37438
072	97125	40348	87083	31417	21815	39250	75237	62047	15501	29578
073	21826	41134	47143	34072	64638	85902	49139	06441	03856	54552
074	73135	42742	95719	09035	85794	74296	08789	88156	64691	19202
075	07638	77929	03061	18072	96207	44156	23821	99538	04713	66994
076	60528	83441	07954	19814	59175	20695	05533	52139	61212	06455
077	83596	35655	06958	92983	05128	09719	77433	53783	92301	50498
078	10850	62746	99599	10507	13499	06319	53075	71839	06410	19362
079	39820	98952	43622	63147	64421	80814	43800	09351	31024	73167
080	59580	06478	75569	78800	88835	54486	23768	06156	04111	08408
081	38508	07341	23793	48763	90822	97022	17719	04207	95954	49953
082	30692	70668	94688	16127	56196	80091	82067	63400	05462	69200
083	65443	95659	18288	27437	49632	24041	08337	65676	96299	90836
084	27267	50264	13192	72294	07477	44606	17985	48911	97341	30358
085	91307	06991	19072	24210	36699	53728	28825	35793	28976	66252
086	68434	94688	84473	13622	62126	98408	12843	82590	09815	93146
087	48908	15877	54745	24591	35700	04754	83824	52692	54130	55160
088	06913	45197	42672	78601	11883	09528	63011	98901	14974	40344
089	10455	16019	14210	33712	91342	37821	88325	80851	43667	70883

TABLE B.9 *(Continued)*

090	12883	97343	65027	61184	04285	01392	17974	15077	90712	26769
091	21778	30976	38807	36961	31649	42096	63281	02023	08816	47449
092	19523	59515	65122	59659	86283	68258	69572	13798	16435	91529
093	67245	52670	35583	16563	79246	86686	76463	34222	26655	90802
094	60584	47377	07500	37992	45134	26529	26760	83637	41326	44344
095	53853	41377	36066	94850	58838	73859	49364	73331	96240	43642
096	24637	38736	74384	89342	52623	07992	12369	18601	03742	83873
097	83080	12451	38992	22815	07759	51777	97377	27585	51972	37867
098	16444	24334	36151	99073	27493	70939	85130	32552	54846	54759
099	60790	18157	57178	65762	11161	78576	45819	52979	65130	04860
100	03991	10461	93716	16894	66083	24653	84609	58232	88618	19161
101	38555	95554	32886	59780	08355	60860	29735	47762	71299	23853
102	17546	73704	92052	46215	55121	29281	59076	07936	27954	58909
103	32643	52861	95819	06831	00911	98936	76355	93779	80863	00514
104	69572	68777	39510	35905	14060	40619	29549	69616	33564	60780
105	24122	66591	27699	06494	14845	46672	61958	77100	90899	75754
106	61196	30231	92962	61773	41839	55382	17267	70943	78038	70267
107	30532	21704	10274	12202	39685	23309	10061	68829	55986	66485
108	03788	97599	75867	20717	74416	53166	35208	33374	87539	08823
109	48228	63379	85783	47619	53152	67433	35663	52972	16818	60311
110	60365	94653	35075	33949	42614	29297	01918	28316	98953	73231
111	83799	42402	56623	34442	34994	41374	70071	14736	09958	18065
112	32960	07405	36409	83232	99385	41600	11133	07586	15917	06253
113	19322	53845	57620	52606	66497	68646	78138	66559	19640	99413
114	11220	94747	07399	37408	48509	23929	27482	45476	85244	35159
115	31751	57260	68980	05339	15470	48355	88651	22596	03152	19121
116	88492	99382	14454	04504	20094	98977	74843	93413	22109	78508
117	30934	47744	07481	83828	73788	06533	28597	20405	94205	20380
118	22888	48893	27499	98748	60530	45128	74022	84617	82037	10268
119	78212	16993	35902	91386	44372	15486	65741	14014	87481	37220
120	41849	84547	46850	52326	34677	58300	74910	64345	19325	81549
121	46352	33049	69248	93460	45305	07521	61318	31855	14413	70951
122	11087	96294	14013	31792	59747	67277	76503	34513	39663	77544
123	52701	08337	56303	87315	16520	69676	11654	99893	02181	68161
124	57275	36898	81304	48585	68652	27376	92852	55866	88448	03584
125	20857	73156	70284	24326	79375	95220	01159	63267	10622	48391
126	15633	84924	90415	93614	33521	26665	55823	47641	86225	31704
127	92694	48297	39904	02115	59589	49067	66821	41575	49767	04037
128	77613	19019	88152	00080	20554	91409	96277	48257	50816	97616
129	38688	32486	45134	63545	59404	72059	43947	51680	43852	59693
130	25163	01889	70014	15021	41290	67312	71857	15957	68971	11403
131	65251	07629	37239	33295	05870	01119	92784	26340	18477	65622
132	36815	43625	18637	37509	82444	99005	04921	73701	14707	93997
133	64397	11692	05327	82162	20247	81759	45197	25332	83745	22567
134	04515	25624	95096	67946	48460	85558	15191	18782	16930	33361

TABLE B.9   *(Continued)*

135	83761	60873	43253	84145	60833	25983	01291	41349	20368	07126
136	14387	06345	80854	09279	43529	06318	38384	74761	41196	37480
137	51321	92246	80088	77074	88722	56736	66164	49431	66919	31678
138	72472	00008	80890	18002	94813	31900	54155	83436	35352	54131
139	05466	55306	93128	18464	74457	90561	72848	11834	79982	68416
140	39528	72484	82474	25593	48545	35247	18619	13674	18611	19241
141	81616	18711	53342	44276	75122	11724	74627	73707	58319	15997
142	07586	16120	82641	22820	92904	13141	32392	19763	61199	67940
143	90767	04235	13574	17200	69902	63742	78464	22501	18627	90872
144	40188	28193	29593	88627	94972	11598	62095	36787	00441	58997
145	34414	82157	86887	55087	19152	00023	12302	80783	32624	68691
146	63439	75363	44989	16822	36024	00867	76378	41605	65961	73488
147	67049	09070	93399	45547	94458	74284	05041	49807	20288	34060
148	79495	04146	52162	90286	54158	34243	46978	35482	59362	95938
149	91704	30552	04737	21031	75051	93029	47665	64382	99782	93478
150	94015	46874	32444	48277	59820	96163	64654	25843	41145	42820
151	74108	88222	88570	74015	25704	91035	01755	14750	48968	38603
152	62880	87873	95160	59221	22304	90314	72877	17334	39283	04149
153	11748	12102	80580	41867	17710	59621	06554	07850	73950	79552
154	17944	05600	60478	03343	25852	58905	57216	39618	49856	99326
155	66067	42792	95043	52680	46780	56487	09971	59481	37006	22186
156	54244	91030	45547	70818	59849	96169	61459	21647	87417	17198
157	30945	57589	31732	57260	47670	07654	46376	25366	94746	49580
158	69170	37403	86995	90307	94304	71803	26825	05511	12459	91314
159	08345	88975	35841	85771	08105	59987	87112	21476	14713	71181
160	27767	43584	85301	88977	29490	69714	73035	41207	74699	09310
161	13025	14338	54066	15243	47724	66733	47431	43905	31048	56699
162	80217	36292	98525	24335	24432	24896	43277	58874	11466	16082
163	10875	62004	90391	61105	57411	06368	53856	30743	08670	84741
164	54127	57326	26629	19087	24472	88779	30540	27886	61732	75454
165	60311	42824	37301	42678	45990	43242	17374	52003	70707	70214
166	49739	71484	92003	98086	76668	73209	59202	11973	02902	33250
167	78626	51594	16453	94614	39014	97066	83012	09832	25571	77628
168	66692	13986	99837	00582	81232	44987	09504	96412	90193	79568
169	44071	28091	07362	97703	76447	42537	98524	97831	65704	09514
170	41468	85149	49554	17994	14924	39650	95294	00566	70481	06905
171	94559	37559	49678	53119	70312	05682	66986	34099	74474	20740
172	41615	70360	64114	58660	90850	64618	80620	51790	11436	38072
173	50273	93113	41794	86861	24781	89683	55411	85667	77535	99892
174	41396	80504	90670	08289	40902	05069	95083	06783	28102	57816
175	25807	24260	71529	78920	72682	07385	90726	57166	98884	08583
176	06170	97965	88302	98041	21443	41808	68984	83620	89747	98882
177	60808	54444	74412	81105	01176	28838	36421	16489	18059	51061
178	80940	44893	10408	36222	80582	71944	92638	40333	67054	16067
179	19516	90120	46759	71643	13177	55292	21036	82808	77501	97427

TABLE B.9 (*Continued*)

180	49386	54480	23604	23554	21785	41101	91178	10174	29420	90438
181	06312	88940	15995	69321	47458	64809	98189	81851	29651	84215
182	60942	00307	11897	92674	40405	68032	96717	54244	10701	41393
183	92329	98932	78284	46347	71209	92061	39448	93136	25722	08564
184	77936	63574	31384	51924	85561	29671	58137	17820	22751	36518
185	38101	77756	11657	13897	95889	57067	47648	13885	70669	93406
186	39641	69457	91339	22502	92613	89719	11947	56203	19324	20504
187	84054	40455	99396	63680	67667	60631	69181	96845	38525	11600
188	47468	03577	57649	63266	24700	71594	14004	23153	69249	05747
189	43321	31370	28977	23896	76479	68562	62342	07589	08899	05985
190	64281	61826	18555	64937	13173	33365	78851	16499	87064	13075
191	66847	70495	32350	02985	86716	38746	26313	77463	55387	72681
192	72461	33230	21529	53424	92581	02262	78438	66276	18396	73538
193	21032	91050	13058	16218	12470	56500	15292	76139	59526	52113
194	95362	67011	06651	16136	01016	00857	55018	56374	35824	71708
195	49712	97380	10404	55452	34030	60726	75211	10271	36633	68424
196	58275	61764	97586	54716	50259	46345	87195	46092	26787	60939
197	89514	11788	68224	23417	73959	76145	30342	42077	11049	72049
198	15472	50669	48139	36732	46874	37088	73465	09819	58869	35220
199	12120	86124	51247	44302	60883	52109	21437	36786	49226	77837
200	19612	78430	11661	94770	77603	65669	86868	12665	30012	75989
201	39141	77400	28000	64238	73258	71794	31340	26256	66453	37016
202	64756	80457	08747	12836	03469	50678	03274	43423	66677	82556
203	92901	51878	56441	22998	29718	38447	06453	25311	07565	53771
204	03551	90070	09483	94050	45938	18135	36908	43321	11073	51803
205	98884	66209	06830	53656	14663	56346	71430	04909	19818	05707
206	27369	86882	53473	07541	53633	70863	03748	12822	19360	49088
207	59066	75974	63335	20483	43514	37481	58278	26967	49325	43951
208	91647	93783	64169	49022	98588	09495	49829	59068	38831	04838
209	83605	92419	39542	07772	71568	75673	35185	89759	44901	74291
210	24895	88530	70774	35439	46758	70472	70207	92675	91623	61275
211	35720	26556	95596	20094	73750	85788	34264	01703	46833	65248
212	14141	53410	38649	06343	57256	61342	72709	75318	90379	37562
213	27416	75670	92176	72535	93119	56077	06886	18244	92344	31374
214	82071	07429	81007	47749	40744	56974	23336	88821	53841	10536
215	21445	82793	24831	93241	14199	76268	70883	68002	03829	17443
216	72513	76400	52225	92348	62308	98481	29744	33165	33141	61020
217	71479	45027	76160	57411	13780	13632	52308	77762	88874	33697
218	83210	51466	09088	50395	26743	05306	21706	70001	99439	80767
219	68749	95148	94897	78636	96750	09024	94538	91143	96693	61886
220	05184	75763	47075	88158	05313	53439	14908	08830	60096	21551
221	13651	62546	96892	25240	47511	58483	87342	78818	07855	39269
222	00566	21220	00292	24069	25072	29519	52548	54091	21282	21296
223	50958	17695	58072	68990	60329	95955	71586	63417	35947	67807
224	57621	64547	46850	37981	38527	09037	64756	03324	04986	83666

TABLE B.9 *(Continued)*

225	09282	25844	79139	78435	35428	43561	69799	63314	12991	93516
226	23394	94206	93432	37836	94919	26846	02555	74410	94915	48199
227	05280	37470	93622	04345	15092	19510	18094	16613	78234	50001
228	95491	97976	38306	32192	82639	54624	72434	92606	23191	74693
229	78521	00104	18248	75583	90326	50785	54034	66251	35774	14692
230	96345	44579	85932	44053	75704	20840	86583	83944	52456	73766
231	77963	31151	32364	91691	47357	40338	23435	24065	08458	95366
232	07520	11294	23238	01748	41690	67328	54814	37777	10057	42332
233	38423	02309	70703	85736	46148	14258	29236	12152	05088	65825
234	02463	65533	21199	60555	33928	01817	07396	89215	30722	22102
235	15880	92261	17292	88190	61781	48898	92525	21283	88581	60098
236	71926	00819	59144	00224	30570	90194	18329	06999	26857	19238
237	64425	28108	16554	16016	00042	83229	10333	36168	65617	94834
238	79782	23924	49440	30432	81077	31543	95216	64865	13658	51081
239	35337	74538	44553	64672	90960	41849	93865	44608	93176	34851
240	05249	29329	19715	94082	14738	86667	43708	66354	93692	25527
241	56463	99380	38793	85774	19056	13939	46062	27647	66146	63210
242	96296	33121	54196	34108	75814	85986	71171	15102	28992	63165
243	98380	36269	60014	07201	62448	46385	42175	88350	46182	49126
244	52567	64350	16315	53969	80395	81114	54358	64578	47269	15747
245	78498	90830	25955	99236	43286	91064	99969	95144	64424	77377
246	49553	24241	08150	89535	08703	91041	77323	81079	45127	93686
247	32151	07075	83155	10252	73100	88618	23891	87418	45417	20268
248	11314	50363	26860	27799	49416	83534	19187	08059	76677	02110
249	12364	71210	87052	50241	90785	97889	81399	58130	64439	05614
250	59467	58309	87834	57213	37510	33689	01259	62486	56320	46265
251	73452	17619	56421	40725	23439	41701	93223	41682	45026	47505
252	27635	56293	91700	04391	67317	89604	73020	69853	61517	51207
253	86040	02596	01655	09918	45161	00222	54577	74821	47335	08582
254	52403	94255	26351	46527	68224	91083	85057	72310	34963	83462
255	49465	46581	61499	04844	94626	02963	41482	83879	44942	61915
256	94365	92560	12363	30246	02086	75036	88620	91088	67691	67762
257	34261	08769	91830	23313	18256	28850	37639	92748	57791	71328
258	37110	66538	39318	15626	44324	82827	08782	65960	58167	01305
259	83950	45424	72453	19444	68219	64733	94088	62006	89985	36936
260	61630	97966	76537	46467	30942	07479	67971	14558	22458	35148
261	01929	17165	12037	74558	16250	71750	55546	29693	94984	37782
262	41659	39098	23982	29899	71594	77979	54477	13764	17315	72893
263	32031	39608	75992	73445	01317	50525	87313	45191	30214	19769
264	90043	93478	58044	06949	31176	88370	50274	83987	45316	38551

TABLE B.9 *(Continued)*

265	79418	14322	91065	07841	36130	86602	10659	40859	00964	71577
266	85447	61079	96910	72906	07361	84338	34114	52096	66715	51091
267	86219	81115	49625	48799	89485	24855	13684	68433	70595	70102
268	71712	88559	92476	32903	68009	58417	87962	11787	16644	72964
269	29776	63075	13270	84758	49560	10317	28778	23006	31036	84906
270	81488	17340	74154	42801	27917	89792	62604	62234	13124	76471
271	51667	37589	87147	24743	48023	06325	79794	35889	13255	04925
272	99004	70322	60832	76636	56907	56534	72615	46288	36788	93196
273	68656	66492	35933	52293	47953	95495	95304	50009	83464	28608
274	38074	74083	09337	07965	65047	36871	59015	21769	30398	44855
275	01020	80680	59328	08712	48190	45332	27284	31287	66011	09376
276	86379	74508	33579	77114	92955	23085	92824	03054	25242	16322
277	48498	09938	44420	13484	52319	58875	02012	88591	52500	95795
278	41800	95363	54142	17482	32705	60564	12505	40954	46174	64130
279	63026	96712	79883	39225	52653	69549	36693	59822	22684	31661
280	88298	15489	16030	42480	15372	38781	71995	77438	91161	10192
281	07839	62735	99218	25624	02547	27445	69187	55749	32322	15504
282	73298	51108	48717	92926	75705	89787	96114	99902	37749	96305
283	12829	70474	00838	50385	91711	80370	56504	56857	80906	09018
284	76569	61072	48568	36491	22587	44363	39592	61546	90181	37348
285	41665	41339	62106	44203	06732	76111	79840	67999	32231	76869
286	58652	49983	01669	27464	79553	52855	25988	18087	38052	17529
287	13607	00657	76173	43357	77334	24140	53860	02906	89863	44651
288	55715	26203	65933	51087	98234	40625	45545	63563	89148	82581
289	04110	66683	99001	09796	47349	65003	66524	81970	71262	14479
290	31300	08681	58068	44115	40064	77879	23965	69019	73985	19453
291	26225	97543	37044	07494	85778	35345	61115	92498	49737	64599
292	07158	82763	25072	38478	57782	75291	62155	52056	04786	11585
293	71251	25572	79771	93328	66927	54069	58752	26624	50463	77361
294	29991	96526	02820	91659	12818	96356	49499	01507	40223	09171
295	83642	21057	02677	09367	38097	16100	19355	06120	15378	56559
296	69167	30235	06767	66323	78294	14916	19124	88044	16673	66102
297	86018	29406	75415	22038	27056	26906	25867	14751	92380	30434
298	44114	06026	97553	55091	95385	41212	37882	46864	54717	97038
299	53805	64150	70915	63127	63695	41288	38192	72437	75075	18570

Source: Reprinted from the Rand Corporation, *A Million Random Digits with 100,000 Normal Deviates,* Free Press, New York, 1955, with the permission of the Rand Corporation and the publisher.

TABLE B.10
Significance levels of ρ, the Spearman rank-correlation coefficient

N	.10	.05	.02	.01	.001
4	1.000				
5	.900	1.000	1.000		
6	.829	.886	.943	1.000	
7	.714	.786	.893	.929	1.000
8	.643	.738	.833	.881	.976
9	.600	.700	.783	.833	.933
10	.564	.648	.745	.794	.903
11	.536	.618	.709	.755	.873
12	.503	.587	.678	.727	.846
13	.484	.560	.648	.703	.824
14	.464	.538	.626	.679	.802
15	.446	.521	.604	.654	.779
16	.429	.503	.582	.635	.762

Note: All *p* values are two-tailed in this table. For *N* greater than 16 see Table B.6.

Source: Reproduced from J. H. Zar, *Biostatistical Analysis* (2d ed.), Prentice-Hall, Englewood Cliffs, NJ, 1984, p. 577, with the permission of the author and publisher.

TABLE B.11
Significance levels of $F_{MAX} = S^2_{MAX}/S^2_{MIN}$ in a set of k independent variances, each based on $n-1$ degrees of freedom

$n-1$ \ k	2	3	4	5	6	7	8	9	10	11	12
2	39.0 / 199.	87.5 / 448.	142. / 729.	202. / 1036.	266. / 1362.	333. / 1705.	403. / 2063.	475. / 2432.	550. / 2813.	626. / 3204.	704. / 3605.
3	15.4 / 47.5	27.8 / 85.	39.2 / 120.	50.7 / 151.	62.0 / 184.	72.9 / 216.	83.5 / 249.	93.9 / 281.	104. / 310.	114. / 337.	124. / 361.
4	9.60 / 23.2	15.5 / 85.	20.6 / 49.	25.2 / 59.	29.5 / 69.	33.6 / 79.	37.5 / 89.	41.1 / 97.	44.6 / 106.	48.0 / 113.	51.4 / 120.
5	7.15 / 14.9	10.8 / 22.	13.7 / 28.	16.3 / 33.	18.7 / 38.	20.8 / 42.	22.9 / 46.	24.7 / 50.	26.5 / 54.	28.2 / 57.	29.9 / 60.
6	5.82 / 11.1	8.38 / 15.5	10.4 / 19.1	12.1 / 22.	13.7 / 25.	15.0 / 27.	16.3 / 30.	17.5 / 32.	18.6 / 34.	19.7 / 36.	20.7 / 37.
7	4.99 / 8.89	6.94 / 12.1	8.44 / 14.5	9.70 / 16.5	10.8 / 18.4	11.8 / 20.	12.7 / 22.	13.5 / 23.	14.3 / 24.	15.1 / 26.	15.8 / 27.
8	4.43 / 7.50	6.00 / 9.9	7.18 / 11.7	8.12 / 13.2	9.03 / 14.5	9.78 / 15.8	10.5 / 16.9	11.1 / 17.9	11.7 / 18.9	12.2 / 19.8	12.7 / 21.
9	4.03 / 6.54	5.34 / 8.5	6.31 / 9.9	7.11 / 11.1	7.80 / 12.1	8.41 / 13.1	8.95 / 13.9	9.45 / 14.7	9.91 / 15.3	10.3 / 16.0	10.7 / 16.6

10	3.72 5.85	4.85 7.4	5.67 8.6	6.34 9.6	6.92 10.4	7.42 11.1	7.87 11.8	8.28 12.4	8.66 12.9	9.01 13.4	9.34 13.9
12	3.28 4.91	4.16 6.1	4.79 6.9	5.30 7.6	5.72 8.2	6.09 8.7	6.42 9.1	6.72 9.5	7.00 9.9	7.25 10.2	7.48 10.6
15	2.86 4.07	3.54 4.9	4.01 5.5	4.37 6.0	4.68 6.4	4.95 6.7	5.19 7.1	5.40 7.3	5.59 7.5	5.77 7.8	5.93 8.0
20	2.46 3.32	2.95 3.8	3.29 4.3	3.54 4.6	3.76 4.9	3.94 5.1	4.10 5.3	4.24 5.5	4.37 5.6	4.49 5.8	4.59 5.9
30	2.07 2.63	2.40 3.0	2.61 3.3	2.78 3.4	2.91 3.6	3.02 3.7	3.12 3.8	3.21 3.9	3.29 4.0	3.36 4.1	3.39 4.2
60	1.67 1.96	1.85 2.2	1.96 2.3	2.04 2.4	2.11 2.4	2.17 2.5	2.22 2.5	2.26 2.6	2.30 2.6	2.33 2.7	2.36 2.7
∞	1.00 1.00	1.00 1.00	1.00 1.00	1.00 1.00	1.00 1.00	1.00 1.00	1.00 1.00	1.00 1.00	1.00 1.00	1.00 1.00	1.00 1.00

Note: The upper value in each cell is the .05 level; the lower value is the .01 level.

Source: Reproduced from E. S. Pearson and H. O. Hartley (Eds.), *Biometrika Tables for Statisticians,* 1956, p. 179, with the permission of *Biometrika* Trustees.

TABLE B.12

Significance levels of Cochran's $g = S^2_{MAX}/\Sigma S^2$ in a set of k independent variances, each based on $n - 1$ degrees of freedom

$n-1$	k = 2	3	4	5	6	7	8	9	10	15	20
1	.9985	.9669	.9065	.8412	.7808	.7271	.6798	.6385	.6020	.4709	.3894
	.9999	.9933	.9676	.9279	.8828	.8376	.7945	.7544	.7175	.5747	.4799
2	.9750	.8709	.7679	.6838	.6161	.5612	.5157	.4775	.4450	.3346	.2705
	.9950	.9423	.8643	.7885	.7218	.6644	.6152	.5727	.5358	.4069	.3297
3	.9392	.7977	.6841	.5981	.5321	.4800	.4377	.4027	.3733	.2758	.2205
	.9794	.8831	.7814	.6957	.6258	.5685	.5209	.4810	.4469	.3317	.2654
4	.9057	.7457	.6287	.5441	.4803	.4307	.3910	.3584	.3311	.2419	.1921
	.9586	.8335	.7212	.6329	.5635	.5080	.4627	.4251	.3934	.2882	.2288
5	.8772	.7071	.5895	.5065	.4447	.3974	.3595	.3286	.3029	.2195	.1735
	.9373	.7933	.6761	.5875	.5195	.4659	.4226	.3870	.3572	.2593	.2048
6	.8534	.6771	.5598	.4783	.4184	.3726	.3362	.3067	.2823	.2034	.1602
	.9172	.7606	.6410	.5531	.4866	.4347	.3932	.3592	.3308	.2386	.1877

7	.8332 .8988	.6530 .7335	.5365 .6129	.4564 .5259	.3980 .4608	.3535 .4105	.3185 .3704	.2901 .3378	.2666 .3106	.1911 .2228	.1501 .1748
8	.8159 .8823	.6333 .7107	.5175 .5897	.4387 .5037	.3817 .4401	.3384 .3911	.3043 .3522	.2768 .3207	.2541 .2945	.1815 .2104	.1422 .1646
9	.8010 .8674	.6167 .6912	.5017 .5702	.4241 .4854	.3682 .4229	.3259 .3751	.2926 .3373	.2659 .3067	.2439 .2813	.1736 .2002	.1357 .1567
16	.7341 .7949	.5466 .6059	.4366 .4884	.3645 .4094	.3135 .3529	.2756 .3105	.2462 .2779	.2226 .2514	.2032 .2297	.1429 .1612	.1108 .1248
36	.6602 .7067	.4748 .5153	.3720 .4057	.3066 .3351	.2612 .2858	.2278 .2494	.2022 .2214	.1820 .1992	.1655 .1811	.1144 .1251	.0879 .0960
144	.5813 .6062	.4031 .4230	.3093 .3251	.2513 .2644	.2119 .2229	.1833 .1929	.1616 .1700	.1446 .1521	.1308 .1376	.0889 .0934	.0675 .0709

Note: The upper value in each cell is the .05 level; the lower value is the .01 level.

Source: Reproduced from B. J. Winer, *Statistical Principles in Experimental Design*, 2d ed., McGraw-Hill, New York, 1971, p. 876, with the permission of the author and publisher.

TABLE B.13
Arcsin transformation ($a = 2$ arcsin $\sqrt{X}$)

X	a	X	a	X	a	X	a	X	a
.001	.0633	.041	.4078	.36	1.2870	.76	2.1177	.971	2.7993
.002	.0895	.042	.4128	.37	1.3078	.77	2.1412	.972	2.8053
.003	.1096	.043	.4178	.38	1.3284	.78	2.1652	.973	2.8115
.004	.1266	.044	.4227	.39	1.3490	.79	2.1895	.974	2.8177
.005	.1415	.045	.4275	.40	1.3694	.80	2.2143	.975	2.8240
.006	.1551	.046	.4323	.41	1.3898	.81	2.2395	.976	2.8305
.007	.1675	.047	.4371	.42	1.4101	.82	2.2653	.977	2.8371
.008	.1791	.048	.4418	.43	1.4303	.83	2.2916	.978	2.8438
.009	.1900	.049	.4464	.44	1.4505	.84	2.3186	.979	2.8507
.010	.2003	.050	.4510	.45	1.4706	.85	2.3462	.980	2.8578
.011	.2101	.06	.4949	.46	1.4907	.86	2.3746	.981	2.8650
.012	.2195	.07	.5355	.47	1.5108	.87	2.4039	.982	2.8725
.013	.2285	.08	.5735	.48	1.5308	.88	2.4341	.983	2.8801
.014	.2372	.09	.6094	.49	1.5508	.89	2.4655	.984	2.8879
.015	.2456	.10	.6435	.50	1.5708	.90	2.4981	.985	2.8960
.016	.2537	.11	.6761	.51	1.5908	.91	2.5322	.986	2.9044
.017	.2615	.12	.7075	.52	1.6108	.92	2.5681	.987	2.9131
.018	.2691	.13	.7377	.53	1.6308	.93	2.6062	.988	2.9221
.019	.2766	.14	.7670	.54	1.6509	.94	2.6467	.989	2.9315
.020	.2838	.15	.7954	.55	1.6710	.95	2.6906	.990	2.9413
.021	.2909	.16	.8230	.56	1.6911	.951	2.6952	.991	2.9516
.022	.2978	.17	.8500	.57	1.7113	.952	2.6998	.992	2.9625
.023	.3045	.18	.8763	.58	1.7315	.953	2.7045	.993	2.9741
.024	.3111	.19	.9021	.59	1.7518	.954	2.7093	.994	2.9865
.025	.3176	.20	.9273	.60	1.7722	.955	2.7141	.995	3.0001
.026	.3239	.21	.9521	.61	1.7926	.956	2.7189	.996	3.0150
.027	.3301	.22	.9764	.62	1.8132	.957	2.7238	.997	3.0320
.028	.3363	.23	1.0004	.63	1.8338	.958	2.7288	.998	3.0521
.029	.3423	.24	1.0239	.64	1.8546	.959	2.7338	.999	3.0783
.030	.3482	.25	1.0472	.65	1.8755	.960	2.7389		
.031	.3540	.26	1.0701	.66	1.8965	.961	2.7440		
.032	.3597	.27	1.0928	.67	1.9177	.962	2.7492		
.033	.3654	.28	1.1152	.68	1.9391	.963	2.7545		
.034	.3709	.29	1.1374	.69	1.9606	.964	2.7598		
.035	.3764	.30	1.1593	.70	1.9823	.965	2.7652		
.036	.3818	.31	1.1810	.71	2.0042	.966	2.7707		
.037	.3871	.32	1.2025	.72	2.0264	.967	2.7762		
.038	.3924	.33	1.2239	.73	2.0488	.968	2.7819		
.039	.3976	.34	1.2451	.74	2.0715	.969	2.7876		
.040	.4027	.35	1.2661	.75	2.0944	.970	2.7934		

Source: Reproduced from B. J. Winer, *Statistical Principles in Experimental Design,* 2d ed., McGraw-Hill, New York, 1971, p. 872, with the permission of the author and publisher.

GLOSSARY

A-B design   Simplest $N = 1$ design, in which the dependent variable is measured repeatedly throughout the pretreatment or baseline period (the A phase) and the treatment period (the B phase).

A-B-A design $N = 1$ design in which there are repeated measures prior to the treatment (the A phase), during the treatment (the B phase), and then with treatment withdrawn (the final A phase).

A-B-A-B design $N = 1$ design in which there are two types of occasions (B to A and A to B) for demonstrating the effects of the treatment variable.

A-B-BC-B design $N = 1$ design in which there are repeated measurements prior to the introduction of the treatments (the A phase), then during treatment B, during the combination of treatments B and C, and finally during treatment B alone; its purpose is to tease out the effect of B both in combination with C and apart from C.

Abscissa   The horizontal axis of a distribution.

Activity   Any intentional act, behavior, or incident that is aimed at affecting the status of events; a natural unit of ethnographic fieldwork.

Aesthetics   A sense of the beautiful; just as art is grounded in beauty, scientists are conscious of the aesthetics of their theoretical and mathematical propositions.

After-only design   A standard experimental design in which subjects' reactions are measured after the treatment has been administered.

Aggregate reliability   See *Effective reliability.*

Aggregating sources of variance   Combining terms that are sufficiently similar, with similarity defined as, e.g., $F < 2$.

Alias   A source of variation completely confounded with another.

Alpha (α) Probability of a type I error; synonyms include *significance level* and *p value.*

Alpha coefficient   A measure (proposed by Lee J. Cronbach) of internal-consistency reliability.

Alternate hypothesis   The experimental hypothesis, symbolized as H_1.

Analysis of covariance   Analysis of variance with the dependent variable adjusted for one or more covariates or predictor variables.

Analysis of variance   Subdivision of the total variance of a set of scores into its components.

Analytic survey   A sample survey the purpose of which is to explore the relations among variables.

Anova   Analysis of variance.

Antirealism   The assertion that scientific theories do not give a literally true account of the world; a view associated with Pierre Duhem, Thomas Kuhn, and Imre Lakatos.

a priori method   Reasoning from cause to effect, or from a general to a particular instance, independently of any scientific observation.

Arcsin transformation   Transformation for proportions making equal differences equally detectable.

Area probability sampling   A type of survey sampling in which the subclasses are geographical areas.

Arithmetic mean   Arithmetic average.

Armor's theta   An index of test reliability based on the eigenvalue of the first (unrotated) principal component.

Artifacts   Specific threats to validity, or confounded aspects of the scientist's observations.

Assumed probability   A probability that is taken for granted, for which there is scientific evidence for belief that a particular relationship or phenomenon is likely to occur or prove true.

Attenuation   Reduction.

Autocorrelation   The relation of observations or measures with one another; see also *Regular autocorrelation* and *Seasonal autocorrelation*.

Average deviation   The average distance from the mean of all scores.

Average error   An index of the variability of a set of data around the most typical value.

Back-translation   Method used in cross-cultural research in which the researcher has one bilingual person translate the questionnaire items from source to target language, and then has another bilingual person independently translate them back into the source language. The researcher then compares the original with the twice-translated version to see whether anything important was lost in the translation.

Baseline   See *Behavioral baseline*.

Before-after design   A standard research design in which subjects' reactions are measured both before and after they have undergone the experimental manipulation or a control substitute.

Behavioral baseline   A comparison base, usually defined as the continuous, and continuing, performance of a single individual in small-N research.

Behavioral science   The term is used in this book as an umbrella concept to refer to all disciplines in which empirical methods are employed in the study of motivation, cognition, and behavior.

Behaviorism   The point of view which states that the behavioral sciences should focus on the study of the relations among observable stimuli and responses; also called *methodological behaviorism* and *pure empiricism* when cognitive functioning is disallowed as a legitimate area of scientific analysis.

BESD   Binomial effect-size display.

Beta (β)   Probability of a type II error.

Between-subjects designs   Statistical designs in which the sampling units (e.g., the research participants) are exposed to one treatment each.

Bias   Net systematic error.

Bimodal   A distribution showing two modes.

Binomial effect-size display (BESD)   Procedure for the display of the practical importance of a correlation (r) of any particular magnitude.

Biosocial experimenter effects   Experimenter artifacts that are a function of biosocial attributes of the experimenter.

Birge's ratio   A reliability coefficient that gives an estimate of the degree to which measurement estimates differ from one another by more than random errors.

Blind controls   Research participants who are unaware of their experimental status.

Blocking   Subdividing sampling units to increase precision, to detect interactions between independent and blocking variables, or to do both.

Bonferroni procedure   Redefining the alpha level of significance to protect against post hoc selection of largest effects.

Box-Jenkins procedure   Statistical procedure to assess an underlying model of serial effects in an interrupted time-series design; also called *ARIMA (autoregressive integrated moving average procedure)*.

Bucket theory of science   Karl Popper's characterization of positivism; the idea that the wine of knowledge is presumed to flow pure and simple from patiently and industriously gathered facts.

Built-in contrasts   Contrasts that are obtained as a natural consequence of an experimental design, such as any source of variance in a 2^k factorial design (not including error terms), or any other effect with a single *df*.

Canonical correlation   Correlation between two or more predictor variables and two or more dependent variables.

Category scale   A recording scale usually in the form of a checklist or tally sheet.

Causal inference   The act or process of inferring that X causes Y.

Ceiling   The maximum score attainable on a test.

Central tendency   Location of the bulk of a distribution measured by means, medians, modes, trimmed means, etc.

Central tendency error   A type of response set in which the respondent is reluctant to give extreme ratings and instead tends to rate in the direction of the mean of the total group.

Characteristic root   Sum of squared factor loadings.

Chi-square (χ^2)   A statistic used to test the degree of agreement between the data actually obtained and that expected under a particular hypothesis (e.g., the null hypothesis).

Chi-square corner cells test   Chi-square test performed on the four corners of a table of counts.

Cluster analysis   Formal procedures for grouping variables or sampling units.

Coefficient of correlation   Index of correlation, typically Pearson r or related product-moment correlation.

Coefficient of determination   Proportion of variance "accounted for" (r^2).

Coefficient of nondetermination   Proportion of variance "not accounted for" (k^2, or $1 - r^2$).

Cogito ergo sum   "I think, therefore I am"; principle of Cartesian skepticism.

Cohen's d   A measure of effect size in σ units.

Cohen's f   Effect-size estimate used with F tests of significance.

Cohen's g   The difference between any proportion and .50.

Cohen's h   The difference between two proportions after each has been transformed via arcsin.

Cohen's kappa See *Kappa*.

Cohen's *q* The difference between two Pearson *r*'s after they have been transformed to Fisher's *z*.

Cohen's *w* Effect-size estimate used with chi-square tests of significance.

Coherence of theories The degree to which ideas that make up a theory "stick together."

Cohort A collection of individuals who were born in the same general period.

Cohort-sequential design Research in which several cohorts are studied with the initial measurements taken in successive years.

Column effects Column means minus grand mean.

Combined category chi-square test Chi-square test performed on redefined tables of counts in which adjacent rows, columns, or both have been meaningfully combined.

Complex multiple partial correlation Canonical correlation performed on variables from which the effects of third-party variables have been removed.

Component loading See *Factor loadings*.

Concurrent validity The extent to which test results are correlated with some criterion in the present.

Confidence interval Region in which a population parameter is likely to be found.

Confounded variables Variables that are correlated with one another.

Consensus tests Checks for consensus among *F* tests formed from largest and smallest relevant error terms.

Consequentialism Judging actions as right or wrong depending on their consequences.

Construct An abstract variable, constructed from ideas or images, which serves as an explanatory term.

Construct validation The procedure by which a means for the measurement of a construct is devised and then related to subjects' performance in a variety of other spheres as the construct would predict or imply.

Construct validity A type of test or research validity that addresses the psychological qualities contributing to the relation between *X* and *Y*.

Content analysis A method of categorizing subjective information based on frequency of occurrence.

Content validity A type of test validity that addresses whether the test adequately samples the relevant material it purports to cover.

Contextualism A world view (or cosmology) that states that events acquire meaning from, as well as impart meaning to, the context in which they are situated.

Contingency table A table in which the data are displayed as counts.

Contrasts Tests of focused questions in which specific predictions can be tested by comparing (or contrasting) them with the obtained data.

Control group A condition against which the effects of the experimental or test conditions are compared.

Conventionalism The philosophical view (associated with Pierre Duhem and W.V. O. Quine) that states that scientific theories evolve by convention on the basis of considerations such as simplicity; also called the *Duhem-Quine thesis*.

Convergent validity Validity supported by substantial correlation between conceptually similar measures.

Corner cells test See *Chi-square corner cells test*.

Corrected range Crude range plus one unit.

Correction for continuity   A procedure for decreasing the absolute difference between obtained and expected frequencies to adjust for the difference between discrete and continuous distributions.

Correlated data   Observations that are not independent of one another.

Correlated replicators   The nonindependence of the researchers who replicate one another's results.

Correlation   Degree of relation between variables.

Counterbalancing   Presenting treatment conditions in a sequence that controls for confounding.

Covariance   Average of the sum of products of deviations from the mean, i.e., $(x - \bar{x})(y - \bar{y})$.

Covariation rule   The principle that in order to demonstrate causality, what is labeled as the "cause" must be shown to be positively correlated with what is labeled as the "effect."

Covary   To have variations (in one variable) that are correlated with variations in another variable.

Criterion variable   An outcome variable, or a variable that was predicted.

Critical incident technique   Open-ended questions that instruct the respondent to describe an observable action (a) the purpose of which was fairly clear to the respondent and (b) the consequences of which were sufficiently definite to leave little doubt about its effects.

Crossed contrasts   Contrasts formed from the crossing of contrasts in two or more main effects.

Crossed sampling units   Sampling units observed under two or more conditions of a study.

Crossed-line interaction   Interaction residuals showing an ascending linear trend for one subgroup and a descending linear trend for another subgroup.

Cross-lagged correlations   Correlations between two sets of variables for which one is treated as a lagged value of the outcome variable.

Cross-lagged panel design   A relational research design employing cross-lagged correlations, cross-sectional correlations repeated over time, and test-retest correlations.

Cross-sectional design   Research that takes a slice of time and compares subjects on one or more variables simultaneously.

Cross-sequential design   Research in which different cohorts are observed over several periods, with the initial measurements taken in the same period.

Crude range   Highest score minus lowest score.

Cubic trend   Curvilinear relation between two variables in which the line changes direction twice.

Curvilinear (quadratic) correlation   The correlation between scores on one variable and extremeness of scores on the other variable.

D   The difference between scores or ranks.

$\bar{D}$ The mean of a set of *D*'s.

d   See *Cohen's d*.

Deception research   Any method of research in which the subjects are misled (*active deception*) or not informed (*passive deception*) about the nature of the investigation.

Deductive-statistical explanation   A claim based on arguments resulting in a conclusion that *has* to be true if the premises are true; the basis of "universal" laws, i.e., principles that are *always* true.

Degrees of freedom   The number of observations minus the number of restrictions limiting the observations' freedom to vary.

Demand characteristics   The mixture of various hints and cues that govern the subject's perception of his or her role and of the experimenter's hypothesis.

Deontology   The view that certain actions are categorically immoral or unethical no matter what their consequences.

Dependent variable   A variable the changes in which are viewed as dependent on changes in one or more other (independent) variables.

Descriptive inquiry   A method of research that seeks to map out what happens behaviorally, i.e., to tell "how things are."

Determinism   The assertion that there are causal laws for behaviors and actions; also called *strict determinism* when causal laws are presumed for *every* behavior or action.

df   Degrees of freedom.

df **between conditions**   Degrees of freedom for the means of conditions.

df **error**   Degrees of freedom for the denominator of the F ratio.

df **means**   Degrees of freedom for the numerator of the F ratio.

df **within conditions**   Degrees of freedom for observations within conditions.

Diachronic research   Research in which an event or behavior is observed in such a way as to uncover changes that occur over a period of time.

Difference in success rates   See *Binomial effect-size display.*

Diffuse tests of significance   Significance tests addressing unfocused (diffuse) questions, as in chi-square with $df > 1$ or F with numerator $df > 1$.

Dimensional analysis   Set of redescriptors of relations among objects in terms of measures of similarity or dissimilarity.

Discovery   A term in philosophy of science referring to the origin, creation, or invention of ideas for scientific justification.

Discriminant function   Special case of multiple correlation with a dichotomous dependent variable.

Discriminant validity   Validity supported by lack of correlation between conceptually unrelated measures.

Disguised measures   Measuring instruments used to study behavior indirectly (e.g., projective tests) or unobtrusively (e.g., nonreactive measures).

Dispersion   Spread or variability.

Distance analysis   Set of redescriptors of relations among objects in terms of measures of similarity or dissimilarity.

Distribution   The relative frequencies as we move over varying values of the independent variable.

Drunkard's search   An effort to gather scientific data in a place that is convenient, but not relevant, resulting in wasted or vitiated effort on the part of the researcher.

Duhem-Quine thesis   See *Conventionalism.*

Dummy-coding   Giving arbitrary numerical values (often 0 or 1) to the two levels of a dichotomous variable.

Edgington method of adding probabilities   Procedure for combining p values of a set of studies.

Effective reliability   The composite, or aggregate, reliability of two or more judges' ratings.

Effects   See *Residuals.*

Effect size   The magnitude of an experimental effect; i.e., the size of the relation between X and Y.

Efficient cause   The propelling or instigating condition, i.e., the X that sets in motion or alters Y.

Eigenvalue   Sum of squared factor loadings.

Empirical method   Any procedure employing controlled experience, observation, or experiment to map out the nature of reality.

Enumerative survey   A survey the purpose of which is to count (enumerate) a representative sample from the population from which the sampling units were taken.

Equal-appearing intervals method   An attitude-scale construction method in which values are obtained for statements or items on the assumption that the underlying intervals are equidistant; also called *Thurstone scale*.

Errors   Deviations of scores from the mean of the group or condition.

Error term   The denominator of an F ratio in the analysis of variance.

Eta   Index of correlation not limited to linear relationships.

Eta^2   Proportion of variance accounted for.

Ethics   The system of moral values by which behavior is judged.

Ethnography   That type of field observation in which a society's culture is studied.

Evaluation apprehension   The research subject's fear of being (negatively) evaluated by the experimenter.

Expectancy control design   An experimental design in which the expectancy variable is permitted to operate separately from the primary independent variable.

Expected frequencies   Counts expected under various conditions if certain hypotheses (e.g., the null hypothesis) were true.

Experimental group   A group or condition in which the subjects are assigned the experimental treatment.

Experimental inquiry   Any method of research that seeks to describe what happens behaviorally when something of interest to the experimenter is introduced into the situation, i.e., to tell "how things are and how they got to be that way."

Experimental realism   The degree of psychological impact of an experimental manipulation on the research subjects.

Experimenter-expectancy effect   Experimenter artifact which results when the hypothesis held by the experimenter leads unintentionally to behavior toward the subjects which, in turn, increases the likelihood that the hypothesis will be confirmed; also called a *self-fulfilling prophecy*.

Extended range   Crude range plus one unit.

External validity   The degree of generalizability.

f   See *Cohen's f*.

Factor analysis   The rewriting of a set of variables into a new set of orthogonal factors.

Factor loadings   Correlations between variables and factors serving as their redescriptors.

Fallacy of period centrism   See *Period centrism fallacy*.

Fallibilistic indeterminacy   The idea that facts and theories are fallible, and therefore we cannot attain absolute certainty or closure about the complex nature of the world.

False precision   When something relatively vague is reported as if the measurement instrument were sensitive to very slight differences.

Falsifiability   The principle (advanced by Karl Popper) that a theoretical system is "scientific" only if it is stated in such a way that it can, if incorrect, be falsified by empirical tests.

F-distributions   Family of distributions centered at $(df)/(df - 2)$ (where df are for the denominator of the F ratio) and ranging from zero to positive infinity.

File drawer problem   Completed, but unreported, studies serving to complicate the quantitative summary of research domains.

Final cause   The end reason for which a person or thing tends naturally to strive; also called the *teleological factor*.

Fisher exact probability test   Test of significance for a 2×2 table of counts based on exact probability rather than reference to a distribution.

Fisher method of adding logs   Procedure for combining p values of a set of studies.

Fisher's z transformation   Transformation for Pearson r's, making equal differences equally detectable.

Fixed effects   Levels of a factor chosen because of our specific interest rather than their representativeness of a population of levels of a factor.

Focused tests of significance   Tests of significance addressing precise questions, as in any 1-df contrast.

Forced-choice   Item format that requires the respondent to select a single item from a presented set of choices, even when the respondent finds none (or more than one) of the choices acceptable. Often used as a method of preventing respondents from "sitting on the fence" with neutral responses.

Formal cause   The implicit form or meaning of something.

Fractional factorials   Design in which higher-order interactions are intentionally confounded with lower-order effects.

F-ratios   Ratios of mean squares that are distributed as F when the null hypothesis is true.

Frequency distribution   A set of data scores arranged according to incidence of occurrence.

F-test   A test of significance employed to judge the tenability of the null hypothesis of no relation between two or more variables, or of no difference between two variabilities.

g   See *Cohen's g*.

Good subjects   Research participants who attempt to "help the cause of science" by providing responses that will validate the experimenter's hypothesis.

Grand mean   Mean of means, or the mean of all observations.

Graphic scale   A type of rating scale in the form of a straight line with cue words attached.

h   See *Cohen's h*.

H_0   Null hypothesis.

H_1   Alternate, or experimental, hypothesis.

Halo effect   A type of response set in which the bias results from the judge's forming a favorable impression of someone with regard to some central trait and then tending to paint a rosier picture of the person on other characteristics.

Harmonic mean   The reciprocal of the arithmetic mean of values that have been transformed to their reciprocals.

Hawthorne effect   The notion that the mere fact of being observed experimentally can influence the behavior of those being observed.

Heterogeneity   Dissimilarity among the elements of a set.

Hidden nesting   The concealed nonindependence of observations brought about by sampling without regard to sources of similarity in the persons sampled.

Hierarchical structure   A system in which one thing is ranked above another.

Higher-order interaction Residuals remaining after all main effects and all lower-order interactions relevant to the higher-order interaction have been subtracted.

History A plausible threat to internal validity when an event or incident that takes place between the premeasurement and the postmeasurement contaminates the results of research not employing randomization.

Homogeneity Similarity among the elements of a set.

Homogeneity of covariances Degree of similarity of covariances found between any two levels of a repeated-measures factor.

Hypothesis A research idea that can serve as a premise or supposition to organize certain facts and thereby guide observations.

IID Normal Assumptions underlying use of t and F tests, that errors be independently and identically distributed in a normal distribution.

Incomplete factorial design Design in which higher-order interactions are intentionally confounded with lower-order effects.

Independent variable A variable on which the dependent variable depends. In experiments, a variable manipulated by the experimenter to determine whether there are effects on another variable, the dependent variable.

Indirect measures Measures of behavior in which the subject is aware of being measured but is unaware of the particular consequences of his or her responses, e.g., the Rorschach test.

Inductive-statistical explanation Claim based on arguments resulting in a conclusion that is *probably* true if the premises are true; also called a *probabilistic assertion*.

Inferential validity A summary term referring to the fact that a particular laboratory relation between two variables has a high degree of internal and external validity.

Initial thinking The first stage in the development of a scientific hypothesis, characterized by the relative vagueness of ideas or first impressions.

Instrumentation A plausible threat to internal validity when changes in the measuring instrument (e.g., deterioration of the instrument) bias the results of research not employing randomization.

Intentional effect A type of noninteractional experimenter effect that results in error owing to the researcher's dishonesty in reporting data.

Interactional experimenter effects Effects of the experimenter that operate by affecting the actual response of the subjects.

Interaction effects Condition means minus grand mean, row effects, and column effects.

Internal-consistency reliability See *Reliability of components*.

Internal manipulation check See *Manipulation checks*.

Internal validity The degree of validity of statements made about whether X causes Y.

Internal-validity rule The principle that in demonstrations of causality, plausible rival explanations of the relation between X and Y must be able to be ruled out.

Interpreter effect A type of noninteractional experimenter effect that results in error during the interpretation of data phase of the research process.

Interrupted time-series designs Research in which the effects of a treatment are inferred from comparing outcome measures obtained at different time intervals before and after the treatment is introduced.

Interval estimates The extent to which point estimates are likely to be in error, e.g., owing to variability in the composition of the population.

Intraclass correlation Procedure for estimating the average intercorrelation among the repeated observations obtained from a set of sampling units.

Item analysis A procedure for selecting items, e.g., for a Likert attitude scale.

Joint method J.S. Mill's method of agreement and difference, which tells us that X is both necessary and sufficient for the occurrence of Y.

Justification A term used by philosophers of science to refer to the evaluation, defense, truth, or confirmation of a hypothesis.

k Coefficient of alienation or "noncorrelation."

k^2 Coefficient of nondetermination.

Kappa A statistic (proposed by Jacob Cohen) to indicate the proportion of agreements between raters after chance agreement has been removed; also called *Cohen's kappa*, and symbolized as κ.

Kuder-Richardson formula 20 A traditional equation for measuring internal-consistency reliability; also called *K-R 20*.

L Sum of the products of condition totals and contrast weights.

Lambda (λ) Weights derived from theory serving to define a contrast.

Latent root Sum of squared factor loadings.

Latin square A square of letters or numbers in which each letter or number appears once and only once in each row and in each column.

Leaves The trailing digits of a stem-and-leaf display.

Leniency error A type of response set in which the judge tends to rate someone who is very familiar, or someone with whom the judge is ego-involved, more positively than the person deserves.

Likert scale See *Summated ratings*.

Linear trend Straight-line relation between two variables.

Loading See *Factor loadings*.

Location measures Measures of central tendency.

Logical error in rating A type of response set in which the judge gives similar ratings for variables or traits that seem logically related.

Logical positivism See *Positivism*.

Log-linear model An approach to the analysis of tables analogous to the analysis of variance.

Longitudinal design Any research design in which the subjects are studied over a period of time.

M The mean of a set of scores.

$\overline{M}$ Grand mean.

Manipulation checks Measures of the effectiveness of experimental treatments, which may involve questioning a new group of subjects (*external manipulation check*) or questioning the research participants themselves (*internal manipulation check*).

Matched pairs Pairs of observations made on the same sampling units.

Material cause The substance out of which something is made or from which it comes about.

Maturation A plausible threat to internal validity that occurs when the results of research not employing randomization are contaminated by the participants' having, e.g., grown older or wiser or stronger or more experienced between the pretest and the posttest.

Mean The arithmetic average of a set of scores.

Mean polishing   Removing grand mean, row, and column effects to expose residuals defining the interaction.

Mechanistic theory   The theory that social causation is comparable to a complex machine and that human nature is a matter of social engineering.

Median   The midmost score of a distribution.

Meta-analysis   The quantitative analysis of the results of sets of studies of a particular research question.

Metaphor   A word or phrase applied to a concept or phenomenon that it does not literally denote.

Method of adding logs   Procedure for combining independent probabilities.

Method of adding probabilities   Procedure for combining independent probabilities.

Method of adding t's   Procedure for combining independent probabilities.

Method of adding weighted Z's   Procedure for combining independent probabilities.

Method of adding Z's   Procedure for combining independent probabilities.

Method of agreement   If X, then Y—which implies X is a sufficient condition of Y.

Method of authority   When an idea is held to be true merely because it is approved by some authority.

Method of concomitant variation   Refers to related changes in amount or degree between two factors; stated as $Y = f(X)$, which means that variations in Y are functionally related to variations in X.

Method of difference   If not-X, then not-Y—which implies that X is a necessary condition of Y.

Method of meaningful diagonals   Forming a concept to summarize the data found on the diagonals of a two-way table of means or of residuals.

Method of meaningful differences   Reducing a two-dimensional display of residuals or means to a one-dimensional display.

Method of tenacity   Clinging tenaciously to an idea because it brings peace of mind.

Method of testing mean p   Procedure for combining independent probabilities.

Method of testing mean Z   Procedure for combining independent probabilities.

Methodological behaviorism   See *Behaviorism*.

Mixed longitudinal designs   Research in which several cohorts are followed, and age effects, time effects, and cohort effects are examined periodically.

Mode   The score occurring with greatest frequency.

Modeling effects   Experimenter artifacts that are a function of the example set by the experimenter.

MS   Mean square.

MS **between**   Mean square between conditions.

MS **error**   Mean square used as denominator of F ratios.

MS **within**   Mean square within conditions.

Multidimensional scaling (unfolding)   Set of redescriptors of relations among objects in terms of measures of similarity or dissimilarity.

Multilevel analysis of variance   Analysis of variance with two or more independent variables and one dependent variable.

Multiple confirmation   The use of two or more independent measures of the same behavior and the comparison of the results.

Multiple correlation   Correlation between two or more predictor variables and a single dependent variable.

Multiple discriminant function Special case of canonical correlation with dichotomous dependent variables.

Multiple-partial correlation Multiple correlation performed on variables from which the effects of third-party variables have been removed.

Multiple path analysis Canonical correlation with time-ordered predictor variables.

Multitrait-multimethod matrix A table of intercorrelations the purpose of which is to triangulate on the convergent and discriminant validity of a construct.

Multivariate analysis of covariance Analysis of covariance for the case of multiple dependent variables.

Multivariate multilevel analysis of variance Analysis of variance with two or more independent and two or more dependent variables.

Multivariate procedures Statistical procedures involving two or more independent (predictor) variables, two or more dependent (criterion) variables, or both.

Mundane realism The extent to which laboratory events are likely to occur in a naturalistic setting.

N The number of scores in a study.

n The number of scores in one condition or subgroup of a study.

$\bar{n}_h$ The harmonic mean n.

Naturalistic observation Any research that looks at behavior in its usual natural environment.

Necessary condition A requisite or essential condition.

Negative synergistic effects Synergistic effects serving to lower scores.

Negativistic subject The research participant who approaches the investigation with an uncooperative attitude.

Nested sampling units Sampling units observed under only one condition of a study.

Nonequivalent-groups designs Nonrandomized research in which responses of a treatment group and a control group are compared on measures collected at the beginning and end of the research.

Noninteractional experimenter effects Experimenter artifacts that occur without affecting the actual response of the human or animal subjects.

Nonorthogonal contrasts Correlated contrasts.

Nonparametric procedures Statistical procedures that are less dependent on the shape of the population distribution from which the observations are drawn.

Nonreactive observation Any observation that does not affect the thing being observed.

Nonresponse bias Error that is due to nonresponse or nonparticipation.

Normal distribution Bell-shaped curve that is completely described by its mean and standard deviation.

Null hypothesis The hypothesis that there is no relation between two or more variables, symbolized as H_0.

Numerical scale A rating scale in which the judges work with a sequence of defined numbers.

Oblique rotations Factor analytic rotations that are nonorthogonal.

Observed frequencies Counts obtained under various conditions.

Observer effect Experimenter artifact that results in overstatements or understatements of some criterion value during the observation and recording phase of the research process.

Occam's razor The principle that explanations should be as parsimonious as possible.

Omnibus tests of significance Significance tests addressing unfocused questions, as in χ^2 with $df > 1$ or F with numerator $df > 1$.

One-group pre-post design A preexperimental design in which the reactions of only one group of subjects are measured before and after exposure to the treatment.

One-shot case study A preexperimental design in which the reactions of only one group of subjects are measured after the event or treatment has occurred.

One-tailed test Test of significance in which the null hypothesis is rejected only if the results are significant in one of the two possible directions.

Open-ended item See *Unconstructed items.*

Operational definition The meaning of a variable in terms of the operations necessary to measure it in any concrete situation, or in terms of the experimental methods involved in its determination.

Ordinal data Objects or events that can be ranked from high to low on some characteristic.

Ordinate The vertical axis of a distribution.

Organismic interactions Treatments showing different effects for different subgroups.

Orthogonal contrasts Uncorrelated contrasts.

Orthogonal polynomial contrasts Sets of orthogonal contrasts in which linear, quadratic, and higher-order trends can be evaluated.

Orthogonal relationship Relationship in which correlation equals zero.

Orthogonal rotations Factor analytic rotations in which axes are kept at right angles to one another.

Overall F test An F test with $df > 1$ in the numerator, which serves as appropriate protection for subsequent contrasts.

Paradoxical incident An occurrence characterized by seemingly self-contradictory aspects.

Paradox of sampling That the appropriateness of a sample is validated by the method used to arrive at its appropriateness.

Paradox of usage That the usage of words is validated by the method based on how the words are actually used.

Parameters Population values.

Parsimony of theories The degree to which the propositions of a theory are "sparing" or "frugal"; see also *Occam's razor.*

Partial aggregation Aggregation of only a subset of all relevant sources of variance.

Partial correlation The correlation between two variables when the influence of other variables on their relationship has been eliminated statistically.

Participant observation A method of observation in which a group or a community is studied from within by a researcher who makes careful records of the behavior as it proceeds.

Partitioning tables Subdividing tables of counts into a set of 2×2 tables each of which addresses a precise question.

Path analysis Multiple regression with time-ordered predictor variables.

Payoff potential The scientist's subjective estimate of the likelihood that the research idea actually corresponds with reality.

Pearson r Standard index of linear relationship.

Percentile Location of a score in a distribution defining the point below which a given percentage of the cases fall; e.g., a score at the 90th percentile falls at a point such that 90 percent of the scores fall at or below that score.

Period centrism fallacy The mistake of assuming that the results of an analysis of one particular period are generalizable to other periods.

Phi coefficient (ϕ) Pearson r where both variables are dichotomous.

Placebo control group A control condition in which a substance without any pharmacological effect is given as a "drug."

Planned contrasts Contrasts intended before the data were examined.

Plausibility stage The second stage in the development of a research hypothesis, during which the scientist evaluates the plausibility of his or her initial lead or idea.

Plausible rival hypothesis A proposition, or set of propositions, that provides a reasonable alternative to the working hypothesis.

Point biserial correlation (r_{pb}) Pearson r for which one of the variables is continuous and the other is dichotomous.

Point estimates Estimates of some particular characteristic of the population, e.g., the number of times an event occurs.

PONS Profile of Nonverbal Sensitivity; a test for measuring sensitivity to nonverbal cues.

Pooling sources of variance Combining terms that are not too markedly different.

Population The universe of elements from which sample elements are drawn, or the universe of elements to which we want to generalize.

Positive synergistic effects Synergistic effects serving to raise scores.

Positivism The philosophical view that states that only by shoring up explanations with positive facts is it possible to attain an exact understanding of objective reality.

Postdictive validity The extent to which the results of a test correlate with some criterion in the past.

Post hoc contrasts Contrasts computed only after the data were examined.

Power of a test The probability when doing significance testing of not making a type II error, or $1 - \beta$.

Practical validity Social utility of established relationships.

Pragmatism The idea that the meaning of conceptions is to be found in their practical applications (associated with Charles S. Peirce, William James, John Dewey, George Herbert Mead, and the foundation of modern contextualism).

Preanalysis of an experiment The statistical analysis of the data predicted by a theory to clarify how the predictions will be tested in the data-analytic model.

Precision Sharpness or exactness of observations or measures.

Predictive validity The extent to which a test can predict future outcomes.

Preexperimental design Any research design in which there is such a total absence of control that it is of minimal value in establishing causality.

Pre-post control group design A before-after experimental design.

Pretest sensitization The confounding of pretesting and X, the independent variable of interest.

Principal components analysis The rewriting of a set of variables into a new set of orthogonal components.

Probabilistic assertions Claims based on inductive-statistical reasoning.

Probability The mathematical chance of an event's occurring.

Probability sampling In survey sampling, a selection procedure in which every unit in the population has a known nonzero probability of being chosen.

Product-moment correlation Standard index of linear relationship, or Pearson's r.

Projective tests Psychological tests that operate on the principle that the subject will project some unconscious aspect of his or her life experience and emotions onto ambiguous stimuli in the spontaneous responses that come to mind, e.g., the Rorschach and TAT tests.

Protected *t* test The *t* test computed under the umbrella of an overall *F* to minimize capitalizing on post hoc selection of largest effects.

Proximity analysis Set of redescriptors of relations among objects in terms of measures of similarity or dissimilarity.

Pseudosubjects Confederates of the experimenter who play the role of research subjects.

Psychosocial experimenter effects Experimenter artifacts that are a function of psychosocial attributes of the experimenter, e.g., the experimenter's personality.

Pure longitudinal designs Research in which a cohort is followed over time.

***p*-value** Probability value or level obtained in a test of significance; also called *alpha* and *significance level*.

q See *Cohen's q*.

Q-sort A rating procedure in which the judge sorts stimuli into piles to resemble a bell-shaped distribution.

Quadratic trend Curvilinear relation between two variables in which the line changes direction once as in a U or ∩ curve).

Quartile range The range of scores found between the 75th and 25th percentiles.

Quasi-control subjects Participants who reflect on the context in which an experiment is conducted and speculate on ways in which the context might influence their own and research subjects' behavior.

Quasi experiment Any design that resembles an experimental design (in that there are treatments, outcome measures, and experimental units) but in which there is no random assignment to create the comparisons from which treatment-caused changes are inferred.

r Pearson's product-moment correlation.

***r*^{2}** Pearson's correlation squared, also called *proportion of variance accounted for,* or *coefficient of determination*.

***r*$_{pb}$** See *point biserial correlation*.

Random assignment In experimentation, the assignment of treatments to research participants at random.

Random effects Levels of a factor chosen as representative of a population of levels of a factor.

Random errors The effects of uncontrolled variables that cannot be specifically identified; such effects are, theoretically speaking, self-canceling in that the average of the errors will probably equal zero.

Randomization Random assignment of treatment conditions to sampling units.

Randomized response technique Method to eliminate evasive answers by using a randomizing instrument (e.g., casting a die) to select how the subject will respond concerning sensitive questions while still providing the investigator usable data for the entire sample.

Random sample A sample chosen by chance procedures and with known probabilities of selection so that every individual in the population will have the same likelihood of being selected.

Range Distance between the highest and lowest score.

Rating scale   The common name for a variety of measuring instruments in which the observer or judge gives a numerical value, either explicitly or implicitly, to certain judgments or assessments.

Reactive observation   An observation that affects what is being observed or measured.

Realism   The assertion that scientific theories give (or probably give) a literally true account of the world; a view associated with Rudolf Carnap, Ronald Giere, and Karl Popper.

Rectangular arrays   Generalizations of Latin squares to $t \times t!$ dimensions, where t = number of treatments.

Redescriptors   Multivariate procedures serving to redescribe a set of variables, often in a smaller set of variables.

Regression analysis   Loosely equivalent to correlational analysis; more technically refers to relations of changes in level of Y to changes in level of X.

Regression toward the mean   A mathematical concept that refers to the relation between two paired variables, X and Y, for which cases at one extreme on X (the independent variable) will, on the average over time, be less extreme on the other variable.

Regular autocorrelation   The dependency of adjacent observations on one another in time-series analysis.

Relational inquiry   Any method of research that seeks to tell "how things are in relation to other things."

Reliability   The degree to which observations or measures are consistent or stable.

Reliability coefficient   A generic name for indices of reliability.

Reliability of components   Reliability based on the intercorrelations among all the single test items or subtests, or other components; also called *internal-consistency reliability*.

Repeated measurements   Measurements made on the same sampling units.

Repeated-measures designs   See *Within-subjects designs*.

Replicability   The ability to repeat or duplicate a scientific observation, usually an experimental observation.

Representative research design   Any design that involves sampling of both subjects and stimuli.

Residuals   Effects left over when appropriate components are subtracted from scores or means.

Response   The consequence of, or reaction to, a stimulus.

Response set   Set in which a person's answers to questions or other responses are determined by a consistent mental set.

Response variable   The dependent variable.

Rho (ρ)   Spearman rank correlation.

Role play   A type of simulation in which subjects act out a given scenario; known as *emotional role play* when a high degree of experimental realism is achieved by increasing the subjects' emotional involvement.

Rotation of factors or components   Rotation of axes on which variables have been located, with the aim of making the factors or components more interpretable.

Row effects   Row means minus grand mean.

S   Square root of the unbiased estimator of the population value of σ^2.

S^2   Unbiased estimator of the population value of σ^2.

Sample   The subset of the population for whom we have obtained observations.

Sample selection bias   Systematic error resulting from the nature of the sampling units.

Sampling plan A design, scheme of action, or procedure that specifies how the participants are to be selected in a survey study.

Sampling stability The concept that all samples produced by the same sampling plan will yield essentially the same results.

Sampling units The elements that make up the sample, e.g., people, schools, cities.

Sampling with replacement A type of random sampling in which the selected names are placed in the selection pool again and may be reselected on subsequent draws; this procedure is contrasted with *sampling without replacement,* in which a previously selected name cannot be chosen again and must be discarded on any later draw.

Scheffé test Significance test appropriate for use when the contrast has been formulated after examining the data.

Searchlight theory of science Karl Popper's characterization of his own (antipositivistic) viewpoint, which conceives of scientific observation as an intensely active process in which observations are planned and prepared by risky theories and hypotheses which are like "searchlights" that shine on events.

Seasonal autocorrelation The dependency of observations separated by one period or cycle in time-series analysis.

Secondary analysis The reanalysis of an existing data base.

Selection A plausible threat to the internal validity of research not employing randomization when different kinds of research subjects have been selected to take part in one treatment group than have been selected for another group.

Self-fulfilling prophecy The prediction of an event that leads individuals to behave in a way that increases the likelihood that the event will occur as prophesied; the prophet thus acts to fulfill his or her own prophecy.

Self-report methods Methods of data collection in which the research participants describe their own behavior or state of mind, e.g., interviews, questionnaires, and self-recorded diaries.

Semantic differential A type of rating method in which connotative (or subjective) meaning is judged in terms of several dimensions, traditionally the dimensions of evaluation, potency, and activity.

Sentence-completion test A type of projective test in which the subject responds by completing an incomplete sentence.

Serendipity The occurrence of discoveries in the course of investigations designed for another purpose.

Σ Instruction telling us to sum (or add) a set of scores.

σ The standard deviation of a set of scores.

σ^2 The variance of a set of scores.

Significance level The level of alpha; also called *p value.*

Significance test Statistical test giving information on the tenability of the null hypothesis of no relation between two or more variables.

Significance testing The use of statistics and probabilities to evaluate a data base in order to make a decision about the rejectability or acceptability of the null hypothesis.

Sign test Test of significance of the preponderance of positive versus negative difference scores for matched-pair data.

Simple random selection A type of sampling plan in which the participants are selected individually on the basis of a table of random digits.

Simulation experiment An experiment based on a model in order to learn what will happen under conditions that mimic the environment in a definite way.

Single-case designs Repeated-measures designs in which $N = 1$.

Situational experimenter effects Experimenter artifacts that are a function of situationally determined experimenter attributes.

Skewness A characteristic of distributions in which extreme scores are concentrated on one side of the mean.

Smallest-space analysis Set of redescriptors of relations among objects in terms of measures of similarity or dissimilarity.

Small-N designs Repeated-measures designs in which the treatment effect is replicated within the same subject or small number of subjects; see also *Single-case designs*.

S^2 means The variance of means around the grand mean.

Social experimentation The application of experimental or quasi-experimental methods to the analysis of community problems and to the development, testing, and assessment of workable interventions to reduce the problems.

Solomon design A four-group experimental design developed by Richard L. Solomon as a means of assessing (1) pretest sensitization effects and (2) initial performance without contamination by pretesting.

Spearman-Brown formula A traditional equation for measuring the overall internal-consistency reliability of a test from a knowledge of the reliability of its components.

Spearman rank correlation Pearson r computed on scores in ranked form.

S^2 pooled Variance collected from two or more samples.

Spread Dispersion or variability.

Stability coefficient A reliability coefficient that tells us about the consistency of what is measured from time to time, or the consistency of the observer from time to time; see also *Test-retest method*.

Standard deviation An index of the variability of a set of data around the mean value in a distribution.

Standard normal curve Normal curve with mean $= 0$ and $\sigma = 1$.

Standard normal deviate Z-score location on a standard normal curve.

Standard score Score converted to a standard deviation unit.

Stationary Reflecting an absence of secular trend in time-series data.

Statistical conclusion validity The degree to which the presumed independent variable X and the presumed dependent variable Y are related.

Statistical power See *Power of a test*.

Statistical significance testing See *Significance testing*.

Stem The leading digits of a stem-and-leaf display.

Stem-and-leaf display The plot of a distribution in which the original data are preserved with any desired precision.

Stouffer method of adding Z's Procedure for combining the p values of a set of studies.

Stratified random sampling Probability sampling plan in which a separate sample is randomly selected within each homogeneous stratum (or layer) of the population.

Strict determinism See *Determinism*.

Strong inference A type of research approach or design in which one hypothesis or fact vies against another.

Structured items Questions with clear-cut response options.

SS Sum of squares.

SS between Sum of squares between conditions.

SS total Total sum of squares.

SS within Sum of squares within conditions.

Summated ratings   A method of attitude-scale construction developed by Rensis Likert, which uses *item analysis* to select the best items.

Symmetry   A characteristic of distributions in which the portions to the right and left of the mean are mirror images of each other.

Synchronic research   Any study in which an event is observed as it occurs at one period in time, not using information about its development or long-term consequences or changes.

Synchronous correlations   Correlations that indicate the degree of relationship of variables at a moment in time.

Synergistic effects   Nonadditive effects of several treatments.

Systematic errors   The effects of uncontrolled variables that often can be specifically identified; such effects are, theoretically speaking, not self-canceling (in contrast to the self-canceling nature of random errors).

Systematic pluralism   An approach to understanding that stresses the necessity of multiple methods and theories, each associated with a plan of action with particular objectives.

Systematic selection plans   Method of selection of sampling units in which particular intervals determine the units to be selected after a random start.

Table analysis   Statistical analysis of frequency counts cast into tabular form.

Tacit knowledge   Facts or truths that we know but cannot easily communicate verbally.

t **distributions**   Family of distributions, centered at zero and ranging from negative to positive infinity.

Teleologic factor   See *Final cause.*

Temporal erosion   Decay in the strength of a relationship over lapses of time.

Temporal-precedence rule   The principle that in demonstrations of causality, what is labeled as the "cause" must be shown to have occurred prior to the "effect."

Test of significance   Statistical test giving information on the tenability of the null hypothesis of no relation between two or more variables.

Testing error   Error whereby familiarity with a test or scale artificially enhances performance.

Testing the grand mean   Evaluating whether the grand mean differs from zero or some other value of theoretical interest.

Test-retest method   A means of evaluating reliability (stability) in test construction, in which the correlation coefficient is computed on data obtained from the same test but from results gotten at different times.

Theoretical definition   The meaning of a variable in relatively abstract terms; also called the *conceptual definition* of a variable.

Theta   An index (proposed by David J. Armor) of internal-consistency reliability.

Thurstone scale   See *Equal-appearing intervals method.*

Time-sequential design   A quasi-experimental design in which subjects of different ages are observed at several different times.

Tolerance for future null effects   Number of filed (unavailable) studies with mean effect size of zero required to bring the combined probability of the available and unavailable studies to a nonsignificant level.

Total aggregation   Aggregation of all relevant sources of variance.

Trimmed mean   The mean of a distribution from which the highest and lowest X percent of the scores have been dropped.

Trimmed range   Range of a distribution remaining after the highest and lowest X percent of the scores have been dropped.

True experimental designs   Research designs characterized by random assignment of treatment conditions to sampling units.

t **test**   A test of significance employed to judge the tenability of the null hypothesis of no relation between two variables.

Two-tailed test   Test of significance in which the null hypothesis is rejected if the results are significant in either of the two possible directions.

Type I error   The error in rejecting the null hypothesis when it is true.

Type II error   The error in failing to reject the null hypothesis when it is false.

Universal laws   See *Deductive-statistical explanation.*

Unobtrusive measures   Measurements or observations that are used to study behavior when the subjects are unaware of being measured or observed.

Unplanned contrasts   Contrasts computed only after the data have been examined.

Unstructured items   Questions that offer the respondent an opportunity to express feelings, motives, or behavior quite spontaneously; also called *open-ended items.*

Unweighted means analysis   Analysis weighting all means equally even if sample sizes differ.

Validity   The degree to which what is observed or measured is the same as what was purported to be observed or measured.

Values   The standards or principles by which the worth of something is judged.

Variables   Attributes of sampling units that can take on two or more values.

Variance   The mean of the squared deviations of scores from their means.

Varimax rotation   Common method of orthogonal factor rotation that tries to make loadings within each factor as close to zero or to 1.0 as possible.

Visualizability   The idea that models of knowledge, to be influential in science, must be perceptible in a way that makes sense given the perceiver's presuppositions.

Volunteer bias   The systematic error resulting when participants who volunteer respond differently than individuals in the general population would respond.

w   See *Cohen's w.*

Winer method of adding *t*'s   Procedure for combining *p* values of a set of studies.

Within-subjects designs   Statistical designs in which the sampling units (e.g., the research participants) receive two or more measurements; also called *repeated-measures designs.*

Word association test   A type of projective test in which the subject, read a list of words, responds with the first word that comes to mind after each stimulus word.

X   Any score; also a symbol for the cause or independent variable in the expression $Y = f(X)$.

$\overline{X}$ The mean of a set of scores.

$\overline{\overline{X}}$ Grand mean.

X **axis**   The horizontal axis of a distribution; also called the *abscissa.*

Yates correction for continuity   Specific correction for continuity in which the absolute difference between obtained and expected frequencies is decreased by .5.

Y **axis**   The vertical axis of a distribution; also called the *ordinate.*

Yea-saying   A type of response set in which the person answers consistently in the affirmative.

Z   Standard normal deviate.

Zeitgeist   The general temper or ambience characteristic of a particular period of history.

Z **score**   Score converted to standard deviation unit.

REFERENCES

Adair, J. G. (1973). *The Human Subject: The Social Psychology of the Psychological Experiment.* Boston. Little, Brown.

_____ (1984). The Hawthorne effect: A reconsideration of the methodological artifact. *Journal of Applied Psychology, 69,* 334–345.

_____, Dushenko, T. W., and Lindsay, R. C. L. (1984). Ethical regulations and their impact on research practice. *American Psychologist, 40,* 59–72.

Adcock, C. J. (1960). A note on combining probabilities. *Psychometrika, 25,* 303–305.

Adorno, T. W., Frenkel-Brunswik, E., Levinson, D. J., and Sanford, R. N. (1950). *The Authoritarian Personality.* New York: Harper and Row.

Aiken, L. S., and Rosnow, R. L. (1973). Role expectations for psychological research participation. Unpublished manuscript, Temple University, Philadelphia.

Alexander, R. A., Scozzaro, M. J., and Borodkin, L. J. (1989). Statistical and empirical examination of the chi-square test for homogeneity of correlations in meta-analysis. *Psychological Bulletin, 106,* 329–331.

Allport, G. W., and Postman, L. (1947). *The Psychology of Rumor.* New York: Holt.

Altmann, J. (1974). Observational study of behavior: Sampling methods. *Behaviour, 49,* 227–267.

Alwin, D. (1974). An analytic comparison of four approaches to the interpretation of relationships in the multitrait-multimethod matrix. In H. Costner (Ed.), *Sociological Methodology 1973–74.* San Francisco: Jossey-Bass.

American Association for the Advancement of Science (1988). *Project on Scientific Fraud and Misconduct.* Washington, D. C.: American Association for the Advancement of Science.

American Psychological Association (1974). *Publication Manual of the American Psychological Association* (2d ed.). Washington, D. C.: American Psychological Association.

_____ (1983). *Publication Manual of the American Psychological Association* (3d ed.). Washington, D.C.: American Psychological Association.

_____ (1985). *Standards for Educational and Psychological Testing.* Washington, D. C.: American Psychological Association.

Anderson, J. W. (1981). The methodology of psychological biography. *Journal of Interdisciplinary History, 11,* 455–475.

Andrich, D. (1988). *Rasch Models for Measurement.* Beverly Hills, Calif.: Sage.

Apel, K. (1982). C. S. Peirce and the post-Tarskian problem of an adequate explication of the meaning of truth: Towards a transcendental-pragmatic theory of truth, part II. *Transactions of the Charles S. Peirce Society, 18,* 3–17.

633

Arellano-Galdames, F. J. (1972). *Some Ethical Problems in Research on Human Subjects.* Unpublished doctoral dissertation, University of New Mexico, Albuquerque.

Armistead, N. (Ed.) (1974). *Reconstructing Social Psychology.* Harmondsworth, Eng.: Penguin.

Armor, D. J. (1974). Theta reliability and factor scaling. In H. L. Costner (Ed.), *Sociological Methodology 1973–1974.* San Francisco: Jossey-Bass.

_____ and Couch, A. S. (1972). *Data-Text Primer: An Introduction to Computerized Social Data Analysis.* New York: Free Press.

Aronson, E., and Carlsmith, J. M. (1968). Experimentation in social psychology. In G. Lindzey and E. Aronson (Eds.), *The Handbook of Social Psychology* (2d ed.), (vol. 2, pp. 1–79). Reading, Mass.: Addison-Wesley.

Asch, S. (1952). *Social Psychology.* Englewood Cliffs, N. J.: Prentice-Hall.

Atwell, J. E. (1981). Human rights in human subjects research. In A. J. Kimmel (Ed.), *New Directions for Methodology of Social and Behavioral Science: Ethics of Human Subject Research,* no. 10, (pp. 81–90). San Francisco: Jossey-Bass.

Averill, J. R. (1982). *Anger and Aggression.* New York: Springer-Verlag.

Axinn, S. (1966). Fallacy of the single risk. *Philosophy of Science, 33,* 154–162.

Babbie, E. R. (1975). *The Practice of Social Research.* Belmont, Calif.: Wadsworth.

Back, K.W., Hood, T. C., and Brehm, M. L. (1963). The subject role in small group experiments. Revision of paper presented at Southern Sociological Society convention, Durham, N. C., April.

Baenninger, R. (1974). Some consequences of aggressive behavior: A selective review of the literature on other animals. *Aggressive Behavior, 1,* 17–37.

_____ (1980). Comparative social perspectives on aggression. *Contemporary Psychology, 25,* 978–979.

_____ (1987). Vanishing species: The disappearance of animals from western art. *Anthrozoos, 1,* 85–89.

_____ (1988). Personal communication to R. L. Rosnow, February 16.

_____, Estes, R. D., and Baldwin, S. (1977). Anti-predator behavior of baboons and impalas toward a cheetah. *Journal of East African Wildlife, 15,* 327–329.

Bailey, K. D. (1974). Cluster analysis. In D. R. Heise (Ed.), *Sociological Methodology 1975* (pp. 59–128). San Francisco: Jossey-Bass.

Bakan, D. (1976). *On Method: Toward a Reconstruction of Psychological Investigation.* San Francisco: Jossey-Bass.

Balaam, L. N. (1963). Multiple comparisons—A sampling experiment. *Australian Journal of Statistics, 5,* 62–84.

Bales, R. F. (1950a). A set of categories for analysis of small group interaction. *American Sociological Review, 15,* 257–263.

_____ (1950b). *Interaction Process Analysis: A Method for the Study of Small Groups.* Cambridge, Mass.: Addison-Wesley.

_____ and Cohen, S. P. (1979). *Symlog: A System for the Multiple Level Observation of Groups.* New York: Free Press.

Banaji, M. R., and Crowder, R. G. (1989). The bankruptcy of everyday memory. *American Psychologist, 44,* 1185–1193.

Barber, B. (1961). Resistance by scientists to scientific discovery. *Science, 134,* 596–602.

_____ and Inkeles, A. (Eds.) (1971). *Stability and Social Change.* Boston: Little, Brown.

Barefoot, J. C. (1969). Anxiety and volunteering. *Psychonomic Science, 16,* 283–284

Barlow, D., and Hayes, S. (1979). Alternating treatments design: One strategy for comparing the effects of two treatments in a single subject. *Journal of Applied Behavioral Analysis, 12,* 199–210.

Barnes, M. L., and Rosenthal, R. (1985). Interpersonal effects of experimenter attractiveness, attire, and gender. *Journal of Personality and Social Psychology, 48,* 435–446.

Baron, R. A. (1977). *Human Aggression.* New York: Plenum.

Baron, R. M. (1977). Role playing and experimental research. *Personality and Social Psychology Bulletin, 3,* 505–513.

Barrass, R. (1978). *Scientists Must Write.* London: Chapman & Hall.

Battig, W. F. (1962). Parsimony in psychology. *Psychological Reports, 11,* 555–572.

Baughman, E. E., and Dahlstrom, W. G. (1968). *Negro and White Children: A Psychological Study in the Rural South.* New York: Academic Press.

Baumrind, D. (1964). Some thoughts on ethics of research: After reading Milgram's "Behavioral Study of Obedience." *American Psychologist, 19,* 421–423.

Becker, H. S., and Geer, B. (1960). Participant observation: The analysis of qualitative field data. In R. N. Adams and J. J. Preiss (Eds.), *Human Organization Research.* Homewood, Ill.: Dorsey.

Beecher, H. K. (1966). Documenting the abuses. *Saturday Review,* July 2, pp. 45–46.

————— (1970). *Research and the Individual.* Boston: Little Brown.

Bem, D. (1987). Writing the empirical journal article. In M. P. Zanna and J. M. Darley (Eds.), *The Compleat Academic: A Practical Guide for the Beginning Social Scientist* (pp. 171–201). New York: Random House.

Bentler, P. M. (1987). Structural modeling and the scientific method: Comments on Freedman's critique. *Journal of Educational Statistics, 12,* 151–157.

Berelson, B. (1952). *Content Analysis in Communication Research.* Glencoe, Ill.: Free Press.

————— (1954). Content analysis. In G. Lindzey (Ed.), *Handbook of Social Psychology* (vol. 1, pp. 488–522). Reading, Mass.: Addison-Wesley.

Berger, J. O., and Berry, D. A. (1988). Statistical analysis and the illusion of objectivity. *American Scientist, 76,* 159–165.

Berk, R. A. (1983). An introduction to sample selection bias in sociological data. *American Sociological Review, 48,* 386–398.

————— and Ray, S. C. (1982). Selection biases in sociological data. *Social Science Research, 11,* 352–398.

Bernard, H. B. and Killworth, P. D. (1970). Informant accuracy in social network data II. *Human Communication Research, 4,* 3–18.

————— and Killworth, P. D. (1980). Informant accuracy in social network data IV: A comparison of clique-level structure in behavioral and cognitive network data. *Social Networks, 2,* 191–218.

Beveridge, W. I. B. (1957). *The Art of Scientific Investigation.* New York: Vintage.

Bhaskar, R. (1983). Beef, structure, and place: Notes from a critical naturalist perspective. *Journal for the Theory of Social Behaviour, 13,* 81–97.

Billow, R. M. (1977). Metaphor: A review of the psychological literature. *Psychological Bulletin, 84,* 81–92.

Birnbaum, A. (1954). Combining independent tests of significance. *Journal of the American Statistical Association, 49,* 559–574.

Bishop, G. F., Oldendick, R. W., and Tuchfarber, A. J. (1982). Political information processing: Question order and context effects. *Political Behavior, 4,* 177–200.

Bishop, Y. M. M., Fienberg, S. E., and Holland, P. W. (1975). *Discrete Multivariate Analysis: Theory and Practice.* Cambridge, Mass.: M. I. T. Press.

Black, B. W., Schumpert, J., and Welch, F. (1972). A "partial reinforcement extinction effect" in perceptual-motor performance: Coerced versus volunteer subject populations. *Journal of Experimental Psychology, 92,* 143–145.

Blumberg, M. (1980). Job switching in autonomous work groups: An exploratory study in a Pennsylvania coal mine. *Academy of Management Journal, 23,* 287–306.

————— and Pringle, C. D. (1983). How control groups can cause loss of control in action research: The case of Rushton coal mine. *Journal of Applied Behavioral Science, 19,* 409–425.

Bok, S. (1978). *Lying: Moral Choice in Public and Private Life.* New York: Pantheon.

Boring, E. G. (1950). *A History of Experimental Psychology* (2d ed.). New York: Appleton-Century-Crofts.

————— (1954). The nature and history of experimental controls. *American Journal of Psychology, 67,* 573–589.

————— (1969). Perspective: Artifact and control. In R. Rosenthal and R. L. Rosnow (Eds.), *Artifact in Behavioral Research* (pp. 1–11). New York: Academic Press.

Boruch, R. F., and Cecil, J. S. (1979). *Assuring the Confidentiality of Social Research Data.* Philadelphia: University of Pennsylvania Press.

Box, G. E. P. (1953). Non-normality and tests on variances. *Biometrika, 40,* 318–335.

_____, Hunter, W. G., and Hunter, J. S. (1978). *Statistics for Experimenters.* New York: Wiley.

_____ and Jenkins, G. M. (1970). *Time-Series Analysis: Forecasting Control.* San Francisco: Holden-Day.

Bradburn, N. M. (1982). Question-wording effects in surveys. In R. Hogarth (Ed.), *New Directions for Methodology of Social and Behavioral Science: Question Framing and Response Consistency,* no. 11 (pp. 65–76). San Francisco: Jossey-Bass.

_____ (1983). Response effects. In P. H. Rossi, J. D. Wright, and A. B. Anderson (Eds.), *Handbook of Survey Research* (pp. 289–328). New York: Academic Press.

_____, Rips, L. J., and Shevell, S. K. (1987). Answering autobiographical questions: The impact of memory and inference on surveys. *Science, 236,* 157–161.

Bradley, J.V. (1968). *Distribution-Free Statistical Tests.* Englewood Cliffs, N. J.: Prentice-Hall.

Brady, J.V. (1958). Ulcers in "executive" monkeys. *Scientific American, 199,* 95–100.

_____, Bigelow, G., Emurian, H., and Williams, D. M. (1974). Design of a programmed environment for experimental analysis of social behavior. In D. H. Carson (Ed.), *Man-Environment Interactions: Evaluations and Applications. 7: Social Ecology* (pp. 187–208). Milwaukee, Wis.: Environmental Design Research Associates.

_____ and Emurian, H. (1979). Behavior analysis of motivational and emotional interactions in a programmed environment. In H. E. Howe, Jr., and R. A. Dienstbier (Eds.), *Nebraska Symposium on Motivation 1978: Human Emotion* (vol. 26). Lincoln: University of Nebraska Press.

_____, Porter, R.W., Conrad, D. G., and Mason, J.W. (1958). Avoidance behavior and the development of gastroduodenal ulcers. *Journal for the Experimental Analysis of Behavior, 1,* 69–72.

Braver, M. C.W., and Braver, S. L. (1988). Statistical treatment of the Solomon four-group design: A meta-analytic approach. *Psychological Bulletin, 104,* 150–154.

Brehm, J. (1966). *A Theory of Psychological Reactance.* New York: Academic Press.

Bresnahan, J. L., and Shapiro, M. M. (1966). A general equation and technique for the exact partitioning of chi-square contingency tables. *Psychological Bulletin, 66,* 252–262.

Brewer, M. B., and Collins, B. E. (Eds.) (1981). *Scientific Inquiry and the Social Sciences.* San Francisco: Jossey-Bass.

Bridgman, P.W. (1927). *The Logic of Modern Physics.* New York: Macmillan.

_____ (1945). Some general principles of operational analysis. *Psychological Review, 52,* 246–249.

Bridgstock, M. (1982). A sociological approach to fraud in science. *Australian and New Zealand Journal of Sociology, 18,* 364–383.

Brinberg, D., and Kidder, L. H. (Eds.) (1982). *Forms of Validity in Research.* San Francisco: Jossey-Bass.

Brinton, J. E. (1961). Deriving an attitude scale from semantic differential data. *Public Opinion Quarterly, 25,* 289–295.

Broome, J. (1984). Selecting people randomly. *Ethics, 95,* 38–55.

Brower, D. (1948). The role of incentive in psychological research. *Journal of General Psychology, 39,* 145–147.

Browne, M.W. (1984). The decomposition of multitrait-multimethod matrices. *British Journal of Mathematical and Statistical Psychology, 37,* 1–21.

Brunswik, E. (1947). *Systematic and Representative Design of Psychological Experiments.* Berkeley: University of California Press.

Bryk, A. S., and Raudenbush, S.W. (1988). Heterogeneity of variance in experimental studies: A challenge to conventional interpretations. *Psychological Bulletin, 104,* 396–404.

Buckhout, R. (1965). Need for approval and attitude change. *Journal of Psychology, 60,* 123–128.

Bunge, M. (1982). Demarcating science from pseudoscience. *Fundamenta Scientiae, 3,* 369–388.

Buranelli, V. (1975). *The Wizard from Vienna: Franz Anton Mesmer.* New York: Coward, McCann and Geoghegan.

Burnham, J. R. (1966). Experimenter bias and lesion labeling. Unpublished manuscript, Purdue University, West Lafayette, Ind.

Buss, A. H. (1971). Aggression pays. In J. L. Singer (Ed.), *The Control of Aggression and Violence.* New York: Academic Press.

Buss, A. R. (1979). *A Dialectical Psychology.* New York: Halsted.

Camilli, G., and Hopkins, K. D. (1978). Applicability of chi-square to 2×2 contingency tables with small expected cell frequencies. *Psychological Bulletin, 85,* 163–167.

Campbell, D.T. (1950). The indirect assessment of attitudes. *Psychological Bulletin, 47,* 15–38.

––––––––– (1963). From description to experimentation: Interpreting trends as quasi-experiments. In C.W. Harris (Ed.), *Problems in Measuring Change.* Madison: University of Wisconsin Press.

––––––––– (1974). Evolutionary epistemology. In P. A. Schilpp (Ed.), *The Philosophy of Karl R. Popper* (vol. 14, I & II, pp. 413-464). LaSalle, Ill.: Open Court.

––––––––– and Boruch, R. F. (1975). Making the case for randomized assignment to treatments by considering the alternatives: Six ways in which quasi-experimental evaluations in compensatory education tend to underestimate effects. In C. A. Bennett and A. A. Lumsdaine (Eds.), *Evaluation and Experiment.* New York: Academic Press.

––––––––– and Fiske, D.W. (1959). Convergent and discriminant validation by the multitrait-multimethod matrix. *Psychological Bulletin, 56,* 81–105.

––––––––– and O'Connell, E. J. (1967). Methods factors in multitrait-multimethod matrices: Multiplicative rather than additive? *Multivariate Behavioral Research, 2,* 409–426.

––––––––– and ––––––––– (1982). Methods as diluting trait relationships rather than adding irrelevant systematic variance. In D. Brinberg and L. H. Kidder (Eds.), *Forms of Validity in Research* (pp. 93–111). San Francisco: Jossey-Bass.

––––––––– and Stanley, J. C. (1966). *Experimental and Quasi-Experimental Designs for Research.* Chicago: Rand McNally.

Cannell, C. F., Miller, P.V., and Oksenberg, L. (1981). Research on interviewing techniques. In S. Leinhardt (Ed.), *Sociological Methodology* (pp. 389–437). San Francisco: Jossey-Bass.

Cannon, W. B. (1945). *The Way of an Investigator.* New York: Norton.

Carlsmith, J. M., Ellsworth, P. C., and Aronson, E. (1976). *Methods of Research in Social Psychology.* Reading, Mass.: Addison-Wesley.

Carmer, S. G., and Swanson, M. R. (1973). An evaluation of ten pairwise multiple comparison procedures by Monte Carlo methods. *Journal of the American Statistical Association, 68,* 66–74.

Cassell, J. (1982). Harms, benefits, wrongs, and rights of fieldwork. In J. E. Sieber (Ed.), *The Ethics of Social Research: Fieldwork, Regulation, and Publication* (vol. 1, pp. 7–31). New York: Springer-Verlag.

Centers for Disease Control Vietnam Experience Study (1988). Health status of Vietnam veterans: 1. Psychosocial characteristics. *Journal of the American Medical Association, 259,* 2701–2707.

Chamberlin, T. C. (1897). The method of multiple working hypotheses. *Journal of Geology, 5,* 838–848.

Chambers, J. M., Cleveland, W. S., Kleiner, B., and Tukey, P. A. (1983). *Graphical Methods for Data Analysis.* Belmont, Calif.: Wadsworth International Group.

Cicchetti, D.V., Showalter, D., and Tyrer, P. J. (1985). The effect of number of rating scale categories on levels of interrater reliability: A Monte Carlo investigation. *Applied Psychological Measurement, 9,* 31–36.

Cicourel, A.V. (1982). Interviews, surveys, and the problem of ecological validity. *American Sociologist, 17,* 11–20.

Clark, R.W. (1971). *Einstein: The Life and Times.* New York: World.

Cleveland, W. S. (1985). *The Elements of Graphing Data.* Monterey, Calif.: Wadsworth.

––––––––– and McGill, R. (1985). Graphical perception and graphical methods for analyzing scientific data. *Science, 229,* 828–833.

Cochran, W. G. (1950). The comparison of percentages in matched samples. *Biometrika, 37,* 256–266.

––––––––– (1954). Some methods for strengthening the common chi-square tests. *Biometrics, 10,* 417–451.

––––––––– (1963). *Sampling Techniques* (2d ed.) New York: Wiley.

––––––––– and Cox, G. M. (1957). *Experimental Designs* (2d ed.). New York: Wiley. (First corrected printing, 1968.)

_____, Mosteller, F., and Tukey, J.W. (1953). Statistical problems of the Kinsey report. *Journal of the American Statistical Association, 48,* 673–716.

Cohen, D. (1980). British Society takes stand on Burt: Tackles practical problems. *APA Monitor, 11*(5), 1, 9.

Cohen, J. (1960). A coefficient of agreement for nominal scales. *Educational and Psychological Measurement, 20,* 37–46.

_____ (1962). The statistical power of abnormal-social psychological research: A review. *Journal of Abnormal and Social Psychology, 65,* 145–153.

_____ (1965). Some statistical issues in psychological research. In B. B. Wolman (Ed.), *Handbook of Clinical Psychology* (pp. 95–121). New York: McGraw-Hill.

_____ (1968). Weighted kappa: Nominal scale agreement with provision for scaled disagreement or partial credit. *Psychological Bulletin, 70,* 213–220.

_____ (1969). *Statistical Power Analysis for the Behavioral Sciences.* New York: Academic Press.

_____ (1977). *Statistical Power Analysis for the Behavioral Sciences* (rev. ed.). New York: Academic Press.

_____ (1982). Set correlation as a general multivariate data-analytic method. *Multivariate Behavioral Research, 17,* 301–341.

_____ (1988). *Statistical Power Analysis for the Behavioral Sciences* (2d ed.). Hillsdale, N. J.: Erlbaum.

_____ and Cohen, P. (1983). *Applied Multiple Regression/Correlation Analysis for the Behavioral Sciences* (2d ed.). Hillsdale, N.J.: Erlbaum.

Cohen, M. R. (1959). *Reason and Nature: An Essay on the Meaning of Scientific Method.* New York: Dover. (First published 1931, Harcourt Brace.)

Collins, H. M. (1978). Science and the rule of replicability: A sociological study of scientific method. Paper presented at annual meeting of the American Association for the Advancement of Science in symposium on "Replication and Experimenter Effect," Washington, D.C.

Columbo, J. (1982). The critical period concept: Research, methodology, and theoretical issues. *Psychological Bulletin, 91,* 260–275.

Comrey, A. L. (1973). *A First Course in Factor Analysis.* New York: Academic Press.

Conant, J. B. (1957). Introduction. In J. B. Conant and L. K. Nash (Eds.), *Harvard Case Studies in Experimental Science* (vol. 1, pp. vii–xvi). Cambridge, Mass.: Harvard University Press.

Conover, W. J. (1974). Some reasons for not using the Yates continuity correction on 2 × 2 contingency tables. *Journal of the American Statistical Association, 69,* 374–376.

_____ (1980). *Practical Nonparametric Statistics* (2d ed.). New York: Wiley.

Conrath, D.W. (1973). Communications environment and its relationship to organizational structure. *Management Science, 20,* 586–603.

_____, Higgins, C. A., and McClean, R. J. (1983). A comparison of the reliability of questionnaire versus diary data. *Social Networks, 5,* 315–322.

Converse, J. M. (1987). *Survey Research in the United States.* Berkeley: University of California Press.

_____ and Presser, S. (1986). *Survey Questions: Handcrafting the Standardized Questionnaire.* Beverly Hills, Calif.: Sage.

Cook, N. R., and Ware, J. H. (1983). Design and analysis methods for longitudinal research. *Annual Review of Public Health, 4,* 1–23.

Cook, T. D., and Campbell, D.T. (1976). The design and conduct of quasi-experiments and true experiments in field settings. In M. D. Dunnette (Ed.), *Handbook of Industrial and Organizational Psychology* (pp. 223–326). Chicago: Rand McNally.

_____ and _____ (1979). *Quasi-Experimentation: Design and Analysis Issues for Field Settings.* Chicago: Rand McNally.

Cooley, W.W., and Lohnes, P. R. (1971). *Multivariate Data Analysis.* New York: Wiley.

_____ and_____ (1985). *Multivariate Data Analysis.* Malabar, Fla.: Krieger.

Coombs, C. H., Dawes, R. M., and Tversky, A. (1970). *Mathematical Psychology: An Elementary Introduction.* Englewood Cliffs, N.J.: Prentice-Hall.

Cooper, H. M. (1984). *The Integrative Research Review: A Systematic Approach.* Beverly Hills, Calif.: Sage.

_____ (1989). *Integrating Research: A Guide for Literature Reviews* (2d ed.) Newbury Park, Calif.: Sage.

_____ and Rosenthal, R. (1980). Statistical versus traditional procedures for summarizing research findings *Psychological Bulletin, 87,* 442–449.

Cooper, J. (1976). Deception and role playing: On telling the good guys from the bad guys. *American Psychologist, 31,* 605–610.

Cooper, W. H. (1981). Ubiquitous halo. *Psychological Bulletin, 90,* 218–244.

Coren, S., and Porac, C. (1977). Fifty centuries of right-handedness: The historical record. *Science, 198,* 631–632.

Cornell, F. G., and McLoone, E. P. (1963). Design of sample surveys in education. *Review of Educational Research, 33,* 523–532.

Corrozi, J. F., and Rosnow, R. L. (1968). Consonant and dissonant communications as positive and negative reinforcements in opinion change. *Journal of Personality and Social Psychology, 8,* 27–30.

Cotter, P. R., Cohen, J., and Coulter, P. B. (1982). Race-of-interviewer effects in telephone interviews. *Public Opinion Quarterly, 46,* 278–284.

Couch, A., and Keniston, K. (1960). Yeasayers and naysayers: Agreeing response set as a personality variable. *Journal of Abnormal and Social Psychology, 60,* 151–174.

Cox, D. E., and Sipprelle, C. N. (1971). Coercion in participation as a research subject. *American Psychologist, 26,* 726–728.

Cox, D. R. (1957). The use of a concomitant variable in selecting an experimental design. *Biometrika, 44,* 150–158.

_____ (1958). *Planning of Experiments.* New York: Wiley.

Crabb, P. B., and Rosnow, R. L. (1988). What is aggressive? Some contextual factors in judging international behavior. *Aggressive Behavior, 14,* 105–112.

Cronbach, L. J. (1946). Response sets and test validity. *Educational and Psychological Measurement, 6,* 475–494.

_____ (1950). Further evidence on response sets and test design. *Educational and Psychological Measurement, 10,* 3–31.

_____ (1951). Coefficient alpha and the internal consistency of tests. *Psychometrika, 16,* 297–334.

_____ (1960). *Essentials of Psychological Testing* (2d ed.). New York: Harper.

_____, Gleser, G. C., Nanda, N., and Rajaratnam, N. (1972). *The Dependability of Behavioral Measurements: Theory of Generalizability for Scores and Profiles.* New York: Wiley.

_____ and Meehl, P. E. (1955). Construct validity in psychological tests. *Psychological Bulletin, 52,* 281–302.

_____ and Quirk, T. J. (1971). Test validity. In L. C. Deighton (Ed.), *Encyclopedia of Education* (vol. 9, pp. 165–175). New York: Macmillan and Free Press.

Crowne, D. P. (1979). *The Experimental Study of Personality.* Hillsdale, N.J.: Erlbaum.

_____ and Marlowe, D. (1964). *The Approval Motive: Studies in Evaluative Dependence.* New York: Wiley.

Cureton, E. E., and D'Agostino, R. B. (1983). *Factor Analysis: An Applied Approach.* Hillsdale, N.J.: Erlbaum.

Dabbs, J. M., and Janis, I. L. (1965). Why does eating while reading facilitate opinion change?—An experimental inquiry. *Journal of Experimental Social Psychology, 1,* 133–144.

D'Agostino, R. B. (1971). A second look at analysis of variance on dichotomous data. *Journal of Educational Measurement, 8,* 327–333.

Danziger, K. (1985). The methodological imperative in psychology. *Philosophy of the Social Sciences, 15,* 1–13.

Darley, J. M. (1980). The importance of being earnest—and ethical. *Contemporary Psychology, 25,* 14–15.

Darroch, R. K., and Steiner, I. D. (1970). Role playing: An alternative to laboratory research? *Journal of Personality, 38,* 302–311.

Dawes, R. M. (1969). "Interaction effects" in the presence of asymmetrical transfer. *Psychological Bulletin, 71,* 55–57.

_____ and Corrigan, B. (1974). Linear models in decision making. *Psychological Bulletin, 81,* 95–106.

Dean, C. (1977). Are serendipitous discoveries a part of normal science? The case of the pulsars. *Sociological Review, 25,* 73–86.

De Jong-Gierveld, J., and Kamphuis, F. (1985). The development of a Rasch-type loneliness scale. *Applied Psychology Measurement, 9,* 289–299.

Delgado, R., and Leskovac, H. (1986). Informed consent in human experimentation: Bridging the gap between ethical thought and current practice. *UCLA Law Review, 34,* 67–130.

DePaulo, B. M., and Rosenthal, R. (1979). Age changes in nonverbal decoding skills: Evidence for increasing differentiation. *Merrill-Palmer Quarterly, 25,* 145–150.

DeVore, I., and Hall, K. R. L. (1965). Baboon ecology. In I. DeVore (Ed.), *Primate Behavior* (pp. 20–52). New York: Holt.

_____ and Washburn, S. L. (1963). Baboon ecology and human evolution. In F. C. Howell and F. Bourliere (Eds.), *African Ecology and Human Evolution* (pp. 335–367). New York: Viking Fund.

DiNitto, D. (1983). Time-series analysis: An application to social welfare policy. *Journal of Applied Behavioral Science, 19,* 507–518.

Director, S. M. (1979). Underadjustment bias in the evaluation of manpower training. *Evaluation Quarterly, 3,* 190–218.

Dohrenwend, B. S. (1965). Some effects of open and closed questions on respondents' answers. *Human Organization, 24,* 175–184.

_____ (1969). Interviewer biasing effects: Toward a reconciliation of findings. *Public Opinion Quarterly, 33,* 121–125.

_____, Colombotos, J., and Dohrenwend, B. P. (1968). Social distance and interviewer effects. *Public Opinion Quarterly, 32,* 410–422.

_____ and Dohrenwend, B. P. (1968). Sources of refusals in surveys. *Public Opinion Quarterly, 32,* 74–83.

_____ and Richardson, S. A. (1963). Directiveness and nondirectiveness in research interviewing: A reformulation of the problem. *Psychological Bulletin, 60,* 475–485.

Dollard, J. (1953). The Kinsey report on women: A strangely flawed masterpiece. *New York Herald Tribune,* Sept. 13, sect. 6, p. 3.

Dorfman, D. D. (1978). The Cyril Burt question: New findings. *Science, 201,* 1177–1186.

Downs, C.W., Smeyak, G. P., and Martin, E. (1980). *Professional Interviewing.* New York: Harper & Row.

Duhem, P. (1954). *The Aim and Structure of Physical Theory.* Princeton, N.J.: Princeton University Press.

Eagly, A. H. (1978). Sex differences in influenceability. *Psychological Bulletin, 85,* 86–116.

Easley, J. A. (1971). Scientific method as an educational objective. In L. C. Deighton (Ed.), *The Encyclopedia of Education* (vol. 8, pp. 150–157). New York: Free Press and Macmillan.

_____ and Tatsuoka, M. M. (1968). *Scientific Thought: Cases from Classical Physics.* Boston: Allyn & Bacon.

Ebbinghaus, H. (1885). *Über das Gedächtnis: Untersuchungen zur experimentellen Psychologie.* Leipzig, Germany: Duncker & Humblot.

_____ (1913). *Memory: A Contribution to Experimental Psychology* (trans. by H. A. Ruger and C. E. Bussenius). New York: Teachers College, Columbia University.

Edgington, E. S. (1972a). An additive model for combining probability values from independent experiments. *Journal of Psychology, 80,* 351–363.

_____ (1972b). A normal curve method for combining probability values from independent experiments. *Journal of Psychology, 82,* 85–89.

Edwards, A. L. (1957). *Techniques of Attitude Scale Construction.* New York: Appleton-Century-Crofts.

_____ (1972). *Experimental Design in Psychological Research* (4th ed.). New York: Holt.

Eisenhart, C., Hastay, M.W., and Wallis, W. A. (Eds.) (1947). *Techniques of Statistical Analysis.* New York: McGraw-Hill.

Entwisle, D. R. (1961). Interactive effects of pretesting. *Educational and Psychological Measurement, 21,* 607–620.

Erikson, K. (1987). On writing social science. *Social Science, 72,* 95–98.

Eron, L. D. (1963). Relationship of television viewing habits and aggressive behavior in children. *Journal of Abnormal and Social Psychology, 67,* 193–196.

———— and Huesmann, L. R. (1980). Sohn should let sleeping dogs lie. *American Psychologist, 36,* 231–233.

————, ————, Lefkowitz, M. M., and Walder, L. O. (1972). Does television violence cause aggression? *American Psychologist, 27,* 253–263.

————, Walder, L. O., and Lefkowitz, M. M. (1971). *Learning of Aggression in Children.* Boston: Little, Brown.

Esposito, J. L., Agard, E., and Rosnow, R. L. (1984). Can confidentiality of data pay off? *Personality and Individual Differences, 5,* 477–480.

———— and Rosnow, R. L. (1984). Cognitive set and message processing: Implications of prose memory research for rumor theory. *Language and Communication, 4,* 301–315.

Everitt, B. S. (1977). *The Analysis of Contingency Tables.* New York: Wiley.

Farr, R. M., and Moscovici, S. (1984). *Social Representations.* Cambridge, Eng.: Cambridge University Press.

Fear, D. E. (1978). *Technical Writing* (2d ed.). New York: Random House.

Federighi, E. T. (1959). Extended tables of the percentage points of Student's *t*-distribution. *Journal of the American Statistical Association, 54,* 683–688.

Feinstein, A. R. (1988). Scientific standards in epidemiological studies of the menace of daily life. *Science, 242,* 1257–1263.

Feldman, R. E. (1968). Response to compatriot and foreigner who seek assistance. *Journal of Personality and Social Psychology, 10,* 202–214.

Festinger, L. (1957). *A Theory of Cognitive Dissonance.* Evanston, Ill.: Row, Peterson.

Feyerabend, P. (1975). *Against Method: Outline of an Anarchistic Theory of Knowledge.* London, Eng.: New Left Books.

Fidler, D. S., and Kleinknecht, R. E. (1977). Randomized response versus direct questioning: Two data-collection methods for sensitive information. *Psychological Bulletin, 84,* 1045–1049.

Fienberg, S. E. (1977). *The Analysis of Cross-Classified Categorical Data.* Cambridge, Mass.: M.I.T. Press.

Filion, F. L. (1975–1976). Estimating bias due to nonresponse in mail surveys. *Public Opinion Quarterly, 39,* 482–492.

Fillenbaum, S. (1966). Prior deception and subsequent experimental performance: The "faithful" subject. *Journal of Personality and Social Psychology, 4,* 532–537.

Firth, R. (1956). Rumor in a primitive society. *Journal of Abnormal and Social Psychology, 53,* 122–132.

Fishbein, M., and Azjen, I. (1975). *Belief, Attitude, Intention and Behavior: An Introduction to Theory and Research.* Reading, Mass.: Addison-Wesley.

Fisher, R. A. (1935). *The Design of Experiments.* London, Eng.: Oliver and Boyd.

———— (1938). *Statistical Methods for Research Workers* (7th ed.). London, Eng.: Oliver and Boyd.

———— (1960). *Design of Experiments* (7th ed.). Edinburgh, Scotland: Oliver and Boyd.

Fiske, D. W. (1982). Convergent-discriminant validation in measurements and research strategies. In D. Brinberg & L. H. Kidder (Eds.), *Forms of Validity in Research* (pp. 77–92). San Francisco: Jossey-Bass.

———— and Shweder, R. A. (Eds.) (1986). *Metatheory and Social Science: Pluralisms and Subjectivities.* Chicago: University of Chicago Press.

Flacks, R. (1967). The liberated generation: An exploration of the roots of social protest. *Journal of Social Issues, 23,* 52–75.

Flanagan, J. C. (1954). The critical incident technique. *Psychological Bulletin, 51,* 327–358.

Fleiss, J. L., and Cohen, J. (1973). The equivalence of weighted kappa and the intraclass correlation coefficient as measures of reliability. *Educational and Psychological Measurement, 33,* 613–619.

————, ————, and Everitt, B. S. (1969). Large sample standard errors of kappa and weighted kappa. *Psychological Bulletin, 72,* 323–327.

Foa, U. G. (1968). Three kinds of behavioral change. *Psychological Bulletin, 70,* 460–473.

———— and Foa, E. B. (1974). *Societal Structures of the Mind.* Springfield, Ill.: Charles C. Thomas.

Forsyth, D. R. (1980). A taxonomy of ethical ideologies. *Journal of Personality and Social Psychology, 39,* 175–184.

———— and Pope, W. R. (1984). Ethical ideology and judgments of social psychological research: Multidimensional analysis. *Journal of Personality and Social Psychology, 46,* 1365–1375.

Forward, J., Canter, R., and Kirsh, N. (1976). Role enactment and deception methodologies. *American Psychologist, 31,* 595–604.

Fraser, D. A. S. (1957). *Nonparametric Methods in Statistics.* New York: Wiley.

Freedman, D. A. (1987a). As others see us: A case study in path analysis. *Journal of Educational Statistics, 12,* 101–128.

———— (1987b). A rejoinder on models, metaphors, and fables. *Journal of Educational Statistics, 12,* 206–223.

Freedman, J. L. (1969). Role playing: Psychology by consensus. *Journal of Personality and Social Psychology, 13,* 107–114.

French, J. R. P. (1953). Experiments in field settings. In L. Festinger and D. Katz (Eds.), *Research Methods in the Behavioral Sciences* (pp. 98–135). New York: Holt.

Frey, J. H. (1986). An experiment with a confidentiality reminder in a telephone survey. *Public Opinion Quarterly 50,* 267–269.

Friedman, C. J., and Gladden, J. W. (1964). Objective measurement of social role concept via the semantic differential. *Psychological Reports, 14,* 239–247.

Friedman, H. (1968). Magnitude of experimental effect and a table for its rapid estimation. *Psychological Bulletin, 70,* 245–251.

Fruchter, B. (1954). *Introduction to Factor Analysis.* Princeton, N.J.: Van Nostrand.

Frye, N. (1957). *The Anatomy of Criticism.* Princeton, N.J.: Princeton University Press.

———— (1963). *Fables of Identity.* New York: Harcourt, Brace & World.

Fung, S. S. K., Kipnis, D., and Rosnow, R. L. (1987). Synthetic benevolence and malevolence as strategies of relational compliance-gaining. *Journal of Social and Personal Relationships, 4,* 129–141.

Furno, O. F. (1966). Sample survey designs in education: Focus on administrative utilization. *Review of Educational Research, 37,* 552–565.

Galtung, J. (1972). A structural theory of aggression. In I. K. Feierabend, R. L. Feierabend, and T. R. Gurr (Eds.), *Anger, Violence, and Politics* (pp. 85–97). Englewood Cliffs, N.J.: Prentice-Hall.

Gardner, G. T. (1978). Effects of federal human subject regulations on data obtained in environmental stressor research. *Journal of Personality and Social Psychology, 36,* 628–634.

Gardner, H. (1986). *The Mind's New Science: A History of the Cognitive Revolution.* New York: Basic Books.

Garfield, E. (1989a). Art and science. Part 1. The art-science connection. *Current Contents, 21(8),* 3–10.

———— (1989b). Art and science. Part 2. Science for art's sake. *Current Contents, 21(9),* 3–8.

Geller, D. M. (1978). Involvement in role-playing simulation: A demonstration with studies on obedience. *Journal of Personality and Social Psychology, 36,* 219–235.

Geller, N. L. (1983). Statistical strategies for animal conservation. In J. A. Sechzer (Ed.), *The Role of Animals in Biomedical Research* (pp. 20–31). New York: New York Academy of Sciences.

Georgoudi, M. (1981). Modern dialectics in social psychology: A reappraisal. *European Journal of Social Psychology, 13,* 77–93.

———— and Rosnow, R. L. (1985a). Notes toward a contextualist understanding of social psychology. *Personality and Social Psychology Bulletin, 11,* 5–22.

———— and ———— (1985b). The emergence of contextualism. *Journal of Communication, 35,* 76–88.

Gergen, K. J. (1973a). Codification of research ethics: Views of a doubting Thomas. *American Psychologist, 28,* 907–912.

_____ (1973b). Social psychology as history. *Journal of Personality and Social Psychology, 26,* 309–320.

_____ (1978). Experimentation in social psychology: A reappraisal. *European Journal of Social Psychology, 8,* 507–527.

_____ (1985). The social constructionist movement in modern psychology. *American Psychologist, 40,* 266–275.

_____ and Gergen, M. (1986). Narrative form and the construction of psychological science. In T. R. Sarbin, (Ed.), *Narrative Psychology: The Storied Nature of Human Conduct* (pp. 22–44). New York: Praeger.

Gergen, M., Suls, J. M., Rosnow, R. L., and Lana, R. E. (1989). *Psychology: A Beginning.* San Diego: Harcourt Brace Jovanovich.

Gibbons, J. D. (1985). *Nonparametric Statistical Inference* (2d ed.). New York: Marcel Dekker.

Giddens, A. (Ed.) (1974). *Positivism and Sociology.* London, Eng.: Heinemann.

Gigerenzer, G. (1987). Probabilistic thinking and the fight against subjectivity. In L. Krüger, G. Gigerenzer, and M. S. Morgan (Eds.), *The Probabilistic Revolution* (vol. 2, pp. 11–33). Cambridge, Mass.: Bradford/M.I.T. Press.

_____ and Murray, D. J. (1987). *Cognition as Intuitive Statistics.* Hillsdale, N.J.: Erlbaum.

_____, Swijtink, Z., Porter, T., Daston, L., Beatty, J., and Krüger, L. (1989). *The Empire of Chance: How Probability Changed Science and Everyday Life.* Cambridge, Eng.: Cambridge University Press.

Gilbert, J. P., McPeek, B., and Mosteller, F. (1977). Statistics and ethics in surgery and anesthesia. *Science, 198,* 684–689.

Gillespie, R. (1988). The Hawthorne experiments and the politics of experimentation. In J. Morawski (Ed.), *The Rise of Experimentation in American Psychology* (pp. 114–137). New Haven, Conn.: Yale University Press.

Gillie, O. (1978). Sir Cyril Burt and the great IQ fraud. *New Statesman,* Nov. 24.

_____ (1979). Burt's missing ladies. *Science, 204,* 1035–1039.

Gilmore, D. D. (1987). *Aggression and Community: Paradoxes of Andalusian Culture.* New Haven, Conn.: Yale University Press.

Glass, D. C., and Singer, J. F. (1972). *Urban Stress: Experiments on Noise and Social Stressors.* New York: Academic Press.

Glass, G.V. (1976). Primary, secondary, and meta-analysis of research. Paper presented at the meeting of the American Educational Research Association, San Francisco, April.

_____ (1980). Summarizing effect sizes. In R. Rosenthal (Ed.), *New Directions for Methodology of Social and Behavioral Science: Quantitative Assessment of Research Domains,* no. 5. San Francisco: Jossey-Bass.

_____, McGaw, B., and Smith, M. L. (1981). *Meta-Analysis in Social Research.* Beverly Hills, Calif.: Sage.

Gniech, G. (1986). *Störeffekte in psychologischen Experimenten.* Stuttgart, Germany: W. Kohlhammer.

Goldstein, J. H., Rosnow, R. L., Goodstadt, B. E., and Suls, J. M. (1972). The"good subject" in verbal operant conditioning research. *Journal of Experimental Research in Personality, 6,* 29–33.

Goode, W. J., and Hatt, P. K. (1952). *Methods in Social Research.* New York: McGraw-Hill.

Goodenough, W. H. (1980). Ethnographic field techniques. In H. C. Triandis and J.W. Berry (Eds.), *Handbook of Cross-Cultural Psychology: Methodology* (vol. 2, pp. 29–55). Boston: Allyn and Bacon.

Goodstadt, B., and Kipnis, D. (1970). Situational influences on the use of power. *Journal of Applied Psychology, 54,* 201–207.

Gorden, R. L. (1969). *Interviewing: Strategy, Techniques and Tactics.* Homewood, Ill.: Dorsey.

Gordon, M. E. and Gross, R. H. (1978). A critique of methods for operationalizing the concept of fakeability. *Educational and Psychological Measurement, 38,* 771–782.

Gorsuch, R. L. (1983). *Factor Analysis* (2d ed.). Hillsdale, N.J.: Erlbaum.

Gottman, J. M. (1981). *Time-Series Analysis: A Comprehensive Introduction for Social Scientists.* Cambridge, Eng.: Cambridge University Press.

Goyder, J. C. (1982). Further evidence on factors affecting response rates to mailed question-naires. *American Sociological Review, 47,* 550–553.

Graham, J. R., and Lilly, R. S. (1984). *Psychological Testing.* Englewood Cliffs, N.J.: Prentice-Hall.

Gray, B. H., Cooke, R. A., and Tannenbaum, A. S. (1978). Research involving human subjects. *Science, 201,* 1094–1101.

Green, B. F., Jr., and Tukey, J. W. (1960). Complex analysis of variance: General problems. *Psychometrika, 25,* 127–152.

Green, D. R. (1963). Volunteering and the recall of interrupted tasks. *Journal of Abnormal and Social Psychology, 66,* 397–401.

Greenberg, M. S. (1967). Role playing: An alternative to deception? *Journal of Personality and Social Psychology, 7,* 152–157.

Greenwald, A. G. (1975). Consequences of prejudice against the null hypothesis. *Psychological Bulletin, 82,* 1–20.

_____ and Ronis, D. L. (1978). Twenty years of cognitive dissonance: Case study of the evolution of a theory. *Psychological Review, 85,* 53–57.

Grey, R. J., and Kipnis, D. (1976). Untangling the performance appraisal dilemma: The influence of perceived organizational context on evaluative processes. *Journal of Applied Psychology, 61,* 329–335.

Grinnell, F. (1987). *The Scientific Attitude.* Boulder, Colo.: Westview.

Gross, A. E., and Fleming, I. (1982). Twenty years of deception in social psychology. *Personality and Social Psychology Bulletin, 8,* 402–408.

Gross, A. G. (1983). A primer on tables and figures. *Journal of Technical Writing and Communication, 13,* 33–55.

Groth-Marnet, G. (1984). *Handbook of Psychological Assessment.* New York: Van Nostrand.

Gruenberg, B. C. (1929). *The Story of Evolution.* New York: Van Nostrand.

Guilford, J. P. (1954). *Psychometric Methods* (2d ed.). New York: McGraw-Hill.

_____ and Fruchter, B. (1978). *Fundamental Statistics in Psychology and Education.* (6th ed.). New York: McGraw-Hill.

Gustafson, L. A., and Orne, M. T. (1965). Effects of perceived role and role success on the detection of deception. *Journal of Applied Psychology, 49,* 412–417.

Guttman, L. (1966). Order analysis of correlation matrices. In R. B. Cattell (Ed.), *Handbook of Multivariate Experimental Psychology* (pp. 438–458). Chicago: Rand McNally.

Haber, M. (1986). An exact unconditional test for the 2 × 2 comparative trial. *Psychological Bulletin, 99,* 129–132.

Hagenaars, J. A., and Cobben, N. P. (1978). Age, cohort and period: A general model for the analysis of social change. *Netherlands Journal of Sociology, 14,* 58–91.

Hall, J. A. (1979). Gender, gender roles, and nonverbal communication skills. In R. Rosenthal (Ed.), *Skill in Nonverbal Communication: Individual Differences* (pp. 32–67). Cambridge, Mass.: Oelgeschlager, Gunn and Hain.

_____ (1980). Gender differences in nonverbal communication skills. In R. Rosenthal (Ed.), *New Directions for Methodology of Social and Behavioral Science: Quantitative Assessment of Research Domains,* no. 5. (pp. 63–77). San Francisco: Jossey-Bass.

_____ (1984a). *Instructor's Manual to Accompany Rosenthal/Rosnow: Essentials of Behavioral Research.* New York: McGraw-Hill.

_____ (1984b). *Nonverbal Sex Differences.* Baltimore: Johns Hopkins University Press.

Hamilton, V. L. (1976). Role play and deception: A re-examination of the controversy. *Journal for the Theory of Social Behaviour, 6,* 233–250.

Hanson, N. R. (1958). *Patterns of Discovery.* Cambridge, Eng.: Cambridge University Press.

_____ (1971). The idea of a logic of discovery. In S. Toulmin and H. Woolf (Eds.), *What I Do Not Believe and Other Essays.* Dordrecht, Holland: D. Reidel.

Harlow, H. F. (1959). Love in infant monkeys. In S. Coopersmith (Ed.), *Frontiers of Psychological Research* (pp. 92–98). San Francisco: Freeman

_____ and Harlow, M. K. (1965). The affectional systems. In A. M. Schrier, H. F. Harlow, and F. Stollnitz (Eds.), *Behavior of Nonhuman Primates: Modern Research Trends* (vol. 2, pp. 287–334). New York: Academic Press.

_____ and _____ (1966). Learning to love. *American Scientist, 54,* 244–272.

_____ and _____ (1970). The young monkeys. In P. Cramer (Ed.), *Readings in Developmental Psychology Today* (pp. 93–97). Del Mar, Calif.: CRM Books.

Harner, M J. (1970). Population pressures and the social evolution of agriculturists. *Southwestern Journal of Anthropology, 26,* 67–86.

Harré, R. (1980). *Social Being: A Theory for Social Psychology.* Totowa, N.J.: Rowman & Littlefield.

_____ and Secord, P. (1972). *The Explanation of Social Behaviour.* Oxford, Eng.: Blackwell.

Harris, M J., and Rosenthal, R. (1985). Mediation of interpersonal expectancy effects: 31 meta-analyses. *Psychological Bulletin 97,* 363–386.

_____ and_____ (1986). *Human Performance Research: An Overview.* Background paper commissioned by the National Research Council, Washington, D.C.: National Academy Press.

Harris, R. J. (1975). *A Primer of Multivariate Statistics.* New York: Academic Press.

_____ (1985). *A Primer of Multivariate Statistics* (2d ed.). New York: Academic Press.

Hartmann, G.W. (1936). A field experiment on the comparative effectiveness of "emotional" and "rational" political leaflets in determining election results. *Journal of Abnormal and Social Psychology, 31,* 99–114.

Haviland, J. B. (1977). Gossip as competition in Zinacantan. *Journal of Communication, 27,* 186–191.

Hays, W. L. (1981). *Statistics* (3d ed.). New York: Holt.

Hayes, S. C. (1987). A contextual approach to therapeutic change. In N. Jacobson (Ed.), *Psychotherapists in Clinical Practice: Cognitive and Behavioral Perspectives.* (pp. 327–387). New York: Guilford.

_____ (1988). Contextualism and the next wave of behavioral psychology. *Behavior Analysis, 23,* 7–22.

_____ and Brownstein, A. J. (1986). Mentalism, behavior-behavior relations, and a behavior-analytic view of the purposes of science. *The Behavior Analyst, 9,* 175–190.

Hearnshaw, L. S. (1979). *Cyril Burt, Psychologist.* Ithaca, N.Y.: Cornell University Press.

Heberlein, T. A., and Baumgartner, R. (1978). Factors affecting response rates to mailed questionnaires: A quantitative analysis of the published literature. *American Sociological Review, 43,* 447–462.

Heckman, J. J. (1980). Sample selection bias as a specification error. In J. P. Smith (Ed.), *Female Labor Supply: Theory and Estimation* (pp. 206–248). Princeton, N.J.: Princeton University Press.

Hedges, L.V. (1987). How hard is hard science, how soft is soft science? *American Psychologist, 42,* 443–455.

_____ and Olkin, I. (1985). *Statistical Methods for Meta-Analysis.* New York: Academic Press.

Heider, F. (1944). Social perception and phenomenal causality. *Psychological Review, 51,* 358–374.

_____ (1958). *The Psychology of Interpersonal Relations.* New York: Wiley.

Hempel, C. G., and Oppenheim, P. (1965). *Aspects of Scientific Explanation and Other Essays in the Philosophy of Science.* New York: Free Press.

Hendrick, C. (Ed.) (1977). Role-playing as a methodology for social research: A symposium. *Personality and Social Psychology Bulletin, 3,* 454–522.

Heritage, J. (1984). *Garfinkel and Ethnomethodology.* Cambridge, Eng.: Polity Press.

Hersen, M. and Barlow, D. H. (1976). *Single-Case Experimental Designs: Strategies for Studying Behavior Change.* Oxford, Eng.: Pergamon.

Higbee, K. L., and Wells, M. G. (1972). Some research trends in social psychology during the 1960s. *American Psychologist, 27,* 963–966.

Highland, R.W., and Berkshire, J. A. (1951). *A Methodological Study of Forced-Choice Performance Rating.* (Res. rep. 51-9.) San Antonio, Tex.: Human Resources Research Center.

Hilgard, E. R. (1980). Introduction. In G. J. Bloch (Ed.), *Mesmerism: A Translation of the Original Medical and Scientific Writings of F. A. Mesmer, M.D.* Los Altos, Calif.: Kaufmann.

Hineline, P. N. (1986). Re-tuning the operant-respondent distinction. In T. Thompson and M. D. Zeiler (Eds.), *Analysis and Interpretation of Behavioral Units* (pp. 55–79). Hillsdale, N.J.: Erlbaum.

Hodgkinson, H. (1970). Student protest: An institutional and national profile. *The Record (Columbia University Teachers' College), 71,* 537–555.

Hoffman, R. R., and Nead, J. M. (1983). General contextualism, ecological sciences and cognitive research. *Journal of Mind and Behavior, 4,* 507–560.

Holden, C. (1979). Ethics in social science research. *Science, 206,* 537–540.

Hollander, M., and Wolfe, D. A. (1973). *Nonparametric Statistical Methods.* New York: Wiley.

Holsti, O. R. (with the collaboration of J. K. Loomba and R. C. North) (1968). Content analysis. In G. Lindzey and E. Aronson (Eds.), *The Handbook of Social Psychology* (2d ed.)(vol. 2, pp. 596–692). Reading, Mass.: Addison-Wesley.

_____ (1969). *Content Analysis for the Social Sciences and Humanities.* Reading, Mass.: Addison-Wesley.

Holton, G., and Morison, R. S. (1978). *Limits of Scientific Inquiry.* New York: Norton.

Horowitz, I. A. (1969). Effects of volunteering, fear arousal, and number of communications on attitude change. *Journal of Personality and Social Psychology, 11,* 34–37.

_____ and Rothschild, B. H. (1970). Conformity as a function of deception and role playing. *Journal of Personality and Social Psychology, 14,* 224–226.

Horowitz, I. L. (1979). Methods and strategies in evaluating equity research. *Social Indicators Research, 6,* 1–22.

Horst, P., and Edwards, A. L. (1982). Analysis of nonorthogonal designs: The 2^k factorial experiment. *Psychological Bulletin, 91,* 190–192.

Houts, A. C., Cook, T. D., and Shadish, W., Jr. (1986). The person-situation debate: A critical multiplist perspective. *Journal of Personality, 54,* 52–105.

Hovey, H. B. (1928). Effects of general distraction on the higher thought processes. *American Journal of Psychology, 40,* 585–591.

Howard, D. (1987). Questions of realism. *Science, 238,* 409–410.

Hoyt, C. (1941). Test reliability estimated by analysis of variance. *Psychometrika, 6,* 153–160.

Hsu, L. M. (1980). Tests of differences in p levels as tests of differences in effect sizes. *Psychological Bulletin, 88,* 705–708.

Hsu, T. C., and Feldt, L. S. (1969). The effect of limitations on the number of criterion score values on the significance level of the *F*-test. *American Educational Research Journal, 6,* 515–527.

Huber, P. J. (1981). *Robust Statistics.* New York: Wiley.

Huck, S. W., and Sandler, H. M. (1979). *Rival Hypotheses.* New York: Harper & Row.

Hume, D. (1739–1740). *A Treatise of Human Nature.* Oxford, Eng.: Clarendon Press. (Republished 1978 by Oxford University Press.)

Humphreys, L. (1975). *Tearoom Trade: Inpersonal Sex in Public Places* (2d ed.). Chicago: Aldine.

Hunter, J. E., and Schmidt, F. L. (1990). *Methods of Meta-Analysis: Correcting Error and Bias in Research Findings.* Newbury Park, Calif.: Sage.

Hurvich, L. W. (1969). Hering and the scientific establishment. *American Psychologist, 24,* 497–514.

Hyman, H. (1954). *Interviewing in Social Research.* Chicago: University of Chicago Press.

_____ and Sheatsley, P. B. (1954). The scientific method. In D. P. Geddes (Ed.), *An Analysis of the Kinsey Reports.* New York: New American Library.

Israel, J., and Tajfel, H. (Eds.) (1972). *The Context of Social Psychology.* London, Eng.: Academic Press.

Jackson, D. N. (1969). Multimethod factor analysis in the evaluation of convergent and discriminant validity. *Psychological Bulletin, 72,* 30–49.

Jackson, R. W. B. (1939). Reliability of mental tests. *British Journal of Psychology, 29,* 267–287.

Jaeger, M. E., and Rosnow, R. L. (1988). Contextualism and its implications for psychological inquiry. *British Journal of Psychology, 79,* 63–75.

Janis, I. L., Kaye, D., and Kirschner, P. (1965). Facilitating effects of "eating-while-reading" on responsiveness to persuasive communications. *Journal of Personality and Social Psychology, 1,* 181–186.

_____ and Mann, L. (1965). Effectiveness of emotional role-playing in modifying smoking habits and attitudes. *Journal of Experimental Research in Personality, 1,* 84–90.

Jenkins, J. J. (1974). Remember that old theory of learning? Well, forget it! *American Psychologist, 11,* 785–795.

Jensen, A. R. (1965). A review of the Rorschach. In O. K. Buros (Ed.), *Sixth Mental Measurement Yearbook* (pp. 501–509). Highland Park, N.H.: Gryphon.

_____ (1978). Sir Cyril Burt in perspective. *American Psychologist, 33,* 499–503.

Johnson, C. G. (1982). Risks in the publication of fieldwork. In J. E. Sieber (Ed.), *The Ethics of Social Research: Fieldwork, Regulation, and Publication* (vol. 1, pp. 71–91). New York: Springer-Verlag.

Jones, E. E., and Nisbett, R. E. (1972). The actor and the observer: Divergent perceptions of the causes of behavior. In E. E. Jones, D. E. Kanouse, H. H. Kelley, R. E. Nisbett, S. Valins, and B. Weiner (Eds.), *Attribution: Perceiving the Causes of Behavior.* Morristown, N.J.: General Learning Press.

_____ and Sigall, H. (1971). The bogus pipeline: A new paradigm for measuring affect and attitude. *Psychological Bulletin, 76,* 349–364.

Jones, F. P. (1964). Experimental method in antiquity. *American Psychologist, 19,* 419.

Jones, L.V., and Fiske, D.W. (1953). Models for testing the significance of combined results. *Psychological Bulletin, 50,* 375–382.

Judd, C. M., and Kenny, D. A. (1981). *Estimating the Effects of Social Interventions.* Cambridge, Eng.: Cambridge University Press.

_____ and McClelland, G. H. (1989). *Data Analysis: A Model-Comparison Approach.* New York: Harcourt Brace Jovanovich.

Jung, J. (1969). Current practices and problems in the use of college students for psychological research. *Canadian Psychologist, 10,* 280–290.

Kahane, H. (1986). *Logic and Philosophy: A Modern Introduction* (5th ed.). Belmont, Calif.: Wadsworth.

Kahn, R. L., and Cannell, C. F. (1965). *The Dynamics of Interviewing.* New York: Wiley.

Kalleberg, A. L., and Kluegel, J. R. (1975). Analysis of the multitrait-multimethod matrix: Some limitations and an alternative. *Journal of Applied Psychology, 60,* 1–9.

Kamin, L. (1974). *The Science and Politics of IQ.* Potomac, Md.: Erlbaum.

Kaplan, A. (1964). *The Conduct of Inquiry: Methodology for Behavioral Science.* Scranton, Pa.: Chandler.

Kaplowitz, S. A., and Shlapentokh, V. (1982). Possible falsification of survey data: An analysis of a mail survey in the Soviet Union. *Public Opinion Quarterly, 46,* 1–23.

Kassarjian, H. H., and Nakanishi, M. (1967). A study of selected opinion measurement techniques. *Journal of Marketing Research, 4,* 148–153.

Katz, J. (1972). *Experimentation with Human Beings.* New York: Russell Sage.

Kazdin, A. E., and Tuma, A. H. (Eds.) (1982). *Single-Case Research Designs.* San Francisco: Jossey-Bass.

Kelman, H. C. (1968). *A Time to Speak: On Human Values and Social Research.* San Francisco: Jossey-Bass.

_____ (1972). The rights of the subject in social research: An analysis in terms of relative power and legitimacy. *American Psychologist, 27,* 989–1016.

Kendall, P. C., and Norton-Ford, J. D. (1982). *Clinical Psychology.* New York: Wiley.

Keniston, K. (1967). The sources of student dissent. *Journal of Social Issues, 23,* 108–137.

_____ (1969). You have to grow up in Scarsdale to know how bad things really are. *New York Times Magazine,* Apr. 27.

Kennedy, J. J. (1983). *Analyzing Qualitative Data.* New York: Praeger.

_____ and Bush, A. J. (1988). Focused comparisons in logit model contingency table analysis. Paper presented at the meeting of the American Educational Research Association, New Orleans, April.

Kenny, D. A. (1973). Cross-lagged and synchronous common factors in panel data. In A. S. Goldenberger & O. D. Duncan (Eds.), *Structural Equation Models in the Social Sciences.* New York: Seminar Press.

_____ (1979). *Correlation and Causality.* New York: Wiley.

_____ and Judd, C. M. (1986). Consequences of violating the independence assumption in analysis of variance. *Psychological Bulletin, 99,* 422–431.

Kerin, R. A., and Peterson, R. A. (1983). Scheduling telephone interviews. *Journal of Advertising Research, 23,* 41–47.

Kidder, L. H. (1972). On becoming hypnotized: How skeptics become convinced: A case of attitude change? *Journal of Abnormal Psychology, 80,* 317–322.

Kim, J. -O. (1975). Factor analysis. In N. H. Nie, C. H. Hull, J. G. Jenkins, K. Steinbrenner, and D. H. Bent, *SPSS: Statistical Package for the Social Sciences* (2d ed.) (pp. 468–514). New York: McGraw-Hill.

_____ and Mueller, C.W. (1978). *Introduction to Factor Analysis: What It Is and How To Do It.* Beverly Hills, Calif.: Sage. (University Paper Series 07-013.)

Kim, K. H., and Roush, F.W. (1980). *Mathematics for Social Scientists.* New York: Elsevier.

Kimble, G. A. (1989). Psychology from the standpoint of a generalist. *American Psychologist, 44,* 491–499.

Kimmel, A. J. (1979). Ethics and human subjects research: A delicate balance. *American Psychologist, 34,* 633–635.

_____ (Ed.) (1981). *Ethics of Human Subject Research.* San Francisco: Jossey-Bass.

_____ (1988). *Ethics and Values in Applied Social Research.* Beverly Hills, Calif.: Sage.

King, L. A., King, D.W., and Klockars, A. J. (1983). Dichotomous and multipoint scales using bipolar adjectives. *Applied Psychological Measurement, 7,* 173–180.

Kinsey, A. C., Pomeroy, W. B., and Martin, C. E. (1948). *Sexual Behavior in the Human Male.* Philadelphia: Saunders.

_____, _____, _____, and Gebhard, P. H. (1953). *Sexual Behavior in the Human Female.* Philadelphia: Saunders.

Kipnis, D. (1976). *The Powerholders.* Chicago: University of Chicago Press.

_____ (1984). The uses of power in organizations and in interpersonal settings. In S. Oskamp (Ed.), *Applied Social Psychology Annual* (vol. 5, pp. 179–210). Beverly Hills, Calif.: Sage.

_____ and Cosentino, J. (1969). Use of leadership powers in industry. *Journal of Applied Psychology, 53,* 460–466.

Kish, L. (1965). *Survey Sampling.* New York: Wiley.

Kleinmuntz, B., and McLean, R. S. (1968). Computers in behavioral science: Diagnostic interviewing by digital computer. *Behavioral Science, 13,* 75–80.

Knorr-Cetina, K. D. (1981). *The Manufacture of Knowledge: An Essay on the Constructivist and Contextual Nature of Science.* Oxford, Eng.: Pergamon.

Koch, S. (1959). General introduction to the series. In S. Koch (Ed.), *Psychology: A Study of a Science* (vol. 1, pp. 1–18). New York: McGraw-Hill.

Kolata, G. B. (1986). What does it mean to be random? *Science, 231,* 1068–1070.

Kordig, D. R. (1978). Discovery and justification. *Philosophy of Science, 45,* 110–117.

Koshland, D. E., Jr. (1988). Science, journalism, and whistle-blowing. *Science, 240,* 585.

Kothandapani, V. (1971). Validation of feeling, belief, and intention to act as three components of attitude and their contribution to prediction of contraceptive behavior. *Journal of Personality and Social Psychology, 19.* 321–333.

Kotses, H., Glaus, K. D., and Fisher, L. E., (1974). Effects of subject recruitment procedure on heart rate and skin conductance measures. *Biological Psychology, 2,* 59–66.

Kourany, J. A. (Ed.) (1987). *Scientific Knowledge.* Belmont,Calif.: Wadsworth.

Kraemer, H. C., and Thiemann, S. (1987). *How Many Subjects? Statistical Power Analysis in Research.* Newbury Park, Calif. Sage.

Krippendorff, K. (1980). *Content Analysis: An Introduction to Its Methodology.* Beverly Hills, Calif.: Sage.

Kruskal, J. B., and Wish, M. (1978). *Multidimensional Scaling.* Beverly Hills, Calif.: Sage.

Kuder, G. F., and Richardson, M.W. (1937). The theory of the estimation of test reliability. *Psychometrika, 2, 151–160.*

Labaw, P. (1980). *Advanced Questionnaire Design.* Cambridge, Mass.: Abt Books.

Lamb, W. K., and Whitla, D. K. (1983). *Meta-Analysis and the Integration of Research Findings: A Trend Analysis and Bibliography Prior to 1983.* Unpublished manuscript, Harvard University, Cambridge, Mass.

Lamberth, J., and Byrne, D. (1971). Similarity-attraction or demand characteristics? *Personality: An International Journal, 2,* 77–91.

Laming, D. R. J. (1967). On procuring human subjects. *Quarterly Journal of Experimental Psychology, 19,* 64–69.

Lana, R. E. (1969). Pretest sensitization. In R. Rosenthal and R. L. Rosnow (Eds.), *Artifact in Behavioral Research* (pp. 119–141). New York: Academic Press.

_____ (1986). Descartes, Vico, contextualism and social psychology. In R. L. Rosnow and M. Georgoudi (Eds.), *Contextualism and Understanding in Behavioral Science: Implications for Research and Theory* (pp. 67–85). New York: Praeger.

_____ and Rosnow, R. L. (1972). *Introduction to Contemporary Psychology.* New York: Holt.

Lancaster, H. O. (1961). The combination of probabilities: An application of orthogonal functions. *Australian Journal of Statistics, 3,* 20–33.

Lance, C. E., and Woehr, D. J. (1986). Statistical control of halo: Clarification from two cognitive models of the performance appraisal process. *Journal of Applied Psychology, 71,* 679–685.

Latané, B., and Darley, J. M. (1970). *The Unresponsive Bystander: Why Doesn't He Help?* New York: Appleton-Century-Crofts.

Laudan, L. (1977). *Progress and Its Problems: Towards a Theory of Scientific Growth.* Berkeley: University of California Press.

Lautenschlager, G. J. (1986). Within-subject measures for the assessment of individual differences in faking. *Educational and Psychological Measurement, 46,* 309–316.

Lavrakas, P. J. (1987). *Telephone Survey Methods: Sampling, Selection, and Supervision.* Beverly Hills, Calif.: Sage.

Lazarsfeld, P. F. (1978). Some episodes in the history of panel analysis. In D. B. Kandel (Ed.), *Longitudinal Research for Drug Abuse.* New York: Hemisphere Press.

_____ and Henry, N.W. (1968). *Latent Structure Analysis.* Boston: Houghton Mifflin.

Lehmann, E. L. (1975). *Nonparametrics: Statistical Methods Based on Ranks.* San Francisco: Holden-Day.

Lessac, M. S., and Solomon, R. L. (1969). Effects of early isolation on the later adaptive behavior of beagles. *Developmental Psychology, 1,* 14–25.

Levi, P. (1984). *The Periodic Table.* New York: Schocken Books.

Levin, J., and Arluke, A. (1987). *Gossip: The Inside Scoop.* New York: Plenum.

_____ and Kimmel, A. J. (1977). Gossip columns: Media small talk. *Journal of Communication, 27,* 169–175.

Levin, S. (1974). Behind every great man is a woman, behind every great woman there is none: A look at *Who's Who in America.* Unpublished data, Harvard University, Cambridge, Mass.

LeVine, R. A. (1981). Knowledge and fallibility in anthropological research. In M. B. Brewer and B. E. Collins (Eds.), *Scientific Inquiry and the Social Sciences* (pp. 172–193). San Francisco: Jossey-Bass.

_____ and Campbell, D.T. (1972). *Ethnocentrism: Theories of Conflict, Ethnic Attitudes, and Group Behavior.* New York: Wiley.

Lieberman, L. R., and Dunlap, J.T. (1979). O'Leary and Borkovec's conceptualization of placebo: The placebo paradox. *American Psychologist, 34,* 553–554.

Light, R. J., and Pillemer, D. B. (1984). *Summing Up: The Science of Reviewing Research.* Cambridge, Mass.: Harvard University Press.

_____ and Smith, P.V. (1971). Accumulating evidence: Procedures for resolving contradictions among different research studies. *Harvard Educational Review, 41,* 429–471.

Likert, R. A. (1932). A technique for the measurement of attitudes. *Archives of Psychology, 140,* 1–55.

Lindquist, E. F. (1953). *Design and Analysis of Experiments in Psychology and Education.* Boston: Houghton Mifflin.

Lindzey, G., and Aronson, E. (Eds.) (1968–1969). *The Handbook of Social Psychology* (2d ed.). Reading, Mass.: Addison-Wesley.

_____ and Borgatta, E. F. (1954). Sociometric measurement. In G. Lindzey (Ed.), *Handbook of Social Psychology* (pp.405–448). Cambridge, Mass.: Addison-Wesley.

Link, S.W. (1982). Correcting response measures for guessing and partial information. *Psychological Bulletin, 92,* 469–486.

Linsky, A. S. (1975). Stimulating responses to mailed questionnaires: A review. *Public Opinion Quarterly, 39,* 83–101.

Lipsey, M.W. (1990). *Design Sensitivity: Statistical Power for Experimental Research.* Newbury Park, Calif.: Sage.

London, P. (1970). The rescuers: Motivational hypotheses about Christians who saved Jews from the Nazis. In J. Macaulay and L. Berkowitz (Eds.) *Altruism and Helping Behavior: Social Psychological Studies of Some Antecedents and Consequences* (pp. 241–250). New York: Academic Press.

Lord, F. M., and Novick, M. R. (1968). *Statistical Theories of Mental Test Scores.* Reading, Mass.: Addison-Wesley.

Lorenz, K. (1971). *On Aggression.* New York: Bantam Books.

Lotz, J. (1968). Social science research and northern development. *Arctic, 21,* 291–294.

Lovejoy, A. O. (1936). *The Great Chain of Being: A Study of the History of an Idea.* Cambridge, Mass.: Harvard University Press.

Luchins, A. S., and Luchins, E. H. (1965). *Logical Foundations of Mathematics for Behavioral Scientists.* New York: Holt.

Lunney, G. H. (1970). Using analysis of variance with a dichotomous dependent variable: An empirical study. *Journal of Educational Measurement, 7,* 263–269.

McAskie, M. (1978). Carelessness or fraud in Sir Cyril Burt's kinship data? A critique of Jensen's analysis. *American Psychologist, 33,* 496–498.

McClelland, D. (1961). *The Achieving Society.* Princeton, N.J.: Van Nostrand.

McCormick, T. (1982). Content analysis: The social history of a method. *Studies in Communication, 2,* 143–178.

McGinniss, J. (1969). *The Selling of the President 1968.* New York: Trident.

McGuigan, F. J. (1963). The experimenter: A neglected stimulus object. *Psychological Bulletin, 60,* 421–428.

McGuire, W. J. (1964). Inducing resistance to persuasion: Some contemporary approaches. In L. Berkowitz (Ed.), *Advances in Experimental Social Psychology* (vol. 1, pp. 191–229). New York: Academic Press.

_____ (1973). The yin and yang of progress in social psychology: Seven koan. *Journal of Personality and Social Psychology, 26,* 446–456.

_____ (1976). Historical comparisons: Testing psychological hypotheses with cross-era data. *International Journal of Psychology, 11,* 161–183.

_____ (1983). A contextual theory of knowledge: Its implications for innovation and reform in psychological research. In L. Berkowtiz (Ed.), *Advances in Experimental Social Psychology* (vol. 16). New York: Academic Press.

_____ (1986). A perspectivist looks at contextualism and the future of behavioral science. In R. L. Rosnow and M. Georgoudi (Eds.), *Contextualism and Understanding in Behavioral Science: Implications for Research and Theory* (pp. 271–301). New York: Praeger.

McMillin, E. (1970). The history and philosophy of science: A taxonomy. In R. Stuewer (Ed.), *Historical and Philosophical Perspectives of Science.* Minneapolis: University of Minnesota Press.

McNemar, Q. (1946). Opinion-attitude methodology. *Psychological Bulletin, 43,* 289–374.

_____ (1960). At random: Sense and nonsense. *American Psychologist, 15,* 295–300.

_____ (1969). *Psychological Statistics* (4th ed.). New York: Wiley.

Maher, B. A. (1978). Stimulus sampling in clinical research: Representative design reviewed. *Journal of Consulting and Clinical Psychology, 46,* 643–647.

Mahler, I. (1953). Attitudes toward socialized medicine. *Journal of Social Psychology, 38,* 273–282.

Mahoney, M. J. (1976). *Scientist as Subject: The Psychological Imperative.* Cambridge, Mass.: Ballinger.

_____ (1978). Experimental methods and outcome evaluation. *Journal of Consulting and Clinical Psychology, 46,* 660–672.

Manicas, P.T., and Secord, P. F. (1983). Implications for psychology of the new philosophy of science. *American Psychologist, 38,* 399–413.

Mann, L. (1967). The effects of emotional role playing on smoking attitudes and behavior. *Journal of Experimental Social Psychology, 3,* 334–348.

_____ and Janis, I. L. (1968). A follow-up study on the long-term effects of emotional role playing. *Journal of Personality and Social Psychology, 8,* 339–342.

Marascuilo, L. A., and McSweeney, M. (1977). *Nonparametric and Distribution-Free Methods for the Social Sciences.* Monterey, Calif.: Brooks/Cole.

Margolis, J., Manicas, P.T., Harré, R., and Secord, P. F. (Eds.) (1986). *Psychology: Designing the Discipline.* Oxford, Eng.: Blackwell.

Marlatt, G. A., Demming, B., and Reid, J. B. (1973). Loss of drinking in alcoholics: An experimental design. *Journal of Abnormal Psychology, 81,* 233–241.

Martin, P., and Bateson, P. (1986). *Measuring Behavior: An Introductory Guide.* Cambridge, Eng.: Cambridge University Press.

Martin, R. M., and Marcuse, F. L. (1958). Characteristics of volunteers and nonvolunteers in psychological experimentation. *Journal of Consulting Psychology, 22,* 475–479.

Maslow, A. H. (1942). Self-esteem (dominance feelings) and sexuality. *Journal of Social Psychology, 16,* 259–293.

_____ and Sakoda, J. M. (1952). Volunteer-error in the Kinsey study. *Journal of Abnormal and Social Psychology, 47,* 259–262.

Matarazzo, J. D., Wiens, A. N., and Saslow, G. (1965). Studies in interview speech behavior. In L. Krasner and L. P. Ullman (Eds.), *Research in Behavior Modification* (pp. 179–210). New York: Holt.

Mayer, L. S., and Carroll, S. S. (1987). Testing for lagged, cotemporal, and total dependence in cross-lagged panel analysis. *Sociological Methods and Research, 16,* 187–217.

Mead, G. H. (1927). 1927 class lectures in social psychology. In D. L. Miller (Ed.), *The Individual and the Social Self: Unpublished Work of George Herbert Mead.* Chicago: University of Chicago Press.

Medawar, P. B. (1969). *Induction and Intuition in Scientific Thought.* (Jayne Lectures for 1968.) Philadelphia: American Philosophical Society.

_____ (1979). *Advice to a Young Scientist.* New York: Harper & Row.

Medley, D. M., and Mitzel, H. E. (1963). Measuring classroom behavior by systematic observations. In N. L. Gage (Ed.), *Handbook of Research on Teaching* (pp. 247–328). Chicago: Rand McNally.

Melton, G. B., Levine, R. J., Koocher, G. P., Rosenthal, R., and Thompson, W. C. (1988). Community consultation in socially sensitive research: Lessons from clinical trials of treatments for AIDS. *American Psychologist, 43,* 573–581.

Meng, X-L., Rosenthal, R., and Rubin, D. B. (1990). *Comparing correlated correlation coefficients.* Manuscript submitted for publication.

Menges, R. J. (1973). Openness and honesty versus coercion and deception in psychological research. *American Psychologist, 28,* 1030–1034.

Merton, R. K. (1948). The self-fulfilling prophecy. *Antioch Review, 8,* 193–210.

_____ (1968). *Social Theory and Social Structure* (enlarged ed.). New York: Free Press.

Michaels, J.W. (1983). Systematic observation as a measurement strategy. *Sociological Focus, 16,* 217–226.

Milgram, S. (1963). Behavioral study of obedience. *Journal of Abnormal and Social Psychology, 67,* 371–378.

_____ (1964). Issues in the study of obedience: A reply to Baumrind. *American Psychologist, 19,* 848–852.

_____ (1965). Some conditions of obedience and disobedience to authority. *Human Relations, 18,* 57–76.

_____ (1975). *Obedience to Authority: An Experimental View.* New York: Harper Colophon Books.

_____ (1977). *The Individual in a Social World: Essays and Experiments.* Reading, Mass.: Addison-Wesley.

Miller, A. G. (1972). Role playing: An alternative to deception? *American Psychologist, 27,* 623–636.

Miller, A. I. (1978). Visualization lost and regained: The genesis of the quantum theory in the period 1913–1927. In J. Wechsler (Ed.), *On Aesthetics in Science* (pp. 73–96). Cambridge, Mass.: M.I.T. Press.

Miller, G. A., Bregman, A. S., and Norman, D. A. (1965). The computer as a general purpose device for the control of psychological experiments. In R.W. Stacy and B. D. Waxman (Eds.), *Computers in Biomedical Research* (vol. 1, pp. 467–490). New York: Academic Press.

Miller, P.V., and Cannell, C. F. (1982). A study of experimental techniques for telephone interviewing. *Public Opinion Quarterly, 46,* 250–269.

Minturn, E. B., Lansky, L. M., and Dember, W. N. (1972). The interpretation of levels of significance by psychologists: A replication and extension. Paper presented at the meeting of the Eastern Psychological Association.

Mishler, E. G. (1979). Meaning in context: Is there any other kind? *Harvard Educational Review, 49,* 1–19.

Mitroff, I. (1974). Norms and counter-norms in a select group of the Apollo moon scientists: A case study of the ambivalence of scientists. *American Sociological Review, 39,* 579–595.

Mixon, D. (1971). Behavior analysis treating subjects as actors rather than organisms. *Journal for the Theory of Social Behaviour, 1,* 19–31.

Mizes, J. S., Fleece, E. L., and Roos, C. (1984). Incentives for increasing return rates: Magnitude levels, response bias, and format. *Public Opinion Quarterly, 48,* 794–800.

Mook, D. G. (1983). In defense of external invalidity. *American Psychologist, 38,* 379–387.

Morawski, J. G. (Ed.) (1988). *The Rise of Experimentation in American Psychology.* New Haven, Conn.: Yale University Press.

Morris, E. K. (1988). Contextualism: The world view of behavior analysis. *Journal of Experimental Child Psychology, 46,* 289–323.

Morrison, D. F. (1976). *Multivariate Statistical Methods* (2d ed.). New York: McGraw-Hill.

Moses, L. E. (1986). *Think and Explain with Statistics.* Reading, Mass.: Addison-Wesley.

Mosteller, F. (1968). Association and estimation in contingency tables. *Journal of the American Statistical Association, 63,* 1–28.

——— and Bush, R. R. (1954). Selected quantitative techniques. In G. Lindzey and E. Aronson (Eds.), *Handbook of Social Psychology* (vol. 1, pp. 328–331). Cambridge, Mass.: Addison-Wesley.

——— and Rourke, R. E. K. (1973). *Sturdy Statistics: Nonparametrics and Order Statistics.* Reading, Mass.: Addison-Wesley.

Mulaik, S. A. (1972). *The Foundations of Factor Analysis.* New York: McGraw-Hill.

Mullen, B. (1989). *Advanced BASIC Meta-Analysis.* Hillsdale, N.J.: Erlbaum.

Mullen, B., and Rosenthal, R. (1985). *BASIC Meta-Analysis: Procedures and Programs.* Hillsdale, N.J.: Erlbaum.

Myers, J. L. (1979). *Fundamentals of Experimental Design* (3d ed.). Boston: Allyn and Bacon.

Nederhof, A. J. (1981). *Some Sources of Artifact in Social Science Research: Nonresponse, Volunteering and Research Experience of Subjects.* Leiden, Netherlands: Pasmans.

Nelson, N., Rosenthal, R., and Rosnow, R. L. (1986). Interpretation of significance levels and effect sizes by psychological researchers. *American Psychologist, 41,* 1299–1301.

Nie, N. H., Hull, C. H., Jenkins, J. G., Steinbrenner, K., and Bent, D. H. (1975). *SPSS: Statistical Package for the Social Sciences* (2d ed.). New York: McGraw-Hill.

Nijsse, M. (1988). Testing the significance of Kendall's τ and Spearman's r_s. *Psychological Bulletin, 103,* 235–237.

Nisbet, R. (1976). *Sociology as an Art Form.* London, Eng.: Oxford University Press.

Noether, G. E. (1967). *Elements of Nonparametric Statistics.* New York: Wiley.

Norman, D. A. (1973). Memory, knowledge, and the answering of questions. In R. S. Solso (Ed.), *Contemporary Issues in Cognitive Psychology: The Loyola Symposium* (pp. 135–165). Washington, D.C.: Winston.

Oppenheim, A. N. (1966). *Questionnaire Design and Attitude Measurement.* New York: Basic Books.

Orne, M.T. (1959). The nature of hypnosis: Artifact and essence. *Journal of Abnormal and Social Psychology, 58,* 277–299.

_____ (1962). On the social psychology of the psychological experiment: With particular reference to demand characteristics and their implications. *American Psychologist, 17,* 776–783.

_____ (1969). Demand characteristics and the concept of quasi-controls. In R. Rosenthal and R. L. Rosnow (Eds.), *Artifact in Behavioral Research* (pp. 143–179). New York: Academic Press.

_____ (1970). Hypnosis, motivation and the ecological validity of the psychological experiment. In W. J. Arnold and M. M. Page (Eds.), *Nebraska Symposium on Motivation.* Lincoln: University of Nebraska Press.

_____, Sheehan, P. W., and Evans, F. J. (1968). Occurrence of posthypnotic behavior outside the experimental setting. *Journal of Personality and Social Psychology, 9,* 189–196.

Osgood, C. E., Suci, G. J., and Tannenbaum, P. H. (1957). *The Measurement of Meaning.* Urbana: University of Illinois Press.

Oskamp, S. (1977). *Attitudes and Opinions.* Englewood Cliffs, N.J.: Prentice-Hall.

OSS Assessment Staff (1948). *Assessment of Men: Selection of Personnel for the Office of Strategic Services.* New York: Rinehart.

Ostrom, C. W., Jr. (1978). *Time-Series Analysis: Regression Techniques.* Beverly Hills, Calif.: Sage.

Overall, J. E. (1965). Reliability of composite ratings. *Educational and Psychological Measurement, 25,* 1011–1022.

_____ (1980). Continuity correction for Fisher's exact probability test. *Journal of Educational Statistics, 5,* 177–190.

_____, Goldstein, B. J., and Brauzer, B. (1971). Symptomatic volunteers in psychiatric research. *Journal of Psychiatric Research, 9,* 31–43.

_____, Rhoades, H. M., and Starbuck, R. R. (1987). Small sample tests for homogeneity of response probabilities in 2 × 2 contingency tables. *Psychological Bulletin, 102,* 307–314.

_____ and Spiegel, D. K. (1969). Concerning least squares analysis of experimental data. *Psychological Bulletin, 72,* 311–322.

_____, Spiegel, D. K., and Cohen, J. (1975). Equivalence of orthogonal and nonorthogonal analysis of variance. *Psychological Bulletin, 82,* 182–186.

Paine, R. (1970). Lappish decisions, partnerships, information management, and sanctions—A nomadic pastoral adaptation. *Ethnology, 9,* 52–67.

Pareek, U., and Rao, T. V. (1980). Cross-cultural surveys and interviewing. In H. C. Triandis and J. W. Berry (Eds.), *Handbook of Cross-Cultural Psychology: Methodology* (vol. 2, pp. 127–179). Boston: Allyn and Bacon.

Parker, K. C. H., Hanson, R. K., and Hunsley, J. (1988). MMPI, Rorschach, and WAIS: A meta-analytic comparison of reliability, stability, and validity. *Psychological Bulletin, 103,* 367–373.

Parten, M. (1950). *Surveys, Polls and Samples.* New York: Harper.

Pearson, E. S., Hartley, H. O. (Eds.) (1956). *Biometrika Tables for Statisticians.* New York: Cambridge University Press.

Pearson, K. (1902). On the mathematical theory of errors of judgment with special reference to the personal equation. *Philosophical Transactions of the Royal Society of London, 198,* 235–299.

Peek, C. J. (1977). A critical look at the theory of placebo. *Biofeedback and Self-Regulation, 2,* 327–335.

Pelz, D. C., and Andrew, F. M. (1964). Detecting causal priorities in panel study data. *American Sociological Review, 29,* 836–848.

Pepitone, A. (1976). Toward a normative and comparative biocultural social psychology. *Journal of Personality and Social Psychology, 4,* 641–653.

Pepper, S. C. (1942). *World Hypotheses: A Study of Evidence.* Berkeley: University of California Press.

_____ (1967). *Concept and Quality: A World Hypothesis.* LaSalle, Ill.: Open Court.

Peterson, R. E. (1968a). *The Scope of Organized Student Protest in 1967–68.* Princeton, N.J.: Princeton University Press.

_____ (1968b). The student left in American higher education. *Daedalus, 97,* 293–317.

Pfungst, O. (1911). *Clever Hans (The Horse of Mr. Von Osten)*. New York: Henry Holt. (Reissued 1965 by Holt, New York.)

Pillemer, D. B., and Light, R. J. (1980). Benefiting from variation in study outcomes. In R. Rosenthal (Ed.), *New Directions for Methodology of Social and Behavioral Science: Quantitative Assessment of Research Domains,* no. 5 (pp. 1–11). San Francisco: Jossey-Bass.

Platt, J. (1981a). Evidence and proof in documentary research: 1. Some specific problems of documentary research. *Sociological Review, 29,* 31–52.

———— (1981b). Evidence and proof in documentary research: 2. Some shared problems in documentary research. *Sociological Review, 29,* 53–66.

Platt, J. R. (1964). Strong inference. *Science, 146,* 347–353.

Polanyi, M. (1963). The potential theory of adsorption. *Science, 141,* 1010–1013.

———— (1966). *The Tacit Dimension.* New York: Doubleday Anchor.

Polkinghorne, D. E. (1988). *Narrative Knowing and the Human Studies.* Albany: State University of New York Press.

Pollard, P., and Richardson, J.T. E. (1987). On the probability of making type I errors. *Psychological Bulletin, 102,* 159–163.

Popper, K. R. (1934). *Logik der Forschung.* Vienna, Austria: Springer-Verlag.

———— (1961). *The Logic of Scientific Inquiry.* New York: Basic Books.

———— (1963). *Conjectures and Refutations.* London, Eng.: Routledge.

———— (1972). *Objective Knowledge: An Evolutionary Approach.* Oxford, Eng.: Oxford University Press.

Powell, K. E., Thompson, P. D., Caspersen, C. J., and Kendrick, J. S. (1987). Physical activity and the incidence of coronary heart disease. *Annual Review of Public Health, 8,* 253–287.

Pratt, J.W., and Gibbons, J. D. (1981). *Concepts of Nonparametric Theory.* New York: Springer-Verlag.

Ramul, K. (1963). Some early measurements and ratings in psychology. *American Psychologist, 18,* 653–659.

RAND Corporation (1955). *A Million Random Digits with 100,000 Normal Deviates.* New York: Free Press.

Rasch, G. (1960). *Probabilistic Models For Some Intelligence and Attainment Tests.* Copenhagen, Denmark: Danish Institute for Educational Research. (Expanded edition 1980, University of Chicago Press.)

———— (1966). An item analysis which takes individual differences into account. *British Journal of Mathematical and Statistical Psychology, 19,* 49–57.

Reed, S. K. (1988). *Cognition: Theory and Applications* (2d ed.). Pacific Grove, Calif.: Brooks/Cole.

Reichenbach, H. (1938). *Experience and Prediction.* Chicago: University of Chicago Press.

Reilly, F. E. (1970). *Charles Peirce's Theory of Scientific Method.* New York: Fordham University Press.

Remington, R. E. and Strongman, K.T. (1972). Operant facilitation during a pre-reward stimulus: Differential effects in human subjects. *British Journal of Psychology, 63,* 237–242.

Remmers, H. H. (1963). Rating methods in research on teaching. In N. L. Gage (Ed.), *Handbook of Research on Teaching* (pp. 329–378). Chicago: Rand McNally.

Rescher, N. (1984). *The Limits of Science.* Berkeley: University of California Press.

Resnick, J. H., and Schwartz, T. (1973). Ethical standards as an independent variable in psychological research. *American Psychologist, 28,* 134–139.

Reynolds, P. D. (1975). Value dilemmas in the professional conduct of social science. *International Social Science Journal, 27,* 563–611.

Riecken, H.W. (1975). Social experimentation. *Society,* July–August, pp. 34–41.

Roberts, L. (1988). Vietnam's psychological toll. *Science, 241,* 159–161.

Robinson, W. S. (1957). The statistical measurement of agreement. *American Sociological Review, 22,* 17–25.

Roethlisberger, F. J., and Dickson, W. J. (1939). *Management and the Worker.* Cambridge, Mass.: Harvard University Press.

Rogosa, D. (1987). Causal models do not support scientific conclusions: A comment in support of Freedman. *Journal of Educational Statistics, 12,* 185–195.

Rosen, E. (1951). Differences between volunteers and non-volunteers for psychological studies. *Journal of Applied Psychology, 35,* 185–193.

Rosenberg, M. J. (1969). The conditions and consequences of evaluation apprehension. In R. Rosenthal and R. L. Rosnow (Eds.), *Artifact in Behavioral Research* (pp. 279–349). New York: Academic Press.

Rosengren, K. E. (Ed.) (1981). *Advances in Content Analysis.* Beverly Hills, Calif.: Sage.

Rosenhan, D. (1973). On being sane in insane places. *Science, 179,* 250–258.

Rosenthal, M. C. (1985). Bibliographic retrieval for the social and behavioral scientist. *Research in Higher Education, 22,* 315–333.

Rosenthal, R. (1966). *Experimenter Effects in Behavioral Research.* New York: Appleton-Century-Crofts.

_____ (1967). Covert communication in the psychological experiment. *Psychological Bulletin, 67,* 356–367.

_____ (1969). Interpersonal expectation. In R. Rosenthal and R. L. Rosnow (Eds.), *Artifact in Behavioral Research* (pp. 181–277). New York: Academic Press.

_____ (1973a). Estimating effective reliability in studies that employ judges' ratings. *Journal of Clinical Psychology, 29,* 342–345.

_____ (1973b). *On the Social Psychology of the Self-Fulfilling Prophecy: Further Evidence for Pygmalion Effects and Their Mediating Mechanisms,* no. 53. New York: MSS Modular Publications.

_____ (1973c). The Pygmalion effect. *Psychology Today, 7,* 56–63.

_____ (1976). *Experimenter Effects in Behavioral Research* (enlarged ed.). New York: Irvington Press.

_____ (1977). Biasing effects of experimenters. *ETC: A Review of General Semantics, 34,* 253–264.

_____ (1978a). Combining results of independent studies. *Psychological Bulletin, 85,* 185–193.

_____ (1978b). How often are our numbers wrong? *American Psychologist, 33,* 1005–1008.

_____ (1979a). The "file drawer problem" and tolerance for null results. *Psychological Bulletin, 86,* 638–641.

_____ (Ed.) (1979b). *Skill in Nonverbal Communication: Individual Differences.* Cambridge, Mass.: Oelgeschlager, Gunn & Hain.

_____ (Ed.) (1980a). *New Directions for Methodology of Social and Behavioral Science: Quantitative Assessment of Research Domains,* no. 5. San Francisco: Jossey-Bass.

_____ (1980b). Summarizing significance levels. In R. Rosenthal (Ed.), *New Directions for Methodology of Social and Behavioral Science: Quantitative Assessment of Research Domains,* no. 5 (pp. 33–46). San Francisco: Jossey-Bass.

_____ (1982). Conducting judgment studies. In K. R. Scherer and P. Ekman (Eds.), *Handbook of Methods in Nonverbal Behavior Research* (pp. 287–361). New York: Cambridge University Press.

_____ (1983). Meta-analysis: Toward a more cumulative social science. In L. Bickman (Ed.), *Applied Social Psychology Annual* (vol. 4, pp. 65–93.). Beverly Hills, Calif.: Sage.

_____ (1984). *Meta-Analytic Procedures for Social Research.* Beverly Hills, Calif.: Sage.

_____ (1985a). Designing, analyzing, interpreting and summarizing placebo studies. In L. White, B. Tursky, and G. E. Schwartz (Eds.), *Placebo: Theory, Research, and Mechanisms* (pp. 110–136). New York: Guilford Press.

_____ (1985b). From unconscious experimenter bias to teacher expectancy effects. In J. B. Dusek (Ed.), *Teacher Expectancies* (pp. 37–65). Hillsdale, N.J.: Erlbaum.

_____ (1986). Meta-analytic procedures and the nature of replication: The Ganzfeld debate. *Journal of Parapsychology, 50,* 315–336.

_____ (1987a). *Judgment Studies: Design, Analysis, and Meta-Analysis.* Cambridge, Eng.: Cambridge University Press.

_____ (1987b). Pygmalion effects: Existence, magnitude, and social importance. *Educational Researcher, 16,* 37–41.

_____ (1990a). How are we doing in soft psychology? *American Psychologist, 45,* 775–777.

_____ (1990b). Replication in behavioral research. *Journal of Social Behavior and Personality, 5,* 1–30.

_____ (in press). Evaluation of procedures and results. In K.W. Wachter and M.L. Straf (Eds.), *The Future of Meta-Analysis.* New York: Russell Sage.

_____, Blanck, P.D., and Vannicelli, M. (1984). Speaking to and about patients: Predicting therapists' tone of voice. *Journal of Consulting and Clinical Psychology, 52,* 679–686.

_____ and DePaulo, B.M. (1979a). Sex differences in accommodation in nonverbal communication. In R. Rosenthal (Ed.), *Skill in Nonverbal Communication: Individual Differences* (pp. 68–103). Cambridge, Mass.: Oelgeschlager, Gunn & Hain.

_____ and _____ (1979b). Sex differences in eavesdropping on nonverbal cues. *Journal of Personality and Social Psychology, 37,* 273–285.

_____ and Fode, K.L. (1963). The effect of experimenter bias on the performance of the albino rat. *Behavioral Science, 8,* 183–189.

_____ and Gaito, J. (1963). The interpretation of levels of significance by psychological researchers. *Journal of Psychology, 55,* 33–38.

_____ and _____ (1964). Further evidence for the cliff effect in the interpretation of levels of significance. *Psychological Reports, 15,* 570.

_____ and Hall, J.A. (1981). Critical values of z for combining independent probabilities. *Replications in Social Psychology, 1*(2), 1–6.

_____, _____, DiMatteo, M.R., Rogers, P.L., and Archer, D. (1979). *Sensitivity to Nonverbal Communication: The PONS Test.* Baltimore: Johns Hopkins University Press.

_____ and Jacobson, L. (1968). *Pygmalion in the Classroom.* New York: Holt.

_____ and Lawson, R. (1964). A longitudinal study of the effects of experimenter bias on the operant learning of laboratory rats. *Journal of Psychiatric Research, 2,* 61–72.

_____ and Rosnow, R.L. (Eds.) (1969). *Artifact in Behavioral Research.* New York: Academic Press.

_____ and _____ (1975). *The Volunteer Subject.* New York: Wiley.

_____ and _____ (1984). Applying Hamlet's question to the ethical conduct of research: A conceptual addendum. *American Psychologist, 39,* 561–563.

_____ and _____ (1985). *Contrast Analysis: Focused Comparisons in the Analysis of Variance.* Cambridge, Eng.: Cambridge University Press.

_____ and Rubin, D.B. (1978). Interpersonal expectancy effects: The first 345 studies. *Behavioral and Brain Sciences, 3,* 377–386.

_____ and _____ (1979a). Comparing significance levels of independent studies. *Psychological Bulletin, 86,* 1165–1168.

_____ and _____ (1979b). A note on percent variance explained as a measure of the importance of effects. *Journal of Applied Social Psychology, 9,* 395–396.

_____ and _____ (1980a). Comparing within- and between-subjects studies. *Sociological Methods and Research, 9,* 127–136.

_____ and _____ (1980b.). Summarizing 345 studies of interpersonal expectancy effects. In R. Rosenthal (Ed.), *New Directions for Methodology of Social and Behavioral Science: Quantitative Assessment of Research Domains,* no. 5 (pp. 79–95). San Francisco: Jossey-Bass.

_____ and _____ (1982a). A simple general purpose display of magnitude of experimental effect. *Journal of Educational Psychology, 74,* 166–169.

_____ and _____ (1982b). Comparing effect sizes of independent studies. *Psychological Bulletin, 92,* 500–504.

_____ and _____ (1983). Ensemble-adjusted p values. *Psychological Bulletin, 94,* 540–541.

_____ and _____ (1984). Multiple contrasts and ordered Bonferroni procedures. *Journal of Educational Psychology, 76,* 1028–1034.

_____ and _____ (1985). Statistical analysis: Summarizing evidence versus establishing facts. *Psychological Bulletin, 97,* 527–529.

_____ and _____ (1986). Meta-analytic procedures for combining studies with multiple effect sizes. *Psychological Bulletin, 99,* 400–406.

_____ and _____ (1988). Comment: Assumptions and procedures in the file drawer problem. *Statistical Science, 3,* 120–125.

_____ and _____ (1989). Effect size estimation for one-sample multiple-choice-type data: Design, analysis, and meta-analysis. *Psychological Bulletin, 106,* 332–337.

_____ and _____ (in press). Further issues in effect size estimation for one-sample multiple-choice-type data. *Psychological Bulletin.*

Rosenzweig, S. (1933). The experimental situation as a psychological problem. *Psychological Review, 40,* 337–354.

_____ (1977). Outline of a denotative definition of aggression. *Aggressive Behavior, 3,* 379–383.

_____ (1981). The current status of the Rosenzweig picture-frustration study as a measure of aggression in personality. In P. F. Brain and D. Benton (Eds.), *Multidisciplinary Approaches to Aggression Research* (pp. 113–125). New York: Elsevier.

_____ (1986). *Freud and Experimental Psychology: The Emergence of Idiodynamics.* New York: McGraw-Hill.

Rosnow, R. L. (1968). A "spread of effect" in attitude formation. In A. G. Greenwald, T. C. Brock, and T. M. Ostrom (Eds.), *Psychological Foundations of Attitudes* (pp. 89–107). New York: Academic Press.

_____ (1978). The prophetic vision of Giambattista Vico: Implications for the state of social psychological theory. *Journal of Personality and Social Psychology, 36,* 1322–1331.

_____ (1980). Psychology of rumor. *Psychological Bulletin, 87,* 578–591.

_____ (1981). *Paradigms in Transition: The Methodology of Social Inquiry.* New York: Oxford University Press.

_____ (1983). Von Osten's horse, Hamlet's question, and the mechanistic view of causality: Implications for a post-crisis social psychology. *Journal of Mind and Behavior, 4,* 319–338.

_____ (1988). Rumor as communication: A contextualist approach. *Journal of Communication, 38,* 12–28.

_____ (1990) Teaching research ethics through role-play and discussion. *Teaching of Psychology, 17,* 179–181.

_____ and Aiken, L. S. (1973). Mediation of artifacts in behavioral research. *Journal of Experimental Social Psychology, 9,* 181–201.

_____ and Arms, R. L. (1968). Adding versus averaging as a stimulus-combination rule in forming impressions of groups. *Journal of Personality and Social Psychology, 10,* 363–369.

_____ and Davis, D. J. (1977). Demand characteristics and the psychological experiment. *ETC: A Review of General Semantics, 34,* 301–313.

_____, Esposito, J. L., and Gibney, L. (1988). Factors influencing rumor spreading: Replication and extension. *Language and Communication, 8,* 29–42.

_____ and Fine, G. A. (1974). Inside rumors. *Human Behavior, 3*(8), 64–68.

_____ and _____ (1976). *Rumor and Gossip: The Social Psychology of Hearsay.* New York: Elsevier.

_____ and Georgoudi, M. (1985). "Killed by idle gossip": The psychology of small talk. In B. Rubin (Ed.), *When Information Counts: Grading the Media* (pp. 59–73). Lexington, Mass.: Heath.

_____ and _____ (Eds.) (1986). *Contextualism and Understanding in Behavioral Science: Implications for Research and Theory.* New York: Praeger.

_____, Goodstadt, B. E., Suls, J. M., and Gitter, A. G. (1973). More on the social psychology of the experiment: When compliance turns to self-defense. *Journal of Personality and Social Psychology, 27,* 337–343.

_____ and Robinson, E. J. (Eds.) (1967). *Experiments in Persuasion.* New York: Academic Press.

_____ and Rosenthal, R. (1970). Volunteer effects in behavioral research. In K. H. Craik et al., *New Directions in Psychology,* no. 4 (pp. 211–277). New York: Holt.

_____ and _____ (1976). The volunteer subject revisited. *Australian Journal of Psychology, 28,* 97–108.

_____ and _____ (1988). Focused tests of significance and effect size estimation in counseling psychology. *Journal of Counseling Psychology, 35,* 203–208.

_____ and _____ (1989a). Definition and interpretation of interaction effects. *Psychological Bulletin, 105,* 143–146.

_____ and _____ (1989b). Statistical procedures and the justification of knowledge in psychological science. *American Psychologist, 44,* 1276–1284.

_____ and Rosnow, M. (1986). *Writing Papers in Psychology: A Student Guide.* Belmont, Calif.: Wadsworth.

_____ and Suls, J. M. (1970). Reactive effects of pretesting in attitude research. *Journal of Personality and Social Psychology, 15,* 338–343.

_____, Wainer, H., and Arms, R. L. (1970). Personality and group impression formation as a function of the amount of overlap in evaluative meaning of the stimulus elements. *Sociometry, 33,* 472–484.

Ross, S., Krugman, A. D., Lyerly, S. B., and Clyde, D. J. (1962). Drugs and placebos: A model design. *Psychological Reports, 10,* 383–392.

Rossi, P. H., Wright, J. D., and Anderson, A. B. (1983). Sample surveys: History, current practice, and future prospects. In P. H. Rossi, J. D. Wright, and A. B. Anderson (Eds.), *Handbook of Survey Research* (pp. 1–20). New York: Academic Press.

Rozelle, R. M., and Campbell, D. T. (1969). More plausible rival hypotheses in the cross-lagged panel correlation technique. *Psychological Bulletin, 71,* 74–80.

Rozin, P. (1967). Specific aversions as a component of specific hungers. *Journal of Comparative and Physiological Psychology, 64,* 237–242.

_____ (1969). Adaptive food sampling patterns in vitamin deficient rats. *Journal of Comparative and Physiological Psychology, 69,* 126–132.

Rozynko, V. V. (1959). Social desirability in the sentence completion test. *Journal of Consulting Psychology, 23,* 280.

Rubin, D. B. (1981). Personal communication to R. Rosenthal, Jan. 4.

Ruch, F. L. (1942). A technique for detecting attempts to fake performance on a self-inventory type of personality test. In Q. McNemar and M. A. Merrill (Eds.), *Studies in Personality.* New York: McGraw-Hill.

Ruehlmann, W. (1977). *Stalking the Feature Story.* Cincinnati, Ohio: Writer's Digest.

Rummell, R. J. (1970). *Applied Factor Analysis.* Evanston, Ill.: Northwestern University Press.

Russell, B. (1957). *Understanding History.* New York: Philosophical Library.

Ryder, N. B. (1965). The cohort as a concept in the study of social change. *American Sociological Review, 30,* 843–861.

Sabini, J., and Silver, M. (1982). *Moralities of Everyday Life.* New York: Oxford University Press.

Sambursky, S. (Ed.) (1975). *Physical Thought from the Presocratics to the Quantum Physicists.* New York: Pica Press.

Sarbin, T. R. (1977). Contextualism: A world view for modern psychology. In J. K. Cole and A. W. Landfield (Eds.), *Nebraska Symposium on Motivation* (vol. 24). Lincoln: University of Nebraska Press.

_____ (Ed.) (1986). *Narrative Psychology: The Storied Nature of Human Conduct.* New York: Praeger.

Sasson, R., and Nelson, T. M. (1969). The human experimental subject in context. *Canadian Psychologist, 10,* 409–437.

Schachter, S. (1959). *The Psychology of Affiliation: Experimental Studies of the Sources of Gregariousness.* Stanford, Calif.: Stanford University Press.

Schaie, K. W. (1965). A general model for the study of developmental problems. *Psychological Bulletin, 64,* 92–107.

Scheffé H. (1959). *The Analysis of Variance.* New York: Wiley.

Schuler, H. (1981). Ethics in Europe. In A. J. Kimmel (Ed.), *Ethics of Human Subject Research* (pp. 41–48). San Francisco: Jossey-Bass.

_____ (1982). *Ethical Problems in Psychological Research.* New York: Academic Press.

Schultz, D. P. (1969). The human subject in psychological research. *Psychological Bulletin, 72,* 214–228.

Schuman, H., Kalton, G., and Ludwig, J. (1983). Context and contiguity. *Public Opinion Quarterly, 47,* 112–115.

Sechzer, J. A. (Ed.) (1983). *The Role of Animals in Biomedical Research* (vol. 406). New York: New York Academy of Sciences.

Sedlmeier, P., and Gigerenzer, G. (1989). Do studies of statistical power have an effect on the power of studies? *Psychological Bulletin, 105,* 309–316.

Shapiro, A. K., and Morris, L. A. (1978). The placebo effect in medical and psychological thera-pies. In J. L. Garfield and A. E. Bergin (Eds.), *Handbook of Psychotherapy and Behavioral Change: An Empirical Analysis* (2d ed.) (pp. 369–410). New York: Wiley.

Shaw, M. E., and Wright, J. M. (1967). *Scales for the Measurement of Attitudes.* New York: McGraw-Hill.

Shea, J. D. C., and Jones, J. (1982). A model for the use of attitude scales across cultures. *International Journal of Psychology, 17,* 331–343.

Shenker, I. (1971). Struggling with perennial and elusive problem: Defining aggression. *The New York Times,* Dec. 9, p. 14.

Shepard, R. N., Romney, A. K., and Nerlove, S. B. (Eds.) (1972). *Multidimensional Scaling* (2 vols.). New York: Seminar Press.

Shibutani, T. (1966). *Improvised News: A Sociological Theory of Rumor.* Indianapolis, Ind.: Bobbs-Merrill.

Shoham-Salomon, V., and Rosenthal, R. (1987). Paradoxical interventions: A meta-analysis. *Journal of Consulting and Clinical Psychology, 55,* 22–28.

Shotter, J. (1984). *Social Accountability and Selfhood.* Oxford, Eng.: Blackwell.

————— (1986). Psychological theories as rhetorical construction. Paper presented at Case Studies in the Rhetoric of the Human Sciences Conference, Temple University, Philadelphia.

Sidman, M. (1960). *Tactics of Scientific Research: Evaluating Experimental Data in Psychology.* New York: Basic Books.

Sieber, J. E. (Ed.) (1982). *The Ethics of Social Research* (vols. 1 and 2). New York: Springer-Verlag.

Siegel, S. (1956). *Nonparametric Statistics.* New York: McGraw-Hill.

————— and Castellan, N. J. (1988). *Nonparametric Statistics for the Behavioral Sciences* (2d ed.). New York: McGraw-Hill.

Sigall, H., Aronson, E., and Van Hoose, T. (1970). The cooperative subject: Myth or reality? *Journal of Experimental Social Psychology, 6,* 1–10.

Silverman, I. (1977). *The Human Subject in the Psychological Experiment.* New York: Pergamon.

Simon, H. A. (1983). Fitness requirements for scientific theories. *British Journal of Philosophy of Science, 34,* 355–365.

Simon, W. M. (1972). *European Positivism in the Nineteenth Century.* Ithaca, New York: Cornell University Press.

Simonton, D. K. (1976). The sociopolitical context of philosophical beliefs: A transhistorical causal analysis. *Social Forces, 54,* 513–523.

————— (1984). *Genius, Creativity, and Leadership.* Cambridge, Mass.: Harvard University Press.

Singer, J. L. (Ed.) (1971). *The Control of Aggression.* New York: Academic Press.

Skagested, P. (1981). Hypothetical realism. In M. B. Brewer and B. E. Collins (Eds.), *Scientific Inquiry and the Social Sciences* (pp. 77–97). San Francisco: Jossey-Bass.

Skinner, B. F. (1980). *Notebooks* (edited by R. Epstein). Englewood Cliffs, N.J.: Prentice-Hall.

————— (1987). Whatever happened to psychology as a science of behavior? *American Psychologist, 42,* 780–786.

Smart, R. G. (1966). Subject selection bias in psychological research. *Canadian Psychologist, 7a,* 115–121.

Smith, C. (1980). *Selecting a Source of Local Television News in the Salt Lake City SMSA: A Multivariate Analysis of Cognitive and Affective Factors for 384 Randomly-Selected News Viewers.* Unpublished doctoral dissertation, Temple University School of Communication, Philadelphia.

Smith, C. P. (1983). Ethical issues: Research on deception, informed consent, and debriefing. In L. Wheeler and P. Shaver (Eds.), *Review of Personality and Social Psychology* (vol. 4, pp. 297–328). Beverly Hills, Calif.: Sage.

Smith, M. B. (1988). Beyond Aristotle and Galileo: Toward a contextualized psychology of persons. *Theoretical and Philosophical Psychology, 8,* 2–15.

Smith, M. L. (1980). Integrating studies of psychotherapy outcomes. In R. Rosenthal (Ed.), *New Directions for Methodology of Social and Behavioral Science: Quantitative Assessment of Research Domains,* no. 5 (pp. 47–61). San Francisco: Jossey-Bass.

————— and Glass, G.V (1977). Meta-analysis of psychotherapy outcome studies. *American Psychologist, 32,* 752–760.

_____, _____, and Miller, T. I. (1980). *Benefits of Psychotherapy.* Baltimore: Johns Hopkins University Press.

Smith, R. J. (1977). Electroshock experiment at Albany violates ethics guidelines. *Science, 198,* 383–386.

Smith, T.W. (1984). Estimating nonresponse bias with temporary refusals. *Sociological Perspectives, 27,* 473–489.

Snedecor, G.W. and Cochran, W. G. (1967). *Statistical Methods* (6th ed.). Ames: Iowa State University Press.

_____ and _____ (1980). *Statistical Methods* (7th ed). Ames: Iowa State University Press.

_____ and _____ (1989). *Statistical Methods* (8th ed.) Ames: Iowa State University Press.

Snider, J. G. (1962). Profiles of some stereotypes held by ninth-grade pupils. *Alberta Journal of Educational Research, 8,* 147–156.

_____ and Osgood, C. E. (Eds.) (1969). *Semantic Differential Technique: A Sourcebook.* Chicago: Aldine.

Sobal, J. (1982). Disclosing information in interview introductions: Methodological consequences of informed consent. *Sociology and Social Research, 66,* 348–361.

Sockloff, A. L., and Edney, J. N. (May, 1972). *Some Extension of Student's t and Pearson's r Central Distributions.* Temple University Measurement and Research Center. Technical Report 72-5.

Solomon, R. L. (1949). An extension of control group design. *Psychological Bulletin, 46,* 137–150.

_____ and Lessac,M. S. (1968). A control group design for experimental studies of developmental processes. *Psychological Bulletin, 70,* 145–150.

Sommer, R. (1968). Hawthorne dogma. *Psychological Bulletin, 70,* 592–595.

Sorokin, P. A. (1964). *Social and Cultural Mobility.* New York: Free Press.

Spacks, P. M. (1985). *Gossip.* New York: Knopf.

Sperling, G., and Melchner, M. J. (1976). Estimating item and order information. *Journal of Mathematical Psychology, 13,* 192–213.

Spradley, J. P. (1980). *Participant Observation.* New York: Holt.

Stanley, J. (1971). Test reliability. In L. C. Deighton (Ed.), *Encyclopedia of Education* (vol. 9, pp. 143–153). New York: Macmillan and Free Press.

Stanovich, K. E. (1986). *How to Think Straight about Psychology.* Glenview, Ill.: Scott, Foresman.

Steering Committee of the Physicians' Health Study Research Group (1988). Preliminary report: Findings from the aspirin component of the ongoing physicians' health study. *New England Journal of Medicine, 318,* 262–264.

Steiger, J. H. (1980). Tests for comparing elements of a correlation matrix. *Psychological Bulletin, 87,* 245–251.

Stephenson, W. (1953). *The Study of Behavior: Q-Technique and Its Methodology.* Chicago: University of Chicago Press.

_____ (1980). Newton's fifth rule and Q methodology: Application to educational psychology. *American Psychologist, 35,* 882–889.

Sterling, T. D. (1959). Publication decisions and their possible effects on inferences drawn from tests of significance—or vice versa. *Journal of the American Statistical Association, 54,* 30–34.

Stockman, N. (1983). *Antipositivist Theories of the Sciences.* Dordrecht, Holland: D. Reidel.

Stone, P., Dunphy, D., Smith, M., and Ogilvie, D. (1966). *The General Inquirer: A Complete Approach to Content Analysis.* Cambridge, Mass.: M.I.T. Press.

Straits, B. C., and Wuebben, P. L. (1973). College students' reactions to social scientific experimentation. *Sociological Methods and Research, 1,* 355–386.

Strube, M. J. (1985). Combining and comparing significance levels from nonindependent hypothesis tests. *Psychological Bulletin, 97,* 334–341.

Sudman, S. (1983). Applied sampling. In P. H. Rossi, J. D. Wright, and A. B. Anderson (Eds.), *Handbook of Survey Research* (pp. 145–194). New York: Academic Press.

_____ and Bradburn, N. M. (1974). *Response Effects in Surveys: A Review and Synthesis.* Chicago: Aldine.

_____, Sirken, M. G. and Cowan, C. D. (1988). Sampling rare and elusive populations. *Science, 240,* 991–996.

Sullivan, D. S., and Deiker, T. E. (1973). Subject-experimenter perceptions of ethical issues in human research. *American Psychologist, 28,* 587–591.

Suls, J. M. and Rosnow, R. L. (1981). The delicate balance between ethics and artifacts in behavioral research. In A. J. Kimmel (Ed.), *Ethics of Human Subject Research* (pp. 55–67). San Francisco: Jossey-Bass.

_____ and _____ (1988). Concerns about artifacts in psychological experiments. In J. Morawski (Ed.), *The Rise of Experimentation in American Psychology* (pp. 163–187). New Haven, Conn.: Yale University Press.

Surber, C. F. (1984). Issues in using quantitative rating scales in developmental research. *Psychological Bulletin, 95,* 226–246.

Susman, G. I. (1976). *Autonomy at Work: A Sociotechnical Analysis of Participative Management.* New York: Praeger.

Symonds, P. M. (1925). Notes on rating. *Journal of Applied Psychology, 9,* 188–195.

Tannenbaum, P. H., and Noah, J. E. (1959). Sportugese: A study of sports page communication. *Journalism Quarterly, 36,* 163–170.

Tedeschi, J. T., and Gallup, G. G., Jr. (1977). Human subjects research. *Science, 198,* 1099–1100.

_____ and Rosenfeld, P. (1981). The experimental research controversy at SUNYA: A case study. In A. J. Kimmel (Ed.), *Ethics of Human Subject Research* (pp. 5–18). San Francisco: Jossey-Bass.

Tesch, F. (1977). Debriefing research participants: Though this be method there is madness to it. *Journal of Personality and Social Psychology, 35,* 217–224.

Thomas, C. B., Hall, J. A., Miller, F. D., Dewhirst, J. R., Fine, G. A., Taylor, M., and Rosnow, R. L. (1979). Evaluation apprehension, social desirability, and the interpretation of test correlations. *Social Behavior and Personality, 7,* 193–197.

Thurstone, L. L. (1929). Theory of attitude measurement. *Psychological Bulletin, 36,* 222–241.

_____ (1929–1934). *The Measurement of Social Attitudes.* Chicago: University of Chicago Press.

Thyer, B. A., and Curtis, G. C. (1983). The repeated pretest-posttest single-subject experiment: A new design for empirical clinical practice. *Journal of Behavior Therapy and Experimental Psychiatry, 14,* 311–315.

Tinsley, H. E. A., and Weiss, D. J. (1975). Interrater reliability and agreement of subjective judgments. *Journal of Counseling Psychology, 22,* 358–376.

Tolman, E. C. (1959). Principles of purposive behavior. In S. Koch (Ed.), *Psychology: A Study of a Science* (vol. 2, pp. 92–157). New York: McGraw-Hill.

Torgerson, W. S. (1958). *Theory and Methods of Scaling.* New York: Wiley.

Toulmin, S., and Leary, D. E. (1985). The cult of empiricism in psychology and beyond. In S. Koch and D. E. Leary (Eds.), *A Century of Psychology as a Science: Retrospections and Assessments.* New York: McGraw-Hill.

Triandis, H. C. (1964). Exploratory factor analyses of the behavioral component of social attitudes. *Journal of Abnormal and Social Psychology, 68,* 420–430.

_____ (1971). *Attitude and Attitude Change.* New York: Wiley.

_____ et al. (Eds.) (1980). *Handbook of Cross-Cultural Psychology* (vols. 1–6). Boston: Addison-Wesley.

Trist, E. L., and Bamforth, K. W. (1951). Some social and psychological consequences of the long wall method of coal-getting. *Human Relations, 4,* 3–38.

_____, Higgin, G. W., Murray, H., and Pollock, A. B. (1963). *Organizational Choice: Capabilities of Groups at the Coal Face under Changing Technologies.* London, Eng.: Tavistock.

Tufte, E. R. (1983). *The Visual Display of Quantitative Information.* Cheshire, Conn.: Graphics Press.

Tukey, J. W. (1977). *Exploratory Data Analysis.* Reading, Mass.: Addison-Wesley.

Tunis, S. L., and Rosnow, R. L. (1983). Heuristic model of synthetic behavior: Rationale, validation and implications. *Journal of Mind and Behavior, 4,* 165–178.

Upton, G. J. G. (1978). *The Analysis of Cross-Tabulated Data.* New York: Wiley.

Van de Geer, J. P. (1971). *Introduction to Multivariate Analysis for the Social Sciences.* San Francisco: Freeman.

Vaught, R. S. (1977). What if subjects can't be randomly assigned? *Human Factors, 19,* 227–234.

Veroff, J. (1983). Contextual determinants of personality. *Personality and Social Psychology Bulletin, 9,* 331–343.

Wachter, K.W. (1988). Disturbed by meta-analysis? *Science, 241,* 1407–1408.

_____ and Straf, M. L. (Eds.) (in press). *The Future of Meta-Analysis.* New York: Russell Sage.

Wainer, H. (1984). How to display data badly. *The American Statistician, 38,* 137–147.

_____ and Thissen, D. (1981). Graphical data analysis. *Annual Review of Psychology, 32,* 191–241.

Walker, H. M., and Lev, J. (1953). *Statistical Inference.* New York: Holt.

Wallace, D. (1954). A case for-and-against mail questionnaires. *Public Opinion Quarterly, 18,* 40–52.

Wallace, D. L. (1959). Bounds on normal approximations to Student's and the chi-square distributions. *Annals of Mathematical Statistics, 30,* 1121–1130.

Wallace, W. A. (1972). *Causality and Scientific Explanation.* Ann Arbor: University of Michigan Press.

Wallis, W. A., and Roberts, H.V. (1956). *Statistics: A New Approach.* New York: Free Press.

Warner, S. B., Jr., and Fleisch, S. (1977). *Measurements for Social History.* Beverly Hills, Calif.: Sage.

Warner, S. L. (1965). Randomized response: A survey response for eliminating evasive answers. *Journal of the American Statistical Association, 60,* 63–69.

Warwick, D. P., and Lininger, C. A. (1975). *The Sample Survey: Theory and Practice.* New York: McGraw-Hill.

Waterman, A. S. (1988). On the use of psychological theory and research in the process of ethical inquiry. *Psychological Bulletin, 103,* 283–298.

Watson, J. B. (1913). Psychology as a behaviorist views it. *Psychological Bulletin, 20,* 158–177.

Watson, P., and Workman, E. (1981). The non-concurrent multiple baseline across-individuals: An extension of the traditional multiple baseline design. *Journal of Behavior Therapy and Experimental Psychiatry, 12,* 257–259.

Weaver, C. (1972). *Human Listening.* Indianapolis, Ind.: Bobbs-Merrill.

Webb, E. J., Campbell, D.T., Schwartz, R. F., and Sechrest, L. (1966). *Unobtrusive Measures: Nonreactive Research in the Social Sciences.* Chicago: Rand McNally.

_____, _____, _____, _____, and Grove, J. B. (1981). *Nonreactive Measures in the Social Sciences* (2d ed.). Boston: Houghton Mifflin.

Webber, R. A. (1970). Perception of interactions between superiors and subordinates. *Human Relations, 23,* 235–248.

Weber, R. P. (1985). *Basic Content Analysis.* Beverly Hills, Calif.: Sage.

Weimann, G. (1982). The prophecy that never fails: On the uses and gratifications of horoscope reading. *Sociological Inquiry, 52,* 274–290.

Weinstein, D. (1979). Fraud in science. *Social Science Quarterly, 59,* 639–652.

Weisberg, R.W. (1986). *Creativity: Genius and Other Myths.* New York: Freeman.

Weiss, C. H. (1970). Interaction in the research interview: The effects of rapport on response. *Proceedings of the American Statistical Association: Social Statistics Section,* pp. 17–20.

Welkowitz, J., Ewen, R. B., and Cohen, J. (1976). *Introductory Statistics for the Behavioral Sciences* (2d ed.). New York: Academic Press.

_____, _____, and _____ (1982). *Introductory Statistics for the Behavioral Sciences* (3d ed.). New York: Academic Press.

Weschler, L. (1988). Onward and upward with the arts. *The New Yorker,* Jan. 18, 33–56.

West, S. G., and Gunn, S. P. (1978). Some issues on ethics and social psychology. *American Psychologist, 33,* 30–38.

_____ and Wicklund, R. A. (1980). *A Primer of Social Psychological Theories.* Monterey, Calif.: Brooks/Cole.

Wheelwright, P. (Ed.) (1951). *Aristotle.* New York: Odyssey Press.

White, R. K. (1984). *Fearful Warriors.* New York: Free Press.

Whiteley, J. M., Burkhart, M. Q., Harway-Herman, M., and Whiteley, R. M. (1975). Counseling and student development. *Annual Review of Psychology, 26,* 337–366.

Wickens, T. D., and Keppel, G. (1983). On the choice of design and of test statistic in the analysis of experiments with sampled materials. *Journal of Verbal Learning and Verbal Behavior, 22,* 296–309.

Wicker, A.W., and Bushweiler, G. (1970). Perceived fairness and pleasantness of social exchange situations: Two factorial studies of inequity. *Journal of Personality and Social Psychology, 15,* 63–75.

Wickesberg, A. K. (1968). Communication networks in a business organization structure. *Journal of the Academy of Management, 11,* 253–262.

Wicklund, R. A. (1974). *Freedom and Reactance.* Potomac, Md.: Erlbaum.

Wilkins, L., and Richter, C. P. (1940). A great craving for salt by a child with corticoadrenal insufficiency. *Journal of the American Medical Association, 114,* 866–868.

Wilkins, W. (1984). Psychotherapy: The powerful placebo. *Journal of Consulting and Clinical Psychology, 52,* 570–573.

Wilkinson, B. (1951). A statistical consideration in psychological research. *Psychological Bulletin, 48,* 156–158.

Williams, E. J. (1959). The comparison of regression variables. *Journal of the Royal Statistical Society, Series B, 21,* 396–399.

Willis, R. H. and Willis, Y. A. (1970). Role playing versus deception: An experimental comparison. *Journal of Personality and Social Psychology, 16,* 472–477.

Winer, B. J. (1971). *Statistical Principles in Experimental Design* (2d ed.). New York: McGraw-Hill.

Wohlwill, J. R. (1970). Methodology and research strategy in the study of developmental change. In L. Goulet and P. Baltes (Eds.), *Life-Span Developmental Psychology* (pp. 92–191). New York: Academic Press.

Wood, R. (1978). Fitting the Rasch model: A heady tale. *British Journal of Mathematical and Statistical Psychology, 31,* 27–32.

Woodrum, E. (1984). "Mainstreaming" content analysis in social science: Methodological advantages, obstacles, and solutions. *Social Science Research, 13,* 1–19.

Wright, B. D., and Master, G. N. (1982). *Rating Scale Analysis: Rasch Measurement.* Chicago: Mesa Press.

Wrightsman, L. S. (1969). Wallace supporters and adherence to "law and order." *Journal of Personality and Social Psychology, 13,* 17–22.

Yardley, K. M. (1984). A critique of role play terminology in social psychology experimentation. *British Journal of Social Psychology, 23,* 113–120.

Young, F.W., and Hamer, R. M. (Eds.) (1987). *Multidimensional Scaling: History, Theory, and Applications.* Hillsdale: N.J.:Erlbaum.

Zajonc, R. F. (1965). Social facilitation. *Science, 13,* 17–22.

Zar, J. H. (1984). *Biostatistical Analysis* (2d ed.). Englewood Cliffs, N.J.: Prentice-Hall.

Zechmeister, E. B., and Nyberg, S. E. (1982). *Human Memory: An Introduction to Research and Theory.* Monterey, Calif.: Brooks/Cole.

Zelen, M., and Joel, L. S. (1959). The weighted compounding of two independent statistical tests. *Annals of Mathematical Statistics, 30,* 885–895.

Zillman, D. (1979). *Hostility and Aggression.* Hillsdale, N.J.: Erlbaum.

NAME INDEX

SUBJECT INDEX